The Despatches of Lord French

Field-Marshal Viscount French, O.M.

The Despatches of Lord French

Mons
The Marne
The Aisne
Flanders
Neuve Chapelle
The Second Battle of Ypres
Loos
Hohenzollern Redoubt

And a complete list
of the Officers and Men
Mentioned

The Naval & Military Press Ltd

Published by

The Naval & Military Press Ltd
Unit 5 Riverside, Brambleside
Bellbrook Industrial Estate
Uckfield, East Sussex
TN22 1QQ England

Tel: +44 (0)1825 749494

www.naval-military-press.com
www.nmarchive.com

In reprinting in facsimile from the original, any imperfections are inevitably reproduced and the quality may fall short of modern type and cartographic standards.

Contents

	Page
Mons	1
The Marne	15
The Aisne	27
Mentioned in Despatches	47
Flanders	91
Mentioned in Despatches	127
The Winter Campaign	205
Neuve Chapelle	229
Mentioned in Despatches	253
The Second Battle of Ypres	357
Loos	389
Mentioned in Despatches	415
Hohenzollern Redoubt	603

Illustrations

	Page
Field-Marshal Viscount French, G.C.B., O.M.	*Frontispiece*
General Sir Horace Smith-Dorrien, G.C.B.	10
Field-Marshal Sir Douglas Haig, G.C.B.	216
General Sir E. H. H. Allenby, K.C.B.	400

Maps*

The General Concentration of the Opposing Forces on the morning of August 22nd, 1914.	3
The Battle of Mons, on August 23rd, 1914, and subsequent retreat to the Oise (24th to 28th August).	12
The Battle of the Marne and advance to the Aisne.	17
The Second Battle of Ypres.	359
Map to illustrate Sir John French's Despatch of July 12th, 1915.	368
The Battle of Loos, September 25th, 1915.	391

*These Maps are reproduced, by permission, from "The Fortnightly Review."

THE details of The First Expeditionary Force on the following pages are reprinted, by permission of Major A. Corbett-Smith, R.F.A., from his book "The Retreat from Mons," Published by Messrs. Cassells.

THE FIRST EXPEDITIONARY FORCE

General Officer Commanding-in-Chief the British Forces.
Field-Marshal Sir J. D. P. French.
Chief of the General Staff.
Lieutenant-General Sir A. J. Murray.
Adjutant-General:
Major-General Sir C. F. N. Macready.
Quartermaster-General:
Major-General Sir W. R. Robertson.

First Army Corps

General Officer Commanding-in-Chief.
Lieutenant-General Sir Douglas Haig.

1ST DIVISION.
General Officer Commanding—Major-General S. H. Lomax.

1ST INFANTRY BRIGADE.
Brigade Commander—Brigadier-General F. I. Maxse.

1st Batt. Coldstream Guards.	1st Batt. R. Highlanders.
1st Batt. Scots Guards.	2nd Batt. R. Munster Fusiliers.

2ND INFANTRY BRIGADE.
Brigade Commander—Brigadier-General E. S. Bulfin.

2nd Batt. R. Sussex Regt.	1st Batt. Northampton Regt.
1st Batt. N. Lancs. Regt.	2nd Batt. K. R. Rifle Corps.

3RD INFANTRY BRIGADE.
Brigade Commander—Brigadier-General H. J. S. Landon. R. War. R.

1st Batt. R. W. Surrey Regt.	1st Batt. Gloucester Regt.
1st Batt. S. Wales Borderers.	2nd Batt. Welsh Regt.

CAVALRY (attached)
C Squadron 15th Hussars.

ROYAL ENGINEERS.
23rd and 26th Field Companies.

ROYAL ARTILLERY.
R.F.A. Batteries—113, 114, 115, 116, 117, 118, 46, 51, 54;
(Howitzer) 30, 40, 57.
Heavy Battery R.G.A.—26.
An Ammunition Column and an Ammunition Park.

2ND DIVISION.
General Officer Commanding—Major-General C. C. Monro.

4TH INFANTRY BRIGADE.
Brigade Commander—Brigadier-General R. Scott-Kerr.

2nd Batt. Grenadier Guards.	3rd Batt. Coldstream Guards.
2nd Batt. Coldstream Guards.	1st Batt. Irish Guards.

5TH INFANTRY BRIGADE.
Brigade Commander—Brigadier-General R. C. B. Haking.
2nd Batt. Worcester Regt. 2nd Batt. Highland L.I.
2nd Batt. Oxford and Bucks L.I. 2nd Batt. Connaught Rangers.

6TH INFANTRY BRIGADE.
Brigade Commander—Brigadier-General R. H. Davies.
1st Batt. Liverpool Regt. 1st Batt. R. Berks. Regt.
2nd Batt. S. Staffs. Regt. 1st Batt. K.R. Rifle Corps.

CAVALRY (attached)
B Squadron 15th Hussars.

ROYAL ENGINEERS.
5th and 11th Field Companies.

ROYAL ARTILLERY.
R.F.A. Batteries—22, 50, 70, 15, 48, 71, 9, 16, 17;
(Howitzer) 47, 56, 60.
Heavy Battery R.G.A.—35.
An Ammunition Column and an Ammunition Park.

CAVALRY.

A DIVISION (FOUR BRIGADES).
General Officer Commanding—Major-General E. H. H. Allenby.

1ST BRIGADE.
Brigade Commander—Brigadier-General C. J. Briggs.
2nd Dragoon Guards. 5th Dragoon Guards.
11th Hussars.

2ND BRIGADE.
Brigade Commander—Brigadier-General H. de B. De Lisle.
4th Dragoon Guards. 9th Lancers.
18th Hussars.

3RD BRIGADE.
Brigade Commander—Brigadier-General H. de la Poer Gough.
4th Hussars. 5th Lancers.
16th Lancers.

4TH BRIGADE.
Brigade Commander—Brigadier-General Hon. C. E. Bingham.
Household Cavalry (composite Regiment).
6th Dragoon Guards. 3rd Hussars.
And—

5TH BRIGADE.
Brigade Commander—Brigadier-General Sir P. W. Chetwode.
12th Lancers. 20th Hussars.
2nd Dragoons.

ROYAL HORSE ARTILLERY.
Batteries "D," "E," "I," "J," "L."

Second Army Corps.

General Officer Commanding-in-Chief—General Sir H. L. Smith-Dorrien.

3RD DIVISION.
General Officer Commanding—Major-General H. I. W. Hamilton.

7TH INFANTRY BRIGADE.
Brigade Commander—Brigadier-General F. W. N. McCrachen.
3rd Batt. Worcester Regt.
2nd Batt. S. Lancs. Regt.
1st Batt. Wilts. Regt.
2nd Batt. R. Irish Rifles.

8TH INFANTRY BRIGADE.
Brigade Commander—Brigadier-General B. J. C. Doran.
2nd Batt. R. Scots.
2nd Batt. R. Irish Regt.
4th Batt. Middlesex Regt.
1st Batt. Gordon Highlanders.

9TH INFANTRY BRIGADE
Brigade Commander—Brigadier-General F. C. Shaw.
1st Batt. Northumberland Fusiliers.
1st Batt. Lincolnshire Regt.
1st Batt. R. Scots Fusiliers.
4th Batt. R. Fusiliers.

CAVALRY (attached)
A Squadron 15th Hussars.

ROYAL ENGINEERS.
56th and 57th Field Companies.

ROYAL ARTILLERY.
R.F.A. Batteries—107, 108, 109, 6, 23, 49, 29, 41, 45;
(Howitzer) 128, 129, 130.
Heavy Battery R.G.A.—48.
An Ammunition Column and an Ammunition Park.

5TH DIVISION
General Officer Commanding—Major-General Sir C. Fergusson.

13th INFANTRY BRIGADE.
Brigade Commander—Brigadier-General G. J. Cuthbert.
2nd Batt. K.O. Scottish Bords.
2nd Batt. Yorks. L.I.
1st Batt. R.W. Kent Regt.
2nd Batt. W. Riding Regt.

14TH INFANTRY BRIGADE.
Brigade Commander—Brigadier-General S. P. Rolt.
2nd Batt. Suffolk Regt.
1st Batt. East Surrey Regt.
1st Batt. Duke of Cornwall's L.I.
2nd Batt. Manchester Regt.

15TH INFANTRY BRIGADE.
Brigade Commander—Brigadier-General Count A. E. W. Gleichen.
1st Batt. Norfolk Regt.
1st Batt. Bedford Regt.
1st Batt. Cheshire Regt.
1st Batt. Dorset Regt.

CAVALRY (attached).
A Squadron 19th Hussars.

ROYAL ENGINEERS.
17th and 59th Field Companies.

ROYAL ARTILLERY.
R.F.A. Batteries—11, 52, 80, 119, 120, 121, 122, 123, 124;
(Howitzer) 37, 61, 65.
Heavy Battery R.G.A.—108.
An Ammunition Column and an Ammunition Park.

19TH INFANTRY BRIGADE.
Brigade Commander—Major-General L. G. Drummond.

2nd Batt. R. Welsh Fusiliers.   1st Batt. Middlesex Regt.
1st Batt. Scottish Rifles.   2nd Batt. Argyll and Sutherland Highlanders.

ROYAL FLYING CORPS.
Aeroplane Squadrons Nos. 2, 3, 4 and 5.

ARMY SERVICE CORPS.
Horsed and Mechanical Transport.

ROYAL ARMY MEDICAL CORPS.
There came into line at Le Cateau on August 25th the—

4TH DIVISION.
General Officer Commanding—Major-General T. D. O. Snow.

10TH INFANTRY BRIGADE.
Brigade Commander—Brigadier-General J. A. L. Haldane.

1st Batt. R. Warwickshire Regt.   1st Batt. R. Irish Fusiliers.
2nd Batt. Seaforth Highlanders.   2nd Batt. R. Dublin Fusiliers.

11TH INFANTRY BRIGADE.
Brigade Commander—Brigadier-General A. G. Hunter-Weston.

1st Batt. Somersetshire L.I.   1st Batt. Hampshire Regt.
1st Batt. E. Lancs. Regt.   1st Batt. Rifle Brigade.

12TH INFANTRY BRIGADE.
Brigade Commander—Brigadier-General H. F. M. Wilson.

1st Batt. R. Lancs. Regt.   2nd Batt. R. Inniskilling Fusiliers.
2nd Batt. Lancashire Fusiliers.   2nd Batt. Essex Regt.

CAVALRY (attached)
B Squadron 19th Hussars.

ROYAL ENGINEERS
7th and 9th Field Companies.

ROYAL ARTILLERY
R.F.A. Batteries—39, 68, 88 (xiv Brigade) ; 125, 126, 127 (xxix. Brigade) ; 27, 134, 135 (xxxii. Brigade); 31, 35, 55 (xxxvii. Brigade).
Heavy Battery R.G.A.—31.

LINES OF COMMUNICATION AND ARMY TROOPS.
1st Batt. Devonshire Regt.   1st Batt. Cameron Highlanders.

I
MONS

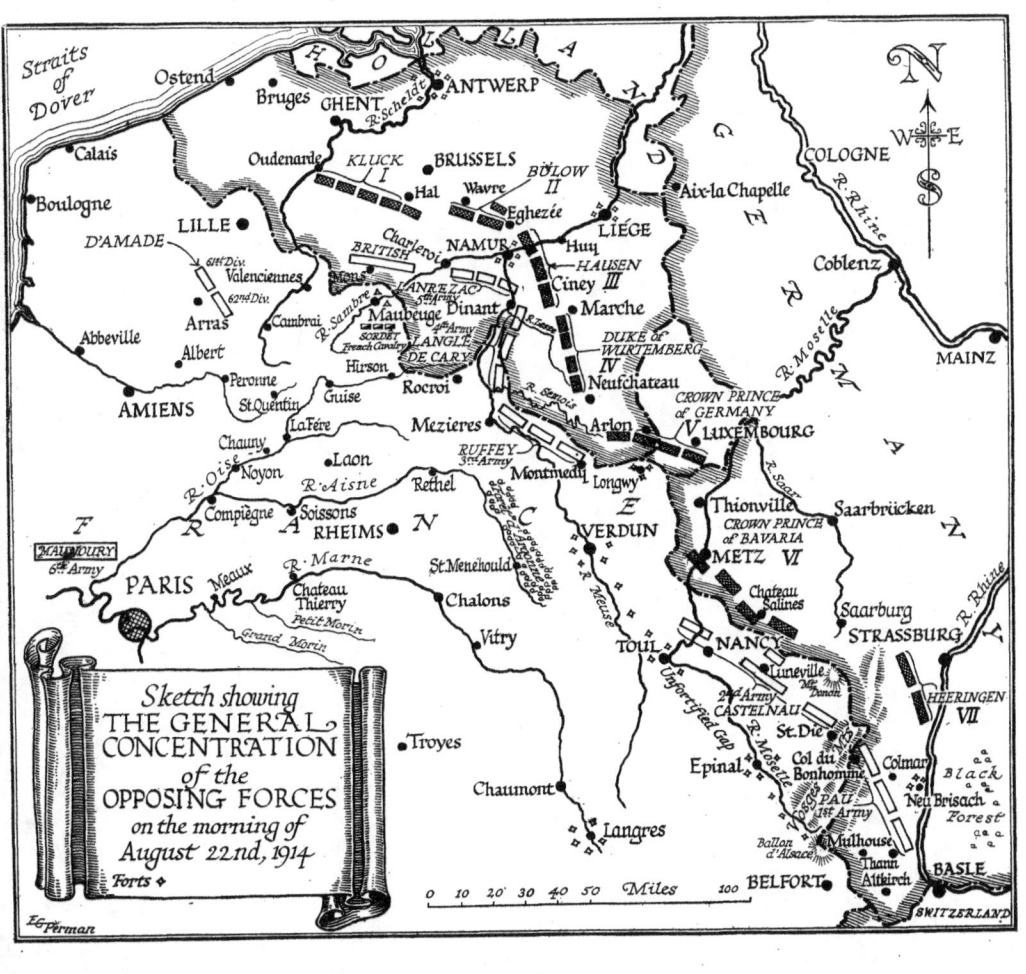

I : France, *7th September*, 1914.

To Field-Marshal Earl Kitchener of Khartoum, K.P., G.C.B., O.M., etc.

My Lord,

I HAVE the honour to report the proceedings of the Field Force under my command up to the time of rendering this despatch.

1. The transport of the troops from England both by sea and by rail was effected in the best order and without a check. Each unit arrived at its destination in this country well within the scheduled time.

The concentration was practically complete on the evening of Friday, the 21st ultimo, and I was able to make dispositions to move the Force during Saturday, the 22nd, to positions I considered most favourable from which to commence operations which the French Commander-in-Chief, General Joffre, requested me to undertake in pursuance of his plans in prosecution of the campaign.

The line taken up extended along the line of the canal from Conde on the west, through Mons and Binche on the east. This line was taken up as follows :—

From Conde to Mons inclusive was assigned to the Second Corps, and to the right of the Second Corps from Mons the First Corps was posted. The 5th Cavalry Brigade was placed at Binche.

In the absence of my Third Army Corps I desired to keep the Cavalry Division as much as possible as a reserve to act on my outer flank, or move in support of any threatened part of the line. The forward reconnaissance was entrusted to Brigadier-General Sir Philip Chetwode

MONS

with the 5th Cavalry Brigade, but I directed General Allenby to send forward a few squadrons to assist in this work.

During the 22nd and 23rd these advanced squadrons did some excellent work, some of them penetrating as far as Soignies, and several encounters took place in which our troops showed to great advantage.

2. At 6 a.m., on August 23rd, I assembled the Commanders of the First and Second Corps and Cavalry Division at a point close to the position, and explained the general situation of the Allies, and what I understood to be General Joffre's plan. I discussed with them at some length the immediate situation in front of us.

From information I received from French Headquarters I understood that little more than one, or at most two, of the enemy's Army Corps, with perhaps one Cavalry Division, were in front of my position; and I was aware of no attempted outflanking movement by the enemy. I was confirmed in this opinion by the fact that my patrols encountered no undue opposition in their reconnoitring operations. The observation of my aeroplanes seemed also to bear out this estimate.

About 3 p.m. on Sunday, the 23rd, reports began coming in to the effect that the enemy was commencing an attack on the Mons line, apparently in some strength, but that the right of the position from Mons and Bray was being particularly threatened.

The Commander of the First Corps had pushed his flank back to some high ground south of Bray, and the 5th Cavalry Brigade evacuated Binche, moving slightly south: the enemy thereupon occupied Binche.

The right of the 3rd Division, under General Hamilton, was at Mons, which formed a somewhat dangerous salient; and I directed the Commander of the Second Corps to be careful not to keep the troops on this salient too long, but, if threatened seriously, to draw back the

RETREAT TO THE MAUBEUGE POSITION

centre behind Mons. This was done before dark. In the meantime, about 5 p.m., I received a most unexpected message from General Joffre by telegraph, telling me that at least three German Corps, viz., a reserve corps, the 4th Corps and the 9th Corps, were moving on my position in front, and that the Second Corps were engaged in a turning movement from the direction of Tournay. He also informed me that the two reserve French divisions and the 5th French Army on my right were retiring, the Germans having on the previous day gained possession of the passages of the Sambre between Charleroi and Namur.

3. In view of the possibility of my being driven from the Mons position, I had previously ordered a position in rear to be reconnoitred. This position rested on the fortress of Maubeuge on the right and extended west to Jenlain, south-east of Valenciennes, on the left. The position was reported difficult to hold, because standing crops and buildings made the siting of trenches very difficult, and limited the field of fire in many important localities. It nevertheless afforded a few good artillery positions.

When the news of the retirement of the French and the heavy German threatening on my front reached me, I endeavoured to confirm it by aeroplane reconnaissance; and as a result of this I determined to effect a retirement to the Maubeuge position at daybreak on the 24th.

A certain amount of fighting continued along the whole line throughout the night, and at daybreak on the 24th the 2nd Division from the neighbourhood of Harmignies made a powerful demonstration as if to retake Binche. This was supported by the artillery of both the 1st and 2nd Divisions, whilst the 1st Division took up a supporting position in the neighbourhood of Peissant. Under cover of this demonstration the Second Corps retired on the line Dour-Quarouble-Frameries. The 3rd Division on the right of the Corps suffered considerable loss in this operation from the enemy, who had retaken Mons.

The Second Corps halted on this line, where they partially entrenched themselves, enabling Sir Douglas Haig with the First Corps gradually to withdraw to the new position ; and he effected this without much further loss, reaching the line Bavai-Maubeuge about 7 p.m. Towards mid-day the enemy appeared to be directing his principal effort against our left.

I had previously ordered General Allenby with the Cavalry to act vigorously in advance of my left front and endeavour to take the pressure off.

About 7.30 a.m. General Allenby received a message from Sir Charles Fergusson, commanding 5th Division, saying that he was very hard pressed and in urgent need of support. On receipt of this message General Allenby drew in the Cavalry and endeavoured to bring direct support to the 5th Division.

During the course of this operation General De Lisle, of the 2nd Cavalry Brigade, thought he saw a good opportunity to paralyse the further advance of the enemy's infantry by making a mounted attack on his flank. He formed up and advanced for this purpose, but was held up by wire about 500 yards from his objective, and the 9th Lancers and 18th Hussars suffered severely in the retirement of the Brigade.

The 19th Infantry Brigade, which had been guarding the Line of Communications, was brought up by rail to Valenciennes on the 22nd and 23rd. On the morning of the 24th they were moved out to a position south of Quarouble to support the left flank of the Second Corps.

With the assistance of the Cavalry Sir Horace Smith-Dorrien was enabled to effect his retreat to a new position ; although, having two corps of the enemy on his front and one threatening his flank, he suffered great losses in doing so.

THE FOURTH DIVISION

At nightfall the position was occupied by the Second Corps to the west of Bavai, the First Corps to the right. The right was protected by the Fortress of Maubeuge, the left by the 19th Brigade in position between Jenlain and Bry, and the Cavalry on the outer flank.

4. The French were still retiring, and I had no support except such as was afforded by the Fortress of Maubeuge; and the determined attempts of the enemy to get round my left flank assured me that it was his intention to hem me against that place and surround me. I felt that not a moment must be lost in retiring to another position.

I had every reason to believe that the enemy's forces were somewhat exhausted, and I knew that they had suffered heavy losses. I hoped, therefore, that his pursuit would not be too vigorous to prevent me effecting my object.

The operation, however, was full of danger and difficulty, not only owing to the very superior force in my front, but also to the exhaustion of the troops.

The retirement was recommenced in the early morning of the 25th to a position in the neighbourhood of Le Cateau, and rearguards were ordered to be clear of the Maubeuge-Bavai-Eth Road by 5.30 a.m.

Two Cavalry Brigades with the Divisional Cavalry of the Second Corps, covered the movement of the Second Corps. The remainder of the Cavalry Division with the 19th Brigade, the whole under the command of General Allenby, covered the west flank.

The 4th Division commenced its detrainment at Le Cateau on Sunday, the 23rd, and by the morning of the 25th eleven battalions and a Brigade of Artillery with Divisional Staff were available for service.

I ordered General Snow to move out to take up a position with his right south of Solesmes, his left resting on the Cambrai-Le Cateau Road south of La Chaprie. In this position the Division rendered great help to the effective retirement of the Second and First Corps to the new position.

Although the troops had been ordered to occupy the Cambrai-Le Cateau-Landrecies position, and the ground had, during the 25th, been partially prepared and entrenched, I had grave doubts—owing to the information I received as to the accumulating strength of the enemy against me—as to the wisdom of standing there to fight.

Having regard to the continued retirement of the French on my right, my exposed left flank, the tendency of the enemy's western corps (II.) to envelop me, and, more than all, the exhausted condition of the troops, I determined to make a great effort to continue the retreat till I could put some substantial obstacle, such as the Somme or the Oise, between my troops and the enemy, and afford the former some opportunity of rest and reorganisation. Orders were, therefore, sent to the Corps Commanders to continue their retreat as soon as they possibly could towards the general line Vermand-St. Quentin-Ribemont.

The Cavalry, under General Allenby, were ordered to cover the retirement.

Throughout the 25th and far into the evening, the First Corps continued its march on Landrecies, following the road along the eastern border of the Forêt De Mormal, and arrived at Landrecies about 10 o'clock. I had intended that the Corps should come further west so as to fill up the gap between Le Cateau and Landrecies, but the men were exhausted and could not get further in without rest.

The enemy, however, would not allow them this rest, and about 9.30 p.m. a report was received that the 4th Guards Brigade in Landrecies was heavily attacked by the troops of the 9th German Army Corps who were coming through the forest on the north of the town. This brigade fought most gallantly and caused the enemy to suffer tremendous loss in issuing from the forest into the

GENERAL SORDÊT

narrow streets of the town. This loss has been estimated from reliable sources at from 700 to 1,000. At the same time information reached me from Sir Douglas Haig that his 1st Division was also heavily engaged south and east of Maroilles. I sent urgent messages to the Commander of the two French Reserve Divisions on my right to come up to the assistance of the First Corps, which they eventually did. Partly owing to this assistance, but mainly to the skilful manner in which Sir Douglas Haig extricated his Corps from an exceptionally difficult position in the darkness of the night, they were able at dawn to resume their march south towards Wassigny on Guise.

By about 6 p.m. the Second Corps had got into position with their right on Le Cateau, their left in the neighbourhood of Caudry, and the line of defence was continued thence by the 4th Division towards Seranvillers, the left being thrown back.

During the fighting on the 24th and 25th the Cavalry became a good deal scattered, but by the early morning of the 26th General Allenby had succeeded in concentrating two brigades to the south of Cambrai.

The 4th Division was placed under the orders of the General Officer Commanding the Second Army Corps.

On the 24th the French Cavalry Corps, consisting of three divisions, under General Sordêt, had been in billets north of Avesnes. On my way back from Bavai, which was my " Poste de Commandement " during the fighting of the 23rd and 24th, I visited General Sordêt, and earnestly requested his co-operation and support. He promised to obtain sanction from his Army Commander to act on my left flank, but said that his horses were too tired to move before the next day. Although he rendered me valuable assistance later on in the course of the retirement, he was unable for the reasons given to afford me any support on the most critical day of all, viz., the 26th.

At daybreak it became apparent that the enemy was

throwing the bulk of his strength against the left of the position occupied by the Second Corps and the 4th Divisions.

At this time the guns of four German Army Corps were in position against them, and Sir Horace Smith-Dorrien reported to me that he judged it impossible to continue his retirement at daybreak (as ordered) in face of such an attack.

I sent him orders to use his utmost endeavours to break off the action and retire at the earliest possible moment, as it was impossible for me to send him any support, the First Corps being at the moment incapable of movement.

The French Cavalry Corps, under General Sordêt, was coming up on our left rear early in the morning, and I sent an urgent message to him to do his utmost to come up and support the retirement of my left flank; but, owing to the fatigue of his horses he found himself unable to intervene in any way.

There had been no time to entrench the position properly, but the troops showed a magnificent front to the terrible fire which confronted them.

The Artillery, although outmatched by at least four to one, made a splendid fight, and inflicted heavy losses on their opponents.

At length it became apparent that, if complete annihilation was to be avoided, a retirement must be attempted; and the order was given to commence it about 3.30 p.m. The movement was covered with the most devoted intrepidity and determination by the Artillery, which had itself suffered heavily, and the fine work done by the Cavalry in the further retreat from the position assisted materially in the final completion of this most difficult and dangerous operation.

Fortunately the enemy had himself suffered too heavily to engage in an energetic pursuit.

I cannot close the brief account of this glorious stand

GENERAL SIR HORACE SMITH-DORRIEN, G.C.B.
Photograph: Central News.

SIR HORACE SMITH-DORRIEN

of the British troops without putting on record my deep appreciation of the valuable services rendered by General Sir Horace Smith-Dorrien.

I say without hesitation that the saving of the left wing of the Army under my command on the morning of the 26th August could never have been accomplished unless a commander of rare and unusual coolness, intrepidity, and determination had been present to personally conduct the operation.

The retreat was continued far into the night of the 26th and through the 27th and 28th, on which date the troops halted on the line Noyon-Chauny-La Fere, having then thrown off the weight of the enemy's pursuit.

On the 27th and 28th I was much indebted to General Sordêt and the French Cavalry Division which he commands for materially assisting my retirement and successfully driving back some of the enemy on Cambrai.

General D'Amade also, with the 61st and 62nd French Reserve Divisions, moved down from the neighbourhood of Arras on the enemy's right flank and took much pressure off the rear of the British forces.

This closes the period covering the heavy fighting which commenced at Mons on Sunday afternoon, 23rd August, and which really constituted a four days' battle.

At this point, therefore, I propose to close the present despatch.

I deeply deplore the very serious losses which the British Forces have suffered in this great battle; but they were inevitable in view of the fact that the British Army —only two days after a concentration by rail—was called upon to withstand a vigorous attack of five German Army Corps.

It is impossible for me to speak too highly of the skill evinced by the two General Officers commanding Army Corps; the self-sacrificing and devoted exertions of their Staffs; the direction of the troops by Divisional, Brigade

MONS

and Regimental Leaders; the command of the smaller units by their officers; and the magnificent fighting spirit displayed by non-commissioned officers and men.

I wish particularly to bring to your Lordship's notice the admirable work done by the Royal Flying Corps under Sir David Henderson. Their skill, energy and perseverance have been beyond all praise. They have furnished me with the most complete and accurate information which has been of incalculable value in the conduct of the operations. Fired at constantly both by friend and foe, and not hesitating to fly in every kind of weather, they have remained undaunted throughout.

Further, by actually fighting in the air, they have succeeded in destroying five of the enemy's machines.

I wish to acknowledge with deep gratitude the incalculable assistance I received from the General and Personal Staffs at Headquarters during this trying period.

Lieutenant-General Sir Archibald Murray, Chief of the General Staff; Major-General Wilson, Sub-Chief of the General Staff; and all under them have worked day and night unceasingly with the utmost skill, self-sacrifice, and devotion; and the same acknowledgment is due by me to Brig.-Gen. Hon. W. Lambton, my Military Secretary, and the Personal Staff.

In such operations as I have described the work of the Quartermaster-General is of an extremely onerous nature. Major-General Sir William Robertson has met what appeared to be almost insuperable difficulties with his characteristic energy, skill and determination; and it is largely owing to his exertions that the hardships and sufferings of the troops—inseparable from such operations—were not much greater.

Major-General Sir Nevil Macready, the Adjutant-General, has also been confronted with most onerous and difficult tasks in connection with disciplinary arrangements and the preparation of casualty lists. He has been

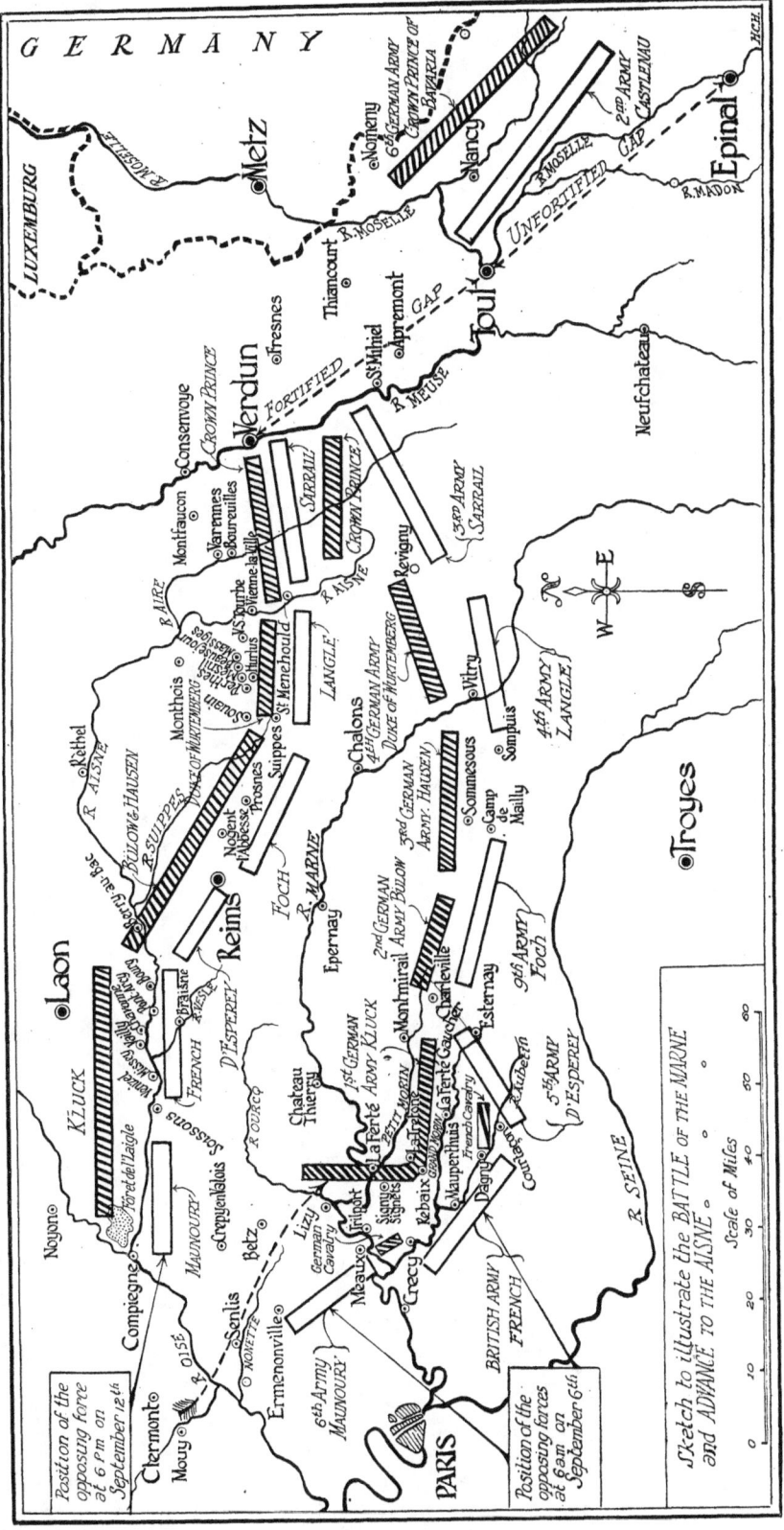

DISTINGUISHED SERVICES

indefatigable in his exertions to meet the difficult situations which arose.

I have not yet been able to complete the list of officers whose names I desire to bring to your Lordship's notice for services rendered during the period under review; and, as I understand it is of importance that this despatch should no longer be delayed, I propose to forward this list, separately, as soon as I can.

I have the honour to be,
  Your Lordship's most obedient servant,
 (*Signed*) J. D. P. FRENCH, Field-Marshal,
  Commander-in-Chief the British Forces in the Field.

II

THE MARNE

II : France, 17*th September*, 1914.

To Field-Marshal Earl Kitchener of Khartoum, K.P., G.C.B., O.M., etc.

My Lord,

IN continuation of my despatch of September 7th, I have the honour to report the further progress of the operations of the Forces under my command from August 28th.

On that evening the retirement of the Force was followed closely by two of the enemy's cavalry columns moving south-east from St. Quentin.

The retreat in this part of the field was being covered by the 3rd and 5th Cavalry Brigades. South of the Somme General Gough, with the 3rd Cavalry Brigade, threw back the Uhlans of the Guards with considerable loss.

General Chetwode, with the 5th Cavalry Brigade, encountered the eastern column near Cérizy, moving south. The Brigade attacked and routed the column, the leading German regiment suffering very severe casualties and being almost broken up.

The 7th French Army Corps was now in course of being railed up from the south to the east of Amiens. On the 29th it nearly completed its detrainment, and the French 6th Army got into position on my left, its right resting on Roye.

The 5th French Army was behind the line of the Oise between La Fère and the Guise.

The pursuit of the enemy was very vigorous; some five or six German corps were on the Somme, facing the 5th Army on the Oise. At least two corps were advancing towards my front, and were crossing the Somme east and west of Ham. Three or four more German corps were opposing the 6th French Army on my left.

THE MARNE

This was the situation at 1 o'clock on the 29th, when I received a visit from General Joffre at my headquarters.

I strongly represented my position to the French Commander-in-Chief, who was most kind, cordial, and sympathetic, as he has always been. He told me that he had directed the 5th French Army on the Oise to move forward and attack the Germans on the Somme, with a view to checking pursuit. He also told me of the formation of the Sixth French Army on my left flank, composed of the 7th Army Corps, four Reserve Divisions, and Sordêt's Corps of Cavalry.

I finally arranged with General Joffre to effect a further short retirement towards the line Compiègne-Soissons, promising him, however, to do my utmost to keep always within a day's march of him.

In pursuance of this arrangement the British Forces retired to a position a few miles north of the line Compiègne-Soissons on the 29th.

The right flank of the German Army was now reaching a point which appeared seriously to endanger my line of communications with Havre. I had already evacuated Amiens, into which place a German reserve division was reported to have moved.

Orders were given to change the base to St. Nazaire, and establish an advance base at Le Mans. This operation was well carried out by the Inspector-General of Communications.

In spite of a severe defeat inflicted upon the 10th Guard and Guard Reserve Corps of the German Army by the 1st and 3rd French Corps on the right of the 5th Army, it was not part of General Joffre's plan to pursue this advantage; and a general retirement on to the line of the Marne was ordered, to which the French Forces in the more eastern theatre were directed to conform.

A new Army (the 9th) had been formed from three corps in the south by General Joffre, and moved into the

THE BEGINNING OF THE OFFENSIVE

space between the right of the 5th and left of the 4th Armies.

Whilst closely adhering to his strategic conception to draw the enemy on at all points until a favourable situation was created from which to assume the offensive, General Joffre found it necessary to modify from day to day the methods by which he sought to attain this object, owing to the development of the enemy's plans and changes in the general situation.

In conformity with the movements of the French Forces, my retirement continued practically from day to day. Although we were not severely pressed by the enemy, rearguard actions took place continually.

On the 1st September, when retiring from the thickly-wooded country to the south of Compiègne, the 1st Cavalry Brigade was overtaken by some German cavalry. They momentarily lost a Horse Artillery battery, and several officers and men were killed and wounded. With the help, however, of some detachments from the 3rd Corps operating on their left, they not only recovered their own guns but succeeded in capturing twelve of the enemy's.

Similarly, to the eastward, the 1st Corps, retiring south, also got into some very difficult forest country, and a somewhat severe rearguard action ensued at Villers-Cotterets, in which the 4th Guards Brigade suffered considerably.

On September 3rd the British Forces were in a position south of the Marne between Lagny and Signy-Signets. Up to this time I had been requested by General Joffre to defend the passages of the river as long as possible, and to blow up the bridges in my front. After I had made the necessary dispositions, and the destruction of the bridges had been effected, I was asked by the French Commander-in-Chief to continue my retirement to a point some 12 miles in rear of the position I then occupied, with a view to taking up a second position behind the Seine. This

THE MARNE

retirement was duly carried out. In the meantime the enemy had thrown bridges and crossed the Marne in considerable force, and was threatening the Allies all along the line of the British Forces and the 5th and 9th French Armies. Consequently several small outpost actions took place.

On Saturday, September 5th, I met the French Commander-in-Chief at his request, and he informed me of his intention to take the offensive forthwith, as he considered conditions were very favourable to success.

General Joffre announced to me his intention of wheeling up the left flank of the 6th Army, pivoting on the Marne and directing it to move on the Ourcq, cross and attack the flank of the 1st German Army, which was then moving in a south-easterly direction east of that river.

He requested me to effect a change of front to my right —my left resting on the Marne and my right on the 5th Army—to fill the gap between that army and the 6th. I was then to advance against the enemy in my front and join in the general offensive movement.

These combined movements practically commenced on Sunday, September 6th, at sunrise; and on that day it may be said that a great battle opened on a front extending from Ermenonville, which was just in front of the left flank of the 6th French Army, through Lizy on the Marne, Mauperthuis, which was about the British centre, Courtecon, which was the left of the 5th French Army, to Esternay and Charleville, the left of the 9th Army under General Foch, and so along the front of the 9th, 4th, and 3rd French Armies to a point north of the fortress of Verdun.

This battle, in so far as the 6th French Army, the British Army, the 5th French Army and the 9th French Army were concerned, may be said to have concluded on the evening of September 10th, by which time the Germans

POSITION OF THE ARMIES

had been driven back to the line Soissons-Reims, with a loss of thousands of prisoners, many guns, and enormous masses of transport.

About the 3rd September the enemy appears to have changed his plans and to have determined to stop his advance South direct upon Paris; for on the 4th September air reconnaissances showed that his main columns were moving in a south-easterly direction generally east of a line drawn through Nanteuil and Lizy on the Ourcq.

On the 5th September several of these columns were observed to have crossed the Marne; whilst German troops, which were observed moving south-east up the left bank of the Ourcq on the 4th, were now reported to be halted and facing that river. Heads of the enemy's columns were seen crossing at Changis, La Ferté, Nogent, Château, Thierry and Mezy.

Considerable German columns of all arms were seen to be converging on Montmirail, whilst before sunset large bivouacs of the enemy were located in the neighbourhood of Coulommiers, south of Rebais, La Ferté-Gaucher and Dagny.

I should conceive it to have been about noon on the 6th September, after the British Forces had changed their front to the right and occupied the line Jouy-Le Chatel-Faremoutiers-Villeneuve Le Comte, and the advance of the 6th French Army north of the Marne towards the Ourcq became apparent, that the enemy realised the powerful threat that was being made against the flank of his columns moving south-east, and began the great retreat which opened the battle above referred to.

On the evening of the 6th September, therefore, the fronts and positions of the opposing armies were roughly as follows :

ALLIES.

6th French Army.—Right on the Marne at Meux, left towards Betz.

THE MARNE

British Forces.—On the line Dagny-Coulommiers-Maison.

5th French Army.—At Courtagon, right on Esternay.

Conneau's Cavalry Corps.—Between the right of the British and the left of the French 5th Army.

Germans.

4th Reserve and 2nd Corps.—East of the Ourcq and facing that river.

9th Cavalry Division.—West of Crecy.

2nd Cavalry Division.—North of Coulommiers.

4th Corps.—Rebais.

3rd and 7th Corps.—South-west of Montmirail.

All these troops constituted the 1st German Army, which was directed against the French 6th Army on the Ourcq, and the British Forces, and the left of the 5th French Army south of the Marne.

The 2nd German Army (IX., X., X.R. and Guard) was moving against the centre and right of the 5th French Army and the 9th French Army.

On the 7th September both the 5th and 6th French Armies were heavily engaged on our flank. The 2nd and 4th Reserve German Corps on the Ourcq vigorously opposed the advance of the French towards that river, but did not prevent the 6th Army from gaining some headway, the Germans themselves suffering serious losses. The French 5th Army threw the enemy back to the line of the Petit Morin river after inflicting severe losses upon them, especially about Montceaux, which was carried at the point of the bayonet.

The enemy retreated before our advance, covered by his 2nd and 9th and Guard Cavalry Divisions, which suffered severely.

Our Cavalry acted with great vigour, especially General De Lisle's Brigade, with the 9th Lancers and 18th Hussars.

THE ENEMY IN FULL RETREAT

On the 8th September the enemy continued his retreat northward, and our Army was successfully engaged during the day with strong rearguards of all arms on the Petit Morin River, thereby materially assisting the progress of the French Armies on our right and left, against whom the enemy was making his greatest efforts. On both sides the enemy was thrown back with very heavy losses. The First Army Corps encountered stubborn resistance at La Trétoire (north of Rebais). The enemy occupied a strong position with infantry and guns on the northern bank of the Petit Morin River; they were dislodged with considerable loss. Several machine guns and many prisoners were captured, and upwards of two hundred German dead were left on the ground.

The forcing of the Petit Morin at this point was much assisted by the Cavalry and the 1st Division, which crossed higher up the stream.

Later in the day a counter attack by the enemy was well repulsed by the First Army Corps, a great many prisoners and some guns again falling into our hands.

On this day (8th September) the Second Army Corps encountered considerable opposition, but drove back the enemy at all points with great loss, making considerable captures.

The Third Army Corps also drove back considerable bodies of the enemy's infantry and made some captures.

On the 9th September the First and Second Army Corps forced the passage of the Marne and advanced some miles to the north of it. The Third Corps encountered considerable opposition, as the bridges at La Ferté was destroyed and the enemy held the town on the opposite bank in some strength, and thence persistently obstructed the construction of a bridge; so the passage was not effected until after nightfall.

During the day's pursuit the enemy suffered heavy loss in killed and wounded, some hundreds of prisoners

THE MARNE

fell into our hands and a battery of eight machine guns were captured by the 2nd Division.

On this day the 6th French Army was heavily engaged west of the River Ourcq. The enemy had largely increased his force opposing them ; and very heavy fighting ensued, in which the French were successful throughout.

The left of the 5th French Army reached the neighbourhood of Chateau Thierry after the most severe fighting, having driven the enemy completely north of the river with great loss.

The fighting of this army in the neighbourhood of Montmirail was very severe.

The advance was resumed at daybreak on the 11th up to the line of the Ourcq, opposed by strong rearguards of all arms. The 1st and 2nd Corps, assisted by the Cavalry Division on the right, the 3rd and 5th Cavalry Brigades on the left, drove the enemy northwards. Thirteen guns, seven machine guns, about 2,000 prisoners, and quantities of transport fell into our hands. The enemy left many dead on the field. On this day the French 5th and 6th Armies had little opposition.

As the 1st and 2nd German Armies were now in full retreat, this evening marks the end of the battle which practically commenced on the morning of the 6th instant ; and it is at this point in the operations that I am concluding the present despatch.

Although I deeply regret to have had to report heavy losses in killed and wounded throughout these operations, I do not think they have been excessive in view of the magnitude of the great fight, the outlines of which I have only been able very briefly to describe, and the demoralisation and loss in killed and wounded which are known to have been caused to the enemy by the vigour and severity of the pursuit.

In concluding this despatch I must call your Lordship's special attention to the fact that from Sunday, August

CEASELESS FIGHTING

23rd, up to the present date (September 17th), from Mons back almost to the Seine, and from the Seine to the Aisne, the Army under my command has been ceaselessly engaged without one single day's halt or rest of any kind.

Since the date to which in this despatch I have limited my report of the operations a great battle on the Aisne has been proceeding. A full report of this battle will be made in an early further despatch.

It will, however, be of interest to say here that, in spite of a very determined resistance on the part of the enemy, who is holding in strength and great tenacity a position peculiarly favourable to defence, the battle which commenced on the evening of the 12th instant has, so far, forced the enemy back from his first position, secured the passage of the river, and inflicted great loss upon him, including the capture of over 2,000 prisoners and several guns.

I have the honour to be,
    Your Lordship's most obedient servant,
      (Signed) J. D. P. FRENCH, Field-Marshal,
Commander-in-Chief the British Forces in the Field.

III

THE AISNE

III : France, *8th October*, 1914

To Field-Marshal Earl Kitchener of Khartoum, K.P., G.C.B., O.M., etc.

My Lord,

I HAVE the honour to report the operations in which the British Forces in France have been engaged since the evening of the 10th September.

1. In the early morning of the 11th the further pursuit of the enemy was commenced; and the three Corps crossed the Ourcq practically unopposed, the Cavalry reaching the line of the Aisne River; the 3rd and 5th Brigades south of Soissons, the 1st, 2nd and 4th on the high ground at Couvrelles and Cerseuil.

On the afternoon of the 12th from the opposition encountered by the 6th French Army to the west of Soissons, by the 3rd Corps south-east of that place, by the 2nd Corps south of Missy and Vailly, and certain indications all along the line, I formed the opinion that the enemy had, for the moment at any rate, arrested his retreat and was preparing to dispute the passage of the Aisne with some vigour.

South of Soissons the Germans were holding Mont de Paris against the attack of the right of the French 6th Army when the 3rd Corps reached the neighbourhood of Buzancy, south-east of that place. With the assistance of the Artillery of the 3rd Corps the French drove them back across the river at Soissons, where they destroyed the bridges.

The heavy artillery fire which was visible for several

THE AISNE

miles in a westerly direction in the valley of the Aisne showed that the 6th French Army was meeting with strong opposition all along the line.

On this day the Cavalry under General Allenby reached the neighbourhood of Braine and did good work in clearing the town and the high ground beyond it of strong hostile detachments. The Queen's Bays are particularly mentioned by the General as having greatly assisted in the success of this operation. They were well supported by the 3rd Division, which on this night bivouacked at Brenelle, south of the river.

The 5th Division approached Missy, but were unable to make headway.

The 1st Army Corps reached the neighbourhood of Vauxcéré without much opposition.

In this manner the Battle of the Aisne commenced.

2. The Aisne Valley runs generally East and West, and consists of a flat-bottomed depression of width varying from half a mile to two miles, down which the river follows a winding course to the West at some points near the southern slopes of the valley and at others near the northern. The high ground both on the north and south of the river is approximately 400 feet above the bottom of the valley, and is very similar in character, as are both slopes of the valley itself, which are broken into numerous rounded spurs and re-entrants. The most prominent of the former are the Chivre spur on the right bank and Sermoise spur on the left. Near the latter place the general plateau of the south is divided by a subsidiary valley of much the same character, down which the small River Vesle flows to the main stream near Sermoise. The slopes of the plateau overlooking the Aisne on the north and south are of varying steepness, and are covered with numerous patches of wood, which also stretch upwards and backwards over the edge on to the top of the high ground. There are several villages and small towns dotted

THE AISNE VALLEY

about in the valley itself and along its sides, the chief of which is the town of Soissons.

The Aisne is a sluggish stream of some 170 feet in breadth, but, being 15 feet deep in the centre, it is unfordable. Between Soissons on the west and Villers on the east (the part of the river attacked and secured by the British Forces) there are eleven road bridges across it. On the north bank a narrow-gauge railway runs from Soissons to Vailly, where it crosses the river and continues eastward along the south bank. From Soissons to Sermoise a double line of railway runs along the south bank, turning at the latter place up the Vesle Valley towards Bazoches.

The position held by the enemy is a very strong one, either for a delaying action or for a defensive battle. One of its chief military characteristics is that from the high ground on neither side can the top of the plateau on the other side be seen except for small stretches. This is chiefly due to the woods on the edges of the slopes. Another important point is that all the bridges are under either direct of high-angle artillery fire.

The tract of country above described, which lies north of the Aisne, is well adapted to concealment, and was so skilfully turned to account by the enemy as to render it impossible to judge the real nature of his opposition to our passage of the river, or to accurately gauge his strength; but I have every reason to conclude that strong rearguards of at least three army corps were holding the passages on the early morning of the 13th.

3. On that morning I ordered the British Forces to advance and make good the Aisne.

The 1st Corps and the Cavalry advanced on the river. The 1st Division was directed on Chanouille viâ the canal bridge at Bourg, and the 2nd Division on Courtecon and Presles viâ Pont-Arcy and on the canal to the north of Braye via Chavonne. On the right the Cavalry and 1st Division met with slight opposition, and found a passage

THE AISNE

by means of the canal which crosses the river by an aqueduct. The Division was therefore able to press on, supported by the Cavalry Division on its outer flank, driving back the enemy in front of it.

On the left the leading troops of the 2nd Division reached the river by 9 o'clock. The 5th Infantry Brigade were only enabled to cross, in single file and under considerable shell fire, by means of the broken girder of the bridge which was not entirely submerged in the river. The construction of a pontoon bridge was at once undertaken, and was completed by 5 o'clock in the afternoon.

On the extreme left the 4th Guards Brigade met with severe opposition at Chavonne, and it was only late in the afternoon that it was able to establish a foothold on the northern bank of the river by ferrying one battalion across in boats.

By nightfall the 1st Division occupied the area Moulins-Paissy-Geny, with posts in the village of Vendresse.

The 2nd Division bivouacked as a whole on the southern bank of the river, leaving only the 5th Brigade on the north bank to establish a bridge head.

The Second Corps found all the bridges in front of them destroyed, except that of Condé, which was in the possession of the enemy, and remained so until the end of the battle.

In the approach to Missy, where the 5th Division eventually crossed, there is some open ground which was swept by heavy fire from the opposite bank. The 13th Brigade was, therefore, unable to advance; but the 14th, which was directed to the east of Venizel at a less exposed point, was rafted across, and by night established itself with its left at St. Marguérite. They were followed by the 15th Brigade; and later on both the 14th and 15th supported the 4th Division on their left in repelling a heavy counter-attack on the Third Corps.

On the morning of the 13th the Third Corps found the

CROSSING THE RIVER

enemy had established himself in strength on the Vregny Plateau. The road bridge at Venizel was repaired during the morning and a reconnaissance was made with a view to throwing a pontoon bridge at Soissons.

The 12th Infantry Brigade crossed at Venizel, and was assembled at Bucy Le Long by 1 p.m., but the bridge was so far damaged that artillery could only be manhandled across it. Meanwhile the construction of a bridge was commenced close to the road bridge at Venizel.

At 2 p.m. the 12th Infantry Brigade attacked in the direction of Chivres and Vregny with the object of securing the high ground east of Chivres as a necessary preliminary to a further advance northwards. This attack made good progress, but at 5.30 p.m. the enemy's artillery and machine-gun fire from the direction of Vregny became so severe that no further advance could be made. The positions reached were held till dark.

The pontoon bridge at Venizel was completed at 5.30 p.m., when the 10th Infantry Brigade crossed the river and moved to Bucy Le Long.

The 19th Infantry Brigade moved to Billy Sur Aisne, and before dark all the artillery of the Division had crossed the river, with the exception of the Heavy Battery and one Brigade of Field Artillery.

During the night the positions gained by the 12th Infantry Brigade to the east of the stream running through Chivres were handed over to the 5th Division.

The section of the Bridging Train allotted to the Third Corps began to arrive in the neighbourhood in Soissons late in the afternoon, when an attempt to throw a heavy pontoon bridge at Soissons had to be abandoned, owing to the fire of the enemy's heavy howitzers.

In the evening the enemy retired at all points and entrenched himself on the high ground about two miles north of the river, along which runs the Chemin-des-Dames. Detachments of Infantry, however, strongly

THE AISNE

entrenched in commanding points down slopes of the various spurs, were left in front of all three corps with powerful artillery in support of them.

During the night of the 13th and on the 14th and following days the Field Companies were incessantly at work night and day. Eight pontoon bridges and one foot bridge were thrown across the river under generally very heavy artillery fire, which was incessantly kept up on to most of the crossings after completion. Three of the road bridges, *i.e.*, Venizel, Missy and Vailly, and the railway bridge east of Vailly were temporarily repaired so as to take foot traffic, and the Villers Bridge made fit to carry weight up to six tons.

Preparations were also made for the repair of the Missy, Vailly and Bourg Bridges so as to take mechanical transport.

The weather was very wet and added to the difficulties by cutting up the already indifferent approaches, entailing a large amount of work to repair and improve.

The operations of the Field Companies during this most trying time are worthy of the best traditions of the Royal Engineers.

4. On the evening of the 14th it was still impossible to decide whether the enemy was only making a temporary halt, covered by rearguard, or whether he intended to stand and defend the position.

With a view to clearing up the situation, I ordered a general advance.

The action of the First Corps on this day under the direction and command of Sir Douglas Haig was of so skilful, bold and decisive a character that he gained positions which alone have enabled me to maintain my position for more than three weeks of very severe fighting on the north bank of the river.

The Corps was directed to cross the line Moulins— Moussy by 7 a.m.

VENDRESSE

On the right the General Officer Commanding the 1st Division directed the 2nd Infantry Brigade (which was in billets and bivouacked about Moulins), and the 25th Artillery Brigade (less one battery), under General Bulfin, to move forward before daybreak, in order to protect the advance of the Division sent up the valley to Vendresse. An officers' patrol sent out by this Brigade reported a considerable force of the enemy near the factory north of Troyon, and the Brigadier accordingly directed two regiments (the King's Royal Rifles and the Royal Sussex Regiment) to move at 3 a.m. The Northamptonshire Regiment was ordered to move at 4 a.m. to occupy the spur east of Troyon. The remaining regiment of the Brigade (the Loyal North Lancashire Regiment) moved at 5.30 a.m. to the village of Vendresse. The factory was found to be held in considerable strength by the enemy, and the Brigadier ordered the Loyal North Lancashire Regiment to support the King's Royal Rifles and the Sussex Regiment. Even with this support the force was unable to make headway, and on the arrival of the 1st Brigade the Coldstream Guards were moved up to support the right of the leading Brigade (the 2nd), while the remainder of the 1st Brigade supported its left.

About noon the situation was, roughly, that the whole of these two brigades were extended along a line running east and west, north of the line Troyon and south of the Chemin-des-Dames. A party of the Loyal North Lancashire Regiment had seized and were holding the factory. The enemy had a line of entrenchments north and east of the factory in considerable strength, and every effort to advance against this line was driven back by heavy shell and machine-gun fire. The morning was wet, and a heavy mist hung over the hills, so that the 25th Artillery Brigade and the Divisional Artillery were unable to render effective support to the advanced troops until about 9 o'clock.

By 10 o'clock the 3rd Infantry Brigade had reached a

THE AISNE

point one mile south of Vendresse, and from there it was ordered to continue the line of the 1st Brigade and to connect with and help the right of the 2nd Division. A strong hostile column was found to be advancing and by a vigorous counter stroke with two of his battalions the Brigadier checked the advance of this column and relieved the pressure on the 2nd Division. From this period until late in the afternoon the fighting consisted of a series of attacks and counter attacks. The counter strokes by the enemy were delivered at first with great vigour, but later on they decreased in strength, and all were driven off with heavy loss.

On the left the 6th Infantry Brigade had been ordered to cross the river and to pass through the line held during the preceding night by the 5th Infantry Brigade and occupy the Courtecon Ridge, whilst a detached force, consisting of the 4th Guards Brigade and the 36th Brigade, Royal Field Artillery, under Brigadier-General Perceval, were ordered to proceed to a point east of the village of Ostel.

The 6th Infantry Brigade crossed the river at Pont-Arcy, moved up the valley towards Braye, and at 9 a.m., had reached the line Tilleul—La Buvelle. On this line they came under heavy artillery and rifle fire, and were unable to advance until supported by the 34th Brigade, Royal Field Artillery, and the 44th Howitzer Brigade and the Heavy Artillery.

The 4th Guards Brigade crossed the river at 10 a.m. and met with very heavy opposition. It had to pass through dense woods; field artillery support was difficult to obtain; but one section of a field battery pushed up to and within the firing line. At 1 p.m. the left of the Brigade was south of the Ostel Ridge.

At this period of the action the enemy obtained a footing between the First and Second Corps, and threatened to cut the communications of the latter.

SIR DOUGLAS HAIG

Sir Douglas Haig was very hardly pressed and had no reserve in hand. I placed the Cavalry Division at his disposal, part of which he skilfully used to prolong and secure the left flank of the Guards Brigade. Some heavy fighting ensued, which resulted in the enemy being driven back with heavy loss.

About 4 o'clock the weakening of the counter attacks by the enemy and other indications tended to show that his resistance was decreasing, and a general advance was ordered by the Army Corps Commander. Although meeting with considerable opposition and coming under very heavy artillery and rifle fire, the position of the corps at the end of the day's operations extended from the Chemin-des-Dames on the right, through Chivy, to Le Cour de Soupir, with the 1st Cavalry Brigade extending to the Chavonne—Soissons road.

On the right the corps was in close touch with the French Moroccan troops of the 18th Corps, which were entrenched in échelon to its right rear. During the night they entrenched this position.

Throughout the Battle of the Aisne this advanced and commanding position was maintained, and I cannot speak too highly of the valuable services rendered by Sir Douglas Haig and the Army Corps under his command. Day after day and night after night the enemy's infantry has been hurled against him in violent counter attack which has never on any one occasion succeeded, whilst the trenches all over his position have been under continuous heavy artillery fire.

The operations of the First Corps on this day resulted in the capture of several hundred prisoners, some field pieces, and machine guns

The casualties were very severe, one brigade alone losing three of its four Colonels.

The 3rd Division commenced a further advance, and had nearly reached the plateau of Aizy when they were driven back by a powerful counter attack, supported by heavy artillery. The division, however, fell back in the best order, and finally entrenched itself about a mile north of Vailly Bridge, effectively covering the passage.

The 4th and 5th Divisions were unable to do more than maintain their ground.

5. On the morning of the 15th, after close examination of the position, it became clear to me that the enemy was making a determined stand ; and this view was confirmed by reports which reached me from the French Armies fighting on my right and left, which clearly showed that a strongly entrenched line of defence was being taken up from the north of Compiègne, eastward and south-eastward, along the whole valley of the Aisne up to and beyond Reims.

A few days previously the Fortress of Maubeuge fell, and a considerable quantity of siege artillery was brought down from that place to strengthen the enemy's position in front of us.

During the 15th shells fell in our position which have been judged by experts to be thrown by eight-inch siege guns with a range of 10,000 yards. Throughout the whole course of the battle our troops have suffered very heavily from this fire, although its effect latterly was largely mitigated by more efficient and thorough entrenching, the necessity for which I impressed strongly upon our Army Corps Commanders. In order to assist them in this work all villages within the area of our occupations were searched for heavy entrenching tools, a large number of which were collected.

In view of the peculiar formation of the ground on the north side of the river between Missy and Soissons, and its extraordinary adaptability to a force on the defensive, the 5th Division found it impossible to maintain its position on the southern edge of the Chivres Plateau, as the enemy in possession of the village of Vregny to the

HEAVY FIGHTING

west was able to bring a flank fire to bear upon it. The Division had, therefore, to retire to a line the left of which was at the village of Marguérite, and thence ran by the north edge of Missy back to the river to the east of that place.

With great skill and tenacity Sir Charles Fergusson maintained this position throughout the whole battle, although his trenches were necessarily on lower ground than that occupied by the enemy on the southern edge of the plateau, which was only 400 yards away.

General Hamilton with the 3rd Division vigorously attacked to the north, and regained all the ground he had lost on the 15th, which throughout the battle has formed a most powerful and effective bridge head.

6. On the 16th the 6th Division came up into line.

It had been my intention to direct the First Corps to attack and seize the enemy's position on the Chemin-des-Dames, supporting it with this new reinforcement. I hoped from the position thus gained to bring effective fire to bear across the front of the 3rd Division which, by securing the advance of the latter, would also take the pressure off the 5th Division and the Third Corps.

But any further advance of the First Corps would have dangerously exposed my right flank. And, further, I learned from the French Commander-in-Chief that he was strongly reinforcing the 6th French Army on my left, with the intention of bringing up the Allied left to attack the enemy's flank and thus compel his retirement. I therefore sent the 6th Division to join the Third Corps with orders to keep it on the south side of the river, as it might be available in general reserve.

On the 17th, 18th and 19th the whole of our line was heavily bombarded, and the First Corps was constantly and heavily engaged. On the afternoon of the 17th the right flank of the 1st Division was seriously threatened. A counter attack was made by the Northamptonshire

THE AISNE

Regiment in combination with the Queen's, and one battalion of the Divisional Reserve was moved up in support. The Northamptonshire Regiment, under cover of mist, crept up to within a hundred yards of the enemy's trenches and charged with the bayonet, driving them out of the trenches and up the hill. A very strong force of hostile infantry was then disclosed on the crest line. This new line was enfiladed by part of the Queen's and the King's Royal Rifles, which wheeled to their left on the extreme right of our infantry line, and were supported by a squadron of cavalry on their outer flank. The enemy's attack was ultimately driven back with heavy loss.

On the 18th, during the night, the Gloucestershire Regiment advanced from their position near Chivy, filled in the enemy's trenches and captured two maxim guns.

On the extreme right the Queen's were heavily attacked, but the enemy were repulsed with great loss. About midnight the attack was renewed on the First Division, supported by artillery fire, but was again repulsed.

Shortly after midnight an attack was made on the left of the 2nd Division with considerable force, which was also thrown back.

At about 1 p.m. on the 19th the 2nd Division drove back a heavy infantry attack strongly supported by artillery fire. At dusk the attack was renewed and again repulsed.

On the 18th I discussed with the General Officer Commanding the Second Army Corps and his Divisional Commanders the possibility of driving the enemy out of Condé, which lay between his two Divisions, and seizing the bridge which has remained throughout in his possession.

As, however, I found that the bridge was closely commanded from all points on the south side and that satisfactory arrangements were made to prevent any issue from it by the enemy by day or night, I decided that it was not necessary to incur the losses which an attack

GENERAL JOFFRE'S NEW PLAN

would entail, as, in view of the position of the Second and Third Corps, the enemy could make no use of Condé, and would be automatically forced out of it by any advance which might become possible for us.

7. On this day information reached me from General Joffre that he had found it necessary to make a new plan, and to attack and envelop the German right flank.

It was now evident to me that the battle in which we had been engaged since the 12th instant must last some days longer until the effect of this new flank movement could be felt and a way opened to drive the enemy from his positions.

It thus became essential to establish some system of regular relief in the trenches, and I have used the infantry of the 6th Division for this purpose with good results. The relieved brigades were brought back alternately south of the river, and, with the artillery of the 6th Division formed a general reserve on which I could rely in case of necessity.

The Cavalry has rendered most efficient and ready help in the trenches, and have done all they possibly could to lighten the arduous and trying task which has of necessity fallen to the lot of the Infantry.

On the evening of the 19th and throughout the 20th the enemy again commenced to show considerable activity. On the former night a severe counter-attack on the 3rd Division was repulsed with considerable loss, and from early on Sunday morning various hostile attempts were made on the trenches of the 1st Division. During the day the enemy suffered another severe repulse in front of the 2nd Division, losing heavily in the attempt. In the course of the afternoon the enemy made desperate attempts against the trenches all along the front of the First Corps, but with similar results.

After dark the enemy again attacked the 2nd Division, only to be again driven back.

THE AISNE

Our losses on these two days were considerable, but the number, as obtained, of the enemy's killed and wounded vastly exceeded them.

As the troops of the First Army Corps were much exhausted by this continual fighting, I reinforced Sir Douglas Haig with a brigade from the reserve, and called upon the 1st Cavalry Division to assist them.

On the night of the 21st another violent counter-attack was repulsed by the 3rd Division, the enemy losing heavily.

On the 23rd the four six-inch howitzer batteries, which I had asked to be sent from home, arrived. Two batteries were handed over to the Second Corps and two to the First Corps. They were brought into action on the 24th with very good results.

Our experiences in this campaign seem to point to the employment of more heavy guns of a larger calibre in great battles which last for several days, during which time powerful entrenching work on both sides can be carried out.

These batteries were used with considerable effect on the 24th and the following days.

8. On the 23rd the action of General de Castelnau's Army on the Allied left developed considerably, and apparently withdrew considerable forces of the enemy away from the centre and east. I am not aware whether it was due to this cause or not, but until the 26th it appeared as though the enemy's opposition in our front was weakening. On that day, however, a very marked renewal of activity commenced. A constant and vigorous artillery bombardment was maintained all day, and the Germans in front of the 1st Division were observed to be "sapping" up to our lines and trying to establish new trenches. Renewed counter-attacks were delivered and beaten off during the course of the day, and in the afternoon a well-timed attack by the 1st Division stopped the enemy's entrenching work.

GALLANTRY AND DEVOTION OF THE FORCES

During the night of 27th-28th the enemy again made the most determined attempts to capture the trenches of the 1st Division, but without the slightest success.

Similar attacks were reported during these three days all along the line of the Allied front, and it is certain that the enemy then made one last great effort to establish ascendancy. He was, however, unsuccessful everywhere, and is reported to have suffered heavy losses. The same futile attempts were made all along our front up to the evening of the 28th, when they died away, and have not since been renewed.

On former occasions I have brought to your Lordship's notice the valuable services performed during this campaign by the Royal Artillery.

Throughout the Battle of the Aisne they have displayed the same skill, endurance and tenacity, and I deeply appreciate the work they have done.

Sir David Henderson and the Royal Flying Corps under his command have again proved their incalculable value. Great strides have been made in the development of the use of aircraft in the tactical sphere by establishing effective communication between aircraft and units in action.

It is difficult to describe adequately and accurately the great strain to which officers and men were subjected almost every hour of the day and night throughout this battle.

I have described above the severe character of the artillery fire which was directed from morning till night, not only upon the trenches, but over the whole surface of the ground occupied by our Forces. It was not until a few days before the position was evacuated that the heavy guns were removed and the fire slackened. Attack and counter-attack occurred at all hours of the night and day throughout the whole position, demanding extreme vigilance, and permitting only a minimum of rest.

THE AISNE

The fact that between the 12th September to the date of this despatch the total numbers of killed, wounded and missing reached the figures amounting to 561 officers, 12,980 men, proves the severity of the struggle.

The tax on the endurance of the troops was further increased by the heavy rain and cold which prevailed for some ten or twelve days of this trying time.

The Battle of the Aisne has once more demonstrated the splendid spirit, gallantry and devotion which animates the officers and men of His Majesty's Forces.

With reference to the last paragraph of my despatch of September 7th, I append the names of officers, non-commissioned officers and men brought forward for special mention by Army Corps commanders and heads of departments for services rendered from the commencement of the campaign up to the present date.

I entirely agree with these recommendations and beg to submit them for your Lordship's consideration.

I further wish to bring forward the names of the following officers who have rendered valuable service :—General Sir Horace Smith-Dorrien and Lieutenant-General Sir Douglas Haig (commanding Second and First Corps respectively) I have already mentioned in the present and former despatches for particularly marked and distinguished service in critical situations.

Since the commencement of the campaign they have carried out all my orders and instructions with the utmost ability.

Lieutenant-General W. P. Pulteney took over the command of the Third Corps just before the commencement of the Battle of the Marne. Throughout the subsequent operations he showed himself to be a most capable commander in the field and has rendered very valuable services.

Major-General E. H. H. Allenby and Major-General H. de la P. Gough have proved themselves to be Cavalry

OFFICERS SPECIALLY MENTIONED

leaders of a high order, and I am deeply indebted to them. The undoubted moral superiority which our Cavalry has obtained over that of the enemy have been due to the skill with which they have turned to the best account the qualities inherent in the splendid troops they command.

In my despatch of 7th September I mentioned the name of Brigadier-General Sir David Henderson and his valuable work in command of the Royal Flying Corps; and I have once more to express my deep appreciation of the help he has since rendered me.

Lieutenant-General Sir Archibald Murray has continued to render me invaluable help as Chief of the Staff and in his arduous and responsible duties he has been ably assisted by Major-General Henry Wilson, Sub-Chief.

Lieutenant-General Sir Nevil Macready and Lieutenant General Sir William Robertson have continued to perform excellent service as Adjutant-General and Quartermaster-General respectively.

The Director of Army Signals, Lieutenant-Colonel J. S. Fowler, has materially assisted the operations by the skill and energy which he has displayed in the working of the important department over which he presides.

My Military Secretary, Brigadier-General the Hon. W. Lambton, has performed his arduous and difficult duties with much zeal and great efficiency.

I am anxious also to bring to your Lordship's notice the following names of officers of my Personal Staff, who throughout these arduous operations have shown untiring zeal and energy in the performance of their duties:

Aides-de-Camp.
Lieutenant-Colonel Stanley Barry.
Lieutenant-Colonel Lord Brooke.
Major Fitzgerald Watt.

Extra Aide-de-Camp.
Captain the Hon. F. E. Guest.

THE AISNE

Private Secretary.
Lieutenant-Colonel Brindsley Fitzgerald.

Major His Royal Highness Prince Arthur of Connaught, K.G., joined my Staff as Aide-de-Camp on the 14th September.

His Royal Highness's intimate knowledge of languages enabled me to employ him with great advantage on confidential missions of some importance, and his services have proved of considerable value.

I cannot close this despatch without informing your Lordship of the valuable services rendered by the Chief of the French Military Mission at my Headquarters, Colonel Victor Huguet, of the French Artillery. He has displayed tact and judgment of a high order in many difficult situations, and has rendered conspicuous service to the Allied cause.

I have the honour to be,

Your Lordship's most obedient Servant,

(*Signed*) J. D. P. FRENCH, Field-Marshal,
Commander-in-Chief the British Forces in the Field

MENTIONED IN DESPATCHES

MENTIONED IN DESPATCHES

GENERAL HEADQUARTERS STAFF, ETC.

Captain A. C. Amy.
Lieutenant-Colonel A. R. C. Atkins.
Major M. H. Babington.
Lieutenant-Colonel J. H. Barefoot.
Major W. H. Bartholomew.
Lieutenant-Colonel W. W. O. Beveridge, D.S.O.
J. F. Bird (Chaplain 1st Class).
Major E. A. Bourke.
Colonel W. G. B. Boyce, C.B.
S. Bradley (Chaplain 3rd Class).
Colonel V. T. Bunbury, C.B., D.S.O.
Major B. B. Burke.
Colonel E. R. C. Butler.
Colonel E. E. Carter, C.M.G., M.V.O.
Colonel A. E. J. Cavendish, C.M.G.
Major (temporary Lieutenant-Colonel) B. E. W. Childs.
Lieutenant-Colonel S. F. Clark.
Captain E. W. Cox.
Major S. L. Cummins, M.D.
Captain W. E. Davies.
Colonel C. T. Dawkins, C.M.G.
Major Hon. H. Dawnay, D.S.O.
Major C. P. Deedes, D.S.O.
Major C. Evans.
Major H. M. G. Fell.
Lieutenant-Colonel R. Ford, D.S.O.
Major J. V. Forrest.
Brigadier-General G. H. Fowke.
Lieutenant-Colonel (temporary Colonel) J. S. Fowler, D.S.O.
H. W. Fox (Chaplain 4th Class).
Major J. S. Gallie.
Brigadier-General F. C. A. Gilpin, C.B.
Major (temporary Lieutenant-Colonel) E. G. Faussett Godfrey.
Captain H. D. Goldsmith.
Major-General E. R. C. Graham, C.B.
L. H. Gwynne (Chaplain 4th Class).
Major R. W. Hare, D.S.O.
Colonel G. M. Harper, D.S.O.
Major A. M. Henniker.
Major E. M. Jack.

MENTIONED IN DESPATCHES

Major G. D. Jebb, D.S.O.
W. Keatinge (Chaplain 1st Class).
Brigadier-General Sir C. W. King, Knt., M.V.O.
Major-General W. F. L. Lindsay, C.B., D.S.O.
Lieutenant-Colonel Lord Loch, M.V.O., D.S.O.
Captain N. Lowe.
Colonel E. H. L. Lynden-Bell.
Major F. Lyon.
Principal Matron Miss E. M. McCarthy.
Colonel G. M. W. Macdonogh.
Major J. G. MacNaught.
E. G. F. Macpherson (Chaplain 1st Class).
Colonel C. M. Mathews, C.B., D.S.O.
Major G. A. Moore.
Major C. D. Myles.
Colonel T. J. O'Donnell, D.S.O.
Captain A. L. Otway.
J. D. S. Parry-Jones (Chaplain 3rd Class).
W. H. F. Pegg (Chaplain 4th Class).
Captain (temporary Major) H. F. P. Percival, D.S.O.
Major P. P. de B. Radcliffe.
Lieutenant G. G. Rawson.
Lieutenant-Colonel J. J. Russell.
Lieutenant-Colonel J. S. M. Shea, D.S.O.
Brevet Colonel F. Smith, D.S.O.
Major E. B. Steel.
Major F. A. Symonds.
J. G. W. Tuckey (Chaplain 1st Class).
Major E. V. Turner.
Major H. Wake, D.S.O.
Colonel R. Wanless O'Gowan.
Major A. H. Waring.
O. S. Watkins (Chaplain 3rd Class).
Major A. L. A. Webb.
Major Lisle Webb.
Surgeon-General (temporary) T. P. Woodhouse.
Captain C. R. Woodroffe.
A. R. Yeoman (Chaplain 3rd Class).
Private F. Annette.
Private W. P. Barsby.
Lance-Corporal W. Carter.
Serjeant J. Cook.
Private W. D. Deane.
Private W. Flaman.
Private L. H. Ginman.
Serjeant A. E. Harland.

MENTIONED IN DESPATCHES

Lance-Serjeant A. Hobbs.
Serjeant E. H. Jesson.
Serjeant-Major G. Leighton.
Serjeant-Major R. J. McKay.
First Class Staff-Serjeant J. T. Main.
Corporal W. R. Price.
Corporal T. Rowland.
Serjeant G. Sadler.
Lance-Corporal J. W. Sloane.
Staff-Serjeant Major W. Taylor.
Serjeant V. Tripp.
Superintending Clerk G. F. W. Willicot.
Captain C. J. Acland Troyte.
Captain H. I. R. Allfrey.
Lieutenant-Colonel N. G. Anderson, D.S.O.
Major B. D. Anley, D.S.O.
Captain E. C. Anstey.
Lieutenant W. M. Armstrong.
Captain H. D. Baird.
Major J. Baker.
Lieutenant-Colonel G. de S. Barrow.
Captain A. W. Bartholomew.
Lieutenant W. O. Bell-Irving.
Brigadier-General Hon. C. Bingham, C.V.O., C.B.
Captain W. A. Blake.
Colonel W. A. T. Bowly.
Captain G. F. Boyd, D.S.O.
Colonel R. C. Boyle.
Brigadier-General C. J. Briggs, C.B.
Captain J. E. S. Brind.
Captain C. F. Brooke.
Lieutenant W. T. Brooks.
Brigadier-General E. S. Bulfin, C.V.O., C.B.
Captain B. F. Burnett-Hitchcock.
Major H. S. Bush.
Major Hon. L. J. P. Butler.
Lieutenant-Colonel A. R. Cameron.
Brevet Lieutenant-Colonel N. J. G. Cameron.
Major J. S. Cawley (dead).
Captain J. Charteris.
Brigadier-General Sir P. Chetwode, D.S.O.
Major A. Chopping.
Major T. E. Clarke.
Lieutenant-Colonel G. Conway-Gordon.
Major B. H. H. Cooke.
Major C. E. Corkran.

MENTIONED IN DESPATCHES

Lieutenant J. H. M. Cornwall.
Major G. N. Cory, D.S.O.
Captain T. S. Cotgrave.
Lieutenant-Colonel G. Cree.
Captain R. A. M. Currie.
Brigadier-General G. J. Cuthbert, C.B.
Lieutenant-Colonel C. Dalton.
Major F. E. Ll. Daniell.
Major J. H. Davidson, D.S.O.
Captain C. M. Davies.
Brigadier-General R. H. Davies, C.B.
Captain O. H. Delano-Osborne.
Brigadier-General H. B. de Lisle, C.B., D.S.O.
Captain E. F. G. Dillon, D.S.O.
Brigadier-General B. J. C. Daran, C.B.
Captain F. H. Dorling.
Brigadier-General J. P. Du Cane, C.B.
Captain F. P. Dunlop.
Colonel B. Dunsterville.
Major H. M. Durand.
Captain G. N. Dyer.
Colonel J. E. Edmonds, C.B.
Lieutenant C. C. Egerton.
Colonel R. Fanshawe, D.S.O.
Major G. J. Farmer.
Major-General Sir C. Fergusson, Bart., C.B., M.V.O., D.S.O.
Lieutenant St. J. ffrench Blake.
Captain E. R. Fitzpatrick.
Brigadier-General G. T. Forestier-Walker, A.D.C.
Captain T. N. C. Frankland.
Lieutenant-Colonel Hon. J. H. Gathorne-Hardy.
Lieutenant R. Giffard.
Captain D. S. Gilkison (killed).
Captain G. H. Gill.
Brigadier-General Count A. E. W. Gleichen, K.C.V.O., C.B., C.M.G., D.S.O.
Brigadier-General F. M. Glubb, C.B., D.S.O.
Major (Local Lieutenant-Colonel) A. F. Gordon, D.S.O.
Captain A. R. G. Gordon.
Colonel Hon. F. Gordon.
Captain Viscount Gort, M.V.O.
Brigadier-General J. E. Gough, C.N.G.
Lieutenant Lord D. M. Graham.
Brigadier-General R. Haking, C.B.
Brigadier-General J. A. L. Haldane, C.B., D.S.O.
Major P. O. Hambro.

MENTIONED IN DESPATCHES

Major-General H. I. W. Hamilton, C.V.O., C.B., D.S.O.
Captain R. S. Hamilton-Grace.
Lieutenant J. Harter.
Brigadier-General J. G. Headlam, C.B., D.S.O.
Brigadier-General W. B. Hickie, C.B.
Colonel H. S. Hickson, M.B.
Captain R. J. T. Hildyard.
Major A. Hinde.
Brigadier-General P. E. F. Hobbs, C.M.G.
Lieutenant-Colonel A. J. Home.
Major Hon. W. P. Hore-Ruthven, D.S.O.
Brigadier-General H. S. Horne, C.B.
Captain H. C. Howard.
Captain R. G. Howard-Vyse.
Brigadier-General A. G. Hunter-Weston, C.B., D.S.O.
Major R. Hutchison.
Captain and Adjutant L. C. Jackson, C.M.G.
Captain J. B. Jenkinson (killed).
Colonel H. S. Jeudwine.
Major R. H. Kearsley.
Brigadier-General H. J. S. Landon, C.B.
Captain B. P. Lefroy.
Captain E. H. G. Leggett.
Major-General S. H. Lomax.
Colonel E. R. Ludlow.
Brigadier-General F. W. N. McCracken, C.B., D.S.O
Captain F. J. A. Mackworth.
Lieutenant-Colonel N. Malcolm, D.S.O.
Colonel R. J. Marker, D.S.O.
Colonel F. S. Maude, C.M.G.
Lieutenant-Colonel F. B. Maurice.
Captain W. J. Maxwell-Scott.
Brigadier-General G. F. Milne, C.B., D.S.O.
Major-General C. C. Monro, C.B.
Lieutenant-Colonel A. A. Montgomery.
Captain A. L. Moulton-Barrett.
Major W. P. Newbiggen, D.S.O.
Captain R. H. Osborne.
Colonel R. S. Oxley.
Lieutenant D. Paige.
Major G. Paley.
Captain W. L. Palmer.
Lieutenant J. Penrose.
Lieutenant C. P. W. Perceval.
Brigadier-General E. M. Perceval, D.S.O.
Major (temporary Lieutenant-Colonel) A. J. B. Percival, D.S.O.

MENTIONED IN DESPATCHES

Colonel R. Porter.
Captain L. A. E. Price-Davies, V.C., D.S.O.
Major F. F. Ready, D.S.O.
Captain W. R. Reid.
Brigadier-General S. R. Rice, C.B.
Brigadier-General S. P. Rolt, C.B.
Lieutenant-Colonel C. F. Romer.
Major E. Ryan.
Colonel W. H. Rycroft, C.B.
Colonel H. N. Sargent, D.S.O.
Lieutenant-Colonel H. T. Sawyer.
Colonel R. H. S. Sawyer.
Lieutenant-Colonel A. L. Schreiber, D.S.O.
Brigadier-General R. Scott-Kerr, C.B., M.V.O., D.S.O.
Brigadier-General F. C. Shaw, C.B.
Major A. B. Smallman.
Major-General T. D'O. Snow, C.B.
Captain R. W. M. Stevens.
Major F. C. Stratton.
Major H. E. Street.
Major H. W. Studd, D.S.O.
Major G. H. F. Tailyour.
Captain E. N. Tandy.
Captain J. J. B. Tapley.
Lieutenant-Colonel F. P. S. Taylor.
Captain F. M. C. Trench.
Colonel J. Vaughan, D.S.O.
Captain J. T. Weatherby.
Major G. A. W. Weir.
Second Lieutenant West.
Captain J. R. Wethered.
Lieutenant R. H. Willan.
Brigadier-General H. F. M. Wilson, C.B.
Brigadier-General F. D. V. Wing, C.B.
Major J. B. Wroughton.
Major J. M. Young.
-Corporal (temporary Serjeant) F. W. Joliffe.
Staff Serjeant-Major S. J. Webster, Army Service Corps.

Royal Flying Corps.

Lieutenant K. P. Atkinson, Royal Field Artillery.
Captain R. A. Roger, Royal Engineers.
Lieutenant I. M. Bonham-Carter, Northumberland Fusiliers.
Captain V. D. Bourke, Oxford and Bucks Light Infantry.
Captain A. B. Burdett, York and Lancaster Regiment.
Brevet Major C. J. Burke, Royal Irish Regiment.

MENTIONED IN DESPATCHES

Lieutenant (temporary Captain) G. I. Carmichael, Royal Field Artillery.
Lieutanant A. Christie, Royal Field Artillery.
Lieutenant E. L. Conran, 2nd County of London Yeomanry.
Captain G. W. P. Dawes, Royal Berkshire Regiment.
Lieutenant L. Dawes, Middlesex Regiment.
Captain E. W. Furse, Royal Field Artillery.
Captain H. C. Jackson, Bedford Regiment.
Lieutenant P. B. Joubert, de la Ferté, Royal Field Artillery.
Lieutenant D. S. Lewis, Royal Engineers.
Brevet Major C. A. H. Longcroft, Welsh Regiment.
Lieutenant Mapplebeck, Royal Flying Corps.
Lieutenant W. G. S. Mitchell, Highland Light Infantry.
Lieutenant M. W. Noel, Liverpool Regiment.
Lieutenant C. E. C. Rabagliati, Yorkshire Light Infantry.
Brevet Major G. R. Raleigh, Essex Regiment.
Brevet Major J. M. Salmond, Royal Lancashire Regiment.
Lieutenant R. G. D. Small, Leinster Regiment.
Lieutenant (temporary Captain), A. H. L. Soames, 3rd Hussars.
Second Lieutenant N. C. Spratte, Royal Flying Corps (S.R.)
Brevet Major (temporary Lieutenant-Colonel) F. H. Sykes.
Captain F. F. Waldron, 19th Hussars.
Second Lieutenant C. W. Wilson, Royal Flying Corps (S.R.)
Flight-Serjeant C. Cullen, Royal Flying Corps.
Flight-Serjeant H. Goodchild, Royal Flying Corps.
Serjeant W. Jones, Royal Flying Corps.
Serjeant M. Keegan, Royal Flying Corps.
Corporal S. Kemp, Royal Flying Corps.
Serjeant-Major E. J. Parker, Royal Flying Corps.
Serjeant-Major J. Ramsay, Royal Flying Corps.
Flight-Serjeant A. M. Saywood, Royal Flying Corps.
Serjeant A. Wilson, Royal Flying Corps.

HOUSEHOLD CAVALRY.

Major Viscount Crichton, M.V.O., D.S.O., Royal Horse Guards.
Captain T. C. Gurney, 2nd Life Guards.
Lieutenant A. L. E. Smith, 1st Life Guards.
Lieutenant D. E. Wallace, 2nd Life Guards.
Corporal of Horse J. Jordon, Royal Horse Guards.
Corporal of Horse A. H. Wilkins, 2nd Life Guards.

2ND DRAGOON GUARDS.

Lieutenant-Colonel H. W. Wilberforce.
Major G. H. A. Ing.
Captain E. S. Chance.
Lieutenant C. A. Heydeman.

MENTIONED IN DESPATCHES

Lieutenant A. J. Lamb, D.S.O.
Lance-Sergeant F. Webb.
Corporal G. Short.
Private J. Goodchild.
Private C. Horne.
Private F. W. Ellicock.

4TH DRAGOON GUARDS.

Lieutenant-Colonel R. L. Mullens.
Major G. T. M. Bridges, D.S.O. (now Lieutenant-Colonel).
Captain C. B. Hornby.
Lieutenant H. L. Jones, 13th Hussars (attached).
Squadron Serjeant-Major W. Sharpe.
Farrier Staff-Serjeant W. Old.
Squadron Serjeant-Major F. Talbot.
Quartermaster-Serjeant C. Syzling.

5TH DRAGOON GUARDS.

Lieutenant-Colonel G. K. Ansell (dead).
Captain E. W. S. Balfour.
Lieutenant V. D. S. Williams.
Regimental Serjeant-Major C. Pooley (now Second Lieutenant).
Squadron Serjeant-Major W. Langford.
Corporal J. Peach.
Serjeant F. Langford.

6TH DRAGOON GUARDS.

Major W. G. Home.
Captain M. N. Kennard.
Lieutenant R. M. Barnsley.
Lieutenant W. T. Gill.
Squadron Serjeant-Major F. J. Gilham.
Serjeant J. Higgins.
Lance-Corporal C. Griffiths.

2ND DRAGOONS.

Lieutenant-Colonel C. B. Bulkeley Johnson.
Major A. Lawson.
Captain W. Long.
Captain W. Duguid-McCombie.
Lieutenant G. F. A. Pigot-Moodie.
Lieutenant J. G. Crabbe.
Second Lieutenant J. G. R. Cooper.
Second Lieutenant E. R. F. Compton.
Lieutenant and Quartermaster D. Coutts.

MENTIONED IN DESPATCHES

Squadron Serjeant-Major Currie.
Serjeant Cranston.
Corporal Clunie.
Private McKleish.

3RD HUSSARS.

Lieutenant-Colonel A. A. Kennedy.
Captain F. J. Du Pre.
Lieutenant C. F. Clarke.
Farrier Quartermaster-Serjeant J. Town.
Serjeant E. Thornhill.
Corporal E. Walker.
Lance-Corporal G. Davidson.
Saddler Corporal W. Townsend.

4TH HUSSARS.

Major P. Howell.
Captain J. K. Gatacre, Indian Army (attached).
Lieutenant K. North.
Lieutenant R. Sherscon, Indian Army (attached).
Lieutenant L. H. Cripps (Special Reserve).
Squadron Serjeant-Major W. Dunsby (since granted a commission).
Squadron Serjeant-Major T. Pateman.
Serjeant T. Scotcher.
Serjeant F. Brown.
Serjeant J. Alexander.
Serjeant A. Sparham.
Lance-Serjeant S. Scopes.
Corporal Wm. Siddons.
Corporal P. Lonergan.
Corporal E. Robbins.
Corporal J. Lynch.
Corporal A. Page.
Corporal A. Laver.
Lance-Corporal W. Ashley.
Private W. Cooper.
Private F. Clark.
Private H. Long.
Private C. Turp.
Private D. Newbury.

5TH LANCERS.

Major J. B. Jardine, D.S.O.
Lieutenant B. W. Robinson.
Lieutenant H. C. Alexander.
Second Lieutenant W. H. Coulter.
Lieutenant T. De Burgh, Indian Army (attached).

MENTIONED IN DESPATCHES

Lieutenant Owen Gough, Indian Army (attached).
Serjeant C. Graham.
Corporal A. Davis.
Corporal R. Ware.
Corporal M. Shutt.
Lance-Corporal E. Wass.
Corporal D. G. Baker.
Corporal E. Grant.
Lance-Corporal G. Inch.
Lance-Corporal D. Mullock.
Serjeant F. D. Wyatt.

9TH LANCERS.

Lieutenant-Colonel D. G. M. Campbell.
Captain D. K. L. Lucas-Tooth (dead).
Captain F. O. Grenfell.
Captain L. Sadleir-Jackson.
Lieutenant R. L. Benson.
Squadron Serjeant-Major H. Durand.
Serjeant W. Turner.
Serjeant G. Davids.

11TH HUSSARS.

Lieutenant Hon. C. Mulholland.
Lieutenant J. S. Ainsworth.
Squadron Serjeant-Major J. Gardner.
Squadron Serjeant-Major G. W. Joslin.
Farrier Staff-Serjeant W. J. Jenkins.
Lance-Corporal A. H. Stevens.

12TH LANCERS.

Lieutenant-Colonel F. Wormald.
Major E. Crawley.
Major C. Fane, D.S.O.
Captain and Adjutant C. E. Bryant.
Lieutenant D. C. H. Richardson.
Lieutenant H. A. Brand.
Lieutenant B. G. Nicholas.
Squadron Serjeant-Major C. Hart.
Squadron Serjeant-Major W. Lockyer.
Squadron Serjeant-Major R. E. Vine.
Private J. Townsend.
Serjeant S. Clarke.

15TH HUSSARS.

Major F. C. Pilkington.
Captain Hon. W. A. Nugent.
Captain A. Courage.

MENTIONED IN DESPATCHES

Captain C. Nelson.
Lieutenant Hon. E. C. Hardinge.
Second Lieutenant G. H. Straker.
Serjeant F. Godden.
Serjeant H. J. Papworth.
Serjeant W. Blishen.
Lance-Serjeant A. J. Earle.
Corporal W. A. Mackay.
Corporal G. Sheppard.
Corporal W. Darley.
Corporal Garforth.
Private F. Aspinall.
Private W. H. Price.
Private W. Pearce.

16TH LANCERS.

Major C. J. Eccles.
Major C. L. K. Campbell.
Captain A. Neave.
Lieutenant E. H. L. Beddington.
Lieutenant E. R. Nash.
Lieutenant J. L. Cheyne.
Lieutenant R. A. J. Beech.
Lieutenant C. E. H. Tempest-Hicks.
Lieutenant D. R. Cross.
Lieutenant R. G. R. Davies.
Lieutenant J. L. Cheyne.
Second Lieutenant L. C. Ramsbottom Isherwood.
Second Lieutenant Lord Woodhouse (attached).
Squadron Serjeant-Major F. Pargeter.
Squadron Serjeant-Major H. C. Archer.
Serjeant W. Lindsay.
Serjeant E. Laurence.
Corporal F. J. Page.
Corporal G. W. Cooper.
Lance-Serjeant A. Roberts.
Saddler-Corporal D. Brown.
Lance-Corporal W. Jewkes.
Lance-Corporal G. Fuller.
Lance-Corporal J. H. Smith.
Lance-Corporal W. Holden.
Lance-Serjeant R. Carr.
Lance-Corporal W. F. Beaumont.

18TH HUSSARS.

Lieutenant G. Gore-Langton.

MENTIONED IN DESPATCHES

Serjeant W. G. Burt.
Shoeing-Smith M. Daly.

19TH HUSSARS.

Major A. W. Parsons.

20TH HUSSARS.

Lieutenant-Colonel G. T. G. Edwards.
Major A. C. Little.
Major M. E. Richardson.
Captain C. G. Mangles.
Lieutenant D. S. Peploe.
Lieutenant and Quartermaster W. Adams.
Serjeant J. L. Beavon.
Serjeant L. H. Halton.
Serjeant E. Clarke.
Corporal H. E. Poole.

MILITARY MOUNTED POLICE.

Serjeant H. Brooks.
Serjeant F. Willis.

NORTH IRISH HORSE.

Major A. W. J. C. Visct. Massereene and Ferrard, D.S.O.
Lieutenant R. A. West.

SOUTH IRISH HORSE.

Major I. W. Burns-Lindow.

ROYAL HORSE ARTILLERY.

Lieutenant-Colonel J. N. Birch.
Captain H. K. Bradbury (dead).
Lieutenant A. H. Burne.
Lieutenant J. D. Campbell (dead).
Lieutenant M. H. Dendy.
Major A. B. Forman.
Major G. Gillson.
Lieutenant J. B. Gough.
Captain W. W. Jelf.
Lieutenant L. H. Mundy (dead).
Lieutenant R. L. Palmer.
Lieutenant G. J. P. St. Clair.
Captain R. H. Sanderson.
Major H. S. Seligman.
Captain H. S. Stanham.
Lieutenant C. L. T. Walwyn.
Corporal S. S. Arkinstall.
Gunner J. B. Carry.

MENTIONED IN DESPATCHES

Serjeant A. Castle.
Driver A. Conie.
Serjeant E. Hodder.
Serjeant H. E. Pitt.
Gunner J. A. Saunders.
Driver W. Smith.
Regimental Serjeant-Major R. Y. K. Walker.
Serjeant J. Wedlock.

ROYAL FIELD ARTILLERY.

Captain E. W. Browne.
Captain J. R. Colville.
Lieutenant G. E. A. Granet.
Lieutenant-Colonel H. E. Hockdale.
Driver Blackwell, 31st Battery.
Driver W. Mills, 88th Battery.
Driver Neil, 88th Battery.
Gunner L. R. Rimington, 88th Battery.
Trumpeter E. T. Steel, 55th Battery.

8TH BRIGADE ROYAL FIELD ARTILLERY.

Lieutenant-Colonel E. J. Duffus.
Major F. A. Wilson, D.S.O.
Captain D. Reynolds.
Lieutenant E. G. Earle.
Serjeant T. Brown.
Trumpeter F. Waldron.
Driver J. H. C. Drain.
Driver F. Luke.
Serjeant Bowers.
Gunner Garlick.
Gunner Baker.
Driver Treloar.
Driver Hall.
Driver Prior.
Gunner Fraser.
Gunner Turner.
Driver Robertson.

14TH BRIGADE ROYAL FIELD ARTILLERY.

Lieutenant-Colonel C. M. Ross-Johnson, D.S.O.
Lieutenant A. Dawson.
Battery Serjeant-Major W. Count.

MENTIONED IN DESPATCHES

15TH BRIGADE ROYAL FIELD ARTILLERY.
Lieutenant-Colonel C. F. Stevens.
Major C. N. B. Ballard.
Captain A. B. Higgon.
Farrier Quartermaster-Serjeant H. J. S. Watts.
Battery Quartermaster-Serjeant V. Hill.
Driver F. S. Brown.

23RD BRIGADE ROYAL FIELD ARTILLERY.
Lieutenant-Colonel A. T. Butler.
Major S. F. Metcalfe.
Captain E. S. Allsup.
Lieutenant E. L. B. Anderson.
Lieutenant D. Hill.
Lieutenant J. C. Forsyth.
Battery Serjeant-Major W. Keegan.
Battery Serjeant-Major W. H. Solman.
Battery Quartermaster-Serjeant G. Peck.
Battery Quartermaster-Serjeant J. Smith.
Battery Quartermaster-Serjeant B. W. Rogers.
Farrier Quartermaster-Serjeant E. Rivett.
Serjeant A. L. Perry.
Corporal A. Johnson.
Corporal G. Norman.

25TH BRIGADE ROYAL FIELD ARTILLERY.
Lieutenant-Colonel W. Gillman.
Major W. Ellershaw.
Lieutenant G. E. W. Franklin.
Battery Serjeant-Major A. Stroudley.
Trumpeter A. C. Cockaday.
Serjeant H. Squelch.
Corporal (now Farrier-Serjeant) S. S. T. Kendall.
Farrier-Serjeant T. Harrison.

26TH BRIGADE ROYAL FIELD ARTILLERY.
Lieutenant-Colonel C. Cunliffe-Owen.
Major G. H. W. Nicholson.
Major H. N. Packard.
Captain T. C. Sinclair.
Gunner W. J. Franklin.
Battery Quartermaster-Serjeant Booth.
Serjeant W. Williams.
Battery Quartermaster-Serjeant G. Oakes.

MENTIONED IN DESPATCHES

27TH BRIGADE ROYAL FIELD ARTILLERY.
Lieutenant-Colonel W. H. Onslow.
Major N. W. Alexander.
Captain G. Masters.
Captain F. F. Congreve.
Lieutenant C. O. D. Preston.
Second Lieutenant H. E. Chapman.
Lieutenant L. E. O. Davidson.
Second Lieutenant R. Staveley.
Battery Quartermaster-Serjeant A. Board.
Bombardier F. Holton.
Driver E. Street.
Driver C. Burkitt.

28TH BRIGADE ROYAL FIELD ARTILLERY.
Lieutenant-Colonel E. C. Cameron.
Major G. H. Saunders.
Captain A. G. Gillman.
Lieutenant A. R. Rainy.
Second Lieutenant R. W. McLeod.
Serjeant W. J. Carnegie.

29TH BRIGADE ROYAL FIELD ARTILLERY.
Major H. G. Lloyd.
Serjeant Sullivan, 127th Battery.

30TH BRIGADE ROYAL FIELD ARTILLERY (HOWITZER).
Lieutenant-Colonel W. C. Staveley.
Major L. T. Ashworth.
Captain A. E. Newland.
Captain H. K. Sadler.
Battery Serjeant-Major A. Hall.
Battery Serjeant-Major A. J. Owen.
Battery Quartermaster-Serjeant F. C. Maskell.
Battery Quartermaster-Serjeant J. J. Bourne.
Battery Quartermaster-Serjeant E. W. Clarke.
Staff Serjeant-Farrier A. R. Benbrook.
Serjeant A. G. Cooney.
Corporal H. W. Stubbs.
Corporal W. Theobald.
Bombardier R. J. Fuller.

32ND BRIGADE ROYAL FIELD ARTILLERY.
Lieutenant-Colonel M. J. MacCarthy.
Major H. E. Vallentin, D.S.O.

MENTIONED IN DESPATCHES

Major C. H. Liveing.
Captain C. A. Mortimore.
Second Lieutenant C. H. Rogers.
Battery Quartermaster-Serjeant Kerr.
Saddler Quartermaster-Serjeant Alger.
Serjeant Jenkins, 27th Battery.
Driver O'Brien, 135th Battery.

34TH BRIGADE ROYAL FIELD ARTILLERY.

Lieutenant-Colonel H. G. Sandilands.
Major H. T. Wynter (killed).
Major H. J. Mackey, M.V.O.
Lieutenant E. J. M. Robertson.
Lieutenant J. E. L. Clarke (dead).
Second Lieutenant H. W. Huggins.
Second Lieutenant A. A. M. Durand.
Brigade Serjeant-Major C. Stammers.
Farrier-Serjeant W. Cook.

36TH BRIGADE ROYAL FIELD ARTILLERY.

Major and Brevet Lieutenant-Colonel C. G. Stewart, D.S.O.
Lieutenant D. R. Macdonald.
Lieutenant A. L. P. Griffith.
Second Lieutenant P. E. Inchbald.
Bombardier W. D. Vellers.

40TH BRIGADE ROYAL FIELD ARTILLERY.

Lieutenant-Colonel R. J. G. Elkington.
Major G. W. S. Brooke.
Major C. St. M. Ingham.
Captain R. A. Anstruther.
Captain E. L. Ellington.
Battery Serjeant-Major H. Grant.
Battery Serjeant-Major C. J. Newcombe.
Battery Serjeant-Major A. Moore.
Serjeant J. Clarke.
Driver F. Price.
Driver H. J. King.
Driver W. Dickerson.

41ST BRIGADE ROYAL FIELD ARTILLERY.

Lieutenant D. D. Rose (dead).
Driver W. Chadwick.
Gunner F. Powe.
Driver W. Austen.

MENTIONED IN DESPATCHES

42ND BRIGADE ROYAL FIELD ARTILLERY.

Lieutenant-Colonel G. H. Geddes.
Major T. Bruce.
Captain H. L. Nevill, D.S.O.
Lieutenant P. S. Myburgh.
Serjeant G. Mallinson.
Bombardier G. Langley.
Gunner R. Townhill.
Gunner W. Scott.
Driver F. Marshall.
Driver A. Amy.
Driver J. Nicholson.
Corporal J. P. Gallivan.

43RD BRIGADE ROYAL FIELD ARTILLERY.

Major E. B. Macnaghten.
Captain F. W. Robinson.
Captain R. Longstaff.
Serjeant W. Clarke.
A. Bombardier W. Whitby.

44TH BRIGADE ROYAL FIELD ARTILLERY.

Lieutenant-Colonel D. Arbuthnot.
Lieutenant J. P. Knight.
Brigade Quartermaster-Serjeant W. H. Jillard.
Gunner A. Belford.
Driver C. Kerridge.

DIVISIONAL AMMUNITION COLUMN.

Captain and Adjutant H. Cornes.
Captain G. M. A. Gregory.
Captain E. White.
Regimental Serjeant-Major R. R. W. Bell.
Staff-Serjeant-Farrier W. Salter, Royal Garrison Artillery
Quartermaster-Serjeant H. Cutbush, Divisional Ammunition Column
Corporal D. Dixon, 36th Brigade Ammunition Column.
Gunner J. Henderson, Royal Garrison Artillery.

ROYAL GARRISON ARTILLERY.

Brevet-Colonel G. Franks.
Serjeant S. Elvin.

48TH (HEAVY) BATTERY ROYAL GARRISON ARTILLERY.

Major C. F. Phipps.

MENTIONED IN DESPATCHES

Captain J. B. Walker.
Serjeant Teasdale.
Corporal G. Smale.
Gunner Keeble.
Gunner J. Bryant.

108TH (HEAVY) BATTERY ROYAL GARRISON ARTILLERY.

Major C. De Sausmarez, D.S.O.
Captain Sir F. N. Elphinstone-Dalrymple, Bt.
Battery Quartermaster-Serjeant W. E. Warren.

ROYAL ENGINEERS.

Captain P. R. Bald.
Lieutenant R. L. Bond.
Major M. G. E. Bowman-Manifold, D.S.O.
Lieutenant-Colonel R. H. H. Boys, D.S.O.
Captain H. E. Day.
Captain W. G. S. Dobbie.
Captain R. V. Howell Doherty.
Captain G. F. Evans.
Lieutenant R. B. Flint.
Captain H. G. Gandy.
Lieutenant A. E. Grasset.
Major A. B. R. Hildebrand.
Major F. G. Howard, M.V.O.
Captain and Adjutant L. C. Jackson, C.M.G.
Captain W. H. Johnston.
Captain O. L. Jordan, 1st Field Squadron.
Lieutenant G. le Q. Martel.
Lieutenant C. G. Martin.
Captain J. J. H. Nation.
Lieutenant R. F. B. Naylor.
Lieutenant C. L. Y. Parker.
Lieutenant J. A. C. Pennycuick.
Captain R. M. Powell, Royal Garrison Artillery (attached).
Captain C. H. Prickett.
Major H. L. Pritchard.
Major C. Russell-Brown.
Major E. Sandys.
Major C. W. Singer.
Lieutenant G. B. F. Smyth.
Colonel J. A. S. Tulloch.
Major G. Walker.
Lieutenant J. Watson.
Captain W. N. Webber.

MENTIONED IN DESPATCHES

Captain J. White.
Lieutenant-Colonel C. S. Wilson.
Lieutenant R. G. Wright.
Captain T. Wright.
Pioneer R. Arthur (killed).
Company Quartermaster-Serjeant W. Barnham.
Sapper L. Bloomfield.
Corporal A. Box.
Quartermaster-Serjeant W. P. Britton.
Corporal C. A. Brocklebank.
Serjeant J. Buckle.
Sapper H. S. Bunyard.
Corporal C. W. Cadman, Motor Cyclist.
Serjeant W. Carvell.
Serjeant E. Chidgey.
Serjeant F. Colvin.
Pioneer E. Cottington.
Sapper E. Doney.
Lance-Corporal R. Dorey.
Serjeant R. Eyres.
Pioneer R. Fielding.
Serjeant H. E. Gallagher.
Corporal J. Geraghty.
Serjeant E. J. Goodhart.
Corporal S. W. Hallett.
Serjeant W. Hayward.
Serjeant E. W. Hinton.
Corporal T. G. Hobson.
Corporal D. Humphries, Motor Cyclist.
Lance-Corporal R. Hyne.
Sapper J. Jack.
Lance-Corporal C. A. Jarvis.
Sapper M. J. Keane.
Pioneer L. Layton.
Corporal W. Lewis.
Serjeant H. E. Mallows.
Sapper S. Middleton.
Sapper C. W. Moreton.
Corporal T. P. Morris.
Serjeant W. F. Norrington.
Serjeant F. Paine.
Co. Serjeant-Major A. G. Palmer.
Sapper R. W. Pardy.
Corporal (since promoted Second Lieutenant) C. F. Portal.
Corporal A. J. S. Proston.
Serjeant J. Quinlan.

MENTIONED IN DESPATCHES

Serjeant J. Quinney.
Serjeant A. Q. Roberts.
Sapper J. R. Roberts.
Serjeant E. J. Runyeard.
Corporal H. Salt.
Corporal T. J. Scaife.
Corporal H. U. Scrutton.
Corporal J. A. Scrutton.
Serjeant A. E. Smith.
Sapper A. J. Sourbutts.
Corporal S. F. C. Stackard.
Second Corporal W. Steele.
Serjeant E. G. Taylor.
Company Serjeant-Major G. Tibble.
Second Corporal C. Todd.
Corporal H. Trepas.
Serjeant W. Weeks.
Company Serjeant-Major M. R. G. Williams.
Sapper W. Winchester.
Serjeant J. Wood.

FOOT GUARDS.

2ND BATTALION GRENADIER GUARDS.

Captain A. Gosselin.
Lieutenant Hon. W. A. Cecil (killed).
Lieutenant R. W. Welby (killed).
Serjeant-Major E. Ludlow.
Corporal F. Parsons.
Lance-Corporal P. McDonnell.
Private C. Rule.

1ST BATTALION COLDSTREAM GUARDS.

Lieut.-Colonel J. Ponsonby, D.S.O.
Captain W. St. A. Warde-Aldam.
Lieutenant and Adjutant G. Campbell.
Lieutenant J. C. Wynne Finch.
Company Quartermaster-Serjeant J. Duggan.
Serjeant A. White.
Lance-Corporal N. Mitchell.
Serjeant T. Harris.
Corporal (temporary Serjeant) T. Fletcher.

2ND BATTALION COLDSTREAM GUARDS.

Lieutenant-Colonel C. E. Pereira.
Major R. A. Markham.

MENTIONED IN DESPATCHES

Captain F. Hardy.
Captain G. B. S. Follett.
Serjeant-Major J. Clancey.
Company Serjeant-Major G. Link.
Serjeant W. Watson.
Lance-Corporal A. Brown.
Private F. W. Dodson.

3RD BATTALION COLDSTREAM GUARDS.

Lieutenant-Colonel G. P. T. Fielding, D.S.O.
Major T. G. Matheson.
Captain A. Tritton.
Lieutenant and Adjutant A. Smith.
Second Lieutenant C. M. Cotrell Dormer.
Lieutenant J. L. Huggan, Royal Army Medical Corps (killed).
C. S. M. Jackson.
Company Serjeant-Major J. Ivey.
Serjeant M. Marks.
Lance-Serjeant W. Small.
Lance-Corporal B. Prentice.
Private E. Godding.
Private E. Batey.
Private G. Wyatt.
Private A. Thomas.
Private H. Chidler.

1ST BATTALION SCOTS GUARDS.

Lieutenant-Colonel H. C. Lowther, C.M.G., D.S.O.
Captain and Adjutant A. L. Stephen, D.S.O.
Company Quartermaster-Serjeant G. Blake.
Private D. Boyle.
Serjeant-Major T. Tate.

1ST BATTALION IRISH GUARDS.

Lieutenant-Colonel Hon. G. Morris (killed).
Major H. F. Crichton (killed).
Lieutenant Hon. H. W. Gough.
Lieutenant H. J. S. Shields, Royal Army Medical Corps.
Company Serjeant-Major Rodgers.
Drill-Serjeant A. Winspear.
Serjeant A. McEnroy.
Corporal P. Sheridan.
Private J. Carney.

MENTIONED IN DESPATCHES

2ND BATTALION ROYAL SCOTS.

Lieutenant-Colonel H. McMicking, D.S.O.
Major F. J. Duncan, D.S.O.
Captain C. L. Price.
Captain R. P. Morrison.
Lieutenant G. E. Hall.
Lieutenant M. Henderson.
Company Quartermaster-Serjeant J. Lamond.
Company Quartermaster-Serjeant J. A. Carleton.
Serjeant-Major J. H. Martin.
Serjeant J. Gallagher.
Serjeant C. Whaley.
Lance-Corporal I. Voyes.

1ST BATTALION ROYAL WEST SURREY REGIMENT.

Lieutenant-Colonel D. Warren (killed).
Captain C. F. Watson, D.S.O.
Captain R. G. Clarke.
Captain F. C. Longbourne.
Serjeant Graham.
Corporal Hammond.
Lance-Corporal Debell.
Private Lawrence.
Private E. Austin.
Drummer Wise.
Drummer Green.

1ST BATTALION ROYAL LANCASTER REGIMENT.

Major R. G. Parker.
Captain C. H. Grover.
Captain W. A. T. B. Somerville.
Lieutenant T. J. Uzielli.
Captain H. Clutterbuck.
Serjeant-Major Dakin.
Corporal Wright.

1ST BATTALION NORTHUMBERLAND FUSILIERS.

Lieutenant-Colonel H. S. Ainslie.
Major C. Yatman, D.S.O.
Captain H. S. Toppin.
Captain W. N. Herbert.
Lieutenant G. O. Sloper.
Second Lieutenant E. F. Boyd.
Captain M. Leckie, Royal Army Medical Corps (attached).
Company Serjeant-Major D. Condon.

MENTIONED IN DESPATCHES

Serjeant A. Laws.
Serjeant J. E. Fenemore.
Serjeant J. Squires.
Lance-Corporal S. Bently.
Private V. Gorton.

1st Battalion Royal Warwickshire Regiment.

Major A. J. Poole.
Major W. C. Christie.
Captain C. F. Burnard.
Serjeant P. Thornton.

4th Battalion Royal Fusiliers.

Lieutenant-Colonel N. R. McMahon, D.S.O.
Major T. R. Mallock, D.S.O.
Captain L. F. Ashburner, M.V.O., D.S.O.
Captain L. W. Le M. Carey.
Lieutenant F. W. A. Steele.
Lieutenant M. J. Dease.
Lieutenant G. O'D. F. Thomas O'Donel.
Serjeant-Major E. W. Tyler.
Company Serjeant-Major G. D. Attewell.
Serjeant H. Savill.
Serjeant M. W. Lindsay.
Serjeant W. F. Osborne.
Lance-Corporal W. Evans.
Lance-Corporal G. Moore.
Private S. Godley.

1st Battalion The King's (Liverpool) Regiment.

Lieutenant-Colonel W. S. Bannatyne.
Captain J. H. S. Batten.
Captain and Adjutant E. Hudson.
Lieutenant D. G. H. H. Scott-Tucker.
Serjeant-Major T. H. Cuddy.
Company Serjeant-Major M. Swannick.
Serjeant M. Fitznolan.
Lance-Corporal J. Blackburn.

2nd Battalion South Staffordshire Regiment.

Lieutenant-Colonel C. S. Davidson.
Captain M. B. Savage.
Private J. Littlewood.
Private A. Mutlow.

MENTIONED IN DESPATCHES

Lance-Corporal H. Watkins.
Serjeant W. Gascoyne.

1st Battalion Norfolk Regiment.

Lieutenant Colonel C. R. Ballard.
Major H. R. Done.
Captain C. E. Luard, D.S.O.
Lieutenant G. C. Lyle.
Captain T. R. Bowlby.
Company Serjeant-Major A. Haymes.
Serjeant R. Francis.
Serjeant C. Pryer.
Corporal H. Smith.
Private P. S. Nicholson.
Private H. Stevens.
Company Serjeant-Major W. Selves (5th Cyclist Company).
Serjeant Rushbrook (5th Cyclist Company).

1st Battalion Lincolnshire Regiment.

Major C. Toogood, D.S.O.
Captain F. W. Greatwood.
Captain H. C. W. Hoskyns.
Captain R. E. Drake.
Lieutenant C. O. Holmes.
Captain G. A. Kempthorne, Royal Army Medical Corps (attached).
Serjeant-Major A. Stapleton.
Serjeant F. Davis.
Serjeant W. Garrett.
Lance-Corporal H. Barlow.
Lance-Corporal A. Brett.
Lance-Corporal S. Yorks.
Private E. J. Stroulger.
Private W. Nix.

2nd Battalion Suffolk Regiment.

Lieutenant-Colonel C. A. H. Brett, D.S.O. (dead).
Serjeant-Major R. Burton.
Company Quartermaster-Serjeant W. Curtis.
Drummer L. Jones.

1st Battalion Somerset Light Infantry.

Major C. B. Prowse.
Captain L. A. Jones-Mortimer.
Captain W. Watson.
Corporal F. Wilcox.

MENTIONED IN DESPATCHES

1st Battalion Bedford Regiment.

Lieutenant-Colonel C. R. J. Griffith, D.S.O.
Captain R. J. McCloughin.
Lieutenant C. E. G. Shearman.
Lieutenant A. G. Corah (Cyclist Company).
Serjeant P. Hunt.
Serjeant R. Hawkins.
Corporal E. Higdon.
Private S. Seaman.
Private W. Jackson.
Dr. H. Chequer.

2nd Battalion Royal Irish Regiment.

Lieutenant-Colonel St. John A. Cox.
Major E. H. E. Daniell, D.S.O.
Lieutenant F. H. L. Rushton.
Regimental Quartermaster-Serjeant T. W. Fitzpatrick.
Serjeant Boyd.
Serjeant-Major J. F. Plunkett.
Serjeant J. Burne.
Lance-Corporal J. Delaney.
Private N. Fernie.
Private J. Doherty.

2nd Battalion Lancashire Fusiliers.

Captain A. H. Spooner.
Major C. J. Griffin.
Private Wilcox.

2nd Battalion Royal Inniskilling Fusiliers.

Major C. A. Wilding.
Lance-Corporal Parkinson.
Private Kelly, " B " Company.

2nd Battalion Royal Scots Fusiliers.

Lieutenant-Colonel W. D. Smith.
Major A. M. H. Forbes.
Captain G. C. Briggs.
Captain J. D. Tullis.
Captain H. G. B. Miller.
Captain T. B. Traill.
Lieutenant B. H. Badham.
Lieutenant C. J. Lyon.
Second Lieutenant E. L. L. Anderson.

MENTIONED IN DESPATCHES

Regimental Quartermaster-Serjeant R. Harrison.
Lance-Corporal G. Mack.

1st Battalion Cheshire Regiment.

Lieutenant-Colonel D. C. Boger.
Captain J. L. Shore.
Captain W. S. Rich.
Lieutenant W. G. R. Elliot.
Company Serjeant-Major J. W. Francis.
Serjeant Edge.
Serjeant W. A. Norris.
Private Burns.
Lance-Corporal A. Smith.
Private F. MacCarthy.

2nd Battalion Royal Welch Fusiliers.

Private F. Jackson.
Private E. Edwards.

1st Battalion South Wales Borderers.

Lieutenant-Colonel H. E. B. Leach.
Major W. L. Lawrence.
Captain W. O. Prichard.
Lieutenant and Adjutant C. J. Patterson.
Lieutenant J. C. Coker (killed).
Serjeant G. Duffy.
Private H. Godfrey.
Private H. Cudlip.

2nd Battalion King's Own Scottish Borderers.

Lieutenant-Colonel C. N. Stephenson.
Major A. E. Haig.
Major E. S. De Coke.
Captain G. W. Smith.
Lieutenant J. R. Hamilton-Dalrymple.
Serjeant-Major N. MacWhinne.
Company Serjeant-Major R. Fuller.
Company Quartermaster-Serjeant Geggie.
Serjeant Kirkwood.
Serjeant P. Welsh.

1st Battalion Scottish Rifles.

Captain T. S. Riddell-Webster.

MENTIONED IN DESPATCHES

1st Battalion Gloucestershire Regiment.

Lieutenant-Colonel A. C. Lovett.
Captain and Adjutant A. H. Radice.
Second Lieutenant W. F. Watkins (Special Reserve).
Company Serjeant-Major W. Hodges.
Drummer C. Fluck.
Private Law.
Private T. Orr.

2nd Battalion Worcestershire Regiment.

Lieutenant-Colonel C. B. Westmacott.
Lieutenant C. Deakin.
Lance-Corporal J. Davis.
Private W. Sheldon.
Private E. Murrell.
Private W. Starting.

3rd Battalion Worcestershire Regiment.

Major W. R. Chichester.
Captain C. V. Beresford.
Captain L. C. Dorman.
Lieutenant S. A. Gabb.
Second Lieutenant S. A. Goldsmid.
Company Serjeant-Major M. J. Murphy.
Company Serjeant-Major F. Workman.
Company Serjeant-Major H. J. Farley.
Serjeant L. T. Vicarage.
Serjeant J. Johnson.
Lance-Corporal W. McNally.
Lance-Corporal R. Whittington.
Corporal J. Jewsbury.
Lance-Corporal J. Bingham.
Private W. Malone.
Private W. Heritage.
Private J. Ware.

1st Battalion East Lancashire Regiment.

Lieutenant-Colonel L. St. G. Le Marchant, D.S.O.
Corporal J. Lismore.

1st Battalion East Surrey Regiment.

Lieutenant-Colonel J. R. Longley.
Major H. S. Tew.
Captain E. M. Wolfe Flanagan.

MENTIONED IN DESPATCHES

Captain Hon. A. R. Hewitt.
Captain M. J. Minogue.
Captain F. A. Bowring.
Serjeant-Major G. E. Hyson.
Company Quartermaster-Serjeant W. J. Woolger.
Serjeant R. Hunt.
Serjeant M. L. Hill.
Serjeant H. Hunt.
Private J. Wilkins.

1ST BATTALION DUKE OF CORNWALL'S LIGHT INFANTRY.

Lieutenant-Colonel M. N. Turner.
Major T. H. F. Price.
Major J. H. T. Cornish Bowden.
Captain C. B. Woodham.
Lieutenant A. N. Acland.
Lieutenant A. J. S. Hammans.
Company Serjeant-Major J. S. Woolcot.
Company Serjeant-Major C. Willis.
Serjeant L. M. Timbury.
Corporal A. J. Richardson.
Corporal W. Evans.
Corporal R. Stevens.

2ND BATTALION WEST RIDING REGIMENT.

Lieutenant-Colonel J. A. C. Gibbs.
Major P. B. Strafford.
Major E. N. Townsend.
Major K. A. Macleod.
Captain C. O. Denman-Jubb.
Captain J. C. Burnett (O.C. Cyclist Company).
Second Lieutenant H. K. O'Kelly.
Company Quartermaster-Serjeant J. E. Wiggins.
Corporal H. Waller.
Private T. Ford.
Private J. Robertshaw.
Private E. Hammond.
Private H. Sanson.

2ND BATTALION ROYAL SUSSEX REGIMENT.

Major E. W. B. Green.
Captain C. E. Bond, D.S.O.
Lieutenant V. E. C. Dashwood.
Lance-Serjeant C. Clay.
Serjeant T. Diplock.
Private J. Still.

MENTIONED IN DESPATCHES

1st Battalion Hampshire Regiment.

Brevet-Colonel S. C. F. Jackson, D.S.O.
Captain Hon. L. C. W. Palk.
Captain P. M. Connelan.
Lieutenant B. B. von B. im Thurn.
Private J. Holloway.

1st Battalion Dorsetshire Regiment.

Lieutenant-Colonel L. J. Bols, D.S.O.
Captain H. S. Williams.
Lieutenant C. H. Woodhouse.
Lieutenant C. F. M. Margetts.
Serjeant E. A. Hill.
Private T. Skipsey.
Private R. Gent.
Private W. Shoufield.
Private J. Iles.
Lance-Corporal B. Lawrence (5th Cyclist Company).

2nd Battalion South Lancashire Regiment.

Captain W. B. Ritchie.
Lieutenant L. A. Clemens.
Lieutenant B. V. Fulcher.
Lieutenant S. T. Boast (Quartermaster).
Serjeant-Major T. Roberts.
Serjeant W. Harrison.
Serjeant J. Boast.
Company Serjeant-Major J. Murphy.
Serjeant A. Leavers.
Corporal J. Jones.
Corporal P. McQuiggan.
Private S. Riddell.
Serjeant F. Winser.

2nd Battalion The Welsh Regiment.

Lieutenant-Colonel C. B. Morland.
Captain and Adjutant W. H. Ferrar.
Captain C. R. Berkeley, D.S.O.
Lieutenant C. A. S. Carleton.
Lieutenant G. D. Melville.
Company Quartermaster-Serjeant J. B. Cownie.
Company Serjeant-Major G. Hunter.
Serjeant A. Smedley.
Private W. Fuller.

MENTIONED IN DESPATCHES

1st Battalion Royal Highlanders.
Major J. T. C. Murray.
Captain Hon. M. C. A. Drummond.
Lieutenant and Adjutant G. Rowan-Hamilton.
Lieutenant R. C. Anderson.
Serjeant J. Duncan.
Lance-Corporal A. Dewar.
Private J. Reilly.

2nd Oxfordshire and Buckinghamshire Light Infantry.
Lieutenant-Colonel H. R. Davies.
Captain G. Blewitt.
Private W. R. Carter.
Private G. F. Payne.
Private A. Kippax.
Lance-Corporal H. Apsey.

2nd Battalion Essex Regiment.
Lieutenant-Colonel F. G. Anley.
Major G. M. Tufnell.
Captain and Adjutant L. O. W. Jones.
Serjeant Purchase.
Corporal Downes.

1st Battalion Loyal North Lancashire Regiment.
Major A. Burrows.
Captain L. T. Allason.
Lieutenant E. J. W. Spread.
Lieutenant J. G. W. Hyndson.
Serjeant-Major W. Waterhouse.
Lance-Corporal F. J. Bowler.
Private F. Lemar.
Private J. Poole.
Drummer G. Gale.

1st Battalion Northamptonshire Regiment.
Lieutenant-Colonel E. O. Smith.
Lieutenant G. St. G. Robinson.
Lieutenant E. J. Needham.
Second Lieutenant L. H. B. Burlton.
Company Serjeant-Major H. F. Pitcher.
Serjeant F. Johnson.

MENTIONED IN DESPATCHES

1st Royal Berkshire Regiment.

Lieutenant-Colonel M. D. Graham.
Captain L. H. Birt.
Lieutenant C. St. Q. O. Fullbrook-Leggatt.
Private A. Ross.
Private E. Philps.

1st Battalion Royal West Kent Regiment.

Lieutenant-Colonel A. Martyn.
Major M. P. Buckle, D.S.O.
Captain R. M. G. Tulloch.
Lieutenant G. B. Legard.
Serjeant-Major H. S. Doe.
Company Serjeant-Major W. Penny.
Serjeant J. Powell.
Serjeant J. Saward.
Lance-Corporal J. Ryan.
Private G. Biggs.

2nd Battalion King's Own Yorkshire Light Infantry.

Lieutenant-Colonel R. C. Bond, D.S.O.
Major C. A. L. Yate.
Major H. E. Trevor.
Major C. E. Heathcote.
Captain J. E. Simpson.
Lieutenant W. de E. Williams.
Lieutenant C. E. D. King.
Company Serjeant-Major E. Millen.
Company Quartermaster-Serjeant Wall.
Serjeant C. J. Marchant.
Corporal A. Medley.
Lance-Corporal F. W. Holmes.
Lance-Corporal C. Warrilow.
Private H. Fendley.
Private H. Normanton.

1st Battalion Middlesex Regiment.

Lieutenant-Colonel B. E. Ward.
Major R. J. Ross.
Lieutenant W. Jefferd.
Corporal J. G. Johnson.

4th Battalion Middlesex Regiment.

Lieutenant-Colonel C. P. A. Hull.
Major H. W. E. Finch.

MENTIONED IN DESPATCHES

Captain G. Oliver.
Lieutenant L. F. Sloane-Stanley.
Company Serjeant-Major R. Sayers.
Serjeant E. E. Jackson.
Serjeant G. Varnham.
Corporal C. Tyler.

1st KING'S ROYAL RIFLE CORPS.

Lieutenant-Colonel E. Northey.
Lieutenant H. H. Prince Maurice of Battenberg.
Captain F. G. Willan.
Lieutenant A. L. Bonham Carter.
Second Lieutenant H. W. Butler.
Second Lieutenant A. H. Wilkie.
Second Lieutenant T. N. Hone.
Captain H. S. Ranken, Royal Army Medical Corps (attached).
Company Serjeant-Major F. Dickerson.
Company Serjeant-Major C. F. Schoon.
Rifleman E. Revell.
Rifleman P. Warr (killed).

2nd BATTALION KING'S ROYAL RIFLE CORPS.

Lieutenant-Colonel E. Pearce-Serocold.
Major L. F. Phillips.
Major H. C. Warre, D.S.O.
Major R. G. Jelf.
Captain W. A. I. Kay.
Lieutenant R. J. H. Purcell.
Lieutenant J. H. S. Dimmer.
Second Lieutenant O. H. C. Balfour.
Company Serjeant-Major F. Dean.
Company Serjeant-Major Walton.
Corporal Chevis.
Rifleman Varley.
Rifleman Stagg.

2nd BATTALION WILTSHIRE REGIMENT.

Lieutenant-Colonel A. W. Hasted.
Lieutenant T. H. Wand-Tetley.
Captain W. I. Cordon (Quartermaster).
Company Quartermaster-Serjeant W. G. Lister.
Serjeant A. Lodder.
Lance-Corporal C. Street.

MENTIONED IN DESPATCHES

2ND BATTALION MANCHESTER REGIMENT.

Lieutenant-Colonel H. L. James.
Captain F. S. Nisbet (dead).
Captain H. Knox.
Lieutenant J. H. L. Reade.
Lieutenant J. S. Harper.
Company Serjeant-Major Wood.
Company Quartermaster-Serjeant J. Morris.
Serjeant Winterbottom.
Serjeant M. Richards.
Serjeant Rice.
Private Hodges.

2ND BATTALION HIGHLAND LIGHT INFANTRY.

Lieutenant-Colonel A. A. Wolfe-Murray.
Lieutenant A. P. D. Telfer-Smollett.
Lieutenant Sir A. C. Gibson Craig, Bart. (killed).
Serjeant J. Nicholson.
Private J. Webber.
Private J. Campbell.
Private G. Wilson.

2ND BATTALION SEAFORTH HIGHLANDERS.

Lieutenant-Colonel Sir Evelyn Bradford, Bart.

1ST BATTALION GORDON HIGHLANDERS.

Lieutenant-Colonel F. H. Neish.
Serjeant J. Boyce.
Serjeant J. Dunbar.
Private A. Ross.

1ST BATTALION CAMERON HIGHLANDERS.

Lieutenant D. Cameron.
Second Lieutenant R. N. Stewart.
Company Serjeant-Major D. Tavendale.
Serjeant J. Ford.
Private K. Boag.
Private D. Hill.

2ND BATTALION ROYAL IRISH RIFLES.

Lieutenant-Colonel W. D. Bird, D.S.O.
Major C. R. Spedding, D.S.O.
Captain C. L. Master.
Captain C. M. L. Becher.

MENTIONED IN DESPATCHES

Captain H. R. Goodman.
Lieutenant S. S. Dillon.
Lieutenant V. L. S. Cowley.
Lieutenant A. N. Whitfield.
Captain S. E. Lewis, Royal Army Medical Corps (attached).
Serjeant E. Henry.
Lance-Corporal H. Murray.
Lance-Corporal J. Behan.
Private J. O'Connor.

2ND BATTALION ROYAL IRISH FUSILIERS.

Second Lieutenant W. H. Liesching.
Company-Serjeant-Major E. Scrafield.
Serjeant Wilson, " C " Company.
Drummer Corrigan.

2ND BATTALION CONNAUGHT RANGERS.

Lieutenant R. I. Thomas (killed).
Second Lieutenant R. L. Spreckley (killed).
Serjeant-Major W. Bluen (? Bruen).
Serjeant M. Duffy.

2ND BATTALION ARGYLL AND SUTHERLAND HIGHLANDERS.

Captain H. Hyslop.
Lieutenant R. M. G. Aytoun.
Second Lieutenant Ian McA. Stewart.
Company Serjeant-Major F. Walker.
Lance-Serjeant J. Taylor.

2ND BATTALION ROYAL DUBLIN FUSILIERS.

Lieutenant T. J. Leahy.
Company Serjeant-Major Hall.
Serjeant Ray.

1ST BATTALION RIFLE BRIGADE.

Major S. H. Rickman.
Major G. N. Salmon.
Captain Hon. F. R. D. Prittie.
Captain G. J. Brownlow.
Captain Hon. R. G. G. Morgan-Grenville.
Captain H. L. Riley.
Lieutenant H. F. Campbell.
Company Quartermaster-Serjeant Hedges.
Serjeant Roberts.
Corporal J. Smith.

MENTIONED IN DESPATCHES

ARMY SERVICE CORPS.

Captain L. C. Bearne.
Major H. Cracroft.
Captain O. B. R. Dickey.
Lieutenant-Colonel E. C. F. Gillespie.
Captain G. Harding.
Captain A. Herklots.
Captain R. R. B. Jackson.
Major T. P. Johnson.
Second Lieutenant C. W. R. Langmaid.
Major J. G. Lecky.
Lieutenant-Colonel A. G. Master.
Second Lieutenant C. J. Martin.
Major A. Northen.
Captain A. F. G. Pery-Knox-Gore.
Captain H. W. P. Stokes.
Lieutenant-Colonel E. F. Taylor.
Captain G. E. Toynbee.
Lieutenant C. L. St. J. Tudor.
Captain G. M. Young.
Staff Serjeant-Major W. Badcock.
Staff Serjeant-Major M. Burke.
Corporal E. W. Castle.
Mechanic Staff-Serjeant Curtis.
Private E. J. Edwards.
Corporal E. H. W. Fillmore.
Lance-Corporal R. Hill.
Staff-Serjeant F. G. Hogan.
Mechanic Serjeant-Major T. Hopper.
Corporal Lomax.
Lance-Corporal B. Main.
Driver S. Martin, No. 1 Cavalry Field Ambulance.
Serjeant F. Myatt.
Mechanic Serjeant-Major B. W. Nicholson.
Corporal C. J. Saunders.
Company Serjeant-Major S. J. Simmons.
Company Serjeant-Major T. Smith.
Serjeant H. Tovell.
Driver Vickers.
Staff Serjeant-Major V. B. Walter.
Staff Serjeant-Major S. J. Webster.
Driver Winser.

ROYAL ARMY MEDICAL CORPS.

Major E. T. F. Birrell.
Lieutenant L. G. Bourdillon.

MENTIONED IN DESPATCHES

Major S. G. Butler.
Captain E. D. Caddell.
Major R. V. Cowey.
Lieutenant R. V. Dolbey.
Major H. Ensor, D.S.O.
Major T. E. Fielding.
Major R. L. V. Foster.
Major T. H. J. C. Goodwin, D.S.O.
Major J. Grech.
Lieutenant C. Hairsine (Special Reserve).
Lieutenant C. Helm.
Major H. A. Hinge.
Lieutenant H. L. Hopkins (Civil Surgeon).
Lieutenant W. M. Howells.
Captain E. B. Lathbury.
Captain M. Leckie.
Major O. W. Lloyd.
Captain J. T. McEntire.
Lieutenant-Colonel L. A. Mitchell.
Lieutenant-Colonel J. C. Morgan.
Captain J. F. Murphy (Special Reserve).
Captain W. M. Nimmo (attached 1st Battalion Loyal North Lancs. Regiment).
Captain C. P. O'Brien-Butler (attached 5th Lancers).
Captain A. C. Osburn.
Lieutenant R. A. Preston.
Major C. W. Profeit.
Captain F. C. Sampson.
Captain H. Stewart.
Captain G. W. W. Ware.
Lieutenant Wyler (Civil Surgeon).
Serjeant H. Amsden.
Serjeant-Major H. J. Anderson.
Lance-Corporal T. Bennett.
Staff-Serjeant A. C. Blair.
Private Burstall.
Corporal F. J. Chatting.
Corporal R. H. Coad.
Serjeant-Major T. E. Coggin.
Serjeant-Major R. R. Cox.
Private Cuffley.
Private H. W. Fann.
Staff-Serjeant J. Gardiner.
Private R. A. Goodwin.
Serjeant-Major A. T. Hasler.
Lance-Corporal J. Jonas.

MENTIONED IN DESPATCHES

Private Leech.
Corporal G. W. Lefever, Army Service Corps (attached).
Serjeant J. W. Lockwood.
Serjeant-Major C. R. Loft.
Private R. Mears.
Serjeant E. Nicholas.
Private H. G. Noble.
Serjeant R. J. Nolan, Army Service Corps (attached).
Corporal F. F. Pettit.
Corporal B. Plume.
Serjeant H. M. Prince.
Staff-Serjeant A. T. Rayer.
Driver D. Rideout, Army Service Corps (attached).
Staff-Serjeant A. Spowage.
Quartermaster-Serjeant E. Steel.
Private G. Stevens.
Private R. V. Sworn.
Private Turner.
Quartermaster-Serjeant G. B. Walker.
Lance-Corporal Wass.

Army Veterinary Corps.

Captain W. I. Macauley.
Captain Oliver.
Captain F. W. Pawlett (T.F.).
Lieutenant-Colonel W. D. Smith.
Captain E. J. Wadley.

Chaplains.

Rev. Monsignor F. Bickerstaffe-Drew, Roman Catholic.
Rev. J. M. Connor, Presbyterian.
Rev. T. S. Goudge, Church of England.
Rev. W. Ketinge, Roman Catholic.
Rev. E. G. S. Macpherson, Church of England.
Rev. H. C. Meeke, Presbyterian.
Rev. O. S. Watkins, Wesleyan.
Rev. A. R. Yeoman, M.A., Chaplain to the Forces, Presbyterian.

SUPPLEMENTARY LIST, ISSUED DECEMBER 4th

Officers.

Colonel J. J. Asser, Commandant, No. 3 Base.
Lieutenant H. Beddingfield, R.A.M.C.
Lieutenant G. C. Binsteed, 2nd Batt. Essex.
Major B. W. B. Bowdler, R.E. (Headquarters Staff).
Lieutenant C. N. Champion de Crespigny, 2nd Dragoon Guards (killed).
Second Lieutenant J. K. C. Cross, 2nd Batt. Lancs. Fus.
Captain H. C. Forster, 4th Batt. Royal Fusiliers.
Captain F. D. Hammond, Railway Staff Officer.
Lieutenant H. D. Harvey-Kelly, R.I. Regt., R. Flying Corps.
Captain Sir F. E. W. Hervey-Bathurst, Staff A.D.C. to Inspector-General of Communications.
Major H. C. T. Hildyard, Railway Staff.
Lieutenant Lord H. W. Holm-Patrick, 16th Lancers (S.R.)
Major C. F. Hunter, 4th Dragoon Guards.
Captain (now Major) W. E. Ironside, Staff No. 3 Base.
Major M. R. de B. James, Staff, No. 2 Base.
Major R. M. Johnson, Royal Artillery.
Brevet-Major H. C. Johnson, D.S.O., King's Royal R.
Colonel F. W. Kerr, D.S.O., Staff (killed).
Major W. M. St. G. Kirke, R.A. (Headquarters Staff).
Second Lieutenant H. Lane, 1st Batt. Somerset L.I.
Captain R. T. Lee, Railway Staff.
Captain E. R. Lloyd, 2nd Batt. Royal Inniskilling Fus.
Lieutenant-Colonel J. G. C. Longmore, A.S.C.
Lieutenant-Colonel M. L. MacEwen, 16th Lancers.
Lieutenant-Colonel (temporary Colonel) A. G. Marrable, Commandant No. 2 Base.
Lieutenant G. A. P. Maxwell, Railway Staff.
Captain R. K. McGillycuddy, 4th Dragoon Guards.
Lieutenant W. H. C. Mansfield, Shropshire L.I. Royal Flying Corps.
Lieutenant R. F. H. Massy-Westropp, 2nd Batt. Royal Dublin Fusiliers.
Colonel A. D. Miller, D.S.O., Staff, Advanced Base.
Lieutenant I. F. R. Miller, 2nd Batt. Royal Inniskilling Fusiliers (Special Reserve).
Brigadier-General J. Moore, Staff.
Captain O. H. L. Nicholson, D.S.O., Staff, No. 1 Base.
Lieutenant F. A. Nicholson, 15th Hussars.
Captain P. B. O'Connor, Railway Staff.
Captain R. Ommanney, Royal Engineers Staff (killed).

MENTIONED IN DESPATCHES

Second Lieutenant G. F. Page, 2nd Batt. Lancs. Fusiliers.
Lieutenant-Colonel A. Parker, 5th Lancers.
Lieutenant T. T. Pitman, 11th Hussars.
Captain G. M. Ponsonby, 2nd Batt. Royal Inniskilling Fusiliers (killed).
Major-General Sir F. S. Robb, K.C.V.O., C.B., Inspector General of Communications.
Brigadier-General A. E. Sandbach, Commandant No. 1 Base.
Major Hon. W. D. Sclater-Booth, R.H.A., " L " Batt.
Captain E. V. M. Shelley, 1st Batt. Royal Warwicks.
Second Lieutenant M. B. Smith, 1st Batt. Coldstream Guards.
Brigadier-General A. M. Stuart, Staff, Director of Works.
Lieutenant H. C. Thompson, 2nd Batt. R. Inniskilling Fusiliers.
Colonel A. G. Thompson, C.B., Commandant, Advanced Base.
Colonel S. Westcott, Staff, R.A.M.C.
Lieutenant-Colonel F. M. Wilson, Assistant Director of Supplies.
Lieutenant L. S. Woodgate, 1st Batt. Royal Lancs. (killed).
Captain J. E. S. Woodman, 2nd Batt. Lancs. Fusiliers.

Warrant Officers, Non-Commissioned Officers and Men.

Serjeant R. W. Allsopp, 1st Batt. Beds.
Serjeant W. E. Archer, 1st Batt. Somerset L.I.
Lance-Corporal W. Barnes, 1st Batt. Royal Warwicks.
Private J. Beesley, 2nd Batt. Lancs. Fusiliers.
Corporal E. Binnie, 2nd Batt. Essex Regt.
Serjeant J. Bradford, 1st Batt. Royal Lancs.
Acting-Corporal J. Brooks, 1st Batt. Rifle Brigade
Serjeant W. Brueton, 2nd Batt. Lancs. Fusiliers.
Private W. Bryant, 2nd Dragoon Guards.
Serjeant S. Caldwell, 9th Lancers (killed).
Corporal C. Cox, 113th Battery R.F.A.
Bombardier W. Culley, 70th Battery R.F.A.
B.-S.-M. G. T. Dorrell, " L " Battery R.H.A.
Gunner J. Dykes, 113th Battery R.F.A.
Private S. Everson, 1st Batt. Royal Lancs.
Serjeant J. G. V. Ewings, 2nd Batt. Lancs. Fusiliers.
Serjeant G. Ferguson, 113th Battery R.F.A.
Serjeant W. Fowler, 1st Batt. Royal Lancs.
Serjeant J. A. J. Fox, 3rd Batt. Coldstream Guards.
Serjeant J. A. Fraser, 2nd Dragoon Guards.
Shoeing-Smith G. Freeman, 1st Sec. 4th D.A.C., R.F.A.
Private E. French, 2nd Batt. Essex Regiment.
Serjeant J. Gaynor, 2nd Batt. Royal Inniskilling Fusiliers.
Serjeant J. Grundy, 2nd Batt. Lancs. Fusiliers.
Bombardier E. G. Harlock, 113th Battery R.F.A.
Co.-Serjeant-Major P. Heaney, 1st Batt. Royal Lancs.

MENTIONED IN DESPATCHES

Private S. Hodgert, R.A.M.C.
Serjeant E. Howes, 19th Hussars.
Lance-Corporal R. Jarvis, 2nd Dragoon Guards.
Serjeant-Major D. S. Jillings, Royal Flying Corps.
Corporal J. Jones, 1st Batt. Liverpool Regiment.
Farrier-Staff-Serjeant H. Knight, 19th Hussars.
Serjeant F. Lelliott, 1st Batt. Royal Lancs.
Serjeant D. Nelson, " L " Battery R.H.A.
Serjeant R. Neville, 2nd Batt. Royal Irish Fusiliers.
Corporal J. C. Pike, 1st Batt. Royal Lancs.
St. Quartermaster-Serjeant C. E. Quarrier, Headquarters Staff.
Private F. Randerson, 1st Batt. Royal Lancs.
Private W. Richons, R.A.M.C.
Serjeant J. Rowley, 1st Batt. Royal Lancs.
Lance-Corporal R. Russell, 1st Batt. Coldstream Guards.
Co. Serjeant-Major W. Sharples, 2nd Batt. Lancs.
Serjeant W. Sharpley, 2nd Batt. Essex.
Regimental Serjeant-Major C. Shergold, Royal Canadian Engineers.
Private G. Swinscoe, 2nd Batt. Lancashire Fusiliers.
Private T. Tinker, 2nd Batt. Royal Lancs.
Private G. Turner, 1st Batt. Royal Lancs.
Co. Serjeant-Major E. Walker, 1st Batt. E. Surreys.
Co. Quartermaster-Serjeant J. W. Welsh, 2nd Batt. Lancs. Fusiliers.
Shoeing-Smith T. J. White, 113th Battery R.F.A.
Serjeant C. Willcox, 1st Batt. Somerset L.I.

IV
FLANDERS

IV : France, 20*th November*, 1914.

To Field-Marshal Earl Kitchener of Khartoum, K.P., G.C.B., O.M., etc.

My Lord,

I HAVE the honour to submit a further despatch recounting the operations of the Field Force under my command throughout the battle of Ypres-Armentières.

Early in October a study of the general situation strongly impressed me with the necessity of bringing the greatest possible force to bear in support of the northern flank of the Allies, in order to effectively outflank the enemy and compel him to evacuate his positions.

At the same time the position on the Aisne, as described in the concluding paragraphs of my last despatch, appeared to me to warrant a withdrawal of the British Forces from the positions they then held.

The enemy had been weakened by continual abortive and futile attacks, whilst the fortification of the position had been much improved.

I represented these views to General Joffre, who fully agreed.

Arrangements for withdrawal and relief having been made by the French General Staff, the operation commenced on the 3rd October ; and the 2nd Cavalry Division under General Gough, marched for Compiègne *en route* for the new theatre.

The Army Corps followed in succession at intervals of a few days, and the move was completed on the 19th October, when the First Corps, under Sir Douglas Haig, completed its detrainment at St. Omer.

FLANDERS

That this delicate operation was carried out so successfully is in great measure due to the excellent feeling which exists between the French and British Armies; and I am deeply indebted to the Commander-in-Chief and the French General Staff for their cordial and most effective co-operation.

As General Foch was appointed by the Commander-in-Chief to supervise the operations of all the French troops north of Noyon, I visited his headquarters at Doullens on 8th October and arranged joint plans of operations as follows:

> The Second Corps to arrive on the line Aire-Bethune on the 11th October, to connect with the right of the French 10th Army and, pivoting on its left, to attack in flank the enemy who were opposing the 10th French Corps in front.
>
> The Cavalry to move on the northern flank of the Second Corps and support its attack until the Third Corps, which was to detrain at St. Omer on the 12th, should come up. They were then to clear the front and to act on the northern flank of the Third Corps in a similar manner, pending the arrival of the First Corps from the Aisne.
>
> The 3rd Cavalry Division and 7th Division, under Sir Henry Rawlinson, which were then operating in support of the Belgian Army, and assisting its withdrawal from Antwerp, to be ordered to co-operate as soon as circumstances would allow.
>
> In the event of these movements so far overcoming the resistance of the enemy as to enable a forward movement to be made, all the Allied Forces to march in an easterly direction. The road running from Bethune to Lille was to be the dividing line between the British and French Forces, the right of the British Army being directed on Lille.

THE BEGINNING OF THE BATTLE

2. The great battle, which is mainly the subject of this despatch, may be said to have commenced on October 11th, on which date the 2nd Cavalry Division, under General Gough, first came into contact with the enemy's cavalry who were holding some woods to the north of the Bethune-Aire Canal. These were cleared of the enemy by our cavalry, which then joined hands with the Divisional Cavalry of the 6th Division in the neighbourhood of Hazebrouck. On the same day the right of the 2nd Cavalry Division connected with the left of the Second Corps which was moving in a north-easterly direction after crossing the above-mentioned canal.

By the 11th October Sir Horace Smith-Dorrien had reached the line of the canal between Aire and Bethune. I directed him to continue his march on the 12th, bringing up his left in the direction of Merville. Then he was to move East to the line Laventie-Lorgies, which would bring him on the immediate left of the French Army and threaten the German flank.

On the 12th this movement was commenced. The 5th Division connected up with the left of the French Army north of Annequin. They moved to the attack of the Germans who were engaged at this point with the French; but the enemy once more extended his right in some strength to meet the threat against his flank. The 3rd Division, having crossed the canal, deployed on the left of the 5th; and the whole Second Corps again advanced to the attack, but were unable to make much headway owing to the difficult character of the ground upon which they were operating, which was similar to that usually found in manufacturing districts, and was covered with mining works, factories, buildings, etc. The ground throughout this country is remarkably flat, rendering effective artillery support very difficult.

Before nightfall, however, they had made some advance and had successfully driven back hostile counter attacks with great loss to the enemy and destruction of some of his machine guns.

On and after the 13th October the object of the General Officer Commanding the Second Corps was to wheel to his right, pivoting on Givenchy to get astride the La Bassée-Lille Road in the neighbourhood of Fournes, so as to threaten the right flank and rear of the enemy's position on the high ground south of La Bassée.

This position of La Bassée has throughout the battle defied all attempts at capture, either by the French or the British.

On this day Sir Horace Smith-Dorrien could make but little progress. He particularly mentions the fine fighting of the Dorsets, 'whose Commanding Officer, Major Roper, was killed. They suffered no less than 400 casualties, 130 of them being killed, but maintained all day their hold on Pont Fixe. He also refers to the gallantry of the Artillery.

The fighting of the Second Corps continued throughout the 14th in the same direction. On this day the Army suffered a great loss, in that the Commander of the 3rd Division, General Hubert Hamilton, was killed.

On the 15th the 3rd Division fought splendidly, crossing the dykes, with which this country is intersected, with planks ; and driving the enemy from one entrenched position to another in loop-holed villages, till at night they pushed the Germans off the Estaires-La Bassée Road, and establishing themselves on the line Pont de Ham—Croix Barbée.

On the 16th the move was continued until the left flank of the Corps was in front of the village of Aubers, which was strongly held. This village was captured on the 17th by the 9th Infantry Brigade ; and at dark on the same day the Lincolns and Royal Fusiliers carried the village of Herlies at the point of the bayonet after a fine attack, the Brigade being handled with great dash by Brigadier-General Shaw.

CONTINUOUS FIGHTING

At this time, to the best of our information, the Second Corps were believed to be opposed by the 2nd, 4th, 7th and 9th German Cavalry Divisions, supported by several battalions of Jaegers and a part of the 14th German Corps.

On the 18th powerful counter-attacks were made by the enemy all along the front of the Second Corps, and were most gallantly repulsed; but only slight progress could be made.

From the 19th to the 31st October the Second Corps carried on a most gallant fight in defence of their position against very superior numbers, the enemy having been reinforced during that time by at least one Division of the 7th Corps, a brigade of the 3rd Corps and the whole of the 14th Corps, which had moved north from in front of the French 21st Corps.

On the 19th the Royal Irish Regiment, under Major Daniell, stormed and carried the village of Le Pilly, which they held and entrenched. On the 20th, however, they were cut off and surrounded, suffering heavy losses.

On the morning of the 22nd the enemy made a very determined attack on the 5th Division, who were driven out of the village of Violaines, but they were sharply counter-attacked by the Worcesters and Manchesters, and prevented from coming on.

The left of the Second Corps being now somewhat exposed, Sir Horace Smith-Dorrien withdrew the line during the night to a position he had previously prepared, running generally from the eastern side of Givenchy, east of Neuve Chapelle to Fauquissart.

On the 24th October the Lahore Division of the Indian Army Corps, under Major-General Watkis, having arrived, I sent them to the neighbourhood of Lacon to support the Second Corps.

Very early on this morning the enemy commenced a heavy attack, but, owing to the skilful manner in which the artillery was handled and the targets presented by the enemy's infantry as it approached, they were unable to come to close quarters. Towards the evening a heavy attack developed against the 7th Brigade, which was repulsed, with very heavy loss to the enemy, by the Wiltshires and the Royal West Kents. Later, a determined attack on the 18th Infantry Brigade drove the Gordon Highlanders out of their trenches, which were retaken by the Middlesex Regiment, gallantly led by Lieutenant-Colonel Hull.

The 8th Infantry Brigade (which had come into line on the left of the Second Corps) was also heavily attacked, but the enemy was driven off.

In both these cases the Germans lost very heavily, and left large numbers of dead and prisoners behind them.

The Second Corps was now becoming exhausted, owing to the constant reinforcements of the enemy, the length of line which it had to defend and the enormous losses which it had suffered.

3. By the evening of the 11th October the Third Corps had practically completed its detrainment at St. Omer, and was moved east to Hazebrouck, where the Corps remained throughout the 12th.

On the morning of the 13th the advanced guard of the Corps, consisting of the 19th Infantry Brigade and a Brigade of Field Artillery, occupied the position of the line Strazeele Station—Caestre—St. Sylvestre.

On this day I directed General Pulteney to move towards the line Armentières-Wytschaete; warning him, however, that should the Second Corps require his aid he must be prepared to move South-East to support it.

A French Cavalry Corps, under General Conneau, was operating between the Second and Third Corps.

The Fourth German Cavalry Corps, supported by some Jaeger Battalions, was known to be occupying the position in the neighbourhood of Meteren; and they

THE THIRD CORPS

were believed to be further supported by the advanced guard of another German Army Corps.

In pursuance of his orders, General Pulteney proceeded to attack the enemy in his front.

The rain and fog which prevailed prevented full advantage being derived from our much superior artillery. The country was very much enclosed and rendered difficult by heavy rain.

The enemy were, however, routed; and the position taken at dark, several prisoners being captured.

During the night the Third Corps made good the attacked position and entrenched it.

As Bailleul was known to be occupied by the enemy, arrangements were made during the night to attack it; but reconnaissances sent out on the morning of the 14th showed that they had withdrawn, and the town was taken by our troops at 10 a.m. on that day, many wounded Germans being found and taken in it.

The Corps then occupied the line St. Jans Cappel-Bailleul.

On the morning of the 15th the Third Corps were ordered to make good the line of the Lys from Armentières to Sailly, which, in the face of considerable opposition and very foggy weather, they succeeded in doing, the 6th Division at Sailly-Bac St. Maur and the 4th Division at Nieppe.

The enemy in its front having retired, the Third Corps on the night of the 17th occupied the line Bois Grenier-Le Gheir.

On the 18th the enemy were holding a line from Radinghem on the south, through Perenchies and Frelinghien on the north, whence the German troops which were opposing the Cavalry Corps occupied the east bank of the river as far as Wervick.

On this day I directed the Third Corps to move down the valley of the Lys and endeavour to assist the Cavalry

FLANDERS

Corps in making good its position on the right bank. To do this it was necessary first to drive the enemy eastward towards Lille. A vigorous offensive in the direction of Lille was assumed, but the enemy was found to have been considerably reinforced, and but little progress was made.

The situation of the Third Corps on the night of the 18th was as follows:

The 6th Division was holding the line Radingham-La Vallée - Emnetières - Capinghem - Premesques-Railway Line 300 yards east of Halte. The 4th Division were holding the line from L'Epinette to the river at a point 400 yards south of Frelinghein, and thence to a point half a mile south-east of Le Gheir. The Corps Reserve was at Armentières Station, with right and left flanks of Corps in close touch with French Cavalry and the Cavalry Corps.

Since the advance from Bailleul the enemy's forces in front of the Cavalry and Third Corps had been strongly reinforced, and on the night of the 17th they were opposed by three or four divisions of the enemy's cavalry, the 19th Saxon Corps and at least one division of the 7th Corps. Reinforcements for the enemy were known to be coming up from the direction of Lille.

4. Following the movements completed on the 11th October, the 2nd Cavalry Division pushed the enemy back through Flêtre and Le Coq de Paille, and took Mont des Cats, just before dark, after stiff fighting.

On the 14th the 1st Cavalry Division joined up, and the whole Cavalry Corps, under General Allenby, moving north, secured the high ground above Berthen, overcoming considerable opposition.

With a view to a further advance east, I ordered General Allenby, on the 15th, to reconnoitre the line of the River Lys, and endeavour to secure the passages on the opposite bank, pending the arrival of the Third and Fourth Corps.

THE OPERATIONS NEAR GHENT & ANTWERP

During the 15th and 16th this reconnaissance was most skilfully and energetically carried out in the face of great opposition, especially along the lower line of the river.

These operations were continued throughout the 17th, 18th, and 19th; but, although valuable information was gained, and strong forces of the enemy held in check, the Cavalry Corps was unable to secure passages or to establish a permanent footing on the eastern bank of the river.

5. At this point in the history of the operations under report it is necessary that I should return to the co-operation of the forces operating in the neighbourhood of Ghent and Antwerp under Lieutenant-General Sir Henry Rawlinson, as the action of his force about this period exercised, in my opinion, a great influence on the course of the subsequent operations.

This force, consisting of the 3rd Cavalry Division, under Major-General the Hon. Julian Byng, and the 7th Division, under Major-General Capper, was placed under my orders by telegraphic instructions from your Lordship.

On receipt of these instructions I directed Sir Henry Rawlinson to continue his operations in covering and protecting the withdrawal of the Belgian Army, and subsequently to form the left column in the eastward advance of the British Forces. These withdrawal operations were concluded about the 16th October, on which date the 7th Division was posted to the east of Ypres on a line extending from Zandvoorde through Gheluvelt to Zonnebeke. The 3rd Cavalry Division was on its left towards Langemarck and Poelcappelle.

In this position Sir Henry Rawlinson was supported by the 87th French Territorial Division in Ypres and Vlamertinghe, and by the 89th French Territorial Division at Poperinghe.

On the night of the 16th I informed Sir Henry Rawlinson of the operations which were in progress by the

FLANDERS

Cavalry Corps and the Third Corps, and ordered him to conform to those movements in an easterly direction, keeping an eye always to any threat which might be made against him from the north-east.

A very difficult task was allotted to Sir Henry Rawlinson and his command. Owing to the importance of keeping possession of all the ground towards the north which we already held, it was necessary for him to operate on a very wide front, and, until the arrival of the First Corps in the northern theatre—which I expected about the 20th—I had no troops available with which to support or reinforce him.

Although on this extended front he had eventually to encounter very superior forces, his troops, both Cavalry and Infantry, fought with the utmost gallantry, and rendered very signal service.

On the 17th four French Cavalry Divisions deployed on the left of the 3rd Cavalry Division, and drove back advanced parties of the enemy beyond the Forêt d'Houthulst.

As described above, instructions for a vigorous attempt to establish the British Forces east of the Lys were given on the night of the 17th to the Second, Third and Cavalry Corps.

I considered, however, that the possession of Menin constituted a very important point of passage, and would much facilitate the advance of the rest of the Army. So I directed the General Officer Commanding the Fourth Corps to advance the 7th Division upon Menin, and endeavour to seize that crossing on the morning of the 18th.

The left of the 7th Division was to be supported by the 3rd Cavalry Brigade, and further north by the French Cavalry in the neighbourhood of Roulers.

Sir Henry Rawlinson represented to me that large hostile forces were advancing upon him from the east and north-east, and that his left flank was severely threatened.

PROTECTING THE CHANNEL PORTS

I was aware of the threats from that direction, but hoped that at this particular time there was no greater force coming from the north-east than could be held off by the combined efforts of the French and British Cavalry and the Territorial troops supporting them until the passage at Menin could be seized and the First Corps brought up in support.

Sir Henry Rawlinson probably exercised a wise judgment in not committing his troops to this attack in their somewhat weakened condition; but the result was that the enemy's continued possession of the passage at Menin certainly facilitated his rapid reinforcement of his troops and thus rendered any further advance impracticable.

On the morning of the 20th October the 7th Division and 3rd Cavalry Division had retired to their old position extending from Zandvoorde through Kruiseik and Gheluvelt to Zonnebeke.

6. On the 19th October the First Corps, coming from the Aisne, had completed its detrainment and was concentrated between St. Omer and Hazebrouck.

A question of vital importance now arose for decision.

I knew that the enemy were by this time in greatly superior strength on the Lys, and that the Second, Third, Cavalry, and Fourth Corps were holding a much wider front than their numbers and strength warranted.

Taking these facts alone into consideration it would have appeared wise to throw the First Corps in to strengthen the line; but this would have left the country north and east of Ypres and the Ypres Canal open to a wide turning movement by the 3rd Reserve Corps and at least one Landwehr Division which I knew to be operating in that region. I was also aware that the enemy was bringing large reinforcements up from the East which could only be opposed for several days by two or three French Cavalry Divisions, some French Territorial troops, and the Belgian Army.

FLANDERS

After the hard fighting it had undergone the Belgian Army was in no condition to withstand, unsupported, such an attack; and unless some substantial resistance could be offered to this threatened turning movement, the Allied flank must be turned and the Channel Ports laid bare to the enemy.

I judged that a successful movement of this kind would be fraught with such disastrous consequences that the risk of operating on so extended a front must be undertaken; and I directed Sir Douglas Haig to move with the First Corps to the north of Ypres.

From the best information at my disposal I judged at this time that the considerable reinforcements which the enemy had undoubtedly brought up during the 16th, 17th and 18th had been directed principally on the line of the Lys and against the Second Corps at La Bassée; and that Sir Douglas Haig would probably not be opposed north of Ypres by much more than the 3rd Reserve Corps, which I knew to have suffered considerably in its previous operations, and perhaps one or two Landwehr Divisions.

At a personal interview with Sir Douglas Haig on the evening of the 19th October I communicated the above information to him, and instructed him to advance with the First Corps through Ypres to Thourout. The object he was to have in view was to be the capture of Bruges and subsequently, if possible, to drive the enemy towards Ghent. In case of an unforeseen situation arising, or the enemy proving to be stronger than anticipated, he was to decide, after passing Ypres, according to the situation, whether to attack the enemy lying to the North or the hostile forces advancing from the East: I had arranged for the French Cavalry to operate on the left of the First Corps and the 3rd Cavalry Division, under General Byng, on its right.

The Belgian Army were rendering what assistance they could by entrenching themselves on the Ypres Canal and the Yser River ; and the troops, although in the last stage of exhaustion, gallantly maintained their positions buoyed up with the hope of substantial British and French support.

I fully realised the difficult task which lay before us, and the onerous rôle which the British Army was called upon to fulfil.

That success has been attained, and all the enemy's desperate attempts to break through our line frustrated, is due entirely to the marvellous fighting power and the indomitable courage and tenacity of officers, non-commissioned officers and men.

No more arduous task has ever been assigned to British soldiers ; and in all their splendid history there is no instance of their having answered so magnificently to the desperate calls which of necessity were made upon them.

Having given these orders to Sir Douglas Haig, I enjoined a defensive rôle upon the Second and Third and Cavalry Corps, in view of the superiority of force which had accumulated in their front. As regards the Fourth Corps, I directed Sir Henry Rawlinson to endeavour to conform generally to the movements of the First Corps.

On the 20th October they reached the line from Elverdinghe to the cross roads one and a half miles north-west of Zonnebeke.

On the 21st the Corps was ordered to attack and take the line Poelcappelle-Passchendaele.

Sir Henry Rawlinson's Command was moving on the right of the First Corps, and French troops, consisting of Cavalry and Territorials, moved on their left under the orders of General Bidon.

The advance was somewhat delayed owing to the roads being blocked ; but the attack progressed favourably in face of severe opposition, often necessitating the use of the bayonet.

Hearing of heavy attacks being made upon the 7th

FLANDERS

Division and the 2nd Cavalry Division on his right, Sir Douglas Haig ordered his reserve to be halted on the north-eastern outskirts of Ypres.

Although threatened by a hostile movement from the Forêt d'Houthulst, our advance was successful until about 2 o'clock in the afternoon, when the French Cavalry Corps received orders to retire west of the canal.

Owing to this and the demands made on him by the Fourth Corps, Sir Douglas Haig was unable to advance beyond the line Zonnebeke-St. Julien-Langemarck-Bixschoote.

As there was reported to be congestion with French troops at Ypres, I went there on the evening of the 21st and met Sir Douglas Haig and Sir Henry Rawlinson. With them I nterviewed General De Mitry, Commanding the French Cavalry, and General Bidon, Commanding the French Territorial Divisions.

They promised me that the town would at once be cleared of the troops, and that the French Territorials would immediately move out and cover the left of the flank of the First Corps.

I discussed the situation with the General Officers Commanding the First and Fourth Army Corps, and told them that, in view of the unexpected reinforcements coming up of the enemy, it would probably be impossible to carry out the original rôle assigned to them. But I informed them that I had that day interviewed the French Commander-in-Chief, General Joffre, who told me that he was bringing up the 9th French Army Corps to Ypres, that more French troops would follow later, and that he intended—in conjunction with the Belgian troops—to drive the Germans East. General Joffre said that he would be unable to commence this movement before the 24th; and I directed the General Officers Commanding the First and Fourth Corps to strengthen their positions as much as possible, and be prepared to hold their ground

A BRILLIANT ATTACK

for two or three days, until the French offensive movement on the North could develop.

It now became clear to me that the utmost we could do to ward off any attempts of the enemy to turn our flank to the North, or to break in from the eastward was to maintain our present very extended front, and to hold fast our positions until French reinforcements could arrive from the South.

During the 22nd the necessity of sending support to the Fourth Corps on his right somewhat hampered the General Officer Commanding the First Corps; but a series of attacks all along his front had been driven back during the day with heavy loss to the enemy. Late in the evening the enemy succeeded in penetrating a portion of the line held by the Cameron Highlanders north of Pilkem.

At 6 a.m. on the morning of the 23rd a counter-attack to recover the lost trenches was made by the Queen's Regiment, the Northamptons and the King's Royal Rifles under Major-General Bulfin. The attack was very strongly opposed and the bayonet had to be used. After severe fighting during most of the day the attack was brilliantly successful, and over six hundred prisoners were taken.

On the same day an attack was made on the 3rd Infantry Brigade. The enemy advanced with great determination, but with little skill, and consequently the loss inflicted on him was exceedingly heavy; some fifteen hundred dead were seen in the neighbourhood of Langemarck. Correspondence found subsequently on a captured German Officer stated that the effectives of this attacking Corps were reduced to 25 per cent. in the course of the day's fighting.

In the evening of this day a division of the French 9th Army Corps came up into line and took over the portion of the line held by the 2nd Division, which, on the 24th, took up the ground occupied by the 7th Division from Poelzelhoek to the Becelaere-Passchendaele Road.

FLANDERS

On the 24th and 25th October repeated attacks by the enemy were brilliantly repulsed.

On the night of the 24th-25th the 1st Division was relieved by French Territorial troops and concentrated about Zillebeke.

During the 25th the 2nd Division, with the 7th on its right and the French 9th Corps on its left, made good progress towards the North-East, capturing some guns and prisoners.

On the 27th October I went to the headquarters of the First Corps at Hooge to personally investigate the condition of the 7th Division.

Owing to constant marching and fighting, ever since its hasty disembarkation, in aid of the Antwerp Garrison, this division had suffered great losses, and were becoming very weak. I therefore decided temporarily to break up the Fourth Corps and place the 7th Division with the First Corps under the command of Sir Douglas Haig.

The 3rd Cavalry Division was similarly detailed for service with the First Corps.

I directed the Fourth Corps Commander to proceed, with his Staff, to England, to watch and supervise the mobilisation of the 8th Division, which was then proceeding.

On receipt of orders, in accordance with the above arrangement, Sir Douglas Haig redistributed the line held by the First Corps as follows :

    (*a*) 7th Division from the Chateau east of Zandvoorde to the Menin Road.

    (*b*) 1st Division from the Menin Road to a point immediately west of Reytel Village.

    (*c*) 2nd Division to near Moorslede-Zonnebeke Road.

On the early morning of the 29th October a heavy attack developed against the centre of the line held by the First Corps, the principal point of attack being the cross roads one mile east of Gheluvelt. After severe fighting

THE EMPEROR'S ORDER

—nearly the whole of the Corps being employed in counter-attack—the enemy began to give way at about 2 p.m.; and by dark the Kruiseik Hill had been recaptured and the 1st Brigade had re-established most of the line north of the Menin Road.

Shortly after daylight on the 30th another attack began to develop in the direction of Zandvoorde, supported by heavy artillery fire. In face of this attack the 3rd Cavalry Division had to withdraw to the Klein Zillebeke ridge. This withdrawal involved the right of the 7th Division.

Sir Douglas Haig describes the position at this period as serious, the Germans being in possession of Zandvoorde Ridge.

Subsequent investigation showed that the enemy had been reinforced at this point by the whole German Active Fifteenth Corps.

The General Officer Commanding First Corps ordered the line Gheluvelt to the corner of the canal to be held at all costs. When this line was taken up the 2nd Brigade was ordered to concentrate in rear of the 1st Division and the 4th Brigade line. One battalion was placed in reserve in the woods one mile south of Hooge.

Further precautions were taken at night to protect this flank, and the Ninth French Corps sent three battalions and one Cavalry Brigade to assist.

The First Corps' communications through Ypres were threatened by the advance of the Germans towards the canal; so orders were issued for every effort to be made to secure the line then held, and, when this had been thoroughly done, to resume the offensive.

An order taken from a prisoner who had been captured on this day purported to emanate from the German General, Von Beimling, and said that the Fifteenth German Corps, together with the 2nd Bavarian and Thirteenth Corps, were entrusted with the task of breaking through the line to Ypres; and that the Emperor himself considered

FLANDERS

the success of this attack to be one of vital importance to the successful issue of the war.

Perhaps the most important and decisive attack (except that of the Prussian Guard on 15th November) made against the First Corps during the whole of its arduous experiences in the neighbourhood of Ypres took place on the 31st October.

General Moussy, who commanded the detachment which had been sent by the French Ninth Corps on the previous day to assist Sir Douglas Haig on the right of the First Corps, moved to the attack early in the morning, but was brought to a complete standstill, and could make no further progress.

After several attacks and counter-attacks during the course of the morning along the Menin—Ypres-road, south-east of Gheluvelt, an attack against that place developed in great force, and the line of the 1st Division was broken. On the south the 7th Division and General Bulfin's detachment were being heavily shelled. The retirement of the 1st Division exposed the left of the 7th Division, and owing to this the Royal Scots Fusiliers, who remained in their trenches, were cut off and surrounded. A strong infantry attack developed against the right of the 7th Division at 1.30 p.m.

Shortly after this the Headquarters of the 1st and 2nd Divisions were shelled. The General Officer Commanding 1st Division was wounded, three Staff Officers of the 1st Division and three of the 2nd Division were killed. The General Officer Commanding the 2nd Division also received a severe shaking, and was unconscious for a short time. General Landon assumed command of the 1st Division.

On receiving a report about 2.30 p.m. from General Lomax that the 1st Division had moved back and that the enemy was coming on in strength, the General Officer Commanding the First Corps issued orders that the line,

MOST CRITICAL MOMENT IN THE BATTLE

Frezenberg-Westhoek-bend of the main road Klein-Zillebeke-bend of canal, was to be held at all costs.

The 1st Division rallied on the line of the woods east of the bend of the road, the German advance by the road being checked by enfilade fire from the north.

The attack against the right of the 7th Division forced the 22nd Brigade to retire, thus exposing the left of the 2nd Brigade. The General Officer Commanding the 7th Division used his reserve, already posted on his flank, to restore the line; but, in the meantime, the 2nd Brigade, finding their left flank exposed, had been forced to withdraw. The right of the 7th Division thus advanced as the left of the 2nd Brigade went back, with the result that the right of the 7th Division was exposed, but managed to hold on to its old trenches till nightfall.

Meantime, on the Menin road, a counter-attack delivered by the left of the 1st Division and the right of the 2nd Division against the right flank of the German line was completely successful, and by 2.30 p.m. Gheluvelt had been retaken with the bayonet, the 2nd Worcestershire Regiment being to the fore in this, admirably supported by the 42nd Brigade, Royal Field Artillery. The left of the 7th Division, profiting by their capture of Gheluvelt, advanced almost to its original line; and connection between the 1st and 7th Divisions was re-established. The recapture of Gheluvelt released the 6th Cavalry Brigade, till then held in support of the 1st Division. Two regiments of this brigade were sent at once to clear the woods to the south-east, and close the gap in the line between the 7th Division and 2nd Brigade. They advanced with much dash, partly mounted and partly dismounted; and, surprising the enemy in the woods, succeeded in killing large numbers and materially helped to restore the line. About 5 p.m. the French Cavalry Brigade also came up to the cross-roads just east of Hooge, and at

FLANDERS

once sent forward a dismounted detachment to support our 7th Cavalry Brigade.

Throughout the day the extreme right and left of the First Corps' line held fast, the left being only slightly engaged, while the right was heavily shelled and subjected to slight infantry attacks. In the evening the enemy were steadily driven back from the woods on the front of the 7th Division and 2nd Brigade; and by 10 p.m. the line as held in the morning had practically been reoccupied.

During the night touch was restored between the right of the 7th Division and left of the 2nd Brigade, and the Cavalry were withdrawn into reserve, the services of the French Cavalry being dispensed with.

As a result of the day's fighting eight hundred and seventy wounded were evacuated.

I was present with Sir Douglas Haig at Hooge between 2 and 3 o'clock on this day, when the 1st Division were retiring. I regard it as the most critical moment in the whole of this great battle. The rally of the 1st Division and the recapture of the village of Gheluvelt at such a time was fraught with momentous consequences. If any one unit can be singled out for especial praise it is the Worcesters.

7. In the meantime the centre of my line, occupied by the Third and Cavalry Corps, was being heavily pressed by the enemy in ever-increasing force.

On the 20th October advanced posts of the 12th Brigade of the 4th Division, Third Corps, were forced to retire, and at dusk it was evident that the Germans were likely to make a determined attack. This ended in the occupation of Le Gheir by the enemy.

As the position of the Cavalry at St. Yves was thus endangered, a counter-attack was decided upon and planned by General Hunter-Weston and Lieutenant-Colonel Anley. This proved entirely successful, the Germans being driven back with great loss and the

COURAGE BEYOND ALL PRAISE

abandoned trenches reoccupied. Two hundred prisoners were taken and about forty of our prisoners released.

In these operations the staunchness of the King's Own Regiment and the Lancashire Fusiliers was most commendable. These two battalions were very well handled by Lieutenant-Colonel Butler of the Lancashire Fusiliers.

I am anxious to bring to special notice the excellent work done throughout this battle by the Third Corps under General Pulteney's command. Their position in the right central part of my line was of the utmost importance to the general success of the operations. Besides the very undue length of front which the Corps was called upon to cover (some 12 or 13 miles), the position presented many weak spots, and was also astride of the River Lys, the right bank of which from Frelinghein downwards was strongly held by the enemy. It was impossible to provide adequate reserves, and the constant work in the trenches tried the endurance of officers and men to the utmost. That the Corps was invariably successful in repulsing the constant attacks, sometimes in great strength, made against them by day and by night is due entirely to the skilful manner in which the Corps was disposed by its Commander, who has told me of the able assistance he has received throughout from his Staff, and the ability and resource displayed by Divisional, Brigade and Regimental leaders in using the ground and the means of defence at their disposal to the very best advantage.

The courage, tenacity, endurance and cheerfulness of the men in such unparalleled circumstances are beyond all praise.

During the 22nd and 23rd and 24th October frequent attacks were made along the whole line of the Third Corps, and especially against the 16th Infantry Brigade; but on all occasions the enemy was thrown back with loss.

During the night of the 25th October the Leicestershire Regiment were forced from their trenches by shells

FLANDERS

blowing in the pits they were in; and after investigation by the General Officers Commanding the 16th and 18th Infantry Brigades it was decided to throw back the line temporarily in this neighbourhood.

On the evening of the 29th October the enemy made a sharp attack on Le Gheir, and on the line to the north of it, but were repulsed.

About midnight a very heavy attack developed against the 19th Infantry Brigade south of Croix Maréchal. A portion of the trenches of the Middlesex Regiment was gained by the enemy and held by him for some hours till recaptured with the assistance of the detachment from the Argyll and Sutherland Highlanders from Brigade Reserve. The enemy in the trenches were all bayonetted or captured. Later information from prisoners showed that there were twelve battalions opposite the 19th Brigade. Over two hundred dead Germans were left lying in front of the Brigade's trenches, and forty prisoners were taken.

On the evening of the 30th the line of the 11th Infantry Brigade in the neighbourhood of St. Yves was broken. A counter-attack carried out by Major Prowse with the Somerset Light Infantry restored the situation. For his services on this occasion this officer was recommended for special reward.

On the 31st October it became necessary for the 4th Division to take over the extreme right of the 1st Cavalry Division's trenches, although this measure necessitated a still further extension of the line held by the Third Corps.

8. On October 20th, while engaged in the attempt to force the line of the River Lys, the Cavalry Corps was attacked from the South and East. In the evening the 1st Cavalry Division held the line St. Yves-Messines: the 2nd Cavalry Division from Messines through Garde Dieu along the Wambeck to Houthem and Kortewilde.

CAVALRY IN THE TRENCHES

At 4 p.m. on the 21st October, a heavy attack was made on the 2nd Cavalry Division, which was compelled to fall back to the line Messines-9th kilo stone on the Warneton-Oostaverne Road-Hollebeke.

On the 22nd I directed the 7th Indian Infantry Brigade, less one battalion, to proceed to Wulverghem in support of the Cavalry Corps. General Allenby sent two battalions to Wytschaete and Voormezeele to be placed under the orders of General Gough, Commanding the 2nd Cavalry Division.

On the 23rd, 24th and 25th several attacks were directed against the Cavalry Corps and repulsed with loss to the enemy.

On the 26th October I directed General Allenby to endeavour to regain a more forward line, moving in conjunction with the 7th Division. But the latter being apparently quite unable to take the offensive, the attempt had to be abandoned.

On October 20th heavy infantry attacks, supported by powerful artillery fire, developed against the 2nd and 3rd Cavalry Divisions, especially against the trenches about Hollebeke, held by the 3rd Cavalry Brigade. At 1.30 p.m. this Brigade was forced to retire, and the 2nd Cavalry Brigade, less one regiment, was moved across from the 1st Cavalry Division to a point between Oostaverne and St. Eloi in support of the 2nd Cavalry Division.

The 1st Cavalry Division in the neighbourhood of Messines was also threatened by a heavy infantry column.

General Allenby still retained the two Indian Battalions of the 7th Indian Brigade, although they were in a somewhat exhausted condition.

After a close survey of the positions and consultations with the General Officer Commanding the Cavalry Corps, I directed four battalions of the Second Corps, which had lately been relieved from the trenches by the Indian Corps, to move to Neuve Eglise under General Shaw, in

FLANDERS

support of General Allenby. The London Scottish Territorial Battalion was also sent to Neuve Eglise.

It now fell to the lot of the Cavalry Corps, which had been much weakened by constant fighting, to oppose the advance of two nearly fresh German Army Corps for a period of over forty-eight hours, pending the arrival of a French reinforcement. Their action was completely successful. I propose to send shortly a more detailed account of the operation.

After the critical situation in front of the Cavalry Corps, which was ended by the arrival of the head of the French 16th Army Corps, the 2nd Cavalry Division was relieved by General Conneau's French Cavalry Corps and concentrated in the neighbourhood of Bailleul.

The 1st Cavalry Division continued to hold the line of trenches east of Wulverghem.

From that time to the date of this despatch the Cavalry Divisions have relieved one another at intervals, and have supported by their artillery the attacks made by the French throughout that period on Hollebeke, Wytschaete and Messines.

The Third Corps in its opposition on the right of the Cavalry Corps continued throughout the same period to repel constant attacks against its front, and suffered severely from the enemy's heavy artillery fire.

The artillery of the 4th Division constantly assisted the French in their attacks.

The General Officer Commanding Third Corps brings specially to my notice the excellent behaviour of the East Lancashire Regiment, the Hampshire Regiment and the Somersetshire Light Infantry in these latter operations; and the skilful manner in which they were handled by General Hunter-Weston, Lieutenant-Colonel Butler and the Battalion Commanders.

9. The Lahore Division arrived in its concentration area in rear of the Second Corps on the 19th and 20th October.

THE INDIAN TROOPS

I have already referred to the excellent work performed by the battalions of this Division which were supporting the Cavalry. The remainder of the Division from the 25th October onwards were heavily engaged in assisting the 7th Brigade of the Second Corps in fighting round Neuve Chappelle. Another brigade took over some ground previously held by the French 1st Cavalry Corps, and did excellent service.

On the 28th October especially the 47th Sikhs and the 20th and 21st Companies of the 3rd Sappers and Miners distinguished themselves by their gallant conduct in the attack on Neuve Chappelle, losing heavily in officers and men.

After the arrival of the Meerut Division at Corps Headquarters the Indian Army Corps took over the line previously held by the Second Corps, which was then partially drawn back into reserve. Two and a half brigades of British Infantry and a large part of the Artillery of the Second Corps still remained to assist the Indian Corps in defence of this line. Two and a half battalions of these brigades were returned to the Second Corps when the Ferozepore Brigade joined the Indian Corps after its support of the Cavalry further North.

The Secunderabad Cavalry Brigade arrived in the area during the 1st and 2nd November, and the Jodhpur Lancers came about the same time. They were all temporarily attached to the Indian Corps.

Up to the date of the present despatch the line held by the Indian Corps has been subjected to constant bombardment by the enemy's heavy artillery, followed up by infantry attacks.

On two occasions these attacks were severe.

On the 13th October the 18th Gurkha Rifles of the Bareilly Brigade were driven from their trenches, and on the 2nd November a serious attack was developed against a portion of the line west of Neuve Chappelle. On this

FLANDERS

occasion the line was to some extent pierced, and was consequently slightly bent back.

The situation was prevented from becoming serious by the excellent leadership displayed by Colonel Norie, of the 2nd Gurkha Rifles.

Since their arrival in this country, and their occupation of the line allotted to them, I have been much impressed by the initiative and resource displayed by the Indian troops. Some of the ruses they have employed to deceive the enemy have been attended with the best results, and have doubtless kept superior forces in front of them at bay.

The Corps of Indian Sappers and Miners have long enjoyed a high reputation for skill and resource. Without going into detail, I can confidently assert that throughout their work in this campaign they have fully justified that reputation.

The General Officer Commanding the Indian Army Corps describes the conduct and bearing of these troops in strange and new surroundings to have been highly satisfactory, and I am enabled, from my own observation, to fully corroborate his statement.

Honorary Major-General H. H. Sir Pratap Singh Bahadur, G.C.S.I., G.C.V.O., K.C.B., A.D.C., Maharaja-Regent of Jodhpur ; Honorary Lieutenant H. H. The Maharaja of Jodhpur ; Honorary Colonel H. H. Sir Ganga Singh Bahadur, G.C.S.I., G.C.I.E., A.D.C., Maharaja of Bikanir ; Honorary Major H. H. Sir Madan Singh Bahadur, K.C.S.I., K.C.I.E., Maharaja-Dhiraj of Kishengarh ; Honorary Captain The Honourable Malik Umar Hayat Khan, C.I.E., M.V.O., Tiwana ; Honorary Lieutenant Raj-Kumar Hira Singh of Panna ; Honorary Lieutenant Maharaj-Kumar Hitendra Narayan of Cooch Behar ; Lieutenant Malik Mumtaz Mahomed Khan, Native Indian Land Forces ; Resaldar Khwaja Mahomed Khan Bahadur, Queen Victoria's Own Corps of Guides ;

EMPEROR SENDS UP THE PRUSSIAN GUARD

Honorary Captain Shah Mirza Beg, are serving with the Indian contingents.

10. Whilst the whole of the line has continued to be heavily pressed, the enemy's principal efforts since the 1st November have been concentrated upon breaking through the line held by the First British and 9th French Corps, and thus gaining possession of the town at Ypres.

From the 2nd November onwards the 27th, the 15th and parts of the Bavarian 13th and 2nd German Corps, besides other troops, were all directed against this northern line.

About the 10th instant, after several units of these Corps had been completely shattered in futile attacks, a division of the Prussian Guard, which had been operating in the neighbourhood of Arras, was moved up to this area with great speed and secrecy. Documents found on dead officers prove that the Guard had received the Emperor's special commands to break through and succeed where their comrades of the line had failed.

They took a leading part in the vigorous attacks made against the centre on the 11th and 12th; but, like their comrades, were repulsed with enormous loss.

Throughout this trying period Sir Douglas Haig, ably assisted by his Divisional and Brigade Commanders, held the line with marvellous tenacity and undaunted courage.

Words fail me to express the admiration I feel for their conduct, or my sense of the incalculable services they rendered. I venture to predict that their deeds during these days of stress and trial will furnish some of the most brilliant chapters which will be found in the military history of our time.

The First Corps was brilliantly supported by the 3rd Cavalry Division under General Byng. Sir Douglas Haig has constantly brought this officer's eminent services to my notice. His troops were repeatedly called upon to restore the situation at critical points, and to fill gaps in the line caused by the tremendous losses which occurred.

Both Corps and Cavalry Division Commanders particularly bring to my notice the name of Brigadier-General Kavanagh, Commanding the 7th Cavalry Brigade, not only for his skill but his personal bravery and dash. This was particularly noticeable when the 7th Cavalry Brigade was brought up to support the French troops when the latter were driven back near the village of Klein Zillebeke on the night of the 7th November. On this occasion I regret to say Colonel Gordon Wilson, Commanding the Royal Horse Guards, and Major the Hon. Hugh Dawnay, Commanding the 2nd Life Guards, were killed.

In these two officers the Army has lost valuable cavalry leaders.

Another officer whose name was particularly mentioned to me was that of Brigadier-General FitzClarence, V.C., Commanding the 1st Guards Brigade. He was, unfortunately, killed in the night attack of the 11th November. His loss will be severely felt.

The First Corps Commander informs me that on many occasions Brigadier-General the Earl of Cavan, Commanding the 4th Guards Brigade, was conspicuous for the skill, coolness and courage with which he led his troops, and for the successful manner in which he dealt with many critical situations.

I have more than once during this campaign brought forward the name of Major-General Bulfin to Your Lordship's notice. Up to the evening of the 2nd November, when he was somewhat severely wounded, his services continued to be of great value.

On the 5th November I despatched eleven battalions of the Second Corps, all considerably reduced in strength, to relieve the infantry of the 7th Division, which was then brought back into general reserve.

Three more battalions of the same Corps, the London Scottish and Hertfordshire Battalions of Territorials, and

THE FLYING CORPS AND THE TERRITORIAL

the Somersetshire and Leicestershire Regiments of Yeomanry, were subsequently sent to reinforce the troops fighting to the east of Ypres.

General Byng in the case of the Yeomanry Cavalry Regiments and Sir Douglas in that of the Territorial Battalions speak in high terms of their conduct in the field and of the value of their support.

The battalions of the Second Corps took a conspicuous part in repulsing the heavy attacks delivered against this part of the line. I was obliged to despatch them immediately after their trying experiences in the southern part of the line and when they had had a very insufficient period of rest; and, although they gallantly maintained these northern positions until relieved by the French, they were reduced to a condition of extreme exhaustion.

The work performed by the Royal Flying Corps has continued to prove of the utmost value to the success of the operations.

I do not consider it advisable in this despatch to go into any detail as regards the duties assigned to the Corps and the nature of their work, but almost every day new methods for employing them, both strategically and tactically, are discovered and put into practice.

The development of their use and employment has indeed been quite extraordinary, and I feel sure that no effort should be spared to increase their numbers and perfect their equipment and efficiency.

In the period covered by this despatch Territorial Troops have been used for the first time in the Army under my command.

The units actually engaged have been the Northumberland, Northamptonshire, North Somerset, Leicestershire and Oxfordshire Regiments of Yeomanry Cavalry; and the London Scottish, Hertfordshire, Honourable Artillery Company and the Queen's Westminster Battalions of Territorial Infantry.

FLANDERS

The conduct and bearing of these units under fire, and the efficient manner in which they carried out the various duties assigned to them, have imbued me with the highest hope as to the value and help of Territorial Troops generally.

Units which I have mentioned above, other than these, as having been also engaged have by their conduct fully justified these hopes.

Regiments and battalions as they arrive come into a temporary camp of instruction, which is formed at Headquarters, where they are closely inspected, their equipment examined, so far as possible perfected, and such instruction as can be given to them in the brief time available in the use of machine guns, etc., is imparted.

Several units have now been sent up to the front besides those I have already named, but have not yet been engaged.

I am anxious in this despatch to bring to Your Lordship's special notice the splendid work which has been done throughout the campaign by the Cyclists of the Signal Corps.

Carrying despatches and messages at all hours of the day and night in every kind of weather, and often traversing bad roads blocked with transport, they have been conspicuously successful in maintaining an extraordinary degree of efficiency in the service of communications.

Many casualties have occurred in their ranks, but no amount of difficulty or danger has ever checked the energy and ardour which has distinguished their Corps throughout the operations.

11. As I close this despatch there are signs in evidence that we are possibly in the last stages of the battle of Ypres-Armentières.

For several days past the enemy's artillery fire has considerably slackened, and infantry attack has practically ceased.

THE MILITARY SITUATION

In remarking upon the general military situation of the Allies as it appears to me at the present moment, it does not seem to be clearly understood that the operations in which we have been engaged embrace nearly all the Continent of Central Europe from East to West. The combined French, Belgian and British Armies in the West, and the Russian Army in the East are opposed to the united forces of Germany and Austria acting as a combined army between us.

Our enemies elected at the commencement of the war to throw the weight of their forces against the armies in the West, and to detach only a comparatively weak force, composed of very few first-line troops and several corps of the second and third lines, to stem the Russian advance till the Western Forces could be completely defeated and overwhelmed.

Their strength enabled them from the outset to throw greatly superior forces against us in the West. This precluded the possibility of our taking a vigorous offensive, except when the miscalculations and mistakes made by their commanders opened up special opportunities for a successful attack and pursuit.

The battle of the Marne was an example of this, as was also our advance from St. Omer and Hazebrouck to the line of the Lys at the commencement of this battle. The rôle which our armies in the West have consequently been called upon to fulfil has been to occupy strong defensive positions, holding the ground gained and inviting the enemy's attack ; to throw these attacks back, causing the enemy heavy losses in his retreat and following him up with powerful and successful counter-attacks to complete his discomfiture.

The value and significance of the rôle fulfilled since the commencement of hostilities by the Allied Forces in the West lies in the fact that at the moment when the Eastern Provinces of Germany are in imminent danger of being

FLANDERS

overrun by the numerous and powerful armies of Russia, nearly the whole of the active army of Germany is tied down to a line of trenches extending from the Fortress of Verdun on the Alsatian Frontier round to the sea at Nieuport, east of Dunkirk (a distance of 260 miles), where they are held, much reduced in numbers and morale by the successful action of our troops in the West.

I cannot speak too highly of the valuable services rendered by the Royal Artillery throughout the battle.

In spite of the fact that the enemy has brought up guns in support of his attacks of great range and shell power ours have succeeded throughout in preventing the enemy from establishing anything in the nature of an artillery superiority. The skill, courage and energy displayed by their commanders have been very marked.

The General Officer Commanding Third Corps, who had special means of judging, makes mention of the splendid work performed by a number of young Artillery Officers, who in the most gallant manner pressed forward in the vicinity of the firing line in order that their guns might be able to shoot at the right targets at the right moment.

The Royal Engineers have, as usual, been indefatigable in their efforts to assist the infantry in field fortification and trench work.

I deeply regret the heavy casualties which we have suffered; but the nature of the fighting has been very desperate, and we have been assailed by vastly superior numbers. I have every reason to know that throughout the course of the battle we have placed at least three times as many of the enemy *hors de combat* in dead, wounded and prisoners.

Throughout these operations General Foch has strained his resources to the utmost to afford me all the support he could; and an expression of my warm gratitude is also due to General D'Urbal, Commanding the 8th French

THE SUPPORT FROM THE FRENCH

Army on my left, and General Maud'huy, Commanding the 10th French Army on my right.

I have many recommendations to bring to Your Lordship's notice for gallant and distinguished service performed by officers and men in the period under report. These will be submitted shortly, as soon as they can be collected.

I have the honour to be,
    Your Lordship's most obedient servant,
(*Signed*) J. D. P. FRENCH, Field-Marshal,
Commander-in-Chief the British Forces in the Field.

V
MENTIONED IN DESPATCHES

V: France, 14*th January*, 1915.

To Field-Marshal Earl Kitchener of Khartoum, K.P., G.C.B., O.M., etc.

My Lord,

IN accordance with the last paragraph of my Despatch of the 20th November, 1914, I have the honour to bring to notice names of those whom I recommend for gallant and distinguished service in the field.

I have the honour to be,
>Your Lordship's most obedient Servant,
>(*Signed*) J. D. P. FRENCH, Field-Marshal,
>*Commander-in-Chief the British Forces in the Field.*

ROYAL NAVY.

Rear-Admiral the Hon. H. L. A. Hood, C.B., M.V.O., D.S.O.
Wing Commander C. R. Samson, D.S.O.
Squadron Commander R. B. Davies.
Flight Lieutenant C. H. Collett, D.S.O.
Flight Lieutenant R. E. C. Peirse.
Acting Commander A. S. Littlejohns.
Lieutenant E. S. Wise.
Lieutenant D. C. G. Shoppee.
Captain J. P. De Montmorency.
Rear-Admiral E. G. Shortland, R.N. (retired).
Captain Sir M. MacGregor, Bt., R.N. (retired).
Captain C. W. G. Crawford, R.N. (retired).
Paymaster-in-Chief C. Alton, C.B., R.N. (retired).
Fleet Paymaster V. H. T. Weekes, R.N.
Fleet Paymaster F. H. Berty, R.N. (retired).

GENERAL HEADQUARTERS STAFF, ETC.

Captain G. J. Acland Troyte.
Major R. B. Airey.
Lieutenant-General C. A. Anderson, C.B.
Colonel (temporary) N. G. Anderson, D.S.O.
Major (temporary Colonel) W. H. Anderson.

MENTIONED IN DESPATCHES

Major B. D. L. G. Anley, D.S.O.
Lieutenant-Colonel W. M. H. Armstrong.
Lieutenant J. Arnott.
A.C.O. and Hon. Lieutenant A. H. Badcock.
Captain R. R. C. Baggallay.
Major J. Baker.
Captain W. D. Barber.
Captain R. V. Barker (killed in action).
Major F. P. Barnes.
Lieutenant-Colonel (temporary Brigadier-General) G. de S. Barrow.
Major A. W. Bartholomew.
Major S. E. C. H. Beamish.
Major J. D. Belgrave.
Chaplain, 1st Class, Rev. F. B. D. Bickerstaffe-Drew.
Honorary Colonel H. H. Sir Ganga Singh Bahadar, G.C.S.I., G.C.I.E., A.D.C., Maharajah of Bikanir.
Colonel (temporary Brigadier-General) Hon. C. E. Bingham, C.V.O., C.B.
Lieutenant-Colonel J. F. N. Birch.
Chaplain, 3rd Class, Rev. H. W. Blackburne, M.A.
Major E. H. Blamey.
Lieutenant C. A. Bolton.
Colonel (temporary Brigadier-General) W. H. Bowes.
Major J. de V. Bowles.
Captain W. A. T. Bowly.
Chaplain (Acting) A. H. Boyd.
Colonel R. C. Boyle.
Lieutenant-Colonel R. H. H. Boys, D.S.O.
Captain (temporary) F. P. Braithwaite.
Colonel (temporary Brigadier-General) C. A. Bray, C.B., C.M.G.
Lieutenant-Colonel (temporary Colonel) G. T. M. Bridges, D.S.O.
Colonel (temporary Brigadier-General) C. J. Briggs, C.B.
Major J. E. S. Brind.
Major B. N. Brooke.
Lieutenant-Colonel H. F. Brooke.
Lieutenant (temporary Captain) W. H. Brooke.
Major E. Brown.
Major J. C. Browne.
Major J. H. Brunskill, M.B.
Colonel (temporary Brigadier-General) R. U. H. Buckland, A.D.C.
Major-General E. S. Bulfin, C.V.O., C.B.
Captain B. F. Burnett-Hitchcock, D.S.O.
Major (temporary Lieutenant-Colonel) J. T. Burnett-Stuart, D.S.O.
Major Hon. L. J. P. Butler.
Captain P. R. Butler.
Lieutenant-Colonel (temporary Brigadier-General) R. H. K. Butler.

MENTIONED IN DESPATCHES

Major-General Hon. J. H. G. Byng, C.B., M.V.O.
Major H. M. Caddell.
Major (temporary Lieutenant-Colonel) A. R. Cameron.
Colonel (temporary Brigadier-General) W. Campbell, D.S.O.
Captain W. H. McN. Campbell.
Lieutenant-Colonel F. G. E. Cannot.
Colonel (temporary Brigadier-General) J. E. Capper, C.B.
Major-General T. Capper, C.B., D.S.O.
Major-General P. M. Carnegy, C.B.
Honorary Brigadier-General (temporary Brigadier-General) F. C. Carter, C.B.
Captain W. F. S. Casson.
Major C. S. H. Viscount Castlereagh, M.V.O.
Colonel (temporary Brigadier-General) F. R. Earl of Cavan, M.V.O.
Major H. C. Cavendish.
Major J. R. E. Charles, D.S.O.
Major F. M. Chenevix-Trench (killed in action).
Colonel (temporary Brigadier-General) A. A. Chichester, D.S.O.
Captain H. S. Clay.
Major-General F. T. Clayton, C.B.
Major G. S. Clive.
Colonel A. S. Cobbe, V.C., D.S.O., A.D.C.
Colonel (temporary Brigadier-General) A. W. G. L. Cole, C.B., D.S.O.
Major Hon. R. H. Collins, D.S.O.
Captain R. J. Collins.
Major G. Conder.
Lieutenant W. la T. Congreve.
Colonel (temporary Brigadier-General) W. N. Congreve, V.C., C.B., M.V.O.
Quartermaster and Hon. Lieutenant J. Connor.
Major C. E. Corkran.
Major G. N. Cory, D.S.O.
Captain J. H. D. Costeker, D.S.O.
Lieutenant-Colonel E. A. W. Courtney.
Major Sir T. A. A. M. Cunninghame, Bt., D.S.O.
Major H. T. Cunningham.
Captain R. A. M. Currie.
Brigadier-General A. G. Dallas.
Lieutenant-Colonel C. Dalton (died of wounds received in action).
Major (temporary Lieutenant-Colonel) A. C. Daly.
Major F. E. LL. Daniell.
Major W. H. V. Darell.
Captain A. E. Davidson.
Major J. H. Davidson, D.S.O.
Captain C. M. Davies.
Major-General F. J. Davies, C.B.

MENTIONED IN DESPATCHES

Lieutenant-Colonel P. M. Davies.
Chaplain, 1st Class, Rev. E. R. Day, M.A.
Lieutenant-Colonel A. E. Delavoye.
Colonel (temporary Major-General) H. de B. De Lisle, C.B., D.S.O.
Chaplain, 3rd Class, Rev. J. Dey.
Captain J. K. Dick-Cunyngham, D.S.O.
Major G. J. Dickson.
Captain J. G. Dill.
Captain E. FitzG. Dillon.
Captain S. H. Dix.
Lieutenant-Colonel C. S. Dodgson.
Colonel (temporary Brigadier-General) B. J. C. Doran, C.B.
Colonel (temporary Brigadier-General) W. R. B. Doran, C.B., D.S.O
Major W. S. Douglas (died of wounds received in action).
Captain W. Drysdale.
Colonel N. W. H. Du Boulay.
Colonel (temporary Brigadier-General) J. P. Du Cane, C.B.
Captain J. G. Dugdale, D.S.O.
Major (temporary Lieutenant-Colonel) F. C. Dundas.
Major St. J. L. H. Du Plat Taylor, D.S.O.
Lieutenant C. C. Egerton.
Colonel (temporary Brigadier-General) R. G. Egerton, C.B.
Captain H. J. Elles.
Major H. Ensor, D.S.O., M.B.
Colonel R. H. Ewart, C.I.E., D.S.O., A.D.C.
Major P. V. Le G. Falle.
Colonel (temporary Brigadier-General) R. Fanshawe, D.S.O.
Major (temporary Lieutenant-Colonel) G. J. Farmar.
Lieutenant-Colonel N. C. Ferguson, C.M.G., M.B.
Major H. C. Fernyhough, D.S.O.
Lieutenant C. W. M. Firth.
Major B. D. Fisher.
Colonel (temporary Brigadier-General) C. Fitzclarence, V.C. (killed in action).
Brevet Lieutenant-Colonel W. C. de M. Earl Fitzwilliam, K.C.V.O. D.S.O.
Chaplain, 3rd Class, Rev. H. J. Fleming.
Lieutenant-Colonel A. Forbes.
Colonel (temporary Brigadier-General) G. T. Forestier-Walker, A.D.C.
Lieutenant-Colonel T. Fraser.
Major H. F. E. Freeland, M.V.O.
Colonel W. T. Furse, D.S.O.
Major (temporary Lieutenant-Colonel) M. F. Gage.
Major C. E. Galwey (Reserve of Officers).

MENTIONED IN DESPATCHES

Hon. Brigadier-General F. S. Garratt, C.B., D.S.O.
Brevet Lieutenant-Colonel Hon. J. F. Gathorne-Hardy.
Colonel R. J. Geddes, D.S.O., M.B.
Major E. Gibb, D.S.O.
Colonel (temporary Brigadier-General) Count A. E. W. Gleichen, K.C.V.O., C.B., C.M.G., D.S.O.
Colonel (temporary Brigadier-General) F. M. Glubb, C.B., D.S.O.
Captain (temporary Major) J. C. L. Godfray.
Captain A. L. Godman.
Major (temporary Lieutenant-Colonel) A. F. Gordon, D.S.O.
Colonel (temporary Brigadier-General) Hon. F. Gordon, D.S.O.
Captain J. S. S. P. V. Gort, Viscount, M.V.O.
Major F. W. Gosset.
Major-General H. De la P. Gough, C.B.
Captain C. A. L. Graham.
Captain C. P. Graham.
Captain A. S. Grant, D.S.O.
Major C. J. C. Grant.
Major R. F. S. Grant, M.V.O., D.S.O.
Captain G. C. Grazebrook.
Major J. E. Green.
Lieutenant-Colonel W. H. Greenly, D.S.O.
Chaplain, 4th Class, Rev. P. W. Guinness, D.S.O., B.A.
Captain R. H. Haining.
Major-General J. A. L. Haldane, C.B., D.S.O.
Major-General H. I. W. Hamilton, C.V.O., C.B., D.S.O. (killed in action).
Captain R. S. Hamilton-Grace.
Major C. H. Harington, D.S.O.
Major P. J. Harris.
Captain C. H. Hart.
Lieutenant J. F. Harter.
Lieutenant-Colonel P. O. Hazelton.
Colonel (temporary Brigadier-General) J. E. W. Headlam, C.B., D.S.O.
Colonel E. H. Hemming.
Major E. Henderson.
Lieutenant J. G. Henderson.
Major R. Henvey.
Captain C. P. Heywood.
Major D. J. J. Hill.
Major H. Hill, M.V.O.
Major R. F. A. Hobbs, D.S.O.
Colonel (temporary Brigadier-General) A. E. A. Holland, M.V.O., D.S.O.

MENTIONED IN DESPATCHES

Brevet Lieutenant-Colonel H. C. Holman, D.S.O.
Brevet Colonel M. P. C. Holt, D.S.O.
Major Hon. W. P. Hore Ruthven (Master of Ruthven), D.S O.
Brevet Lieutenant-Colonel (temporary Colonel) A. R. Hoskins D.S.O
Colonel (temporary Brigadier-General) H. Hudson, C.B., C.I.E.
Lieutenant-Colonel T. R. C. Hudson.
Major G. W. G. Hughes.
Lieutenant-Colonel G. Humphreys, D.S.O.
Captain E. T. Humphreys.
Colonel (temporary Brigadier-General) A. H. Hussey.
Major R. Hutchison.
Honorary Major General Sir Pratap Singh Bahadar, G.C.S.I., G.C.V.O. K.C., A.D.G., Maharajah of Idar, Jodhpore Lancers.
Colonel (temporary Brigadier-General) E. C. Ingouville-Williams C.B., D.S.O.
Major F. S. Irvine, M.B.
Major C. V. Isacke.
Brevet Lieutenant-Colonel H. Isacke.
Colonel (temporary Brigadier-General) H. K. Jackson, D.S.O.
Major L. C. Jackson, C.M.G.
Colonel C. W. Jacob.
Captain A. H. C. James.
Captain G. M. James (killed in action).
Major (temporary Lieutenant-Colonel) G. D. Jebb, D.S.O.
Major J. L. Jesse.
Colonel H. S. Jeudwine.
Honorary Lieutenant H. H. Raj Rajeshwar Maharaja Shiraja Sumer Singh Bahadar, Maharajah of Jodhpore, Jodhpore Lancers.
Colonel (temporary Brigadier-General) F. E. Johnson, D.S.O.
Major R. H. Johnson.
Lieutenant-Colonel H. B. Jones.
Colonel (temporary Brigadier-General) C. T. McM. Kavanagh, C.V.O., C.B., D.S.O.
Major R. H. Kearsley.
Major-General H. D'U. Keary, C.B., D.S.O.
Major-General J. L. Keir, C.B.
Captain G. C. Kelly.
Lieutenant-Colonel G. C. Kemp.
Colonel F. W. Kerr, D.S.O. (killed in action).
Major J. C. M. Kerr.
Major K. J. Kincaid-Smith, D.S.O.
Lieutenant (temporary Captain) C. E. D. King.
Major W. M. St. G. Kirke.
Honorary Major H. H. Sir Madan-Singh Bahadar, K.C S.I., Maharajah Dhiraj of Kishengarh.
Major-General H. J. S. Lansdon, C.B.

MENTIONED IN DESPATCHES

Captain B. J. Lang.
Captain A. P. Y. Langhorne, D.S.O.
Colonel (temporary Brigadier-General) S. T. B. Lawford.
Honorary Lieutenant-Colonel J. F. Laycock, D.S.O.
Captain B. P. Lefroy, D.S.O.
Captain C. G. Liddell.
Captain W. G. Lindsell.
Colonel A. L. Lynden-Bell, C.M.G.
Chaplain (Acting) Rev. J. Lynn, B.A., B.D.
Captain A. G. Lyttleton.
Quartermaster and Hon. Captain D. McCallum.
Captain D. H. B. McCalmont.
Major-General F. W. N. McCracken, C.B., D.S.O.
Captain K. McL. McKenzie.
Inspector of Mechanical Transport and Hon. Lieutenant J. C. Mackie
Major C. W. Macleod.
Major-General (temporary Lieutenant-General) Sir C. F. N. Macready, K.C.B.
Captain H. C. Maitland Makgill Crichton.
Colonel (temporary Brigadier-General) E. Makins, D.S.O.
Lieutenant Malik Mumtaz Muhammad Khan.
Hon. Captain Hon. Malik Umar Hayat Khan, C.I.E., M.V.O., Tiwana.
Captain R. H. Mangles, D.S.O.
Lieutenant-Colonel (temporary Colonel) R. J. Marker, D.S.O. (died of wounds received in action).
Major H. de C. Martelli.
Major E. E. Martin, F.R.C.V.S.
Major J. F. Martin, M.B.
Colonel (temporary Brigadier-General) F. S. Maude, C.M.G., D.S.O.
Brevet Lieutenant-Colonel (temporary Colonel) F. B. Maurice.
Major-General (temporary Lieutenant-General) R. C. Maxwell, C.B.
Captain W. J. Maxwell-Scott.
Captain and Brevet Major R. S. May.
Major C. C. M. Maynard, D.S.O.
Captain R. C. Mayne.
Major M. Meares.
Colonel J. Meek, M.D.
Colonel (temporary Brigadier-General) H. F. Mercer, C.B., A.D.C.
Colonel (temporary Brigadier-General) G. F. Milne, C.B., D.S.O.
Captain St. J. E. Montagu.
Major (temporary Colonel) A. A. Montgomery.
Major (temporary Colonel) H. M. de F. Montgomery.
Colonel (temporary Brigadier-General) R. A. K. Montgomery, C.B., D.S.O.
Lieutenant-Colonel S. G. Moores.
Major C. K. Morgan, M.B.

MENTIONED IN DESPATCHES

Major-General T. L. N. Morland, C.B., D.S.O.
Captain E. L. Moss.
Captain A. L. Moulton-Barrett.
Captain J. L. Mowbray.
Lieutenant-Colonel (temporary Brigadier-General) R. L. Mullens.
Major-General (temporary Lieutenant-General) Sir A. J. Murray, K.C.B., C.V.O., D.S.O.
Lieutenant-Colonel V. Murray.
Colonel (temporary Brigadier-General) H. C. Nanton.
Brevet Colonel F. J. Nason, D.S.O.
Captain N. Neill (killed in action).
Major C. C. Newnham.
Second Lieutenant R. H. A. Newsome.
Colonel M. W. O'Keefe, M.D.
Major R. Ommanney (killed in action).
Captain F. C. O'Rorke, F.R.C.V.S.
Inspector of Mechanical Transport, 2nd Class, and Hon. Captain A.D. Owen.
Colonel (temporary Brigadier-General) W. L. H. Paget, C.B., M.V.O.
Captain D. Paige.
Captain G. de la P. B. Pakenham.
Hon. Lieutenant Raj Kumar Hira Singh of Panna.
Quartermaster and Hon. Captain E. A. Parker.
Colonel (temporary Brigadier-General) H. D. E. Parsons, C.M.G.
Major (temporary Lieutenant-Colonel) A. W. Peck.
Chaplain (Acting) Rev. Hon. M. B. Peel.
Captain R. Earl of Pembroke and Montgomery, M.V.O.
Major (temporary Lieutenant-Colonel) A. J. B. Perceval, D.S.O.
Lieutenant-Colonel C. J. Perceval, D.S.O.
Colonel (temporary Brigadier-General) E. M. Perceval, D.S.O.
Major J. W. P. Peters.
Colonel (temp. Brigadier-General) E. J. Phipps-Hornby, V.C., C.B.
Colonel (temporary Brigadier-General) R. J. Pinney.
Second Lieutenant P. J. G. Pipon, I.C.S.
Captain W. W. Pitt-Taylor, D.S.O.
Major C. O. Place, D.S.O.
Brevet Lieutenant-Colonel Sir F. E. G. Ponsonby, K.C.V.O., C.B.
Surgeon-General (temporary) R. Porter, M.B.
Lieutenant (temporary Captain) C. C. H. Potter.
Colonel S. H. Powell.
Captain P. A. Prescott-Roberts.
Lieutenant-Colonel (temporary Colonel) W. Price, C.M.G., V.D.
Lieutenant Hon. N. J. A. Primrose.
Major S. W. H. Rawlins.
Major-General (temporary Lieutenant-General) Sir H. S. Rawlinson, Bart., C.V.O., C.B.

MENTIONED IN DESPATCHES

Chaplain (Acting) Rev. B. S. Rawlinson.
Major F. F. Ready, D.S.O.
Captain W. R. Reid.
Captain L. F. Renny.
Major-General (temporary Lieutenant-General) Sir W. R. Robertson, K.C.V.O., C.B., D.S.O.
Captain H. S. Rogers.
Brevet Lieutenant-Colonel (temporary Colonel) C. F. Romer.
Lieutenant-Colonel H. Rose.
Chaplain, 4th Class, Rev. B. W. Rowan, B.A.
Colonel (temporary Brigadier-General) H. G. Ruggles-Brise, M V.O.
Major Hon. A. V. F. Russell, M.V.O.
Lieutenant J. N. O. Rycroft.
Colonel (temporary Brigadier-General) W. H. Rycroft, C.B.
Lieutenant-Colonel Hon. C. J. Sackville-West.
Captain L. W. de V. Sadlier-Jackson, D.S.O.
Major-General A. E. Sandbach, C.B., D.S.O.
Colonel R. H. S. Sawyer, M.B., F.R.C.S.I.
Captain H. V. Scott.
Lieutenant-Colonel and Honorary Colonel Right Honourable J. E B Seely, D.S.O., T.D.
Captain W. H. E. Segrave, D.S.O.
Honorary Captain Shah Mirza Beg.
Major-General F. C. Shaw, C.B.
Colonel H. P. Shekleton, C.B.
Captain E. V. M. Shelley.
Colonel (temporary Brigadier-General) A. H. Short.
Brevet Lieutenant-Colonel T. H. Shoubridge, D.S.O.
Principal Chaplain Rev. J. M. Simms, D.D., K.H.C.
Lieutenant (temporary) E. C. Simpson.
Surgeon-General Sir A. T. Knight, Sloggett, C.B., C.M.G., K.H S
Chaplain, 4th Class, Rev. F. F. S. Smithwick, B.A.
Major E. M. de Smidt.
Major (temporary) Rt. Hon. F. E. Smith.
Colonel (temporary Brigadier-General) G. B. Smith.
Captain G. N. T. Smyth-Osborne.
Major J. M. Stapylton.
Major R. A. Steel.
Brevet Major I. Stewart.
Lieutenant G. H. Straker.
Major H. E. Street.
Captain G. A. Sullivan.
Colonel W. T. Swan, M.B.
Lieutenant-Colonel (temporary) E. D. Swinton, D.S.O.
Hon. Lieutenant Maharajah Kumar Gopal Saran Narain Singh of Takari.

MENTIONED IN DESPATCHES

Major E. N. Tandy.
Lieutenant-Colonel F. P. S. Taylor.
Captain M. G. Taylor.
Honorary Captain Hon. W. G. Thesiger, D.S.O.
Colonel W. A. Thompson.
Major C. B. Thomson.
Lieutenant J. B. Thomson.
Captain A. F. A. N. Thorne.
Captain G. Thorpe.
Colonel G. F. N. Tinley, C.B.
Major R. H. D. Tompson, D.S.O.
Colonel F. H. Treherne, F.R.C.S.Edin.
Major W. H. Trevor.
Lieutenant-Colonel J. A. S. Tulloch.
Captain J. E. Turner.
Lieutenant-Colonel P. G. Twining, M.V.O.
Lieutenant-Colonel (temporary Brigadier-General) J. H. Twiss.
Colonel (temporary Brigadier-General) J. D. T. Tyndale-Biscoe.
Major R. F. Uniacke.
Major L. R. Vaughan.
Colonel (temporary Brigadier-General) F. W. G. Wadeson.
Chaplain (Acting) Rev. P. N. Waggett.
Captain B. Walcot.
Major H. A. Walker.
Captain J. D. G. Walker, D.S.O.
Captain R. F. H. Wallace.
Colonel R. Wanless-O'Gowan.
Brevet Major C. F. Watson, D.S.O.
Lieutenant-Colonel C. D. R. Watts.
Colonel (temporary Brigadier-General) H. E. Watts, C.B.
Captain J. T. Weatherby.
Chaplain, 3rd Class, Rev. H. M. Webb-Peploe, M.A.
Lieutenant-Colonel (temporary Brigadier-General) C. B. Westmacott.
Major H. R. A. Duke of Westminster, G.C.V.O.
Colonel R. D. Whigham, D.S.O.
Honorary Brigadier-General W. L. White, C.B.
Captain C. G. Wickham, D.S.O.
Lieutenant-General Sir J. Willcocks, K.C.B., K.C.S.I., K.C.M.G., D.S.O.
Lieutenant J. L. Willcocks.
Colonel (temporary Brigadier-General) H. B. Williams, D.S.O.
Lieutenant-Colonel C. S. Wilson.
Major F. W. Wilson, F.R.C.V.S.
Major-General F. D. V. Wing, C.B.
Captain Hon. M. A. Wingfield.
Chaplain, 4th Class, Rev. D. P. Winnifrith, M.A.

MENTIONED IN DESPATCHES

Captain R. Wyllie.
Captain C. M. Yates.
Major A. Young (died of wounds received in action).
Staff-Serjeant S. Farnham.
Superintending Clerk G. Hockley, R.E.
Staff Serjeant-Major P. E. Keller.
Mechanician Serjeant-Major G. W. Martin.

Intelligence Corps.

Second Lieutenant (temporary) C. Agnew.
Major J. L. Baird, C.M.G., M.P., Scottish Horse.
Captain G. H. Bell, South Lancashire Regiment.
Second Lieutenant (temporary) W. L. Blennerhasset.
Second Lieutenant (temporary) L. O. Bosworth.
Second Lieutenant (temporary) G. D. E. Chapman.
Second Lieutenant (temporary) F. P. Cockerell.
Captain J. H. M. Cornwall.
Captain J. A. F. Cuffe, Royal Marine Light Infantry.
Captain (temporary Major) J. A. Dunnington-Jefferson, Royal Fusiliers.
Second Lieutenant (temporary) R. B. FitzGerald.
Second Lieutenant (temporary) W. G. Gabain.
Second Lieutenant (temporary) J. S. Hay.
Second Lieutenant (temporary) F. E. Hotblack.
Captain F. W. Hunt, Indian Army (killed in action).
Second Lieutenant (temporary) E. H. King.
Captain R. Lambert, D.S.O.
Lieutenant D. C. M. Lawrie, 8th Hussars.
Second Lieutenant (temporary) F. O. Morris.
Second Lieutenant (temporary) C. Sandeman.
Second Lieutenant (temporary) C. M. Smith.
Lieutenant A. M. Smith-Cumming, Seaforth Highlanders (deceased).
Second Lieutenant (temporary) E. H. Smythe.
Lieutenant (temporary Captain) W. L. Spiers, 11th Hussars.
Second Lieutenant (temporary) A. Waley.
Second Lieutenant (temporary) G. Wood.
Serjeant-Major (now temporary Lieutenant) T. Curry.
Serjeant L. Kirchner.

Royal Flying Corps.

Lieutenant (temporary Captain) R. O. Abercromby, Gordon Highlanders.
Brevet Major H. J. W. Becke, Notts and Derby Regiment.
Captain A. E. Borton, Royal Highlanders.
Lieutenant (temporary Captain) H. le M. Brock, Royal Warwickshire Regiment.
Major A. D. Carden, Royal Engineers.

MENTIONED IN DESPATCHES

Lieutenant (temporary Captain) E. F. Chinnery, Coldstream Guards (since killed in action).
Captain R. Cholmondeley, Rifle Brigade.
Captain F. J. L. Cogan, R.A.
Lieutenant (temporary Captain) E. R. L. Corballis, Royal Dublin Fusiliers.
Major (temporary Lieutenant-Colonel) J. F. A. Higgins, D.S.O., Royal Artillery.
Captain H. H. Hughes Hallett, North Staffordshire Regiment.
Lieutenant G. N. Humphreys, (S.R.).
Lieutenant (temporary Captain) B. T. James, R.E.
Second Lieutenant O. G. W. G. Lywood, Norfolk Regiment.
Captain (temporary Major) A. C. H. Maclean, Royal Scots.
Second Lieutenant G. J. Malcolm, Royal Artillery.
Captain A. C. E. Marsh, Royal Artillery.
Captain R. B. Martyn, Wiltshire Regiment.
Major H. Musgrave, Royal Engineers.
Lieutenant (temp. Captain) H. J. A. Roche, Royal Munster Fusiliers (since killed).
Major W. G. H. Salmond, Royal Artillery.
Lieutenant A. Shekleton, Royal Munster Fusiliers.
Captain (temporary Major) G. S. Shephard, Royal Fusiliers.
Lieutenant F. G. Small, Connaught Rangers.
Second Lieutenant F. G. Small, Connaught Rangers.
Second Lieutenant L. A. Strange, Dorset Regiment.
Captain G. E. Todd, Welsh Regiment.
Second Lieutenant V. H. M. Wadham, Hampshire Regiment.

1st LIFE GUARDS.

Major Hon. A. F. Stanley, D.S.O.
Captain Lord H. W. Grosvenor.
Captain L. H. Hardy.
Captain Hon. E. H. Wyndham.
Captain Hon. E. S. Wyndham, D.S.O.
Lieutenant A. L. E. Smith.
Serjeant J. Roantree.
Corporal F. Lidster.
Trooper G. Swain.
Trooper S. Whittaker.

2nd LIFE GUARDS.

Major Hon. H. Dawnay, D.S.O. (killed in action).
Captain T. G. J. Torrie (Ind. Cav. attached).
Lieutenant S. G. Menzies, D.S.O.
Corporal of Horse R. Glynn.
Corporal H. Tingey.

MENTIONED IN DESPATCHES

ROYAL HORSE GUARDS.
Lieutenant-Colonel G. C. Wilson, M.V.O. (killed in action).
Major H. W. Earl of Erne, M.V.O., D.S.C.
Major Lord D. Tweedmouth, M.V.O., D.S.O.
Captain G. V. S. Bowlby.
Captain A. W. Foster.
Captain Lord A. R. Innes-Ker, D.S.O.
Lieutenant Lord A. St. C. Sutherland-Leveson-Gower.
Second Lieutenant (temporary) C. Kerr.

2ND DRAGOON GUARDS.
Captain H. W. Hall.
Lieutenant G. Sartorius (Ind. Cav. attached).
Serjeant C. C. Wallace.

3RD DRAGOON GUARDS.
Captain P. D. Stewart.
Captain E. Wright (killed in action).
Lieutenant E. W. Chapman (killed in action).
Captain E. R. Coles.
Lieutenant H. A. Grimshaw.
Lieutenant C. E. R. Holroyd-Smyth (Reserve of Officers).
Second Lieutenant W. G. Bagnell (Special Reserve).
Shoeing Smith R. Brydon.
Serjeant T. H. Chalmers.
Corporal A. Kendrick.
Lance-Corporal F. Hill.

4TH DRAGOON GUARDS.
Major H. S. Sewell.
Major A. Solly-Flood, D.S.O.
Captain C. B. Hornby.
Lieutenant (temporary Captain) J. W. Aylmer.
Lieutenant (temporary) A. C. G. Harrison (attached).
Second Lieutenant (temporary) N. Thwaites (attached).
Second Lieutenant L. M. E. Dent, D.S.O. (6th Dragoon Guards, Special Reserve).
Serjeant-Cook H. F. Allaby.
Serjeant J. Baldwin.
Serjeant W. J. Calloway.
Serjeant T. Phillips.
Lance-Corporal L. S. Bull.
Lance-Corporal E. Fisher.

5TH DRAGOON GUARDS.
Captain E. W. S. Balfour.
Captain J. E. D. Holland.

MENTIONED IN DESPATCHES

6TH DRAGOON GUARDS.
Captain M. N. Kennard.
Squadron Serjeant-Major F. Gillham.
Corporal A. J. Furze.
Private S. Absolom.
Private J. R. Cline.
Private H. W. C. Lambert.
Private J. Merrilees.
Private P. W. Nash.
Private W. E. Wright.

7TH DRAGOON GUARDS.
Private C. Cook.

1ST (ROYAL) DRAGOONS.
Lieutenant-Colonel G. F. Steele.
Major T. P. Dorington.
Captain R. Houston.
Lieutenant (temporary Captain) Hon. J. H. F. Grenfell, D.S.O.
Lieutenant H. M. P. Hewitt.
Lieutenant A. Waterhouse.
Serjeant J. Waldrond.
Corporal R. Kelman.
Private A. Bartlett.
Private G. W. MacDonald.
Private J. C. Yeaman.

2ND DRAGOONS.
Lieutenant (temporary Captain) H. D. Denison-Pender.
Second Lieutenant O. T. D. Osmond-Williams, D.S.O.
Quartermaster and Hon. Lieutenant D. Coutts.

3RD HUSSARS.
Major H. Combe.
Second Lieutenant (temporary Lieutenant) D. P. B. Taylor.

4TH HUSSARS.
Lieutenant-Colonel P. Howell.
Captain T. W. Pragnell.
Lieutenant K. C. North (killed in action).
Lieutenant J. R. V. Sherston (Ind. Cav. attached).
Corporal A. Ewens.
Lance-Corporal J. Slater.
Private J. Bennett.
Private F. Herbert.
Private C. Pooley.
Private T. F. Temple.

MENTIONED IN DESPATCHES

5TH LANCERS.
Major J. B. Jardine, D.S.O.
Captain Hon. H. C. Alexander, D.S.O.
Captain B. W. Robinson.
Lieutenant W. H. Coulter.

7TH HUSSARS.
Captain E. G. K. Cross, Special Reserve.

9TH LANCERS.
Major E. H. E. Abadie, D.S.O.
Major H. M. Durand, D.S.O.
Lieutenant R. L. Benson.
Lieutenant G. H. Phipps-Hornby.

10TH HUSSARS.
Major Hon. W. G. S. Cadogan, M.V.O. (killed in action).
Major Hon. C. B. O. Mitford.
Captain C. H. Peto (killed in action).
Lieutenant C. B. Wilson (Reserve of Officers).
Lance-Corporal W. Barnes.

11TH HUSSARS.
Lieutenant-Colonel T. T. Pitman.
Captain M. L. Lakin (Special Reserve).
Captain A. B. Lawson.
Captain Hon. C. H. G. Mulholland.

12TH LANCERS.
Major C. Fane, D.S.O.
Major G. W. Hobson (Reserve of Officers).
Captain C. E. Bryant.
Lieutenant J. Leslie (Special Reserve).
Lieutenant D. C. H. Richardson.
Second Lieutenant M. C. Wroughton (Special Reserve) (killed in action).
Serjeant E. Edwards.
Lance-Corporal S. Gregory.

14TH HUSSARS.
Major J. G. Browne (attached 3rd Dragoon Guards).

15TH HUSSARS.
Major F. C. Pilkington.
Captain A. Courage.

MENTIONED IN DESPATCHES

Lieutenant H. F. Brace.
Lieutenant (temporary) P. P. Curtis (attached).
Lieutenant C. H. Liddell.
Lieutenant C. J. L. Stanhope.
Serjeant C. Ryland.
Serjeant R. C. Scarterfield.
Corporal W. P. R. Witt.
Lance-Corporal C. Bradford.
Private D. T. Holmes.

16TH LANCERS.

Lieutenant-Colonel C. J. Eccles.
Major C. L. K. Campbell.
Captain C. M. Dixon (Special Reserve).
Captain A. W. Macarthur-Onslow (killed in action).
Lieutenant D. R. Cross.
Second Lieutenant C. J. Aris, D.S.O.
Lance-Serjeant F. J. Page.
Private E. House.

18TH HUSSARS.

Lieutenant G. W. Gore-Langton.
Lieutenant (temporary Captain) W. Holdsworth.

19TH HUSSARS.

Major A. W. Parsons.
Major C. R. McClure (killed in action).
Lieutenant E. G. Davidson.
Squadron Serjeant-Major E. Holland.
Serjeant J. E. Linthwaite.
Corporal H. Neve.
Corporal C. Rush.
Private W. Canham.

20TH HUSSARS.

Major G. T. R. Cook.
Captain J. C. Darling.
Captain G. A. Sanford.
Lieutenant J. K. McConnel, D.S.O.
Lieutenant W. A. Silvertop.
Corporal T. Buck.
Serjeant W. Lucking.
Lance-Corporal R. Jardine.
Private A. Webster.

MENTIONED IN DESPATCHES

MILITARY MOUNTED POLICE.
Lance-Corporal J. Matkin.
Serjeant G. Royle.
Serjeant L. C. Smyrk.

NORTH IRISH HORSE.
Major A. W. J. C. Viscount Massereene and Ferrard, D.S.O.
Corporal J. Wright.
Private R. McIlwane.

SOUTH IRISH HORSE.
Lieutenant J. Roche-Kelly.
Private J. E. Wright.
Private J. Johnston.

NORTHAMPTONSHIRE YEOMANRY.
Lieutenant-Colonel H. Wickham.

NORTHUMBERLAND HUSSARS.
Lieutenant-Colonel P. B. Cookson.
Major H. Sidney.
Captain S. Burrell.
Captain W. A. Kennard, 13th Hussars (Adjutant).
Second Lieutenant P. Eustace-Smith.
Second Lieutenant E. R. Joicey.
Second Lieutenant C. M. Laing.
Squadron Serjeant-Major M. Halliday.
Serjeant G. Allison.
Serjeant A. Armstrong.
Serjeant R. Cooke-Jones.
Serjeant E. Nicholson.
Corporal J. Cruickshank.
Lance-Corporal J. R. Hall.
Trooper T. Blair.

OXFORDSHIRE HUSSARS.
Second Lieutenant (temporary Captain) F. A. Gill.

NORTH SOMERSET YEOMANRY.
Lieutenant-Colonel G. C. Glyn, D.S.O.
Major G. Lubbock.
Captain E. L. Gibbs.
Second Lieutenant R. C. B. Gibbs.
Second Lieutenant L. C. Gibbs.
Serjeant A. E. Cleall.
Corporal K. G. Jenkins.
Private E. Evans.
Private V. C. Tutton.

MENTIONED IN DESPATCHES

Royal Horse Artillery.
Major H. P. Burnyeat.
Lieutenant D. J. Cochrane.
Major W. S. D. Craven.
Lieutenant H. L. Davies (" F " Battery) (killed in action).
Major R. G. Finlayson.
Major A. B. Forman, D.S.O.
Major O. M. Harris (" N " Battery).
Major W. H. Kay.
Major J. W. F. Lamont.
Captain E. B. Maxwell.
Captain E. F. Norton.
Major J. S. Ollivant, D.S.O.
Lieutenant-Colonel H. C. C. Uniacke.
Major G. H. A. White.
Quartermaster-Serjeant H. A. Hibbert.
Battery Serjeant-Major W. H. Lane.

Royal Field Artillery.
Lieutenant-Colonel E. W. Alexander (27th Brigade).
Captain H. Allen (Siege Artillery).
Captain R. W. Allen (29th Battery).
Lieutenant-Colonel A. T. Anderson.
Lieutenant E. L. B. Anderson, D.S.O. (108th Battery).
Major A. G. Arbuthnot, D.S.O. (24th Battery).
Lieutenant-Colonel D. Arbuthnot (44th Brigade).
Major H. W. Atlay (15th Brigade).
Lieutenant-Colonel C. N. B. Ballard (15th Brigade).
Lieutenant A. G. Bates (31st Battery).
Major H. T. Belcher, D.S.O.
Major A. B. Bethell (29th Battery).
Lieutenant-Colonel H. Biddulph (Divisional Ammunition Column).
Lieutenant R. Blewitt, D.S.O. (54th Battery).
Captain S. A. Boddam-Whetham.
Major H. H. Bond (17th Battery).
Lieutenant-Colonel H. J. Brock.
Captain Lord A. E. Browne, Reserve of Officers (28th Brigade).
Major T. Bruce (41st Battery).
Major L. M. Bucknill (105th Battery).
Captain H. F. Burke (Siege Artillery).
Lieutenant-Colonel A. T. Butler (23rd Brigade).
Lieutenant-Colonel G. G. S. Carey (39th Brigade).
Major H. E. Carey (108th Battery).
Major C. R. B. Carrington (16th Battery).
Major J. Carruthers, M.V.O. (134th Battery).
Lieutenant-Colonel G. N. Cartwright (55th Battery).

MENTIONED IN DESPATCHES

Lieutenant F. C. Chaytor (106th Battery).
Lieutenant-Colonel H. W. A. Christie (12th Battery).
Major J. Chrystie (Siege Artillery) (killed in action).
Major H. C. S. Clarke (70th Battery).
Captain J. H. M. Cornwall.
Lieutenant A. F. B. Cottrell (54th Battery).
Second Lieutenant A. N. Coxe (105th Battery) (died of wounds received in action).
Lieutenant H. W. Crippin (87th Battery).
Captain F. L. M. Crossman (32nd Brigade).
Colonel C. Cunliffe Owen.
Second Lieutenant F. H. N. Davidson (27th Brigade).
Captain L. E. O. Davidson (27th Brigade).
Major P. P. E. de Berry (93rd Battery).
Second Lieutenant M. E. Dennis (106th Battery).
Captain D. S. Dodgson (Siege Artillery) (killed in action).
Captain P. B. Dresser (25th Battery).
Lieutenant-Colonel E. J. Duffus (8th Brigade).
Second Lieutenant E. G. Earle (8th Brigade).
Lieutenant J. D. Edge (61st Battery).
Lieutenant R. H. Eliott (45th Battery).
Lieutenant-Colonel R. J. G. Elkington.
Major C. L. Evans (Siege Artillery).
Major W. Evans, D.S.O. (25th Battery).
Major C. N. Ewart (Siege Artillery).
Colonel (temporary Brigadier-General) E. A. Fanshawe.
Lieutenant-Colonel D. J. M. Fasson.
Lieutenant S. F. M. Ferguson (23rd Brigade).
Lieutenant-Colonel R. Fitzmaurice (Divisional Ammunition Column).
Major Hon. D. A. Forbes, M.V.O. (Divisional Ammunition Column).
Lieutenant-Colonel C. H. Ford (Divisional Ammunition Column).
Colonel R. F. Fox, D.S.O. (24th Battery).
Second Lieutenant N. W. W. Freer.
Lieutenant R. C. Freer (40th Battery).
Lieutenant B. A. H. Gage (7th Battery).
Lieutenant H. Gardner.
Lieutenant-Colonel G. H. Geddes (25th Brigade).
Lieutenant-Colonel J. G. Geddes.
Major L. Godman (15th Battery).
Lieutenant-Colonel A. H. S. Goff.
Lieutenant-Colonel L. A. C. Gordon (4th Brigade).
Second Lieutenant W. B. Gosset (5th Battery) (killed in action).
Captain C. R. Gover (25th Battery).
Second Lieutenant F. Graham, D.S.O. (51st Battery).
Lieutenant-Colonel L. Graham.
Major H. A. Hamilton.

MENTIONED IN DESPATCHES

Captain R. T. Hammick (23rd Brigade).
Lieutenant K. B. Harbord (24th Brigade).
Lieutenant Colonel R. S. Hardman.
Second Lieutenant J. B. Harman (29th Battery) (killed in action).
Second Lieutenant L. A. Hawes (Siege Artillery).
Lieutenant A. G. Hewson (15th Brigade).
Lieutenant-Colonel L. J. Hext (109th Battery).
Major H. W. Hill (105th Battery).
Lieutenant E. J. T. Housden.
Second Lieutenant H. W. Huggins, D.S.O.
Second Lieutenant C. A. Jardine, D.S.O. (127th Battery).
Major W. Jennings (Ammunition Column).
Lieutenant-Colonel H. Johnstone (30th Brigade).
Major H. Karslake, D.S.O. (129th Battery).
Major G. R. V. Kinsman (28th Brigade).
Lieutenant J. P. Knight, D.S.O. (44th Brigade).
Lieutenant-Colonel H. A. Lake (Divisional Ammunition Column).
Lieutenant-Colonel E. P. Lambert (35th Brigade).
Lieutenant-Colonel C. E. Lawrie, D.S.O. (24th Brigade).
Captain K. W. Lee (12th Battery).
Major J. E. C. Livingstone-Learmonth (8th Brigade).
Lieutenant K. M. Loch (68th Battery).
Captain W. F. Lumsden (Siege Artillery).
Lieutenant-Colonel S. Lushington, C.M.G. (41st Brigade).
Lieutenant H. S. MacDonald (2nd Brigade).
Second Lieutenant A. H. MacIlwaine (43rd Battery).
Major G. B. Mackenzie (Siege Artillery).
Major E. B. Macnaghten (30th Battery).
Lieutenant J. D. G. MacNeece.
Lieutenant W. E. Maitland-Dougall, D.S.O. (50th Battery).
Lieutenant G. E. Mansfield (86th Battery).
Lieutenant S. W. Marriott, Army Veterinary Department (attached 34th Brigade).
Second Lieutenant J. H. Moriarty (Siege Artillery).
Lieutenant R. F. Morrison (129th Battery).
Second Lieutenant T. J. Moss (70th Battery).
Major M. Muirhead (Brigade Ammunition Column).
Lieutenant P. H. Murray.
Major A. E. Newland (130th Battery).
Lieutenant G. F. Nixon (129th Battery) (killed in action).
Second Lieutenant R. W. Oldfield (58th Battery).
Lieutenant-Colonel W. H. Onslow (27th Brigade).
Captain U. E. Osmaston (54th Battery).
Major P. J. Paterson (2nd Battery).
Lieutenant-Colonel E. J. R. Peel (54th Battery).
Captain C. C. Phillips (106th Battery).

MENTIONED IN DESPATCHES

Lieutenant G. A. Pinney.
Lieutenant G. B. Pollard (27th Brigade) (killed in action).
Lieutenant-Colonel F. Potts.
Captain W. C. Rait-Kerr, D.S.O. (57th Battery) (killed in action).
Major J. V. Ramsden (27th Brigade).
Lieutenant-Colonel F. T. Ravenhill.
Captain B. F. Rhodes (107th Battery).
Second Lieutenant J. H. K. Richardson (8th Brigade).
Major J. B. Riddell (42nd Brigade).
Captain F. M. Rideout (Siege Artillery).
Major H. C. Rochfort-Boyd (9th Battery).
Captain R. C. Rome (15th Brigade).
Captain H. A. L. Rose.
Major W. C. E. Rudkin, D.S.O. (15th Brigade).
Lieutenant-Colonel C. F. Rugge-Price.
Lieutenant-Colonel G. H. Sanders (28th Brigade).
Lieutenant-Colonel H. G. Sandilands (34th Brigade).
Lieutenant-Colonel W. B. R. Sandys (28th Brigade).
Lieutenant E. C. A. Schreiber, D.S.O. (115th Battery).
Lieutenant-Colonel F. L. Sharp (43rd Brigade).
Major W. A. Short (68th Battery).
Second Lieutenant G. P. Simpson (31st Battery).
Major H. C. Simpson.
Lieutenant-Colonel C. O. Smeaton (Siege Artillery).
Lieutenant W. H. W. Smith (108th Battery).
Lieutenant R. A. E. Smyth (5th Battery).
Lieutenant-Colonel E. W. Spedding (29th Brigade).
Lieutenant-Colonel W. C. Staveley (30th Brigade).
Major E. A. Steel (37th Brigade).
Lieutenant R. H. Studdert (28th Brigade).
Major Hon. H. E. Thellusson (Brigade Ammunition Column).
Brevet-Colonel W. A. M. Thompson (12th Brigade).
Captain J. F. P. Thorburn (28th Brigade).
Second Lieutenant R. H. Towell (41st Battery).
Lieutenant F. A. Trenchard.
Second Lieutenant J. A. Tucker (5th Battery).
Captain T. R. Ubsdell, Reserve of Officers.
Major L. D. Vernon, D.S.O.
Captain J. C. Walford, D.S.O.
Major H. Ward (134th Battery).
Major H. D. O Ward (49th Battery)
Major A. E. Wardrop (117th Battery).
Major L. E. Warren (58th Battery).
Captain S. R. Wason (130th Battery).

MENTIONED IN DESPATCHES

Lieutenant-Colonel R. A. C. Wellesley (29th Brigade).
Captain W. M. M. O'D. Welsh (59th Battery).
Lieutenant-Colonel H. D. White-Thomson, D.S.O.
Second Lieutenant C. T. Whitehouse (15th Battery).
Lieutenant-Colonel E. H. Willis (94th Battery).
Major F. A. Wilson, D.S.O. (8th Brigade).
Major L. M. Wilson (27th Brigade).
Second Lieutenant K. E. Wingfield Digby.
Lieutenant E. A. Woods.
Captain H. G. Young.
Bombardier A. Adie (47th Battery).
Farrier-Serjeant G. A. Albutt (58th Battery).
Serjeant N. W. Anderson (127th Battery).
Bombardier C. L. Baserga (126th Battery).
Farrier Staff-Serjeant M. Baxter (35th Battery).
Gunner H. Blake (134th Battery).
Serjeant J. Boyd (66th Battery).
Bombardier E. S. Brereton (125th Battery).
Battery Quartermaster-Serjeant H. G. Bugg (28th Brigade, Ammunition Column).
Regimental Serjeant-Major T. H. Bull (35th Brigade).
Corporal V. C. Buxey (47th Battery).
Bombardier A. Clarkson (44th Brigade).
Bombardier A. Collins (116th Battery).
Gunner G. Cowell (93rd Battery).
Bombardier W. Curry (41st Brigade).
Bombardier E. F. Davies (15th Battery).
Corporal J. Dean (134th Battery).
Serjeant W. E. Dickers (68th Battery).
Farrier-Serjeant J. Downie (52nd Battery).
Driver F. C. Faulkner (23rd Brigade).
Corporal A. J. Flint (109th Battery).
Serjeant G. Fox (135th Battery).
Bombardier E. J. Girding (68th Battery).
Regimental Serjeant-Major J. W. Goddard (4th Divisional Ammunition Column).
Serjeant P. W. Greest (115th Battery).
Serjeant H. W. Hines (17th Battery).
Battery Serjeant-Major H. R. Homan (65th Battery).
Bombardier W. Hook (29th Battery).
Bombardier W. S. How (93rd Battery).
Serjeant T. W. Howes (54th Battery).
Corporal Huston (17th Battery).

MENTIONED IN DESPATCHES

Regimental Serjeant-Major A. Ibbitson (30th Brigade).
Staff Serjeant-Farrier R. Keenan (4A Reserve Brigade).
Bombardier G. W. Kemp (25th Battery).
Battery Quartermaster-Serjeant W. E. Kenning (134th Battery).
Battery Quartermaster-Serjeant J. W. Kitchen (37th Brigade Ammunition Column).
Bombardier J. Lambert (31st Battery).
Serjeant C. H. Lee (123rd Battery).
Bombardier H. Mildenhall (109th Battery).
Bombardier F. Morris (47th Battery).
Corporal A. Morris (32nd Brigade Headquarters).
Bombardier A. Moyniham (37th Battery).
Havildar Major Multani Ram (attached to Meerut Divisional Ammunition Column).
Bombardier W. Neale (47th Battery).
Corporal J. E. Petty (109th Battery).
Gunner G. L. Pond (115th Battery).
Regimental Serjeant-Major W. Potter (2A Reserve Brigade).
Bombardier Z. Print (70th Battery).
Gunner H. Reeve (108th Battery).
Bombardier T. Richardson (37th Battery).
Fitter Corporal B. Rogers (42nd Brigade Ammunition Column).
Driver A. Saxby (25th Battery).
Bombardier J. Scales (30th Brigade Headquarters).
Gunner A. H. Squires (28th Brigade).
Acting Bombardier F. W. Swinerd (58th Battery).
Corporal W. Taylor.
Battery Quartermaster-Serjeant G. W. Thompson (60th Battery).
Driver A. Tibbles (15th Battery).
Gunner N. Todd (88th Battery).
Battery Serjeant-Major T. E. Wardle (8th Brigade).
Corporal C. R. Watson (70th Battery).
Gunner C. J. J. West (68th Battery).
Bombardier E. Wilfred (80th Battery).
Battery Serjeant-Major C. Wilkins (126th Battery) (now Second Lieutenant).
Serjeant F. Wilkinson (58th Battery).

Royal Garrison Artillery.

Captain C. Bovill.
Major A. Ellershaw (111th Battery).
Captain W. A. Erskine (108th Heavy Battery).
Major P. L. Holbrooke (4th Siege Battery).

MENTIONED IN DESPATCHES

Lieutenant C. P. J. Layard (110th Heavy Battery).
Captain A. M. Matthews (109th Heavy Battery).
Major H. W. M. Parker, Reserve of Officers (112th Battery).
Colonel H. de T. Phillips.
Major C. F. Phipps (48th Heavy Battery).
Major F. C. Poole, D.S.O., Reserve of Officers (114th Heavy Battery).
Captain R. M. Powell.
Captain F. M. Rideout (3rd Siege Battery).
Lieutenant-Colonel T. A. Tancred (3rd Heavy Battery).
Major G. E. Tyrrell (108th Heavy Battery).
Farrier-Quartermaster-Serjeant H. Crouch (48th Heavy Battery).
Corporal F. Fulger (2nd Siege Company).
Quartermaster-Serjeant W. Hales.
Farrier-Serjeant A. H. Hewett (108th Heavy Battery).
Serjeant R. J. Leete (48th Heavy Battery).
Acting Bombardier C. Mison (48th Heavy Battery).
Corporal J. Sargent (108th Heavy Battery).
Staff-Serjeant-Farrier H. A. Shields (25th Heavy Battery) (died of wounds received in action).
Gunner R. C. Wainwright (48th Heavy Battery).
Gunner F. Wilcox (3rd Siege Battery).

HONOURABLE ARTILLERY COMPANY (T.F.).

Lieutenant G. F. T. Murname.
Private A. L. Laskie.

ROYAL ENGINEERS.

Major G. H. Addison.
Quartermaster and Hon. Lieutenant R. J. Barnes, Postal Section, Special Reserve.
Major P. K. Betty.
Major G. H. Boileau.
Captain J. C. Bowles.
Major D. Brady.
Major F. M. Browne.
Lieutenant H. M. Cadell.
Lieutenant E. E. Calthrop.
Lieutenant G. Cheetham.
Lieutenant V. A. C. Clery.
Captain A. E. J. Collins (killed in action).
Quartermaster and Hon. Captain W. H. Dale.
Captain H. E. Day.
Second Lieutenant A. Dewar, Special Reserve.
Captain W. G. S. Dobbie.
Captain G. E. B. Dobbs.

MENTIONED IN DESPATCHES

Captain R. V. Doherty-Holwell.
Major W. S. Douglas (died of wounds received in action).
Captain J. A. Edgeworth.
Captain K. E. Edgeworth.
Captain C. O'R. Edwards
Lieutenant C. E. Fishbourne, Special Reserve.
Lieutenant R. B. Flint, D.S.O.
Lieutenant-Colonel E. G. Godfrey-Faussett.
Captain G. F. B. Goldney.
Lieutenant K. I. Gourlay.
Captain G. C. Gowlland.
Major A. H. W. Grubb, D.S.O.
Lieutenant W. F. Hanna.
Major G. C. Harvey, Royal Anglesey, Special Reserve.
Captain J. T. Heath.
Major F. G. Howard, M.V.O.
Major D. M. FitzG. Hoysted.
Lieutenant F. G. Hyland.
Lieutenant F. G. Hyland.
Captain W. H. Johnston, V.C.
Lieutenant W. A. FitzG. Kerrich.
Captain E. F. W. Lees.
Lieutenant J. A. Leventhorpe.
Major R. S. McClintock.
Lieutenant G. E. Mansergh.
Lieutenant G. le Q. Martel.
Lieutenant K. J. Martin, D.S.O.
Lieutenant-Colonel A. T. Moore.
Major H. T. G. Moore.
Captain C. G. Moores (died of wounds received in action).
Lieutenant E. L. Morris.
Captain P. Neame.
Major W. P. E. Newbigging, D.S.O., Manchester Regiment (attached)
Major C. N. North (killed in action).
Captain E. A. Osborne, D.S.O.
Captain A. L. Owen.
Captain W. E. Pain.
Captain A. N. Paxton.
Second Lieutenant G. S. T. Pilcher (Intelligence Corps) (attached).
Lieutenant C. E. R. Pottinger.
Captain C. H. Prickett.
Major H. L. Pritchard, D.S.O.
Captain H. G. Pyne.
Captain H. E. F. Rathbone.
Captain G. G. Rawson.
Quartermaster and Hon. Lieutenant W. Reid.

MENTIONED IN DESPATCHES

Second Lieutenant H. F. T. Renny-Tailyour (killed in action).
Major L. St. V. Rose (killed in action).
Lieutenant-Colonel W. H. Rotherham.
Major C. Russell-Brown.
Major A. F. Sargeaunt.
Lieutenant-Colonel A. L. Schrieber, D.S.O.
Major C. W. Singer.
Major G. E. Smith, C.M.G.
Major H. C. Smith.
Captain V. P. Smith.
Captain G. B. F. Smyth, D.S.O.
Major A. G. Stevenson, D.S.O.
Major C. B. O. Symons.
Major E. V. Turner.
Lieutenant A. Tyler (killed in action).
Major C. E. G. Vesey.
Second Lieutenant C. H. H. Vulliamy.
Major G. Walker.
Lieutenant H. C. B. Wemyss, D.S.O.
Lieutenant C. A. West.
Captain F. C. Westland.
Major J. R. White.
Captain B. H. Wilbraham.
Captain G. C. Williams.
Second Lieutenant M. R. Wingate.
Lieutenant J. S. Yule.
Lance-Corporal Allen.
Serjeant C. J. Amphlett.
Serjeant E. W. Anderson.
Superintending Clerk J. Armstrong.
Corporal H. J. Banyard.
Pioneer A. Barrett.
Corporal F. Barry.
Company Quartermaster-Serjeant A. Beck.
Corporal B. Benton.
Serjeant H. Bird.
Serjeant B. Blower.
Serjeant J. T. Bridges.
Second Corporal J. Brown.
Sapper A. E. Bullen.
Corporal P. J. Bullock.
Company Serjeant-Major J. J. Bulman.
Second Corporal (Acting Corporal) W. Bultitude.
Sapper W. Burgess.
Quartermaster-Serjeant C. H. Burrage.
Corporal E. L. Bury.

MENTIONED IN DESPATCHES

Serjeant W. Butler.
Sapper F. Callegiri.
Serjeant J. Campbell.
Serjeant T. Carey.
Corporal B. F. Carter.
Sapper F. V. Christian.
Corporal W. Clark.
Company Serjeant-Major A. B. Coe.
Second Corporal C. Collings.
Serjeant T. Comins.
Sapper J. Coombe.
Quartermaster-Serjeant F. Coombes.
Serjeant H. E. Cooper.
Driver W. H. Cooper.
Lance-Corporal (Acting Second Corporal) G. Crane.
Lance-Corporal A. Dagnall.
Lance-Corporal A. Davidson.
Corporal T. B. L. Disney.
Serjeant T. G. Dixon.
Sapper W. Dodd.
Serjeant L. Domoney.
Sapper J. Donald.
Serjeant A. Doree.
Pioneer F. Dunford.
Corporal T. J. Evans.
Second Corporal F. C. Eynott (Acting Serjeant)
Corporal H. L. F. Fegan.
Serjeant J. Ferguson.
Second Corporal C. Freshwater.
Sapper V. Fry.
Serjeant A. Gadsby.
Lance-Corporal J. Graham.
Lance-Corporal W. Guinan.
Lance-Corporal W. Gunning.
Serjeant H. Haggertay.
Serjeant W. Hales.
Pioneer W. J. Hargreaves.
Corporal A. J. Harris.
Serjeant G. S. Harris.
Pioneer R. Haward.
Corporal R. B. Hawes.
Company Quartermaster-Serjeant J. Hayman.
Second Corporal T. Hodgson.
Corporal R. H. Holyoake.
Serjeant A. Hooper.
Company Serjeant-Major H. W. Hose.

MENTIONED IN DESPATCHES

Serjeant W. Hutt.
Superintending Clerk C. H. Hutton.
Serjeant A. E. Ives.
Corporal J. James.
Corporal B. H. Jeffery.
Sapper R. Johnson.
Serjeant M. Keane.
Corporal C. Kearton.
Second Corporal G. Kemp.
Pioneer S. Kershaw.
Serjeant C. W. King.
Corporal F. Langton.
Sapper E. A. Lashmar.
Corporal A. Lazzell.
Lance-Corporal W. Leach.
Quartermaster-Serjeant E. A. Lewis.
Acting Serjeant H. Locke.
Sapper T. McCreddin.
Farrier Serjeant McDowell.
Serjeant T. Mansell.
Serjeant-Major W. G. Mansell.
Corporal E. Marsden (deceased).
Serjeant G. Marshall.
Serjeant E. Mills.
Acting Corporal L. Morris.
Corporal T. P. Norris.
Second Corporal W. Nunn.
Sapper J. O'Laughlin (deceased).
Company Quartermaster-Serjeant F. Owen.
Pioneer F. Oxer.
Corporal H. J. Payn.
Serjeant G. Perry.
Serjeant E. Phillips.
Sapper G. Reddaway.
Corporal W. Roberts.
Corporal W. Rouse.
Sapper J. Rowland.
Corporal M. Ryan.
Superintending Clerk H. Simpson.
Company Quartermaster-Serjeant R. Sinclair.
Sapper E. A. Singleton.
Serjeant J. Smeeth.
Sapper H. Stokes.
Serjeant J. Stooke.
Serjeant W. Swain.
Superintending Clerk G. H. Taylor.

MENTIONED IN DESPATCHES

Corporal S. Taylor.
Serjeant J. Thorne.
Second Corporal W. Trump.
Serjeant A. Upton.
Shoeing Smith Corporal R. J. Wheals.
Sapper H. Whitting.
Corporal A. Wilkinson.
Corporal J. Wood.
Serjeant C. J. Woode.
Pioneer L. G. Woolgar.
Corporal S. P. Wright.
Serjeant F. Wyatt.
Pioneer R. Wylie.

3RD SIGNAL COMPANY.

Lieutenant R. W. Dammers (Notts and Derby Regiment).
Lieutenant C. Deakin (Worcester Regiment).

1ST BATTALION GRENADIER GUARDS.

Brevet Lieutenant-Colonel M. Earle, D.S.O.
Major L. R. V. Colby (killed in action).
Major H. St. L. Stucley (killed in action).
Major Honourable A. O. W. C. Weld Forester, M.V.O. (killed in action).
Captain R. E. K. Leatham.
Captain G. E. C. Rasch.
Captain Lord R. Wellesley (killed in action).
Lieutenant M. A. A. Darby.
Lieutenant Lord C. N. Hamilton, D.S.O.
Lieutenant G. E. Hope.
Quartermaster and Hon. Lieutenant J. Teece.
Serjeant-Major J. E. Parkin
Lance-Corporal T. W. Francis.

2ND BATTALION GRENADIER GUARDS.

Lieutenant-Colonel W. R. A. Smith.
Lieutenant H. F. B. Lord Congleton (killed in action).
Serjeant W. E. Jaques.
Lance-Corporal A. W. Sapsford.
Private W. A. Chapman.
Private E. W. Curtis.
Private P. H. Smith.

1ST BATTALION COLDSTREAM GUARDS.

Major Hon. L. d'H. Hamilton, M.V.O.
Quartermaster and Hon. Lieutenant J. Boyd.

MENTIONED IN DESPATCHES

Serjeant W. Brown.
Serjeant T. C. Buck.
Lance-Serjeant E. A. Bushell.
Lance-Serjeant G. A. Troke.
Private F. D. Benson.
Private C. S. Chaplin (deceased).
Private A. Head.
Private T. Paxton.
Private C. Penwell.

2ND BATTALION COLDSTREAM GUARDS.

Lieutenant-Colonel C. E. Pereira.
Major P. A. Macgregor, D.S.O.
Major R. A. Markham (died of wounds received in action).
Lieutenant L. M. Gibbs.
Captain A. Leigh-Bennett.
Quartermaster and Hon. Capt. S. Wright.
Serjeant W. J. Black.
Private J. Saville.
Private B. Wells.

3RD BATTALION COLDSTREAM GUARDS.

Lieutenant-Colonel G. P. T. Feilding, D.S.O.
Major T. G. Matheson.
Captain A. G. Tritton.
Captain Hon. E. W. M. M. Brabazon, D.S.O.
Captain R. L. Dawson (killed in action).
Lieutenant R. E. A. Viscount Feilding, D.S.O., Special Reserve.
Private A. E. Friend.

1ST BATTALION SCOTS GUARDS.

Captain C. E. de la Pasture.
Captain C. F. P. Hamilton (died of wounds received in action).
Captain R. G. Stracey (killed in action).
Lieutenant Sir I. Colquhoun, Bt.
Lieutenant G. A. Lloyd (killed in action).
Quartermaster and Hon. Lieutenant D. Kinlay.
Company Serjeant-Major J. Barwick.
Serjeant J. Macdonald.
Serjeant J. Turner.
Private J. Clancy.
Private G. Locke.

2ND BATTALION SCOTS GUARDS.

Major A. B. E. Cator, D.S.O.

MENTIONED IN DESPATCHES

Captain C. V. Fox, D.S.O.
Captain G. C. B. Paynter, D.S.O.
Captain G. H. Loder.
Captain H. Taylor (killed in action).
Lieutenant (temporary Captain) Sir F. L. F. Fitz-Wygram, Bt.
Lieutenant Sir E. H. W. Hulse, Bt.
Second Lieutenant (temporary Lieutenant) G. C. L. Ottley (died of wounds received in action).
Second Lieutenant (temporary Lieutenant) E. C. T. Warner.
Quartermaster and Hon. Lieutenant T. Ross.
Serjeant-Major J. Moneur.
Serjeant T. Mitchell.
Corporal J. McLellan.
Private J. Fergusson.
Private J. Finlayson.
Private J. Robertson.

Irish Guards.

Lieutenant-Colonel Lord R. Le N. Ardee.
Major Hon. J. F. Hepburn-Stuart-Forbes-Trefusis.
Major H. A. Herbert-Stepney (killed in action).
Captain Lord F. G. Montagu Douglas Scott, D.S.O., Grenadier Guards (attd.).
Captain N. A. Orr-Ewing, D.S.O., Scots Guards (attached).
Lieutenant G. M. Maitland, Special Reserve.
Lieutenant N. L. Woodroffe (killed in action).
Drill-Serjeant A. Winspear.
Serjeant T. Corry.
Serjeant D. Voyles.

INFANTRY.

2nd Battalion Royal Scots.

Major F. J. Duncan, D.S.O.
Major H. B. Dyson.
Captain Hon. H. L. Bruce, 3rd Bn. (attd.).
Captain A. E. Croker.
Captain H. D. Saward.
Captain F. C. Tanner, D.S.O.
Captain H. G. F. Boyle, 3rd Bn. Border Regt. (attd.).
Lieutenant B. de L. Cazenove, 3rd Bn. (attd.).
Lieutenant E. P. Combe.
Lieutenant G. C. C. Strange.
Second Lieutenant (temporary Lieutenant) D. J. McDougall.
Second Lieutenant (temporary Lieutenant) T. S. Robson-Scott.
Quartermaster and Honorary Captain A. E. Everingham.

MENTIONED IN DESPATCHES

Regimental Quartermaster-Serjeant O. W. Clarke.
Serjeant J. Farrell.
Serjeant W. O. McCarthy.
Corporal R. Sangster.
Corporal S. Smith.
Lance-Corporal M. Gorman.
Private D. Anderson.
Lance-Corporal A. Austin.
Private W. Beveridge.
Private J. Burke.
Private W. Harper.
Private D. Hill.
Private W. Hodge.
Private A. Lawrie.
Drummer W. Thompson.
Private G. Vaughan.

1ST BATTALION ROYAL WEST SURREY REGIMENT.
Captain and Brevet Major C. F. Watson, D.S.O.
Captain R. F. S. Stanley-Creek, D.S.O.
Lieutenant (temporary Captain) J. D. Boyd, D.S.O.
Acting Serjeant A. C. Barnes.

2ND BATTALION ROYAL WEST SURREY REGIMENT
Lieutenant-Colonel M. C. Coles.
Major H. C. Whinfield.
Captain W. H. Alleyne.
Captain H. F. Lewis.
Captain F. S. Montague-Bates, E. Surrey Regiment (attd.).
Lieutenant R. K. Ross.
Lieutenant H. C. Williams.
Second Lieutenant (temporary Lieutenant) D. G. Ramsay, R. Sussex Regiment (attached) (killed in action).
Corporal J. Lamond.
Private S. Constant.
Private A. Knowles.

1ST BATTALION EAST KENT REGIMENT.
Colonel H. de la M. Hill.
Lieutenant G. F. Hamilton.
Lieutenant G. R. Thornhill.
Corporal H. W. Hills.
Private J. Hills.

1ST BATTALION ROYAL LANCASTER REGIMENT.
Major J. H. Morrah (killed in action).

MENTIONED IN DESPATCHES

Major R. G. Parker.
Captain W. A. T. B. Somerville.
Lieutenant C. E. R. Bridson, 3rd Battalion (attd.).
Serjeant J. Borders.
Lance-Corporal L. C. W. Hoggard.
Lance-Corporal J. Rawlinson.
Private E. Mann.

1st Battalion Northumberland Fusiliers.

Major C. Yatman, D.S.O.
Captain R. M. St. J. Booth.
Captain E. B. Gordon.
Lieutenant L. A. Barrett.
Lieutenant C. F. Nunneley, 3rd Battalion (attached).
Lieutenant R. T. Vachell.
Lieutenant F. E. Watkin (killed in action).
Lance-Corporal W. M. Stafford.

1st Battalion Royal Warwickshire Regiment.

Lieutenant-Colonel A. J. Poole.
Major W. C. Christie (killed in action).
Captain J. A. M. Bannerman.
Captain C. A. C. Bentley (killed in action).
Captain B. M. Montgomery, D.S.O.
Captain F. C. P. Williams Freeman (Reserve of Officers).
Lieutenant (temporary Captain) H. J. I. Walker.
Lieutenant E. V. Briscoe.
Quartermaster and Honorary Captain T. H. Harwood.
Private J. Cook.
Private J. Moore.
Private W. T. Russell.

2nd Battalion Royal Warwickshire Regiment.

Lieutenant-Colonel W. L. Loring (killed in action).
Major G. N. B. Forster.
Major P. J. Foster.
Captain F. B. Follett.
Captain E. G. Sydenham.
Lieutenant (temporary Captain) J. P. Duke.
Quartermaster and Honorary Lieutenant W. N. Hyde.

1st Battalion Royal Fusiliers.

Major B. G. Price, D.S.O.
Captain W. W. Chard.

MENTIONED IN DESPATCHES

Lieutenant H. M. Marshall.
Second Lieutenant (temporary Lieutenant) R. F. Cooper.
Corporal F. Bailey.

4TH BATTALION ROYAL FUSILIERS.

Lieutenant-Colonel (temporary Brigadier-General) N. R. McMahon, D.S.O. (killed in action).
Major T. R. Mallock, D.S.O.
Captain L. F. Ashburner, M.V.O., D.S.O.
Captain L. W. Le M. Carey.
Captain H. C. Forster.
Captain G. O'D. E. Thomas-O'Donel.
Lieutenant O. S. Cooper.
Lieutenant F. W. A. Steele.
Second Lieutenant C. T. Maclean, 7th Battalion (attached).
Company Serjeant-Major T. H. Crabb.
Acting Company Serjeant-Major W. G. Foster.
Serjeant G. F. Greenhill.

1ST BATTALION THE KING'S (LIVERPOOL REGIMENT).

Lieutenant-Colonel W. S. Bannatyne (killed in action).
Major C. J. Steavenson.
Captain P. Hudson.
Lieutenant J. H. A. Ryan.
Company Serjeant-Major J. Connolly (killed in action).
Private S. Halliwell.
Private H. H. Marsh.

10TH (SCOTTISH) BATTALION LIVERPOOL REGIMENT.

Captain (temporary Major) A. S. Anderson.
Company Serjeant-Major J. W. Dunham.

1ST BATTALION NORFOLK REGIMENT.

Lieutenant-Colonel (temporary Brigadier-General) C. R. Ballard.
Major H. R. Done.
Captain R. H. Brudenell-Bruce.
Captain W. C. K. Megaw.
Lieutenant E. H. T. Broadwood.
Second Lieutenant F. C. Boosey.
Second Lieutenant (temporary Lieutenant) R. W. Patteson.
Quartermaster and Honorary Lieutenant E. Smith.
Serjeant-Major J. Haggar.
Company Serjeant-Major J. G. Lawrence.
Serjeant (now Second Lieutenant, Welsh Regiment) J. W. Betts.
Lance-Corporal W. Golder.

MENTIONED IN DESPATCHES

Lance-Corporal E. Pearson.
Private C. W. Benns.
Private J. Lomas.
Private W. F. Riches.

1st Battalion Lincolnshire Regiment.

Lieutenant-Colonel W. E. B. Smith.
Captain G. K. Butt.
Captain E. James, 3rd Battalion (attached).
Captain R. H. Johnson.
Captain E. Tatchell, Reserve of Officers.
Captain L. de O. Tollemache.
Lieutenant (temporary Captain) F. H. Blackwood, D.S.O.
Second Lieutenant C. G. Shaw, Notts and Derby Regiment, S.R. (attd.).
Acting Serjeant-Major H. Parish.
Acting Company Serjeant-Major F. Maddison.
Corporal S. W. Jacobs.
Lance-Corporal W. Clay.
Private J. Cox.
Lance-Corporal A. Brownley.
Private P. J. Hatcliffe.
Private H. Holberry.
Private G. H. Phillips.

2nd Battalion Lincolnshire Regiment.

Lieutenant-Colonel G. B. McAndrew.
Lieutenant E. H. Impey.

1st Battalion Devonshire Regiment.

Lieutenant-Colonel E. G. Williams.
Captain B. H. Besly (killed in action).
Captain E. O. St. C. G. Quicke, 3rd Battalion (attd.) (killed in action).
Captain P. R. Worrall.
Lieutenant T. O. B. Ditmas (killed in action).
Lieutenant C. F. W. Lang.
Lieutenant R. E. Hancock, D.S.O. (killed in action).
Serjeant W. Booker.
Private J. E. B. Binmore.
Private H. A. Tillyer.
Lance-Corporal H. Truffery.

2nd Battalion Devonshire Regiment.

Lieutenant-Colonel J. O. Travers, D.S.O.

MENTIONED IN DESPATCHES

2ND BATTALION SUFFOLK REGIMENT.

Lieutenant-Colonel H. F. H. Clifford.
Captain E. F. Hausberg, 3rd Battalion (attached).
Captain W. B. Squirl-Dawson, 3rd Battalion (attached).
Captain A. H. W. Temple (Reserve of Officers) (killed in action).
Lieutenant E. C. T. B. Williams.
Second Lieutenant (temporary Lieutenant) H. P. Sparks.
Co. Serjeant-Major J. C. Parsons.
Co. Serjeant-Major A. Stannard.
Corporal C. Shaw.
Drummer L. Jones.
Lance-Corporal W. R. Laflin.
Private B. Barber.
Private L. Jones.

1ST BATTALION SOMERSETSHIRE LIGHT INFANTRY.

Brevet Lieutenant-Colonel C. B. Prowse.
Captain L. A. Jones-Mortimer.
Captain W. Watson.
Captain A. H. Yatman.
Lieutenant R. L. Moore (died of wounds).
Second Lieutenant V. A. Braithwaite.
Serjeant-Major J. Bond.
Company Quartermaster-Serjeant F. E. Day.
Serjeant C. Wilcox.
Serjeant J. Anglin.
Serjeant H. Delamere.
Private W. E. Venning.
Private P. Gunner.

1ST BATTALION WEST YORKSHIRE REGIMENT.

Captain W. H. A. De la Pryme.
Lieutenant J. Lawson-Smith (killed in action).
Lieutenant F. L. Wright.
Serjeant E. J. Rendell.
Lance-Corporal M. Burke.

2ND BATTALION WEST YORKSHIRE REGIMENT.

Lieutenant-Colonel G. F. Phillips.

1ST BATTALION EAST YORKSHIRE REGIMENT.

Major B. W. Bogle.
Major W. H. Young.
Captain D. F. Anderson.

MENTIONED IN DESPATCHES

Captain H. R. S. Brown, Reserve of Officers.
Lieutenant (temporary Captain) J. A. Markham.
Corporal A. H. Frost.
Lance-Corporal J. D. Burton.
Lance-Corporal C. E. A. Ptolomy.

1st Battalion Bedfordshire Regiment.

Lieutenant-Colonel C. R. J. Griffith, D.S.O.
Major W. Allason.
Major E. I. de S. Thorpe.
Captain C. E. Goff, Liverpool Regiment (attached).
Captain J. Macready.
Captain J. MacM. Milling.
Lieutenant W. St. J. Coventry.
Lieutenant J. S. Davenport.
Second Lieutenant A. G. R. Garrod, 3rd Leicestershire Regiment (attached).
Second Lieutenant L. W. Rendell (killed in action).
Company Serjeant-Major M. J. McGinn.
Company Serjeant-Major W. Sharp.
Company Serjeant-Major E. Watson.
Private H. C. Cattle.

2nd Battalion Bedfordshire Regiment.

Major R. P. Stares (killed in action).
Major J. M. Traill (commanding) (killed in action).
Captain C. C. Foss.
Captain S. C. Garnett-Botfield (died of wounds received in action).
Lieutenant W. Pastarf (killed in action).
Lieutenant E. E. Punchard (killed in action).
Second Lieutenant D. L. de T. Fernandes (killed in action).
Regimental Serjeant-Major F. W. Thurley.
Company Serjeant-Major F. W. Bliss.
Company Serjeant-Major J. Coe.
Company Serjeant-Major L. Flint.
Company Serjeant-Major J. Guerin.

1st Battalion Leicestershire Regiment.

Colonel H. L. Croker.
Captain E. S. W. Tidswell.
Captain W. C. Wilson.
Lieutenant H. L. Bayfield.
Lieutenant T. Prain (killed in action).
Lieutenant (temporary Captain) J. T. Waller.
Company Serjeant-Major (now Second Lieutenant) J. Redwood.

MENTIONED IN DESPATCHES

Serjeant R. Heath.
Corporal W. H. Moreby.
Private S. Burfield.
Private W. Keightley.

2ND BATTALION LEICESTERSHIRE REGIMENT.

Lieutenant-Colonel C. G. Blackader, D.S.O.
Lieutenant-Colonel H. Gordon.
Captain H. A. Grant (killed in action).
Second Lieutenant M. W. Seton-Browne (killed in action).
Serjeant P. Foister.
Corporal G. Gray.
Private W. O. Chamberlain (died of wounds received in action).
Private E. W. Chatten.
Lance-Corporal F. E. Garton.
Lance-Corporal J. Taylor.

2ND BATTALION ROYAL IRISH REGIMENT.

Major E. H. E. Daniell, D.S.O.
Captain G. O. M. Furnell.
Captain H. G. Gregorie.
Captain M. C. C. Harrison.
Lieutenant D. P. Laing.
Lieutenant E. G. D. M. Phillips.
Second Lieutenant H. G. O. Downing.
Company Serjeant-Major H. E. Cooper.
Company Quartermaster-Serjeant H. Heaton.
Acting Corporal W. Atley.
Acting Corporal W. Turnbull.
Lance-Corporal J. Lynch.
Lance-Corporal C. Whelan.
Private T. Barry.
Private C. Duggan.
Private J. Gowton.
Private W. Roberts.

2ND BATTALION YORKSHIRE REGIMENT.

Lieutenant-Colonel C. A. C. King (killed in action).
Captain C. G. Jeffery (died of wounds received in action).
Captain B. S. Moss-Blundell.
Captain L. Peel.
Lieutenant H. G. Brooksbank.
Lieutenant H. S. Kreyer, D.S.O.
Lieutenant F. C. Ledgard.
Lieutenant A. E. G. Palmer.
Quartermaster and Hon. Lieutenant E. Pickard.

MENTIONED IN DESPATCHES

2ND BATTALION LANCASHIRE FUSILIERS.
Lieutenant (temporary Captain) A. J. W. Blencowe.
Captain R. Luker.
Captain A. H. Spooner.
Captain J. E. S. Woodman, D.S.O.
Company Serjeant-Major Clague.

1ST BATTALION ROYAL SCOTS FUSILIERS.
Lieutenant-Colonel (temporary Brigadier-General) W. D. Smith.
Captain C. J. C. Barrett (killed in action).
Captain Hon. J. Boyle.
Captain S. F. A. A. Hurt (killed in action).
Captain Hon. R. S. Stuart.
Captain T. B. Traill, D.S.O.
Lieutenant D. G. C. Critchley-Salmonson.
Second Lieutenant S. Mann.
Company Quartermaster-Serjeant G. Brown (killed in action).
Lance-Corporal A. Humberstone.
Lance-Corporal R. Ferrier.
Private J. Blythe.
Private W. Burt.
Private J. Fleming.
Private C. Morgan (killed in action).
Private S. Melvon.

2ND BATTALION ROYAL SCOTS FUSILIERS.
Lieutenant-Colonel A. G. B. Smith.
Captain A. G. Bruce.
Captain R. M. Burgoyne.
Captain R. V. G. Horn.
Captain H. W. V. Stewart, D.S.O.
Captain J. C. Whigham.
Lieutenant K. C. Thomson.
Second Lieutenant G. B. Bayley, 2nd King's Own Scottish Borderers (attached) (killed in action).
Second Lieutenant (temporary Lieutenant) W. G. Clutterbuck.
Company Serjeant-Major (now Second Lieutenant) M. D. Evans.
Serjeant J. Christie.
Private A. Coleman.
Private J. Dodds.
Lance-Corporal J. Smith.

1ST BATTALION CHESHIRE REGIMENT.
Captain J. A. Busfield, Reserve of Officers.
Captain F. L. Lloyd, Reserve of Officers.
Captain F. H. Mahony (died of wounds received in action).
Captain W. S. Rich (died of wounds received in action).

MENTIONED IN DESPATCHES

Captain J. L. Shore.
Lieutenant T. L. Frost.
Second Lieutenant G. R. L. Anderson, 3rd Battalion (attached) (killed in action).
Second Lieutenant H. N. Atkinson, D.S.O., 3rd Battalion (attached).
Quartermaster and Hon. Lieutenant J. C. Sproule.
Company Serjeant-Major T. McCreary.
Corporal J. A. Davies.
Private F. Appleton.
Private R. Chantler.
Private A. S. Heath.
Private E. Hughes.
Private J. Thompson.
Private D. Wright.
Drummer W. Hammond (killed in action).

1ST BATTALION ROYAL WELSH FUSILIERS.

Lieutenant-Col. H. O. S. Cadogan.
Major R. E. P. Gabbett.
Captain J. R. M. Minshull Ford, 2nd Battalion (atttached).
Captain E. O. Skaife.
Lieutenant A. E. C. T. Dooner.
Lieutenant B. C. H. Poole.
Quartermaster and Honorary Captain E. A. Parker.
Corporal R. Farmar.
Private G. Beech.
Private S. A. Britton.
Private J. Butler.
Private A. T. Dunn.
Private J. Evans.
Private A. E. Forest.
Private P. Goode.
Private T. W. Lewis.
Private J. O. Morton.
Private R. J. Phillips.
Private J. Whalin.

2ND BATTALION ROYAL WELSH FUSILIERS.

Lieutenant-Colonel H. Delmé-Radcliffe.
Major O. De L. Williams.
Captain R. N. Phillips.
Captain C. I. Stockwell.
Second Lieutenant M. Murphy.
Second Lieutenant W. G. Fletcher (O.T.C.) (attached).
Serjeant J. T. Wilde.
Private S. Edwards.

MENTIONED IN DESPATCHES

1st Battalion South Wales Borderers.
Major A. J. Reddie.
Captain G. B. C. Ward.
Lieutenant (temporary Captain) H. M. B. Salmon.
Lieutenant C. K. Steward.
Company Serjeant Major H. Hicks.
Lance-Corporal A. Jeffries.
Corporal F. Smith.
Lance-Corporal W. Day.
Private W. Melham.
Private A. Ravenhill.

2nd Battalion King's Own Scottish Borderers.
Major E. S. D'E. Coke.
Captain C. E. W. Bland, 3rd Battalion (attached).
Captain J. C. W. Connell.
Captain R. C. Y. Dering.
Captain A. J. Henryson-Caird, 3rd Battalion (attached).
Lieutenant R. Gibson, 3rd Battalion (attached).
Lance-Serjeant T. Lawrie.
Serjeant S. Ramsden.
Lance-Corporal J. Farquharson.
Lance-Corporal K. Maxwell.
Private G. S. Connell.
Private J. Dick.
Private R. Renny.

1st Battalion Scottish Rifles.
Lieutenant-Colonel P. R. Robertson.
Captain A. G. Ritchie (died of wounds received in action).
Captain R. H. W. Rose (killed in action).
Captain J. C. Stormonth-Darling.
Lieutenant (temporary Captain) R. C. Money.
Corporal T. W. Taylor (killed in action).
Lance-Corporal H. McCann.

2nd Battalion Scottish Rifles.
Lieutenant-Colonel W. M. Bliss.
Lieutenant R. N. O'Connor.

5th Battalion Scottish Rifles (Territorial Force).
Lieutenant-Colonel R. J. Douglas.
Lieutenant (temporary Captain) A. M. Alexander.

Royal Inniskilling Fusiliers.
Lieutenant G. E. Sampson, D.S.O.

MENTIONED IN DESPATCHES

2ND BATTALION ROYAL INNISKILLING FUSILIERS.

Lieutenant-Colonel C. A. Wilding.
Captain G. R. V. Steward.
Second Lieutenant J. G. B. Thomas (died of wounds received in action)
Serjeant S. Crec (deceased).

1ST BATTALION GLOUCESTERSHIRE REGIMENT.

Captain A. St. J. Blunt, 1st Battalion York and Lancs. (attached).
Captain R. E. Rising, D.S.O. (died of wounds received in action).
Lieutenant (temporary Captain) H. E. de R. Wetherall.
Lieutenant D. Baxter.
Company Serjeant Major A. Long.
Lance-Corporal T. New.
Private F. Dutton.
Private A. Faulkes.
Private M. C. Parry.
Private E. C. Robbins.
Private O. J. Taylor.
Private J. Williams.

WORCESTERSHIRE REGIMENT.

Major E. B. Hankey.
Major W. J. J. Sweetman, 6th Battalion (attached).
Captain E. L. Bowring.
Captain and Adjutant B. C. S. Clarke.
Captain R. J. Ford.
Captain P. S. G. Wainman, 6th Battalion (attached).
Lieutenant F. G. Gilson, 6th Battalion (attached).
Lieutenant G. A. Slaughter.
Second Lieutenant (temporary Lieutenant) F. C. F. Biscoe.
Second Lieutenant F. G. O. Curtler.
Second Lieutenant C. H. Ralston.
Serjeant J. Baxter.
Serjeant W. Plant.
Lance-Serjeant J. Clem.
Lance-Serjeant T. Hall.
Corporal C. E. Stewart.
Lance-Corporal J. Offord.
Private J. Danks.
Private C. Robbins.

1ST BATTALION WORCESTERSHIRE REGIMENT.

Lieutenant-Colonel A. E. Lascelles.
Lieutenant F. C. Roberts.

MENTIONED IN DESPATCHES

3RD BATTALION WORCESTERSHIRE REGIMENT.
Lieutenant-Colonel B. F. B. Stuart.
Captain T. H. Hughes (killed in action).
Captain A. C. Johnston.
Captain A. S. Nesbitt (killed in action).
Captain W. A. Underhill (killed in action).
Lieutenant A. Northey (killed in action).
Quartermaster and Hon. Captain A. Whitty.
Company Serjeant-Major P. T. Blond.
Serjeant A. Lemon.
Corporal H. Bird.
Lance-Corporal J. Hughes.
Private J. Hamlett.
Private S. Pearman.
Private W. R. Such.

1ST BATTALION EAST LANCASHIRE REGIMENT.
Lieutenant-Colonel G. H. Lawrence.
Lieutenant (temporary Captain) F. E. Belchier.
Lieutenant F. D. Hughes (killed in action).
Lieutenant E. B. M. Delmege.
Second Lieutenant R. W. Palmer, Special Reserve (attached).
Second Lieutenant L. D. Waud (killed in action).
Serjeant-Major A. Ebsworth.
Serjeant F. Noden (killed in action).
Private Taylor.
Private H. Topping.

2ND BATTALION EAST LANCASHIRE REGIMENT.
Lieutenant-Colonel C. L. Nicholson.
Lieutenant T. H. Daw.
Company Serjeant-Major W. Bright.
Serjeant A. F. Bullen.
Corporal R. H. Wilson.

1ST BATTALION EAST SURREY REGIMENT.
Lieutenant-Colonel J. R. Longley.
Major W. H. Paterson.
Major H. S. Tew.
Captain M. J. Minogue.
Lieutenant T. H. Darwell.
Lieutenant R. A. F. Montanaro.
Lieutenant G. R. P. Roupell.
Serjeant W. Parkes.
Lance-Serjeant H. Bousfield.

MENTIONED IN DESPATCHES

Lance-Corporal G. D. Bosten.
Lance-Corporal H. Gutsall.
Private C. W. Burton.
Private J. Hudson.
Private A. F. Quesnel.
Private H. J. Ward.
Private W. Glock.

DUKE OF CORNWALL'S LIGHT INFANTRY.
Lieutenant O. Edgcumbe Pearce.

1ST BATTALION DUKE OF CORNWALL'S LIGHT INFANTRY.
Captain M. Crawley-Boevey.
Captain T. A. Kendall, 3rd Battalion (attached).
Captain G. F. Phillips.
Captain A. H. Romilly (killed in action).
Captain C. B. Woodham.
Lieutenant (temporary Captain) A. N. Acland.
Lieutenant (temporary Captain) W. P. Buckley, D.S.O.
Lieutenant A. J. S. Hammans.
Lieutenant H. C. C. Lloyd.
Quartermaster and Hon. Lieutenant W. T. Price.
Serjeant H. W. Springett.
Private H. Cox.
Lance-Corporal G. J. Denton.
Lance-Corporal W. H. Stoneman.
Private W. F. Kilminster.
Private S. T. Westall.
Bandsman T. E. Rendle.

2ND BATTALION WEST RIDING REGIMENT.
Captain B. J. Barton, Reserve of Officers.
Captain E. R. Taylor.
Captain H. K. Umfreville (Reserve of Officers).
Lieutenant R. O'D. Carey.
Lieutenant R. J. A. Henniker.
Lieutenant E. N. F. Hitchins.
Lieutenant F. R. Thackeray.
Lieutenant J. H. L. Thompson (died of wounds received in action).
Company Quartermaster-Serjeant E. Gilbard.
Company Quartermaster-Serjeant J. Parker.
Company Serjeant-Major A. Hanson.
Company Serjeant-Major W. Lister.
Company Serjeant-Major J. Regan.
Serjeant A. Pain.
Lance-Corporal F. Carrington.

MENTIONED IN DESPATCHES

2ND BATTALION BORDER REGIMENT.

Lieutenant-Colonel L. I. Wood.
Major J. T. I. Bosanquet.
Major G. E. Warren.
Captain C. G. W. Andrews (killed in action).
Captain H. A. Askew (killed in action).
Captain H. V. Gerrard (killed in action).
Lieutenant M. S. N. Kennedy, 3rd Battalion (attached).
Lieutenant G. W. H. Hodgson (killed in action).
Lieutenant (temporary Captain) W. Watson.
Company Serjeant-Major (now Second Lieutenant) B. Hutton.
Private A. Acton.
Private W. Balman.
Private T. Bennett.
Private G. F. Burton.
Drummer W. Fitzsimons.
Private G. Jones.
Private A. E. Reader.
Private C. Rivers.
Private C. Robinson.
Private T. Shepheard.
Private J. Smith.

2ND BATTALION ROYAL SUSSEX REGIMENT.

Lieutenant-Colonel H. T. Crispin (killed in action).
Lieutenant-Colonel E. W. B. Green.
Captain E. F. Villiers, D.S.O.
Captain R. H. Waithman.
Lieutenant V. E. C. Dashwood.
Lieutenant G. H. B. De Chair.
Lieutenant V. E. C. De Chair.
Lieutenant L. H. K. Finch.
Lieutenant C. F. Verrall (killed in action).
Serjeant S. Burgess.
Private F. Hollingdale.
Private W. A. Tester.

1ST BATTALION HAMPSHIRE REGIMENT.

Major Hon. L. C. W. Palk.
Major G. H. Parker (killed in action).
Captain P. M. Connellan (killed in action).
Captain B. B. von B. im Thurn.
Captain G. F. Perkins.
Corporal R. Bird.
Lance-Corporal F. Drinkwater.

MENTIONED IN DESPATCHES

1ST BATTALION SOUTH STAFFORDSHIRE REGIMENT.

Lieutenant-Colonel R. M. Ovens.
Major A. C. Buckle.
Captain C. B. Adams.
Captain S. Bonner.
Captain J. S. S. Dunlop (killed in action).
Captain J. F. Vallentin (killed in action).
Lieutenant C. E. C. Bartlett.
Quartermaster and Hon. Captain F. H. White.
Corporal A. Baker.

2ND BATTALION SOUTH STAFFORDSHIRE REGIMENT.

Lieutenant-Colonel C. S. Davidson.
Major P. C. L. Routledge.
Captain S. G. Johnson.
Captain A. F. G. Kilby.
Captain M. B. Savage.
Captain C. H. Thomas (died of wounds received in action).
Lieutenant J. L. Dent, D.S.O.
Lieutenant (temporary Captain) F. H. Gunner, D.S.O.
Lieutenant J. Sharpe.
Second Lieutenant B. J. H. Scott (killed in action).

DORSETSHIRE REGIMENT.

Lieutenant C. W. M. Firth.

1ST BATTALION DORSETSHIRE REGIMENT.

Lieutenant-Colonel L. J. Bols, D.S.O.
Major W. A. C. Fraser.
Major R. T. Roper (killed in action).
Major C. Saunders.
Captain A. L. Ransome.
Captain F. H. B. Rathborne.
Captain A. R. M. Roy (died of wounds received in action).
Captain E. K. Twiss, I.A. (attached).
Lieutenant C. O. Lilly.
Second Lieutenant (temporary Lieutenant) C. G. Butcher.
Second Lieutenant G. S. Shannon, Special Reserve (attached).
Serjeant A. Boater.
Serjeant C. Gambling.
Corporal W. J. Cannings.
Corporal W. Kerr.
Lance-Corporal O. V. Ball.
Lance-Corporal R. Gough.
Private W. H. Curtis.

MENTIONED IN DESPATCHES

Private W. Dolman.
Private F. W. Inker.
Private F. Wheatcroft.
Drummer W. T. Prowse.

2ND BATTALION SOUTH LANCASHIRE REGIMENT.

Captain L. A. Clemens.
Lieutenant B. V. Fulcher (killed in action).
Quartermaster and Hon. Lieutenant S. T. Boast.
Serjeant J. Stephenson.
Private J. Coady.
Private C. Knowles.
Private O. J. Wolff.

THE WELSH REGIMENT.

Captain D. P. Dickinson (Signalling Off.).

2ND BATTALION WELSH REGIMENT.

Lieutenant-Colonel C. B. Morland (died of wounds received in action).
Captain T. P. Aldworth, 3rd Battalion West Kent Regiment (attached.)
Captain W. S. Evans.
Captain H. C. Rees, D.S.O.
Second Lieutenant W. G. Hewett.
Company Serjeant-Major F. O'D. Collins.
Company Quartermaster-Serjeant M. Flavin.
Serjeant W. J. Burder.
Lance-Serjeant W. J. Peoples.
Acting-Serjeant E. R. Harvey.
Lance-Corporal A. Beard.
Corporal G. H. Taylor.
Private L. Pullen.

1ST BATTALION BLACK WATCH (ROYAL HIGHLANDERS).

Captain H. F. S. Amery.
Captain V. M. Fortune.
Lieutenant (temporary Captain) F. Anderson.
Quartermaster-Serjeant C. A. Scott.
Serjeant J. McVey.
Lance-Corporal C. Roy.
Lance-Corporal G. Simmonite.
Lance-Corporal D. Wilson.

2ND BATTALION BLACK WATCH (ROYAL HIGHLANDERS).

Major W. J. St. J. Harvey.
Major A. G. Wauchope, D.S.O.

MENTIONED IN DESPATCHES

Lieutenant (temporary Captain) J. N. Inglis.
Company Serjeant-Major (now Second Lieutenant) J. Kennedy.
Lance-Corporal A. Venters.
Lance-Corporal T. Swan.
Private J. Daniels.
Private J. McIntosh.
Private R. Madill.
Private M. Stark.
Private Steward.
Private W. P. Watters.

5TH BATTALION BLACK WATCH (ROYAL HIGHLANDERS).
Lieutenant-Colonel H. Scrymgeour-Wedderburn.

2ND BATTALION OXFORDSHIRE AND BUCKINGHAMSHIRE LIGHT INFANTRY
Lieutenant-Colonel H. R. Davies.
Captain H. M. Dillon.
Captain A. H. Harden (killed in action).
Captain E. H. Kirkpatrick.
Lieutenant C. S. Baines, D.S.O.
Lieutenant (temporary Captain) and Adjutant R. B. Crosse, D.S.O.
Lieutenant H. V. Pendavis, D.S.O., 3rd Battalion (attached).
Lieutenant A. V. Spencer, D.S.O., 3rd Battalion (attached).
Second Lieutenant F. Pepys, D.S.O. (killed in action).
Second Lieutenant J. B. M. Ward (killed in action).
Serjeant W. H. Fossey.
Serjeant A. G. Waters.
Serjeant R. L. Wood.
Lance-Corporal W. J. Dobson.
Lance-Corporal R. Kerswell.
Lance-Corporal E. Radley.
Private G. W. Atkins.
Private F. W. Hart.
Private J. Salmon.
Private W. A. Wheeler.

2ND BATTALION ESSEX REGIMENT.
Bervet Major F. W. Moffitt.
Captain L. O. W. Jones.
Lieutenant J. V. Atkinson.
Acting Company Serjeant-Major W. Chapman.
Serjeant G. J. Gale.
Lance-Corporal A. Vince.

1ST BATTALION NOTTINGHAMSHIRE AND DERBYSHIRE REGIMENT.
Brevet Colonel W. R. Marshall.
Captain D. W. A. Campbell, 4th South Staffordshire Regiment (attd.)
   (killed in action).

MENTIONED IN DESPATCHES

2ND BATTALION NOTTINGHAMSHIRE AND DERBYSHIRE REGIMENT.

Major P. Leveson-Gower.
Major R. F. J. Taylor.
Captain G. de C. Glover, South Staffs. Regiment (attached).
Captain C. J. W. Hobbs.
Second Lieutenant H. L. C. Smith, S.R. (attached).
Second Lieutenant (temporary Lieutenant) J. D'A. Whicher.
Second Lieutenant (temporary Lieutenant) H. B. D. Wilcox.
Serjeant A. W. Grant.
Serjeant G. H. Hillier.
Serjeant F. Sentance.
Corporal C. T. Howarth.
Private A. Doughty.
Private J. Morley.

1ST BATTALION LOYAL NORTH LANCASHIRE REGIMENT.

Major A. J. Carter, D.S.O. (killed in action).
Captain (temporary Major) H. G. Powell, Reserve of Officers.
Captain and Adjutant J. F. Allen (killed in action).
Lieutenant D. H. Garden, 3rd Battalion East Kent Regiment (attd.).
Second Lieutenant J. G. W. Hyndson.
Quartermaster and Hon. Lieutenant E. Wilkinson (killed in action).
Serjeant G. Fowler.
Corporal G. Timms.
Private J. McDermott.
Private F. S. Oaker.

1ST BATTALION NORTHAMPTONSHIRE REGIMENT.

Captain G. M. Bentley (died of wounds).
Captain J. H. Farrar, 3rd Battalion (attached).
Quartermaster and Hon. Lieutenant A. Hofman.
Serjeant A. G. McNaught.
Private W. Pipet.
Serjeant A. Taylor.
Lance-Corporal A. Richardson.
Private J. F. Charman.

2ND BATTALION NORTHAMPTONSHIRE REGIMENT.

Lieutenant-Colonel C. S. Prichard, D.S.O.

1ST BATTALION ROYAL BERKSHIRE REGIMENT.

Lieutenant-Colonel M. D. Graham.
Major H. M. Finch.
Captain C. H. T. Lucas.
Captain O. Steele (killed in action).
Lieutenant G. Belcher, 3rd Battalion (attached).

MENTIONED IN DESPATCHES

Lieutenant and Adjutant C. St. Q. O. Fullbrook-Leggatt, D.S.O.
Lieutenant A. A. H. Hanbury-Sparrow, D.S.O.
Lieutenant (temporary Captain) A. G. F. Isaac.
Lieutenant L. C. Nicholson, D.S.O., 3rd Battalion (attached) (died of wounds).
Second Lieutenant T. A. Knott (died of wounds).
Second Lieutenant J. H. Stokes, 3rd Battalion Royal West Kent Regt. (attached).
Second Lieutenant J. Vesey.
Serjeant E. Ward.
Corporal G. G. Titchener.
Lance-Corporal A. E. Burchell.
Private S. J. Raisey.
Private A. G. Wood.

2ND BATTALION ROYAL BERKSHIRE REGIMENT.

Lieutenant-Colonel E. Feetham.

1ST BATTALION ROYAL WEST KENT REGIMENT.

Lieutenant-Colonel A. Martyn.
Major P. M. Buckle, D.S.O. (killed in action).
Major P. M. Robinson, C.M.G.
Captain H. D. Buchanan Dunlop.
Captain G. B. Legard (killed in action).
Captain R. M. G. Tulloch.
Lieutenant (temporary Captain) W. V. Palmer.
Lieutenant H. B. H. White, D.S.O.
Lieutenant P. F. Wilberforce-Bell.
Second Lieutenant (temporary Lieutenant) J. R. Russell, D.S.O.
Quartermaster and Honorary Lieutenant H. G. Rogers.
Company Serjeant-Major A. Reynolds.
Serjeant W. G. File.
Serjeant W. Marslin.
Serjeant H. A. Palmer.
Serjeant M. P. Stroud.
Lance-Corporal P. E. Eldridge (killed in action).
Lance-Corporal J. Gilbert.
Private F. G. Floyd.
Private G. Ward.

2ND BATTALION YORKSHIRE LIGHT INFANTRY.

Lieutenant-Colonel W. M. Withycombe.
Major C. E. Heathcote.
Captain H. F. G. Carter.
Captain M. F. Day.

MENTIONED IN DESPATCHES

Captain A. B. Smyth.
Captain H. T. Watson, 3rd Liverpool Regiment (attached).
Captain W. d'E. Williams.
Lieutenant (temporary Captain) C. E. D. King.
Serjeant R. Turner.
Serjeant W. Whitaker.
Serjeant E. J. Whiteway.
Lance-Corporal R. H. Bell.
Lance-Corporal A. Quantrill.
Private J. Cecil.
Private W. Wardman.

1st Battalion Shropshire Light Infantry.

Lieutenant-Colonel C. P. Higginson, D.S.O.
Major E. B. Luard.
Captain P. C. Huth, D.S.O.
Captain B. E. Murray.
Captain P. Prince.
Lieutenant F. H. R. Maunsell.
Serjeant-Major S. G. Moore.
Company Serjeant-Major J. H. Busby.
Company Serjeant-Major E. Jones.
Private W. Church.
Private W. Dobinson.
Private W. G. Griggs.
Private D. Hurley.

1st Battalion Middlesex Regiment.

Lieutenant-Colonel F. G. M. Rowley.
Lieutenant-Colonel B. E. Ward (died of wounds).
Captain E. S. Gibbons, D.S.O.
Captain G. H. Hastings.
Captain H. P. Osborne.
Lieutenant N. Y. L. Welman, D.S.O.
Second Lieutenant (temporary Lieutenant) R. H. Brodie.
Regimental Quartermaster-Serjeant J. S. Goggin.
Serjeant E. F. James.
Corporal F. C. McClelland.
Corporal S. Walker.
Private W. F. Hatten.
Private R. Oldfield.

2nd Battalion Middlesex Regiment.

Lieutenant-Colonel R. H. Hayes.

MENTIONED IN DESPATCHES

4TH BATTALION MIDDLESEX REGIMENT.

Lieutenant-Colonel (temporary Brigadier-General) C. P. A. Hull.
Major H. Storr, Reserve of Officers.
Captain G. Oliver.
Second Lieutenant G. N. U. Cursons.
Second Lieutenant (temporary Lieutenant) L. H. V. Fraser.
Quartermaster and Hon. Lieutenant M. W. Farrow.
Quartermaster-Serjeant A. W. Andrews.
Company Quartermaster-Serjeant L. Allingham.
Company Serjeant-Major W. Stannett.
Company Serjeant-Major A. Smith.
Serjeant A. J. Walker.
Lance-Corporal G. A. Allison.
Lance-Corporal E. H. Jones.
Lance-Corporal S. Peach.
Lance-Corporal W. Wright.

1ST BATTALION KING'S ROYAL RIFLE CORPS.

Captain E. B. Denison.
Captain G. C. Kelly.
Captain F. L. Pardoe, D.S.O.
Lieutenant H. H. Prince M. V. D. of Battenberg, K.C.V.O. (died of wounds received in action).
Second Lieutenant J. Casey (killed in action).

2ND BATTALION KING'S ROYAL RIFLE CORPS.

Lieutenant-Colonel E. Serocold Peace.
Major L. F. Philips.
Major H. C. Warre, D.S.O.
Captain C. K. Howard-Bury, 6th Battalion (attached).
Second Lieutenant R. A. Persse, Rifle Brigade (attached) (killed in action).
Serjeant H. Trotter.
Lance-Corporal G. H. Foote.
Lance-Corporal J. Nelson.

1ST BATTALION WILTSHIRE REGIMENT.

Major T. Roche (killed in action).
Captain C. D. V. Cary-Barnard, D.S.O.
Captain W. H. Mosley.
Captain P. S. Rowan.
Lieutenant (temporary Captain) G. S. Browne (died of wounds).
Lieutenant H. W. C. Lloyd, D.S.O.
Lieutenant (temporary Captain) B. H. Goodhart.
Second Lieutenant G. E. George, 3rd Battalion (attached).

MENTIONED IN DESPATCHES

Serjeant D. Haddrell.
Company Serjeant-Major A. J. Poolman.
Serjeant G. A. F. Wyatt.
Private A. H. Mead.
Private F. E. Russell.

2ND BATTALION WILTSHIRE REGIMENT.

Lieutenant-Colonel J. F. Forbes.
Lieutenant (temporary Captain) J. M. Ponsford.

1ST BATTALION MANCHESTER REGIMENT.

Lieutenant-Colonel E. P. Strickland, C.M.G., D.S.O.
Second Lieutenant (temporary Lieutenant) S. D. Connell (killed in action).
Company Serjeant-Major R. Wilson.
Corporal T. Duffy.
Lance-Corporal W. Coleshill.
Lance-Corporal F. Crooks.
Private A. A. Metcalfe.
Private J. Mitchell.

2ND BATTALION MANCHESTER REGIMENT.

Captain W. K. Evans.
Lieutenant A. J. Scully.
Lieutenant E. R. Vanderspar.
Second Lieutenant G. Dickson, 3rd Battalion (attached).
Second Lieutenant J. Leach, V.C.
Second Lieutenant R. T. Miller, 3rd Battalion (attached).
Second Lieutenant G. W. Williamson, 3rd Battalion (attached).
Quartermaster and Hon. Lieutenant W. L. Connery.
Serjeant J. Hogan, V.C.
Serjeant H. Massey.
Serjeant T. Ruddy.
Serjeant F. Snow.
Corporal C. W. Mutters.
Private W. Cleaver.

1ST BATTALION NORTH STAFFORDSHIRE REGIMENT.

Lieutenant-Colonel V. W. de Falbe, D.S.O.
Captain F. C. T. Ewald.
Lieutenant C. F. Gordon.
Lieutenant J. W. L. S. Hobart.
Lieutenant A. R. A. Leggett (killed in action).
Company Serjeant-Major E. J. Keeling.
Company Quartermaster-Serjeant F. W. Gould.

MENTIONED IN DESPATCHES

Serjeant E. R. Shelley.
Serjeant E. Lawless.
Private J. C. Barnes.
Private F. Hoyle.
Private W. Walton.

2ND BATTALION YORK AND LANCASTER REGIMENT.

Lieutenant-Colonel E. C. Cobbold.
Major G. E. Bayley.
Major F. E. B. Isherwood.
Lance-Corporal T. Matthews.

2ND BATTALION DURHAM LIGHT INFANTRY.

Major J. A. Crosthwaite.
Major W. Northey, D.S.O.
Lieutenant R. B. Bradford.
Lieutenant J. A. Churchill.
Lieutenant (temporary Captain) C. R. Congreve, D.S.O.
Lieutenant W. E. Parke (killed in action).
Lance-Corporal O. Bolam.
Lance-Corporal J. Hunter.
Private D. Metcalfe.
Private H. Salt.

2ND BATTALION HIGHLAND LIGHT INFANTRY.

Lieutenant-Colonel A. A. Wolfe-Murray.
Major E. R. Hill.
Major R. E. S. Prentice.
Captain W. L. Brodie, V.C.
Captain K. L. Buist.
Captain and Adjutant J. H. Hope.
Captain C. R. G. Mayne, D.S.O.
Captain F. S. Thackeray.
Lieutenant (temporary Captain) I. D. Dalrymple.
Second Lieutenant C. C. Mylles, Sp. R. (attached).
Serjeant J. Buchanan.
Serjeant J. Nisbet.
Lance-Corporal D. Hunt.
Lance-Corporal J. McGill.
Lance-Corporal W. Stewart.
Private A. Adams.
Private A. Angus.
Private J. Martin.
Private D. Sidey.

MENTIONED IN DESPATCHES

1st Battalion Seaforth Highlanders.

Lieutenant-Colonel A. B. Ritchie.
Captain R. Horn.
Captain H. W. C. Wicks.
Lieutenant I. M. McL. Macandrew (killed in action).
Company Serjeant-Major B. Kenney.
Company Serjeant-Major R. Sutherland.
Serjeant Piper D. Mathieson.
Corporal W. Macneil.
Lance-Corporal C. Leahy.

2nd Battalion Seaforth Highlanders.

Lieutenant-Colonel R. S. Vandeleur.
Major E. Campion.
Major C. I. Stockwell (died of wounds received in action).
Captain H. F. Baillie.
Lieutenant D. B. Burt-Marshall.
Lieutenant (temporary Captain) Hon. E. O. Campbell.
Lieutenant (temporary Captain) F. L. Fraser.
Lieutenant J. A. D. Perrins.
Second Lieutenant (temporary Captain) L. N. Fyfe Jamieson.
Quartermaster and Honorary Captain J. Davidson.
Company Serjeant-Major S. Munro.
Serjeant F. G. Marchant.
Lance-Corporal F. J. Bush.
Private W. Ferguson.
Private A. Ferguson.
Private J. Hampton.
Private J. McIntosh.
Private J. MacWilliams.

1st Battalion Gordon Highlanders.

Brevet Major A. W. F. Baird, D.S.O.
Major J. P. Grant, 3rd Seaforth Highlanders (attached).
Major C. J. Simpson.
Captain H. P. Burn.
Captain D. F. Campbell, D.S.O., 3rd Royal Highlanders (attached).
Captain W. M. K. Marshall.
Lieutenant G. R. V. Hume-Gore.
Lieutenant W. H. Paterson, 4th A. and S. Highlanders (attached).
Lieutenant D. R. Turnbull, D.S.O.
Second Lieutenant J. Bartholomew, 3rd Battalion (attached).
Second Lieutenant G. M. Monteith, 3rd Battalion (attached).
Serjeant A. (now Second Lieutenant) Pirie.
Serjeant J. McKenna.

MENTIONED IN DESPATCHES

Serjeant J. McLeod.
Serjeant L. Lowry.
Lance-Serjeant D. McAteer.
Private J. Gordon.
Private J. Innes.
Private J. McGowan.
Private R. A. Mackenzie.
Private A. McVean.
Private R. Third.

2ND BATTALION GORDON HIGHLANDERS.

Lieutenant-Colonel H. P. Uniacke.
Captain J. R. E. Stansfield, D.S.O.
Captain J. L. G. Burnett.
Lieutenant J. A. O. Brooke (killed in action).
Lieutenant J. H. Fraser (killed in action).
Lieutenant (temporary Captain) J. M. Hamilton.
Second Lieutenant W. Robertson.
Quartermaster and Hon. Captain J. Mackie.
Band-Serjeant W. E. Fuller.
Serjeant W. Reid.
Lance-Corporal R. B. B. Archer.
Lance-Corporal A. R. Nicol.
Piper B. Stewart.
Private A. Calder.
Private J. Christie.
Private T. Hepburn.
Private W. B. McGlinchy.
Private D. McLeod.
Private W. Kenny.

CAMERON HIGHLANDERS.

Lieutenant A. C. Allan (Signalling Officer).

1ST BATTALION CAMERON HIGHLANDERS.

Lieutenant-Colonel D. L. MacEwen.
Major E. Craig-Brown.
Quartermaster and Hon. Major A. P. Yeadon.
Regimental Serjeant-Major S. Axten.
Serjeant J. Miller.
Corporal J. Cameron.
Private J. Campbell.
Private J. White.
Private J. Cowe.
Pnr. J. Johnston.

MENTIONED IN DESPATCHES

1ST BATTALION ROYAL IRISH RIFLES.
Lieutenant-Colonel G. B. Laurie.

2ND BATTALION ROYAL IRISH RIFLES.
Lieutenant L. Browne, 4th Battalion (attached).
Second Lieutenant G. V. FitzGerald, 3rd Battalion Leinster Regiment (attached).
Second Lieutenant M. C. Kearne.
Second Lieutenant J. Martin (was Regimental Serjeant-Major).
Lance-Corporal W. McFarlane.
Rifleman L. Carolan.
Rifleman A. Gare.
Rifleman A. McGrath.
Rifleman C. Morley.

1ST BATTALION ROYAL IRISH FUSILIERS.
Lieutenant-Colonel A. R. Burrowes.
Captain G. Bull.
Captain M. B. C. Carbery (killed in action).
Captain C. J. Elkan, Reserve of Officers.
Captain R. J. Kentish, D.S.O.
Second Lieutenant C. E. Cooke, 3rd Battalion (attached).
Lieutenant E. J. McN. Penrose.
Lieutenant R. P. Power.
Quartermaster and Hon. Lieutenant T. E. Bunting.
Company Serjeant-Major J. Butler.
Serjeant F. W. Borley.
Lance-Corporal E. Carty (killed).
Private J. Copeland.
Private J. S. Morrow (killed).

1ST BATTALION CONNAUGHT RANGERS.
Lieutenant-Colonel H. S. L. Ravenshaw.
Major W. A. Hamilton.
Major S. J. Murray.
Captain R. G. Eyre.
Lieutenant (temporary Captain) J. E. Hume.
Captain R. L. Payne.
Lance-Corporal (now Serjeant) T. Kelly.
Private John McGovern.

2ND BATTALION CONNAUGHT RANGERS.
Major W. N. S. Alexander.
Captain H. J. N. Davis.
Captain E. G. Hamilton.
Second Lieutenant L. N. Aveling.
Second Lieutenant F. D. Foott.

MENTIONED IN DESPATCHES

2ND BATTALION ARGYLL AND SUTHERLAND HIGHLANDERS.

Major H. B. Kirk.
Captain H. H. G. Hyslop.
Captain G. Thorpe.
Lieutenant H. J. D. Clark.
Lieutenant J. A. Liddell, 3rd Battalion (attached).
Serjeant-Major H. Kerr.
Private J. Campbell.
Private J. Haddon.

2ND BATTALION LEINSTER REGIMENT.

Lieutenant (temporary Captain) J. V. Macartney.
Second Lieutenant (temporary Lieutenant) H. C. Berne.
Second Lieutenant (temporary Lieutenant) G. N. G. Young.

2ND BATTALION ROYAL MUNSTER FUSILIERS.

Lieutenant-Colonel A. M. Bent.

2ND BATTALION ROYAL DUBLIN FUSILIERS.

Lieutenant-Colonel A. Loveband.
Captain N. P. Clarke.
Captain T. H. C. Frankland.
Captain R. M. Watson.
Captain S. G. de C. Wheeler.
Lieutenant F. C. G. Campbell, 4th Pathans (attached).
Quartermaster and Hon. Major J. Burke.
Serjeant-Major F. W. Hatt.
Company Serjeant-Major E. Henderson.
Serjeant C. E. O'Hagan.
Corporal Cooke.

THE RIFLE BRIGADE.

Major R. Haig, 6th Battalion (attached).

1ST BATTALION RIFLE BRIGADE.

Major S. H. Rickman.
Major G. N. Salmon.
Captain G. J. Brownlow.
Captain G. W. Liddell.
Captain Hon. R. G. G. Morgan-Grenville (Master of Kinloss) (killed in action).
Captain Hon. F. R. D. Prittie, (killed in action).
Captain H. L. Riley.
Lieutenant H. F. Campbell.

MENTIONED IN DESPATCHES

Lieutenant F. W. L. Gull.
Lieutenant (temporary Captain) J. Micklem.
Second Lieutenant A. S. L. Daniell, 5th Battalion (attached) (killed in action).
Second Lieutenant C. J. Gasson, South Lancs. Regiment (attached).
Quartermaster and Hon. Lieutenant G. Mitchell.
Company Serjeant-Major W. Halliwell.
Serjeant E. Eaves.
Acting Serjeant B. Daldry.
Acting Corporal G. E. Chambers.

2ND BATTALION RIFLE BRIGADE.

Lieutenant-Colonel R. B. Stephens.
Captain E. Durham.
Captain J. E. V. Isaac, D.S.O., Reserve of Officers.
Serjeant M. W. Thompson.

3RD BATTALION RIFLE BRIGADE.

Captain A. K. Hargreaves.
Captain N. J. B. Leslie (killed in action).
Captain S. A. Sherston.
Lieutenant D. B. Landale (killed in action).
Second Lieutenant J. H. Smith.
Company Serjeant-Major H. Ellse.
Company Quartermaster-Serjeant C. H. Dowden.
Serjeant W. Fowler.
Corporal C. W. Arnold.
Corporal H. W. Simpson.
Serjeant A. F. Wheeler.
Rifleman A. Appleton.
Rifleman G. S. Lancaster.
Rifleman A. Lawler.

2ND BATTALION MONMOUTHSHIRE REGIMENT.

Lieutenant-Colonel E. B. Cuthbertson, M.V.O.
Captain H. J. Miers.
Second Lieutenant J. E. Paton (killed in action).
Serjeant J. Noble.
Serjeant F. Collins.

5TH (CITY OF LONDON) BATT. LONDON REGT. (LONDON RIFLE BRIGADE).

Lieutenant-Colonel W. D., Earl Cairns.
Captain A. C. Oppenheim, King's Royal Rifle Corps (Adjutant).
Second Lieutenant W. L. Willett.
Corporal T. H. Jenkins.
Private R. E. Peck.

MENTIONED IN DESPATCHES

9TH (COUNTY OF LONDON) BATTALION LONDON REGIMENT (QUEEN VICTORIA'S RIFLES).

Captain S. V. Shea.
Colour-Serjeant A. Sherriff.

13TH (COUNTY OF LONDON) KENSINGTON BATTN. LONDON REGIMENT.

Lieutenant-Colonel F. G. Lewis.

14TH (COUNTY OF LONDON) BATTALION LONDON REGIMENT (LONDON SCOTTISH).

Lance-Corporal H. G. Latham.
Private A. S. Lambert.
Private C. Winterbottom.

1ST BATTALION HERTFORDSHIRE REGIMENT.

Lieutenant-Colonel T. W. Viscount Hampden.

ARMY SERVICE CORPS.

Major A. W. Alexander.
Major C. R. T. Annesley.
Captain (temporary Major) G. K. Archibald.
Lieutenant-Colonel F. S. Atkinson.
Captain B. B. Barrett.
Captain M. H. F. Berkeley.
Captain V. O. Beuttler.
Captain W. T. R. Browne.
Major H. G. Burrard.
Second Lieutenant H. B. B. Butler.
Major J. C. M. Canny, D.S.O.
Captain (temporary Major) L. A. L. Carter.
Major A. M. Cockshott.
Major H. W. A. Collum.
Second Lieutenant H. Cowan.
Major H. Cracroft.
Second Lieutenant N. Crail.
Captain (temporary Major) D. W. Cunningham.
Major P. C. de la Pryme.
Major E. F. Falkner.
Major G. H. Harvey.
Major T. Hazlerigg.
Quartermaster and Hon. Captain J. A. Hebb.
Second Lieutenant (temporary Captain) T. S. Jackson, Special Reserve (attached).
Major H. A. Johnson.

MENTIONED IN DESPATCHES

Major (temporary Lieutenant-Colonel) H. O. Knox, Reserve of Officers.
Captain (temporary Major) T. J. R. Langmaid.
Major J. G. Lecky.
Major A. R. Liddell.
Major E. J. McAllister.
Major W. A. M. G. Maconochie-Welwood.
Major M. Moore.
Major L. M. S. Page.
Major D. Parsons.
Major J. H. B. Peyton.
Lieutenant-Colonel G. E. Pigott, D.S.O.
Major F. J. Reid.
Major W. P. Robinson.
Major W. E. Roe.
Lieutenant-Colonel C. M. Ryan, D.S.O.
Major W. Scott-Elliot.
Lieutenant-Colonel A. K. Seccombe, D.S.O.
Major H. A. Stewart.
Second Lieutenant (temporary Lieutenant) N. S. Thomas (Special Reserve).
Captain (temporary Major) G. E. Toynbee.
Major C. D. E. Upton.
Major A. M. Wilson.
Major F. W. Wright.
Farrier-Serjeant T. Ahern.
Staff Quartermaster-Serjeant C. H. Atkins.
Serjeant J. Baird.
Serjeant H. Basten.
Mechanical Serjeant-Major A. F. Bateman.
Serjeant J. Batty.
Company Quartermaster-Serjeant M. T. Bearman.
Farrier Staff-Serjeant S. C. Blackwell.
Staff Quartermaster-Serjeant A. E. J. Booth.
Mechanical Staff-Serjeant W. Buckle.
Company Quartermaster-Serjeant G. J. Carter.
Company Serjeant-Major J. Carter.
Farrier Staff-Serjeant H. Chidgey.
Staff Serjeant-Major J. Connell.
Serjeant H. Craib (specially enlisted).
Corporal P. Cross.
Company Serjeant-Major E. Cruttenden.
Serjeant R. Curzon-Hope.
Driver H. G. Dockree.
Staff-Serjeant F. W. Dorling.
Serjeant C. Dove.
Serjeant M. Eyles.

MENTIONED IN DESPATCHES

Staff-Serjeant-Major H. G. H. (now Quartermaster and Hon. Lieut.) Fogg.
Lance-Serjeant R. Forbes.
Serjeant G. Foster.
Serjeant-Major H. G. Francis.
S. Quartermaster-Serjeant W. J. Franks.
Farrier S. Serjeant J. L. Goode.
Serjeant G. Gould.
Company Quartermaster-Serjeant L. Hall.
Company Serjeant-Major W. S. Hall.
S. Serjeant-Major L. Hancock.
Company Quartermaster-Serjeant F. C. Hankel.
Serjeant C. H. Hanson.
S. Serjeant-Major W. H. Heard.
Company Serjeant-Major E. J. Hector.
S. Serjeant-Major P. Hulbert.
Mech. Serjeant-Major H. G. Hulste.
Farrier Quartermaster-Serjeant S. W. Izzard.
Corporal A. Jamieson.
Mechanical S. Serjeant C. Leggott.
Private S. C. Levermore.
Company Quartermaster-Serjeant W. F. Norris.
Serjeant (Acting Regimental Serjeant-Major) E. Packman.
Corporal S. H. Parker.
Private G. Parsons.
Farrier-Serjeant L. Partridge.
Lance-Corporal T. A. Peet.
Mech. S. Serjeant F. G. Porton.
S. Serjeant R. B. Pryer.
Mech. Serjeant-Major J. Radcliffe.
Company Serjeant-Major T. H. Ranson.
S. Serjeant-Major H. Rayner.
S. Serjeant-Major J. W. Rose.
Corporal P. Rowden.
S. Serjeant-Major W. R. Rowden.
Company Serjeant-Major G. H. Ruse.
Corporal D. H. Salisbury.
Company Serjeant-Major P. Scott.
S. Serjeant-Major W. A. Scott.
Serjeant F. V. Sibbald.
Acting Company Serjeant-Major A. J. Smith.
Farrier-Serjeant J. Stock.
Corporal S. Stone.
Serjeant-Major W. J. Stroud.
Serjeant A. E. Taylor.
Serjeant A. E. Warner.

MENTIONED IN DESPATCHES

Mech. Serjeant-Major H. H. (now Quartermaster and Hon. Lieutenant) Way.
Private A. A. Webb.
Serjeant J. T. Wellington.
Company Serjeant-Major G. White.
Mech. Serjeant-Major A. G. Woodhams.
Serjeant C. H. York.

MEDICAL SERVICES.

Major J. H. Barbour, M.B.
Major H. R. Bateman.
Major M. C. Beatty, M.B.
Lieutenant-Colonel A. W. Bewley.
Major R. B. Black, M.B., Reserve of Officers.
Colonel (temporary) Sir A. A. Bowlby, Kt., C.M.G., F.R.C.S.
Colonel (temporary) Sir J. R. Bradford, K.C.M.G , F.R.S., M.D.
Lieutenant-Colonel G. W. Brazier-Creagh, C.M.G.
Lieutenant-Colonel (temporary Colonel) C. H. Burtchaell, M.B.
Captain J. H. Campbell, M.B.
Quartermaster and Hon. Major A. J. Chalk.
Major B. R. Dennis, M.B.
Captain P. Dwyer, M.B.
Major W. F. Ellis.
Major C. R. Evans.
Major P. Evans, M.B.
Major M. H. G. Fell.
Lieutenant (temporary) J. M. Glasse, M.B.
Major C. M. Goodbody (I.M.S.).
Lieutenant-Colonel F. W. Hardy, M.B.
Major L. W. Harrison, M.B.
Quartermaster and Hon. Lieutenant A. Huntingford.
Colonel F. W. C. Jones, M.B.
Major F. Kiddle, M.B.
Lieutenant-Colonel C. B. Lawson, M.B.
Major J. W. Leake.
Brevet Colonel Sir W. B. Leishman, Kt., F.R.S., M.B., F.R.C.P., K.H.P.
Lieutenant-Colonel A. J. Luther.
Lieutenant-Colonel S. Macdonald, M.B.
Major J. R. McMunn.
Surgeon-General W. G. Macpherson, C.M G , M.B., K.H.P.
Colonel (temporary) G. H. Makins, C.B., F.R.C.S.
Captain S. H. Middleton-West, F.R.C.S. (I.M.S.).
Lieutenant-Colonel L. T. M. Nash.

MENTIONED IN DESPATCHES

Major R. A. Needham, M.B. (I.M.S.).
Major H. L. W. Norrington.
Colonel (temporary Surgeon-General) T. J. O'Donnell, D.S.O.
Major S. De C. O'Grady, M.B.
Quartermaster and Hon. Lieutenant J. W. Osborne.
G. H. Pile, Esq. (British Red Cross Society) (recommended by G.O.C. II. Corps).
Major W. M. Power.
Major J. J. W. Prescott, D.S.O.
Major L. M. Purser, M.B.
Captain J. M. B. Rahilly, M.B.
Captain C. Ryles, M.B.
Lieutenant-Colonel B. H. Scott.
Lieutenant-Colonel D. D. Shanahan.
Lieutenant-Colonel W. H. Starr.
Major F. A. Stephens.
Captain G. G. Tabuteau.
Major C. G. Thomson.
Major W. F. Tyndale, C.M.G., M.D.
Major T. B. Unwin, M.B.
Major F. Wall (I.M.S.).
Quartermaster and Hon. Captain J. Watkins, Reserve of Officers.
Major B. Watts.
Serjeant-Major A. Baker.
Serjeant-Major J. Banks.
Private C. A. Barnes.
S. Serjeant E. G. W. Barnes.
S. Serjeant A. Bell.
Serjeant-Major A. Bennett.
Driver F. Burnham, A.S.C. (attached).
Staff-Serjeant A. W. Currie.
Corporal B. Davidson.
Serjeant-Major F. Davis.
Corporal A. Day.
Quartermaster-Serjeant A. A. Dell.
Serjeant-Major J. J. Earp.
Staff-Serjeant J. R. Edwards.
Serjeant W. A. Gerrie.
Quartermaster-Serjeant E. J. Gosling.
Corporal W. Greenhalgh.
Serjeant H. C. Hughes.
Serjeant-Major F. G. Hurran.
Serjeant E. Kemp, A.S.C. (attached).
Quartermaster-Serjeant P. le Poidevin.
Staff-Serjeant W. C. Leppington.
Private T. McEnnery.

MENTIONED IN DESPATCHES

Quartermaster-Serjeant W. A. Muirhead.
Serjeant J. W. F. Munden.
Quartermaster-Serjeant J. E. Newton.
Quartermaster-Serjeant W. E. Perritt.
Serjeant-Major H. J. Reeve.
Private F. Robinson.
Serjeant-Major P. Snow.
Serjeant W. J. Spiers.
Quartermaster-Serjeant A. Springett.
Corporal T. A. Tunnicliffe.
Private W. H. Vogel.
Staff-Serjeant Yates, A.S.C. (attached).

ROYAL ARMY MEDICAL CORPS.

Lieutenant T. H. Balfour, M.B.
Lieutenant H. C. Bazett, M.B., F.R.C.S., Special Reserve.
Major E. W. Bliss.
Captain S. C. Bowle.
Lieutenant (temporary) R. B. Taylor.
Captain T. W. Browne.
Quartermaster and Honorary Lieutenant E. J. Buckley.
Lieutenant (temporary) A. E. Bullock.
Lieutenant (temporary) A. E. Carrington, M.B.
Captain V. T. Carruthers, M.B., F.R.C.S.
Captain H. St. M. Carter, M.D.
Lieutenant J. P. Charles, M.B.
Major R. W. Clements, M.B.
Lieutenant-Colonel R. J. Copeland, M.B.
Lieutenant F. G. Cowtan.
Major V. J. Crawford.
Lieutenant-Colonel G. S. Crawford, M.D.
Lieutenant F. C. Davidson, M.B.
Captain J. S. Dunne, D.S.O., F.R.C.S.I.
Major FitzG. G. FitzGerald.
Lieutenant-Colonel B. Forde, M.B.
Major A. C. Fox.
Captain A. D. Fraser, M.B.
Lieutenant F. P. Freeman, Special Reserve.
Captain E. M. Glanvill, M.B. (killed in action).
Lieutenant (temporary) J. R. C. Greenlees, M.B.
Major A. R. Greenwood.
Lieutenant (temporary) E. H. Griffin, M.D.
Captain J. B. Grogan.
Lieutenant J. FitzG. Gwynne, M.B.
Lieutenant J. Hare, M.B.
Lieutenant C. Helm.

MENTIONED IN DESPATCHES

Captain V. C. Honeybourne.
Major A. W. Hooper, D.S.O.
Major W. E. Hudleston.
Lieutenant (temporary) W. W. Ingram, M.B.
Lieutenant (temporary) J. L. Jackson, M.B.
Lieutenant (temporary) P. W. James, M.B.
Captain C. Kelly, M.D.
Lieutenant E. C. Lang, M.B.
Captain P. A. Jones Lloyd, M.B.
Captain W. F. M. Loughnan.
Lieutenant D. M. Lyon, M.B., Special Reserve.
Lieutenant W. McK. H. McCullagh, M.B., Special Reserve.
Major A. J. MacDougall, M.B.
Lieutenant-Colonel G. S. McLoughlin, D.S.O., M.B.
Captain C. McQueen.
Lieutenant (temporary) A. Martin, M.D , F.R.C.S.
Lieutenant (temporary) V. C. Martin-Leake.
Lieutenant (temporary) J. B. Mathews.
Major G. T. K. Maurice.
Captain A. A. Meaden.
Lieutenant (temporary) F. W. Milne.
Lieutenant-Colonel A. Milne-Thomson (T.F.).
Major H. W. S. Nickerson, V.C., M.B.
Captain J. J. O'Keefe, M.B.
Major G. J. A. Ormsby, M.D.
Lieutenant E. Percival, M.D.
Captain E. C. Phelan, M.B.
Lieutenant R. B. Philippo.
Captain T. McC. Phillips (died of wounds).
Lieutenant-Colonel R. Pickard, M.D. (T.F.).
Lieutenant I. M. Pirrie, M.B., Special Reserve.
Lieutenant R. E. Pirrie, M.B. (killed in action).
Captain E. T. Potts, M.D.
Lieutenant R. B. Price, M.B.
Major C. W. Profeit, M.B.
Captain W. B. Purdon, M.B.
Major M. MacG. Rattray, M.B.
Major F. G. Richards.
Lieutenant M. Richardson, M.B. (died of wounds).
Captain F. E. Roberts.
Captain H. G. Robertson, M.B.
Major N. J. C. Rutherford, M.B.
Captain P. Sampson, D.S.O.
Captain T. H. Scott, M.B.
Major J. P. Silver, M.B.
Major E. W. Slayter, M.B.

MENTIONED IN DESPATCHES

Lieutenant-Colonel A. B. Soltau, M.D. (T.F.).
Captain S. J. Steward, D.S.O., M.D., Special Reserve.
Lieutenant (temporary) J. S. Stewart, M.B.
Major H. S. Thurston.
Lieutenant W. Tyrrell, M.B., Special Reserve.
Lieutenant (temporary) J. R. Waddy.
Major F. S. Walker, F.R.C.S.I.
Captain S. J. A. H. Walshe, M.B., Special Reserve.
Lieutenant-Colonel A. A. Watson, Special Reserve (Lieutenant R.A.M.C., T.F.).
Lieutenant N. T. Whitehead, M.B.
Lieutenant (temporary) J. S. Williamson.
Captain H. T. Wilson.
Major J. H. R. Winder, M.D.
Captain W. G. Wright.
Serjeant-Major H. J. Anderson.
Private C. Arnold.
Staff-Serjeant E. Barlow.
Corporal C. W. Barlow.
Private B. Bethell.
Private A. Briggs.
Private E. G. Brogden.
Staff-Serjeant A. Buckner.
Corporal A. Bunker.
Staff-Serjeant A. J. Canty.
Serjeant T. B. Carter.
Private Clements.
Quartermaster-Serjeant H. Dawson.
Private H. Dodsworth.
Private W. Edwards.
Quartermaster-Serjeant R. D. Elliott.
Serjeant-Major R. J. Fleming.
Corporal J. Flynn.
Private R. Forman.
Staff-Serjeant A. I. Harper.
Private C. A. G. Harris.
Private H. Higgins.
Private T. G. Hill.
Serjeant A. O. Hort.
Serjeant-Major L. Hubbard.
Corporal W. Hughes.
Private W. Humphreys.
Bugler F. W. T. Hurley.
Private E. Jones.
Quarter-Master Serjeant J. H. Jones.
Private E. Jordan.

MENTIONED IN DESPATCHES

Serjeant W. Lawson.
Private E. Lord.
Serjeant T. J. Moffatt.
Quartermaster-Serjeant F. C. Morrison.
Private T. Page.
Staff-Serjeant W. H. Parr.
Private E. C. Partridge.
Serjeant C. T. Pepper.
Staff-Serjeant G. P. Pursey.
Serjeant A. R. Robinson.
Private A. W. Sams.
Private J. Sheehan.
Private J. F. Simmons.
Serjeant-Major W. H. Storey.
Staff-Serjeant G. Stubbs.
Private L. P. Unwin.
Serjeant E. H. White.
Private P. Wild.
Staff-Serjeant W. A. Wilson.
Serjeant F. Woodward.

Army Veterinary Corps.

Lieutenant (temporary Captain) R. E. Beilby (T.F.).
Captain T. Bone.
Captain L. Daniels.
Major W. B. Edwards.
Major R. H. Holmes, F.R.C.V.S.
Captain B. L. Lake.
Captain H. S. Mosley.
Major A. Olver, F.R.C.V.S.
Captain J. W. Rainey (Reserve of Officers).
Lieutenant E. Sewell, Special Reserve.
Lieutenant J. J. M. Soutar.
Serjeant-Major W. Beckett.
Staff-Serjeant H. L. Chavasse.
Serjeant A. Diemer.
Serjeant W. H. Harrison.
Serjeant-Major F. A. Nason.
Serjeant-Major A. J. Warburton.

Queen Alexandra's Imperial Military Nursing Service and Its Military and Civil Reserves.

Matron M. M. Blakely, Q.A.I.M.N.S.
Sister M. Clements, Q.A.I.M.N.S.
Sister S. Coulters, Civil Hosp. Res. (Manchester R. Infirmary).
Matron J. E. Dods, Q.A.I.M.N.S.

MENTIONED IN DESPATCHES

Sister F. E. Filkin, Q.A.I.M.N.S. Res.
Matron F. M. Hodgins, Q.A.I.M.N.S.
Sister V. N. Kiddle, Civil Hosp. Res. (Guy's Hosp.).
Sister G. Knowles, Q.A.I.M.N.S.
Sister E. M. Lyde, Q.A.I.M.N.S.
Matron M. Mark, Q.A.I.M.N.S.
Sister E. J. Minns, Q.A.I.M.N.S.
Matron R. Osborne, Q.A.I.M.N.S.
Sister A. M. Phillips, Q.A.I.M.N.S.
Matron H. W. Reid, Q.A.I.M.N.S.
Matron G. M. Richards, Q.A.I.M.N.S.
Matron A. B. Smith, R.R.C., Q.A.I.M.N.S.
Sister G. M. Smith, Q.A.I.M.N.S.
Matron L. E. C. Steen, Q.A.I.M.N.S.
Sister M. R. Stewart-Richardson, Q.A.I.M.N.S., Res.
Sister H. Stuart, Q.A.I.M.N.S.
Sister M. M. Tunley, Q.A.I.M.N.S.
Sister E. Tulley, Civil Hosp. Res. (R. Infirmary, Edinburgh).
Sister A. L. Walker, Q.A.I.M.N.S.
Matron M. Wilson, R.R.C , Q.A.I.M.N.S.

ARMY ORDNANCE DEPARTMENT.

Lieutenant-Colonel J. F. Bernard.
Inspector of Ord. Machinery, 1st Class, and Hon. Major C. W. Everett.
A.C.O. and Hon. Lieutenant J. H. Keyes.

Army Ordnance Corps.

Armt. Serjeant-Major S. W. Brown.
Armt. Serjeant-Major J. Byrom.
Sub-Condr. B. Fuller.
Condr. P. Hadland.
Condr. J. M. (now A.C.O. and Hon. Lieutenant) Lynam.
Sub-Condr. A. C. Maile.
Sub-Condr. J. (now A.C.O. and Hon. Lieut.) Watson.

Army Pay Corps.

Staff Serjeant-Major R. Cleland.

Corps of Military Police.

Serjeant G. A. Day.

MENTIONED IN DESPATCHES
INDIAN ARMY.

4TH CAVALRY.
Ressidar Udmi Ram.

3/4TH POONA HORSE.
Major G. M. Molloy.
Lieutenant F. A. de Pass (killed in action).
Risaldar Rathore Hamir Singh.
Sowar Abdullah Khan.
Sowar Fateh Khan.
Sowar Firman Shah.

1ST SAPPERS AND MINERS.
Captain A. J. G. Bird.
Captain E. H. Kelly.
Captain R. G. G. Robson.
Lieutenant E. O. Wheeler.
Subadar Gauri Shanker Dube.
Jemadar Abdul Aziz.
Col Havildar Chagatta, I.O.M.
Company Serjeant-Major N. Gibbons.
Sapper Suba Singh.

3RD SAPPERS AND MINERS.
Captain B. C. Battye.
Captain A. L. Paris.
Captain J. S. Richardson.
Lieutenant F. E. Buller.
Lieutenant M. A. R. G. Fitzmaurice.
Captain F. P. Nosworthy.
Lieutenant R. S. Rait-Kerr.
Subadar Malla Singh.
Jemadar Ganga Charan Dikshit.
Jemadar Ismail Khan.
Company Serjeant-Major H. J. White.
Serjeant E. L. Hill.

LAHORE SIGNAL COMPANY.
Lieutenant FitzA. Drayson, Border Regiment.
Corporal R. S. Stoneham, Bombay Vol. Rifles.

MEERUT SIGNAL COMPANY.
Serjeant J. G. Brewer.

MENTIONED IN DESPATCHES

SIGNAL CORPS.

Captain H. S. E. Franklin, 1/5th Sikhs.
Regimental Serjeant-Major A. Sergeant, Indian Unattached List.

6TH JAT LIGHT INFANTRY.

Lieutenant-Colonel H. J. Roche.
Major P. H. Dundas.
Lieutenant E. C. Liptrott (deceased).
Jemadar Lakhi Ram.
Havildar Badlu.
Havildar Harpul.
Havildar Mula.
Sepoy Bagmal.
Sepoy Risal.

9TH BHOPAL INFANTRY.

Captain G. D. Martin.
Subadar Major Bhure Singh.
Havildar Amar Singh.

15TH LUDHIANA SIKHS.

Major C. A. Vivian.
Captain J. A. S. Daniell, 14th K.G.O. Sikhs (attached).
Lieutenant G. L. Betham.
Jemadar Bir Singh.
Jemadar Wazir Singh.
Naik Bishn Singh.

34TH SIKH PIONEERS.

Major G. H. F. Kelly.
Captain J. F. Mackain (killed in action).
Captain G. E. H. Wilson.
Subadra Sher Singh.
Havildar Narayan Singh.
Subadra Sher Singh.
Havildar Narayan Singh.
Havildar Pala Singh.
Naik Bir Singh.
L/Naik Tota Singh.
Sepoy Gopal Singh.
Sepoy Ishar Singh.
Sepoy Katha Singh.
Sepoy Sant Singh.

MENTIONED IN DESPATCHES

1/39TH GARHWAL RIFLES.
Lieutenant-Colonel E. R. R. Swiney.
Captain J. T. H. Lane.
Captain F. G. E. Lumb.
Subadar Dan Sing Negi.
L/Naik Kiyali Gusain.
Bglr. Bhola Bisht.
Rifleman Dhan Sing Negi.
Rifleman Ghantu Rawat.
Rifleman Keshi Bisht.
Rifleman Kutalu Bisht.
Rifleman Partab Rana.
Rifleman Riachand Negi.

2/39TH GHARWAL RIFLES.
Lieutenant-Colonel D. H. Drake-Brockman.
Major G. H. Taylor.
Jemadar Lachman Sing Rawat.
Havildar Bir Sing Danu.
Havildar Diwan Singh Padhujar, A Company.
Havildar Ranjir Sing Pandir, C Company.
Naik Kedar Sing Mahar.
Rifleman Kesar Sing Rana.
Rifleman Madan Sing Rawat.
Rifleman Nain Sing Rawat.

47TH SIKHS.
Major S. R. Davidson.
Captain R. J. McCleverty (killed in action).
Captain A. M. Brown.
Lieutenant G. S. Brunskill.
Havildar Bhagat Singh.
C. Havildar Bhola Singh.
Naik Jaget Singh.
Sepoy Bhuta Singh.
Sepoy Kesar Singh.

57TH WILDE'S RIFLES.
Lieutenant-Colonel F. W. B. Gray, D.S.O.
L/Naik Lalak.
Sepoy Alvas Khan.
Sepoy Mir Badshah.
Sepoy Mir Badshah.
Sepoy Mir Baz.

MENTIONED IN DESPATCHES

58TH VAUGHAN'S RIFLES.

Major C. E. D. Davidson-Houston.
Captain H. L. C. Baldwin (deceased).
Captain W. McM. Black (killed in action).
Captain E. S. C. Willis, D.S.O.
Lieutenant S. Gordon, I.M.S.
Jemadar Hamid.
Jemadar Indar Singh.
Jemadar Sihel Singh.
Havildar Indar Singh.
Havildar Lashkar.
Havildar Sunday Singh.
Naik Baidullah.

59TH SCINDE RIFLES.

Captain B. E. Anderson.
Captain H. N. Lee (killed in action).
Havildar Niaz Gul.

107TH PIONEERS.

Captain W. P. M. D. McLaughlin.
Subadar Hashmat Dad Khan.
Subadar Labh Singh.
Subadar Zaman Khan.
Havildar Baghat Singh.

129TH BALUCHIS.

Lieutenant-Colonel W. M. Southey.
Major G. G. P. Humphreys (killed in action).
Captain W. F. Adair (killed in action).
Captain R. F. Dill, D.S.O.
Subadar Adam Khan.
Subadar Zaman Khan.
Havildar Sobatkhan.
Naik Zammir.
L/Naik Hobabgul.
Sepoy Kassib.
Sepoy Lafar Khan.
Sepoy Lal Sher.
Sepoy Redigui.
Sepoy Said Ahmed.

2/2ND GURKHA RIFLES.

Lieutenant-Colonel C. E. de M. Norie, D.S.O.
Major F. H. Norie (attached, interpreter).

MENTIONED IN DESPATCHES

Captain G. M. McCleverty.
Lieutenant E. J. Corse-Scott.
Subadar Karak Sing Rana.
Jemadar Amian Thapa.
Havildar Janglai Gurung.
Havildar Judhia Sarki.
Havildar Ran Patti Gurung.
Naik Gamer Sing Bura.
Naik Patiram Thapa.
Naik Ram Pershad Thapa.
L/Naik Sher Singh Ghale.
Rifleman Kalu Gurung.

2/3RD GURKHA RIFLES.

Lieutenant-Colonel W. R. Brakspear.
Captain R. D. Alexander.
Lieutenant H. F. C. McSwiney.
Jemadar Harak Bahadur Gurung.
Rifleman Gaj Bir Bisht.
Rifleman Ganpati Thapa.
Rifleman Ran Bahadur Sahi.

2/8TH GURKHA RIFLES.

Captain G. C. B. Buckland, D.S.O.

1/9TH GURKHA RIFLES.

Captain G. D. Pike.
Subadar Haridhoj Khattri.
L/Naik Jaman Singh Khattri.
Rifleman Gajbir Bisht.
Rifleman Ran Bahadur Sahi.

SUPPLY AND TRANSPORT SERVICES.

Lieutenant-Colonel J. P. C. Hennessy.
Major Lutf Ali Khan.
Staff-Serjeant F. G. Levings (9th Mule Corps.).
Private D. E. Watkins (Meerut Divn. Supply Co.).

MEDICAL SERVICES.

Lieutenant-Colonel A. H. Moorhead, M.B., I.M.S.
Major J. M. Sloan, D.S.O., M.B.
Captain A. W. M. Harvey, M.B., I.M.S.
Captain J. B. Jones, M.B.
3rd Class Assistant Surgeon F. Braganza, B.A.

MENTIONED IN DESPATCHES

1st Class Sub. Assistant Surgeon Muhammad Umar.
1st Class Sub. Assistant Surgeon Wahidyar Khan.
Serjeant J. Sharland, 2nd East Surrey Regiment (attached 130th I.F.A.)
Havildar Bihari, No. 8 Company, A.B. Corps.
Naik Achroo, 8th Battalion, Field Ambulance.
L/Naik Surjoo.
Private Fenner, 3rd K.R.R. (attached 19th Brigade, F.A.).
Driver Ingrey, A.S.C. (attached 111th Indian Field Ambulance).
Stretcher-Bearer Jaganaut, 111th I.F.A.,
Bearer Ram Sabatu.

III

THE WINTER CAMPAIGN

III : France, *2nd February*, 1915.

To Field-Marshal Earl Kitchener of Khartoum, K.P., G.C.B., O.M., etc.

My Lord,

I HAVE the honour to forward a further report on the operations of the Army under my command.

1. In the period under review the salient feature was the presence of His Majesty the King in the Field. His Majesty arrived at Headquarters on the 30th November, and left on the 5th December.

At a time when the strength and endurance of the troops had been tried to the utmost throughout the long and arduous Battle of Ypres-Armentières, the presence of His Majesty in their midst was of the greatest possible help and encouragement.

His Majesty visited all parts of the extensive area of operations and held numerous inspections of the troops behind the line of trenches.

On the 16th November Lieutenant His Royal Highness the Prince of Wales, K.G., Grenadier Guards, joined my Staff as Aide-de-Camp.

2. Since the date of my last report the operations of the Army under my command have been subject almost entirely to the limitations of weather.

History teaches us that the course of campaigns in Europe, which have been actively prosecuted during the months of December and January, have been largely influenced by weather conditions. It should, however, be thoroughly understood throughout the country that the most recent development of armaments and the latest methods of conducting warfare have added greatly to the difficulties and drawbacks of a vigorous winter campaign.

THE WINTER CAMPAIGN

To cause anything more than a waste of ammunition long-range artillery fire requires constant and accurate observation ; but this most necessary condition is rendered impossible of attainment in the midst of continual fog and mist.

Again, armies have now grown accustomed to rely largely on aircraft reconnaissance for accurate information of the enemy ; but the effective performance of this service is materially influenced by wind and weather.

The deadly accuracy, range, and quick-firing capabilities of the modern rifle and machine-gun require that a fire-swept zone be crossed in the shortest possible space of time by attacking troops. But if men are detained under the enemy's fire by the difficulty of emerging from a water-logged trench, and by the necessity of passing over ground knee-deep in holding mud and slush, such attacks become practically prohibitive owing to the losses they entail.

During the exigencies of the heavy fighting which ended in the last week of November the French and British Forces had become somewhat mixed up, entailing a certain amount of difficulty in matters of supply and in securing unity of command.

By the end of November I was able to concentrate the Army under my command in one area, and, by holding a shorter line, to establish effective reserves.

By the beginning of December there was a considerable falling off in the volume of artillery fire directed against our front by the enemy. Reconnaissance and reports showed that a certain amount of artillery had been withdrawn. We judged that the cavalry on our front, with the exception of one Division of the Guard, had disappeared.

There did not, however, appear to have been any great diminution in the numbers of infantry holding the trenches.

3. Although both artillery and rifle fire were exchanged with the enemy every day, and sniping went on

RAIDING PARTIES

more or less continuously during the hours of daylight, the operations which call for special record or comment are comparatively few.

During the last week in November some successful minor night operations were carried out in the 4th Corps.

On the night of the 23rd-24th November a small party of the 2nd Lincolnshire Regiment, under Lieutenant E. H. Impey, cleared three of the enemy's advanced trenches opposite the 25th Brigade and withdrew without loss.

On the night of the 24th-25th Captain J. R. Minshull Ford, Royal Welsh Fusiliers, and Lieutenant E. L. Morris, Royal Engineers, with 15 men of the Royal Engineers and Royal Welsh Fusiliers, successfully mined and blew up a group of farms immediately in front of the German trenches on the Touquet-Bridoux Road which had been used by German snipers.

On the night of the 26th-27th November a small party of the 2nd Scots Guards, under Lieutenant Sir E. H. W. Hulse, Bt., rushed the trenches opposite the 20th Brigade ; and after pouring a heavy fire into them returned with useful information as to the strength of the Germans and the position of machine guns.

The trenches opposite the 25th Brigade were rushed the same night by a patrol of the 2nd Rifle Brigade, under Lieutenant E. Durham.

On the 23rd November the 112th Regiment of the 14th German Army Corps succeeded in capturing some 800 yards of the trenches held by the Indian Corps, but the General Officer Commanding the Meerut Division organized a powerful counter-attack, which lasted throughout the night. At daybreak on the 24th November the line was entirely re-established.

The operation was a costly one, involving many casualties, but the enemy suffered far more heavily.

We captured over 100 prisoners, including 3 officers, as well as 3 machine guns and 2 trench mortars.

THE WINTER CAMPAIGN

On December 7th the concentration of the Indian Corps was completed by the arrival of the Sirhind Brigade from Egypt.

On December 9th the enemy attempted to commence a strong attack against the 3rd Corps, particularly in front of the trenches held by the Argyll and Sutherland Highlanders and the Middlesex Regiment.

They were driven back with heavy loss, and did not renew the attempt. Our casualties were very slight.

During the early days of December certain indications along the whole front of the Allied Line induced the French Commanders and myself to believe that the enemy had withdrawn considerable forces from the Western Theatre.

Arrangements were made with the Commander of the 8th French Army for an attack to be commenced on the morning of December 14th.

Operations began at 7 a.m. by a combined heavy artillery bombardment by the two French and the 2nd British Corps.

The British objectives were the Petit Bois and the Maedelsteed Spur, lying respectively to the west and south-west of the village of Wytschaete.

At 7.45 a.m. the Royal Scots, with great dash, rushed forward and attacked the former, while the Gordon Highlanders attacked the latter place.

The Royal Scots, commanded by Major F. J. Duncan D.S.O., in face of a terrible machine-gun and rifle fire, carried the German trench on the west edge of the Petit Bois capturing two machine guns and 53 prisoners, including one officer.

The Gordon Highlanders, with great gallantry, advanced up the Maedelsteed Spur, forcing the enemy to evacuate their front trench. They were, however, losing heavily, and found themselves unable to get any further. At nightfall they were obliged to fall back to their original position

OFFENSIVE OPERATIONS

Captain C. Boddam-Whetham and Lieutenant W. F. R. Dobie showed splendid dash, and with a few men entered the enemy's leading trenches; but they were all either killed or captured.

Lieutenant G. R. V. Hume-Gore and Lieutenant W. H. Paterson also distinguished themselves by their gallant leading.

Although not successful, the operation was most creditable to the fighting spirit of the Gordon Highlanders, most ably commanded by Major A. W. F. Baird, D.S.O.

As the 32nd French Division on the left had been unable to make any progress, the further advance of our infantry into the Wytschaete Wood was not practicable.

Possession of the western edge of the Petit Bois was, however, retained.

The ground was devoid of cover and so water-logged that a rapid advance was impossible, the men sinking deep in the mud at every step they took.

The artillery throughout the day was very skilfully handled by the C.R.A.'s of the 3rd, 4th, and 5th Divisions: Major-General F. D. V. Wing, C.B., Brigadier-General G. F. Milne, C.B., D.S.O., and Brigadier-General J. E. W. Headlam, C.B., D.S.O.

The casualties during the day were about 17 officers and 407 other ranks. The losses of the enemy were very considerable, large numbers of dead being found in the Petit Bois and also in the communicating trenches in front of the Gordon Highlanders, in one of which a hundred were counted by a night patrol.

On this day the artillery of the 4th Division, 3rd Corps, was used in support of the attack, under orders of the General Officer Commanding 2nd Corps.

The remainder of the 3rd Corps made demonstrations against the enemy with a view to preventing him from detaching troops to the area of operations of the 2nd Corps.

THE WINTER CAMPAIGN

From the 15th to the 17th December the offensive operations which were commenced on the 14th were continued, but were confined chiefly to artillery bombardment.

The infantry advance against Wytschaete Wood was not practicable until the French on our left could make some progress to afford protection to that flank.

On the 17th it was agreed that the plan of attack as arranged should be modified; but I was requested to continue demonstrations along my line in order to assist and support certain French operations which were being conducted elsewhere.

4. In his desire to act with energy up to his instructions to demonstrate and occupy the enemy, the General Officer Commanding the Indian Corps decided to take the advantage of what appeared to him a favourable opportunity to launch attacks against the advanced trenches in his front on the 18th and 19th December.

The attack of the Meerut Division on the left was made on the morning of the 19th with energy and determination, and was at first attended with considerable success, the enemy's advanced trenches being captured. Later on, however, a counter-attack drove them back to their original position with considerable loss.

The attack of the Lahore Division commenced at 4.30 a.m. It was carried out by two companies each of the 1st Highland Light Infantry and the 1st Battalion, 4th Gurkha Rifles, of the Sirhind Brigade, under Lieutenant-Colonel R. W. H. Ronaldson. This attack was completely successful, two lines of the enemy's trenches being captured with little loss.

Before daylight the captured trenches were filled with as many men as they would hold. The front was very restricted, communication to the rear impossible.

At daybreak it was found that the position was practically untenable. Both flanks were in the air, and a supporting

CAPTURE OF GIVENCHY

attack, which was late in starting, and, therefore, conducted during daylight, failed, although attempted with the greatest gallantry and resolution.

Lieutenant-Colonel Ronaldson held on till dusk, when the whole of the captured trenches had to be evacuated, and the detachment fell back to its original line.

By the night of the 19th December nearly all the ground gained during the day had been lost.

From daylight on the 20th December the enemy commenced a heavy fire from artillery and trench mortars on the whole front of the Indian Corps. This was followed by infantry attacks, which were in especial force against Givenchy, and between that place and La Quinque Rue.

At about 10 a.m. the enemy succeeded in driving back the Sirhind Brigade, and capturing a considerable part of Givenchy, but the 57th Rifles and 9th Bhopals, north of the canal, and the Connaught Rangers, south of it, stood firm.

The 15th Sikhs of the Divisional Reserve were already supporting the Sirhind Brigade. On the news of the retirement of the latter being received, the 47th Sikhs were also sent up to reinforce General Brunker. The 1st Manchester Regiment, 4th Suffolk Regiment, and two battalions of French Territorials under General Carnegy were ordered to launch a vigorous counter-attack from Pont Fixe through Givenchy to retake by a flank attack the trenches lost by the Sirhind Brigade.

Orders were sent to General Carnegy to divert his attack on Givenchy Village, and to re-establish the situation there.

A battalion of the 58th French Division was sent to Annequin in support.

About 5 p.m. a gallant attack by the 1st Manchester Regiment and one company of the 4th Suffolk Regiment had captured Givenchy, and had cleared the enemy out of the two lines of trenches to the north-east. To the east

THE WINTER CAMPAIGN

of the village the 9th Bhopal Infantry and 57th Rifles had maintained their positions, but the enemy were still in possession of our trenches to the north of the village.

General Macbean, with the Secunderabad Cavalry Brigade, 2nd Battalion, 8th Gurkha Rifles, and the 47th Sikhs, was sent up to support General Brunker, who at 2 p.m. directed General Macbean to move to a position of readiness in the second line trenches from Maris northward, and to counter-attack vigorously if opportunity offered.

Some considerable delay appears to have occurred, and it was not until 1 a.m. on the 21st that the 47th Sikhs and the 7th Dragoon Guards, under the command of Lieutenant-Colonel H. A. Lempriere, D.S.O., of the latter regiment, were launched in counter-attack.

They reached the enemy's trenches, but were driven out by enfilade fire, their gallant Commander being killed.

The main attack by the remainder of General Macbean's force, with the remnants of Lieutenant-Colonel Lempriere's detachment (which had again been rallied), was finally pushed in at about 4.30 a.m., and also failed.

In the northern section of the defensive line the retirement of the 2nd Battalion, 2nd Gurkha Rifles, at about 10 a.m. on the 20th, left the flank of the 1st Seaforth Highlanders, on the extreme right of the Meerut Division line, much exposed. This battalion was left shortly afterwards completely in the air by the retirement of the Sirhind Brigade.

The 58th Rifles, therefore, were ordered to support the left of the Seaforth Highlanders, to fill the gap created by the retirement of the Gurkhas.

During the whole of the afternoon strenuous efforts were made by the Seaforth Highlanders to clear the trenches to their right and left. The 1st Battalion, 9th Gurkha Rifles, reinforced the 2nd Gurkhas near the orchard where the Germans were in occupation of the

SUPPORT FOR THE INDIAN CORPS

trenches abandoned by the latter regiment. The Garhwal Brigade was being very heavily attacked, and their trenches and loopholes were much damaged; but the brigade continued to hold its front and attack, connecting with the 6th Jats on the left of the Dehra Dun Brigade.

No advance in force was made by the enemy, but the troops were pinned to their ground by heavy artillery fire, the Seaforth Highlanders especially suffering heavily.

Shortly before nightfall the 2nd Royal Highlanders on the right of the Seaforth Highlanders had succeeded in establishing touch with the Sirhind Brigade; and the continuous line (though dented near the orchard) existed throughout the Meerut Division.

Early in the afternoon of December 20th orders were sent to the 1st Corps, which was then in general army reserve, to send an infantry brigade to support the Indian Corps.

The 1st Brigade was ordered to Bethune, and reached that place at midnight on 20th-21st December. Later in the day Sir Douglas Haig was ordered to move the whole of the 1st Division in support of the Indian Corps.

The 3rd Brigade reached Bethune between 8 a.m. and 9 a.m. on the 21st, and on the same date the 2nd Brigade arrived at Lacon at 1 p.m.

The 1st Brigade was directed on Givenchy, *via* Pont Fixe, and the 3rd Brigade, through Gorre, on the trenches evacuated by the Sirhind Brigade.

The 2nd Brigade was directed to support; the Dehra Dun Brigade being placed at the disposal of the General Officer Commanding Meerut Division.

At 1 p.m. the General Officer Commanding 1st Division directed the 1st Brigade in attack from the west of Givenchy in a north-easterly direction, and the 3rd Brigade from Festubert in an east-north-easterly direction, the object being to pass the position originally held by us and to capture the German trenches 400 yards to the east of it.

THE WINTER CAMPAIGN

By 5 p.m. the 1st Brigade had obtained a hold in Givenchy, and the ground south as far as the canal; and the 3rd Brigade had progressed to a point half a mile west of Festubert.

By nightfall the 1st South Wales Borderers and the 2nd Welsh Regiment of the 3rd Brigade had made a lodgment in the original trenches to the north-east of Festubert, the 1st Gloucestershire Regiment continuing the line southward along the track east of Festubert.

The 1st Brigade had established itself on the east side of Givenchy.

By 3 p.m. the 3rd Brigade was concentrated at Le Touret, and was ordered to retake the trenches which had been lost by the Dehra Dun Brigade.

By 10 p.m. the support trenches west of the orchard had been carried, but the original fire trenches had been so completely destroyed that they could not be occupied.

This operation was performed by the 1st Loyal North Lancashire Regiment and the 1st Northamptonshire Regiment, supported by the 2nd King's Royal Rifle Corps, in reserve.

Throughout this day the units of the Indian Corps rendered all the assistance and support they could in view of their exhausted condition.

At 1 p.m. on the 22nd Sir Douglas Haig took over command from Sir James Willcocks. The situation in the front line was then approximately as follows:

> South of the La Bassée Canal the Connaught Rangers of the Ferozepore Brigade had not been attacked. North of the canal a short length of our original line was still held by the 9th Bhopals and the 57th Rifles of the same brigade. Connecting with the latter was the 1st Brigade holding the village of Givenchy and its eastern and northern approaches. On the left of the 1st Brigade was the 3rd Brigade. Touch had been lost between the left of the former and the right of the

FIELD-MARSHAL SIR DOUGLAS HAIG, G.C.B.
Photograph : Central News.

RESTORING THE LINE

latter. The 3rd Brigade held a line along, and in places advanced to, the east of the Festubert Road. Its left was in communication with the right of the Meerut Division line, where troops of the 2nd Brigade had just relieved the 1st Seaforth Highlanders. To the north, units of the 2nd Brigade held an indented line west of the orchard, connecting with half of the 2nd Royal Highlanders, half of the 41st Dogras and the 1st Battalion, 9th Gurkha Rifles. From this point to the north the 6th Jats and the whole of the Garhwal Brigade occupied the original line which they had held from the commencement of the operations.

The relief of most units of the southern sector was effected on the night of 22nd December. The Meerut Division remained under the orders of the 1st Corps, and was not completely withdrawn until the 27th December.

In the evening the position at Givenchy was practically re-established, and the 3rd Brigade had re-occupied the old line of trenches.

During the 23rd the enemy's activities ceased, and the whole position was restored to very much its original condition.

In my last despatch I had occasion to mention the prompt and ready help I received from the Lahore Division under the command of Major-General H. B. B. Watkis, C.B., which was thrown into action immediately on arrival, when the British Forces were very hard pressed during the battle of Ypres-Armentières.

The Indian troops have fought with the utmost steadfastness and gallantry whenever they have been called upon. Weather conditions were abnormally bad, the snow and floods precluding any active operations during the first three weeks of January.

5. At 7.30 a.m. on the 25th January, the enemy began to shell Bethune, and at 8 a.m. a strong hostile infantry attack developed south of the canal, preceded by a heavy

THE WINTER CAMPAIGN

bombardment of artillery, minenwerfers and, possibly, the explosion of mines, though the latter is doubtful.

The British line south of the canal formed a pronounced salient from the canal on the left, thence running forward toward the railway triangle and back to the main La Bassée-Bethune Road, where it joined the French. This line was occupied by half a battalion of the Scots Guards, and half a battalion of the Coldstream Guards, of the 1st Infantry Brigade. The trenches in the salient were blown in almost at once; and the enemy's attack penetrated this line. Our troops retired to a partially prepared second line, running approximately due north and south from the canal to the road, some 500 yards west of the railway triangle. This second line had been strengthened by the construction of a keep half way between the canal and the road. Here the other two half battalions of the above-mentioned regiments were in support.

These supports held up the enemy, who, however, managed to establish himself in the brick stacks and some communication trenches between the keep, the road and the canal—and even beyond and west of the keep on either side of it.

The London Scottish had in the meantime been sent up in support, and a counter-attack was organized with the 1st Royal Highlanders, part of the 1st Cameron Highlanders, and the 2nd King's Royal Rifle Corps, the latter regiment having been sent forward from the Divisional Reserve.

The counter-attack was delayed in order to synchronize with a counter-attack north of the canal, which was arranged for 1 p.m.

At 1 p.m. these troops moved forward, their flanks making good progress near the road and the canal, but their centre being held up. The 2nd Royal Sussex Regiment was then sent forward, late in the afternoon, to

ENEMY ATTACK ON GIVENCHY

reinforce. The result was that the Germans were driven back far enough to enable a somewhat broken line to be taken up, running from the culvert on the railway, almost due south to the keep, and thence south-east to the main road.

The French left near the road had also been attacked and driven back a little, but not to so great an extent as the British right. Consequently, the French left was in advance of the British right and exposed to a possible flank attack from the north.

The Germans did not, however, persevere further in their attack.

The above-mentioned line was strengthened during the night, and the 1st Guards Brigade, which had suffered severely, was withdrawn into reserve and replaced by the 2nd Infantry Brigade.

While this was taking place another, and equally severe, attack was delivered north of the canal against the village of Givenchy.

At 8.15 a.m., after a heavy artillery bombardment with high explosive shells, the enemy's infantry advanced under the effective fire of our artillery, which, however, was hampered by the constant interruption of telephonic communication between the observers and batteries. Nevertheless, our artillery fire, combined with that of the infantry in the fire trenches, had the effect of driving the enemy from his original direction of advance, with the result that his troops crowded together on the north-east corner of the village and broke through into the centre of the village as far as the keep, which had been previously put in a state of defence. The Germans had lost heavily, and a well-timed local counter-attack, delivered by the reserves of the 2nd Welsh Regiment and 1st South Wales Borderers, and by a company of the 1st Royal Highlanders (lent by the 1st Brigade as a working party—this company was at work on the keep at the time), was completely

THE WINTER CAMPAIGN

successful, with the result that, after about an hour's street fighting, all who had broken into the village were either captured or killed; and the original line round the village was re-established by noon.

South of the village, however, and close to the canal, the right of the 2nd Royal Munster Fusiliers fell back in conformity with the troops south of the canal; but after dark that regiment moved forward and occupied the old line.

During the course of the attack on Givenchy the enemy made five assaults on the salient at the north-east of the village about French Farm, but was repulsed every time with heavy loss.

6. On the morning of the 29th January attacks were made on the right of the 1st Corps, south of the canal in the neighbourhood of La Bassée.

The enemy (part of the 14th German Corps), after a severe shelling, made a violent attack with scaling ladders on the keep, also to the north and south of it. In the keep and on the north side the Sussex Regiment held the enemy off, inflicting on him serious losses. On the south side the hostile infantry succeeded in reaching the Northamptonshire Regiment's trenches; but were immediately counter-attacked and all killed. Our artillery co-operated well with the infantry in repelling the attack.

In this action our casualties were inconsiderable, but the enemy lost severely, more than 200 of his killed alone being left in front of our position.

7. On the 1st February a fine piece of work was carried out by the 4th Brigade in the neighbourhood of Cuinchy.

Some of the 2nd Coldstream Guards were driven from their trenches at 2.30 a.m., but made a stand some twenty yards east of them in a position which they held till morning.

A counter-attack, launched at 3.15 a.m. by one company of the Irish Guards and half a company of the

THE COLDSTREAM AND IRISH GUARDS

2nd Coldstream Guard, proved unsuccessful, owing to heavy rifle fire from the east and south.

At 10.5 a.m., acting under orders of the 1st Division, a heavy bombardment was opened on the lost ground for ten minutes; and this was followed immediately by an assault by about 50 men of the 2nd Coldstream Guards with bayonets, led by Captain A. Leigh Bennett, followed by 30 men of the Irish Guards, led by Second Lieutenant F. F. Graham, also with bayonets. These were followed by a party of Royal Engineers with sand bags and wire.

All the ground which had been lost was brilliantly retaken; the 2nd Coldstream Guards also taking another German trench and capturing two machine guns.

Thirty-two prisoners fell into our hands.

The General Officer Commanding 1st Division describes the preparation by the artillery as " splendid, the high explosive shells dropping in the exact spot with absolute precision."

In forwarding his report on this engagement, the General Officer Commanding First Army writes as follows :

Special credit is due—

(i) To Major-General Haking, Commanding 1st Division, for the prompt manner in which he arranged this counter-attack and for the general plan of action, which was crowned with success.

(ii) To the General Officer Commanding the 4th Brigade (Lord Cavan) for the thorough manner in which he carried out the orders of the General Officer Commanding the Division.

(iii) To the regimental officers, non-commissioned officers and men of the 2nd Coldstream Guards and Irish Guards, who, with indomitable pluck, stormed two sets of barricades, captured three German trenches, two machine guns, and killed or made prisoners many of the enemy.

THE WINTER CAMPAIGN

8. During the period under report the Royal Flying Corps has again performed splendid service.

Although the weather was almost uniformly bad and the machines suffered from constant exposure, there have been only thirteen days on which no actual reconnaissance has been effected. Approximately, one hundred thousand miles have been flown.

In addition to the daily and constant work of reconnaissance and co-operation with the artillery, a number of aerial combats have been fought, raids carried out, detrainments harassed, parks and petrol depôts bombed, etc.

Various successful bomb-dropping raids have been carried out, usually against the enemy's aircraft material. The principle of attacking hostile aircraft whenever and wherever seen (unless highly important information is being delivered) has been adhered to, and has resulted in the moral fact that enemy machines invariably beat immediate retreat when chased.

Five German aeroplanes are known to have been brought to the ground, and it would appear probable that others, though they have managed to reach their own lines, have done so in a considerably damaged condition.

9. In my despatch of 20th November, 1914, I referred to the reinforcements of Territorial Troops which I had received, and I mentioned several units which had already been employed in the fighting line.

In the positions which I held for some years before the outbreak of this war I was brought into close contact with the Territorial Force, and I found every reason to hope and believe that, when the hour of trial arrived, they would justify every hope and trust which was placed in them.

The Lords Lieutenant of Counties and the Associations which worked under them bestowed a vast amount of labour and energy on the organization of the Territorial

THE TERRITORIALS AND O.T.C.

Force; and I trust it may be some recompense to them to know that I, and the principal Commanders serving under me, consider that the Territorial Force has far more than justified the most sanguine hopes that any of us ventured to entertain of their value and use in the field. Commanders of Cavalry Divisions are unstinted in their praise of the manner in which the Yeomanry regiments attached to their brigades have done their duty, both in and out of action. The service of Divisional Cavalry is now almost entirely performed by Yeomanry, and Divisional Commanders report that they are very efficient.

Army Corps Commanders are loud in their praise of the Territorial Battalions which form part of nearly all the brigades at the front in the first line, and more than one of them have told me that these battalions are fast approaching—if they have not already reached—the standard of efficiency of Regular Infantry.

I wish to add a word about the Officers Training Corps. The presence of the Artists' Rifles (28th Battalion, The London Regiment) with the Army in France enabled me also to test the value of this organization.

Having had some experience in peace of the working of the Officers Training Corps, I determined to turn the Artists' Rifles (which formed part of the Officers Training Corps in peace time) to its legitimate use. I therefore established the battalion as a Training Corps for Officers in the field.

The cadets pass through a course, which includes some thoroughly practical training, as all cadets do a tour of 48 hours in the trenches, and afterwards write a report on what they see and notice. They also visit an observation post of a battery or group of batteries, and spend some hours there.

A Commandant has been appointed, and he arranges and supervises the work, sets schemes for practice,

THE WINTER CAMPAIGN

administers the school, and delivers lectures, reports on the candidates.

The cadets are instructed in all branches of military training suitable for platoon commanders.

Machine-gun tactics, a knowledge of which is so necessary for all junior officers, is a special feature of the course of instruction.

When first started the school was able to turn out officers at the rate of 75 a month. This has since been increased to 100.

Reports received from Divisional and Army Corps Commanders on officers who have been trained at the school are most satisfactory.

10. Since the date of my last report I have been able to make a close personal inspection of all the units in the command. I was most favourably impressed by all I saw.

The troops composing the Army in France have been subjected to as severe a trial as it is possible to impose upon any body of men. The desperate fighting described in my last despatch had hardly been brought to a conclusion when they were called upon to face the rigours and hardships of a winter campaign. Frost and snow have alternated with periods of continuous rain.

The men have been called upon to stand for many hours together almost up to their waists in bitterly cold water, only separated by one or two hundred yards from a most vigilant enemy.

Although every measure which science and medical knowledge could suggest to mitigate these hardships was employed, the sufferings of the men have been very great.

In spite of all this they presented, at the inspections to which I have referred, a most soldier-like, splendid, though somewhat war-worn appearance. Their spirit remains high and confident; their general health is excellent, and their condition most satisfactory.

I regard it as most unfortunate that circumstances have

INSPECTING THE ARMY

prevented any account of many splendid instances of courage and endurance, in the face of almost unparalleled hardship and fatigue in war, coming regularly to the knowledge of the public.

Reinforcements have arrived from England with remarkable promptitude and rapidity. They have been speedily drafted into the ranks, and most of the units I inspected were nearly complete when I saw them. In appearance and quality the drafts sent out have exceeded my most sanguine expectations, and I consider the Army in France is much indebted to the Adjutant-General's Department at the War Office for the efficient manner in which its requirements have been met in this most essential respect.

With regard to these inspections, I may mention in particular the fine appearance presented by the 27th and 28th Divisions, composed principally of battalions which had come from India. Included in the former division was the Princess Patricia's Royal Canadian Regiment. They are a magnificent set of men, and have since done excellent work in the trenches.

It was some three weeks after the events recorded in paragraph 4 that I made my inspection of the Indian Corps, under Sir James Willcocks. The appearance they presented was most satisfactory, and fully confirmed my first opinion that the Indian troops only required rest, and a little acclimatizing, to bring out all their fine inherent fighting qualities.

I saw the whole of the Indian Cavalry Corps, under Lieutenant-General Rimington, on a mounted parade soon after their arrival. They are a magnificent body of Cavalry, and will, I feel sure, give the best possible account of themselves when called upon.

In the meantime, at their own particular request, they have taken their turn in the trenches and performed most useful and valuable service.

THE WINTER CAMPAIGN

11. The Rt. Rev. Bishop Taylor Smith, C.V.O., D.D., Chaplain-General to the Forces, arrived at my Headquarters on 6th January, on a tour of inspection throughout the command.

The Cardinal Archbishop of Westminster has also visited most of the Irish Regiments at the front and the principal centres on the line of communications.

In a quiet and unostentatious manner the chaplains of all denominations have worked with devotion and energy in their respective spheres.

The number with the forces in the field at the commencement of the war was comparatively small, but towards the end of last year the Rev. J. M. Simms, D.D., K.H.C., Principal Chaplain, assisted by his Secretary, the Rev. W. Drury, reorganized the branch, and placed the spiritual welfare of the soldier on a more satisfactory footing. It is hoped that the further increase of personnel may be found possible.

I cannot speak too highly of the devoted manner in which all chaplains, whether with the troops in the trenches, or in attendance on the sick and wounded in casualty clearing stations and hospitals on the line of communications, have worked throughout the campaign.

Since the commencement of hostilities the work of the Royal Army Medical Corps has been carried out with untiring zeal, skill and devotion. Whether at the front under conditions such as obtained during the fighting on the Aisne, when casualties were heavy and accommodation for their reception had to be improvised, or on the line of communications, where an average of some 11,000 patients have been daily under treatment, the organization of the Medical Services has always been equal to the demands made upon it.

The careful system of sanitation introduced into the Army has, with the assistance of other measures, kept the troops free from any epidemic, in support of which it is

THE R.A.M.C. AND THE ROYAL ENGINEERS

to be noticed that since the commencement of the war some 500 cases only of enteric have occurred.

The organization for the first time in war of Motor Ambulance Convoys is due to the initiative and organizing powers of Surgeon-General T. J. O'Donnell, D.S.O., ably assisted by Major P. Evans, Royal Army Medical Corps.

Two of these convoys, composed entirely of Red Cross Society personnel, have done excellent work under the superintendence of Regular Medical Officers.

Twelve Hospital Trains ply between the front and the various bases. I have visited several of the trains when halted in stations, and have found them conducted with great comfort and efficiency.

During the more recent phase of the campaign the creation of Rest Depôts at the front has materially reduced the wastage of men to the line of communications.

Since the latter part of October, 1914, the whole of the medical arrangements have been in the hands of Surgeon-General Sir A. T. Sloggett, C.M.G., K.H.S., under whom Surgeon-General T. P. Woodhouse and Surgeon-General T. J. O'Donnell have been responsible for the organization on the line of communications and at the front respectively.

12. The exceptional and peculiar conditions brought about by the weather have caused large demands to be made upon the resources and skill of the Royal Engineers.

Every kind of expedient has had to be thought out and adopted to keep the lines of trenches and defence work effective.

The Royal Engineers have shown themselves as capable of overcoming the ravages caused by violent rain and floods as they have been throughout in neutralizing the effect of the enemy's artillery.

In this connexion I wish particularly to mention the

THE WINTER CAMPAIGN

excellent services performed by my Chief Engineer, Brigadier-General G. H. Fowke, who has been indefatigable in supervising all such work. His ingenuity and skill have been most valuable in the local construction of the various expedients which experience has shown to be necessary in prolonged trench warfare.

13. I have no reason to modify in any material degree my views of the general military situation, as expressed in my despatch of November 20th, 1914.

14. I have once more gratefully to acknowledge the valuable help and support I have received throughout this period from General Foch, General D'Urbal, and General Maud'huy of the French Army.

I have the honour to be,

    Your Lordship's most obedient Servant,

(*Signed*) J. D. P. FRENCH, Field-Marshal,

Commander-in-Chief the British Forces in the Field.

IV. NEUVE CHAPELLE

V : General Headquarters, 5*th April*, 1915.

To Field-Marshal Earl Kitchener of Khartoum, K.P., G.C.B., O.M., etc.

My Lord,

I HAVE the honour to report the operations of the Forces under my command since the date of my last despatch, 2nd February, 1915.

1. The event of chief interest and importance which has taken place is the victory achieved over the enemy at the Battle of Neuve Chapelle, which was fought on the 10th, 11th and 12th of March. The main attack was delivered by troops of the First Army under the command of General Sir Douglas Haig, supported by a large force of Heavy Artillery, a Division of Cavalry and some Infantry of the general reserve.

Secondary and holding attacks and demonstrations were made along the front of the Second Army under the direction of its Commander, General Sir Horace Smith-Dorrien.

Whilst the success attained was due to the magnificent bearing and indomitable courage displayed by the troops of the 4th and Indian Corps, I consider that the able and skilful dispositions which were made by the General Officer Commanding First Army contributed largely to the defeat of the enemy and to the capture of his position. The energy and vigour with which General Sir Douglas Haig handled his command show him to be a leader of great ability and power.

Another action of considerable importance was brought about by a surprise attack of the Germans made on the 14th March against the 27th Division holding the trenches east of St. Eloi. A large force of artillery was concentrated in this area under cover of mist, and a heavy volume of fire was suddenly brought to bear on the trenches at 5 p.m. This artillery attack was accompanied by two mine explosions; and, in the confusion caused by these and the suddenness of the attack, the position of St. Eloi was captured and held for some hours by the enemy.

Well directed and vigorous counter attacks, in which the troops of the 5th Army Corps showed great bravery and determination, restored the situation by the evening of the 15th.

A more detailed account of these operations will appear in subsequent pages of this despatch.

2. On the 6th February a brilliant action by troops of the 1st Corps materially improved our position in the area south of the La Bassée Canal. During the previous night parties of Irish Guards and of the 3rd Battalion Coldstream Guards had succeeded in gaining ground whence converging fire could be directed on the flanks and rear of certain " brickstacks " occupied by the Germans, which had been for some time a source of considerable annoyance.

At 2 p.m. the affair commenced with a severe bombardment of the " brickstacks " and the enemy's trenches. A brisk attack by the 3rd Coldstream Guards and Irish Guards from our trenches west of the " brickstacks " followed, and was supported by fire from the flanking positions which had been seized the previous night by the same regiments. The attack succeeded, the " brickstacks " were occupied without difficulty, and a line established north and south through a point about forty yards east of the " brickstacks."

The casualties suffered by the 5th Corps throughout the period under review, and particularly during the month of February, have been heavier than those in other parts of the line. I regret this; but I do not think, taking all the circumstances into consideration, that they were unduly numerous. The position then occupied by

THE FIFTH CORPS

the 5th Corps has always been a very vulnerable part of our line; the ground is marshy, and trenches are most difficult to construct and maintain. The 27th and 28th Divisions of the 5th Corps have had no previous experience of European warfare, and a number of the units composing it had only recently returned from service in tropical climates. In consequence, the hardships of a rigorous winter campaign fell with greater weight upon these Divisions than upon any other in the command.

Chiefly owing to these causes, the 5th Corps, up to the beginning of March, was constantly engaged in counter-attack to retake trenches and ground which had been lost.

In their difficult and arduous task, however, the troops displayed the utmost gallantry and devotion; and it is most creditable to the skill and energy of their leaders that I am able to report how well they have surmounted all their difficulties, that the ground first taken over by them is still intact, and held with little greater loss than is incurred by troops in all other parts of the line.

On the 14th February the 82nd Brigade of the 27th Division was driven from its trenches east of St. Eloi; but by 7 a.m. on the 15th all these trenches had been recaptured, fifteen prisoners taken, and sixty German dead counted in front of the trenches. Similarly in the 28th Division trenches were lost by the 85th Brigade and retaken the following night.

During the month of February the enemy made several attempts to get through all along the line, but he was invariably repulsed with loss. A particularly vigorous attempt was made on the 17th February against the trenches held by the Indian Corps, but it was brilliantly repulsed.

On February 28th a successful minor attack was made on the enemy's trenches near St. Eloi by small parties of the Princess Patricia's Canadian Light Infantry. The attack was divided into three small groups, the whole

NEUVE CHAPELLE

under the command of Lieutenant Crabbe: No. 1 Group under Lieutenant Papineau, No. 2 Group under Serjeant Patterson, and No. 3 Group under Co. S.-M. Lloyd.

The head of the party got within fifteen or twenty yards of the German trench and charged; it was dark at the time (about 5.15 a.m.).

Lieutenant Crabbe, who showed the greatest dash and *élan*, took his party over everything in the trench until they had gone down it about eighty yards, when they were stopped by a barricade of sandbags and timber. This party, as well as the others, then pulled down the front face of the German parapet. A number of Germans were killed and wounded, and a few prisoners were taken.

The services performed by this distinguished corps have continued to be very valuable since I had occasion to refer to them in my last despatch. They have been most ably organised, trained and commanded by Lieutenant-Colonel F. D. Farquhar, D.S.O., who, I deeply regret to say, was killed while superintending some trench work on the 20th March. His loss will be deeply felt.

A very gallant attack was made by the 4th Battalion of the King's Royal Rifle Corps of the 80th Brigade on the enemy's trenches in the early hours of March 2nd. The Battalion was led by Major Widdrington, who launched it at 12.30 a.m. (he himself being wounded during its progress), covered by an extremely accurate and effective artillery fire. About sixty yards of the enemy's trench were cleared, but the attack was brought to a standstill by a very strong barricade, in attempting to storm which several casualties were incurred.

3. During the month of February I arranged with General Foch to render the 9th French Corps, holding the trenches on my left, some much-needed rest by sending the three Divisions of the British Cavalry Corps to hold a portion of the French trenches, each division for a period of ten days alternately.

CAVALRY IN THE TRENCHES

It was very gratifying to me to note once again in this campaign the eager readiness which the Cavalry displayed to undertake a rôle which does not properly belong to them in order to support and assist their French comrades.

In carrying out this work leaders, officers and men displayed the same skill and energy which I have had reason to comment upon in former despatches.

The time passed by the Cavalry in the French trenches was, on the whole, quiet and uneventful, but there are one or two incidents calling for remark.

At about 1.45 a.m. on 16th February a half-hearted attack was made against the right of the line held by the 2nd Cavalry Division, but it was easily repulsed by rifle fire, and the enemy left several dead in front of the trenches. The attack was delivered against the second and third trenches from the right of the line of the Division.

At 6 a.m. on the 21st the enemy blew up one of the 2nd Cavalry Division trenches, held by the 16th Lancers, and some adjoining French trenches. The enemy occupied forty yards of our trench and tried to advance, but were stopped. An immediate counter-attack by the supporting squadron was stopped by machine-gun fire. The line was established opposite the gap, and a counter-attack by two squadrons and one company of French reserve was ordered. At 5.30 p.m. 2nd Cavalry Division reported that the counter-attack did not succeed in retaking the trench blown in, but that a new line had been established forty yards in rear of it, and that there was no further activity on the part of the enemy. At 10 p.m. the situation was unchanged.

The Commander of the Indian Cavalry Corps expressed a strong desire that the troops under his command should gain some experience in trench warfare. Arrangements were made, therefore, with the General Officer

NEUVE CHAPELLE

Commanding the Indian Corps, in pursuance of which the various units of the Indian Cavalry Corps have from time to time taken a turn in the trenches, and have thereby gained some valuable experience.

4. About the end of February many vital considerations induced me to believe that a vigorous offensive movement by the Forces under my command should be planned and carried out at the earliest possible moment.

Amongst the more important reasons which convinced me of this necessity were :—The general aspect of the Allied situation throughout Europe, and particularly the marked success of the Russian Army in repelling the violent onslaughts of Marshal von Hindenburg ; the apparent weakening of the enemy in my front, and the necessity for assisting our Russian Allies to the utmost by holding as many hostile troops as possible in the Western Theatre ; the efforts to this end which were being made by the French Forces at Arras and Champagne ; and, perhaps the most weighty consideration of all, the need of fostering the offensive spirit in the troops under my command after the trying and possibly enervating experiences which they had gone through of a severe winter in the trenches.

In a former despatch I commented upon the difficulties and drawbacks which the winter weather in this climate imposes upon a vigorous offensive. Early in March these difficulties became greatly lessened by the drying up of the country and by spells of brighter weather.

I do not propose in this despatch to enter at length into the considerations which actuated me in deciding upon the plan, time and place of my attack, but Your Lordship is fully aware of these.

As mentioned above, the main attack was carried out by units of the First Army, supported by troops of the Second Army and the general reserve.

The object of the main attack was to be the capture of

THE BATTLE OPENS

the village of Neuve Chapelle and the enemy's position at that point, and the establishment of our line as far forward as possible to the east of that place.

The object, nature and scope of the attack, and instructions for the conduct of the operation were communicated by me to Sir Douglas Haig in a secret memorandum dated 19th February.

The main topographical feature of this part of the theatre is a marked ridge which runs south-west from a point two miles south-west of Lille to the village of Fournes, whence two spurs run out, one due west to a height known as Haut Pommereau, the other following the line of the main road to Illies.

The buildings of the village of Neuve Chapelle run along the Rue du Bois-Fauquisart Road. There is a triangle of roads just north of the village. This area consists of a few big houses, with walls, gardens, orchards, etc., and here, with the aid of numerous machine guns, the enemy had established a strong post which flanked the approaches to the village.

The Bois du Biez, which lies roughly south-east of the village of Neuve Chapelle, influenced the course of this operation.

Full instructions as to assisting and supporting the attack were issued to the Second Army.

The battle opened at 7.30 a.m. on the 10th March by a powerful artillery bombardment of the enemy's position at Neuve Chapelle. The artillery bombardment had been well prepared and was most effective, except on the extreme northern portion of the front of attack.

At 8.5 a.m. the 23rd (left) and 25th (right) Brigades of the 8th Division assaulted the German trenches on the north-west of the village.

At the same hour the Garhwal Brigade of the Meerut Division, which occupied the position to the south of Neuve Chapelle, assaulted the German trenches in its front.

NEUVE CHAPELLE

The Garhwal Brigade and the 25th Brigade carried the enemy's lines of entrenchments where the wire entanglements had been almost entirely swept away by our shrapnel fire. The 23rd Brigade, however, on the north-east, was held up by the wire entanglements, which were not sufficiently cut.

At 8.5 a.m. the artillery turned on to Neuve Chapelle, and at 8.35 a.m. the advance of the infantry was continued.

The 25th and Garhwal Brigades pushed on eastward and north-eastward respectively, and succeeded in getting a footing in the village. The 23rd Brigade was still held up in front of the enemy's wire entanglements, and could not progress. Heavy losses were suffered, especially in the Middlesex Regiment and the Scottish Rifles. The progress, however, of the 25th Brigade into Neuve Chapelle immediately to the south of the 23rd Brigade had the effect of turning the southern flank of the enemy's defences in front of the 23rd Brigade.

This fact, combined with powerful artillery support, enabled the 23rd Brigade to get forward between 10 and 11 a.m., and by 11 a.m. the whole of the village of Neuve Chapelle and the roads leading northward and south-westward from the eastern end of that village were in our hands.

During this time our artillery completely cut off the village and the surrounding country from any German reinforcements which could be thrown into the fight to restore the situation by means of a curtain of shrapnel fire. Prisoners subsequently reported that all attempts at reinforcing the front line were checked.

Steps were at once taken to consolidate the position won.

Considerable delay occurred after the capture of the Neuve Chapelle position. The infantry was greatly disorganised by the violent nature of the attack and by its

DELAY IN BRINGING UP RESERVES

passage through the enemy's trenches and the buildings of the village. It was necessary to get units to some extent together before pushing on. The telephonic communication being cut by the enemy's fire rendered communication between front and rear most difficult. The fact of the left of the 23rd Brigade having been held up had kept back the 8th Division, and had involved a portion of the 25th Brigade in fighting to the north out of its proper direction of advance. All this required adjustment. An orchard held by the enemy north of Neuve Chapelle also threatened the flank of an advance towards the Aubers Ridge.

I am of opinion that this delay would not have occurred had the clearly expressed order of the General Officer Commanding First Army been more carefully observed.

The difficulties above enumerated might have been overcome at an earlier period of the day if the General Officer Commanding 4th Corps had been able to bring his reserve brigades more speedily into action.

As it was, the further advance did not commence before 3.30 p.m.

The 21st Brigade was able to form up in the open on the left without a shot being fired at it, thus showing that at the time the enemy's resistance had been paralysed. The Brigade pushed forward in the direction of Moulin Du Pietre.

At first it made good progress, but was subsequently held up by the machine-gun fire from the houses and from a defended work in the line of the German entrenchments opposite the right of the 22nd Brigade.

Further to the south the 24th Brigade, which had been directed on Pietre, was similarly held up by machine-guns in the houses and trenches at the road junction six hundred yards north-west of Pietre.

The 25th Brigade, on the right of the 24th, was also held up by machine-guns from a bridge held by the

NEUVE CHAPELLE

Germans, over the River Des Layes, which is situated to the north-west of the Bois Du Biez.

Whilst two Brigades of the Meerut Division were establishing themselves on the new line, the Dehra Dun Brigade, supported by the Jullundur Brigade of the Lahore Division, moved to the attack of the Bois Du Biez, but were held up on the line of the River Des Layes by the German post at the bridge which enfiladed them and brought them to a standstill.

The defended bridge over the River Des Layes and its neighbourhood immediately assumed considerable importance. Whilst artillery fire was brought to bear, as far as circumstances would permit, on this point, Sir Douglas Haig directed the 1st Corps to despatch one or more battalions of the 1st Brigade in support of the troops attacking the bridge. Three battalions were thus sent to Richebourg St. Vaast. Darkness coming on, and the enemy having brought up reinforcements, no further progress could be made, and the Indian Corps and 4th Corps proceeded to consolidate the position they had gained.

Whilst the operations which I have thus briefly recorded were going on, the 1st Corps, in accordance with orders, delivered an attack in the morning from Givenchy, simultaneously with that against Neuve Chapelle; but, as the enemy's wire was insufficiently cut, very little progress could be made, and the troops at this point did little more than hold fast the Germans in front of them.

On the following day, March 11th, the attack was renewed by the 4th and Indian Corps, but it was soon seen that a further advance would be impossible until the artillery had dealt effectively with the various houses and defended localities which held up the troops along the entire front. Efforts were made to direct the artillery fire accordingly; but owing to the weather conditions, which did not permit of aerial observation, and the fact that

THE ATTACK SUSPENDED

nearly all the telephonic communications between the artillery observers and their batteries had been cut, it was impossible to do so with sufficient accuracy. Even when our troops which were pressing forward occupied a house here and there, it was not possible to stop our artillery fire, and the infantry had to be withdrawn.

The two principal points which barred the advance were the same as on the preceding day—namely, the enemy's position about Moulin de Pietre and at the bridge over the River des Layes.

On the 12th March the same unfavourable conditions as regards weather prevailed, and hampered artillery action.

Although the 4th and Indian Corps most gallantly attempted to capture the strongly fortified positions in their front, they were unable to maintain themselves, although they succeeded in holding them for some hours.

Operations on this day were chiefly remarkable for the violent counter-attacks, supported by artillery, which were delivered by the Germans, and the ease with which they were repulsed.

As most of the objects for which the operations had been undertaken had been attained and as there were reasons why I considered it inadvisable to continue the attack at that time, I directed Sir Douglas Haig on the night of the 12th to hold and consolidate the ground which had been gained by the 4th and Indian Corps, and to suspend further offensive operations for the present.

On the morning of the 12th I informed the General Officer Commanding 1st Army that he could call on the 2nd Cavalry Division, under General Gough, for immediate support in the event of the successes of the First Army opening up opportunities for its favourable employment. This Division and a Brigade of the North Midland Division, which was temporarily attached to it, was moved forward for this purpose.

NEUVE CHAPELLE

The 5th Cavalry Brigade, under Sir Philip Chetwode, reached the Rue Bacquerot at 4 p.m., with a view to rendering immediate support; but he was informed by the General Officer Commanding 4th Corps that the situation was not so favourable as he had hoped it would be, and that no further action by the cavalry was advisable.

General Gough's command, therefore, retired to Estaires.

The artillery of all kinds was handled with the utmost energy and skill, and rendered invaluable support in the prosecution of the attack.

The losses during these three days' fighting were, I regret to say, very severe, numbering—

190 officers and 2,337 other ranks, killed.
359 officers and 8,174 other ranks, wounded.
23 officers and 1,728 other ranks, missing.

But the results attained were, in my opinion, wide and far reaching.

The enemy left several thousand dead on the battle-field, which were seen and counted; and we have positive information that upwards of 12,000 wounded were removed to the north-east and east by train.

Thirty officers and 1,657 other ranks of the enemy were captured.

I can best express my estimate of this battle by quoting an extract from a Special Order of the Day which I addressed to Sir Douglas Haig and the First Army at its conclusion:

"I am anxious to express to you personally my warmest appreciation of the skilful manner in which you have carried out your orders, and my fervent and most heartfelt appreciation of the magnificent gallantry and devoted, tenacious courage displayed by all ranks whom you have ably led to success and victory."

5. Some operations in the nature of holding attacks,

THE ACTION OF ST. ELOI

carried out by troops of the Second Army, were instrumental in keeping the enemy in front of them occupied, and preventing reinforcements being sent from those portions of the front to the main point of attack.

At 12.30 a.m. on the 12th March the 17th Infantry Brigade of the 4th Division, 3rd Corps, engaged in an attack on the enemy which resulted in the capture of the village of L'Epinette and adjacent farms.

Supported by a brisk fire from the 18th Infantry Brigade, the 17th Infantry Brigade, detailed for the attack, assaulted in two columns converging, and obtained the first houses of the village without much loss. The remainder of the village was very heavily wired, and the enemy got away by means of communication trenches while our men were cutting through the wire.

The enemy suffered considerable loss; our casualties being 5 officers and 30 other ranks, killed and wounded.

The result of this operation was that an advance of 300 yards was made on a front of half a mile.

All attempts to retake this position have been repulsed with heavy loss to the enemy.

The General Officer Commanding the Second Corps arranged for an attack on a part of the enemy's position to the south-west of the village of Wytschaete which he had timed to commence at 10 a.m. on the 12th March. Owing to dense fog, the assault could not be made until 4 o'clock in the afternoon.

It was then commenced by the Wiltshires and Worcestershire Regiments, but was so hampered by the mist and the approach of darkness that nothing more was effected than holding the enemy to his ground.

The action of St. Eloi referred to in the first paragraph of this despatch commenced at 5 p.m. on the 14th March by a very heavy cannonade which was directed against our trenches in front of St. Eloi, the village itself and the approaches to it. There is a large mound lying to the

NEUVE CHAPELLE

south-east of the village. When the artillery attack was at its height a mine was exploded under this mound, and a strong hostile infantry attack was immediately launched against the trenches and the mound.

Our artillery opened fire at once, as well as our infantry, and inflicted considerable losses on the enemy during their advance ; but, chiefly owing to the explosion of the mine and the surprise of the overwhelming artillery attack, the enemy's infantry had penetrated the first line of trenches at some points. As a consequence the garrisons of other works which had successfully resisted the assault were enfiladed and forced to retire just before it turned dark.

A counter attack was at once organised by the General Officer Commanding 82nd Brigade, under the orders of the General Officer Commanding 27th Division, who brought up a reserve brigade to support it.

The attack was launched at 2 a.m., and the 82nd Brigade succeeded in recapturing the portion of the village of St. Eloi which was in the hands of the enemy and a portion of the trenches east of it. At 3 a.m. the 80th Brigade in support took more trenches to the east and west of the village.

The counter attack, which was well carried out under difficult conditions, resulted in the recapture of all lost ground of material importance.

It is satisfactory to be able to record that, though the troops occupying the first line of trenches were at first overwhelmed, they afterwards behaved very gallantly in the counter-attack for the recovery of the lost ground ; and the following units earned and received the special commendation of the Army Commander :—The 2nd Royal Irish Fusiliers, the 2nd Duke of Cornwall's Light Infantry, the 1st Leinster Regiment, the 4th Rifle Brigade and the Princess Patricia's Canadian Light Infantry.

A vigorous attack made by the enemy on the 17th to recapture these trenches was repulsed with great loss.

THE ROYAL FLYING CORPS

Throughout the period under review night enterprises by smaller or larger patrols, which were led with consummate skill and daring, have been very active along the whole line. A moral superiority has thus been established, and valuable information has been collected.

I cannot speak too highly of the invincible courage and the remarkable resource displayed by these patrols.

The troops of the 3rd Corps have particularly impressed me by their conduct of these operations.

6. The work of the Royal Flying Corps throughout this period, and especially during the operations of the 10th, 11th, and 12th March, was of the greatest value. Though the weather on March 10th and on the subsequent days was very unfavourable for aerial work, on account of low-lying clouds and mist, a remarkable number of hours flying of a most valuable character were effected, and continuous and close reconnaissance was maintained over the enemy's front.

In addition to the work of reconnaissance and observation of artillery fire, the Royal Flying Corps was charged with the special duty of hampering the enemy's movements by destroying various points on his communications. The railways at Menin, Courtrai, Don and Douai were attacked, and it is known that very extensive damage was effected at certain of these places. Part of a troop train was hit by a bomb, a wireless installation near Lille is believed to have been effectively destroyed, and a house in which the enemy had installed one of his Headquarters was set on fire. These afford other instances of successful operations of this character. Most of the objectives mentioned were attacked at a height of only 100 to 150 feet. In one case the pilot descended to about 50 feet above the point he was attacking.

Certain new and important forms of activity, which it is undesirable to specify, have been initiated and pushed forward with much vigour and success.

NEUVE CHAPELLE

There have been only eight days during the period under review on which reconnaissances have not been made. A total of approximately 130,000 miles have been flown—almost entirely over the enemy's lines.

No great activity has been shown over our troops on the part of the enemy's aircraft, but they have been attacked whenever and wherever met with, and usually forced down or made to seek refuge in their own lines.

7. In my last despatch I referred to the remarkable promptitude and rapidity with which reinforcements arrived in this country from England. In connection with this it is of interest to call attention to the fact that, in spite of the heavy casualties incurred in the fighting between the 10th and 15th March, all deficiencies, both in officers and rank and file, were made good within a few days of the conclusion of the battle.

The drafts for the Indian Contingents have much improved of late, and are now quite satisfactory.

Since the date of my last report the general health of the Army has been excellent; enteric has decreased, and there has been no recurrence on any appreciable scale of the " foot " trouble which appeared so threatening in December and January.

These results are due to the skill and energy which have characterised in a marked degree the work of the Royal Army Medical Corps throughout the campaign, under the able supervision of Surgeon-General T. J. O'Donnell, D.S.O., Deputy Director-General, Medical Services. But much credit is also due to Divisional, Brigade, Regimental and Company Commanders for the close supervision which has been kept over the health of their men by seeing that the precautions laid down for the troops before entering and after leaving the trenches are duly observed, and by the establishment and efficient maintenance of bathing-places and wash-houses, and by the ingenious means universally employed throughout the

THE MEDICAL SERVICES

Forces to maintain the cleanliness of the men, having regard both to their bodies and their clothing.

I have inspected most of these houses and establishments, and consider them models of careful organisation and supervision.

I would particularly comment upon the energy displayed by the Royal Army Medical Corps in the scientific efforts they have made to discover and check disease in its earliest stages by a system of experimental research, which I think has never before been so fully developed in the field.

In this work they have been ably assisted by those distinguished members of the medical profession who are now employed as Military Medical Officers, and whose invaluable services I gratefully acknowledge.

The actual strength of the Force in the field has been increased and the health of the troops improved by a system of " convalescent " hospitals.

In these establishments slight wounds and minor ailments are treated, and men requiring attention and rest are received.

By these means efficient soldiers, whose services would otherwise be lost for a long time, are kept in the country, whilst a large number of men are given immediate relief and rest when they require it without removing them from the area of operations.

This adds materially to the fighting efficiency of the Forces.

The principal convalescent hospital is at St. Omer. It was started and organised by Colonel A. F. L. Bate, Army Medical Service, whose zeal, energy and organising power have rendered it a model hospital of its kind, and this example has materially assisted in the efficient organisation of similar smaller establishments at every Divisional Headquarters.

8. I have already commented upon the number and

severity of the casualties in action which have occurred in the period under report. Here once again I have to draw attention to the excellent work done by Surgeon-General O'Donnell and his officers. No organisation could excel the efficiency of the arrangements—whether in regard to time, space, care and comfort, or transport—which are made for the speedy evacuation of the wounded.

I wish particularly to express my deep sense of the loss incurred by the Army in general, and by the Forces in France in particular, in the death of Brigadier-General J. E. Gough, V.C., C.M.G., A.D.C., late Brigadier-General, General Staff, First Army, which occurred on 22nd February as a result of a severe wound received on the 20th February when inspecting the trenches of the 4th Corps.

I always regarded General Gough as one of our most promising military leaders of the future. His services as a Staff Officer throughout the campaign have been invaluable, and I had already brought his name before Your Lordship for immediate promotion.

I can well understand how deeply these casualties are felt by the nation at large, but each daily report shows clearly that they are being endured on at least an equal scale by all the combatants engaged throughout Europe, friends and foes alike.

In war as it is to-day between civilised nations, armed to the teeth with the present deadly rifle and machine-gun, heavy casualties are absolutely unavoidable. For the slightest undue exposure the heaviest toll is exacted.

The power of defence conferred by modern weapons is the main cause of the long duration of the battles of the present day, and it is this fact which mainly accounts for such loss and waste of life.

Both one and the other can, however, be shortened and lessened if attacks can be supported by the most efficient and powerful force of artillery available ; but an almost

THE ARRIVAL OF THE CANADIANS

unlimited supply of ammunition is necessary and a most liberal discretionary power as to its use must be given to the Artillery Commanders.

I am confident that this is the only means by which great results can be obtained with a minimum of loss.

9. On the 15th February the Canadian Division began to arrive in this country. I inspected the Division, which was under the command of Lieutenant-General E. A. H. Alderson, C.B., on 20th February.

They presented a splendid and most soldier-like appearance on parade. The men were of good physique, hard and fit. I judged by what I saw of them that they were well trained, and quite able to take their places in the line of battle.

Since then the Division has thoroughly justified the good opinion I formed of it.

The troops of the Canadian Division were first attached for a few days by brigades for training in the 3rd Corps trenches under Lieutenant-General Sir William Pulteney, who gave me such an excellent report of their efficiency that I was able to employ them in the trenches early in March.

During the Battle of Neuve Chapelle they held a part of the line allotted to the First Army, and, although they were not actually engaged in the main attack, they rendered valuable help by keeping the enemy actively employed in front of their trenches.

All the soldiers of Canada serving in the Army under my command have so far splendidly upheld the traditions of the Empire, and will, I feel sure, prove to be a great source of additional strength to the forces in this country.

In former despatches I have been able to comment very favourably upon the conduct and bearing of the Territorial Forces throughout the operations in which they have been engaged.

As time goes on, and I see more and more of their work,

whether in the trenches or engaged in more active operations, I am still further impressed with their value.

Several battalions were engaged in the most critical moments of the heavy fighting which occurred in the middle of March, and they acquitted themselves with the utmost credit.

Up till lately the troops of the Territorial Force in this country were only employed by battalions, but for some weeks past I have seen formed divisions working together and I have every hope that their employment in the larger units will prove as successful as in the smaller.

These opinions are fully borne out by the result of the close inspection which I have recently made of the North Midland Division, under Major-General Hon. Montagu-Stuart-Wortley, and the 2nd London Division, under Major-General Barter.

10. General Baron Von Kaulbars, of the Russian General Staff, arrived at my Headquarters on the 18th March. He was anxious to study our aviation system, and I gave him every opportunity of doing so.

The Bishop of London arrived here with his Chaplain on Saturday, March 27th, and left on Monday, April 5th.

During the course of his visit to the Army His Lordship was at the front every day, and I think I am right in saying that there was scarcely a unit in the command which was not at one time or another present at his services or addresses.

Personal fatigue and even danger were completely ignored by His Lordship. The Bishop held several services virtually under shell fire, and it was with difficulty that he could be prevented from carrying on his ministrations under rifle fire in the trenches.

I am anxious to place on record my deep sense of the good effect produced throughout the Army by this self-sacrificing devotion on the part of the Bishop of London, to whom I feel personally very deeply indebted.

THE TRANSPORT SERVICES

I have once more to remark upon the devotion to duty, courage and contempt of danger which has characterised the work of the Chaplains of the Army throughout this campaign.

11. The increased strength of the Force and the gradual exhaustion of the local resources have necessitated a corresponding increase in our demands on the Line of Communications, since we are now compelled to import many articles which in the early stages could be obtained by local purchase. The Directorates concerned have, however, been carefully watching the situation, and all the Administrative Services on the Line of Communications have continued to work with smoothness and regularity, in spite of the increased pressure thrown upon them. In this connection I wish to bring to notice the good service which has been rendered by the Staff of the Base Ports.

The work of the Railway Transport Department has been excellently carried out, and I take this opportunity of expressing my appreciation of the valuable service rendered by the French railway authorities generally, and especially by Colonel Ragueneau, late Director des Chemins de Fer, Lieutenant-Colonel Le Hénaff, Directeur des Chemins de Fer, Lieutenant-Colonel Dumont, Commissaire Militaire, Chemin de Fer du Nord, and Lieutenant-Colonel Frid, Commissaire Regulateur, Armée Anglaise.

The Army Postal Service has continued to work well, and at the present time a letter posted in London is delivered at General Headquarters or at the Headquarters of the Armies and Army Corps on the following evening, and reaches an addressee in the trenches on the second day after posting. The delivery of parcels has also been accelerated, and is carried out with regularity and despatch.

12. His Majesty the King of the Belgians visited the British lines on February 8th and inspected some of the units in reserve behind the trenches.

NEUVE CHAPELLE

During the last two months I have been much indebted to His Majesty and his gallant Army for valuable assistance and co-operation in various ways.

13. His Royal Highness the Prince of Wales is the bearer of this despatch.

His Royal Highness continues to make most satisfactory progress. During the Battle of Neuve Chapelle he acted on my General Staff as a Liaison Officer. Reports from the General Officers Commanding Corps and Divisions to which he has been attached agree in commending the thoroughness in which he performs any work entrusted to him.

I have myself been very favourably impressed by the quickness with which His Royal Highness has acquired knowledge of the various branches of the service, and the deep interest he has always displayed in the comfort and welfare of the men. His visits to the troops, both in the field and in hospitals, have been greatly appreciated by all ranks. His Royal Highness did duty for a time in the trenches with the Battalion to which he belongs.

14. In connection with the Battle of Neuve Chapelle I desire to bring to Your Lordship's special notice the valuable services of General Sir Douglas Haig, K.C.B., K.C.I.E., K.C.V.O., A.D.C., Commanding the 1st Army.

I am also much indebted to the able and devoted assistance I have received from Lieutenant-General Sir William Robertson, K.C.B., K.C.V.O., D.S.O., Chief of the General Staff, in the direction of all the operations recorded in this despatch.

I have many other names to bring to notice for valuable, gallant and distinguished service during the period under review, and these will form the subject of a separate report at an early date. I have the honour to be,

Your Lordship's most obedient servant,

(*Signed*) J. D. P. FRENCH, Field-Marshal,
Commander-in-Chief the British Forces in the Field.

MENTIONED IN DESPATCHES

VI : France, 31st *May*, 1915.

To Field-Marshal Earl Kitchener of Khartoum, K.P., G.C.B., O.M., etc.

My Lord,

IN accordance with the last paragraph of my Despatch of the 5th April, 1915, I have the honour to bring to notice names of those whom I recommend for gallant and distinguished service in the field.

I have the honour to be,
    Your Lordship's most obedient servant,
  (*Signed*) J. D. P. FRENCH, Field-Marshal,
Commander-in-Chief the British Forces in the Field.

MENTIONED IN DESPATCHES.

ROYAL NAVY.

Lieutenant G. Muirhead-Gould.
Lieutenant L. F. Robinson (Armoured train).
Chief Petty Officer E. Ball.
Chief Petty Officer (temporary Sub-Lieutenant, Royal Naval Volunteer Reserve) H. Mewett.

GENERAL HEADQUARTERS STAFF, &c.

Captain G. J. Acland Troyte, King's Royal Rifle Corps.
Captain J. J. Aitken, Army Veterinary Corps.
Lieutenant-General E. A. H. Alderson, C.B.
Major H. L. Alexander, Dorsetshire Regiment.
Captain R. G. Alexander, 11th Lancers.
Major-General (temporary Lieutenant-General) Sir E. H. H. Allenby, K.C.B.
Captain H. I. R. Allfrey, Somersetshire Light Infantry.
Lieutenant-General C. A. Anderson, K.C.B.
Brevet Lieutenant-Colonel N. G. Anderson, D.S.O., Army Service Corps.
Major (temporary Colonel) W. H. Anderson, Cheshire Regiment.

MENTIONED IN DESPATCHES

Major V. Asser, D.S.O., Royal Artillery.
Major (temporary Lieutenant-Colonel) L. W. Atcherley, M.V.O., Reserve of Officers.
Lieutenant-Colonel A. R. C. Atkins, Army Service Corps.
Temporary Colonel J. Atkins, M.B., F.R.C.S.
Captain Hon. H. R. Atkinson.
Major H. B. D. Baird, 12th Cavalry.
Lieutenant A. Barker, Manchester Regiment.
Lieutenent-Colonel (temporary Brigadier-General) G. de S. Barrow, 35th Horse.
Major W. H. Bartholomew, Royal Artillery.
Major J. S. J. Baumgartner, East Lancashire Regiment.
Lieutenant-Colonel J. Beatson Bell, Indian Army.
Captain E. H. L. Beddington, 16th Lancers.
Major B. L. Beddy, Army Service Corps.
Major Baron W. G. Bentinck, C.M.G., D.S.O., Reserve of Officers.
Lieutenant-Colonel W. W. O. Beveridge, D.S.O., M.B., Royal Army Medical Corps.
Temporary Captain H. F. F. Birch, Army Service Corps.
Lieutenant-Colonel E. T. F. Birrell, C.M.G., M.B., Royal Army Medical Corps.
Major W. A. Blake, Wiltshire Regiment.
Major E. P. Blencowe, Army Service Corps.
Lieutenant-Colonel (temporary Brigadier-General) L. J. Bols, C.B., D.S.O., Dorsetshire Regiment.
Captain Hon. G. E. Boscawen, D.S.O., Royal Artillery.
Major (temporary Lieutenant-Colonel) W. K. Bourne, 2nd Lancers.
Captain W. T. Bowly, Dorsetshire Regiment.
Captain H. E. R. R. Braine, Royal Munster Fusiliers.
Lieutenant-Colonel F. J. Brakenridge, Royal Army Medical Corps.
Assistant Commissary and Honorary Lieutenant J. H. Bridge, Indian Army Department.
Lieutenant-Colonel (temporary Colonel) G. T. M. Bridges, D.S.O., 4th Hussars.
Major J. E. S. Brind, Royal Artillery.
Captain B. de L. Brock, 126th Baluchistan Infantry.
Major B. N. Brooke, D.S.O., Grenadier Guards.
Captain A. F. Broke, Royal Artillery.
Captain W. H. Brooke, Yorkshire Light Infantry.
Major E. Brown, D.S.O., Army Veterinary Corps.
Colonel (temporary Brigadier-General) S. D. Browne.
Lieutenant E. G. Bullard, Postal Services.
Lieutenant-Colonel (temporary Brigadier-General) H. E. Burstall, Royal Canadian Artillery.
Colonel C. H. Burtchaell, C.M.G., M.B.
Colonel E. R. C. Butler, F.R.C.V.S.

MENTIONED IN DESPATCHES

Brevet Colonel (temporary-Brigadier-General) R. H. K. Butler, Lancashire Fusiliers.
Major H. M. Caddell, Army Service Corps.
Colonel (temporary Brigadier-General) J. E. Capper, C.B.
Major-General Sir T. Capper, K.C.M.G., C.B., D.S.O.
Lieutenant-Colonel W.M. Carpendale, retired, Indian Army.
Colonel H. Carr, M.D.
Colonel (temporary Brigadier-General) E. E. Carter, C.M.G., M.V.O.
Captain J. B. F. Cartland, Reserve of Officers.
Major A. B. E. Cator, D.S.O., Scots Guards.
Colonel (temporary Brigadier-General) F. R. Cavan, Earl of, C.B., M.V.O.
Major O. K. Chance, 5th Lancers.
Colonel (temporary Brigadier-General) A. J. Chapman, C.B.
Major J. Charteris, Royal Engineers.
Colonel (temporary Brigadier-General) A. A. Chichester, D.S.O.
Brevet Major (temporary Colonel) B. E. W. Childs, Royal Irish Regiment.
Lieutenant-Colonel A. Chopping, Royal Army Medical Corps.
Major W. E. T. Christie, Army Service Corps.
Lieutenant-Colonel G. R. M. Church, Royal Artillery.
Brevet Lieutenant-Colonel T. E. Clarke, Royal Inniskilling Fusiliers.
Colonel (temporary Brigadier-General) A. S. Cobbe, V.C., D.S.O., A.D.C.
Lieutenant-Colonel H. de B. Codrington, Indian Army.
Lieutenant-Colonel Campbell Coffin, Royal Engineers.
Colonel (temporary Brigadier-General) A. W. G. L. Cole, C.B., D.S.O. (died of wounds).
Captain R. J. Collins, Royal Berkshire Regiment.
Major (temporary Colonel) B. H. H. Cooke, Rifle Brigade.
Captain E. W. Cox, Royal Engineers.
Second Lieutenant E. R. Culverwell, Royal Artillery.
Lieutenant-Colonel S. L. Cummins, M.D., Royal Army Medical Corps.
Colonel (temporary Brigadier-General) A. W. Currie, Canadian Contingent.
Captain V. A. H. Daly, West Yorkshire Regiment.
Brevet Lieutenant-Colonel J. H. Davidson, D.S.O., King's Royal Rifle Corps.
Major P. Davidson, D.S.O., M.B., Royal Army Medical Corps.
Major-General F. J. Davies, C.B.
Major W. E. Davies, Rifle Brigade.
Major W. P. L. Davies, Royal Artillery.
Lieutenant-Colonel E. Davis, Reserve of Officers.
Colonel (temporary Brigadier-General) C. T. Dawkins, C.B., C.M.G.
Colonel J. A. Dealy.
Major H. S. de Brett, D.S.O., Royal Artillery.

MENTIONED IN DESPATCHES

Captain C. P. Deedes, D.S.O., Yorkshire Light Infantry.
Colonel F. J. De Gex, C.B.
Lieutenant-Colonel H. D. De Pree, Royal Artillery.
Captain C. J. Deverell, West Yorkshire Regiment.
Brevet Colonel W. V. Dickinson, retired pay.
Captain W. H. Diggle, Grenadier Guards.
Captain J. G. Dill, Leinster Regiment.
Lieutenant-Colonel C. S. Dodgson, Army Service Corps.
Captain J. A. Don, Royal Field Artillery.
Major C. M. Doran, Army Service Corps.
Captain E. P. Dorrien-Smith, D.S.O., Shropshire Light Infantry.
Captain W. S. Douglas, Royal Engineers (killed).
Captain W. J. Dugan, Worcestershire Regiment.
Captain W. F. B. R. Dugmore, D.S.O., Reserve of Officers.
Colonel J. W. Dunlop, C.B.
Major A. M. Duthie, Royal Artillery.
Captain P. Dwyer, M.B., Royal Army Medical Corps.
Captain H. L. Dyce, 9th Hodson's Horse.
Lieutenant-Colonel F. Eassie, D.S.O., Army Veterinary Corps.
Major P. G. Easton, Royal Army Medical Corps.
Colonel J. C. B. Eastwood.
Lieutenant C. C. Egerton, West Riding Regiment (killed).
Lieutenant-Colonel H. Ensor, D.S.O., M.B., Royal Army Medical Corps.
Honorary Colonel H. A. Erskine, C.B., V.D., Northumbrian Divisional Train, A.S.C., Territorial Force.
Lieutenant-Colonel P. Evans, M.B., Royal Army Medical Corps.
Colonel H. J. Everett.
Major C. G. Falcon, Royal Engineers.
Temporary Brigadier-General E. A. Fanshawe, C.B., Royal Artillery.
Temporary Brigadier-General R. Fanshawe, C.B., D.S.O.
Lieutenant-Colonel H. B. Fawcus, M.B., Royal Army Medical Corps.
Lieutenant-Colonel M. H. G. Fell, Royal Army Medical Corps.
Captain R. T. Fellowes, Rifle Brigade.
Colonel N. C. Ferguson, C.M.G., M.B., Royal Army Medical Corps.
Temporary Lieutenant W. Ferguson, Postal Section, Royal Engineers, Special Reserve.
Lieutenant-General Sir C. Fergusson, Bt., K.C.B., M.V.O., D.S.O.
Major V. M. Fergusson, Royal Artillery.
Major W. A. Fetherstonhaugh, 8th Cavalry (Indian Army).
Captain and Brevet Major H. Findlay, East Kent Regiment.
Major G. A. FitzGerald, D.S.O., Reserve of Officers.
Captain (temporary Major) E. R. Fitzpatrick, Loyal N. Lancs. Regt.
Major A. F. Fletcher, 17th Lancers.
Lieutenant-Colonel (temporary Colonel) A. Forbes, Army Ordnance Department.

MENTIONED IN DESPATCHES

Temporary Major-General G. T. Forestier-Walker, C.B., A.D.C.
Lieutenant-Colonel J. V. Forrest, M.B., Royal Army Medical Corps.
Brevet Colonel (temporary Brigadier-General) G. McK. Franks, Royal Artillery.
Captain H. E. Franklyn, Yorkshire Regiment.
Major H. F. Fraser, 21st Lancers.
Captain J. C. Freeland, 35th Sikhs.
Major H. F. E. Freeland, M.V.O., Royal Engineers.
Captain W. H. M. Freestun, Somerset Light Infantry.
Major and Brevet Lieutenant-Colonel G. H. B. Freeth, D.S.O., Lancashire Fusiliers.
Major P. W. Game, Royal Artillery.
Major H. W. Gardiner, Royal Artillery.
Honorary Brigadier-General F. S. Garratt, C.B., D.S.O.
Captain W. C. Garsia, Hampshire Regiment.
Colonel R. J. Geddes, D.S.O., M.B.
Captain E. C. Gepp, 3rd Battalion, Duke of Cornwall's Light Infantry.
Major (temporary Lieutenant-Colonel) E. Gibb, D.S.O., Army Service Corps.
Major G. F. B. Goldney, Royal Engineers.
Captain H. D. Goldsmith.
Lieutenant-Colonel T. H. J. C. Goodwin, D.S.O.
Lieutenant-Colonel A. F. Gordon, D.S.O., Gordon Highlanders.
Captain J. S. S. P. V. Gort, Viscount, M.V.O., Grenadier Guards.
Major-General E. R. C. Graham, C.B.
Captain Lord D. M. Graham, Royal Artillery.
Captain C. P. Graham, D.S.O., Welsh Regiment.
Major Grant, P. G., Royal Engineers.
Major R. F. S. Grant, M.V.O., D.S.O., Rifle Brigade.
Temporary Captain J. A. S. Gray, General List.
Captain G. C. Grazebrook, Royal Inniskilling Fusiliers.
Lieutenant-Colonel W. H. Greenly, C.M.G., D.S.O., 19th Hussars.
Major D. M. Griffith, Royal Engineers.
Major F. G. Griffith, 32nd Lancers.
Captain L. Griffith, 107th Pioneers.
Major J. N. Griffiths, M.P., 2nd King Edward's Horse (attached Royal Engineers).
Major Sir E. I. B. Grogan, Bt., Rifle Brigade.
Colonel R. P. Grove.
Captain R. W. Hadow, Reserve of Officers.
Captain R. H. Haining, Royal Artillery.
Colonel T. W. Hale, Army Ordnance Department.
Major (temporary Lieutenant-Colonel) P. O. Hambro, 15th Hussars.
Captain M. A. Hamer, 129th Baluchis.
Lieutenant-Colonel R. S. Hamilton, Army Ordnance Department.
Major (temporary Lieutenant-Colonel) G. T. Hamilton, Royal Artillery.

MENTIONED IN DESPATCHES

Captain F. D. Hammond, Royal Engineers.
Lieutenant-Colonel R. H. Hare, M.V.O., D.S.O., Royal Garriso Artillery.
Major R. W. Hare, D.S.O., Norfolk Regiment.
Major (Brevet Lieutenant-Colonel) R.N. Harvey, D.S.O., Roya Engineers.
Captain H. R. Headlam, York and Lancaster Regiment.
Captain Hon. A. M. Henley, 5th Lancers.
Lieutenant-Colonel J. P. C. Hennessy, Indian Army.
Captain O. C. Herbert, Reserve of Officers.
Colonel T. Heron.
Colonel (temporary Brigadier-General) F. J. Heyworth, D.S.O.
Temporary Captain C. M. Higgins.
Major R. J. T. Hildyard, Royal West Kent Regiment.
Major D. J. J. Hill, Army Ordnance Department.
Major H. Hill, M.V.O., Royal Welsh Fusiliers.
Lieutenant-Colonel E. S. Hoare Nairne, Royal Artillery.
Temporary Brigadier-General P. E. F. Hobbs, C.B., C.M.G.
Major R. F. A. Hobbs, D.S.O., Royal Engineers.
Major C. C. H. Hogg, Royal Engineers.
Colonel (temporary Brigadier-General) A. E. A. Holland, M.V.O D.S.O.
Temporary Lieutenant-Colonel G. E. Holland, C.I.E., D.S.O., Roy Engineers.
Captain L. Holland, Seaforth Highlanders.
Captain H. W. Holland, Inns of Court Officers' Training Corps.
Major S. E. Holland, Rifle Brigade.
Brevet Lieutenant-Colonel H. C. Holman, C.M.G., D.S.O., 16t Cavalry.
Colonel M. P. C. Holt, D.S.O.
Major (temporary Lieutenant-Colonel) A. F. Home, D.S.O., 11t Hussars.
Major G. V. Hordern, King's Royal Rifle Corps.
Major and Brevet Lieutenant-Colonel (temporary Colonel) A. I Hoskins, D.S.O., North Staffordshire Regiment.
Temporary Captain Hon. G. Howard, Royal Marines.
Captain H. C. L. Howard, 16th Lancers.
Captain R. G. H. Howard-Vyse, Royal Horse Guards.
Temporary Captain E. B. Howell.
Major A. S. Humphreys, Army Service Corps.
Captain A. J. Hunter, King's Royal Rifle Corps.
Major R. Hutchison, 4th Dragoon Guards.
Captain A. B. Incledon-Webber, Royal Irish Fusiliers.
Colonel (temporary Brigadier-General) E. C. Ingouville-William C.B., D.S.O.
Major W. E. Ironside, Royal Artillery.

MENTIONED IN DESPATCHES

Major F. S. Irvine, M.B., Royal Army Medical Corps.
Captain J. E. V. Isaac, D.S.O., Reserve of Officers (missing, believed killed).
Major R. H. Isacke, Reserve of Officers.
Major E. M. Jack, Royal Engineers.
Colonel (temporary Brigadier-General) C. W. Jacob.
Captain A. H. C. James, D.S.O., South Staffordshire Regiment.
Captain G. M. James, East Kent Regiment (killed).
Lieutenant-Colonel M. R. de B. James, Army Service Corps.
Lieutenant-Colonel (temporary Brigadier-General) W. B. James, C.I.E., M.V.O., Indian Army.
Major (temporary Lieutenant-Colonel) G. D. Jebb, D.S.O., Bedfordshire Regiment.
Captain A. C. Jeffcoat, D.S.O., Royal Fusiliers.
Brevet Colonel H. J. W. Jerome, C.B., retired pay, attached Royal Engineers.
Major R. H. Johnson, Royal Artillery.
Major R. M. Johnson, Royal Artillery.
Major-General H. D'U. Keary, C.B., D.S.O.
Major A. C. Kennedy, Royal Artillery, Indian Ordnance Department.
Captain H. C. B. Kirkpatrick, King's Own Scottish Borderers.
Lieutenant-Colonel R. B. Kirwan, Royal Artillery.
Major H. H. S. Knox, Northamptonshire Regiment.
Major F. C. Larmour, Army Ordnance Department.
Captain P. R. Laurie, 2nd Dragoons.
Colonel (temporary Brigadier-General) S. T. B. Lawford, C.B.
Temporary Captain H. M. Leaf, Royal Marines.
Major T. B. A. Leahy, Army Ordnance Department.
Colonel (temporary Brigadier-General) Lecky, R. St. C.
Brevet Major (temporary Colonel) A. H. Lee, Reserve of Officers.
Captain B. P. Lefroy, D.S.O., Royal Warwickshire Regiment.
Major W. K. Legge, Essex Regiment.
Captain R. A. C. L. Leggett, Reserve of Officers.
Captain G. R. F. Leverson, Northumberland Fusiliers.
Captain C. G. Liddell, Leicestershire Regiment.
Lieutenant C. H. Liddell, 15th Hussars.
Colonel W. A. Liddell.
Colonel A. L. Lindsay.
Lieutenant-Colonel H. A. P. Lindsay, Supplies and Transport Corps.
Temporary Captain J. H. Lloyd, Royal Lancaster Regiment.
Major S. C. Long, Reserve of Officers.
Brevet Colonel (temporary Brigadier-General) J. R. Longley, East Surrey Regiment.
Lieutenant-Colonel J. C. G. Longmore, D.S.O., Army Service Corps.
Brevet Lieutenant-Colonel J. A. Longridge, 43rd Regiment.
Captain C. C. Lucas, Royal Artillery.

MENTIONED IN DESPATCHES

Captain R. M. Luckock, Royal Lancaster Regiment.
Major R. C. W. Lukin, 9th Hodson's Horse.
Major R. K. Lynch-Staunton, Royal Artillery.
Colonel (temporary Brigadier-General) A. L. Lynden-Bell, C.M.G.
Lieutenant-Colonel F. Lyon, D.S.O., Royal Artillery.
Lieutenant-Colonel (temporary-Brigadier General) H. J. M. Macandrew, D.S.O., Indian Army.
Captain (local Captain in Army) J. T. McColl, Commonwealth Forces.
Colonel (temporary Brigadier-General) G. M. W. Macdonogh, C.B.
Captain H. E. Macfarlane, 19th Hussars.
Major A. A. McHardy, D.S.O., Royal Artillery.
Major C. W. Macleod, Army Service Corps.
Colonel R. L. R. MacLeod.
Surgeon-General W. G. Macpherson, C.B,. C.M.G., M.B., K.H.P.
Maitland Makgill Crichton, H. C., Royal Scots Fusiliers.
Captain C. Mansel-Jones, V.C., Reserve of Officers.
Temporary Lieutenant-Colonel G. C. A. Marescaux, Rear-Admiral, retired.
Lieutenant-Colonel (temporary Brigadier-General) A. G. Marrable, Yorkshire Light Infantry.
Major F. J. Marshall, Seaforth Highlanders.
Captain G. Masters, Royal Engineers.
Colonel C. M. Mathew, C.B., D.S.O.
Colonel (temporary Brigadier-General) F. S. Maude, C.B., C.M.G., D.S.O.
Brevet Lieutenant-Colonel (temporary Brigadier-General) F. B. Maurice, C.B., Nottinghamshire and Derbyshire Regiment.
Captain G. A. R. Maxwell.
Major-General H. F. Mercer, C.B.
Colonel (temporary Brigadier-General) M. S. Mercer.
Captain Hon. G. V. A. Monckton-Arundell, 1st Life Guards.
Brevet Colonel R. C. Money, Reserve of Officers.
Major General (temporary Lieutenant-General) C. C. Monro, K.C.B.
Brevet Lieutenant-Colonel (temporary Colonel) H. M. de F. Montgomery, Royal Artillery.
Colonel (temporary-Brigadier-General) R. A.K. Mongtomery, C.B., D.S.O.
Colonel S. G. Moores.
Lieutenant-Colonel C. K. Morgan, M.B., Royal Army Medical Corps.
Major-General T. L. N. Morland, C.B., D.S.O.
Colonel C. G. Morrison.
Captain E. E. J. Morrison, Reserve of Officers, Scottish Rifles.
Captain A. L. Moulton-Barrett, Dorsetshire Regiment.
Major J. L. Mowbray, Royal Artillery.
Lieutenant-Colonel V. Murray, Royal Engineers.
Captain (temporary Major) H. Needham, Gloucestershire Regiment.

MENTIONED IN DESPATCHES

Lieutenant-Colonel A. C. Newsom, Army Veterinary Corps.
Colonel J. S. Nicholson, C.B., C.M.G., D.S.O.
Brevet Major O. H. L. Nicholson, D.S.O., West Yorkshire Regiment.
Temporary Lieutenant P. E. Noble, Northumberland Hussars.
Brevet Colonel C. E. de M. Norie, D.S.O., 2nd Gurkhas.
Captain O. H. North, Lancashire Fusiliers.
Surgeon-General T. J. O'Donnell, D.S.O.
Captain C. Ogston, Gordon Highlanders.
Captain E. A. B. Orr, Royal Berkshire Regiment.
Captain R. H. Osborne, 20th Hussars.
Captain L. C. Owen, Royal Engineers.
Colonel (temporary Brigadier-General) W. L. H. Paget, C.B., M.V.O.
Captain A. E. S. L. Paget, M.V.O., 11th Hussars.
Captain D. Paige, Royal Artillery.
Major A. T. Paley, Rifle Brigade.
Captain A. E. G. Palmer, Yorkshire Regiment.
Captain W. L. Palmer, 10th Hussars.
Lieutenant-Colonel F. S. Penny, M.B., Royal Army Medical Corps.
Colonel (temporary Brigadier-General) E. M. Perceval, C.B., D.S.O.
Major H. F. P. Percival, D.S.O., Army Service Corps.
Honorary Colonel A. I. Earl Percy, Tyne Electrical Royal Engineers (Captain, Grenadier Guards, Special Reserve).
Colonel (temporary Brigadier-General) Petrie, R. D.
Captain G. F. Phillips, Duke of Cornwall's Light Infantry.
Colonel (temporary Brigadier-General) Phipps-Hornby, E. J., V.C., C.B.
Colonel (temporary Brigadier-General) R. J. Pinney.
Captain W. W. Pitt-Taylor, D.S.O., Rifle Brigade.
Lieutenant-General Sir H. C. O. Plumer, K.C.B.
Surgeon-General R. Porter, M.B.
Colonel S. H. Powell.
Lieutenant-Colonel (temporary Colonel in Army) W. W. Price, C.M.G., V.D., Postal Section, Royal Engineers, Special Reserve.
Major H. E. ap R. Pryce, 18th Infantry (Indian Army).
Captain H. M. Pryce-Jones, Coldstream Guards.
Major-General (temporary Lieutenant-General) W. P. Pulteney, K.C.B., D.S.O.
Major (temporary Lieutenant-Colonel) P. P. de B. Radcliffe, Royal Artillery.
Lieutenant E. Ramsden, 5th Lancers.
Major-General (temporary Lieutenant-General) Sir H. S. Rawlinson, Bt., K.C.B., C.V.O.
Brevet Colonel C. Rawnsley, D.S.O., Reserve of Officers.
Major F. F. Ready, D.S.O., Royal Berkshire Regiment.
Lieutenant-Colonel H. L. Reed, V.C., Royal Artillery.
Captain L. F. Renny, Royal Dublin Fusiliers.

MENTIONED IN DESPATCHES

Major-General S. R. Rice, C.B.
Honorary Major C. E. F. Rich (Captain, 3rd Battalion, Lincolnshire Regiment).
Lieutenant H. G. Riley, Army Pay Department.
Captain M. B. H. Ritchie, M.B., Royal Army Medical Corps.
Major W. Robertson, Royal Engineers.
Captain D. J. Robinson, 46th Punjabis.
Major S. W. Robinson, Royal Artillery.
Captain H. S. Rogers, Shropshire Light Infantry.
Major W. K. Russell, Royal Engineers.
Captain T. G. Ruttledge, Connaught Rangers.
Captain H. T. Ryan, F.R.C.V.S., Army Veterinary Corps.
Colonel (temporary Brigadier-General) W. H. Rycroft, C.B., C.M.G.
Brevet Colonel F. J. Ryder (Remount Service).
Major P. B. Sangster, 2nd Lancers.
Colonel (temporary Brigadier-General) H. N. Sargent, D.S.O.
Major J. A. Scarlett, Royal Artillery.
Lieutenant-Colonel G. P. Schofield, Royal Engineers.
Colonel (temporary Brigadier-General) A. B. Scott, C.B., D.S.O.
Captain H. V. Scott, Rifle Brigade.
Major (temporary Lieutenant-Colonel) C. R. Scott-Elliott, 81st Pioneers.
Captain W. H. E. Segrave, D.S.O., Highland Light Infantry.
Captain (temporary Major) R. Shelton, Army Service Corps.
Captain E. Sheppard, 19th Hussars.
Lieutenant-Colonel (temporary Colonel) G. S. Sheppard, Military Accounts Department.
Brevet Lieutenant-Colonel O. C. Sherwood, Reserve of Officers.
Lieutenant-Colonel A. F. Sillem.
Major H. C. Smith, Royal Engineers.
Lieutenant-Colonel (temporary Brigadier-General) W. E. B. Smith, C.M.G., Lincolnshire Regiment.
Captain G. N. T. Smyth-Osbourne, Devonshire Regiment.
Major-General T. D'O. Snow, C.B.
Lieutenant-Colonel (temporary Brigadier-General) W. M. Southey, C.M.G., 129th Baluchis.
Lieutenant (temporary Captain) E. L. Spiers, 11th Hussars.
Lieutenant-Colonel H. S. McC. Stannell, retired pay.
Captain H. W. Stenhouse, Royal West Surrey Regiment.
Brevet Major I. Stewart, Scottish Rifles.
Major J. H. K. Stewart, 2/39 Garhwal Rifles.
Major W. M. Stewart, Cameron Highlanders.
Major G. H. Stobart, Reserve of Officers.
Colonel (temporary Brigadier-General) A. Stokes, D.S.O.
Lieutenant G. H. Straker, 15th Hussars.
Major A. G. Stuart, 40th Pathans.

MENTIONED IN DESPATCHES

Captain G. A. Sullivan, Oxfordshire and Buckinghamshire Light Infantry.
Colonel W. T. Swan, M.B.
Major (temporary Lieutenant-Colonel) E. D. Swinton, D.S.O., Royal Engineers.
Major C. G. R. Sydney-Turner, Army Service Corps.
Brevet Lieutenant-Colonel (temporary Colonel) F. H. Sykes, 15th Hussars.
Lieutenant-Colonel (temporary Brigadier-General) H. A. L. Tagart, D.S.O., 15th Hussars.
Captain J. J. B. Tapley, Army Veterinary Corps.
Brevet Colonel H. d'A. P. Taylor, Reserve of Officers.
Brevet Lieutenant-Colonel H. S. H. Prince Alexander A. F. W. A. G. of Teck, G.C.B., G.C.V.O., D.S.O.
Temporary Captain F. W. Tennant, General List.
Major R. L. B. Thompson, Royal Engineers.
Captain A. F. A. N. Thorne, Grenadier Guards.
Captain G. Thorpe, D.S.O., Argyll and Sutherland Highlanders.
Captain S. H. J. Thunder, Northamptonshire Regiment.
Captain E. G. L. Thurlow, Somerset Light Infantry.
Major H. L. Tomkins, D.S.O., 28th Punjabis.
Captain H. A. Tomkinson, 1st Dragoons.
Surgeon-General F. H. Treherne, C.M.G., F.R.C.S.Edin.
Major W. H. Trevor, East Kent Regiment.
Major E. V. Turner, Royal Engineers.
Captain J. E. Turner, Scottish Rifles.
Colonel (temporary Brigadier-General) R. E. W. Turner, V.C., D.S.O.
Lieutenant-Colonel P. G. Twining, M.V.O., Royal Engineers.
Lieutenant-Colonel (temporary Brigadier-General) J. H. Twiss, Royal Engineers.
Captain W. L. O. Twiss, 9th Gurkhas.
Captain F. St. J. Trywhitt, Worcester Regiment.
Major (temporary-Lieutenant-Colonel) P. Umfreville.
Lieutenant-Colonel (temporary Brigadier-General) H. C. C. Uniacke, Royal Artillery.
Major (temporary Lieutenant-Colonel) R. F. Uniacke, Royal Inniskilling Fusiliers.
Major (temporary Lieutenant-Colonel) L. R. Vaughan, 7th Gurkhas.
Lieutenant-Colonel R. E. Vaughan, Supplies and Transport Corps.
Captain I. L. B. Vesey, Royal West Surrey Regiment.
Captain J. P. Villiers-Stuart, Indian Army.
Major V. Vivian, M.V.O., Grenadier Guards.
Brevet Colonel C. B. Vyvyan, C.B.
Colonel (temporary Brigadier-General) F. W. G., Wadeson.
Lieutenant-Colonel W. D. Waghorn, Royal Engineers.
Captain B. Walcot, Royal Engineers.

MENTIONED IN DESPATCHES

Major G. H. Walford, Suffolk Regiment (killed).
Major H. A. Walker, Royal Fusiliers.
Captain J. B. Walker, D.S.O., Royal Artillery.
Colonel (temporary-Brigadier-General) W. G. Walker, V.C., C.B.
Captain H. W. L. Waller, Royal Artillery.
Captain M. R. Walsh, Worcester Regiment.
Colonel (temporary Brigadier-General) R. Wanless-O'Gowan.
Major (temporary Lieutenant-Colonel) P. Warren, Postal Section, Royal Engineers, Special Reserve.
Lieutenant H. L. Watkis, 37th Lancers.
Major J. K. Watson, C.V.O., C.M.G., D.S.O., Reserve of Officers.
Colonel (temporary Brigadier-General) H. E. Watts, C.B., C.M.G.
Captain A. P. Wavell, Royal Highlanders.
Brevet Major J. T. Weatherby, Oxfordshire and Buckinghamshire Light Infantry.
Lieutenant-Colonel A. L. A. Webb, Royal Army Medical Corps.
Captain N. W. Webber, Royal Engineers.
Major G. A. Weir, 3rd Dragoon Guards.
Major (temporary Lieutenant-Colonel) M. H. E. Welch, Royal Irish Regiment.
Captain G. F. Wells, Royal Engineers.
Colonel S. Westcott, C.M.G.
Colonel (temporary Brigadier-General) R. D. Whigham, C.B., D.S.O.
Honorary Brigadier-General W. L. White, C.B.
Major W. N. White, Army Service Corps.
Captain C. G. Wickham, D.S.O., Norfolk Regiment.
Major H. B. des V. Wilkinson, Durham Light Infantry.
Lieutenant-General Sir J. Willcocks, K.C.B., K.C.S.I., K.C.M.G., D.S.O.
Lieutenant J. L. Willcocks, Royal Highlanders.
Lieutenant-Colonel F. M. Wilson, Army Service Corps.
Major F. W. Wilson, F.R.C.V.S., Army Veterinary Corps.
Major-General H. F. M. Wilson, C.B.
Temporary Second Lieutenant S. H. C. Woolrych, Intelligence Corps.
Major (temporary Lieutenant-Colonel) C. R. Woodroffe, Royal Artillery
Quartermaster and Honorary Captain R. J. Woods, Reserve of Officers.
Major (temporary Lieutenant-Colonel) J. B. Wroughton, Royal Sussex Regiment.
Major J. M. Young, Army Service Corps.
Honorary Lieutenant (attached Garhwal Brigade) Hitendra Narayan, Maharaj Kumar of Cooch Behar.
Subadar Major Amar Singh, Sardar Bahadur, Sirhind Brigade, Native Indian Land Forces.
Risaldar Major Bahadur Muhi-ud-din Khan.
Staff Serjeant-Major V. H. Courtney (School of Cookery).

MENTIONED IN DESPATCHES

INTELLIGENCE CORPS.

Temporary Captain C. A. Cameron.
Temporary Second Lieutenant R. B. Fitzgerald.
Temporary Lieutenant G. P. Pollitt.
Temporary Lieutenant T. M. Rogers.
Temporary Lieutenant E. H. Smythe.
Temporary Lieutenant R. R. F. West, D.S.O.
Temporary Lieutenant K. T. Gemmell.
Temporary Second Lieutenant A. Ladenburg.
Second Lieutenant W. L. McEwen.
Temporary Lieutenant A. Capel.
Temporary Second Lieutenant W. G. Fletcher (killed).
Temporary Second Lieutenant F. E. Hotblack.
Serjeant L. Gough (Scotland Yard Detective).

ROYAL FLYING CORPS.

Brevet Major B. H. Barrington-Kennett, Grenadier Guards (killed).
Captain R. J. F. Barton, Royal Scots Fusiliers.
Captain (temporary Major) W. D. Beatty, Royal Engineers.
Lieutenant W. C. K. Birch, Yorkshire Regiment.
Brevet Major (temporary Lieutenant-Colonel) H. R. M. Brooke-Popham, Oxfordshire and Buckinghamshire Light Infantry.
Captain T. W. C. Carthew, 4th Battalion Bedfordshire Regiment.
Captain R. G. Cherry, Royal Artillery.
Captain D. S. K. Crosbie, Argyll and Sutherland Highlanders.
Lieutenant G. L. Cruickshank, Gordon Highlanders.
Lieutenant (temporary Captain) W. R. Freeman, Manchester Regiment.
Lieutenant H. M. Hankin, Corps of Guides.
Lieutenant (temporary Captain) L. G. Hawker, D.S.O., Royal Engineers.
Captain (temporary Major) F. V. Holt, D.S.O., Oxfordshire and Buckinghamshire Light Infantry.
Captain G. B. Hynes, Royal Artillery.
Second Lieutenant J. F. Lascelles, Rifle Brigade.
Lieutenant (temporary Captain in Army) C. F. Lee, West Somerset Yeomanry.
Captain E. R. Ludlow-Hewitt, Royal Irish Rifles.
Lieutenant (temporary Captain) R. P. Mills, Royal Fusiliers.
Lieutenant A. E. Morgan, 6th Battalion, Royal Fusiliers (killed).
Captain C. F. de S. Murphy, Royal Berkshire Regiment.
Temporary Lieutenant E. W. Powell.
Lieutenant (temporary Captain) G. F. Pretyman, D.S.O., Somerset Light Infantry.
Lieutenant (temporary Captain) C. E. C. Rabagliati, Yorkshire Light Infantry.
Brevet Major G. H. Raleigh, Essex Regiment (killed).

MENTIONED IN DESPATCHES

Lieutenant W. B. Rhodes-Moorhouse, V.C., Special Reserve (died of wounds).
Lieutenant (temporary Captain) H. J. A. Roche, Royal Munster Fusiliers (killed).
Lieutenant C. B. Spence, Royal Artillery (killed).
Lieutenant (temporary Captain) J. E. Tennant, Scots Guards.
Brevet Lieutenant-Colonel H. M. Trenchard, C.B., D.S.O., Royal Scots Fusiliers.
Lieutenant (temporary Captain) R. M. Vaughan, Royal Inniskilling Fusiliers.
Lieutenant (temporary Captain) F. A. Wanklyn, Royal Artillery.
Corporal A. Barter.
Corporal T. G. Bird.
Corporal C. R. S. Evans.
Flight-Serjeant J. Fulton.
Serjeant E. J. P. Kelly.
Serjeant-Major J. Mead.
Serjeant-Major S. J. Payne.
Serjeant E. C. Rumford.
Serjeant F. F. Traylor.
Serjeant-Major W. Waddington.
Serjeant W. G. Webb.
Serjeant-Major J. Wilkinson.

1ST LIFE GUARDS.

Surgeon-Lieutenant E. D. Anderson.
Acting Corporal A. Fabray.
Acting Corporal C. Stanghan.
Trooper S. J. Clements.

2ND LIFE GUARDS.

Surgeon-Captain E. J. H. Luxmore.
Corporal of Horse E. Button.

ROYAL HORSE GUARDS.

Lieutenant G. V. Naylor-Leyland (killed).
Surgeon-Major B. Pares.
Quartermaster and Honorary Lieutenant C. E. Harford.
Corporal of Horse G. R. Mitchell.
Corporal H. Jordan.

1ST DRAGOON GUARDS.

Acting Serjeant-Major R. M. Holmes.
Private W. Fryer.

MENTIONED IN DESPATCHES

2ND DRAGOON GUARDS.

Major J. A. Browning (killed).
Captain H. W. Hall.
Captain A. D. Sloane, Special Reserve (attached).
Second Lieutenant (temporary Lieutenant) V. H. Misa.
Second Lieutenant F. Milnes.
Acting Serjeant R. J. Chelmsford.
Private J. Jagger.

3RD DRAGOON GUARDS.

Corporal A. H. Rodgers.

4TH DRAGOON GUARDS.

Major H. S. Sewell.
Captain H. S. Hodgkin (attached 1st Battalion Cheshire Regiment).
Second Lieutenant R. J. F. Chance.
Serjeant H. J. Donovan.
Serjeant E. E. Thomas.
Corporal R. A. Stuttard.

5TH DRAGOON GUARDS.

Lieutenant-Colonel W. Q. Winwood, D.S.O.
Captain C. H. Blackburne, D.S.O.
Lieutenant N. W. Curran.
Second Lieutenant C. Pooley.

6TH DRAGOON GUARDS.

Lieutenant-Colonel S. R. Kirby.
Captain and Adjutant P. H. Compton.
Captain P. M. A. Kerans.
Lieutenant V. H. Barnard.
Serjeant J. C. Cullen.
Lance-Corporal W. Meiklejohn.
Private G. G. Gowans.
Private J. Green.
Private A. E. Harris.
Private A. Smith.

7TH DRAGOON GUARDS.

Lieutenant-Colonel H. A. Lempriere, D.S.O. (killed).
Captain J. L. Mansell (missing).
Lieutenant (temporary Captain) F. J. Scott.

1ST (ROYAL) DRAGOONS.

Captain W. H. J. St. L. Atkinson (killed).

MENTIONED IN DESPATCHES

2ND DRAGOONS.
Major A. G. Seymour.
Captain S. J. Hardy (attached to 8th Signal Troop).
Second Lieutenant (now Captain Welsh Guards) O. T. D. Osmond-Williams, D.S.O.
Serjeant J. Pearson.
Lance-Corporal C. Hunter.
Private J. Lorimer (attached to 1st Life Guards).
Private J. McCrone.

3RD HUSSARS.
Lieutenant Colonel (temporary Brigadier-General) A. A. Kennedy, C.M.G.
Captain J. J. Dobie.
Captain D. C. Gilroy, Special Reserve (attached).
Second Lieutenant (temporary Lieutenant) J. H. Eliot.
Serjeant F. Banbury.
Acting Serjeant W. Taylor.
Corporal G. Davidson.
Acting Corporal A. Raison.
Acting Shoeing Smith C. Bailey.

4TH HUSSARS.
Captain B. Blood.
Captain H. K. D. Evans.
Lieutenant (temporary Captain) F. King.
Lieutenant R. J. V. Falkner.
Second Lieutenant M. F. Radclyffe, Special Reserve (attached).
Serjeant F. Baker.
Acting Corporal J. P. Colson.
Private A. V. Bradley.
Private A. H. Hampton.
Private W. Wright.

5TH LANCERS.
Captain and Adjutant A. I. Macdougall.
Captain V. de V. M. Vallance.
Lieutenant J. A. Batten Pooll.
Lieutenant C. H. Stringer.
Quartermaster and Honorary Lieutenant G. J. Burridge.
Serjeant L. Kirby.
Corporal E. C. Jenner.
Acting Corporal H. Eglington.
Private F. W. King (wounded and missing).

7TH HUSSARS.
Major C. H. Rankin, D.S.O.

MENTIONED IN DESPATCHES

9TH LANCERS.

Major D. J. E. Beale-Browne.
Lieutenant (temporary Captain) A. C. S. Bovill.
Captain J. G. Porter.
Lieutenant F. S. Crossley.
Lieutenant L. W. Diggle.
Lieutenant C. W. Norman.
Acting Serjeant-Major A. Wilson.
Serjeant J. Hillman.
Serjeant J. W. Hussey.
Lance-Corporal G. W. Twyford.
Private H. Baker.

10TH HUSSARS.

Lance-Corporal F. H. Jenkins.

11TH HUSSARS.

Captain M. L. Lakin, Special Reserve (attached).
Captain A. B. Lawson.
Lieutenant F. V. Drake (commanding No. 7 Signal Troop).
Lieutenant C. W. Moke Norrie.
Quartermaster and Honorary Lieutenant E. Milson.
Private T. Cross.
Lance-Corporal O. H. Hall.

12TH LANCERS.

Lieutenant (temporary Captain) W. R. Styles.
Lieutenant E. H. Leatham (killed).
Serjeant W. H. Stone.
Serjeant W. J. West.
Corporal S. Gregory.

15TH HUSSARS.

Captain F. A. Nicolson.

16TH LANCERS.

Major W. J. Shannon.
Captain T. L. Horn.
Captain G. Hutton-Riddell, M.V.O., Special Reserve (attached).
Lieutenant H. W. Lord Holmpatrick, Special Reserve (attached).
Lieutenant R. L. Loyd.
Squadron Serjeant-Major F. Norton.
Farrier Staff-Serjeant T. Crossland.
Serjeant W. Pauley.

MENTIONED IN DESPATCHES

Serjeant G. F. Wakefield.
Lance-Corporal A. Barton.
Lance-Corporal W. B. Brooks.
Lance-Corporal W. R. Kennett.
Private A. W. Adam.
Private J. Loscombe.
Private S. Prytherch.

18TH HUSSARS.

Lieutenant-Colonel C. K. Burnett.
Major H. St. V. R. Stewart.
Captain and Adjutant B. Neame.
Captain F. W. Sopper.
Lieutenant Hon. M. F. S. Howard, Reserve of Officers (attached).
Acting Quartermaster-Serjeant B. Brogden.
Serjeant J. Smith.
Acting Lance-Serjeant J. W. Finch.
Acting Lance-Serjeant W. Cox.

19TH HUSSARS.

Captain F. D. Alexander, Special Reserve (attached) (attached to 2nd Signal Squadron, R.E.).
Captain A. S. M. Summers (attached to 16th Lancers).
Lieutenant R. H. N. Settle (attached to 16th Lancers).
Serjeant E. W. Hall (attached to 16th Lancers).

20TH HUSSARS.

Major G. T. R. Cook, D.S.O.
Second Lieutenant (temporary Lieutenant) J. H. Goodhart.
Second Lieutenant (temporary Lieutenant) R. M. Thompson.
Acting-Serjeant W. A. Brown.
Lance-Corporal G. Tester.

21ST LANCERS.

Captain St. J. L. O'B A. ff. Blake (attached to 2nd Signal Squadron, R.E.).

SOUTH IRISH HORSE.

Private L. P. Allen.
Private J. Ardill.
Private P. McCarthy.

NORTH IRISH HORSE.

Squadron Serjeant-Major W. Sewell, A.
Acting Serjeant W. Booker.

MENTIONED IN DESPATCHES

Leicestershire Yeomanry.
Lieutenant-Colonel Hon. P. C. Evans-Freke.
Acting Regimental Serjeant-Major G. C. Parker (Permanent Staff), 19th Hussars.
Squadron Serjeant-Major J. H. Green.
Serjeant J. H. S. Christian.
Serjeant G. W. Cox.

Northamptonshire Yeomanry.
Lieutenant-Colonel H. Wickham.
Major Sir C. B. Lowther, Bt.
Major E. D. Miller, D.S.O.
Captain and Adjutant J. G. Lowther, 11th Hussars.
Captain P. W. Nickalls.
Squadron Serjeant-Major A. J. Ingle.
Lance-Serjeant H. H. Johnson.

Northumberland Hussars.
Temporary Lieutenant-Colonel M. R. C. Backhouse, D.S.O.
Captain Hon. J. N. Ridley.
Regimental Quartermaster-Serjeant J. Elliott.

Oxfordshire Hussars.
Lieutenant-Colonel A. Dugdale.
Major V. Fleming.
Captain G. Bonham-Carter, 19th Hussars (Adjutant) (died of wounds).
Farrier-Serjeant F. T. Cleverly.
Serjeant A. G. Thompson.
Lance-Corporal W. A. S. Bayliss.
Private J. W. Checkley.
Private W. J. E. Napper.
Private F. B. Dallow (killed).

Surrey Yeomanry.
Major G. O. Borwick.
Major C. A. Calvert.
Lieutenant H. J. Bell.
Temporary Lieutenant F. G. D. Colman.
Acting Squadron Serjeant-Major J. C. Rawdon.
Serjeant A. H. Shields.
Private W. H. Barley.

Royal Horse Artillery.
Lieutenant-Colonel H. F. Askwith.
Lieutenant A. G. Bates.
Lieutenant-Colonel A. T. Butler, C.M.G.

MENTIONED IN DESPATCHES

Second Lieutenant C. H. Cameron (killed).
Captain T. H. Carlisle.
Captain C. J. H. Clibborn.
Captain D. J. Cochrane.
Major W. S. D. Craven.
Major E. H. H. Elliot.
Second Lieutenant M. F. Heath-Caldwell.
Captain H. O. Hutchison.
Major E. O. Lewin.
Second Lieutenant A. R. F. Lucas.
Major A. K. Main.
Major W. P. Monkhouse, M.V.O.
Lieutenant-Colonel J. G. Rotton.
Lieutenant-Colonel H. Rouse, D.S.O.
Major N. E. Tilney.
Lieutenant-Colonel H. H. Tudor.
Major A. H. D. West.
Second Lieutenant W. S. Wingate-Gray.
Major H. W. Wynter.
Driver G. Alderton.
Gunner A. Creaser.
Corporal E. W. Haynes.
Corporal K. McCaskill.
Gunner A. Mellor.
Acting Bombardier A. Morgan.
Bombardier W. S. Rotherham.
Gunner S. E. Smith.
Gunner J. F. Strudwick.
Battery Serjeant-Major H. W. Troupe.

ROYAL FIELD ARTILLERY.

Major J. G. B. Allardyce (106th Battery).
Lieutenant-Colonel E. W. Alexander, V.C. (22nd Brigade).
Captain and Adjutant H. M. J. Alves (13th Brigade).
Major E. O. Anderson.
Second Lieutenant R. H. Antrobus.
Lieutenant-Colonel D. Arbuthnot, C.M.G.
Major A. G. Arbuthnot, D.S.O.
Major T. M. Archdale, D.S.O. (44th Battery).
Captain A. S. Archdale (30th Brigade).
Second Lieutenant R. A. Archer (128th Battery).
Lieutenant H. W. H. Armytage.
Captain J. A. Baillie, D.S.O. (Hampshire Royal Garrison Artillery).
Major H. M. Ballingall (29th Brigade).
Lieutenant J. R. Barry.

MENTIONED IN DESPATCHES

Major P. Barton (81st Battery).
Second Lieutenant J. F. Batten.
Lieutenant R. C. N. Bellingham, Special Reserve (37th Battery, attached) (deceased).
Major A. B. Bethell (29th Battery).
Second Lieutenant C. B. J. Bishop (37th Howitzer Battery).
Major D. G. Blois (8th Brigade).
Second Lieutenant J. R. N. Bolton.
Major H. A. Boyd.
Captain Hon. H. G. O. Bridgeman (15th Brigade).
Major and Brevet Lieutenant-Colonel E. W. S. Brooke (6th Battery).
Lieutenant J. R. I. Brooke, Wessex (Hampshire) Royal Garrison Artillery, Territorial Force.
Major and Brevet Lieutenant-Colonel T. Bruce (41st Battery).
Major C. N. Buchanan-Dunlop (12th Battery).
Lieutenant F. W. Burkinshaw (9th Brigade).
Major E. R. Burne.
Major B. A. B. Butler.
Lieutenant G. A. Camell, D.S.O. (44th Battery).
Lieutenant-Colonel and Brevet Colonel G. G. S. Carey (39th Brigade).
Major C. R. B. Carrington (115th Battery).
Second Lieutenant E. Chalker, Special Reserve (attached).
Major W. T. Chambers.
Captain N. R. L. Chance, Special Reserve (attached) (2nd Nottinghamshire and Derbyshire Regiment).
Lieutenant A. A. M. Charles (73rd Battery) (killed).
Major W. E. Clark (16th Battery).
Major H. C. S. Clarke (70th Battery).
Second Lieutenant N. C. Clery.
Lieutenant-Colonel E. R. H. J. Cloeté.
Second Lieutenant G. W. T. Coates (33rd Battery) (killed).
Brevet Colonel C. E. Coghill (Reserve of Officers) (1st Division A.C.).
Major J. R. Colville (55th Battery).
Major A. S. Cotton (15th Battery).
Captain F. L. M. Crossman.
Major B. B. Crozier, D.S.O. (36th Battery).
Captain E. G. L. Cullum.
Captain S. N. Custance (8th Brigade).
Major P. P. E. de Berry (93rd Battery).
Lieutenant J. V. Delahaye (106th Battery).
Second Lieutenant R. A. A. de Stackpoole (1st Battery) (killed).
Captain A. K. Digby, D.S.O. (94th Battery).
Captain and Adjutant R. C. Dodgson (37th Brigade).
Lieutenant N. Donaldson (Reserve of Officers) (killed).
Captain F. J. Duggan (29th Brigade).
Lieutenant K. F. W. Dunn.

MENTIONED IN DESPATCHES

Second Lieutenant W. G. Dyson, Special Reserve (attached 56th Battery).
Second Lieutenant J. D. Edge (8th Brigade).
Captain R. S. Ellis (367th Battery).
Lieutenant-Colonel W. B. Emery.
Captain J. Esmonde-White (27th Brigade).
Major M. J. F. Fitzgerald.
Lieutenant-Colonel R. Fitzmaurice (27th Brigade).
Captain E. C. Fleming (45th Brigade).
Lieutenant A. C. Fluke (killed).
Captain J. C. Fullerton (14th Brigade).
Lieutenant B. A. H. Gage (4th Brigade).
Captain J. A. Geary (6th Battery).
Captain A. J. Gibbs (A.D.C. to C.R.A., 1st Division).
Lieutenant S. Giffard (20th Battery) (killed).
Captain W. W. Gillum (3rd Battery).
Second Lieutenant H. Godsal.
Lieutenant-Colonel A. H. S. Goff (45th Brigade).
Colonel L. A. C. Gordon (4th Brigade).
Lieutenant-Colonel L. G. F. Gordon, D.S.O. (5th Brigade).
Lieutenant-Colonel L. Graham (33rd Brigade).
Captain C. A. L. Graham, D.S.O.
Captain M. Gregory (19th Battery).
Captain E. C. Hall.
Major E. Harding Newman (37th Howitzer Battery).
Second Lieutenant A. L. Harman (23rd Battery).
Second Lieutenant T. M. Hawker (33rd Battery).
Major J. P. V. Hawksley (32nd Brigade).
Major A. E. M. Head (1st Battery).
Major G. J. Henderson (Reserve of Officers).
Captain C. W. Hince (Reserve of Officers, 146th Brigade).
Lieutenant-Colonel G. B. Hinton (26th Brigade).
Major J. W. Hope (103rd Battery).
Lieutenant E. J. T. Housden.
Captain H. H. Hulton (36th Brigade).
Captain H. O. Hutchison (37th Howitzer Battery).
Lieutenant T. J. Hutton (32nd Brigade).
Captain H. H. Joll.
Lieutenant G. L. Kaye (27th Brigade).
Lieutenant-Colonel H. E. T. Kelly (31st Brigade).
Lieutenant-Colonel W. E. Kerrich (Reserve of Officers) (28th Division A.C.).
Second Lieutenant E. Kington.
Major G. R. V. Kinsman (28th Brigade).
Captain J. H. Knight.
Second Lieutenant A. J. L. Knight-Bruce (32nd Battery) (killed).

MENTIONED IN DESPATCHES

Captain C. L. Knyvett.
Captain R. W. Lamb (Reserve of Officers).
Major E. G. Langford (49th Battery).
Second Lieutenant F. R. F. Lankester (1st Battery).
Captain O. M. Lanyon (4th Division).
Major E. H. G. Leggett (4th Division).
Lieutenant C. M. Lister.
Captain C. M. Longmore (1st Division A.C.).
Major R. Longstaff (40th Battery).
Major A. T. McGrath.
Major H. J. A. Mackey, M.V.O.
Lieutenant-Colonel W. R. N. Madocks (40th Battery).
Captain E. B. Maxwell (117th Battery).
Lieutenant A. Maxwell (94th Battery).
Lieutenant-Colonel J. McC. Maxwell (11th Brigade).
Second Lieutenant M. E. Moir (36th Battery).
Second Lieutenant Morgan (37th Howitzer Battery).
Second Lieutenant W. S. Morrison, Special Reserve (attached).
Major A. D. Musgrave.
Lieutenant J. O. Naismith, Special Reserve (attached).
Major H. W. Newcome, D.S.O. (47th Battery).
Lieutenant-Colonel G. H. W. Nicholson (35th Brigade).
Major L. C. L. Oldfield, D.S.O. (35th Battery).
Lieutenant-Colonel R. G. Ouseley, D.S.O. (18th Brigade).
Second Lieutenant H. J. Page, Special Reserve (attached) (30th Battery).
Captain C. T. S. Paul (33rd Brigade).
Lieutenant-Colonel C. F. P. Parry (3rd Battery).
Major W. P. Paynter (14th Battery).
Captain J. Penrose (3rd Signal Troop).
Second Lieutenant R. R. M. Perceval (42nd Brigade).
Lieutenant-Colonel L. M. Phillpotts, D.S.O.
Lieutenant-Colonel Hon. S. Pleydell-Bouverie, 4th Home Counties (Howitzer) Brigade, Territorial Force.
Major C. F. Potter (28th Battery).
Lieutenant-Colonel F. Potts (9th Brigade).
Major E. W. M. Powell, D.S.O. (Reserve of Officers) (48th Battery).
Major R. C. Prance (129th Battery).
Captain C. O'D. Preston (27th Brigade).
Captain J. T. Price (30th Battery).
Major J. V. Ramsden (27th Brigade).
Lieutenant-Colonel F. T. Ravenhill.
Captain A. J. Rendel (73rd Battery).
Captain and Adjutant R. M. Rendel (40th Brigade).
Second Lieutenant H. McA. Richards (1st Battery).
Colonel (temporary Brigadier-General) W. A. Robinson (14th Brigade).

MENTIONED IN DESPATCHES

Major W. L. Y. Rogers.
Major W. C. E. Rudkin, D.S.O. (15th Brigade).
Brevet Colonel G. R. T. Rundle (Reserve of Officers) (146th Brigade).
Captain and Adjutant H. K. Sadler (30th Brigade).
Major C. W. Scott (71st Battery).
Major T. O. Seagram.
Major E. McM. Seddon (Ammunition Column).
Second Lieutenant O. W. Sherwell, Special Reserve (attached).
Second Lieutenant G. T. Spain.
Lieutenant-Colonel E. W. Spedding, C.M.G. (37th Brigade).
Captain F. E. Spencer (33rd Battery).
Second Lieutenant F. B. B. Spragge (25th Brigade).
Second Lieutenant H. M. Stanford (32nd Battery).
Major Hon. G. F. Stanley (58th Battery).
Major E. A. Steel (35th Battery).
Major E. H. Stevenson, D.S.O.
Lieutenant-Colonel D. B. Stewart (36th Battery).
Major W. Stirling (32nd Brigade).
Captain and Adjutant C. E. Stranack (33rd Brigade).
Lieutenant-Colonel W. Strong (15th Brigade).
Lieutenant R. H. Studdert (28th Brigade).
Lieutenant G. Temple.
Major C. B. Thackeray (5th Battery).
Second Lieutenant S. K. Thorburn.
Major G. S. Tovey (23rd Battery).
Captain H. E. O'B. Traill (15th Brigade).
Captain D. le P. Trench (42nd Brigade).
Lieutenant J. L. H. Turner (Royal New Zealand Artillery).
Major D. K. Tweedie.
Lieutenant T. C. Usher, Special Reserve (attached).
Lieutenant C. E. Vivian (Reserve of Officers) (45th Brigade).
Major J. C. Walch (14th Brigade).
Captain C. H. Wallace (45th Battery).
Major E. C. W. D. Walthall, D.S.O.
Major W. M. Warburton.
Major H. Ward (33rd Brigade).
Major H. D. O. Ward (49th Battery).
Major W. R. Warren (73rd Battery).
Major R. W. White.
Second Lieutenant C. T. Whitehouse (15th Battery) (died of wounds).
Major T. E. P. Wickham, D.S.O. (366th Battery).
Major E. R. G. Wilmer (9th Brigade).
Captain E. W. G. Wilson.
Major H. G. Young.
Corporal F. S. Allison.
Bombardier C. Andrews.

MENTIONED IN DESPATCHES

Serjeant J. Ashwell.
Corporal V. A. Baldwin.
Gunner J. F. Bathgate.
Battery Serjeant-Major W. Bennett.
Bombardier E. Brackley.
Gunner B. R. Braines.
Serjeant G. Brierley.
Serjeant W. J. K. Cave.
Corporal H. J. Charman.
Battery Serjeant-Major F. Clarke.
Driver B. G. Cobey (dead).
Trumpeter C. J. Collar.
Corporal C. Collins.
Fitter B. Colloff.
Acting Bombardier T. H. Connor.
Battery Serjeant-Major T. H. Court.
Bombardier A. Cray.
Bombardier W. Croghan.
Corporal S. Cullum.
Bombardier W. J. Dale.
Corporal G. A. Dalzell.
Bombardier E. Dauncey.
Bombardier J. Davies.
Serjeant-Major Artillery Clerk S. H. Dexter.
Bombardier A. L. Dickenson.
Battery Serjeant-Major E. Doolan.
Corporal A. R. Dray.
Company Serjeant-Major F. E. Elliott.
Serjeant A. Farr.
Corporal J. Ferguson.
Serjeant-Major C. H. Flaye.
Acting Bombardier J. Fletcher.
Bombardier V. A. Forsyth.
Gunner J. Francey.
Bombardier G. W. Garling.
Serjeant T. H. Godfree.
Bombardier H. Greatrex.
Serjeant-Cook A. E. Green.
Driver G. W. Haldenby.
Bombardier W. Hammond.
Corporal F. A. Harnor.
Corporal E. H. Harrison.
Gunner R. T. Harrison.
Serjeant-Major (A.C.) T. A. Hartgrove.
Acting Bombardier F. Hawkes.
Driver C. Hill.

MENTIONED IN DESPATCHES

Acting Battery Serjeant-Major T. Hogan.
Corporal A. W. Hoile.
Acting Bombardier Hopwood.
Battery Serjeant-Major J. Hunter.
Bombardier J. D. Ingram.
Acting Bombardier J. O. James.
Corporal E. Jeffries.
Gunner E. G. Jenkins.
Acting Bombardier W. Jennings.
Acting Bombardier E. Joyce.
Battery Quartermaster-Serjeant T. Kane.
Battery Serjeant-Major H. O. Kay.
Gunner J. Keefe.
Gunner J. Lane.
Acting Serjeant J. W. Lark.
Serjeant T. Leahy.
Corporal J. Leech.
Gunner J. Lees.
Bombardier W. J. Lemon.
Staff Serjeant Artificer W. Leslie.
Staff Serjeant Farrier W. Lowth.
Acting Corporal A. Martin.
Serjeant R. Martin.
Gunner H. G. Meadows.
Battery Quartermaster-Serjeant W. Mitton.
Bombardier S. W. Morley (dead).
Bombardier C. T. Morris.
Corporal W. R. C. Norgate.
Bombardier H. O'Hare.
Gunner S. Osman.
Corporal W. Paines.
Acting Bombardier J. W. Palmer.
Saddler Corporal C. H. Peach.
Serjeant J. Pemberton.
Battery Serjeant-Major A. L. Perry.
Acting Bombardier A. W. Petty.
Gunner W. Phyall.
Trumpeter C. Pope.
Corporal T. H. Pope.
Farrier Quartermaster-Serjeant E. J. Poyner.
Farrier Staff Serjeant E. Price.
Farrier Serjeant W. Priddle.
Corporal A. Ransom.
Bombardier G. Read.
Bombardier F. Riches.
Farrier Quartermaster-Serjeant E. G. Rivett.

MENTIONED IN DESPATCHES

Serjeant R. N. Rodgers.
Bombardier S. Salisbury.
Gunner D. H. Saunders.
Regimental Serjeant-Major Sheppard.
Bombardier E. Silver.
Gunner H. C. Silver.
Battery Serjeant-Major C. Syms.
Corporal J. E. Tate.
Serjeant C. Tomkins.
Gunner T. Trobe.
Bombardier W. J. Tulett (dead).
Corporal W. C. Villa.
Serjeant (A.C.) J. E. Wager.
Serjeant R. Watson.
Gunner E. H. Wellard.
Corporal F. H. West.
Corporal A. E. White.
Gunner S. White.
Serjeant F. Wilkinson.
Gunner W. E. B. Willcocks.
Battery Serjeant-Major H. Wilson.
Quartermaster-Serjeant E. A. (A.C.) Wiltshire.

ROYAL GARRISON ARTILLERY.

Major F. E. Andrews.
Captain W. F. Armstrong (7th Mountain Battery).
Lieutenant C. D'A. S. Banks.
Major C. W. Burdon.
Captain H. F. Burke (2nd Siege Battery).
Lieutenant-Colonel P. de S. Burney (Reserve of Officers).
Captain E. L. Caldecott (35th Battery).
Captain W. H. McN. Campbell.
Major C. E. C. G. Charlton (116th Battery).
Second Lieutenant G. M. Churcher.
Major E. F. Creswell.
Captain A. L. Cruickshank (35th Battery).
Captain C. G. F. Davidson.
Captain S. D. Douglas-Jones (24th Battery).
Captain C. A. Eeles (109th Battery).
Major A. Ellershaw.
Lieutenant W. T. A. Everton (8th Heavy Battery Ammunition Column)
Second Lieutenant H. W. F. B. Farrer (113th Battery).
Lieutenant B. E. Floyd.
Lieutenant-Colonel L. D. Fraser.
Temporary Second Lieutenant N. W. Freeman (108th Battery).
Captain W. H. Fry (6th Siege Battery).

MENTIONED IN DESPATCHES

Captain L. Galloway, D.S.O. (31st Heavy Battery).
Second Lieutenant J. A. H. Gammell (114th Battery).
Captain Hon. R. E. Grosvenor.
Captain H. B. L. G. Gunn (8th Heavy Brigade).
Major A. G. Haig.
Major E. L. Hardcastle (1st Siege Battery).
Second Lieutenant E. G. W. W. Harrison (No. 7 Mountain Battery).
Lieutenant A. Hartree.
Major R. L. Haymes (6th Siege Battery).
Major C. L. Hickling.
Major A. R. Hudson (118th Battery).
Captain N. Hudson (No. 11 Anti-Aircraft Section).
Major J. H. H. Jones (5th Siege Battery).
Major C. R. Kelly (113th Battery).
Lieutenant-Colonel K. K. Knapp (7th Mountain Battery).
Captain A. W. Langley (5th Siege Battery).
Major W. Loring.
Major W. H. Macalpine-Leny, D.S.O. (115th Battery).
Captain K. I. McIver (114th Battery).
Captain E. Miles (24th Heavy Battery).
Second Lieutenant D. N. Morgan (No. 7 Mountain Battery).
Second Lieutenant D. J. St. C. Mullaly (1st Siege Battery).
Major V. M. C. Napier (113th Battery).
Captain H. G. Paris (35th Heavy Battery).
Major H. W. M. Parker (Reserve of Officers).
Colonel H. de T. Phillips (8th Heavy Brigade).
Major F. C. Poole, D.S.O. (Reserve of Officers).
Major E. V. D. Riddell (26th Heavy Battery).
Major H. Rowan Robinson.
Captain J. C. J. Smith (26th Heavy Battery).
Captain D. G. T. Sneyd.
Second Lieutenant R. A. Watson (35th Heavy Battery).
Second Lieutenant (late Serjeant) T. Weatherhead.
Major A. C. Wilkinson (35th Heavy Battery).
Captain F. R. Woollcombe.
Major C. E. G. Woollcombe-Adams (114th Battery).
Corporal R. S. R. Ansell (116th Heavy Battery).
Serjeant E. J. Bicknell (116th Heavy Battery).
Gunner P. H. Bolston (116th Heavy Battery).
Serjeant F. Burgess.
Serjeant P. Clune (3rd Siege Battery).
Company Serjeant-Major C. F. Cockfield.
Corporal T. H. Cooper (35th Heavy Battery).
Battery Serjeant-Major T. Cotton (116th Heavy Battery).
Serjeant W. Hall (5th Siege Battery).
Serjeant A. T. Henly (1st Indian Lahore Ammunition Park).

MENTIONED IN DESPATCHES

Acting Bombardier F. H. Heywood (131st Heavy Battery).
Corporal A. T. Kealey (118th Heavy Battery).
Battery Serjeant-Major W. Miller (113th Heavy Battery).
Serjeant J. Moran (118th Heavy Battery).
Bombardier H. Shiner (35th Heavy Battery).
Corporal W. J. Smart (26th Heavy Battery).
Gunner J. Wilson (6th Siege Battery).

Honourable Artillery Company.

Lieutenant-Colonel E. Treffry.
Major A. L. Ward.
Captain M. G. Douglas.
Temporary Captain C. W. Holliday.
Quartermaster and Honorary Lieutenant G. H. Mayhew.

Royal Engineers.

Lieutenant C. C. Adams.
Major G. H. Addison.
Captain C. J. Aston.
Second Lieutenant O. D. Atkinson.
Captain P. R. Bald.
Temporary Captain W. M. Batchelor.
Captain H. H. Bateman.
Captain B. C. Battye.
Major P. K. Betty.
Captain G. T. Biggs, Territorial Force.
Captain C. A. Bird.
Major L. F. Blandy.
Major G. H. Boileau.
Lieutenant R. L. Bond, D.S.O.
Captain J. C. Bowles (killed).
Lieutenant H. A. Broadway (died of wounds).
Major A. Brough.
Major C. M. Browne, D.S.O. (5th Field Company).
Second Lieutenant J. Buckle (59th Field Company).
Lieutenant E. E. Calthorp.
Lieutenant K. MacL. Carnduff.
Second Lieutenant K. McC. Cave.
Captain R. Chenevix-Trench.
Temporary Second Lieutenant W. R. Cloutman.
Major B. W. Y. Danford.
Second Lieutenant B. C. Dening.
Major P. T. Denis de Vitre.
Captain R. V. Doherty Holwell.
Lieutenant F. G. Drew.
Major R. G. Earle.

MENTIONED IN DESPATCHES

Captain K. E. Edgeworth.
Captain C. O'R. Edwards.
Quartermaster and Honorary Lieutenant W. R. Evans.
Lieutenant E. N. Evelegh.
Major C. H. Foulkes, D.S.O.
Captain T. H. Foster.
Lieutenant W. M. Fowle.
Captain H. G. Gandy.
Major A. Gardiner (missing).
Lieutenant (temporary Lieutenant in Army) H. G. Gilchrist, Territorial Force.
Lieutenant K. B. Godsell (17th Field Company).
Lieutenant K. I. Gourlay.
Second Lieutenant G. E. Grimsdale.
Lieutenant W. F. Hanna.
Captain H. W. Herring.
Captain R. C. R. Hill.
Major E. Hingston (killed).
Major D. M. FitzG. Hoysted.
Major C. G. W. Hunter, D.S.O.
Lieutenant A. M. Jackson.
Temporary Lieutenant R. D. James.
Temporary Lieutenant A. A. Jayne.
Major C. R. Johnson, D.S.O.
Captain W. H. Johnston, V.C.
Major D. C. Jones.
Major T. E. Kelsall.
Captain F. H. Kisch.
Lieutenant G. A. Ledingham, Territorial Force.
Lieutenant-Colonel R. P. Lee.
Captain E. F. W. Lees.
Captain H. P. T. Lefroy.
Lieutenant R. A. H. Lewin.
Major H. L. Lewis.
Second Lieutenant N. C. Lowson (Special Reserve).
Lieutenant A. R. Marshall (Special Reserve).
Lieutenant G. Le Q. Martel.
Lieutenant C. G. Martin, V.C., D.S.O.
Major W. F. Maxwell.
Lieutenant E. Moore (Special Reserve).
Temporary Second Lieutenant F. Newhouse.
Captain N. D. Noble.
Second Lieutenant R. D. Pank.
Second Lieutenant A. J. Parkes (Special Reserve).
Second Lieutenant D. M. Parsons (missing).
Captain G. B. Pears.

MENTIONED IN DESPATCHES

Lieutenant J. R. Pinsent.
Quartermaster and Honorary Lieutenant E. H. J. Plowright.
Lieutenant C. E. R. Pottinger (died of wounds).
Captain F. Preedy.
Lieutenant T. C. Richardson (Special Reserve).
Major C. Russell-Brown.
Major A. R. C. Sanders.
Major C. E. P. Sankey.
Major A. F. Sargeaunt.
Second Lieutenant C. M. Simpson.
Captain E. M. Sinauer.
Major C. W. Singer, D.S.O.
Second Lieutenant L. S. Smith (Motor Cyclist Section, Special Reserve).
Captain G. E. Sopwith.
Lieutenant J. H. Stafford.
Major A. D. Stevenson, D.S.O.
Captain T. A. S. Swinburne.
Major C. B. O. Symons.
Second Lieutenant E. F. Tickell.
Major C. E. G. Vesey.
Second Lieutenant N. M. Vibart.
Captain J. Watson.
Lieutenant M. W. T. Webb.
Major J. R. White.
Brevet Major G. C. Williams.
Major F. Wilson, Territorial Force.
Lieutenant B. K. Young.
Corporal J. E. C. Adams.
Acting Second Corporal T. C. Aitcheson, 1st Signal Squadron.
Engineer Clerk, Quartermaster-Serjeant W. J. Arnall.
Quartermaster-Serjeant W. E. Alwin.
Quartermaster-Serjeant J. H. A. Banger.
Second Corporal W. Banham.
Serjeant W. Barnes.
Acting Superintendent Clerk G. H. Batty.
Sapper C. Bayes.
Lance-Corporal (Acting Second Corporal) W. L. Bevan.
Lance-Corporal W. Biggs.
Second Corporal R. T. L. Birch.
Corporal T. McW. Bourke.
Second Corporal E. Bowden.
Sapper R. Brandford.
Sapper W. W. A. Bromley, 7th Field Company.
Acting Corporal G. Brown.
Lance-Corporal R. W. Bullen.

MENTIONED IN DESPATCHES

Serjeant W. Butler.
Pioneer W. Canter.
Acting-Serjeant F. B. Carter.
Serjeant W. Carvell.
Corporal A. Chisholm.
Serjeant J. Clark (30th Fortress Company).
Serjeant S. O. Clements (9th Field Company).
Mechanist Quartermaster-Serjeant T. Collins.
Serjeant H. H. Cook (6th Signal Company).
Sapper F. W. Cropley (23rd Field Company).
Lance-Corporal D. B. Cunningham.
Acting-Serjeant P. H. Dart.
Staff-Serjeant F. G. L. Davey.
Lance-Corporal A. Davidson (7th Field Company).
Acting-Serjeant A. C. Davis.
Serjeant J. Donald (6th Signal Company).
Acting Superintendent Clerk E. J. Drumm.
Sapper W. Ewing.
Quartermaster-Serjeant J. S. Fenton.
Serjeant J. Fergusson (dead).
Second Corporal W. H. Finch.
Serjeant F. M. Florance.
Pioneer W. R. Ford.
Acting-Serjeant T. Foxley.
Lance-Corporal J. Fraher.
Acting Superintendent Clerk H. B. J. Franklin.
Serjeant F. J. Fuller.
Second Corporal J. Galvin (7th Field Company).
Sapper G. E. Gifkins (1st Signal Squadron).
Second Corporal C. Goldman.
Sapper L. E. Gooden.
Engineer Clerk Quartermaster-Serjeant C. F. Grandy.
Second Corporal H. J. Grice.
Lance-Corporal W. J. Hadley.
Corporal J. F. Hadlow.
Lance-Corporal W. J. Hall.
Second Corporal F. C. Heath (56th Company).
Mechanist Staff-Serjeant E. Hennen.
Serjeant W. J. Henwood.
Serjeant H. S. Higgins.
Company Quartermaster-Serjeant M. Higgins.
Serjeant A. J. M. Hill.
Staff-Serjeant G. E. Hogg.
Second Corporal B. Hopcroft.
Corporal A. C. Hopkins.
Lance-Corporal E. Hopkins (1st Signal Squadron).

MENTIONED IN DESPATCHES

Pioneer A. Horley.
Corporal C. G. Hudson.
Second Corporal S. Hughes.
Pioneer E. Hurd.
Superintending Clerk W. R. V. Isaac.
Acting Serjeant-Major (Superintending Clerk) M. Jackson.
Serjeant J. James (dead).
Serjeant H. Jewell (20th Fortress Company).
Second Corporal E. Johnson (dead).
Sapper F. V. Jones.
Engineer Clerk Quartermaster-Serjeant J. W. Jordan.
Sapper R. S. Jordan.
Serjeant C. E. W. Kingsford (9th Field Company).
Corporal M. A. E. W. Keaney.
Sapper J. W. Knight.
Engineer Clerk Quartermaster-Serjeant W. Knott.
Staff-Serjeant F. C. Langton.
Acting Serjeant T. Lawes.
Serjeant P. G. Livesey.
Sapper S. McComb.
Second Corporal J. J. McDonald.
Sapper R. McKenzie.
Staff-Serjeant J. Mackesy.
Corporal H. McNab.
Sapper J. McCutcheon.
Sapper F. Marshall.
Sapper H. Mathieson.
Second Corporal C. Membry.
Engineer Clerk Staff-Serjeant A. S. Meyers.
Company Serjeant-Major J. E. B. Nealon.
Company Quartermaster-Serjeant J. Newland.
Sapper S. Nicholls.
Corporal G. T. Northover.
Pioneer W. Older.
Corporal A. T. Palmer.
Engineer Clerk Lance-Corporal W. J. Pavitt.
Engineer Clerk Staff-Serjeant F. A. Payne.
Engineer Clerk Quartermaster-Serjeant W. W. Popperwell.
Superintending Clerk A. G. Porters.
Serjeant H. Powell.
Company Serjeant-Major W. G. Prescott.
Corporal F. A. H. Preston.
Engineer Clerk Quartermaster-Serjeant H. Pride.
Pioneer C. Ramsay.
Sapper C. Redley.
Corporal J. Redman.

MENTIONED IN DESPATCHES

Superintending Clerk R. J. Reeder.
Sapper G. Reynolds.
Serjeant H. W. Richardson.
Corporal T. J. Riggs.
Serjeant-Major Superintending Clerk F. W. Roberts.
Sapper W. Roberts.
Company Quartermaster-Serjeant W. Sanby.
Sapper E. W. Sangrouber.
Acting Company Serjeant-Major L. J. Santer.
Lance-Corporal R. G. Shaw.
Corporal C. Shearman.
Pioneer T. Shields.
Corporal N. W. Shillito.
Second Corporal L. T. Silvester.
Superintending Clerk H. S. Smith.
Quartermaster-Serjeant A. Snow.
Serjeant R. Spalding.
Sapper E. J. Springer.
Sapper W. Stafford.
Serjeant P. Stanley.
Superintending Clerk G. T. Stroud.
Corporal R. A. Thompson.
Company Serjeant-Major (now Second Lieutenant) S. C. R. Usher.
Lance-Corporal J. T. Vickery.
Sapper H. L. Vile.
Company Quartermaster-Serjeant G. S. Walshaw.
Serjeant G. Waterhouse.
Quartermaster-Serjeant C. Watson.
Sapper T. Wells.
Lance-Corporal A. J. Westwood.
Sapper H. White.
Serjeant R. P. W. White.
Corporal J. Whittaker.
Corporal S. Willcocks.
Corporal A. C. Wilde.
Serjeant C. Williams.
Sapper A. K. Williams.
Sapper J. Wilson.
Second Corporal T. D. Wilson.
Sapper R. Winterbottom.
Company Serjeant-Major A. E. Winton.
Lance-Corporal H. W. Wright.

ROYAL ENGINEERS SPECIAL RESERVE.

Major R. S. Forestier-Walker, Royal Monmouthshire Royal Engineers.
Captain J. A. A. Pickard.

MENTIONED IN DESPATCHES

Lieutenant T. G. B. Forster, Royal Monmouthshire Royal Engineers.
Lieutenant H. E. Moore, Royal Monmouthshire Royal Engineers.
Serjeant R. C. E. Hounsell (Regular Establishment).
Company Serjeant-Major G. B. Bowstead (Postal Section).
Serjeant E. Vinson (Regular Establishment).

ROYAL ENGINEERS, TERRITORIAL FORCE.

1st East Anglian Field Company.
Second Lieutenant C. H. Humphreys.

1st Home Counties Field Company.
Temporary Major C. C. Bryan.
Temporary Captain J. E. Tindall.
Second Corporal J. T. Steadman.
Sapper D. Jiles.
Sapper E. A. Mercer.

2nd Home Counties Field Company.
Temporary Major A. C. Ticehurst.
Lieutenant W. H. C. Challoner.
Sapper J. Bishop.
Sapper A. Breeds.

1st London Field Company.
Company Serjeant-Major F. Flowers (Permanent Staff).
Serjeant E. Black.

1/1st Lowland Field Company.
Major J. M. Arthur.
Lance-Corporal E. Bauchop.
Lance-Corporal R. Parker.

1st South Midland Field Company.
Major E. Gardiner (killed).

1st Northumbrian Field Company.
Major G. C. Pollard, D.S.O.
Lieutenant W. R. Stowell.
Second Corporal J. Tait.

Cheshire Field Company.
Lieutenant A. Leitch
Serjeant J. Armstrong.
Serjeant J. R. Hughes.
Acting Corporal T. Challoner.
Acting Corporal D. Jones.

1st Wessex Field Company.
Captain S. L. Harvey.
Corporal J. H. Giddings (killed).
Lance-Corporal H. Tate.
Sapper H. F. Lewis.

MENTIONED IN DESPATCHES

2nd Wessex Field Company.

Major P. G. Fry.
Captain M. C. M. Wills.
Captain R. B. M. Wills (killed).
Serjeant A. G. Mogg.

Tunnelling Companies.

Second Lieutenant F. P. Lacy, Westmorland and Cumberland Yeomanry.

Wessex Divisional Signal Company.

Major E. H. Varwell.
Lieutenant J. Vicary, 5th Battalion Devonshire Regiment.
Serjeant H. E. Bunting.
Corporal G. H. Parr.
Sapper F. Loney.

Home Counties Divisional Signal Company.

Major H. C. Saunders.

1ST BATTALION GRENADIER GUARDS.

Lieutenant-Colonel L. R. Fisher-Rowe (died of wounds).
Major C. R. Champion de Crespigny.
Major C. W. Duberly (Reserve of Officers) (killed).
Captain Hon. G. H. Douglas-Pennant (Reserve of Officers) (killed).
Captain Hon. R. Lygon, M.V.O. (Reserve of Officers).
Captain W. E. Nicol, D.S.O.
Lieutenant and Adjutant C. V. Fisher-Rowe (Special Reserve).
Quartermaster and Honorary Lieutenant J. Teece.
Company Serjeant-Major W. West.
Company Quartermaster Serjeant W. Hughes.
Company Serjeant-Major C. Jones.
Serjeant J. Langley.
Serjeant J. Smith.
Lance-Corporal R. E. Nash.
Private W. J. Lambourne.
Private H. Lund.

2ND BATTALION GRENADIER GUARDS.

Lieutenant-Colonel W. R. A. Smith, C.M.G. (died of wounds).
Major G. C. Hamilton.
Captain P. A. Clive (Reserve of Officers).
Captain and Adjutant E. J. L. Pike.
Captain E. D. Ridley.
Lieutenant Hon. W. R. Bailey.
Serjeant W. T. Austin.
Serjeant J. H. Blackwell.
Serjeant H. Paradine.

MENTIONED IN DESPATCHES

Serjeant W. Parry.
Private J. Fincham.
Private D. J. Jones (attached 170th Company Royal Engineers).

1st Battalion Coldstream Guards.

Major Hon. C. Heathcote-Drummond-Willoughby (Reserve of Officers)
Captain Hon. J. B. Campbell, D.S.O. (Reserve of Officers).
Captain G. Stewart (Reserve of Officers) (killed).
Lieutenant A. C. M. B. Viscount Acheson (Reserve of Officers).
Second Lieutenant C. G. Mills (Special Reserve) (killed).
Second Lieutenant T. A. Tapp (Special Reserve).
Serjeant G. W. Jackson.
Lance-Serjeant F. Whelan.
Lance-Serjeant R. J. Woollacott.
Corporal W. E. Robinson.
Private A. Hancock.

2nd Battalion Coldstream Guards.

Captain E. B. G. Gregge-Hopwood.
Captain A. Leigh-Bennett, D.S.O.
Lieutenant (temporary Captain) W. T. Towers-Clark.
Quartermaster-Serjeant E. W. Bond.
Company Quartermaster-Serjeant W. Corbett.
Orderly Room Quartermaster-Serjeant A. Webb.
Pioneer-Serjeant A. Helps.
Serjeant E. J. Doel.
Serjeant T. McMullen (dead).
Lance-Serjeant H. E. Pitt (died of wounds).

3rd Battalion Coldstream Guards.

Lieutenant (temporary Captain) P. R. B. Lawrence.
Captain G. E. Vaughan.
Lieutenant Sir R. J. Corbet, Bt. (killed).
Second Lieutenant (temporary Lieutenant) G. F. Whidborne.
Quartermaster and Honorary Lieutenant F. T. Prichard.
Quartermaster-Serjeant D. D. Jones.
Serjeant G. Bryant.
Serjeant J. Fox.
Serjeant F. Hutchings.
Lance-Corporal R. Davies.
Private S. Stratham.
Private J. Waddington.
Private M. Walton.

MENTIONED IN DESPATCHES

1st Battalion Scots Guards.

Lieutenant-Colonel Hon. W. P. Hore Ruthven (Master of Ruthven C.M.G., D.S.O.
Brevet Lieutenant-Colonel B. H. S. Romilly, D.S.O.
Second Lieutenant Hon. R. Coke, D.S.O. (Special Reserve).
Quartermaster and Honorary Lieutenant D. Kinlay.
Company Serjeant-Major J. Macdonald.
Company Serjeant-Major W. Pyper.
Acting-Serjeant R. Spencer.
Acting-Corporal F. Collings.
Private R. Arnott.

2nd Battalion Scots Guards.

Major G. C. B. Paynter, D.S.O.
Major J. J., Earl of Stair.
Captain E. C. T. Warner.
Lieutenant A. H. C. Swinton.
Quartermaster and Honorary Lieutenant T. Ross.
Lance-Corporal J. McVean.
Private A. Kerr (attached Signal Company Royal Engineers).
Private J. Lister.

1st Battalion Irish Guards.

Major Hon. J. F. Hepburn-Stuart-Forbes-Trefusis, D.S.O.
Major P. L. Reid.
Captain Lord D. FitzGerald.
Captain D. J. F. Gough (killed).
Captain E. B. Greer.
Lieutenant R. St. J. Blacker Douglass (killed).
Lieutenant T. Musgrave (Special Reserve) (killed).
Second Lieutenant (on probation) F. F. Graham (Special Reserve).
Second Lieutenant A. C. W. Innes (Special Reserve).
Second Lieutenant (on probation) J. R. Ralli (Special Reserve).
Second Lieutenant (on probation) L. S. Straker (Special Reserve).
Serjeant-Major J. Kirk.
Acting Company Quartermaster-Serjeant H. Carton.
Company Serjeant-Major T. Corry.
Company Serjeant-Major D. A. Moyles.
Serjeant A. Denn.
Serjeant J. Topping (killed).
Acting-Serjeant W. Graham (killed).
Lance-Corporal J. Doran.
Private J. Cleary.
Private A. O'Leary.

MENTIONED IN DESPATCHES

1st Battalion Royal Scots.

Lieutenant-Colonel D. A. Callender.
Captain N. H. S. Fargus.
Captain E. J. F. Johnston (killed).
Lieutenant G. E. Hall.
Lieutenant F. O. St. John (attached 35th Divisional Signal Company).
Second Lieutenant (temporary Lieutenant) N. M. Young (killed).
Second Lieutenant J. Hobbs.
Regimental Quartermaster-Serjeant J. E. Williams.
Serjeant D. Campbell.
Lance-Corporal C. Sachs.
Private A. Clark.
Private W. Hastie.

2nd Battalion Royal Scots.

Captain B. H. H. Perry.
Captain N. S. Stewart.
Lieutenant and Adjutant E. P. Combe.
Lieutenant M. B. Duncan (Special Reserve).
Lieutenant (temporary Captain) G. C. C. Strange.
Quartermaster and Honorary Captain A. E. Everingham.
Acting-Serjeant R. Bruce.
Lance-Corporal C. Malcolm.
Lance-Corporal J. Mullan.
Private E. Brewster.
Private D. Cousins (killed).
Private A. Cuthbertson.
Private J. Gordon.
Private P. Innes.

8th Battalion Royal Scots.

Temporary Lieutenant-Colonel A. V. D. Brook (died of wounds).
Temporary Major W. Gimmell.
Temporary Captain W. A. R. M. McRae.
Captain J. Tait.
Captain T. Todrick (killed).
Temporary Lieutenant R. M. Thorburn.
Private C. Coull.
Private H. Kerr.
Private G. Renton.
Private J. B. Waddell (killed).

Royal West Surrey Regiment.

Second Lieutenant A. R. Abercrombie (attached 1st Battalion East Surrey Regiment).

MENTIONED IN DESPATCHES

2ND BATTALION ROYAL WEST SURREY REGIMENT.

Major H. R. Bottomley (died of wounds).
Captain W. H. Alleyne.
Lieutenant C. H. B. Blount.
Temporary Second Lieutenant C. F. Austin (attached) (killed).
Temporary Second Lieutenant H. Messon (attached) (killed).
Serjeant J. T. Jones.
Private A. C. Dolan.

3RD BATTALION ROYAL WEST SURREY REGIMENT.

Second Lieutenant M. D. Wilson (attached 1st Battalion Lincolnshire Regiment).

EAST KENT REGIMENT.

Captain C. D. K. Greenway (Reserve of Officers) (attached 4th Battalion Middlesex Regiment).
Captain G. Lee.

1ST BATTALION EAST KENT REGIMENT.

Brevet Colonel (temporary Brigadier-General) J. Hasler (killed).
Major R. McDouall, D.S.O.
Captain R. G. D. Groves-Raines.
Captain H. S. Hardy.
Captain and Adjutant L. W. Lucas.
Serjeant P. A. Vincer.
Serjeant J. Ward.
Private F. F. Brown.
Private J. W. W. Morgan.
Private R. W. Mosto.

2ND BATTALION EAST KENT REGIMENT.

Colonel A. D. Geddes (killed).
Captain L. Fort (killed).
Serjeant A. H. Goldfinch.
Corporal F. Driscoll.
Corporal F. G. Fraser.

3RD BATTALION EAST KENT REGIMENT.

Lieutenant D. H. G. Northcote (attached 1st Battalion Wiltshire Regiment) (killed).

1ST BATTALION ROYAL LANCASTER REGIMENT.

Major T. D. Jackson, M.V.O., D.S.O.
Captain A. B. Woodgate, 3rd Battalion (attached).
Second Lieutenant G. R. R. Beaumont (attached to 4th Signal Company, Royal Engineers).

MENTIONED IN DESPATCHES

2ND BATTALION ROYAL LANCASTER REGIMENT.

Major O. C. Borrett.
Major H. H. Wilson.
Lieutenant G. L. Harford (killed).
Lieutenant H. C. E. Jebb.
Company Serjeant-Major G. Kemp (wounded and missing).
Lance-Corporal P. Lynch.
Lance-Corporal E. A. Tuffield.

5TH BATTALION ROYAL LANCASTER REGIMENT.

Lieutenant-Colonel Rt. Hon. Lord R. F. Cavendish (Honorary Colonel 4th Battalion).
Captain F. Eaves.
Lieutenant G. C. Milnes.
Serjeant R. J. Wallbank.
Private C. Cotton.

1ST BATTALION NORTHUMBERLAND FUSILIERS.

Lieutenant B. G. Gunner.
Quartermaster and Honorary Captain A. Landen.
Serjeant A. Kilvington.
Corporal A. C. Waddell.
Drummer F. Addams.
Private G. S. Allen.
Private J. Ovitch.

2ND BATTALION NORTHUMBERLAND FUSILIERS.

Major E. M. Moulton-Barrett.
Captain O. B. Foster.
Captain A. C. Hart (killed).
Lieutenant F. B. Corbet-Singleton.
Lieutenant C. H. Markham.
Company Serjeant-Major E. Vines.
Private J. Fairweather.
Private W. Taylor.

3RD BATTALION NORTHUMBERLAND FUSILIERS.

Lieutenant R. C. H. Roddam (attached 1st Battalion Northumberland Fusiliers).

4TH BATTALION NORTHUMBERLAND FUSILIERS.

Second Lieutenant D. T. Turner.
Company Serjeant-Major J. W. Smith.
Lance-Corporal E. Woodman (killed).
Private A. Brown.

MENTIONED IN DESPATCHES

5TH BATTALION NORTHUMBERLAND FUSILIERS.
Temporary Captain W. G. Graham.
Captain L. C. Soltau-Symons, Durham Light Infantry (formerly Adjutant).
Second Lieutenant R. Ellis.

6TH BATTALION NORTHUMBERLAND FUSILIERS.
Lieutenant A. R. Garton (killed).
Second Lieutenant W. Anderson.
Private C. Ridley.

1ST BATTALION ROYAL WARWICKSHIRE REGIMENT.
Captain C. T. Tomes.
Captain H. J. I. Walker (killed).
Lieutenant (temporary Captain) C. W. C. Wasey.
Quartermaster-Serjeant G. Beck.
Serjeant J. C. Kelly.

2ND BATTALION ROYAL WARWICKSHIRE REGIMENT.
Lieutenant-Colonel W. L. Loring (killed).
Major (temporary Lieutenant-Colonel) R. H. W. Brewis (killed).
Second Lieutenant A. A. Owen, 3rd Battalion (attached) (killed).
Lance-Corporal D. Chowns.
Lance-Corporal H. W. Brown.
Private R. Connell.
Private A. Edwards.
Private H. Grimley.
Private A. E. Phipps.
Private W. Piper.

3RD BATTALION ROYAL WARWICKSHIRE REGIMENT.
Captain L. G. Pilkington.
Lieutenant J. S. T. Weston, attached 1st Battalion Royal Berkshire Regiment.

1/8TH BATTALION ROYAL WARWICKSHIRE REGIMENT.
Temporary Captain S. H. N. Coxon.
Private H. W. Holman.

ROYAL FUSILIERS.
Major W. F. Sweny (Commanding 2nd Battalion East Yorkshire Regiment).

1ST BATTALION ROYAL FUSILIERS.
Lieutenant-Colonel R. Fowler-Butler.
Major A. C. Roberts.
Captain R. Howlett.

MENTIONED IN DESPATCHES

3RD BATTALION ROYAL FUSILIERS.

Lieutenant-Colonel G. L. B. du Maurier, D.S.O. (killed).
Captain E. N. S. Crankshaw.
Captain H. F. Dawes.
Lieutenant R. R. Waddell-Dudley (killed).
Company Serjeant-Major A. E. Smith.
Serjeant H. J. Lawrence.
Drummer C. Franklin.

4TH BATTALION ROYAL FUSILIERS.

Major R. G. Hely-Hutchinson.
Captain M. R. K. Hodgson (killed).
Captain G. M. Lee (Reserve of Officers).
Captain C. A. H. Palairet.
Captain R. H. Pipon.
Second Lieutenant (temporary Lieutenant) R. W. Thornton.
Quartermaster and Honorary Lieutenant F. C. Cross.
Serjeant-Major H. Savill.

1ST BATTALION LIVERPOOL REGIMENT.

Lieutenant-Colonel B. C. M. Carter.
Private G. Caine (died of wounds).
Private T. Dawson.
Private S. Doyle.
Drummer L. Upton.

3RD BATTALION LIVERPOOL REGIMENT.

Captain F. E. Feneran, Liverpool Regiment (attached) (killed).
Lieutenant E. B. Baker (killed).
Lieutenant G. W. Miller, Liverpool Regiment (attached).
Lieutenant H. M. T. Webb (killed).
Lieutenant P. M. Young (killed).
Second Lieutenant T. H. Madden, Liverpool Regiment (attached) (killed).
Second Lieutenant H. P. O'Donoghue, Liverpool Regiment (attached) (killed).
Serjeant A. Evans.
Acting-Corporal W. Cufflin.
Lance-Corporal G. Wagstaff.
Private F. F. Beech.
Private J. Eastwood.
Private T. Smith.
Private J. Welsh.

MENTIONED IN DESPATCHES

10TH (SCOTTISH) BATTALION LIVERPOOL REGIMENT.
Lieutenant-Colonel J. R. Davidson.
Captain R. F. B. Dickinson.
Captain and Adjutant C. P. James (Argyll and Sutherland Highlanders).
Lieutenant (temporary Captain) J. Graham.
Captain B. McKinnell.
Lance-Corporal C. Elliott.
Lance-Corporal B. L. Rawlins (died).
Private D. Carr.
Private A. Jones.
Private J. L. Wallace.

NORFOLK REGIMENT.
Lieutenant R. C. Nixon (attached 5th Signal Company Royal Engineers).

1ST BATTALION NORFOLK REGIMENT.
Major L. N. Jones-Bateman.
Captain J. Bagwell, M.V.O., 3rd Battalion (attached).
Captain W. C. K. Megaw (killed).
Captain P. V. P. Stone.
Second Lieutenant (temporary Lieutenant) R. W. Patteson.
Lieutenant A. F. Todd, 3rd Battalion (attached) (died of wounds).
Serjeant-Major F. Nunley.
Acting Serjeant-Major A. Haymes.
Acting-Serjeant A. E. Hurrel.
Acting-Serjeant J. H. Owen.
Acting-Serjeant E. Pearson.
Lance-Corporal V. A. Taylor.
Private T. S. Moore.
Private V. W. Strong.
Private H. Wilson.

1ST BATTALION LINCOLNSHIRE REGIMENT.
Major H. E. R. Boxer.
Captain J. N. Phillips (Reserve of Officers) (attached) (died of wounds).
Quartermaster and Honorary Lieutenant F. W. Masters.
Acting Company Serjeant-Major A. Ball.
Acting-Serjeant J. FitzSimmonds.
Lance-Corporal J. Rogers (killed).
Acting Lance-Corporal J. Scott.
Private N. D. Tocher.

2ND BATTALION LINCOLNSHIRE REGIMENT.
Lieutenant-Colonel G. B. McAndrew (killed).
Captain R. Bastard, D.S.O.
Captain E. H. Impey.
Captain and Adjutant E. P. Lloyd.

MENTIONED IN DESPATCHES

Lieutenant (temporary Captain) C. G. W. Peake (killed).
Captain F. S. Whinney.
Lieutenant (temporary Captain) W. F. G. Wiseman.
Lieutenant A. W. Wylie (killed).
Quartermaster and Honorary Captain E. W. Skinner.
Company Serjeant-Major C. Newton (killed).
Serjeant R. Hart.
Acting Corporal A. Heightley (killed).
Lance-Corporal G. Battram (killed).
Lance-Corporal C. E. Perry.
Lance-Corporal G. Warrener (killed).
Private D. Dimbleby.
Drummer W. Roworth.

1ST BATTALION DEVONSHIRE REGIMENT.

Lieutenant-Colonel E. G. Williams, C.M.G.
Major J. F. Radcliffe, D.S.O.
Captain and Adjutant L. E. L. Maton.
Lieutenant (temporary Captain) G. E. R. Prior.
Temporary Second Lieutenant A. W. Fisher (attached).
Lieutenant W. A. Fleming.
Second Lieutenant F. W. J. Galton.
Acting Company Serjeant-Major E. F. Thole.
Lance-Corporal G. Crews.
Lance-Corporal W. J. Howard.

2ND BATTALION DEVONSHIRE REGIMENT.

Lieutenant-Colonel J. O. Travers, D.S.O.
Major J. D. Ingles.
Captain H. Eardley-Wilmot.
Captain C. A. Lafone, D.S.O. (killed).
Lieutenant R. O. Bristowe (killed).
Lieutenant F. R. Cobb.
Second Lieutenant (temporary Lieutenant) H. J. H. Cox.
Second Lieutenant G. C. Wright (killed).
Regimental Serjeant-Major W. Pritchard.
Serjeant F. H. Radford.
Lance-Corporal J. Middlewick.
Lance-Corporal W. H. Nosworthy.
Lance-Corporal S. Roberts.
Lance-Corporal B. C. Smith.
Private S. W. Wood.

1ST BATTALION SUFFOLK REGIMENT.

Lieutenant-Colonel W. B. Wallace.
Captain and Adjutant D. V. M. Balders.

MENTIONED IN DESPATCHES

2ND BATTALION SUFFOLK REGIMENT.

Lieutenant (temporary Captain) N. B. Oakes.
Captain E. C. T. B. Williams.
Second Lieutenant (temporary Lieutenant) H. P. Sparks.
Second Lieutenant J. L. H. Smith.
Second Lieutenant H. G. D. Winton (killed).
Second Lieutenant T. S. Wynn.
Serjeant-Major O. W. Parkinson.
Acting-Serjeant H. G. Marshall.
Pioneer-Serjeant J. J. Morrough.
Acting-Serjeant E. Warden.
Private H. Barber.
Private H. W. T. Death.
Private C. H. Goodchild.

3RD BATTALION SUFFOLK REGIMENT.

Major W. O. Cautley, D.S.O., attached 1st Battalion Northamptonshire Regiment (killed).
Lieutenant J. R. M. Vesey.

4TH BATTALION SUFFOLK REGIMENT.

Captain E. L. Brown.
Captain and Adjutant R. Cockburn.

6TH (CYCLIST) BATTALION SUFFOLK REGIMENT.

Captain C. J. F. Cobbold, attached 2nd Battalion.

1ST BATTALION SOMERSET LIGHT INFANTRY.

Lieutenant-Colonel C. W. Compton.
Lieutenant (temporary Captain) and Adjutant W. M. Sutton.
Lieutenant R. H. E. Bennett.
Serjeant W. F. Gibbons (killed).
Private W. Croker.

3RD BATTALION SOMERSET LIGHT INFANTRY.

Second Lieutenant C. E. W. Birkett (Reserve of Officers), attached 1st Battalion King's Royal Rifle Corps.

1ST BATTALION WEST YORKSHIRE REGIMENT.

Lieutenant-Colonel F. W. Towsey.
Major G. G. Lang.
Second Lieutenant R. W. Beacham.
Company Serjeant-Major J. Wood.
Serjeant G. Wood.
Private F. Green.
Private J. Kalaher.

MENTIONED IN DESPATCHES

2ND BATTALION WEST YORKSHIRE REGIMENT.

Captain and Adjutant R. A. Colvin (killed).
Captain Hon. B. M. O. S. Foljambe (Signal Service).
Captain S. G. Francis, D.S.O.
Captain Harington, H.D., D.S.O.
Captain P. L. Ingpen.
Lieutenant (temporary Captain) G. H. G. Perry (died of wounds).
Lieutenant F. J. Harington, D.S.O.
Lieutenant J. F. Ruttledge.
Corporal H. Archer.
Lance-Corporal P. Dewhurst.
Private H. Ferrari.
Private J. Taylor.

3RD BATTALION WEST YORKSHIRE REGIMENT.

Captain W. T. C. Huffam, attached to 1st Battalion.
Lieutenant N. E. Atkinson.

1ST BATTALION EAST YORKSHIRE REGIMENT.

Captain A. R. Kino.
Second Lieutenant J. Brindley.
Serjeant W. Appleton.
Serjeant P. Foster.
Acting-Serjeant H. Jameson.
Serjeant H. A. Pickering.
Private R. H. Rout.

2ND BATTALION EAST YORKSHIRE REGIMENT.

Major C. P. Berthon.
Second Lieutenant N. L. C. De Rinzy.
Serjeant H. J. Parks.
Serjeant H. Rowley.
Private T. J. Ottewell.

1ST BATTALION BEDFORDSHIRE REGIMENT.

Lieutenant-Colonel C. R. J. Griffith, C.M.G., D.S.O.
Major W. Allason, D.S.O.
Captain F. H. Edwards.
Lieutenant (temporary Captain) S. A. Gledstanes (died of wounds).
Second Lieutenant C. Kennedy.
Quartermaster and Honorary Lieutenant A. E. Pierce.
Regimental Serjeant-Major F. Wombwell.
Acting-Serjeant J. Cross.
Serjeant W. Humphries.
Acting-Corporal A. E. Knight.

MENTIONED IN DESPATCHES

2ND BATTALION BEDFORDSHIRE REGIMENT.

Major W. H. Denne, D.S.O.
Major H. C. Jackson.
Major C. C. Onslow.
Captain J. H. G. Baird.
Captain C. B. Cumberlege.
Lieutenant C. H. Willans.
Company Serjeant-Major F. W. Bliss.
Acting Company Serjeant-Major J. Horne (killed).
Acting Lance-Serjeant W. G. Peggs.
Private B. Day.
Private A. Hearn.
Private J. Price.
Private S. Scrivener (killed).

4TH BATTALION BEDFORDSHIRE REGIMENT.

Lieutenant L. T. Despicht (attached 2nd Battalion) South Staffs Regiment.

1ST BATTALION LEICESTERSHIRE REGIMENT.

Major B. C. Dent.
Major H. S. Smith.
Lance-Corporal F. H. J. Spencer.
Lance-Corporal E. Neale.
Private T. Gillett.
Private G. A. Scurr.

2ND BATTALION LEICESTERSHIRE REGIMENT.

Lieutenant-Colonel H. Gordon, D.S.O.
Captain N. A. Morgan.
Captain F. H Romilly, D.S.O.
Captain D. L. Weir.
Pioneer Serjeant J. T. Allen.
Corporal H. Owen.
Lance-Corporal W. Wain.
Lance-Corporal G. Richardson.
Private A. G. Robinson.
Private A. Whitehead.

1ST BATTALION ROYAL IRISH REGIMENT.

Lieutenant-Colonel G. F. R. Forbes (died of wounds).
Major W. H. White (killed).
Lieutenant (temporary Captain) P. J. G. Gordon-Ralph.
Lieutenant (temporary Captain) D. H. Pratt.
Captain T. E. H. Taylor.
Lieutenant A. P. Pargiter.

MENTIONED IN DESPATCHES

Second Lieutenant P. M. R. Anderson, 3rd Battalion (attached) (died of wounds).
Temporary Second Lieutenant R. D. Ford (attached) (killed).
Company Serjeant-Major T. Wilkinson.

2ND BATTALION YORKSHIRE REGIMENT.

Lieutenant-Colonel C. A. C. King (killed).
Lieutenant-Colonel W. L. Alexander (killed).
Captain E. S. Broun (killed).
Captain B. H. Leatham.
Captain W. K. Rollo.
Captain C. R. White, 3rd Battalion (attached).
Lieutenant H. G. Brooksbank (died of wounds).
Lieutenant W. A. A. Chauncy.
Serjeant W. Brett.
Private T. Harrison.
Private G. Thompson.

2ND BATTALION LANCASHIRE FUSILIERS.

Captain A. J. W. Blencowe.
Lieutenant J. W. Evatt.
Lance-Corporal J. Beesley.
Private C. G. Armstrong.

1ST BATTALION ROYAL SCOTS FUSILIERS.

Major D. H. A. Dick, 3rd Battalion (attached).
Captain A. M. MacG. Bell.
Captain A. C. Bolton.
Lieutenant (temporary Captain) D. S. Davidson, D.S.O.
Lieutenant A. Prestwood.
Second Lieutenant J. L. Drummond, 3rd Battalion (attached).
Acting Regimental Serjeant-Major (now Second Lieutenant) Webster.
Quartermaster-Serjeant F. A. Osborn.
Corporal M. Barry.
Private R. Allan.
Private J. Cunningham.
Private R. Farrell.
Private F. Justice, attached Signal Company Royal Engineers.

2ND BATTALION ROYAL SCOTS FUSILIERS.

Major J. H. W. Pollard.
Captain A. G. Bruce.
Captain and Adjutant R. V. G. Horn.
Captain H. Thompson.
Lieutenant N. Kennedy (killed).

MENTIONED IN DESPATCHES

Lieutenant A. Ross-Thompson.
Quartermaster and Honorary Lieutenant A. Spence.
Lance-Corporal D. Currie.
Lance-Corporal J. C. Newberry (killed).
Private J. Boyes.
Private S. Drapir (killed).
Private J. Durward.
Private E. Kirkpatrick (killed).

1st Battalion Cheshire Regiment.

Captain C. de W. Woodyer.
Lieutenant A. Pogson.
Quartermaster and Honorary Lieutenant J. C. Sproule.
Acting Company Quartermaster-Serjeant J. A. Williams.
Corporal W. Douglas.
Private J. Boag.
Private J. J. Brookin.
Private G. Davies.
Private P. Dean.
Private J. Twemlow.

2nd Battalion Cheshire Regiment.

Lieutenant-Colonel T. H. F. Pearse.
Major C. G. E. Hughes.
Major A. B. Stone.
Acting-Serjeant J. F. McWhinnie.

3rd Battalion Cheshire Regiment.

Captain A. E. Harry, attached 1st Battalion.

1/5th Battalion Cheshire Regiment.

Second Lieutenant H. F. Davies.

1st Battalion Royal Welsh Fusiliers.

Lieutenant-Colonel H. O. S. Cadogan (missing).
Captain R. V. Barker (killed).
Temporary Second Lieutenant H. F. Parkes (attached 2nd Battalion) (killed).

2nd Battalion Royal Welsh Fusiliers.

Major O. de L. Williams, D.S.O.
Captain J. A. C. Childe-Freeman.
Captain J. R. M. Minshull-Ford.
Captain and Adjutant C. S. Owen.

MENTIONED IN DESPATCHES

Captain A. L. Samson.
Captain C. E. Wood (killed).
Lieutenant L. A. A. Alston.
Lieutenant J. Cottrell.
Lieutenant P. G. J. Mostyn.

4TH BATTALION ROYAL WELSH FUSILIERS.

Major W. R. Wilson.
Captain T. O. Bury.
Second Lieutenant J. A. Hughes (died of wounds).
Acting Serjeant-Major R. P. Davies.
Lance-Serjeant W. Ledsham.
Private E. Swainson.

1ST BATTALION SOUTH WALES BORDERERS.

Major A. J. Reddie.
Captain A. R. Lord de Freyne, 3rd Battalion (attached) (killed).
Captain H. G. C. Fowler.
Captain A. M. O. J. Lloyd.
Lieutenant H. H. Travers (died of wounds).
Private E. Lowe.
Private M. D. Macauley.
Private W. Norman.

3RD BATTALION SOUTH WALES BORDERERS.

Lieutenant T. R. Allaway (attached to 2nd Battalion Welsh Regiment).
Lieutenant N. P. J. Turner (attached to 2nd Battalion Welsh Regiment).

KING'S OWN SCOTTISH BORDERERS.

Major P. A. V. Stewart.

2ND BATTALION KING'S OWN SCOTTISH BORDERERS.

Lieutenant-Colonel R. D. Sladen, D.S.O.
Captain R. C. Y. Dering (died of wounds).
Captain G. Hilton.
Lieutenant K. McDiarmid, 3rd Battalion (attached) (killed).
Lieutenant E. G. Miles (5th Signal Company, 4th Section, Royal Engineers).
Second Lieutenant R. Gillespie.
Second Lieutenant A. N. Lewis.
Second Lieutenant A. E. Moreton.
Corporal J. E. Evans.
Lance-Corporal F. Jacobson.
Private J. Hargreaves.
Private A. Inglis.
Private D. Nichol.
Private J. Tinlin (killed).

MENTIONED IN DESPATCHES

1st Battalion Scottish Rifles.
Major J. G. Chaplin.
Captain F. A. C. Hamilton.
Regimental Serjeant-Major T. Winderam.
Company Serjeant-Major B. Cliff.
Serjeant H. D. Grant.
Serjeant A. H. Hills.
Serjeant G. F. Jones.

2nd Battalion Scottish Rifles.
Lieutenant-Colonel W. M. Bliss (killed).
Major G. T. C. Carter-Campbell, D.S.O.
Captain E. B. Ferrers.
Captain T. B. G. Foster, attached 1st Battalion Royal Scots Fusiliers.
Lieutenant W. F. Somervail.
Quartermaster and Honorary Lieutenant J. Graham.
Regimental Serjeant-Major J. Chalmers.
Serjeant W. Snowden.
Lance-Corporal E. Collins.
Lance-Corporal S. Lorkin.
Bandsman J. C. Bowman.
Private H. McCabe.
Bandsman F. Robinson.
Private E. Kane.

5th Battalion Scottish Rifles.
Major R. M. Benzie.
Captain W. D. Croft, Scottish Rifles, Adjutant.
Serjeant S. McKnight.
Lance-Corporal G. H. Black.

2nd Battalion Royal Inniskilling Fusiliers.
Captain G. E. Sampson, D.S.O. (Signal Service).
Lieutenant R. G. S. Cox.
Lieutenant R. W. G. Hinds (killed).

Gloucestershire Regiment, Special Reserve.
2nd Lieutenant B. H. Waddy, attached 2nd Battalion Bedfordshire Regiment.

1st Battalion Gloucestershire Regiment.
Captain G. B. Bosanquet.
Captain W. P. Pritchett (died of wounds).
Captain H. C. Richmond (killed).
Second Lieutenant G. C. Firbank.

MENTIONED IN DESPATCHES

Second Lieutenant W. H. Hodges.
Serjeant W. Biddle.
Serjeant H. H. Coles.
Corporal J. Griffen.
Lance-Corporal H. Sheppard.
Private F. Ball.
Private J. Cole, attached 23rd Field Company Royal Engineers.
Private P. T. Long.
Private A. J. Pope.

2ND BATTALION GLOUCESTERSHIRE REGIMENT.

Lieutenant-Colonel G. S. Tulloh (killed).
Captain D. Burgess.
Captain E. G. H. Power.
Captain and Adjutant A. C. Vicary.
Lieutenant W. G. Chapman.
Second Lieutenant H. Rummins.

3RD BATTALION GLOUCESTERSHIRE REGIMENT.

Second Lieutenant H. G. de L. Bush, attached 1st Battalion.

1ST BATTALION WORCESTERSHIRE REGIMENT.

Major J. F. S. Winnington, D.S.O.
Major E. C. F. Wodehouse, D.S.O. (killed).
Captain (temporary Major) J. H. M. Arden, D.S.O. (Reserve of Officers).
Captain C. S. Linton.
Lieutenant E. B. Conybeare.
Lieutenant L. G. Phillips (Signal Service).
Company Serjeant-Major F. G. Morgan.
Corporal J. W. E. Jones.
Lance-Corporal H. A. Evans.
Private F. Baker.
Private H. Hemus.
Private C. Newman.
Private T. Snow.
Private C. Stokes.
Private A. C. Usher.

2ND BATTALION WORCESTERSHIRE REGIMENT.

Major G. C. Lambton, D.S.O.
Serjeant-Major C. C. Tough.
Serjeant L. J. Butler.

3RD BATTALION WORCESTERSHIRE REGIMENT.

Captain E. W. Buckler, 6th Battalion (attached).
Captain G. N. Fitzjohn, Special Reserve (attached).

MENTIONED IN DESPATCHES

Captain A. C. Johnston (attached 3rd Signal Company Royal Engineers)
Captain J. P. S. Maitland (Reserve of Officers).
Second Lieutenant A. Holland, 3rd Battalion Dorsetshire Regiment (attached).
Serjeant-Major C. Hodgkinson.
Serjeant F. Lester.
Lance-Serjeant W. J. Carter (attached 3rd Signal Company Royal Engineers).
Private E. Gray.
Private G. Lillis.
Private C. Norman.

1st Battalion East Lancashire Regiment.
Major E. F. Rutter (killed).
Second Lieutenant J. W. Pendlebury, Special Reserve (attached).
Serjeant J. Mortimer.

2nd Battalion East Lancashire Regiment.
Lieutenant-Colonel C. L. Nicholson.
Major H. Maclear.
Captain and Adjutant K. H. L. Arnott.
Captain W. A. Gallagher (killed).
Lieutenant G. A. Seckham (killed).
Company Serjeant-Major W. Bright (killed).
Acting-Serjeant G. Schoales (killed).
Acting-Corporal M. Cunningham.
Lance-Corporal J. Robinson.
Acting Lance-Corporal G. W. C. Harris (killed).
Acting Lance-Corporal J. McKenzie.
Private W. H. Pearson.

1st Battalion East Surrey Regiment.
Major W. H. Paterson (killed).
Lieutenant (temporary Captain) D. Wynward (killed).
Lieutenant E. G. H. Clarke.
Lieutenant T. H. Darwell.
Serjeant P. Griggs.
Acting-Corporal F. W. Adams (killed).
Private J. Brown.
Private A. E. Elliott.
Private C. Owen (killed).

2nd Battalion East Surrey Regiment.
Captain L. J. Le Fleming.
Second Lieutenant J. A. H. Wood, 4th Battalion (attached).
Private R. W. Dellar, attached Clerical Staff, Meerut Division.
Private R. Hare.
Private L. Townsend.

MENTIONED IN DESPATCHES

3RD BATTALION EAST SURREY REGIMENT.
Lieutenant J. H. L. Haller, attached 1st Battalion (killed).

1ST BATTALION DUKE OF CORNWALL'S LIGHT INFANTRY.
Major H. T. Cantan.
Captain I. B. H. Benn.
Captain C. B. Scott, 3rd Battalion (attached).
Lieutenant O. Pearce Edgcumbe.
Lieutenant A. J. S. Hammans.
Second Lieutenant P. Wills (died of wounds).
Quartermaster and Honorary Lieutenant W. T. Price.
Company Quartermaster-Serjeant F. Gunn.
Company Quartermaster-Serjeant W. T. Miller.
Corporal E. H. Gregory.

2ND BATTALION DUKE OF CORNWALL'S LIGHT INFANTRY.
Captain H. N. B. Harrison, M.V.O. (died of wounds).
Lieutenant R. M. Aston (missing, believed killed).
Lieutenant James E. H. Carkeet.
Lieutenant (Acting Adjutant) E. N. Willyams.
Serjeant T. Gowing.
Private I. Davis.
Private G. Hambridge.

3RD BATTALION DUKE OF CORNWALL'S LIGHT INFANTRY.
Captain A. P. Bosanquet, attached 1st Battalion.

2ND BATTALION WEST RIDING REGIMENT.
Lieutenant-Colonel P. A. Turner.
Major W. E. M. Tyndall, D.S.O.
Captain B. J. Barton, D.S.O. (Reserve of Officers).
Captain E. R. Taylor (killed).
Captain E. N. F. Hitchins, attached 5th Signal Company Royal Engineers.
Lieutenant C. T. Young, 3rd Battalion (attached).
Second Lieutenant T. Hutton.
Serjeant-Major C. Shepherd.
Acting Company Serjeant-Major G. Deacon (dead).
Serjeant J. Nolan.
Corporal G. Fox.
Lance-Corporal T. Outhwaite.
Lance-Corporal E. Drake (killed).

BORDER REGIMENT.
Captain FitzA. Drayson, attached 32nd Signal Co. Royal Engineers.

MENTIONED IN DESPATCHES

2ND BATTALION BORDER REGIMENT.
Lieutenant-Colonel L. I. Wood, C.M.G.
Captain H. A. Askew (killed).
Captain T. H. Beves.
Captain H. F. Chads.
Lieutenant G. P. L. Drake-Brockman.
Lieutenant W. Kerr.
Serjeant-Major V. H. S. Davenport.
Serjeant T. Toner.
Lance-Corporal J. Robinson.
Private W. H. Corkish.

3RD BATTALION BORDER REGIMENT.
Second Lieutenant C. E. H. James, attached 2nd Battalion Welsh Regiment.

2ND BATTALION ROYAL SUSSEX REGIMENT.
Major R. J. A. Terry, M.V.O.
Captain C. E. Bond, D.S.O.
Captain E. F. Villiers, D.S.O.
Lieutenant E. H. Preston.
Quartermaster and Honorary Lieutenant T. A. Jones.
Serjeant J. Batt.
Serjeant W. Dray.
Serjeant J. Richardson.
Serjeant W. Smethurst.
Corporal F. Busby.
Corporal H. Hyland.
Private B. Attree.
Private J. Martin.
Private W. Minns.
Private A. Wedge.

3RD BATTALION ROYAL SUSSEX REGIMENT.
Lieutenant F. J. A Dibdin, attached to 2nd Battalion Welsh Regiment.

5TH BATTALION ROYAL SUSSEX REGIMENT.
Lieutenant-Colonel F. G. Langham, V.D.
Captain G. L. Courthorpe.
Captain F. N. Grant.
Captain T. B. Hornblower.
Corporal W. G. Robins.
Lance-Corporal L. Hill.
Lance-Corporal J. Tunnell.

MENTIONED IN DESPATCHES

1st Battalion Hampshire Regiment.

Captain J. D. M. Beckett.
Captain L. U. Unwin (killed).
Second Lieutenant F. Fidler (killed).

1st Battalion South Staffordshire Regiment.

Major H. E. Walshe, attached 1st Battalion Dorsetshire Regiment.
Captain F. S. N. Savage-Armstrong.
Lieutenant C. W. Evans.
Lieutenant H. L. Mackintosh (killed).
Acting Company Serjeant-Major W. B. Timmins.
Bandsman J. Williams.
Private C. Bonning.
Private W. Neville.
Private F. Winchester.

2nd Battalion South Staffordshire Regiment.

Brevet Lieutenant-Colonel P. C. L. Routledge (killed).
Lieutenant (temporary Captain) J. C. Chaytor.
Lieutenant J. S. Townshend.
Second Lieutenant W. Draycott Wood.
Serjeant A. W. Vizor.
Lance-Corporal H. Bache.
Lance-Corporal B. Fitzpatrick.
Private T. Deakin.
Private J. Kennerley.

4th Battalion South Staffordshire Regiment.

Lieutenant A. V. Whitehead, attached 2nd Battalion East Lancashire Regiment.

Dorsetshire Regiment.

Captain O. M. T. Frost, attached 8th Signal Company Royal Engineers

1st Battalion Dorsetshire Regiment.

Major H. R. N. Cowie, D.S.O.
Captain H. C. C. Batten, 3rd Battalion (attached).
Captain R. E. Partridge.
Captain and Adjutant A. L. Ransome.
Lieutenant (temporary Captain) A. E. Hawkins.
Lieutenant J. G. Clayton, 3rd Battalion (attached).
Second Lieutenant E. D. Le Sauvage.
Second Lieutenant F. J. Morley.
Second Lieutenant C. H. Morris.
Quartermaster and Honorary Lieutenant W. Alderman.

MENTIONED IN DESPATCHES

Serjeant-Major J. Pell.
Serjeant W. J. Cannings.
Lance-Serjeant W. Kerr.
Drummer E. J. Astridge.
Private H. J. Catalinet.
Private W. Handley.

3RD BATTALION DORSETSHIRE REGIMENT.

Captain R. Leycester, attached 2nd Battalion Welsh Regiment.
Lieutenant R. V. Kestell-Cornish, attached 1st Battalion.

2ND BATTALION SOUTH LANCASHIRE REGIMENT.

Lieutenant-Colonel (temporary Colonel) F. A. Dudgeon.
Second Lieutenant (temporary Lieutenant) W. E. N. Burlton.

4TH BATTALION SOUTH LANCASHIRE REGIMENT.

Lieutenant-Colonel B. Fairclough.
Major G. R. Crosfield.

1ST BATTALION WELSH REGIMENT.

Lieutenant-Colonel T. O. Marden.
Captain L. M. B. Salmon.
Lieutenant H. G. Evans-Jones (killed).
Lieutenant H. W. W. Davis (killed).
Company Serjeant-Major S. Oates.
Lance-Corporal J. Garnsworthy.
Lance-Corporal W. Reynolds.
Private T. Scott.

2ND BATTALION WELSH REGIMENT.

Captain W. M. Hore.
Lieutenant W. G. Hewett.
Second Lieutenant J. R. B. Weeding (killed).
Lance-Serjeant W. Harvey.
Acting-Serjeant C. Mack.
Corporal W. J. Martin.
Acting-Serjeant W. Phillips (killed).

1ST BATTALION THE BLACK WATCH (ROYAL HIGHLANDERS).

Lieutenant-Colonel C. E. Stewart.
Major J. G. H. Hamilton, D.S.O.
Captain W. Green.
Lieutenant R. E. Anstruther.
Lieutenant K. Buist (killed).
Lieutenant W. H. C. Edwards (killed).

MENTIONED IN DESPATCHES

Quartermaster and Honorary Lieutenant W. Fowler.
Lance-Corporal (Piper) A. Stewart.
Private W. Fenton.
Private C. McIntosh (killed).
Private M. Peebles.
Private J. Ritchie.
Private W. Tabor.

2ND BATTALION THE BLACK WATCH (ROYAL HIGHLANDERS).

Brevet Lieutenant-Colonel W. J. St. J. Harvey.
Major H. H. Sutherland.
Captain H. F. F. Murray.
Lieutenant N. McMicking.

3RD BATTALION THE BLACK WATCH (ROYAL HIGHLANDERS).

Lieutenant J. M. Richmond, attached 1st Battalion.

1/4TH BATTALION THE BLACK WATCH (ROYAL HIGHLANDERS).

Lieutenant-Colonel H. Walker, T.D.
Captain F. R. Tarleton, Royal Highlanders (Adjutant).
Lieutenant S. H. Stephen, D.S.O.

1/5TH BATTALION THE BLACK WATCH (ROYAL HIGHLANDERS).

Temporary Major H. F. Blair-Imrie.
Lieutenant I. M. Bruce-Gardyne.
Second Lieutenant L. A. Elgood.
Lance-Corporal J. Taylor.
Private J. Davidson.
Private A. Ferrier.
Private W. High.
Private A. Howie (killed).
Private A. Redford.

2ND BATTALION OXFORDSHIRE AND BUCKINGHAMSHIRE LIGHT INFANTRY.

Major A. J. F. Eden.
Captain H. M. Dillon.
Lieutenant (temporary Captain) W. G. Tolson.

ESSEX REGIMENT.

Temporary Lieutenant J. Tomlinson, attached to 1st Battalion Royal Lancaster Regiment.

2ND BATTALION ESSEX REGIMENT.

Captain G. C. Binsteed (killed).
Captain L. O. W. Jones.

MENTIONED IN DESPATCHES
Lieutenant (temporary Captain) P. Pechell.
Quartermaster and Honorary Lieutenant S. Freestone.
Serjeant-Major R. A. Baldwin.
Serjeant F. C. Bloom.
Serjeant Flack.
Acting-Serjeant R. Parish.

3RD BATTALION ESSEX REGIMENT (T.F.)
Second Lieutenant A. G. de la Mare, attached to 1st Battalion North Staffordshire Regiment.

1ST BATTALION NOTTINGHAMSHIRE AND DERBYSHIRE REGIMENT.
Major L. St. H. Morley.
Major C. R. Mortimer.
Captain H. B. Dixon (killed).
Lieutenant G. S. Dobbie.
Lieutenant C. S. C. Kennedy (8th Signal Company).
Lieutenant and Adjutant R. H. Stranger (died of wounds).
Company Serjeant-Major T. W. Phillips.
Company Quartermaster-Serjeant A. Blanchard.
Serjeant J. H. Cox.
Lance-Serjeant W. Murfitt.
Lance-Serjeant J. Pearce.
Lance-Corporal J. Booth.
Lance-Corporal F. Waldron.
Private J. F. Limerick.

2ND BATTALION NOTTINGHAMSHIRE AND DERBYSHIRE REGIMENT.
Second Lieutenant L. W. Peck, Special Reserve (attached).
Quartermaster and Honorary Captain F. Tomlinson.
Acting Company Serjeant Major W. H. Cooke.
Acting Company Serjeant-Major J. Sephton.
Private J. Hodgson.
Private T. Stretton.

6TH BATTALION NOTTINGHAMSHIRE AND DERBYSHIRE REGIMENT.
Second Lieutenant H. F. Severne (killed).

1ST BATTALION LOYAL NORTH LANCASHIRE REGIMENT.
Captain J. Dare.
Captain G. W. Hay, 3rd Battalion (attached).
Captain S. T. Lucey.
Second Lieutenant H. G. Gilliland, 3rd Battalion (attached).
Serjeant-Master Cook W. F. S. Collins.

MENTIONED IN DESPATCHES

5TH BATTALION LOYAL NORTH LANCASHIRE REGIMENT.

Major G. Hesketh.
Captain W. R. H. Dann, Bedfordshire Regiment (Adjutant).
Serjeant-Major A. Watts.
Company Serjeant-Major V. G. Winder.
Corporal N. Ryder.

1ST BATTALION NORTHAMPTONSHIRE REGIMENT.

Major L. G. W. Dobbin.
Captain B. B. Dickson (killed).
Second Lieutenant H. F. Pitcher.
Serjeant (now Second Lieutenant) R. E. Cox.
Acting-Serjeant R. Hinde.
Serjeant W. Pipet.
Serjeant G. W. Pridmore.
Acting-Serjeant J. P. Singleton.

2ND BATTALION NORTHAMPTONSHIRE REGIMENT.

Lieutenant-Colonel C. S. Pritchard, D.S.O. (killed).
Captain A. G. C. Capell (killed).
Captain and Adjutant H. Power (killed).
Company Serjeant-Major R. Carvill (killed).
Serjeant T. Hullett.
Private A. Sleet.

3RD BATTALION NORTHAMPTONSHIRE REGIMENT.

Captain J. H. Farrar, attached 1st Battalion.
Captain G. B. Vernon, attached 1st Battalion.
Second Lieutenant T. C. Fulton.

ROYAL BERKSHIRE REGIMENT.

Lieutenant J. T. Leslie (Signal Section, 25th Brigade).

1ST BATTALION ROYAL BERKSHIRE REGIMENT.

Major C. G. Hill, D.S.O.
Captain L. W. Bird.
Captain A. G. F. Isaac.
Captain M. C. Radford.
Second Lieutenant (temporary Lieutenant) E. E. N. Burney.
Lieutenant and Adjutant C. St. Q. O. Fullbrook-Leggatt, D.S.O.
Quartermaster and Honorary Lieutenant F. S. Boshell.
Acting-Serjeant S. Summers.
Acting-Serjeant E. Harris.
Acting-Corporal W. Jarvis.
Acting-Corporal C. Bates.
Acting-Corporal V. T. Bradley.
Private F. A. Wood (killed).

MENTIONED IN DESPATCHES

2ND BATTALION ROYAL BERKSHIRE REGIMENT.

Colonel (temporary Brigadier-General) E. Feetham.
Captain and Adjutant T. R. Aldworth (killed).
Captain A. E. F. Harris.
Captain W. B. Thornton.
Lieutenant (temporary Captain) D. A. Macgregor (missing, believe killed).
Lieutenant A. D. Gordon.
Quartermaster and Honorary Captain H. S. Lickman.
Company Serjeant-Major E. Addicott.
Company Serjeant-Major R. Embling.
Company Serjeant-Major W. Weston.
Acting-Serjeant S. Smith.
Lance-Corporal W. Rice.

1ST BATTALION ROYAL WEST KENT REGIMENT.

Major P. M. Robinson, C.M.G.
Captain E. F. Moulton-Barrett.
Lieutenant C. M. Payton, 3rd Battalion (attached) (killed).
Second Lieutenant E. B. Walker (killed).
Lieutenant C. H. Wild, 3rd Battalion (attached).
Lance-Corporal F. Brockies.
Lance-Corporal J. Knight.
Lance-Corporal A. Steane (killed).
Private C. Barr.
Private A. J. Chandler.

1ST BATTALION KING'S OWN YORKSHIRE LIGHT INFANTRY.

Major C. R. I. Brooke.
Captain F. J. G. Agg.
Captain C. R. T. Thorp (Signal Service).
Lieutenant A. U. Collis-Browne (killed).
Lance-Serjeant W. Neil.
Corporal E. Fuller.
Private H. Millis.

2ND BATTALION KING'S OWN YORKSHIRE LIGHT INFANTRY.

Lieutenant-Colonel W. M. Withycombe, C.M.G.
Captain G. E. Alt, 3rd Battalion (attached) (killed).
Captain M. F. Day.
Lieutenant T. Wells, 3rd Battalion (attached).
Second Lieutenant H. L. Slingsby.
Quartermaster and Honorary Lieutenant A. E. Bentham.
Serjeant-Major J. Moore.
Lance-Corporal W. Eagling.

MENTIONED IN DESPATCHES

Lance-Corporal A. Holding.
Lance-Corporal A. Quantrill.
Lance-Corporal J. Dearnaley.
Private W. Parker.
Private J. Brearley.
Private F. Carey.
Private G. Mead.

1st Battalion Shropshire Light Infantry.

Major J. A. Strick.
Captain P. L. Hanbury.
Captain and Adjutant H. A. R. Hoffmeister.
Lance-Serjeant G. Rogers.
Private W. E. Holmes.

2nd Battalion Shropshire Light Infantry.

Lieutenant-Colonel R. J. Bridgford, D.S.O.
Major J. H. Bailey.
Captain C. E. Atchison.
Captain H. G. Bryant, D.S.O.
Captain F. J. Leach (died of wounds).
Captain C. M. Vassar Smith.
Lieutenant H. Beacall.
Lieutenant J. O. Farrer.
Lieutenant L. H. Torin.
Lieutenant W. D. Vyvyan (killed).
Regimental Serjeant-Major S. J. C. Baikie.
Acting Company Serjeant-Major H. Hayley.
Serjeant J. Higginson.
Bugler C. Meredith.

3rd Battalion Shropshire Light Infantry.

Captain F. G. P. Philips, attached 1st Manchester Regiment.

1st Battalion Middlesex Regiment.

Captain and Adjutant M. Browne.
Second Lieutenant E. W. Shaw, D.S.O.
Company Serjeant-Major H. Graves.
Company Serjeant-Major W. Reed.

2nd Battalion Middlesex Regiment.

Lieutenant-Colonel R. H. Hayes.
Lieutenant A. G. Cade.
Second Lieutenant A. L. Bishop.
Quartermaster and Honorary Lieutenant H. A. Wiemers.

MENTIONED IN DESPATCHES

Company Quartermaster-Serjeant S. A. Coleopy.
Serjeant W. T. Pavey.
Corporal W. A. Millins.
Lance-Corporal A. J. G. Martindale (dead).
Lance-Corporal H. S. Mitchell.
Private W. Larkins (dead).

3RD BATTALION MIDDLESEX REGIMENT.

Lieutenant-Colonel E. W. R. Stephenson (killed).
Private J. O'Keefe.

4TH BATTALION MIDDLESEX REGIMENT.

Captain H. M. Meyler, 5th Battalion (attached).
Captain and Adjutant T. S. Woollocombe.
Quartermaster and Honorary Captain M. W. Farrow.
Acting Company Serjeant-Major W. T. Vause.
Serjeant C. Law.
Private W. Butler.
Private A. E. Davis.
Private P. W. Lilley.

5TH BATTALION MIDDLESEX REGIMENT.

Lieutenant L. J. Hudleston.
Lieutenant W. S. Meeke, attached to 2nd Battalion Royal Munster Fusiliers.

1ST BATTALION KING'S ROYAL RIFLE CORPS.

Major G. C. Shakerley, D.S.O. (killed).
Captain A. L. Bonham-Carter.
Captain F. L. Pardoe, D.S.O.
Captain and Adjutant W. A. C. Saunders-Knox-Gore, D.S.O.
Captain E. P. Shakerley, 6th Battalion (attached) (killed).
Captain F. G. Willan.
Captain R. H. Woods, 15th Brigade Machine Gun Officer.
Lieutenant G. A. Fisher, 6th Battalion (attached).
Lieutenant H.C. Lloyd.
Second Lieutenant H. Ellse.
Second Lieutenant R. H. Slater.
Quartermaster and Honorary Lieutenant A. Harman.
Serjeant-Major H. Tedder.
Acting Company Serjeant-Major S. Cockayne.
Lance-Corporal H. Campling.
Lance-Corporal J. Higney.
Lance-Corporal J. Reidy.
Rifleman J. Martinelli.
Rifleman C. H. Pocock.
Rifleman F. Reidy.

MENTIONED IN DESPATCHES

2ND BATTALION KING'S ROYAL RIFLE CORPS.

Captain and Adjutant Hon. E. E. M. J. Upton.
Captain L. C. Rattray, 6th Battalion (attached).
Lieutenant R. C. Fetherstonhaugh (died of wounds).
Quartermaster and Honorary Lieutenant A. Robinson.
Second Lieutenant J. F. Amphlett-Morton (killed).
Second Lieutenant C. H. Dowden, D.S.O.
Temporary Second Lieutenant T. B. J. Mahar (attached).
Bandmaster W. J. Dunn.
Serjeant F. Walters.
Corporal E. Rafferty.
Acting-Corporal E. Evans.
Acting-Corporal P. Gould.
Rifleman P. Sullivan.

3RD BATTALION KING'S ROYAL RIFLE CORPS.

Major W. J. Long.
Captain J. B. Brady, 6th Battalion (attached).
Captain and Adjutant J. F. Franks.
Captain W. S. W. Parker-Jervis.
Captain E. F. Ward (Reserve of Officers).
Lieutenant A. H. Brocklehurst.
Lance-Corporal T. P. McDowell.

4TH BATTALION KING'S ROYAL RIFLE CORPS.

Major H. F. W. Bircham.
Lieutenant (temporary Captain) H. O. Curtis.
Captain C. V. L. Poë (missing).
Captain and Adjutant H. C. Ponsonby
Captain H. W. M. Watson.
Lieutenant Hon. W. A. M. Eden (missing).
Lieutenant G. S. Oxley.
Serjeant-Major T. Brasier.
Acting Serjeant-Major W. Green.
Company Serjeant-Major F. O'Connor.
Acting Serjeant R. Adams.
Serjeant H. Butler (killed).
Acting-Corporal R. S. Jackson.
Rifleman E. Marr.

6TH BATTALION KING'S ROYAL RIFLE CORPS.

Second Lieutenant H. H. Marten, attached 2nd Battalion Manchester Regiment (now Second Lieutenant Manchester Regiment).

MENTIONED IN DESPATCHES

1st Battalion Wiltshire Regiment.
Lieutenant-Colonel A. W. Hasted, C.M.G.
Captain R. H. Broome.
Captain and Acting Adjutant B. H. Goodhart.
Captain P. J. V. Viner-Johnson, 3rd Battalion (attached) (killed).
Second Lieutenant A. H. Hales.
Quartermaster and Honorary Major W. I. Cordon.
Company Serjeant-Major A. J. Goulding (killed).
Serjeant P. J. Fulks.
Serjeant H. Marsham.
Lance-Corporal J. Hayes.

2nd Battalion Wiltshire Regiment.
Captain P. S. L. Beaver.
Captain E. L. Makin.
Lieutenant E. L. Francis, 3rd Battalion (attached).
Lieutenant H. M. Hunter, 3rd Battalion (attached) (died of wounds).
Serjeant J. Hounsell.
Corporal E. A. Player.

1st Battalion Manchester Regiment.
Lieutenant-Colonel H. W. E. Hitchins (killed).
Major B. D. L. G. Anley, D.S.O.
Captain and Adjutant J. R. Heelis.
Captain B. V. Mair.
Captain A. K. D. Tillard.
Lieutenant R. H. R. Parminter.
Regimental Serjeant-Major W. Finney.
Company Quartermaster-Serjeant R. J. Stanley (killed).

2nd Battalion Manchester Regiment.
Major R. S. Weston.
Captain W. K. Evans, D.S.O.
Captain N. W. Humphrys.
Captain C. D. Irwin.
Lieutenant H. T. Pomfret, Reserve of Officers (attached).
Quartermaster-Serjeant J. T. Connery.
Serjeant C. Boardman.
Acting-Serjeant E. Kent.
Acting-Serjeant W. H. Robinson (killed).
Serjeant F. Snow.
Private R. Dakin.
Private G. Gilligan.

1st Battalion North Staffordshire Regiment.
Lieutenant C. F. Gordon.
Lieutenant and Adjutant J. W. L. S. Hobart.

MENTIONED IN DESPATCHES

Lieutenant V. V. Pope.
Acting Company Serjeant-Major F. W. Gould.
Company Serjeant-Major A. W. Stapleton.
Acting Corporal A. Hickman.

1st Battalion York and Lancaster Regiment.

Lieutenant-Colonel A. G. Burt (killed).
Major H. K. Colston (missing, believed killed).
Captain P. H. C. Collins.
Lieutenant H. C. M. Howard.
Lieutenant A. L. Kent-Lemon.
Corporal W. H. Hall.

2nd Battalion York and Lancaster Regiment.

Major W. F. Clemson.
Captain F. K. Hardy.
Captain A. V. Jarrett.
Captain G. McD. Pratt.
Serjeant-Major W. Cholerton.
Company Quartermaster-Serjeant J. W. Foster.
Company Serjeant-Major F. Brown.
Lance-Corporal S. McGilton.
Bandsman C. Higgins (dead).

3rd Battalion York and Lancaster Regiment.

Captain C. H. Rowe, attached 2nd Battalion Wiltshire Regiment.

2nd Battalion Durham Light Infantry.

Major J. A. Crosthwaite.
Captain and Adjutant W. H. Godsal.
Lieutenant L. G. Norton.
Second Lieutenant W. F. L. Oliver.
Serjeant-Major J. Watson.
Quartermaster-Serjeant E. Black.
Serjeant T. S. Duddy.
Corporal J. Lowe.
Private J. T. Sproates.

5th Battalion Durham Light Infantry (T.F.).

Acting Quartermaster-Serjeant E. W. Berry.

6th Battalion Durham Light Infantry (T.F.).

Lieutenant T. Welch.

8th Battalion Durham Light Infantry (T.F.).

Lieutenant-Colonel J. Turnbull, V.D.
Captain G. A. Stevens, Royal Fusiliers (Adjutant).
Second Lieutenant E. H. Motum.

MENTIONED IN DESPATCHES

1st Battalion Highland Light Infantry.
Lieutenant-Colonel R. W. H. Ronaldson.
Major and Brevet Lieutenant-Colonel E. R. Hill.
Captain S. (Adjutant) Acklom, attached 9th Battalion.
Captain W. Halswelle (killed).
Captain G. M. Knight.
Captain W. P. Stewart.
Captain H. S. Tarrant (killed).
Lieutenant J. R. Cowan.
Regimental Serjeant-Major A. G. House.

2nd Battalion Highland Light Infantry.
Captain F. S. Thackeray.
Lieutenant (temporary Captain) C. J. Wallace.
Quartermaster and Honorary Captain J. E. Taylor.
Quartermaster-Serjeant E. F. Hayball.
Private D. Tennent.

9th Battalion Highland Light Infantry.
Lieutenant-Colonel C. C. Murray.
Captain A. K. Reid.
Second Lieutenant E. McCosh.
Bugler E. P. McGregor.

1st Battalion Seaforth Highlanders.
Lieutenant-Colonel A. B. Ritchie, C.M.G.
Major A. B. A. Stewart, D.S.O.
Captain A. B. Baillie-Hamilton (killed).
Captain and Adjutant R. Horn.
Captain R. Laing.
Captain Hon. C. H. M. St. Clair (killed).
Quartermaster and Honorary Lieutenant J. Macrae.
Regimental Serjeant-Major A. Sutherland.
Acting-Serjeant J. McIntosh.
Lance-Corporal J. Field (killed).
Private S. Dornan.
Private S. N. McEachearn.
Drummer J. Neill.

2nd Battalion Seaforth Highlanders.
Major (temporary Lieutenant-Colonel) D. A. Carden, attached 7th Battalion Argyll and Sutherland Highlanders.
Captain D. G. Methven (killed).
Second Lieutenant (temporary Lieutenant) J. F. Glass (died of wounds).
Serjeant J. Munro.

MENTIONED IN DESPATCHES

3RD BATTALION SEAFORTH HIGHLANDERS.

Second Lieutenant A. Crum Ewing, attached to 1st Battalion Cameron Highlanders.

4TH BATTALION SEAFORTH HIGHLANDERS.

Lieutenant-Colonel D. J. Mason Macfarlane, T.D.
Major T. W. Cuthbert, D.S.O.
Second Lieutenant (temporary Captain) W. S. Dewar.
Private G. W. Macrae.

1ST BATTALION GORDON HIGHLANDERS.

Major A. W. F. Baird, C.M.G., D.S.O.
Captain H. P. Burn.
Captain E. H. Davidson.
Lieutenant W. F. R. Dobie (missing, believed killed).
Captain L. Gordon.
Lieutenant G. W. A. Alexander.
Acting Transport Serjeant J. Bruce.
Private J. Foreman.
Private T. Clucas (killed).
Private J. McGrady.
Private H. Radcliffe.

2ND BATTALION GORDON HIGHLANDERS.

Lieutenant-Colonel H. P. Uniacke, C.B. (killed).
Brevet Major J. M. Hamilton.
Brevet Major J. R. E. Stansfeld, D.S.O. (Adjutant).
Captain H. M. Sprot.

3RD BATTALION GORDON HIGHLANDERS.

Captain J. Bartholomew, attached 1st Battalion Gordon Highlanders.

4TH BATTALION GORDON HIGHLANDERS.

Lieutenant-Colonel T. Ogilvie.

6TH BATTALION GORDON HIGHLANDERS.

Lieutenant-Colonel C. McLean (Captain, Reserve of Officers) (killed).
Captain J. A. L. Campbell, Argyll and Sutherland Highlanders (Adjutant) (died of wounds).
Captain J. Dawson.
Captain I. G. Fleming.
Captain G. Smith (killed).
Second Lieutenant (temporary Lieutenant) A. S. P. Burn (killed).
Second Lieutenant P. Kynoch-Shand.
Company Quartermaster-Serjeant C. J. Niven (killed).

MENTIONED IN DESPATCHES

Serjeant J. Craig.
Serjeant-Drummer S. Jack.
Lance-Corporal W. Johnston.
Lance-Corporal J. Robb.

1st Battalion Cameron Highlanders.

Major E. Craig-Brown, D.S.O.
Captain Sir T. W. H. J. Erskine, Bt.
Captain R. B. Trotter (killed).
Lieutenant R. N. Stewart.
Quartermaster and Honorary Major A. P. Yeadon.
Acting-Serjeant J. J. Gilchrist.
Corporal G. O. Rose.
Acting-Corporal W. Lewis.
Private W. Blair.
Private J. Coulter.
Private J. Fergie.
Private D. Jamieson.
Private A. McLennan.
Private J. Smith.
Private A. Wood.
Drummer J. MacPherson.

2nd Battalion Cameron Highlanders.

Brevet Lieutenant-Colonel J. Campbell, D.S.O.
Major L. O. Graeme.
Captain I. C. Grant.
Captain and Adjutant A. D. Macpherson.
Lieutenant L. F. Hussey-Macpherson.
Second Lieutenant J. Giffin.
Second Lieutenant D. Grant (killed).
Acting-Serjeant A. Douglas.
Acting-Corporal D. Liddell.
Lance-Corporal A. Roberts.
Private J. Fairley.
Private A. Hendry.
Private H. J. Hersey.
Private S. Hoskyn, attached Lahore Casualty Clearing Station.
Private J. Little.

1/4th Cameron Highlanders (Territorial Force).

Temporary Lieutenant-Colonel A. Fraser, V.D. (killed).
Captain G. B. Duff, Cameron Highlanders (Adjutant).
Second Lieutenant A. Sutherland.

MENTIONED IN DESPATCHES

1st Battalion Royal Irish Rifles.

Lieutenant-Colonel G. B. Laurie (killed).
Captain A. J. Biscoe (died of wounds).
Captain F. R. W. Graham.
Captain A. M. O'Sullivan (killed).
Lieutenant (temporary Captain) A. O'H. Wright (Adjutant) (killed).
Lieutenant W. A. Burges (killed).
Second Lieutenant G. I. Gartlan.
Quartermaster and Honorary Lieutenant G. W. Edwards.
W. Carroll (R.S.M.)
Serjeant P. Breen.
Serjeant R. Stovin.
Corporal J. Quinlan.
Corporal C. Sexton.
Lance-Corporal J. Lennon.
Rifleman R. Brown.
Bandsman P. Kelly.

2nd Battalion Royal Irish Rifles.

Major J. W. Alston (killed).
Captain E. C. Mayne (Reserve of Officers).
Captain T. L. B. Soutry.
Captain R. P. Varwell.
Lieutenant G. S. Norman.
Company Serjeant-Major J. McGibney.
Bandsman H. Palmer.
Private D. Russell.

1st Battalion Royal Irish Fusiliers.

Major R. G. Shuter, D.S.O.
Captain G. Bull.

2nd Battalion Royal Irish Fusiliers.

Lieutenant-Colonel P. R. Wood.
Major P. Gould.
Captain M. J. Furnell.
Captain and Adjutant H. W. D. McCarthy-O'Leary.
Lieutenant R. Egerton.
Lieutenant G. D. C. Elton.
Lieutenant J. F. Hodges.
Quartermaster and Honorary Major J. Shannon.
Private J. Baldwin.
Private E. Brady.
Private J. Carroll.
Private J. Devlin.

MENTIONED IN DESPATCHES

Private W. Hartley.
Private J. Lynch.
Private J. McKenna.
Private F. Macready (killed).

1st Battalion Connaught Rangers.
Lance-Corporal W. Cooper.
Bandsman G. Cole.
Bandsman T. Gillan.
Bandsman J. Horton.

3rd Battalion Connaught Rangers.
Captain M. I. M. Campbell, attached 2nd Battalion Welsh Regiment.

1st Battalion Argyll and Sutherland Highlanders.
Captain and Adjutant A. R. Boyle.
Captain C. H. Patten.
Captain D. M. Porteous, D.S.O. (killed).
Captain J. H. Young.
Second Lieutenant R. Gibb (killed).
Lance-Corporal F. Armit.
Private C. Cleary.
Private A. Gray.
Private D. Stead.

2nd Battalion Argyll and Sutherland Highlanders.
Brevet Lieutenant-Colonel H. B. Kirk.
Lieutenant J. C. Aitken.
Serjeant D. Duncan.

4th Battalion Argyll and Sutherland Highlanders.
Captain R. J. Nicol, attached 2nd Battalion.

7th Battalion Argyll and Sutherland Highlanders.
Lieutenant A. G. Moir (killed).
Second Lieutenant E. F. Yarrow.
Company Serjeant-Major F. Cameron.
Lance-Corporal W. McFarlane.
Private G. Ferguson.

1st Battalion Leinster Regiment.
Lieutenant (temporary Captain) J. V. Meredith (Acting Adjutant).
Lieutenant J. L. Whitty.
Serjeant Griffiths.
Acting-Corporal J. T. Pavitt.
Private E. Costello.
Private M. Fay.
Private A. O'Brien.

MENTIONED IN DESPATCHES

2ND BATTALION LEINSTER REGIMENT.
Lieutenant-Colonel W. T. M. Reeve.
Major G. M. Bullen-Smith.
Second Lieutenant J. F. Marsland.
Bandsman J. Dooley.
Private T. Morrisey.
Private M. Neary.
Private P. Reid.

4TH BATTALION LEINSTER REGIMENT.
Captain H. E. Goodbody, attached 1st Battalion (killed).

ROYAL MUNSTER FUSILIERS.
Captain H. M. Travers, D.S.O., attached 2nd Battalion West Riding Regiment (killed).

2ND BATTALION ROYAL MUNSTER FUSILIERS.
Lieutenant-Colonel A. M. Bent, C.M.G.
Major A. Gorham.
Captain M. W. L. Hawkes, 4th Battalion (attached).
Brevet Major G. J. Ryan, D.S.O. (killed).
Second Lieutenant C. H. Carrigan.
Second Lieutenant T. Price.
Private W. Abbott (killed).
Private J. Dickson.
Private J. A. Smith.

3RD BATTALION ROYAL MUNSTER FUSILIERS.
Lieutenant W. J. Hewett, attached 2nd Battalion (killed).

2ND BATTALION ROYAL DUBLIN FUSILIERS.
Major R. D. Johnson, 3rd Battalion (attached).
Lieutenant J. MacN. Dickie.
Quartermaster-Serjeant J. J. O'Connor.
Company Serjeant-Major A. Graham.
Corporal W. P. Curley.
Corporal P. Murphy (killed).

1ST BATTALION RIFLE BRIGADE.
Major W. W. Seymour.
Captain R. S. Follett.
Lieutenant G. W. Barclay.

2ND BATTALION RIFLE BRIGADE.
Lieutenant-Colonel R. B. Stephens.
Major C. E. Harrison (killed).
Captain and Adjutant T. J. Fitzherbert-Brockholes (killed).

MENTIONED IN DESPATCHES

Captain S. A. Sherston (killed).
Lieutenant E. H. Leigh (killed).
Lieutenant T. P. Pilcher (killed).
Second Lieutenant Hon. H. R. Hardinge (killed).
Quartermaster and Honorary Lieutenant J. H. Alldridge.
Serjeant A. Hard (dead).
Acting-Corporal C. Garner.
Corporal A. Woolnough.
Acting-Corporal J. G. Moore.
Rifleman H. Carpenter.
Rifleman L. Hilliam.
Rifleman E. Jolly.
Rifleman W. Munson.

3RD BATTALION RIFLE BRIGADE.

Captain M. Godolphin-Osborne (died of wounds).
Captain E. R. Meade-Waldo.
Captain R. Pigot.
Captain C. F. T. Swan.
Quartermaster and Honorary Lieutenant L. Eastmead.

4TH BATTALION RIFLE BRIGADE.

Brevet Colonel G. H. Thesiger, C.B., C.M.G.
Major J. Harington.
Captain R. L. H. Collins.
Captain and Adjutant H. G. Moore-Gwyn.
Lieutenant (temporary Captain) L. C. Sackville Stopford.
Lieutenant R. C. Hargreaves.
Second Lieutenant C. Saunders.
Rifleman S. Blackman.
Rifleman F. Middleton.
Rifleman F. Poplett.

6TH BATTALION RIFLE BRIGADE.

Lieutenant G. M. Bradley, attached 2nd Welsh Regiment (missing).
Lieutenant H. Law, attached 2nd Battalion Royal Welsh Fusiliers (now Second Lieutenant Royal Welsh Fusiliers).
Lieutenant R. K. Ledger, attached 1st Battalion Royal Welsh Fusiliers (killed).
Lieutenant K. H. C. Woodroffe, attached 2nd Welsh Regiment (killed).

ARMY CYCLIST CORPS.

Captain R. M. Heath, D.S.O., Middlesex Regiment (8th Divisional Cyclist Company).
Serjeant F. S. Lang, 8th Divisional Cyclist Company.

MENTIONED IN DESPATCHES

Corporal C. Dyson, 1st Divisional Cyclist Company.
Lance-Corporal A. Woolger, 1st Divisional Cyclist Company.
Private S. W. Brown, 8th Divisional Cyclist Company.
Private H. Reeks, 8th Divisional Cyclist Company.
Private G. Whiting, 28th Divisional Cyclist Company.

1/2ND MONMOUTH REGIMENT.

Captain A. H. Edwards.
Temporary Lieutenant A. E. Fraser (killed).
Lieutenant H. J. Walters.
Second Lieutenant R. B. Comely.
Company Serjeant-Major G. S. Mellsop.
Corporal S. Vaughan.

3RD BATTALION MONMOUTH REGIMENT.

Temporary Lieutenant-Colonel H. Worsley-Gough.
Temporary Major W. A. Lewis.
Captain K. F. D. Gattie.
Company Serjeant-Major J. T. Gill.

1ST BATTALION CAMBRIDGESHIRE REGIMENT.

Temporary Major E. T. Saint.
Lance-Corporal F. J. Gatward.
Lance-Corporal W. Rolfe.

2ND BATTALION THE LONDON REGIMENT (ROYAL FUSILIERS).

Temporary Lieutenant-Colonel J. Attenborough.

1/3RD BATTALION THE LONDON REGIMENT (ROYAL FUSILIERS).

Lieutenant-Colonel A. A. Howell.
Captain G. E. Hawes, Royal Fusiliers (Adjutant).
Captain H. A. Moore, D.S.O.
Captain H. R. S. Pulman (killed).

1/4TH BATTALION THE LONDON REGIMENT (ROYAL FUSILIERS).

Second Lieutenant A. R. Moore.

5TH BATTALION THE LONDON REGIMENT (THE LONDON RIFLE BRIGADE).

Temporary Major A. S. Bates.
Captain R. H. Husey.

9TH BATTALION THE LONDON REGIMENT (QUEEN VICTORIA'S RIFLES).

Lieutenant-Colonel R. B. Shipley, T.D.
Captain G. Culme-Seymour, King's Royal Rifle Corps (Adjutant) (killed).

MENTIONED IN DESPATCHES

Captain S. J. M. Sampson.
Second Lieutenant E. P. Cawston.
Second Lieutenant G. H. Woolley, V.C.
Quartermaster and Honorary Major T. O'Shea.
Acting Company Serjeant-Major F. T. A. Brehant.
Serjeant M. Brawn.
Serjeant W. Halfacre.

12TH BATTALION THE LONDON REGIMENT (THE RANGERS).

Lieutenant-Colonel A. D. Bayliffe, T.D.
Captain W. K. Venning, Duke of Cornwall's Light Infantry (Adjutant).

13TH BATTALION THE LONDON REGIMENT.

Lieutenant-Colonel F. G. Lewis, T.D.
Captain Hon. E. Coke, 5th Battalion Rifle Brigade (attached).
Captain A. Prismall (killed).
Captain G. Thompson, Connaught Rangers (Adjutant) (killed).
Lieutenant R. M. MacGregor (killed).
Second Lieutenant R. G. Malby (killed).
Quartermaster and Honorary Lieutenant A. Ridley.
Corporal R. C. Jolliffe.
Lance-Corporal N. Galt.
Drummer W. Forth.
Private V. O. Lander.

14TH BATTALION THE LONDON REGIMENT (LONDON SCOTTISH).

Lieutenant-Colonel B. C. Green, T.D.
Captain C. H. Campbell, Cameron Highlanders (Adjutant).
Temporary Captain J. Paterson.
Temporary Captain H. E. Stebbing.
Lieutenant H. A. H. Newington.
Second Lieutenant D. L. Grant.
Lance-Corporal D. J. Chisholm.

16TH BATTALION THE LONDON REGIMENT (QUEEN'S WESTMINSTER RIFLES).

Lieutenant-Colonel R. Shoolbred, T.D.
Captain H. J. Flower, King's Royal Rifle Corps (Adjutant).
Serjeant E. W. Adams.
Serjeant W. H. Musselwhite.
Corporal R. de R. Roche.
Lance-Corporal P. P. Wheaton.
Rifleman P. H. Tibbs.

28TH BATTALION THE LONDON REGIMENT (ARTISTS' RIFLES).

Lieutenant-Colonel H. A. R. May, V.D.

MENTIONED IN DESPATCHES

1st Battalion Hertfordshire Regiment.

Lieutenant-Colonel T. W. Viscount Hampden.
Major H. P. Croft, M.P.
Major F. Page.
Captain A. G. Clerk.
Captain Hon. N. C. Gathorne-Hardy, Rifle Brigade (Adjutant).
Captain P. E. Longmore.
Captain L. F. Smeatham.
Lieutenant G. E. Whitfield.
Serjeant J. Barber.
Serjeant F. Rayment.
Serjeant A. E. Sandell.
Serjeant R. Shirtcliffe.
Lance-Corporal R. A. Gough.
Private G. F. Curtis.

Motor Machine Gun Section.

Captain H. J. G. Bird, No. 4 Battery (Reserve of Officers).
Temporary Second Lieutenant J. Clough.
Temporary Second Lieutenant J. R. Farrington.

Army Service Corps.

Captain (temporary Major) S. G. Allden.
Lieutenant (temporary Captain) J. C. Armstrong.
Quartermaster and Honorary Lieutenant W. W. Barron.
Major T. E. Bennett.
Captain (temporary Major) J. Blount-Dinwiddle.
Major G. C. G. Blunt.
Major C. T. Boyd.
Captain (temporary Major) M. S. Brander.
Temporary Lieutenant C. W. Breadmore.
Temporary Captain W. W. Briggs.
Lieutenant-Colonel E. W. Brooke.
Quartermaster and Honorary Lieutenant F. W. Burdett.
Captain (temporary Major) C. Burton.
Lieutenant (temporary Captain) H. A. Courtenay.
Lieutenant-Colonel H. Davies.
Second Lieutenant (temporary Lieutenant) C. E. S. Dobbs.
Captain (temporary Major) L. O. A. Dunphy.
Major E. G. Evans.
Temporary Captain N. L. Fawcett.
Major J. H. Fessenden.
Second Lieutenant (temporary Captain) J. T. Field.
Captain (temporary Major) E. H. Fitzherbert.

MENTIONED IN DESPATCHES

Second Lieutenant (temporary Lieutenant) W. V. Foulis.
Lieutenant (temporary Captain) H. M. Gale.
Lieutenant (temporary Captain) H. R. Glen (Special Reserve).
Captain (temporary Major) C. le B. Goldney.
Captain (temporary Major) H. St. G. Hamersley.
Major G. H. Harvey.
Second Lieutenant (temporary Captain) H. J. C. Hawkins.
Major H. R. Hayter.
Lieutenant (temporary Captain) H. P. Henderson.
Lieutenant (temporary Captain) U. S. Holden.
Temporary Captain A. G. Hounsfield.
Major C. R. I. Hull.
Major L. D. Inglefield.
Temporary Lieutenant-Colonel (Colonel, Territorial Force) T. J. Kearns, C.B.
Major P. G. P. Lea.
Temporary Lieutenant F. W. Lloyd.
Quartermaster and Honorary Captain D. McCallum.
Temporary Quartermaster and Honorary Lieutenant J. McLundie.
Temporary Major A. T. S. Magan.
Captain (temporary Major) C. F. Milsom.
Quartermaster and Honorary Lieutenant J. Moore.
Temporary Inspector of Mechanical Transport and Honorary Captain H. Niblett.
Major C. A. Organ.
Lieutenant (temporary Captain) H. D. Parkin.
Second Lieutenant (temporary Lieutenant) L. T. Peach, Special Reserve.
Major A. F. G. Pery-Knox-Gore.
Lieutenant-Colonel J. Puckle, D.S.O.
Temporary Captain J. K. Rashleigh.
Temporary Captain (Captain, Territorial Force) W. P. K. Reynolds.
Temporary Inspector of Mechanical Transport (Captain) E. A. Rose.
Temporary Major H. S. Scott Harden.
Temporary Captain A. Shipwright.
Lieutenant (temporary Captain) G. Simpson.
Captain (temporary Major) F. W. Smyth.
Second Lieutenant (temporary Lieutenant) E. S. Snell, Special Reserve.
Captain (temporary Major) H. J. Solomon.
Quartermaster and Honorary Lieutenant T. G. Spain.
Lieutenant (temporary Captain) F. A. Spencer.
Lieutenant-Colonel W. S. Swabey.
Second Lieutenant (temporary Captain) N. S. Thomas, Special Reserve.
Temporary Lieutenant G. F. B. Vigne.
Temporary Inspector of Mechanical Transport and Honorary Captain J. E. Wilks.
Mechanist Staff-Serjeant O. T. Abbott.

MENTIONED IN DESPATCHES

Saddler Staff-Serjeant F. Albon.
Lance-Corporal H. C. Andrewartha.
Serjeant J. Ashton.
Staff Quartermaster-Serjeant C. R. Aspden.
Staff Quartermaster-Serjeant C. H. Atkins.
Private S. Bailey.
Serjeant L. J. V. Bathurst.
Staff-Serjeant W. D. Bedding.
Staff-Serjeant J. T. Bews.
Staff Serjeant-Major A. E. J. Booth.
Mechanist Staff-Serjeant T. G. Boshier.
Staff Quartermaster-Serjeant T. G. Bunch.
1st Class Staff-Serjeant-Major A. V. Burd.
1st Class Staff Serjeant-Major A. J. Carey.
1st Class Staff Serjeant-Major J. W. Carr.
Driver H. F. Carter.
Staff Quartermaster-Serjeant F. W. Claye.
Mechanist Serjeant-Major G. Clements.
Staff Serjeant-Major J. Connell.
Serjeant F. W. Coombes.
Corporal F. Corbitt.
Mechanist Serjeant-Major G. Dawson.
Farrier-Serjeant G. Denton.
Temporary Mechanist Staff-Serjeant T. Dixon.
Serjeant S. A. Dowrick.
Staff Quartermaster-Serjeant W. Duff.
Serjeant W. F. Dyas.
Staff-Serjeant D. Edgar.
Staff-Serjeant G. T. Elliott.
Staff Quartermaster-Serjeant H. Finlinson.
Staff Quartermaster-Serjeant W. J. Franks.
Company Quartermaster-Serjeant W. J. French.
Staff Serjeant-Major G. H. Gracey.
Company Quartermaster-Serjeant A. Gresham.
Mechanist Staff-Serjeant A. V. Hanaghan.
Staff Serjeant-Major A. Hewett.
Corporal G. A. Hewett.
Corporal T. Hodgkinson.
Serjeant G. W. Horn.
Acting Lance-Corporal W. Hull.
Corporal G. Huws.
Staff Quartermaster Serjeant J. T. Hyrons.
Corporal F. Jackson.
Company Serjeant-Major M. G. Jones.
Staff Serjeant-Major A. W. Kearn.
Serjeant J. Keyes.

MENTIONED IN DESPATCHES

1st Class Staff Serjeant-Major J. C. Kinna.
Staff Serjeant-Major G. Knight.
Serjeant W. B. Marsh.
1st Class Staff Serjeant-Major E. J. Morrison.
Serjeant T. J. Newland.
Driver A. J. Norfolk.
Staff-Serjeant J. J. O'Shea.
Serjeant R. H. H. Page.
Driver J. Pike.
Lance-Corporal G. W. Pilcher.
1st Class Staff Serjeant-Major F. Pilkington.
Serjeant F. C. Pobjee.
Staff Quartermaster-Serjeant T. Pollock.
Company Serjeant-Major H. E. Shannon.
Staff Quartermaster-Serjeant (Acting Staff Serjeant-Major) W. J. Sharp.
Serjeant (Acting Quartermaster-Serjeant) A. H. Sharpe.
Mechanist Staff-Serjeant A. F. Shelton.
Staff-Serjeant J. Short.
Serjeant F. V. Sibbald.
Staff Serjeant-Major S. J. Simmonds.
Staff-Serjeant V. C. Soggee.
Staff Serjeant-Major W. E. Spalding.
Company Serjeant-Major H. N. Stannard.
Staff-Serjeant A. J. Steele.
Serjeant W. A. Stephens.
Farrier-Serjeant J. Stock.
Private H. A. Tillbrook.
Lance-Corporal S. A. Truselle.
Company Quartermaster-Serjeant F. Varney.
Serjeant T. R. C. Wallace.
Staff-Serjeant C. Wallis.
Serjeant L. J. Walter.
Acting Company Serjeant-Major F. Warren.
Mechanist Serjeant-Major F. J. Way.
Staff Serjeant-Major J. H. Webster.
Staff Serjeant-Major W. J. Wesson.
Serjeant B. V. Wheeler.
Mechanist Serjeant-Major A. P. Wills.
Staff Serjeant-Major W. H. Wilson.
Lance-Corporal F. G. Woodason.
Staff Serjeant-Major W. W. Woods.
Staff-Quartermaster-Serjeant A. Woolard.

ARMY SERVICE CORPS (ATTACHED ROYAL ARMY MEDICAL CORPS).
Serjeant J. Bean.
Serjeant F. W. Coombes.

MENTIONED IN DESPATCHES

Serjeant P. F. Maley.
Acting-Serjeant F. L. Saunders.
Serjeant A. Tysall.
Lance-Corporal J. Irwin.
Lance-Corporal A. Littler.
Lance-Corporal J. Williams.
Driver B. Jefferson.
Private G. Sutcliffe.

MEDICAL SERVICE AND ROYAL ARMY MEDICAL CORPS.

Temporary Colonel Sir A. A. Bowlby, K.C.M.G., F.R.C.S.
Temporary Colonel F. F. Burghard, M.D., F.R.C.S.
Temporary Colonel Sir B. E. Dawson, K.C.V.O., M.D.
Temporary Colonel H. M. W. Gray, M.B., F.R.C.S. (Edin.).
Temporary Colonel Sir W. P. Herringham, Knt. M.D.
Temporary Colonel W. T. Lister, M.B., F.R.C.S.
Colonel J. Meek, M.D.
Temporary Colonel G. H. Makins, K.C.N.G., C.B., F.R.C.S.
Temporary Colonel Sir B. G. A. Moynihan, Knt., M.B., F.R.C.S.
Temporary Colonel Sir A. E. Wright, Knt., M.D., F.R.C.S.I., F.R.S.
Colonel C. A. Young.
Major R. B. Ainsworth.
Quartermaster and Honorary Captain W. N. Archibald.
Quartermaster and Honorary Lieutenant A. P. Barnard.
Major B. S. Bartlett.
Captain W. J. E. Bell, M.B.
Quartermaster and Honorary Lieutenant E. Birch.
Captain A. H. Bond.
Major J. S. Bostock, M.B.
Captain W. W. Boyce.
Lieutenant-Colonel M. Boyle, M.B.
Major R. T. Brown, M.D.
Captain C. G. Browne.
Quartermaster and Honorary Captain E. J. Buckley.
Captain W. H. S. Burney.
Major H. H. Burnham, attached 2nd Canadian Artillery Brigade.
Temporary Lieutenant P. Cagney, M.B.
Lieutenant J. W. Cairns, M.D. (Territorial Force).
Lieutenant J. W. Cannon, M.B. (Special Reserve).
Quartermaster and Honorary Lieutenant J. Carr (Territorial Force).
Captain H. St. M. Carter, M.D.
Lieutenant W. McM. Chesney., M.B. (Special Reserve).
Lieutenant T. W. Clarke, M.B. (Special Reserve).
Quartermaster and Honorary Lieutenant T. D. Conway.
Captain M. Coplans, M.D. (Territorial Force).
Major R. V. Cowey.

MENTIONED IN DESPATCHES

Lieutenant D. D. Craig, M.B.
Lieutenant-Colonel G. S. Crawford, M.D.
Captain T. J. Crean, V.C. (Reserve of Officers).
Temporary Lieutenant R. E. Cree, M.B.
Temporary Captain J. Dalrymple.
Captain W. Darling, M.B., F.R.C.S. (Edin.).
Captain G. F. Dawson, M.B.
Lieutenant A. E. L. Devonald (Territorial Force).
Temporary Honorary Captain G. H. Du Cros.
Quartermaster and Honorary Lieutenant H. Dugdale (Territorial Force)
Temporary Captain A. T. Duka, D.S.O.
Quartermaster and Honorary Lieutenant E. W. J. Escott.
Major T. E. Fielding, M.B.
Captain J. R. Foster.
Major R. J. Franklin.
Captain R. Gale, M.B.
Temporary Lieutenant R. W. Galloway, M.B.
Lieutenant A. J. Gilchrist (Special Reserve).
Temporary Lieutenant A. S. Glynn, M.B.
Major C. E. Goddard, M.D. (Territorial Force).
Quartermaster and Honorary Major J. Green.
Quartermaster and Honorary Lieutenant R. H. Green.
Quartermaster and Honorary Lieutenant T. Grenfell.
Major D. L. Harding, F.R.C.S.I.
Quartermaster and Honorary Lieutenant G. W. Harris (Territorial Force).
Temporary Lieutenant C. H. Hart, M.B.
Temporary Lieutenant J. B. Haycraft, M.B.
Lieutenant-Colonel H. Herrick.
Captain F. M. Hewson, F.R.C.S.I.
Temporary Lieutenant F. T. Hill.
Lieutenant A. C. Hincks (Territorial Force).
Captain J. W. Houston, M.B.
Captain F. D. G. Howell.
Captain H. L. Howell.
Temporary Lieutenant T. L. Ingram.
Captain A. E. S. Irvine.
Temporary Lieutenant P. W. James, M.D.
Temporary Lieutenant H. G. Janion.
Captain J. B. Jones, M.B.
Temporary Lieutenant T. H. Just, M.B.
Captain E. J. Kavanagh, M.B.
Lieutenant-Colonel J. F. M. Kelly, M.B.
Captain J. W. Lane, M.D.
Lieutenant-Colonel J. W. Langstaff.
Temporary Lieutenant D. Le Bas.

MENTIONED IN DESPATCHES

Major E. F. Q. L'Estrange.
Lieutenant H. Lightstone (Territorial Force).
Lieutenant A. B. Lindsay, M.B.
Temporary Lieutenant W. H. Lister.
Captain P. A. Lloyd-Jones, M.B.
Lieutenant A. G. H. Lovell, M.B., F.R.C.S.
Quartermaster and Honorary Captain A. Lunney.
Captain W. H. L. McCarthy, M.D. (Special Reserve).
Lieutenant W. T. McCurry (Special Reserve) (killed).
Captain K. B. Macglashan, M.D., F.R.C.S. (Edin.) (Special Reserve).
Lieutenant D. Mackie, M.B. (Special Reserve).
Captain J. N. McLaughlin, M.D. (Special Reserve).
Temporary Lieutenant I. C. Maclean, M.D.
Lieutenant W. F. McLean, M.B. (Special Reserve).
Captain O. W. McSheehy, M.B.
Major J. F. Martin, M.B.
Captain S. Martyn, M.B. (Territorial Force).
Lieutenant W. A. Miller, M.B. (Special Reserve).
Temporary Lieutenant E. H. Moore, D.S.O., M.B.
Lieutenant E. M. Morris (Territorial Force).
Quartermaster and Honorary Captain A. Morrison (Reserve of Officers).
Captain C. W. O'Brien.
Quartermaster and Honorary Major E. P. Offord.
Quartermaster and Honorary Lieutenant J. T. Packard.
Captain C. M. Page, M.B., F.R.C.S. (Special Reserve).
Major S. L. Pallant.
Lieutenant H. S. Pemberton, M.B. (Special Reserve).
Lieutenant-Colonel J. Poe, M.B.
Lieutenant R. A. Preston, M.B.
Lieutenant J. G. Priestly, M.B.
Major F. G. Richards (killed).
Temporary Captain O. Richards, M.D.
Captain T. T. H. Robinson, M.B.
Major H. Rogers, M.B.
Lieutenant-Colonel J. M. Rogers Tilstone (Territorial Force).
Temporary Honorary Lieutenant-Colonel P. Sargent, M.B., F.R.C.S.
Temporary Lieutenant E. Seelley, M.B.
Captain J. J. McI. Shaw, M.B.
Quartermaster and Honorary Major J. B. Short.
Lieutenant-Colonel E. W. Slavter, M.B.
Temporary Lieutenant A. C. S. Smith.
Temporary Lieutenant P. Smith.
Lieutenant L. C. Somervell.
Quartermaster and Honorary Major H. Spackman.
Captain A. D. Stirling, M.B.
Captain J. W. C. Stubbs, M.B.

MENTIONED IN DESPATCHES

Lieutenant-Colonel F. A. Symons, D.S.O., M.B.
Temporary Lieutenant F. J. Thorne, M.B.
Lieutenant-Colonel H. S. Thurston.
Captain J. R. R. Trist (Special Reserve).
Temporary Lieutenant D. C. Turnbull, M.B. (died of wounds).
Captain C. H. Turner.
Captain H. F. Vellacott, F.R.C.S. (Special Reserve).
Quartermaster and Honorary Lieutenant H. A. Ward.
Lieutenant-Colonel A. E. L. Wear, M.D.
Lieutenant-Colonel A. L. A. Webb.
Lieutenant B. H. Wedd, M.D.
Captain A. G. Wells.
Major J. W. West, M.B.
Captain N. T. Whitehead, M.B.
Temporary Lieutenant R. F. Wilkinson.
Temporary Lieutenant C. McM. Wilson, M.D.
Captain H. G. Winter.
Temporary Lieutenant H. F. Woolfenden, M.D., F.R.C.S.
Captain J. L. Wood.
Temporary Lieutenant P. R. Woodhouse, M.B.
Major Sir E. S. Worthington, Knt., M.V.O.
Captain F. Worthington, M.B.
Lieutenant T. W. Wylie, M.B. (Special Reserve).
Quartermaster-Serjeant W. Andrews.
Acting Serjeant-Major W. Argent.
Private P. F. Arnold.
Acting-Corporal F. Avery.
Acting-Corporal G. F. Bardswell.
Serjeant F. P. Barron.
Private P. Batchelor.
Private J. F. Benson.
Private W. T. Blewitt.
Serjeant W. Bowler.
Serjeant H. G. Boxall.
Acting-Corporal G. Burdett.
Staff-Serjeant W. Bush.
Corporal H. Butler.
Private J. Cartwright.
Private S. J. Chase.
Acting-Corporal A. Clark.
Lance-Corporal W. C. Cook.
Staff-Serjeant A. Dady.
Private W. J. Davis.
Private J. G. Deakin.
Serjeant-Major E. B. Dewberry.

MENTIONED IN DESPATCHES

Private F. Emmerson.
Private A. Evans.
Private H. Floyd.
Staff-Serjeant J. G. A. Forbes.
Serjeant-Major G. A. Gibbs.
Serjeant-Major A. Gillespie.
Corporal F. Godfrey.
Private H. Greenwood.
Serjeant A. O. Gregory.
Quartermaster-Serjeant T. Gregson.
Private W. H. Hamer.
Serjeant G. Harris.
Private J. Harrison.
Private E. W. Hayne.
Serjeant G. W. Herbert.
Private P. Horrigan.
Serjeant W. Hutchings.
Staff-Serjeant J. R. Ireson.
Staff-Serjeant (Acting Serjeant-Major) C. Jones.
Private J. Jones.
Quartermaster-Serjeant P. G. Knightley.
Private R. N. Knowles.
Serjeant-Major E. Larner.
Private W. A. Last.
Serjeant A. F. Leaney.
Private W. Matchin.
Serjeant W. H. Mattison.
Serjeant J. N. Mercer.
Serjeant-Major W. Merchant.
Corporal J. Morrison.
Acting Corporal H. F. Mulley.
Quartermaster-Serjeant P. H. Musgrave.
Staff-Serjeant P. J. O'Rourke.
Private E. T. J. Owen.
Quartermaster-Serjeant F. A. Philbrook.
Serjeant R. Pollock.
Quartermaster-Serjeant F. Poole.
Private A. Pooley.
Serjeant J. D. Powell.
Serjeant H. M. Prince.
Quartermaster-Serjeant W. C. Prince.
Staff-Serjeant G. P. Pursey.
Private A. F. Reynolds.
Quartermaster-Serjeant C. E. T. Richardson.
Corporal R. Roberts.

MENTIONED IN DESPATCHES

Staff-Serjeant W. Robertson.
Serjeant H. Russell.
Staff-Serjeant W. Scott.
Serjeant-Major W. H. Scott-Badcock.
Serjeant H. W. Seldon.
Staff-Serjeant E. Sharp.
Serjeant-Major F. M. Sharpe.
Serjeant E. F. Smith.
Serjeant-Major H. Sprinks.
Serjeant-Major E. Steele.
Staff-Serjeant G. P. Steer.
Staff-Serjeant G. Stubbs.
Serjeant H. E. Taylor.
Quartermaster-Serjeant J. H. Thomas.
Serjeant W. B. Thomas.
Private B. P. Thorpe.
Staff-Serjeant W. S. Toye.
Acting Serjeant-Major C. J. Tiunn.
Serjeant-Major G. B. Walker.
Serjeant-Major D. Watt.
Staff-Serjeant W. Whyte.
Private H. Wilkinson.

ROYAL ARMY MEDICAL CORPS (TERRITORIAL FORCE).

Captain R. E. Bickerton, M.B., 84th Field Ambulance.
Major E. B. Bird, 26th Field Ambulance.
Captain W. Blackwood, M.B., 25th Field Ambulance.
Lieutenant R. Burgess, 24th Field Ambulance.
Lieutenant-Colonel D. A. Cameron, M.B., 86th Field Ambulance.
Captain H. A. T. Fairbank, F.R.C.S., 85th Field Ambulance.
Major D. L. Fisher, M.B., 86th Field Ambulance.
Captain W. J. Harrison, M.B., attached 6th Battalion Northumberland Fusiliers.
Quartermaster and Honorary Lieutenant C. W. Hearn, 26th Field Ambulance.
Major W. B. Mackay, M.D., attached 7th Battalion Northumberland Fusiliers.
Lieutenant-Colonel W. S. Sharpe, M.D., 84th Field Ambulance.
Captain E. C. Sprawson, 3rd Division.
Major E. B. Waggett, M.B., 85th Field Ambulance.
Lieutenant V. H. Wardle, 86th Field Ambulance.
Lieutenant-Colonel J. R. Whait, M.B., 85th Field Ambulance.
Serjeant C. W. Abnett, 81st Field Ambulance.
Private H. Boundy, 24th Field Ambulance.
Staff-Serjeant J. T. Boyes.
Lance-Corporal J. Burvill, 82nd Field Ambulance.

MENTIONED IN DESPATCHES

Lance-Serjeant J. Dalton, 1st West Lancashire Field Ambulance.
Serjeant C. D. Dymond, Welsh Border Mounted Brigade.
Staff-Serjeant J. C. Caswell.
Private H. Dominy, 25th Field Ambulance.
Lance-Corporal P. Elcock, 26th Field Ambulance.
Staff-Serjeant W. G. Gotham, 25th Field Ambulance.
Acting Serjeant-Major H. W. Gregory, 26th Field Ambulance.
Corporal W. N. Hodge, 83rd Field Ambulance.
Acting Serjeant-Major A. E. R. House, 24th Field Ambulance.
Serjeant E. Ingleton, 82nd Field Ambulance.
Lance-Corporal E. Meigh, 1st West Lancashire Field Ambulance.
Acting Serjeant-Major T. W. Parsons, 25th Field Ambulance.
Staff-Sergeant S. C. Pocock, 26th Field Ambulance.
Private C. T. Royle, 81st Field Ambulance.
Private J. St. John, 3rd Welsh Field Ambulance.
Private H. C. Sell.
Private H. Stapleton, 83rd Field Ambulance.
Acting-Serjeant R. M. Watchorn, 3rd Welsh Field Ambulance.
Staff-Serjeant J. J. Webster.
Private A. E. Wright, 81st Field Ambulance.

1st London (*City of London*) *Sanitary Company.*
Lieutenant C. N. Draycott.
Corporal (Acting-Serjeant) N. A. Dore.

2nd London Sanitary Company.
Lieutenant J. Clayton.
Lieutenant J. H. N. Price.
Staff-Serjeant W. K. Hadingham.
Staff-Serjeant S. Pickering.

BRITISH RED CROSS SOCIETY.
Mr. F. Alexander.
Captain F. Daniell.
Mr. C. D. Fisher.
Principal Matron Miss N. Fletcher.
Doctor G. R. Fox.
Mrs. Phillips.
Miss A. L. Pierce.
Doctor J. W. Struthers.
Mr. A. C. Valadier.
Mr. G. W. Young.

ARMY VETERINARY CORPS.
Captain E. P. Argyle.
Lieutenant W. A. J. Buchanan, Special Reserve.

MENTIONED IN DESPATCHES

Captain W. J. Dale.
Lieutenant C. Davenport.
Temporary Lieutenant J. M. Dawson.
Captain H. Gamble, F.R.C.V.S.
Captain M. St. G. Glasse.
Major J. J. Griffith, F.R.C.V.S. (attached Royal Field Artillery, 28th Brigade).
Major P. J. Harris.
Major F. W. Hunt.
Lieutenant H. E. A. L. Irwin.
Lieutenant G. C. Lancaster, Special Reserve.
Captain R. W. Mellard.
Lieutenant W. McG. Mitchell, Special Reserve.
Captain W. W. R. Neale.
Veterinary-Major W. A. Pallin, F.R.C.V.S., Royal Horse Guards.
Lieutenant P. B. Riley, Special Reserve.
Temporary Lieutenant J. Sherley.
Captain W. H. Simpson.
Lieutenant F. B. Sneyd, Special Reserve.
Captain W. H. Walker.
Temporary Staff-Serjeant C. Marson.
Serjeant A. Lawie.

Army Chaplains Department.

Rev. W. H. Abbot, Temporary Chaplain to the Forces, 4th Class.
Rev. J. E. Adams, Temporary Chaplain to the Forces, 4th Class.
Rev. F. I. Anderson, Chaplain to the Forces, 3rd Class.
Rev. J. Blackbourne, Chaplain to the Forces, 1st Class.
Rev. H. W. Blackburne, Chaplin to the Forces, 3rd Class.
Rev. A. H. Boyd, Temporary Chaplain to the Forces, 4th Class.
Rev. A. T. Cape, Temporary Chaplain to the Forces, 4th Class.
Rev. G. H. Colbeck, Chaplain to the Forces, 3rd Class.
Rev. W. Drury, Chaplain to the Forces, 3rd Class.
Rev. W. Forrest, Chaplain to the Forces, 2nd Class.
Rev. H. V. Gill, Temporary Chaplain to the Forces, 4th Class.
Rev. F. H. Gillingham, Temporary Chaplain to the Forces, 4th Class.
Rev. P. W. Guinness, D.S.O., Chaplain to the Forces, 4th Class.
Rev. J. Gwynn, Temporary Chaplain to the Forces, 4th Class.
Rev. Canon D. J. S. Hunt, Chaplain to the Territorial Force, 2nd Class.
Rev. W. S. Jaffray, Chaplain to the Forces, 1st Class.
Rev. W. Keatinge, Chaplain to the Forces, 1st Class.
Rev. F. J. King, Chaplain to the Forces, 3rd Class.
Rev. J. C. Kinnear, Chaplain to the Forces, 4th Class.
Rev. S. S. Knapp, Temporary Chaplain to the Forces, 4th Class.
Rev. M. P. McCready, Chaplain to the Forces, 4th Class.
Rev. E. G. F. Macpherson, Chaplain to the Forces, 1st Class.

MENTIONED IN DESPATCHES

Rev. Henry Marshall, Chaplain to the Forces, 4th Class.
Rev. H. C. Meeke, Chaplain to the Forces, 3rd Class.
Rev. J. P. Molony, Temporary Chaplain to the Forces, 4th Class.
Rev. J. C. Moth, Chaplain to the Forces, 3rd Class.
Rev. J. F. O'Shaughnessy, Temporary Chaplain to the Forces, 4th Class.
Rev. H. T. A. Peacey, Temporary Chaplain to the Forces, 4th Class.
Rev. Hon. M. B. Peel, Temporary Chaplain to the Forces, 4th Class.
Rev. A. E. Popham, Temporary Chaplain to the Forces, 4th Class..
Rev. E. J. Powell, Temporary Chaplain to the Forces, 4th Class.
Rev. W. H. Sarchet, Temporary Chaplain to the Forces, 4th Class.
Rev. J. M. Simms, D.D., K.H.C., Principal Chaplain.
Rev.. F. W. Stewart, Chaplain to the Forces, 3rd Class.
Rev. N. S Talbot, Temporary Chaplain to the Forces, 4th Class.
Rev. E. H. Thorold, Chaplain to the Forces, 4th Class.
Rev. J. G. W. Tuckey, Chaplain to the Forces, 1st Class.
Rev. J. R. Walkey, Chaplain to the Forces, 4th Class.
Rev. O. S. Watkins, Temporary Chaplain to the Forces, 2nd Class.

ECCLESIASTICAL ESTABLISHMENT, BENGAL.

Rev. R. J. B. Irwin.
Rev. T. H. Dixon.

ARMY ORDNANCE DEPARTMENT.

Lieutenant-Colonel A. S. Baker.
Commissary of Ordnance and Honorary Major W. W. Blades.
Captain W. H. McN. Campbell, Royal Artillery.
Honorary Major J. R. Collacott, Inspector of Ordnance Machinery, 1st Class.
Assistant Commissary and Honorary Lieutenant G. Cornhill.
Honorary Major P. G. Davies, Inspector of Ordnance Machinery, 1st Class.
Major E. M. de Smidt.
Captain A. C. V. Gibson, Royal Artillery.
Major F. W. R. Hill, D.S.O.
Major C. H. Saunders.
Honorary Captain P. W. M. Sparey, Inspector of Ordnance Machinery, 2nd Class.
Assistant Commissary and Honorary Lieutenant S. N. Smith, temporary Deputy Commissary of Ordnance and Honorary Captain.
Lieutenant-Colonel W. D C. Trimnell.

ARMY ORDNANCE CORPS.

Armament Staff-Serjeant J. J. Callegari (killed).
Staff-Serjeant (Acting Sub-Conductor) L. J. Collins.
Conductor A. M. Collison.

MENTIONED IN DESPATCHES

Acting-Serjeant T. B. Daniels.
Armament Serjeant-Major B. Graves.
Armourer Quartermaster-Serjeant B. Honnor.
Armourer Staff-Serjeant H. J. Horner (killed).
Conductor F. L. Jones.
Acting Staff-Serjeant F. G. Leaney.
Sub-Conductor H. S. Lewarn.
Acting Serjeant W. H. F. Mockler.
Conductor D. Murray.
Armament Staff-Serjeant F. E. Peake.
Conductor H. Seyde.
Armament Serjeant-Major A. Wiltshire.

QUEEN ALEXANDRA'S IMPERIAL MILITARY NURSING SERVICE.

Matron-in-Chief Miss E. M. McCarthy, R.R.C.
Acting Matron Miss A. F. Byers.
Matron Miss F. M. Hodgkins.
Matron Miss H. W. Reid.
Matron Miss G. M. Richards.
Sister Miss G. M. Allen.
Sister Miss S. K. Bills.
Sister Miss J. H. Congleton.
Acting Sister Miss M. C. Corbishley.
Sister Miss H. M. Drage.
Sister Miss H. Hartigan.
Sister Miss G. A. Howe.
Sister Miss E. J. M. Keene.
Sister Miss E. M. Lang.
Acting Sister Miss C. MacK. MacRae.
Acting Sister Miss K. M. Mathews.
Sister Miss G. M. Smith.
Sister Miss M. Steenson.
Sister Miss M. S. Williams.
Staff Nurse Miss D. M. Best.
Staff Nurse Miss M. F. Davies.
Staff Nurse Miss M. M. Roberts.

QUEEN ALEXANDRA'S IMPERIAL MILITARY NURSING SERVICE (RESERVE).

Miss N. Adler.
Miss J. Barclay Smith.
Miss E. G. Barrett.
Miss E. D. Devenish-Meares.
Miss C. Elston.
Miss E. M. Hansard.
Miss B. J. D. Reid.
Miss L. M. Thurling.

MENTIONED IN DESPATCHES

TERRITORIAL FORCE NURSING SERVICE.
Miss M. A. Brander.
Miss A. H. Ivin.
Miss E. A. Jackson.
Miss P. M. Morris.
Miss H. G. Palin.
Miss C. Webber.

CIVIL HOSPITALS RESERVE.
Miss M. W. Bannister, Royal Infirmary, Hull.
Miss I. E. M. Barbier, Royal Infirmary, Bristol.
Miss M. Clark, Royal Southern Hospital, Liverpool.
Miss M. A. Doherty, Dr. Steeven's Hospital, Dublin.
Miss E. Fearnley, St. Thomas's Hospital, London (dead).
Miss E. T. Ferguson, Royal Infirmary, Perth.
Miss F. Harley, St. Thomas's Hospital, London.
Miss A. Healey, Dr. Steeven's Hospital, Dublin.
Miss K. Johnston, City of Dublin Hospital, Dublin.
Miss V. M. Kiddle, Guy's Hospital, London.
Miss M. R. Knight, Westminster Hospital, London.
Miss E. M. Le Sueur, University College Hospital, London.
Miss S. C. McIntosh, Royal Infirmary, Edinburgh.
Miss M. Oakey, General Hospital, Birmingham.
Miss L. O. Peet, Derby Royal Infirmary, Derby.
Miss A. Wainwright, The London Hospital, London.

ARMY PAY CORPS.
Lieutenant-Colonel A. W. B. Buckle, Staff Paymaster.
Major R. S. Hutchison, Paymaster (temporary Staff Paymaster).
Assistant Paymaster and Honorary Lieutenant T. Knapp.
Staff Quartermaster-Serjeant H. M. Courtney.
Serjeant R. S. Horn.

MILITARY PROVOST STAFF CORPS.
Quartermaster-Serjeant F. A. Clements.

MILITARY MOUNTED POLICE.
Lance-Corporal G. Ballard.
Lance-Corporal T. Cannon.
Serjeant C. H. Dale.
Quartermaster-Serjeant T. Harris.
Serjeant A. Huggett.
Lance-Corporal A. Ivens.
Serjeant-Major T. Loughnane.
Serjeant J. McLintock.
Lance-Corporal D. G. S. Porter.
Serjeant W. Sweet.

MENTIONED IN DESPATCHES

CORPS OF MILITARY POLICE.
Serjeant C. W. Drake.
Lance-Corporal W. Mewett.
Serjeant R. Waller.

AUSTRALIAN ARMY MEDICAL CORPS.
Lieutenant-Colonel (temporary Lieutenant-Colonel in Army) W. L'E Eames, C.B.
Serjeant-Major C. R. Williams.
Serjeant P. W. Chapman.

AUSTRALIAN NURSING SERVICE.
Matron Miss I. Greaves.

STAFF, 1ST CANADIAN DIVISION.
Lieutenant-Colonel (temporary Colonel) G. La F. Foster, Canadian Army Medical Corps.
Lieutenant-Colonel R. J. F. Hayter (Major, Cheshire Regiment).
Lieutenant-Colonel G. B. Hughes.
Lieutenant-Colonel H. Kemmis-Betty.
Lieutenant-Colonel (temporary Colonel) T. B. Wood, Royal Artillery
Brevet Lieutenant-Colonel (temporary Colonel) C. F. Romer, C.B. Royal Dublin Fusiliers.
Major C. H. L. Beatty, D.S.O.
Major (temporary Lieutenant-Colonel) G. C. W. Gordon-Hall, Yorkshire Light Infantry.
Captain (temporary Major) H. A. Chisholm, Canadian Army Medical Corps.
Captain R. P. Clark.
Captain E. S. Clifford, D.S.O.
Captain (temporary Lieutenant-Colonel) J. H. MacBrien.
Captain E. W. Pope.
Captain F. B. Ware.

DIVISIONAL ARTILLERY, 1ST CANADIAN DIVISION.
Major F. F. Lambarde (Reserve of Officers).
Second Lieutenant (temporary Lieutenant) G. M. Harbord, Royal Artillery.
Lieutenant A. G. F. Ramsden, Royal Field Artillery, Special Reserve.
Corporal H. Pobjoy.
Driver F. T. Marks.

1ST CANADIAN ARTILLERY BRIGADE.
Captain L. V. M. Cosgrave (Brigade Staff).
Captain D. A. White (2nd Battery).
Corporal L. A. Lamplough (1st Battery) (killed).

MENTIONED IN DESPATCHES

2ND CANADIAN ARTILLERY BRIGADE.
Lieutenant-Colonel J. J. Creelman (Brigade Staff).
Major E. G. Hanson (5th Battery).
Lieutenant H. F. Geary (6th Battery).
Lieutenant H. M. Savage (7th Battery).
Corporal A. S. Hicks (8th Battery).
Corporal S. Shirley (7th Battery) (killed).

3RD CANADIAN ARTILLERY BRIGADE.
Lieutenant-Colonel J. H. Mitchell (Brigade Staff).
Major H. G. Carscallen (11th Battery).
Major W. B. King (10th Battery).
Lieutenant E. A. Greene (9th Battery).
Lieutenant A. C. Ryerson (Ammunition Column).
Lieutenant J. H. Scandrett (12th Battery).
Battery Serjeant-Major R. Wildgoose (9th Battery).
Serjeant W. Barnacal (11th Battery).
Serjeant J. Hayward (Ammunition Column).
Serjeant M. Jacobs (Brigade Staff).

CANADIAN ENGINEERS.
Lieutenant-Colonel C. J. Armstrong.
Major G. B. Wright (3rd Field Company) (killed).
Captain A. Macphail (1st Field Company).
Lieutenant H. F. H. Hertzberg (2nd Field Company).
Serjeant-Major S. A. Ridgwell.
Company Serjeant-Major G. R. Chetwynd (2nd Field Company).
Serjeant G. R. Turner (3rd Field Company).
Second Corporal A. J. L. Evans (1st Field Company).

1ST CANADIAN DIVISIONAL SIGNAL COMPANY.
Major F. A. Lister.
Captain F. C. Kilburn.

CANADIAN DIVISIONAL CYCLIST COMPANY.
Lieutenant J. R. Dennistoun.

PRINCESS PATRICIA'S CANADIAN LIGHT INFANTRY.
Temporary Lieutenant-Colonel H. C. Buller (Captain, Rifle Brigade).
Temporary Lieutenant-Colonel F. D. Farquhar, D.S.O. (Major, Coldstream Guards) (killed).
Major A. H. Gault, D.S.O.
Lieutenant G. W. Colquhoun.
Lieutenant C. E. Crabbe.
Lieutenant H. W. Niven.
Lieutenant T. M. Papineau.
Serjeant H. Laing.

MENTIONED IN DESPATCHES

1st Canadian Battalion.
Major A. E. Kimmins.
Captain J. H. Parks.
Serjeant W. E. Jones.
Private M. J. Aiken.
Private G. Moore.

2nd Canadian Battalion.
Lieutenant-Colonel D. Watson.
Captain E. C. Culling.
Captain A. G. Turner.
Serjeant E. W. Bussell.

3rd Canadian Battalion.
Captain J. H. Lyne-Evans.
Lance-Corporal E. H. Minns.

4th Canadian Battalion.
Captain (temporary Lieutenant-Colonel) A. P. Birchall (Royal Fusiliers) (killed).
Major J. Ballantine.
Captain J. D. Glover (killed).
Corporal G. Rogers.
Private E. Shipman.
Private F. L. Wright.

5th Canadian Battalion.
Lieutenant-Colonel G. S. Tuxford.
Major G. S. T. Pragnell.
Lieutenant J. M. Currie.
Private N. McIvor.

7th Canadian Battalion.
Lieutenant-Colonel W. F. R. Hart-McHarg (killed).
Major V. W. Odlum.
Corporal J. W. Odlum (killed).

8th Canadian Battalion.
Temporary Lieutenant-Colonel L. J. Lipsett (Major, Royal Irish Regiment).
Major H. H. Matthews.
Lieutenant N. G. M. McLeod.
Lieutenant J. M. Scott.
Temporary Lieutenant M. B. W. Smith-Rewse (killed).
Regimental Serjeant-Major W. M. Robertson (missing).
Lance-Corporal J. A. K. Payne (missing).

MENTIONED IN DESPATCHES

10TH CANADIAN BATTALION.

Lieutenant-Colonel R. L. Boyle (died of wounds).
Major J. McLaren (killed).
Captain C. G. Arthur.

13TH CANADIAN BATTALION.

Lieutenant-Colonel F. O. W. Loomis.
Major D. R. McCuaig.
Major E. C. Norsworthy (killed).
Regimental Serjeant-Major (temporary Lieutenant) J. Jeffery.
Company Serjeant-Major J. Trainor.

14TH CANADIAN BATTALION.

Lieutenant-Colonel W. W. Burland.
Lieutenant-Colonel F. S. Meighen.
Company Serjeant-Major A. Hancock.
Serjeant A. E. Hawkins.

15TH CANADIAN BATTALION.

Major W. R. Marshall.
Captain G. M. Alexander.
Regimental-Serjeant-Major J. Keith.
Corporal W. J. Flood.
Private M. K. Kerr.

16TH CANADIAN BATTALION.

Lieutenant-Colonel R. G. E. Leckie.
Major G. Godson Godson.
Captain C. M. Merritt (killed).
Corporal G. C. Heath (dead).
Lance-Corporal A. W. Minchin.
Private J. W. Bizley.

CANADIAN ARMY SERVICE CORPS.

Lieutenant-Colonel W. A. Simson.
Lieutenant R. H. Webb.
Serjeant J. G. Kinsell (attached No. 3 Field Ambulance).
Private J. D. Sharman.

CANADIAN ARMY MEDICAL CORPS.

Lieutenant-Colonel F. S. L. Ford.
Lieutenant-Colonel D. W. McPherson.
Lieutenant-Colonel A. E. Ross.
Lieutenant-Colonel A. T. Shillington.
Lieutenant-Colonel W. L. Watt.

MENTIONED IN DESPATCHES

Major J. L. Duval.
Major E. B. Hardy.
Captain F. C. Bell.
Captain G. P. Brown.
Captain A. S. Donaldson.
Captain J. J. Fraser.
Captain R. H. McGibbon.
Captain T. H. McKillip.
Captain J. D. McQueen.
Captain E. L. Stone.
Lieutenant A. K. Haywood, attached 3rd Canadian Battalion.
Quartermaster-Serjeant G. S. Cooke.
Staff-Serjeant H. G. B. Butt.
Staff-Serjeant A. J. B. Milborne.
Staff-Serjeant A. E. Rotsey.
Serjeant T. M. Brown.
Serjeant J. W. McKay (dead).
Serjeant W. B. Smith.
Lance-Corporal W. McDonald.
Private A. Bartley.
Private R. W. Chester.
Private J. Dalton.
Private C. J. E. Farr.
Private W. J. Holloway.
Private R. L. Head.
Private F. J. Lisney.
Private W. M. Leishman.
Private A. Millen.
Private H. G. Stewart.
Private C. B. Tompkins.
Private E. Trottier.
Private J. G. Youldon.

CANADIAN NURSING SERVICE.

Matron Miss E. Campbell.
Nursing Sister Miss M. P. Richardson.

INDIAN ARMY.

4TH CAVALRY.

Lieutenant-Colonel H. G. Stainforth.
Captain G. Howson.

5TH CAVALRY.

Lieutenant A. G. J. Copeland, attached 32nd (Divisional Signal) Company.

15TH LANCERS.

Lieutenant-Colonel H. C. Ricketts.

MENTIONED IN DESPATCHES

20TH DECCAN HORSE.
Captain A. C. Ross, D.S.O.
Lieutenant F. B. N. Tinley.

22ND CAVALRY (FRONTIER FORCE).
Lieutenant E. A. Somerville, attached 3rd Skinner's Horse.
Lance-Dafador Zahook Ali, attached 3rd Skinner's Horse.

25TH CAVALRY (FRONTIER FORCE).
Lieutenant J. Nethersole, attached 2nd Life Guards.

28TH LIGHT CAVALRY.
Sowar Mohammed Husain, attached Lahore Casualty Clearing Station.

34TH POONA HORSE.
Lieutenant F. A. de Pass, V.C. (killed).

38TH CENTRAL INDIA HORSE.
Captain J. Gourlie, attached 16th Lancers.

QUEEN VICTORIA'S OWN CORPS OF GUIDES (FRONTIER FORCE).
Lieutenant-Colonel P. C. Eliott-Lockhart, D.S.O. (died of wounds).

1ST KING GEORGE'S OWN SAPPERS AND MINERS.
Captain A. J. G. Bird, D.S.O., Royal Engineers (No. 4 Company).
Captain E. F. J. Hill, Royal Engineers (No. 3 Company).
Captain P. C. S. Hobart, Royal Engineers (No. 3 Company).
Lieutenant E. L. Farley, Royal Engineers.
Lieutenant E. O. Wheeler, Royal Engineers (No. 3 Company).

MILITARY WORKS SERVICES.
Captain E. K. Squires, Royal Engineers (attached 3rd Sappers and Miners).

SAPPERS AND MINERS.—NO. 31 (DIVISIONAL SIGNAL) COMPANY.
Captain F. W. Townend, Royal Engineers (died of wounds).

6TH JAT LIGHT INFANTRY.
Captain R. C. Ross.

14TH SIKHS.
Captain J. A. S. Daniell, attached 15th Sikhs.
Lieutenant C. McD. Allardice, attached 47th Sikhs (killed).

15TH SIKHS.
Lieutenant-Colonel J. Hill, D.S.O.
Lieutenant A. E. Barstow.
Lieutenant J. G. Smyth.

MENTIONED IN DESPATCHES

30TH PUNJABIS.
Captain C. J. Torrie, D.S.O. (Commanding 35th Signal Company).

34TH SIKH PIONEERS.
Captain C. E. Hunt.
Captain G. S. M. Hutchinson.

35TH SIKHS.
Lieutenant-Colonel O. G. Gunning, attached 47th Sikhs.

1ST BATTALION 39TH GARHWAL RIFLES.
Lieutenant A. H. Mankelow (killed).
Jemadar Bishan Sing Rowat.
2nd Class Sub-Assistant Surgeon Ramkrishna Ganpat Shinde.

2ND BATTALION 39TH GARHWAL RIFLES.
Lieutenant-Colonel D. H. Drake-Brockman.
Captain D. A. Blair.
Captain G. W. Burton.
Jemadar Ghantu Sing Bisht (killed).
Jemadar Pancham Sing Mahar.
Jemadar Sangram Sing Negi.

41ST DOGRAS.
Lieutenant-Colonel H. W. Cruddas.
Major E. Colson.
Captain W. E. Fleming.
Lieutenant E. L. E. Lindop.

47TH SIKHS.
Lieutenant-Colonel H. L. Richardson.
Captain W. H. Ralston.
Captain E. C. Talbot (died of wounds).
Lieutenant H. S. Cormack, M.B., Indian Medical Service.

52ND SIKHS (FRONTIER FORCE).
Captain P. S. Hore, attached 58th Rifles (killed).

55TH COKE'S RIFLES (FRONTIER FORCE).
Lieutenant F. C. De Butts, attached 31st (Divisional Signal) Company.
Havildar Hazrat Gul, attached 57th Rifles.
Sepoy Mir Kasim, attached 57th Rifles.

57TH WILDE'S RIFLES (FRONTIER FORCE).
Major E. L. Swifte.
Major T. J. Willans.

MENTIONED IN DESPATCHES

Captain and Adjutant W. S. Trail.
Lieutenant E. K. Fowler.
Subadar I. O. M. Arsla Khan Bahadur.
Sepoy Ajab Nur.
Sepoy Jagat Ram.
Sepoy Ram Das.
Sepoy Sher Singh.

58TH VAUGHAN'S RIFLES (FRONTIER FORCE).
Major A. G. Thomson.

59TH SCINDE RIFLES (FRONTIER FORCE).
Lieutenant-Colonel C. C. Fenner (killed).
Major T. L. Leeds.
Captain T. Reed (killed).
Lieutenant J. A. M. Scobie.
Subadar Parbat Chand.

69TH PUNJABIS.
Captain H. H. McGann, attached 1/4th Gurkhas.

84TH PUNJABIS.
Captain F. F. Hodgson, attached 58th Rifles (died of wounds).

96TH BERAR INFANTRY.
Captain C. H. Jardine, attached 9th Bhopal Infantry.

107TH PIONEERS.
Lieutenant-Colonel N. M. C. Stevens.
Captain E. B. Mangin.

113TH INFANTRY.
Captain J. F. Parkin, attached 2/39th Garhwal Rifles.

121ST PIONEERS.
Captain A. T. Sheringham, attached 107th Pioneers.

123RD OUTRAM'S RIFLES
Captain W. Odell, attached 125th Rifles.
Lieutenant C. F. F. Moore, attached 1/4th Gurkhas

129TH BALUCHIS.
Major J. A. Hannyngton, C.M.G.
Major H. W. R. Potter (missing).
Lieutenant F. M. Griffith-Griffin.
Lieutenant H. V. Lewis.

MENTIONED IN DESPATCHES

1st Battalion 1st Gurkha Rifles.
Major C. Bliss, C.I.E. (died of wounds).
Captain W. J. Evans.
Captain G. S. Kennedy (killed).
Captain H. I. Money (killed).

2nd Battalion 2nd Gurkha Rifles.
Major E. R. P. Boileau.
Major D. M. Watt, D.S.O.
Captain A. D. Smith.
Lieutenant E. J. Corse-Scott.
Lance-Naik Bhagat Bahadur Gurung.

2nd Battalion 3rd Gurkha Rifles.
Lieutenant-Colonel V. A. Ormsby.
Major A. B. Tillard, D.S.O.
Captain H. H. Grigg (killed).
Captain J. T. Lodwick, D.S.O.
Subadar Bhim Sing Thapa.
Subadar-Major Gambhir Sing Gurung.

1st Battalion 4th Gurkha Rifles.
Major B. U. Nicolay.
Major D. C. Young (killed).
Captain L. P. Collins, D.S.O.
Captain M. T. Cramer-Roberts.
Captain C. M. T. Hogg.
Captain D. Inglis (killed).

1st Battalion 7th Gurkha Rifles.
Lieutenant L. C. C. Rogers (died of wounds).
Rifleman Dil Rurshad, attached Lahore Casualty Clearing Station.

1st Battalion 9th Gurkha Rifles.
Lieutenant-Colonel G. T. Widdicombe.
Lieutenant R. G. H. Murray.

10th Gurkha Rifles.
Captain L. A. Bethell, attached 2/2nd Gurkha Rifles.

Supply and Transport Corps.
Lieutenant-Colonel C. H. G. Moore, D.S.O.
Major A. K. Heyland.
Major W. F. Smith, Meerut Divisional Train.
Major H. N. Young.

MENTIONED IN DESPATCHES

Captain G. W. Bond, Lahore Divisional Train.
Captain H. F. E. MacMahon.
Conductor R. J. Holmes.
Conductor G. Leitch, 32nd Mule Corps.
Conductor J. A. Morris.
Sub-Conductor A. E. Bantock.
Sub-Conductor C. Franklin.
Sub-Conductor W. L. Stevenson.
Sub-Conductor W. H. Thomas.
Staff-Serjeant H. Burdett, 11th Mule Corps.
Staff-Serjeant B. Grainge, 2nd Mule Corps.
Staff-Serjeant F. G. Levings, 9th Mule Corps.
Staff-Serjeant J. Mitchell.
Staff-Serjeant E. T. Walsh, attached Lahore Casualty Clearing Station.

QUEEN ALEXANDRA'S MILITARY NURSING SERVICE FOR INDIA.

Lady Superintendent Miss P. F. Watt.
Senior Nursing Sister Miss H. A. M. Rait.
Nursing Sister Miss E. Kelso.

INDIAN MEDICAL SERVICE.

Lieutenant F. J. Anderson, 111th Indian Field Ambulance.
Major P. P. Atal (killed).
Lieutenant-Colonel H. J. K. Bamfield.
Major R. M. Barron, 113th Indian Field Ambulance.
Major H. Boulton, M.B., D.A.D.M.S., Meerut Division.
Lieutenant-Colonel C. H. Bowle-Evans, M.B., Lucknow Casualty Clearing Station.
Lieutenant P. F. Gow, M.B.
Lieutenant-Colonel H. C. R. Hime, M.B., Royal Army Medical Corps (attached).
Major H. M. H. Melhuish, 112th Indian Field Ambulance.
Major R. A. Needham, M.B.
Major W. H. Odlum, 112th Indian Field Ambulance.
Captain J. S. O'Neill, M.B.
Lieutenant-Colonel F. R. Ozzard.
Captain D. H. Rai, M.B., attached 6th Jats.
Captain C. H. Reinhold, 111th Indian Field Ambulance.
Captain A. L. Sheppard, M.B.
Captain John Taylor, M.B., attached 1/39th Garhwal Rifles.
Major W. L. Trafford, M.B., F.R.C.S.
Lieutenant-Colonel F. Wall.
Lieutenant-Colonel W. W. White, M.D., 128th Indian Field Ambulance.

MENTIONED IN DESPATCHES

INDIAN SUBORDINATE MEDICAL DEPARTMENT.

Senior Assistant Surgeon and Honorary Lieutenant Macqueen, K.G.S.
1st Class Assistant Surgeon J. A. H. Holmes.
1st Class Assistant Surgeon W. J. S. Maine.
2nd Class Assistant Surgeon M. C. R. Rodgers.
3rd Class Assistant Surgeon B. J. Bouche.
3rd Class Assistant Surgeon A. W. Cummins.
3rd Class Assistant Surgeon H. A. Fox.
3rd Class Assistant Surgeon A. G. L. Fraser.
4th Class Assistant Surgeon A. F. J. D'Arcy.
4th Class Assistant Surgeon E. R. Hill.
4th Class Assistant Surgeon J. W. Perkins.
1st Class Senior Sub-Assistant Surgeon Gauri Shankan.
1st Class Sub-Assistant Surgeon S. Jasudasan.
1st Class Sub-Assistant Surgeon Lachmann Das.
1st Class Sub-Assistant Surgeon Muhammad Raza Khan.
1st Class Sub-Assistant Surgeon Narayan-parshad Sukul.
1st Class Sub-Assistant Surgeon Salagram.
3rd Class Sub-Assistant Surgeon Ganpat Kanoji Rao Rane.
3rd Class Sub-Assistant Surgeon Raj Singh.
3rd Class Sub-Assistant Surgeon Upendra Kumar Ganguli.

INDIAN ARMY BEARER CORPS.

Naik Wadhawa.

MISCELLANEOUS—INDIAN ARMY.

Conductor A. J. Cameron, Chief Clerk, Indian Cavalry Corps.
Conductor G. W. Twiddy, Madras Miscellaneous List.
Sub-Conductor W. Forsyth, India Miscellaneous List.
Sub-Conductor C. G. Jackson, India Miscellaneous List.
Sub-Conductor F. C. Marks, India Miscellaneous List.
Serjeant-Major A. Hirtes, Unattached List, Indian Subordinate Veterinary Establishment.
Staff-Serjeant E. W. Smith, India Miscellaneous List.
Staff-Serjeant F. Church, India Miscellaneous List.

VII. THE SECOND BATTLE OF YPRES

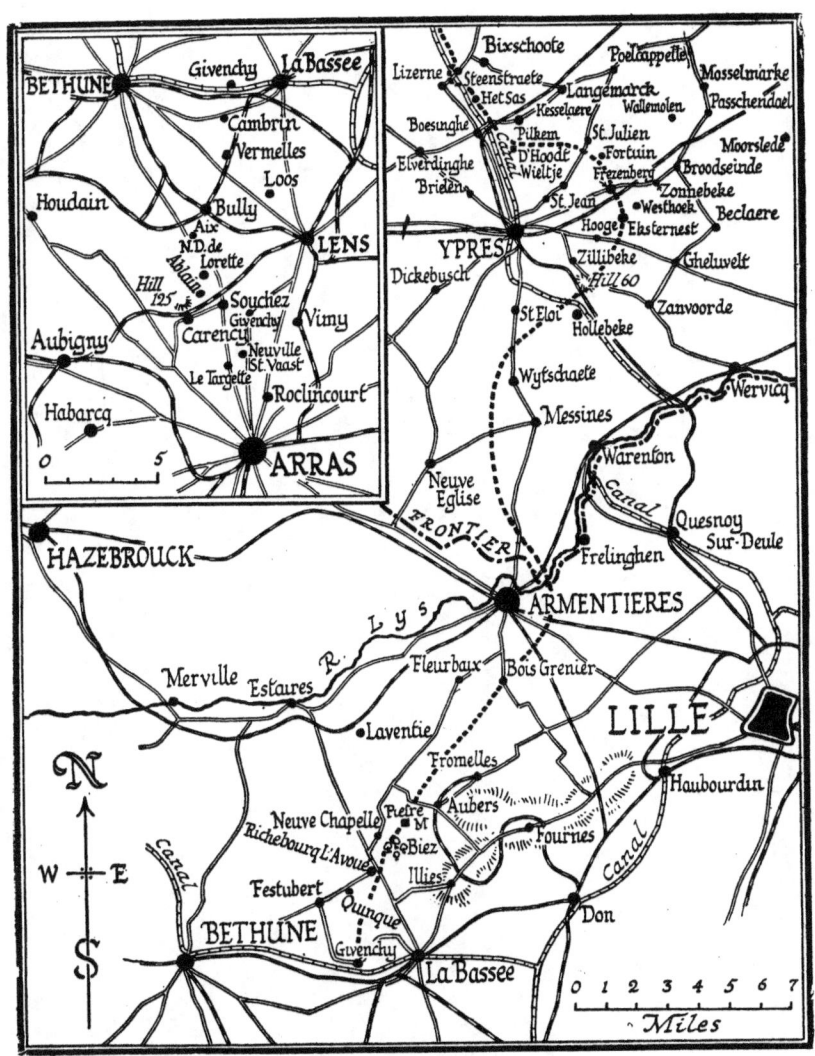

The Second Battle of Ypres.

VII : France, 15th June, 1915.

To Field-Marshal Earl Kitchener of Khartoum, K.P., G.C.B., O.M., etc.

My Lord,

I HAVE the honour to report that since the date of my last despatch (5th April, 1915) the Army in France under my command has been heavily engaged opposite both flanks of the line held by the British Forces.

1. In the North the town and district of Ypres have once more in this campaign been successfully defended against vigorous and sustained attacks made by large forces of the enemy, and supported by a mass of heavy and field artillery, which, not only in number, but also in weight and calibre, is superior to any concentration of guns which has previously assailed that part of the line.

In the South a vigorous offensive has again been taken by troops of the First Army, in the course of which a large area of entrenched and fortified ground has been captured from the enemy, whilst valuable support has been afforded to the attack which our Allies have carried on with such marked success against the enemy's positions to the east of Arras and Lens.

2. I much regret that during the period under report the fighting has been characterised on the enemy's side by a cynical and barbarous disregard of the well-known usages of civilised war and a flagrant defiance of the Hague Convention.

All the scientific resources of Germany have apparently been brought into play to produce a gas of so virulent and poisonous a nature that any human being brought into contact with it is first paralysed and then meets with a lingering and agonising death.

The enemy has invariably preceded, prepared and

THE SECOND BATTLE OF YPRES

supported his attacks by a discharge in stupendous volume of these poisonous gas fumes whenever the wind was favourable.

Such weather conditions have only prevailed to any extent in the neighbourhood of Ypres, and there can be no doubt that the effect of these poisonous fumes materially influenced the operations in that theatre, until experience suggested effective counter-measures, which have since been so perfected as to render them innocuous.

The brain power and thought which has evidently been at work before this unworthy method of making war reached the pitch of efficiency which has been demonstrated in its practice shows that the Germans must have harboured these designs for a long time.

As a soldier I cannot help expressing the deepest regret and some surprise that an Army which hitherto has claimed to be the chief exponent of the chivalry of war should have stooped to employ such devices against brave and gallant foes.

3. On the night of Saturday, April 17th, a commanding hill which afforded the enemy excellent artillery observation toward the West and North-West was successfully mined and captured. This hill, known as Hill 60, lies opposite the northern extremity of the line held by the 2nd Corps.

The operation was planned and the mining commenced by Major-General Bulfin before the ground was handed over to the troops under Lieutenant-General Sir Charles Fergusson, under whose supervision the operation was carried out.

The mines were successfully fired at 7 p.m. on the 17th instant, and immediately afterwards the hill was attacked and gained, without difficulty, by the 1st Battalion Royal West Kent Regiment, and the 2nd Battalion King's Own Scottish Borderers. The attack was well supported by the Divisional Artillery, assisted by French and Belgian batteries.

HILL 60

During the night several of the enemy's counter-attacks were repulsed with heavy loss, and fierce hand-to-hand fighting took place; but on the early morning of the 18th the enemy succeeded in forcing back the troops holding the right of the hill to the reverse slope, where, however, they hung on throughout the day.

On the evening of the 18th these two battalions were relieved by the 2nd Battalion West Riding Regiment, and the 2nd Battalion King's Own Yorkshire Light Infantry, who again stormed the hill under cover of heavy artillery fire, and the enemy was driven off at the point of the bayonet.

In this operation fifty-three prisoners were captured, including four officers.

On the 20th and following days many unsuccessful attacks by the enemy were made on Hill 60, which was continuously shelled by heavy artillery.

On May 1st another attempt to recapture Hill 60 was supported by great volumes of asphyxiating gas, which caused nearly all the men along a front of about 400 yards to be immediately struck down by its fumes.

The splendid courage with which the leaders rallied their men and subdued the natural tendency to panic (which is inevitable on such occasions), combined with the prompt intervention of supports, once more drove the enemy back.

A second and more severe " gas " attack, under much more favourable weather conditions, enabled the enemy to recapture this position on May 5th.

The enemy owes his success in this last attack entirely to the use of asphyxiating gas. It was only a few days later that the means, which have since proved so effective, of counteracting this method of making war were put into practice. Had it been otherwise, the enemy's attack on May 5th would most certainly have shared the fate of all the many previous attempts he had made.

THE SECOND BATTLE OF YPRES

4. It was at the commencement of the Second Battle of Ypres on the evening of the 22nd April, referred to in paragraph 1 of this report, that the enemy first made use of asphyxiating gas.

Some days previously I had complied with General Joffre's request to take over the trenches occupied by the French, and on the evening of the 22nd the troops holding the lines east of Ypres were posted as follows:

From Steenstraate to the east of Langemarck, as far as the Poelcappelle Road, a French Division.

Thence, in a south-easterly direction, toward the Passchendaele-Becelaere Road, the Canadian Division.

Thence a Division took up the line in a southerly direction east of Zonnebeke to a point west of Becelaere, whence another Division continued the line south-east to the northern limit of the Corps on its right.

Of the 5th Corps there were four battalions in Divisional Reserve about Ypres; the Canadian Division had one battalion in Divisional Reserve and the 1st Canadian Brigade in Army Reserve. An Infantry Brigade, which had just been withdrawn, after suffering heavy losses on Hill 60, was resting about Vlamertinghe.

Following a heavy bombardment, the enemy attacked the French Division at about 5 p.m., using asphyxiating gases for the first time. Aircraft reported that at about 5 p.m. thick yellow smoke had been seen issuing from the German trenches between Langemarck and Bixschoote. The French reported that two simultaneous attacks had been made east of the Ypres-Staden Railway, in which these asphyxiating gases had been employed.

What followed almost defies description. The effect of these poisonous gases was so virulent as to render the whole of the line held by the French Division mentioned above practically incapable of any action at all. It was at first impossible for anyone to realise what had actually

THE FIRST GAS ATTACK

happened. The smoke and fumes hid everything from sight, and hundreds of men were thrown into a comatose or dying condition, and within an hour the whole position had to be abandoned, together with about 50 guns.

I wish particularly to repudiate any idea of attaching the least blame to the French Division for this unfortunate incident.

After all the examples our gallant Allies have shown of dogged and tenacious courage in the many trying situations in which they have been placed throughout the course of this campaign it is quite superfluous for me to dwell on this aspect of the incident, and I would only express my firm conviction that, if any troops in the world had been able to hold their trenches in the face of such a treacherous and altogether unexpected onslaught, the French Division would have stood firm.

The left flank of the Canadian Division was thus left dangerously exposed to serious attack in flank, and there appeared to be a prospect of their being overwhelmed and of a successful attempt by the Germans to cut off the British troops occupying the salient to the East.

In spite of the danger to which they were exposed the Canadians held their ground with a magnificent display of tenacity and courage ; and it is not too much to say that the bearing and conduct of these splendid troops averted a disaster which might have been attended with the most serious consequences.

They were supported with great promptitude by the reserves of the Divisions holding the salient and by a Brigade which had been resting in billets.

Throughout the night the enemy's attacks were repulsed, effective counter-attacks were delivered, and at length touch was gained with the French right, and a new line was formed.

The 2nd London Heavy Battery, which had been

THE SECOND BATTLE OF YPRES

attached to the Canadian Division, was posted behind the right of the French Division, and, being involved in their retreat, fell into the enemy's hands. It was recaptured by the Canadians in their counter-attack, but the guns could not be withdrawn before the Canadians were again driven back.

During the night I directed the Cavalry Corps and the Northumbrian Division, which was then in general reserve, to move to the west of Ypres, and placed these troops at the disposal of the General Officer Commanding the Second Army. I also directed other reserve troops from the 3rd Corps and the First Army to be held in readiness to meet eventualities.

In the confusion of the gas and smoke the Germans succeeded in capturing the bridge at Steenstraate and some works south of Lizerne, all of which were in occupation by the French.

The enemy having thus established himself to the west of the Ypres Canal, I was somewhat apprehensive of his succeeding in driving a wedge between the French and Belgian troops at this point. I directed, therefore, that some of the reinforcements sent north should be used to support and assist General Putz, should he find difficulty in preventing any further advance of the Germans west of the canal.

At about 10 o'clock on the morning of the 23rd, connection was finally ensured between the left of the Canadian Division and the French right, about eight hundred yards east of the canal; but as this entailed the maintenance by the British troops of a much longer line than that which they had held before the attack commenced on the previous night, there were no reserves available for counter-attack until reinforcements, which were ordered up from the Second Army, were able to deploy to the east of Ypres.

Early on the morning of the 23rd I went to see General Foch, and from him I received a detailed account of what

A CRITICAL SITUATION

had happened, as reported by General Putz. General Foch informed me that it was his intention to make good the original line and regain the trenches which the French Division had lost. He expressed the desire that I should maintain my present line, assuring me that the original position would be re-established in a few days. General Foch further informed me that he had ordered up large French reinforcements, which were now on their way, and that troops from the North had already arrived to reinforce General Putz.

I fully concurred in the wisdom of the General's wish to re-establish our old line, and agreed to co-operate in the way he desired, stipulating, however, that if the position was not re-established within a limited time I could not allow the British troops to remain in so exposed a situation as that which the action of the previous twenty-four hours had compelled them to occupy.

During the whole of the 23rd the enemy's artillery was very active, and his attacks all along the front were supported by some heavy guns which had been brought down from the coast in the neighbourhood of Ostend.

The loss of the guns on the night of the 22nd prevented this fire from being kept down, and much aggravated the situation. Our positions, however, were well maintained by the vigorous counter-attacks made by the 5th Corps.

During the day I directed two Brigades of the 3rd Corps, and the Lahore Division of the Indian Corps, to be moved up to the Ypres area and placed at the disposal of the Second Army.

In the course of these two or three days many circumstances combined to render the situation east of the Ypres Canal very critical and most difficult to deal with.

The confusion caused by the sudden retirement of the French Division, and the necessity for closing up the gap and checking the enemy's advance at all costs, led to a

THE SECOND BATTLE OF YPRES

mixing up of units and a sudden shifting of the areas of command, which was quite unavoidable. Fresh units, as they came up from the South, had to be pushed into the firing line in an area swept by artillery fire, which, owing to the capture of the French guns, we were unable to keep down.

All this led to very heavy casualties; and I wish to place on record the deep admiration which I feel for the resource and presence of mind evinced by the leaders actually on the spot.

The parts taken by Major-General Snow and Brigadier-General Hull were reported to me as being particularly marked in this respect.

An instance of this occurred on the afternoon of the 24th when the enemy succeeded in breaking through the line at St. Julien.

Brigadier-General Hull, acting under the orders of Lieutenant-General Anderson, organised a powerful counter-attack with his own Brigade and some of the nearest available units. He was called upon to control, with only his Brigade Staff, parts of battalions from six separate divisions which were quite new to the ground. Although the attack did not succeed in retaking St. Julien, it effectually checked the enemy's further advance.

It was only on the morning of the 25th that the enemy were able to force back the left of the Canadian Division from the point where it had originally joined the French line.

During the night, and the early morning of the 25th, the enemy directed a heavy attack against the Division at Broodseinde cross-roads which was supported by a powerful shell fire, but he failed to make any progress.

During the whole of this time the town of Ypres and all the roads to the East and West were uninterruptedly subjected to a violent artillery fire, but in spite of this the supply of both food and ammunition was maintained throughout with order and efficiency.

THE LAHORE DIVISION

During the afternoon of the 25th many German prisoners were taken, including some officers. The hand-to-hand fighting was very severe, and the enemy suffered heavy loss.

During the 26th the Lahore Division and a Cavalry Division were pushed up into the fighting line, the former on the right of the French, the latter in support of the 5th Corps.

In the afternoon the Lahore Division, in conjunction with the French right, succeeded in pushing the enemy back some little distance toward the North, but their further advance was stopped owing to the continual employment by the enemy of asphyxiating gas.

On the right of the Lahore Division the Northumberland Infantry Brigade advanced against St. Julien and actually succeeded in entering, and for a time occupying, the southern portion of that village. They were, however, eventually driven back, largely owing to gas, and finally occupied a line a short way to the South. This attack was most successfully and gallantly led by Brigadier-General Riddell, who, I regret to say, was killed during the progress of the operation.

Although no attack was made on the south-eastern side of the salient, the troops operating to the east of Ypres were subjected to heavy artillery fire from the direction which took some of the battalions, which were advancing North to the attack, in reverse.

Some gallant attempts made by the Lahore Division on the 27th, in conjunction with the French, pushed the enemy further North; but they were partially frustrated by the constant fumes of gas to which they were exposed. In spite of this, however, a certain amount of ground was gained.

The French had succeeded in retaking Lizerne, and had made some progress at Steenstraate and Het Sas; but up to the evening of the 28th no further progress had been made toward the recapture of the original line.

THE SECOND BATTLE OF YPRES

I sent instructions, therefore, to Sir Herbert Plumer, who was now in charge of the operation, to take preliminary measures for the retirement to the new line which had been fixed upon.

On the morning of the 29th I had another interview with General Foch, who informed me that strong reinforcements were hourly arriving to support General Putz, and urged me to postpone issuing orders for any retirement until the result of his attack, which was timed to commence at daybreak on the 30th, should be known. To this I agreed, and instructed Sir Herbert Plumer accordingly.

No substantial advance having been made by the French, I issued orders to Sir Herbert Plumer at one o'clock on May 1st to commence his withdrawal to the new line.

The retirement was commenced the following night, and the new line was occupied on the morning of May 4th.

I am of opinion that this retirement, carried out deliberately with scarcely any loss, and in the face of an enemy in position, reflects the greatest possible credit on Sir Herbert Plumer and those who so efficiently carried out his orders.

The successful conduct of this operation was the more remarkable from the fact that on the evening of May 2nd, when it was only half completed, the enemy made a heavy attack, with the usual gas accompaniment, on St. Julien and the line to the west of it.

An attack on a line to the east of Fortuin was made at the same time under similar conditions.

In both cases our troops were at first driven from their trenches by gas fumes, but on the arrival of the supporting battalions and two brigades of a Cavalry Division, which were sent up in support from about Potijze, all the lost trenches were regained at night.

On the 3rd May, while the retirement was still going on,

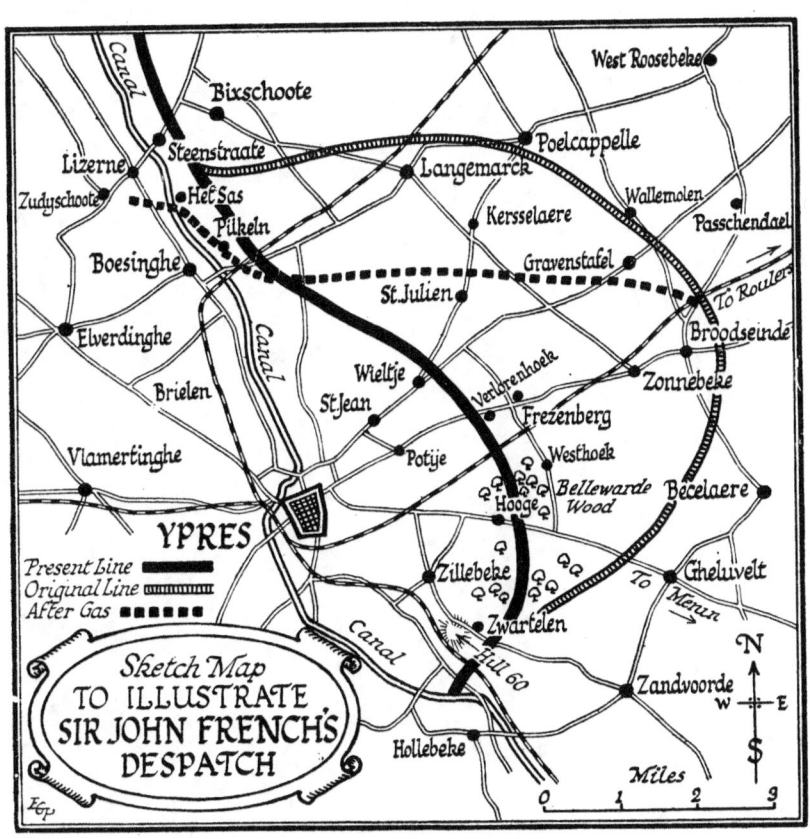

VIOLENT ARTILLERY BOMBARDMENT

another violent attack was directed on the northern face of the salient. This was also driven back with heavy loss to the enemy.

Further attempts of the enemy during the night of the 3rd to advance from the woods west of St. Julien were frustrated entirely by the fire of our artillery.

During the whole of the 4th the enemy heavily shelled the trenches we had evacuated, quite unaware that they were no longer occupied. So soon as the retirement was discovered the Germans commenced to entrench opposite our new line and to advance their guns to new positions. Our artillery, assisted by aeroplanes, caused him considerable loss in carrying out these operations.

Up to the morning of the 8th the enemy made attacks at short intervals, covered by gas, on all parts of the line to the east of Ypres, but was everywhere driven back with heavy loss.

Throughout the whole period since the first break of the line on the night of April 22nd all the troops in this area had been constantly subjected to violent artillery bombardment from a large mass of guns with an unlimited supply of ammunition. It proved impossible whilst under so vastly superior fire of artillery to dig efficient trenches, or to properly reorganise the line, after the confusion and demoralisation caused by the first great gas surprise and the subsequent almost daily gas attacks. Nor was it until after this date (May 8th) that effective preventatives had been devised and provided. In these circumstances a violent bombardment of nearly the whole of the 5th Corps front broke out at 7 a.m. on the morning of the 8th, which gradually concentrated on the front of the Division between north and south of Frezenberg. This fire completely obliterated the trenches and caused enormous losses.

The artillery bombardment was shortly followed by a heavy infantry attack, before which our line had to give way.

THE SECOND BATTLE OF YPRES

I relate what happened in Sir Herbert Plumer's own words :

" The right of one Brigade was broken about 10.15 a.m. ; then its centre, and then part of the left of the Brigade in the next section to the south. The Princess Patricia's Canadian Light Infantry, however, although suffering very heavily, stuck to their fire or support trenches throughout the day. At this time two battalions were moved to General Headquarters, 2nd line astride the Menin road to support and cover the left of their Division.

" At 12.25 p.m. the centre of a Brigade further to the left also broke ; its right battalion, however, the 1st Suffolks, which had been refused to cover a gap, still held on and were apparently surrounded and overwhelmed. Meanwhile, three more battalions had been moved up to reinforce, two other battalions were moved up in support to General Headquarters line, and an Infantry Brigade came up to the grounds of Vlamertinghe Chateau in Corps Reserve.

" At 11.30 a.m. a small party of Germans attempted to advance against the left of the British line, but were destroyed by the 2nd Essex Regiment.

" A counter attack was launched at 3.30 p.m. by the 1st York and Lancaster Regiment, 3rd Middlessx Regiment, 2nd East Surrey Regiment, 2nd Royal Dublin Fusiliers and the 1st Royal Warwickshire Regiment. The counter attack reached Frezenberg, but was eventually driven back and held up on a line running about north and south through Verlorenhoek, despite repeated efforts to advance. The 12th London Regiment on the left succeeded at great cost in reaching the original trench line, and did considerable execution with their machine gun.

" The 7th Argyll and Sutherland Highlanders and the 1st East Lancashire Regiment attacked in a north-easterly direction towards Wieltje, and connected the old trench line with the ground gained by the counter-attack, the line being consolidated during the night.

"During the night orders were received that two Cavalry Divisions would be moved up and placed at the disposal of the 5th Corps, and a Territorial Division would be moved up to be used if required.

"On the 9th the Germans again repeated their bombardment. Very heavy shell fire was concentrated for two hours on the trenches of the 2nd Gloucestershire Regiment and 2nd Cameron Highlanders, followed by an infantry attack which was successfully repulsed. The Germans again bombarded the salient, and a further attack in the afternoon succeeded in occupying 150 yards of trench. The Gloucesters counter-attacked, but suffered heavily, and the attack failed. The salient being very exposed to shell fire from both flanks, as well as in front, it was deemed advisable not to attempt to retake the trench at night, and a retrenchment was therefore dug across it.

"At 3 p.m. the enemy started to shell the whole front of the centre Division, and it was reported that the right Brigade of this Division was being heavily punished, but continued to maintain its line.

"The trenches of the Brigades on the left centre were also heavily shelled during the day and attacked by infantry. Both attacks were repulsed.

"On the 10th instant the trenches on either side of the Menin-Ypres Road were shelled very severely all the morning. The 2nd Cameron Highlanders, 9th Royal Scots, and the 3rd and 4th King's Royal Rifles, however, repulsed an attack made, under cover of gas, with heavy loss. Finally, when the trenches had been practically destroyed and a large number of the garrison buried, the 3rd King's Royal Rifles and 4th Rifle Brigade fell back to the trenches immediately west of Bellewaarde Wood. So heavy had been the shell fire that the proposal to join up the line with a switch through the wood had to be

THE SECOND BATTLE OF YPRES

abandoned, the trees broken by the shells forming an impassable entanglement.

" After a comparatively quiet night and morning (10th-11th) the hostile artillery fire was concentrated on the trenches of the 2nd Cameron Highlanders at a slightly more northern point than on the previous day. The Germans attacked in force and gained a footing in part of the trenches, but were promptly ejected by a supporting company of the 9th Royal Scots. After a second short artillery bombardment the Germans again attacked about 4.15 p.m., but were again repulsed by rifle and machine-gun fire. A third bombardment followed, and this time the Germans succeeded in gaining a trench—or rather what was left of it—a local counter-attack failing. However, during the night the enemy were again driven out. The trench by this time being practically non-existent, the garrison found it untenable under the heavy shell fire the enemy brought to bear upon it, and the trench was evacuated. Twice more did the German snipers creep back into it, and twice more they were ejected. Finally, a retrenchment was made, cutting off the salient which had been contested throughout the day. It was won owing solely to the superior weight and number of the enemy's guns, but both our infantry and our artillery took a very heavy toll of the enemy, and the ground lost has proved of little use to the enemy.

" On the remainder of the front, the day passed comparatively quietly, though most parts of the line underwent intermittent shelling by guns of various calibres.

" With the assistance of the Royal Flying Corps the 31st Heavy Battery scored a direct hit on a German gun, and the North Midland Heavy Battery got on to some German howitzers with great success.

" With the exception of another very heavy burst of shell fire against the right Division early in the morning, the 12th passed uneventfully.

SIR HERBERT PLUMER'S REPORT

"On the night of the 12th-13th the line was re-organised, the centre Division retiring into Army Reserve to rest, and their places being taken in the trenches by the two Cavalry Divisions; the Artillery and Engineers of the centre Division forming with them what was known as the 'Cavalry Force' under the command of General De Lisle.

"On the 13th the various reliefs having been completed without incident, the heaviest bombardment yet experienced broke out at 4.30 a.m., and continued with little intermission throughout the day. At about 7.45 a.m. the Cavalry Brigade astride the railway, having suffered very severely, and their trenches having been obliterated, fell back about 800 yards. The North Somerset Yeomanry on the right of the Brigade, although also suffering severely, hung on to their trenches throughout the day, and actually advanced and attacked the enemy with the bayonet. The Brigade on its right also maintained its position; as did also the Cavalry Division, except the left squadron which, when reduced to sixteen men, fell back, The 2nd Essex Regiment, realising the situation, promptly charged and retook the trench, holding it till relieved by the Cavalry. Meanwhile a counter-attack by two Cavalry Brigades was launched at 2.30 p.m., and succeeded, in spite of very heavy shrapnel and rifle fire, in regaining the original line of trenches, turning out the Germans who had entered it, and in some cases pursuing them for some distance. But a very heavy shell fire was again opened on them, and they were again compelled to retire to an irregular line in rear, principally the craters of shell holes. The enemy in their counter-attack suffered very severe losses.

"The fighting in other parts of the line was little less severe. The 1st East Lancashire Regiment were shelled out of their trenches, but their support company and the 2nd Essex Regiment, again acting on their own initiative,

THE SECOND BATTLE OF YPRES

won them back. The enemy penetrated into the farm at the north-east corner of the line, but the 1st Rifle Brigade, after a severe struggle, expelled them. The 1st Hampshire Regiment also repelled an attack, and killed every German who got within fifty yards of their trenches. The 5th London Regiment, despite very heavy casualties, maintained their position unfalteringly. At the southern end of the line the left Brigade was once again heavily shelled, as indeed was the whole front. At the end of a very hard day's fighting our line remained in its former position, with the exception of the short distance lost by one Cavalry Division. Later, the line was pushed forward, and a new line was dug in a less exposed position, slightly in rear of that originally held. The night passed quietly.

" Working parties of from 1,200 to 1,800 men have been found every night by a Territorial Division and other units for work on rear lines of defence, in addition to the work performed by the garrisons in reconstructing the front line trenches which were daily destroyed by shell fire.

" The work performed by the Royal Flying Corps has been invaluable. Apart from the hostile aeroplanes actually destroyed, our airmen have prevented a great deal of aerial reconnaissance by the enemy, and have registered a large number of targets with our artillery.

" There have been many cases of individual gallantry. As instances may be given the following :

" During one of the heavy attacks made against our infantry gas was seen rolling forward from the enemy's trenches. Private Lynn of the 2nd Lancashire Fusiliers at once rushed to the machine gun without waiting to adjust his respirator. Single-handed he kept his gun in action the whole time the gas was rolling over, actually hoisting it on the parapet to get a better field of fire. Although nearly suffocated by the gas, he poured a stream of lead into the advancing enemy and checked their attack.

He was carried to his dug-out, but, hearing another attack was imminent, he tried to get back to his gun. Twenty-four hours later he died in great agony from the effects of the gas.

"A young subaltern in a cavalry regiment went forward alone one afternoon to reconnoitre. He got into a wood, 1,200 yards in front of our lines, which he found occupied by Germans, and came back with the information that the enemy had evacuated a trench and were digging another—information which proved most valuable to the artillery as well as to his own unit.

"A patrol of two officers and a non-commissioned officer of the 1st Cambridgeshires went out one night to reconnoitre a German trench 350 yards away. Creeping along the parapet of the trench, they heard sounds indicating the presence of six or seven of the enemy. Further on they heard deep snores, apparently proceeding from a dug-out immediately beneath them. Although they knew that the garrison of the trench outnumbered them, they decided to procure an identification. Unfortunately, in pulling out a clasp knife with which to cut off the sleeper's identity disc, one of the officer's revolvers went off. A conversation in agitated whispers broke out in the German trench, but the patrol crept safely away, the garrison being too startled to fire.

"Despite the very severe shelling to which the troops had been subjected, which obliterated trenches and caused very many casualties, the spirit of all ranks remains excellent. The enemy's losses, particularly on the 10th and 13th, have unquestionably been serious. On the latter day they evacuated trenches (in face of the cavalry counterattack) in which were afterwards found quantities of equipment and some of their own wounded. The enemy have been seen stripping our dead, and on three occasions men in khaki have been seen advancing."

The fight went on by the exchange of desultory shell

THE SECOND BATTLE OF YPRES

and rifle fire, but without any remarkable incident until the morning of May 24th. During this period, however, the French on our left had attained considerable success. On the 15th instant they captured Steenstraate and the trenches in Het Sas, and on the 16th they drove the enemy headlong over the canal, finding two thousand German dead. On the 17th they made a substantial advance on the east side of the canal, and on the 20th they repelled a German counter-attack, making a further advance in the same direction, and taking one hundred prisoners.

On the early morning of the 24th a violent outburst of gas against nearly the whole front was followed by heavy shell fire, and the most determined attack was delivered against our position east of Ypres.

The hour the attack commenced was 2.45 a.m. A large proportion of the men were asleep, and the attack was too sudden to give them time to put on their respirators.

The 2nd Royal Irish and the 9th Argyll and Sutherland Highlanders, overcome by gas fumes, were driven out of a farm held in front of the left Division, and this the enemy proceeded to hold and fortify.

All attempts to retake this farm during the day failed, and during the night of the 24th-25th the General Officer Commanding the left Division decided to take up a new line which, although slightly in rear of the old one, he considered to be a much better position. This operation was successfully carried out.

Throughout the day the whole line was subjected to one of the most violent artillery attacks which it had ever undergone; and the 5th Corps and the Cavalry Divisions engaged had to fight hard to maintain their positions. On the following day, however, the line was consolidated, joining the right of the French at the same place as before, and passing through Wieltje (which was strongly fortified) in a southerly direction on to Hooge, where the Cavalry

THE BATTLE OF FESTUBERT

have since strongly occupied the chateau, and pushed our line further east.

5. In pursuance of a promise which I made to the French Commander-in-Chief to support an attack which his troops were making on the 9th May between the right of my line and Arras, I directed Sir Douglas Haig to carry out on that date an attack on the German trenches in the neighbourhood of Rougebanc (north-west of Fromelles) by the 4th Corps, and between Neuve Chapelle and Givenchy, by the 1st and Indian Corps.

The bombardment of the enemy's positions commenced at 5 a.m.

Half-an-hour later the 8th Division of the 4th Corps captured the first line of German trenches about Rougebanc, and some detachments seized a few localities beyond this line. It was soon found, however, that the position was much stronger than had been anticipated, and that a more extensive artillery preparation was necessary to crush the resistance offered by his numerous fortified posts.

Throughout the 9th and 10th repeated efforts were made to make further progress. Not only was this found to be impossible, but the violence of the enemy's machine-gun fire from his posts on the flanks rendered the captured trenches so difficult to hold that all the units of the 4th Corps had to retire to their original position by the morning of the 10th.

The 1st and Indian Divisions south of Neuve Chapelle met with no greater success, and on the evening of the 10th I sanctioned Sir Douglas Haig's proposal to concentrate all our available resources on the southern point of attack.

The 7th Division was moved round from the 4th Corps area to support this attack, and I directed the General Officer Commanding the First Army to delay it long enough to ensure a powerful and deliberate artillery preparation.

THE SECOND BATTLE OF YPRES

The operations of the 9th and 10th formed part of a general plan of attack which the Allies were conjointly conducting on a line extending from the north of Arras to the south of Armentières; and, although immediate progress was not made during this time by the British forces, their attack assisted in securing the brilliant successes attained by the French forces on their right, not only by holding the enemy in their front but by drawing off a part of the German reinforcements which were coming up to support their forces east of Arras.

It was decided that the attack should be resumed on the night of the 12th instant, but the weather continued very dull and misty, interfering much with artillery observation. Orders were finally issued, therefore, for the action to commence on the night of the 15th instant.

On the 15th May I moved the Canadian Division into the 1st Corps area and placed them at the disposal of Sir Douglas Haig.

The infantry of the Indian Corps and the 2nd Division of the 1st Corps advanced to the attack of the enemy's trenches which extended from Richebourg L'Avoué in a south-westerly direction.

Before daybreak the 2nd Division had succeeded in capturing two lines of the enemy's trenches, but the Indian Corps were unable to make any progress owing to the strength of the enemy's defences in the neighbourhood of Richebourg L'Avoué.

At daybreak the 7th Division, on the right of the 2nd, advanced to the attack, and by 7 a.m. had entrenched themselves on a line running nearly North and South, half-way between their original trenches and La Quinque Rue, having cleared and captured several lines of the enemy's trenches, including a number of fortified posts.

As it was found impossible for the Indian Corps to make any progress in face of the enemy's defences Sir Douglas Haig directed the attack to be suspended at this

GOOD PROGRESS MADE

point and ordered the Indian Corps to form a defensive flank.

The remainder of the day was spent in securing and consolidating positions which had been won, and endeavouring to unite the inner flanks of the 7th and 2nd Divisions, which were separated by trenches and posts strongly held by the enemy.

Various attempts which were made throughout the day to secure this object had not succeeded at nightfall in driving the enemy back.

The German communications leading to the rear of their positions were systematically shelled throughout the night.

About two hundred prisoners were captured on the 16th instant.

Fighting was resumed at daybreak; and by 11 o'clock the 7th Division had made a considerable advance, capturing several more of the enemy's trenches. The task allotted to this Division was to push on in the direction of Rue D'Ouvert, Chateau St. Roch and Canteleux.

The 2nd Division was directed to push on when the situation permitted towards the Rue de Marais and Violaines.

The Indian Division was ordered to extend its front far enough to enable it to keep touch with the left of the 2nd Division when they advanced.

On this day I gave orders for the 51st (Highland) Division to move into the neighbourhood of Estaires to be ready to support the operations of the First Army.

At about noon the enemy was driven out of the trenches and posts which he occupied between the two Divisions, the inner flanks of which were thus enabled to join hands.

By nightfall the 2nd and 7th Divisions had made good progress, the area of captured ground being considerably extended to the right by the successful operations of the latter.

THE SECOND BATTLE OF YPRES

The state of the weather on the morning of the 18th much hindered an effective artillery bombardment, and further attacks had, consequently, to be postponed.

Infantry attacks were made throughout the line in the course of the afternoon and evening; but, although not very much progress was made, the line was advanced to the La Quinque Rue-Bethune Road before nightfall.

On the 19th May the 7th and 2nd Divisions were drawn out of the line to rest. The 7th Division was relieved by the Canadian Division and the 2nd Division by the 51st (Highland) Division.

Sir Douglas Haig placed the Canadian and 51st Divisions, together with the artillery of the 2nd and 7th Division, under the command of Lieutenant-General Alderson, whom he directed to conduct the operations which had hitherto been carried on by the General Officer Commanding First Corps; and he directed the 7th Division to remain in Army Reserve.

During the night of the 19th-20th a small post of the enemy in front of La Quinque Rue was captured.

During the night of the 20th-21st the Canadian Division brilliantly carried on the excellent progress made by the 7th Division by seizing several of the enemy's trenches and pushing forward their whole line several hundred yards. A number of prisoners and some machine guns were captured.

On the 22nd instant the 51st (Highland) Division was attached to the Indian Corps, and the General Officer Commanding the Indian Corps took charge of the operations at La Quinque Rue, Lieutenant-General Alderson with the Canadians conducting the operations to the north of that place.

On this day the Canadian Division extended their line slightly to the right and repulsed three very severe hostile counter attacks.

On the 24th and 25th May the 47th Division (2nd

THE RESULT OF THE BATTLE

London Territorials) succeeded in taking some more of the enemy's trenches and making good the ground gained to the east and north.

I had now reason to consider that the battle, which was commenced by the First Army on the 9th May and renewed on the 16th, having attained for the moment the immediate object I had in view, should not be further actively proceeded with ; and I gave orders to Sir Douglas Haig to curtail his artillery attack and to strengthen and consolidate the ground he had won.

In the battle of Festubert above described the enemy was driven from a position which was strongly entrenched and fortified, and ground was won on a front of four miles to an average depth of 600 yards.

The enemy is known to have suffered very heavy losses, and in the course of the battle 785 prisoners and 10 machine guns were captured. A number of machine guns were also destroyed by our fire.

During the period under report the Army under my command has taken over trenches occupied by some other French Divisions.

I am much indebted to General D'Urbal, commanding the 10th French Army, for the valuable and efficient support received throughout the battle of Festubert from three groups of French 75 centimetre guns.

In spite of very unfavourable weather conditions, rendering observations most difficult, our own artillery did excellent work throughout the battle.

6. During the important operations described above, which were carried on by the First and Second Armies, the 3rd Corps was particularly active in making demonstrations with a view to holding the enemy in its front and preventing reinforcements reaching the threatened areas.

As an instance of the successful attempts to deceive the enemy in this respect it may be mentioned that on the afternoon of the 24th instant a bombardment of about an

THE SECOND BATTLE OF YPRES

hour was carried out by the 6th Division with the object of distracting attention from the Ypres salient.

Considerable damage was done to the enemy's parapets and wire; and that the desired impression was produced on the enemy is evident from the German wireless news on that day, which stated " West of Lille the English attempts to attack were nipped in the bud."

In previous reports I have drawn attention to the enterprise displayed by the troops of the 3rd Corps in conducting night reconnaissances, and to the courage and resource shown by officers' and other patrols in the conduct of these minor operations.

Throughout the period under report this display of activity has been very marked all along the 3rd Corps front, and much valuable information and intelligence have been collected.

7. I have much pleasure in again expressing my warm appreciation of the admirable manner in which all branches of the Medical Services now in the field under the direction of Surgeon-General Sir Arthur Sloggett, have met and dealt with the many difficult situations resulting from the operations during the last two months.

The medical units at the front were frequently exposed to the enemy's fire, and many casualties occurred amongst the officers of the regimental Medical Service. At all times the officers, non-commissioned officers and men, and nurses carried out their duties with fearless bravery and great devotion to the welfare of the sick and wounded.

The evacuation of casualties from the front to the Base and to England was expeditiously accomplished by the Administrative Medical Staffs at the front and on the Lines of Communication. All ranks employed in units of evacuation and in Base Hospitals have shown the highest skill and untiring zeal and energy in alleviating the condition of those who passed through their hands.

THE ROYAL FLYING CORPS

The whole organisation of the Medical Services reflects the highest credit on all concerned.

8. I have once more to call your Lordship's attention to the part taken by the Royal Flying Corps in the general progress of the campaign, and I wish particularly to mention the invaluable assistance they rendered in the operations described in this report, under the able direction of Major-General Sir David Henderson.

The Royal Flying Corps is becoming more and more an indispensable factor in combined operations. In cooperation with the artillery, in particular, there has been continuous improvement both in the methods and in the technical material employed. The ingenuity and technical skill displayed by the officers of the Royal Flying Corps, in effecting this improvement, have been most marked.

Since my last despatch there has been a considerable increase both in the number and in the activity of German aeroplanes in our front. During this period there have been more than sixty combats in the air, in which not one British aeroplane has been lost. As these fights take place almost invariably over or behind the German lines, only one hostile aeroplane has been brought down in our territory. Five more, however, have been definitely wrecked behind their own lines, and many have been chased down and forced to land in most unsuitable ground.

In spite of the opposition of hostile aircraft and the great number of anti-aircraft guns employed by the enemy, air reconnaissance has been carried out with regularity and accuracy.

I desire to bring to your Lordship's notice the assistance given by the French Military Authorities, and in particular by General Hirschauer, Director of the French Aviation Service, and his assistants, Colonel Bottieaux and Colonel Stammler, in the supply of aeronautical material, without which the efficiency of the Royal Flying Corps would have been seriously impaired.

THE SECOND BATTLE OF YPRES

9. In this despatch I wish again to remark upon the exceptionally good work done throughout this campaign by the Army Service Corps and by the Army Ordnance Department, not only in the field, but also on the Lines of Communication and at the Base Ports.

To foresee and meet the requirements in the matter of Ammunition, Stores, Equipment, Supplies and Transport has entailed on the part of the officers, non-commissioned officers and men of these Services a sustained effort which has never been relaxed since the beginning of the war, and which has been rewarded by the most conspicuous success.

The close co-operation of the Railway Transport Department, whose excellent work, in combination with the French Railway Staff, has ensured the regularity of the maintenance services, has greatly contributed to this success.

The degree of efficiency to which these Services have been brought was well demonstrated in the course of the Second Battle of Ypres.

The roads between Poperinghe and Ypres, over which transport, supply and ammunition columns had to pass, were continually searched by hostile heavy artillery during the day and night; whilst the passage of the canal through the town of Ypres, and along the roads east of that town, could only be effected under most difficult and dangerous conditions as regards hostile shell fire. Yet, throughout the whole five or six weeks during which these conditions prevailed, the work was carried on with perfect order and efficiency.

10. Since the date of my last report some Divisions of the " New " Army have arrived in this country.

I made a close inspection of one Division, formed up on parade, and have at various times seen several units belonging to others.

These Divisions have as yet had very little experience in actual fighting; but, judging from all I have seen, I

THE ARRIVAL OF THE NEW ARMY

am of opinion that they ought to prove a valuable addition to any fighting force.

As regards the Infantry, their physique is excellent, whilst their bearing and appearance on parade reflects great credit on the officers and staffs responsible for their training. The units appear to be thoroughly well officered and commanded. The equipment is in good order and efficient.

Several units of artillery have been tested in the firing line behind the trenches, and I hear very good reports of them. Their shooting has been extremely good, and they are quite fit to take their places in the line.

The Pioneer Battalions have created a very favourable impression, the officers being keen and ingenious and the men of good physique and good diggers. The equipment is suitable. The training in field works has been good, but, generally speaking, they require the assistance of Regular Royal Engineers as regards laying out of important works. Man for man in digging the battalions should do practically the same amount of work as an equivalent number of sappers, and in rivetting, entanglements, etc., a great deal more than the ordinary infantry battalions.

11. During the months of April and May several divisions of the Territorial Force joined the Army under my command.

Experience has shown that these troops have now reached a standard of efficiency which enables them to be usefully employed in complete divisional units.

Several divisions have been so employed; some in the trenches, others in the various offensive and defensive operations reported in this despatch.

In whatever kind of work these units have been engaged, they have all borne an active and distinguished part, and have proved themselves thoroughly reliable and efficient.

The opinion I have expressed in former despatches as to the use and value of the Territorial Force has been fully justified by recent events.

THE SECOND BATTLE OF YPRES

12. The Prime Minister was kind enough to accept an invitation from me to visit the Army in France, and arrived at my Headquarters on the 30th May.

Mr. Asquith made an exhaustive tour of the front, the hospitals and all the administrative arrangements made by Corps Commanders for the health and comfort of men behind the trenches.

It was a great encouragement to all ranks to see the Prime Minister amongst them; and the eloquent words which on several occasions he addressed to the troops had a most powerful and beneficial effect.

As I was desirous that the French Commander-in-Chief should see something of the British troops, I asked General Joffre to be kind enough to inspect a division on parade.

The General accepted my invitation, and on the 27th May he inspected the 7th Division, under the command of Major General H. de la P. Gough, C.B., which was resting behind the trenches.

General Joffre subsequently expressed to me in a letter the pleasure it gave him to see the British troops, and his appreciation of their appearance on parade. He requested me to make this known to all ranks.

The Moderator of the Church of Scotland, the Right Reverend Dr. Wallace Williamson, Dean of the Order of the Thistle, visited the Army in France between the 7th and 17th May, and made a tour of the Scottish Regiments with excellent results.

13. In spite of the constant strain put upon them by the arduous nature of the fighting which they are called upon to carry out daily and almost hourly, the spirit which animates all ranks of the Army in France remains high and confident.

They meet every demand made upon them with the utmost cheerfulness.

This splendid spirit is particularly manifested by the

THE SPLENDID SPIRIT OF THE WOUNDED men in hospital, even amongst those who are mortally wounded.

The invariable question which comes from lips hardly able to utter a sound is, " How are things going on at the front ? "

14. In conclusion, I desire to bring to Your Lordship's special notice the valuable services rendered by General Sir Douglas Haig in his successful handling of the troops of the First Army throughout the Battle of Festubert, and Lieutenant-General Sir Herbert Plumer for his fine defence of Ypres throughout the arduous and difficult operations during the latter part of April and the month of May.

I have the honour to be,
    Your Lordship's most obedient servant,
(*Signed*) J. D. P. FRENCH, Field-Marshal,
Commander-in-Chief the British Forces in the Field.

VIII
LOOS

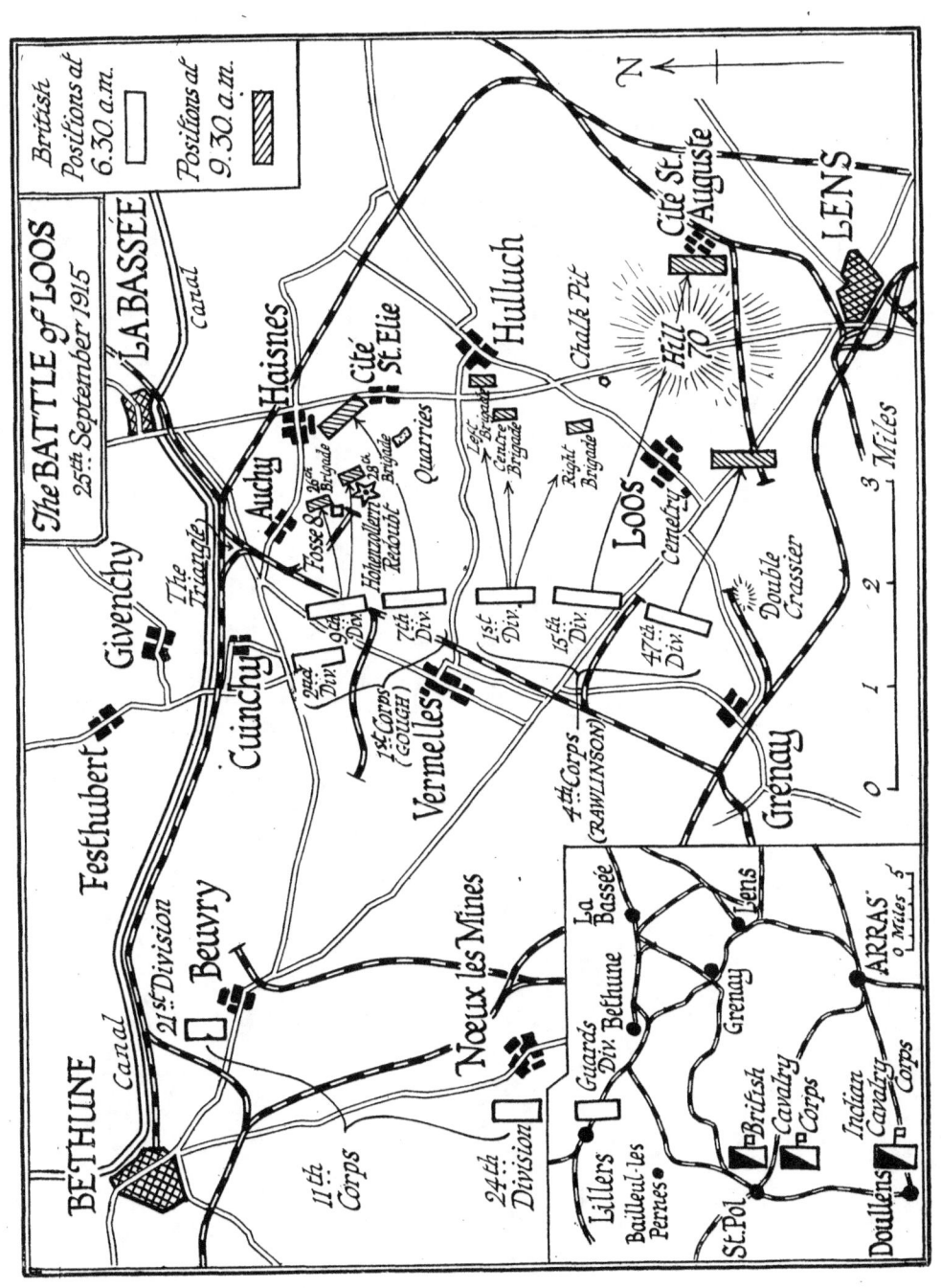

VIII : France, 15*th October*, 1915.

To Field-Marshal Earl Kitchener of Khartoum, K.P., G.C.B., O.M., etc.

My Lord,

I HAVE the honour to report the operations of the Forces under my command since the date of those described in my last despatch dated 15th June, 1915.

1. Those of the greatest importance took place during the last days of the period under report. Nevertheless, the Army under my command was constantly engaged throughout the whole time in enterprises which, although not securing the same important results, have yet had considerable influence on the course of events.

2. On 2nd June the enemy made a final offensive in the Ypres salient with the object of gaining our trenches and position at Hooge. The attack was most determined and was preceded by a severe bombardment. A gallant defence was made by troops of the 3rd Cavalry Division and 1st Indian Division, and our position was maintained throughout.

During the first weeks of June the front of the Second Army was extended to the North as far as the village of Boesinghe.

3. After the conclusion of the Battle of Festubert the troops of the First Army were engaged in several minor operations.

By an attack delivered on the evening of 15th June after a prolonged bombardment the 1st Canadian Brigade obtained possession of the German front line trenches north-east of Givenchy, but were unable to retain them owing to their flanks being too much exposed.

4. On 16th June an attack was carried out by the 5th Corps on the Bellewaarde Ridge, east of Ypres.

LOOS

The enemy's front line was captured, many of his dead and wounded being found in the trenches.

The troops, pressing forward, gained ground as far East as the Bellewaarde Lake, but found themselves unable to maintain this advanced position. They were, however, successful in securing and consolidating the ground won during the first part of the attack, on a front of a thousand yards, including the advanced portion of the enemy's salient north of the Ypres-Menin Road.

During this action the fire of the artillery was most effective, the prisoners testifying to its destructiveness and accuracy. It also prevented the delivery of counter attacks, which were paralysed at the outset.

Over two hundred prisoners were taken, besides some machine-guns, trench material and gas apparatus.

Holding attacks by the neighbouring 2nd and 6th Corps were successful in helping the main attack, whilst the 36th French Corps co-operated very usefully with artillery fire on Pilkem.

Near Hill 60 the 15th Infantry Brigade made four bombing attacks, gaining and occupying about fifty yards of trench.

On 6th July a small attack was made by the 11th Infantry Brigade on a German salient between Boesinghe and Ypres, which resulted in the capture of a frontage of about 500 yards of trench and a number of prisoners.

In the course of this operation it was necessary to move a gun of the 135th Battery Royal Field Artillery, into the front line to destroy an enemy sap-head. To reach its position the gun had to be taken over a high canal embankment, rafted over the canal under fire, pulled up a bank with a slope of nearly 45 degrees, and then dragged over three trenches and a sky line to its position seventy yards from the German lines. This was carried out without loss.

This incident is of minor importance in itself, but I quote it as an example of the daily difficulties which

THE FIRST LIQUID FIRE ATTACK

officers and men in the trenches are constantly called upon to overcome, and of the spirit of initiative and resource which is so marked a feature amongst them.

From the 10th to the 12th of July the enemy made attempts, after heavy shelling, to recapture the lost portion of their line; but our artillery, assisted by that of the French on our left, prevented any serious assault from being delivered. Minor attacks were constant, but were easily repulsed by the garrison of our trenches.

On 19th July an enemy's redoubt at the western end of the Hooge defences was successfully mined and destroyed, and a small portion of the enemy's trenches were captured.

5. Since my last despatch a new device has been adopted by the enemy for driving burning liquid into our trenches with a strong jet.

Thus supported, an attack was made on the trenches of the Second Army at Hooge, on the Menin Road early on 30th July. Most of the infantry occupying these trenches were driven back, but their retirement was due far more to the surprise and temporary confusion caused by the burning liquid than to the actual damage inflicted.

Gallant endeavours were made by repeated counter attacks to recapture the lost section of trenches. These, however, proving unsuccessful and costly, a new line of trenches was consolidated a short distance further back.

Attacks made by the enemy at the same time west of Bellewaarde Lake were repulsed.

On 9th August these losses were brilliantly regained, owing to a successful attack carried out by the 6th Division. This attack was very well executed and resulted in the recapture, with small casualties, not only of the whole of the lost trenches, but, in addition, of four hundred yards of German trench north of the Menin Road.

At the end of this engagement it was estimated that between four and five hundred German dead were lying on the battlefield.

LOOS

Valuable help was rendered by two batteries of French artillery lent by General Hely d'Oissel, commanding 36th French Corps.

6. From the conclusion of the above-mentioned operations until the last week in September there was relative quiet along the whole of the British line, except at those points where the normal conditions of existence comprised occasional shelling or constant mine and bomb warfare. In these trying forms of encounter all ranks have constantly shown the greatest enterprise and courage, and have consistently maintained the upper hand.

The close accord and co-operation which has always existed between the Commander-in-Chief of our Allies and myself has been maintained, and I have had constant meetings with General Joffre, who has kept me informed of his views and intentions, and explained the successive methods by which he hopes to attain his ultimate object.

After full discussion of the military situation a decision was arrived at for joint action, in which I acquiesced.

It was arranged that we should make a combined attack from certain points of the Allied line during the last week in September.

The reinforcements I have received enabled me to comply with several requests which General Joffre has made that I should take over additional portions of the French line.

7. In fulfilment of the role assigned to it in these operations the Army under my command attacked the enemy on the morning of the 25th September.

The main attack was delivered by the 1st and 4th Corps between the La Bassée Canal on the north and a point of the enemy's line opposite the village of Grenay on the south.

At the same time a secondary attack, designed with the object of distracting the enemy's attention and holding his troops to their ground, was made by the 5th Corps on

THE BEGINNING OF THE BATTLE

Bellewaarde Farm, situated to the east of Ypres. Subsidiary attacks with similar objects were delivered by the 3rd and Indian Corps north of the La Bassée Canal and along the whole front of the Second Army.

The object of the secondary attack by the 5th Corps was most effectively achieved, for not only was the enemy contained on that front, but we have reason to believe that reserves were hurried toward that point of the line.

The attack was made at daybreak by the 3rd and 14th Divisions, and at first the greater part of the enemy's front line was taken; but, owing to the powerful artillery fire concentrated against them, the troops were unable to retain the ground, and had to return to their original trenches toward nightfall. The 5th Corps succeeded, however, in capturing two officers and 138 other prisoners.

Similar demonstrations with equally good results were made along the whole front of the Second Army.

With the same object in view, those units of the First Army occupying the line north of the Bethune-La Bassée Canal were detailed to carry out some minor operations.

Portions of the 1st Corps assaulted the enemy's trenches at Givenchy. The Indian Corps attacked the Moulin du Piétre; while the 3rd Corps was directed against the trenches at Le Bridoux.

These attacks started at daybreak and were at first successful all along the line. Later in the day the enemy brought up strong reserves, and after hard fighting and variable fortunes the troops engaged in this part of the line reoccupied their original trenches at nightfall. They succeeded admirably, however, in fulfilling the role allotted to them, and in holding large numbers of the enemy away from the main attack.

The 8th Division of the 3rd Corps and the Meerut Division of the Indian Corps were principally engaged in this part of the line.

LOOS

On the front of the Third Army subsidiary operations of a similar nature were successfully carried out.

The Wing of the Royal Flying Corps attached to this Army performed valuable work by undertaking distant flights behind the enemy's lines and by successfully blowing up railways, wrecking trains and damaging stations on the line of communication by means of bomb attacks.

Valuable assistance was rendered by Vice-Admiral Bacon and a squadron of His Majesty's ships operating off Zeebrugge and Ostend.

8. The general plan of the main attack on the 25th September was as follows :

In co-operation with an offensive movement by the 10th French Army on our right, the 1st and 4th Corps were to attack the enemy from a point opposite the little mining village of Grenay on the south to the La Bassée Canal on the north. The Vermelles-Hulluch Road was to be the dividing line between the two Corps, the 4th Corps delivering the right attack, the 1st Corps the left.

In view of the great length of line along which the British troops were operating it was necessary to keep a strong reserve in my own hand. The 11th Corps, consisting of the Guards, the 21st and 24th Divisions, were detailed for this purpose.

This reserve was the more necessary owing to the fact that the 10th French Army had to postpone its attack until one o'clock in the day ; and, further, that the Corps operating on the French left had to be directed in a more or less south-easterly direction, involving, in case of our success, a considerable gap in our line.

To ensure, however, the speedy and effective support to the 1st and 4th Corps in the case of their success, the 21st and 24th Divisions passed the night of the 24th-25th on the line Beuvry (to the east of Bethune)-Noeux les Mines. The Guards Division was in the neighbourhood of Lillers on the same night.

NOTABLE TACTICAL POINTS

I also directed the General Officer Commanding Second Army to draw the 28th Division back to Bailleul and to hold it in readiness to meet unexpected eventualities.

The British Cavalry Corps, less 3rd Cavalry Division, under General Fanshawe, was posted in the neighbourhood of St. Pol and Bailleul les Pernes; and the Indian Cavalry Corps, under General Rimington, at Doullens; both in readiness to co-operate with the French Cavalry in exploiting any success which might be attained by the combined French and British Forces. Plans for effective co-operation were fully arranged between the Cavalry Commanders of both Armies.

The 3rd Cavalry Division, less one brigade, was assigned to the General Officer Commanding First Army as a reserve, and moved into the area of the 4th Corps on the 21st and 22nd September.

9. Opposite the front of the main line of attack the distance between the enemy's trenches and our own varied from about 100 to 500 yards.

The country over which the advance took place is open and overgrown with long grass and self-sown crops.

From the canal southward our trenches and those of the enemy ran, roughly, parallel up an almost imperceptible rise to the south-west.

From the Vermelles-Hulluch Road southward the advantage of height is on the enemy's side as far as the Bethune-Lens Road. There the two lines of trenches cross a spur in which the rise culminates, and thence the command lies on the side of the British trenches.

Due east of the intersection of spur and trenches, and a short mile away, stands Loos. Less than a mile further south-east is Hill 70, which is the summit of the gentle rise in the ground.

Other notable tactical points in our front were:

"*Fosse* 8" (a thousand yards south of Auchy), which is a coal mine with a high and strongly defended slag heap.

LOOS

"*The Hohenzollern Redoubt.*"—A strong work thrust out nearly five hundred yards in front of the German lines and close to our own. It is connected with their front line by three communication trenches abutting into the defences of Fosse 8.

Cité St. Elie.—A strongly defended mining village lying fifteen hundred yards south of Haisnes.

"*The Quarries.*"—Lying half-way to the German trenches west of Cité St. Elie.

Hulluch.—A village strung out along a small stream, lying less than half a mile south-east of Cité St. Elie and 3,000 yards north-east of Loos.

Half a mile north of Hill 70 is "*Puits 14 bis,*" another coal mine, possessing great possibilities for defence when taken in conjunction with a strong redoubt situated on the north-east side of Hill 70.

10. The attacks of the 1st and 4th Corps were delivered at 6.30 a.m. and were successful all along the line, except just south of the La Bassée Canal.

The enemy met the advance by wild infantry fire of slight intensity, but his artillery fire was accurate and caused considerable casualties.

The 47th Division on the right of the 4th Corps rapidly swung its left forward and occupied the southern outskirts of Loos and a big double slag heap opposite Grenay, known as the Double Crassier. Thence it pushed on, and, by taking possession of the cemetery, the enclosures and chalk pits south of Loos, succeeded in forming a strong defensive flank.

The London Territorial Division acquitted itself most creditably. It was skilfully led and the troops carried out their task with great energy and determination. They contributed largely to our success in this part of the field.

On the left of the 47th Division a Scottish Division of the New Armies (15th Division) assaulted Loos, Hill 70 and Fosse 14 bis.

THE DELIVERY OF THE ATTACK

The attack was admirably delivered, and in a little more than an hour parts of the division occupied Loos and its northern outskirts, Puits 14 bis and Hill 70, whilst some units had pushed on as far as Cité St. Auguste, a mile east of Hill 70.

The 15th Division carried out its advance with the greatest vigour, in spite of its left flank being exposed, owing to the 1st Division on its left having been checked.

About 1 p.m. the enemy brought up strong reserves, and the advanced portions of the division at Fosse 14 bis and on the far side of Hill 70 were driven in. We had, however, secured the very substantial gain of Loos and the western portion of Hill 70.

11. At 9.30 a.m. I placed the 21st and 24th Divisions at the disposal of the General Officer commanding First Army, who at once ordered the General Officer commanding the 11th Corps to move them up in support of the attacking troops.

Between 11 a.m. and 12 noon the central brigades of these divisions filed past me at Bethune and Noeux les Mines respectively. At 11.30 a.m. the heads of both divisions were within three miles of our original trench line.

As the success of the 47th Division on the right of the 4th Corps caused me less apprehension of a gap in our line near that point, I ordered the Guards Division up to Noeux les Mines, and the 28th Division to move in a southerly direction from Bailleul.

12. The 1st Division, attacking on the left, of the 15th was unable at first to make any headway with its right brigade.

The brigade on its left (the 1st) was, however, able to get forward and penetrated into the outskirts of the village of Hulluch, capturing some gun positions on the way.

The determined advance of this brigade, with its right flank dangerously exposed, was most praiseworthy, and combined with the action of divisional reserves, was instrumental in causing the surrender of a German detachment some 500 strong which was holding up the advance of the right brigade in the front system of trenches.

The inability of the right of this division to get forward had, however, caused sufficient delay to enable the enemy to collect local reserves behind the strong second line.

The arrangements, the planning and execution of the attack, and the conduct of the troops of the 4th Corps were most efficient and praiseworthy.

13. In the attack of the 1st Corps the 7th Division was directed on the Quarries. The 9th Division was to capture the Hohenzollern Redoubt and then to push on to Fosse 8.

The assault of the 7th Division succeeded at once, and in a very short time they had reached the western edge of the Quarries, Cité St. Elie and even the village of Haisnes the tendency of the action having been to draw the troops northward.

On the right of the 9th Division the 26th Brigade secured Fosse 8 after heavy fighting, and the 28th Brigade captured the front line of the German trenches east of Vermelles railway. At the latter point the fighting was extremely severe; and this brigade, suffering considerable losses, was driven back to its own trenches.

At nightfall, after a heavy day's fighting and numerous German counter attacks, the line was, roughly, as follows:

From the Double Crassier, south of Loos, by the western part of Hill 70, to the western exit of Hulluch; thence by the Quarries and western end of Cité St. Elie, east of Fosse 8, back to our original line.

Throughout the length of the line heavy fighting was in progress, and our hold on Fosse 8, backed as it is by the strong defences and guns of Auchy, was distinctly precarious.

Heavy rain fell throughout the day, which was very

GENERAL SIR F. H. ALLENBY, K.C.B.
From a drawing by the Official Artist, Francis Dodd.

DEATH OF MAJOR-GENERAL CAPPER

detrimental to efficient observation of fire and reconnaissance by aircraft.

In the course of the night 25th-26th September the enemy delivered a series of heavy counter attacks along most of our new front. The majority of these were repulsed with heavy loss; but in parts of the line, notably near the Quarries, our troops were driven back a certain distance.

At 6 p.m. the Guards Division arrived at Noeux les Mines, and on the morning of the 26th I placed them at the disposal of the General Officer commanding First Army.

14. The situation at the Quarries, described above, was re-adjusted by an attack of the 7th Division on the afternoon of September 26th; and on that evening very heavy attacks delivered by the enemy were repulsed with severe loss.

On the 4th Corps front attacks on Hulluch and on the redoubt on the east side of Hill 70 were put in operation, but were anticipated by the enemy organising a very strong offensive from that direction. These attacks drove in the advanced troops of the 21st and 24th Divisions, which were then moving forward to attack.

Reports regarding this portion of the action are very conflicting, and it is not possible to form an entirely just appreciation of what occurred in this part of the field.

At nightfall there was no change up to Hill 70, except for a small gain of ground south of Loos. From Hill 70 the line bent sharply back to the north-west as far as Loos-La Bassée Road, which it followed for a thousand yards, bearing thence north-eastward to near the west end of Hulluch. Thence northward it was the same as it had been on the previous night.

The night of September 26th-27th was as disturbed as the previous night, for many further counter attacks were made and constant pressure was maintained by the enemy.

LOOS

A dismounted cavalry brigade was thrown into Loos to form a garrison.

On this day I placed the 28th Division at the disposal of the General Officer commanding First Army.

I regret to say that Major-General Sir Thompson Capper, K.C.M.G., C.B., D.S.O., commanding 7th Division, was severely wounded on the 26th, and died on the morning of the 27th. He was a most distinguished and capable leader, and his loss will be severely felt.

15. Soon after dawn on the 27th it became apparent that the brigade holding Fosse 8 was unable to maintain its position, and eventually it was slowly forced back until at length our front at this point coincided with the eastern portion of the Hohenzollern Redoubt.

I regret to say that during this operation Major-General G. H. Thesiger, C.B., C.M.G., A.D.C., commanding the 9th Division, was killed whilst most gallantly endeavouring to secure the ground which had been won.

In the afternoon of this day the Guards Division, which had taken over part of the line to the north of the 4th Corps, almost restored our former line, bringing it up parallel to and slightly west of the Lens-La Bassée Road.

This Division made a very brilliant and successful attack on Hill 70 in the afternoon. They drove the Germans off the top of the hill, but could not take the redoubt, which is on the north-east slopes below the crest. They also took the Chalk Pit which lies north of Puits 14, and all the adjacent woods, but were unable to maintain themselves in the Puits itself, which was most effectively commanded by well-posted machine-guns.

The 47th Division on the right of the Guards captured a wood further to the south and repulsed a severe hostile counter attack.

The 28th was passed in consolidating the ground gained and in making a certain number of internal moves of divisions, in order to give the troops rest and to enable

GENERAL FOCH GIVES SUPPORT

those units whose casualties had been heavy to refill their ranks with reinforcements.

The 47th Division made a little more ground to the south, capturing one field gun and a few machine-guns.

On the evening of this day the situation remained practically unchanged.

16. The line occupied by the troops of the First Army south of the canal became now very much extended by the salient with which it indented the enemy's line.

The French 10th Army had been very heavily opposed, and I considered that the advance they were able to make did not afford sufficient protection to my right flank.

On representing this to General Joffre he was kind enough to ask the Commander of the northern group of French Armies to render me assistance.

General Foch met these demands in the same friendly spirit which he has always displayed throughout the course of the whole campaign, and expressed his readiness to give me all the support he could.

On the morning of the 28th we discussed the situation, and the General agreed to send the 9th French Corps to take over the ground occupied by us extending from the French left up to and including that portion of Hill 70 which we were holding, and also the village of Loos.

This relief was commenced on the 30th September and completed on the two following nights.

17. During the 29th and 30th September and the first days of October fighting was almost continuous along the northern part of the new line, particularly about the Hohenzollern Redoubt and neighbouring trenches, to which the enemy evidently attached great value. His attacks, however, invariably broke down with very heavy loss under the accurate fire of our infantry and artillery.

The Germans succeeded in gaining some ground in and about the Hohenzollern Redoubt but they paid heavily for it in the losses they suffered.

LOOS

Our troops all along the front were busily engaged in consolidating and strengthening the ground won, and the efficient and thorough manner in which the work was carried out reflects the greatest credit upon all ranks. Every precaution was made to deal with the counter attack which was inevitable.

During these operations the weather has been most unfavourable, and the troops have had to fight in rain and mud and often in darkness. Even these adverse circumstances have in no way affected the magnificent spirit continually displayed alike by officers and men. In the Casualty Clearing and Dressing Stations, of which I visited a great number during the course of the action, I found nothing but the most cheery optimism among the wounded.

I have to deplore the loss of a third most valuable and distinguished General of Division during these operations. On the afternoon of 2nd October Major-General F. D. V. Wing, C.B., commanding the 12th Division, was killed.

18. On the afternoon of 8th October our expectations in regard to a counter attack were fulfilled. The enemy directed a violent and intense attack all along the line from Fosse 8 on the north to the right of the French 9th Corps on the south. The attack was delivered by some twenty-eight battalions in first line, with larger forces in support, and was prepared by a very heavy bombardment from all parts of the enemy's front.

At all parts of the line except two the Germans were repulsed with tremendous loss, and it is computed on reliable authority that they left some eight to nine thousand dead lying on the battlefield in front of the British and French trenches.

On the right the attack succeeded in making a small and unimportant lodgment on the Double Crassier held by the French; whilst on the left the trench held by troops of the Guards Division to the north-east of the

ENEMY COUNTER ATTACKS

Hohenzollern Redoubt was temporarily captured. The latter was, however, speedily retaken, and at midnight on the 9th October the line held by the First Army was identically the same as that held before the enemy's attack started.

The main enemy attacks on the front held by our troops had been against the 1st Division in the neighbourhood of the Chalk Pit and the Guards Division in the neighbourhood of the Hohenzollern Redoubt. Both attacks were repulsed, and the enemy lost heavily from machine-gun and artillery fire.

From subsequent information it transpired that the German attack was made by about twelve battalions against the line Loos-Chalk Pit, and that a subsidiary attack by six to eight battalions was made from the direction of the Hohenzollern Redoubt against the Guards Division.

Some eight or ten German battalions were directed against the French 9th Corps.

19. The position assaulted and carried with so much brilliancy and dash by the 1st and 4th Corps on 25th September was an exceptionally strong one. It extended along a distance of some 6,500 yards, consisted of a double line, which included works of considerable strength, and was a network of trenches and bomb-proof shelters. Some of the dug-outs and shelters formed veritable caves thirty feet below the ground, with almost impenetrable head cover. The enemy had expended months of labour upon perfecting these defences.

The total number of prisoners captured during these operations amounted to 57 officers and 3,000 other ranks. Material which fell into our hands included 26 field-guns, 40 machine-guns and 3 minenwerfer.

I deeply regret the heavy casualties which were incurred in this battle, but in view of the great strength of the position, the stubborn defence of the enemy and the powerful artillery by which he was supported, I do not think they were excessive. I am happy to be able to add that the proportion of slightly wounded is relatively very large indeed.

20. Since the date of my last despatch the Army has received strong reinforcements, and every reinforcement has had its quota of Field Artillery. In addition, numerous batteries of heavy guns and howitzers have been added to the strength of the heavy artillery. The arrival of these reinforcements in the field has tested the capacity of the Artillery as a whole to expand to meet the requirements of the Army, and to maintain the high level of efficiency that has characterised this arm throughout the campaign. Our enemy may have hoped, not perhaps without reason, that it would be impossible for us, starting from such small beginnings, to build up an efficient Artillery to provide for the very large expansion of the Army. If he entertained such hopes, he has now good reason to know that they have not been justified by the result.

The efficiency of the Artillery of the New Armies has exceeded all expectations, and during the period under review excellent services have been rendered by the Territorial Artillery.

The necessity to denude the old batteries of Regular Horse and Field Artillery of officers and non-commissioned officers, in order to provide for the expansion referred to, has not in any way impaired their efficiency, and they continue to set an example to all by their high standard and devotion to duty.

I must give a special word of praise to the officers and rank and file of the Royal Garrison Artillery for the admirable way in which they have accustomed themselves to the conditions of active service in the field, to which for the most part they were unaccustomed, and for the manner in which they have applied their general knowledge of gunnery to the special problems arising in trench warfare. The excellence of their training and the accuracy

THE WORK OF THE ARTILLERY

of their shooting have, I feel sure, made a marked impression on the enemy.

21. The work of the Artillery during the daily life in the trenches calls for increasing vigilance and the maintenance of an intricate system of communications in a thorough state of efficiency, in order that the guns may be ever ready to render assistance to the Infantry when necessity arises. A high standard of initiative is also required in order to maintain the moral ascendancy over the enemy, by impeding his working parties, destroying his works and keeping his artillery fire under control.

To the many calls upon them the Artillery has responded in a manner that is altogether admirable.

In the severe offensive actions that have taken place it is not too much to say that the first element of success has been the artillery preparation of the attack. Only when this preparation has been thorough have our attacks succeeded. It is impossible to convey in a despatch an adequate impression of the amount of care and labour involved in the minute and exact preparations that are the necessary preliminaries of a bombardment preparatory to an attack in a modern battle.

The immense number of guns that it is necessary to concentrate, the amount of ammunition to be supplied to them, and the diversity of the tasks to be carried out, demand a very high order of skill in organisation and technical professional knowledge.

22. The successful attacks at Hooge on 9th August and of the First Army on 25th September show that our Artillery officers possess the necessary talents and the rank and file the necessary skill and endurance to ensure success in operations of this character.

Moreover, the repulse of the enemy's attack on 8th October in the neighbourhood of Loos and Hulluch with such heavy losses shows the capacity of the Artillery to concentrate its fire promptly and effectively at a moment's notice for the defence of the front.

I cannot close these remarks on the Artillery without expressing my admiration for the work of the observing officers and the men who work with them. Carrying out their duties, as they do, in close proximity to the front line in observing stations that are the special mark of the enemy's guns, they are constantly exposed to fire, and are compelled to carry on their work, involving the use of delicate instruments and the making of nice calculations, in circumstances of the greatest difficulty and danger. That they have never failed in their duties and that they have suffered very heavy casualties in performing them, are to their lasting credit and honour.

The work of the Artillery in co-operation with the Royal Flying Corps continues to make most satisfactory progress, and has been most highly creditable to all concerned.

The new weapons that have been placed in the field during the period under review have more than fulfilled expectations, and the enemy must be well aware of their accuracy and general efficiency.

23. I have on previous occasions called your Lordship's attention to the admirable work of the Corps of the Royal Engineers.

This work covers a very wide field, demanding a high standard of technical knowledge and skill, as well as unflagging energy ; and throughout the supreme test of war these qualities have never been found wanting, thus reflecting the greatest credit on the organisation of the Corps as a whole, and on the training of the officers and men individually.

The spirit which is imbued in all ranks from the base ports to the front trenches and beyond is the same.

No matter where or how the personnel of the Corps has been employed, devotion to duty and energy have been ever present.

THE WORK OF THE FIELD UNITS

In this despatch I wish particularly to draw attention to the work of the Field Units and Army Troops Companies, which must almost invariably be performed under the most trying circumstances by night as well as by day. Demanding qualities of whole-hearted courage and self-sacrifice, combined with sound judgment and instant action, the work of officers, non-commissioned officers and men has been beyond all praise.

The necessity for skilled labour at the front has been so continuous that Royal Engineer units have frequently been forced to forego those periods of rest which at times it has been possible to grant to other troops; but, in spite of this, they have responded loyally to every call on their services.

Notwithstanding the heavy casualties sustained by all ranks, the esprit de corps of the Royal Engineers is such that the new material is at once animated by the same ideals, and the same devotion to duty is maintained.

24. I desire to call your Lordship's attention to the splendid work carried out by the Tunnelling Companies. These companies, officered largely by mining engineers, and manned by professional miners, have devoted themselves whole-heartedly to the dangerous work of offensive and defensive mining; a task ever accompanied by great and unseen dangers.

It is impossible within the limits of a despatch to give any just idea of the work of these units, but it will be found, when their history comes to be written, that it will present a story of danger, of heroism, and of difficulties surmounted worthy of the best traditions of the Royal Engineers, under whose general direction their work is carried out.

25. Owing to the repeated use by the enemy of asphyxiating gases in their attacks on our positions, I have been compelled to resort to similar methods; and a detachment was organised for this purpose, which took part in

LOOS

the operations commencing on the 25th September for the first time.

Although the enemy was known to have been prepared for such reprisals, our gas attack met with marked success, and produced a demoralising effect in some of the opposing units, of which ample evidence was forthcoming in the captured trenches.

The men who undertook this work carried out their unfamiliar duties during a heavy bombardment with conspicuous gallantry and coolness ; and I feel confident in their ability to more than hold their own should the enemy again resort to this method of warfare.

26. I would again call your Lordship's attention to the work of the Royal Flying Corps.

Throughout the summer, notwithstanding much unfavourable weather, the work of co-operating with the Artillery, photographing the positions of the enemy, bombing their communications and reconnoitring far over hostile territory has gone on unceasingly.

The volume of work performed steadily increases ; the amount of flying has been more than doubled during this period. There have been more than 240 combats in the air, and in nearly every case our pilots have had to seek the enemy behind his own lines, where he is assisted by the fire of his movable anti-aircraft guns ; and in spite of this they have succeeded in bringing down four of the German machines behind our trenches and at least twelve in the enemy's lines, and many more have been seen to dive to earth in a damaged condition or to have retired from the fight. On one occasion an officer of the Royal Flying Corps engaged four enemy machines and drove them off, proceeding on his reconnaissance. On another occasion two officers engaged six hostile machines and disabled at least one of them.

Artillery observation and photography are two of the most trying tasks the Royal Flying Corps is called upon to

UNITS SPECIALLY MENTIONED

perform, as our airmen must remain for long periods within easy range of the enemy's anti-aircraft guns.

The work of observation for the guns from aeroplanes has now become an important factor in artillery fire, and the personnel of the two arms work in the closest co-operation.

As evidence of the dangers our flying officers are called upon to face I may state that on one occasion a machine was hit in no fewer than 300 places soon after crossing the enemy's lines, and yet the officer successfully carried out his mission.

The Royal Flying Corps has on several occasions carried out a continuous bombing of the enemy's communications, descending to 500 feet and under in order to hit moving trains on the railway. This has in some cases been kept up day after day; and during the operations at the end of September, in the space of five days nearly six tons of explosives were dropped on moving trains, and are known to have practically wrecked five, some containing troops, and to have damaged the main railway line in many different places.

For the valuable work carried out by the Royal Flying Corps I am greatly indebted to their commander, Brigadier General H. M. Trenchard, C.B., D.S.O., A.D.C.

27. Throughout the campaign the financial requirements of the Army have been successfully met by the Army Pay Department. The troops have been paid, and all claims against the Army discharged, with unbroken regularity, and the difficulties inseparable from a foreign banking system and a strange currency have been overcome.

The work of the department has been greatly assisted by the Bank of France, the administration of which has spared no effort to help.

29. While the circumstances of this campaign have brought no exceptional strain on horses, great credit is

LOOS

due to all concerned for the excellent arrangements in the Remount Depôts and Veterinary Hospitals.

29. I am pleased to be able once more to report very favourably on the divisions of the New Armies which have arrived in this country since the date of my last report.

It is evident that great trouble and much hard work have been expended on these units during their training at home, and it is found that they have received such sound teaching that a short period of instruction in trench life under fire soon enables them to take their places with credit beside their acclimatised comrades of the older formations.

30. The Territorial Force Units have continued to merit the favourable remarks I have made on them in previous despatches, and have taken a prominent part in many of the active operations in which the Army has been engaged.

31. A new Division has been sent from Canada and has joined the Army in the field. The material of which it is composed is excellent; and the Division will, I am convinced, acquit itself as well in face of the enemy as the 1st Canadian Division has always done.

32. During the period under report I have been very glad once more to receive the Prime Minister at my Headquarters, as well as the Secretary of State for War.

The Prime Minister of Canada and the Minister of Militia and Defence of Canada also came to France for a few days and visited the troops of the Canadian Contingent.

The Chief Rabbi paid a short visit to the front and interested himself in the members of the large Jewish community now serving with the Army in the Field.

33. I cannot conclude the account of these operations without expressing the deep admiration felt by all ranks of the Army under my command for the splendid part

OUR ALLIES

taken by our French Allies in the battle which opened on 25th September. Fortified positions of immense strength, upon which months of skill and labour had been expended, and which extended for many miles, were stormed and captured by our French comrades with a bravery and determination which went far to instil hope and spirit into the Allied Forces.

The large captures of men and material which fell into their hands testified to the completeness of their victory.

The close co-operation between the two Armies of the Allied Powers, which has been so marked a feature throughout the whole campaign, has been as prominent as ever in the work of the last three weeks.

I have already referred to the cordial and willing help rendered by General Foch in the support of the 9th French Corps, and I have also once again to express my deep indebtedness to General d'Urbal, commanding the 10th French Army, operating on my right; and to General Hely d'Oissel, commanding the French Forces in the North.

34. The part taken by the troops of His Majesty the King of the Belgians was very effective in holding the enemy in front of them to his positions.

35. I have many names to bring to your Lordship's notice for valuable, gallant and distinguished service during the period under review, and these will form the subject of a separate report at an early date.

I have the honour to be,
Your Lordship's most obedient servant,
(*Signed*) J. D. P. FRENCH, Field-Marshal,
Commander-in-Chief the British Forces in the Field.

IX
MENTIONED IN DESPATCHES

IX : France, 30th November, 1915.

To Field-Marshal Earl Kitchener of Khartoum, K.P., G.C.B., O.M., etc.

My Lord,

IN accordance with the last paragraph of my Despatch of the 15th October, 1915, I have the honour to bring to notice the names of those whom I recommend for gallant and distinguished service in the field.

I have the honour to be,
> Your Lordship's most obedient servant,
> (*Signed*) J. D. P. FRENCH, Field-Marshal,
> *Commander-in-Chief the British Forces in the Field.*

MENTIONED IN DESPATCHES
Royal Navy.

Commander A. S. Littlejohns.
Commander H. C. Halahan, D.S.O.
Commander J. Man.
Commander A. Rowand, D.S.O.
Captain D. M. Hamilton.
Captain Sir M. Macgregor, Bart.
Acting Captain A. E. H. Marescaux.
Lieutenant N. H. Cragg (killed).
Assistant-Paymaster C. S. Strange.

Royal Marine Artillery.

Major G. L. Raikes.
Captain D. L. Aman.
Captain E. H. Barr.
Temporary Captain G. Evans.
Captain A. L. Forster, D.S.O.
Temporary Captain R. H. Fox.
Captain (temporary Major) W. N. Stokes.
Temporary Captain F. Summers, Royal Marines.
Temporary Lieutenant F. L. Robinson, Royal Marines.
Temporary Lieutenant T. Cuming, Royal Marines.
Second Lieutenant (temporary Lieutenant) D. M. Quill.
Acting Serjeant-Major Warrant Officer, 1st Class, F. Merckel.
Motor Driver F. Baker.

MENTIONED IN DESPATCHES

ROYAL MARINES.

Temporary Captain H. M. Leaf.

ROYAL NAVAL VOLUNTEER RESERVE.

Armoured Cars, etc.

Lieutenant Hon. L. Guest, attached to Royal Naval Division 'Bus Company.
Lieutenant-Commander B. Kerr. Lieutenant G. C. Neilson.
Chief Petty Officer C. C. Ball. Petty Officer E. Smith.

GENERAL HEADQUARTERS STAFF, ETC.

Major R. N. Abadie, King's Royal Rifle Corps.
Major G. J. Acland Troyte, King's Royal Rifle Corps.
Major R. L. Adlercron, Cameron Highlanders.
Second Lieutenant E. S. Agnew, 5th Lancers, Special Reserve.
Brevet Lieutenant-Colonel R. B. Airey, Army Service Corps.
Lieutenant-General E. A. H. Alderson, C.B.
Lieutenant-Colonel (temporary Brigadier-General) E. W. Alexander, V.C., C.M.G., Royal Artillery.
Captain R. G. Alexander, 11th Lancers.
Major C. Allen, West Riding Brigade, Royal Field Artillery.
Brevet Lieutenant-Colonel E. Allen, retired pay.
Major-General (temporary General) Sir E. H. H. Allenby, K.C.B.
Major F. G. Alston, Scots Guards.
Lieutenant-General Sir C. A. Anderson, K.C.B.
Captain D. F. Anderson, D.S.O., East Yorkshire Regiment.
Captain E. L. B. Anderson, D.S.O., Royal Artillery.
Brevet Lieut.-Colonel N. G. Anderson, D.S.O., Army Service Corps.
Brevet Colonel (temporary Brigadier-General) F. G. Anley, Essex Regiment.
Brevet Colonel (temporary Brigadier-General) D. Arbuthnot, C.M.G., Royal Artillery.
Lieutenant M. A. Arbuthnot, 16th Lancers, Special Reserve.
Major R. J. Armes, North Staffordshire Regiment.
Major C. C. Armitage, Royal Artillery.
Temporary Captain E. T. Aspinall.
Major V. Asser, D.S.O., Royal Artillery.
Major (temporary Brigadier-General) L. W. Atcherley, M.V.O., Reserve of Officers.
Temporary Colonel J. Atkins, M.B., F.R.C.S., Army Medical Service.
Lieutenant-Colonel B. Atkinson, Royal Artillery.
Honorary Major-General (temporary Major-General) J. M. Babington, C.B., C.M.G., retired pay.
Captain J. Bagwell, M.V.O., Norfolk Regiment, Special Reserve (Captain retired pay).

MENTIONED IN DESPATCHES

Captain W. M. Baird, Argyll and Sutherland Highlanders, Territorial Force.
Temporary Major C. D'A. B.S. Baker-Carr.
Major-General R. Bannantine-Allason, C.B.
Captain N. C. Bannatyne, 128th Pioneers.
Colonel (temporary Brigadier-General) F. L. Banon.
Captain W. D. Barber, King's Royal Rifle Corps.
Major R. D. Barbor, Army Service Corps.
Temporary Captain Hon. H. Baring.
Major G. H. Barnett, King's Royal Rifle Corps.
Major-General C. St. L. Barter, C.V.O., C.B.
Major A. W. Bartholomew, D.S.O., Royal Artillery.
Captain J. Bartholomew, Gordon Highlanders, Special Reserve.
Major (temporary Lieutenant-Colonel) W. H. Bartholomew, Royal Artillery.
Lieutenant-Colonel W. H. F. Basevi, 91st Punjabis.
Major A. G. Bayley, Oxfordshire and Buckinghamshire Light Infantry.
Major E. A. Beck, Royal Scots Fusiliers.
Major J. D. Belgrave, Royal Artillery.
Captain G. H. Bell, South Lancashire Regiment.
Lieutenant W. O. Bell-Irving, 11th Hussars.
Major C. R. Bekeley, D.S.O., Welsh Regiment.
Lieutenant-Colrnel J. F. Bernard, Army Ordnance Department.
Major W. H. Besant, Norfolk Regiment, Special Reserve (Major, Reserve of Officers).
Captain H. K. Bethell, 7th Hussars.
Temporary-Lieutenant O. C. Bevan, Royal Artillery.
Major S. S. Binny, D.S.O., Reserve of Officers.
Brevet Colonel (temporary Brigadier-General) J. F. N. Birch, Royal Artillery, A.D.C.
Major C. F. Birney, Royal Engineers.
Brevet Colonel (temporary Brigadier-General) C. G. Blackader, D.S.O., Leicestershire Regiment.
Lieutenant-Colonel A. Blair, D.S.O., King's Own Scottish Borderers.
Major E. P. Blencowe, Army Service Corps.
Captain G. Blewitt, Oxfordshire and Buckinghamshire Light Infantry.
Major (temporary Lieutenant-Colonel) G. H. Boileau, D.S.O., Royal Engineers.
Captain J. Bois, Royal Lancaster Regiment.
Major C. Bonham-Carter, Royal West Kent Regiment.
Captain Hon. G. E. Boscawen, D.S.O., Royal Field Artillery.
Major B. W. B. Bowdler, Royal Engineers.
Captain W. A. T. Bowly, Dorsetshire Regiment.
Major A. M. Boyall, D.S.O., West Yorkshire Regiment.
Colonel (temporary Brigadier-General) W. G. B. Boyce, C.B., D.S.O.
Brevet Lieutenant-Colonel G. F. Boyd, D.S.O., Royal Irish Regiment.

MENTIONED IN DESPATCHES

Captain H. Boyd-Rochfort, 21st Lancers.
Colonel (temporary Brigadier-General) R. C. Boyle, C.B.
Major H. E. R. R. Braine, Royal Munster Fusiliers.
Temporary Captain F. P. Braithwaite.
Colonel (temporary Brigadier-General) C. A. Bray, C.B., C.M.G., Army Pay Department.
Colonel (temporary Brigadier-General) E. F. Brereton, D.S.O.
Captain (temporary Major in Army) Hon. M. V. B. Brett, M.V.O., Royal Highlanders (Territorial Force).
Captain C. E. D. Bridge, Royal Artillery.
Lieutenant-Colonel (temporary Brigadier-General) G. T. M. Bridges, C.M.G., D.S.O., 4th Hussars.
Captain E. C. Brierley, Reserve of Officers.
Major-General C. J. Briggs, C.B.
Captain W. H. Brooke, Yorkshire Light Infantry.
Captain W. T. Brooks, Duke of Cornwall's Light Infantry.
Major A. D. M. Browne, Royal Lancaster Regiment.
Major J. C. Browne, Army Service Corps.
Major W. T. R. Browne, Army Service Corps.
Major G. D. Bruce, 61st Pioneers.
Major A. Bryant, Gloucestershire Regiment.
Captain E. N. Buchan, D.S.O., Manchester Regiment.
Major K. G. Buchanan, Seaforth Highlanders.
Colonel (temporary Brigadier-General) R. U. H. Buckland, C.B., A.D.C.
Temporary Captain A. S. Buckland-Cockell.
Major P. P. Budge, Royal Artillery.
Lieutenant-Colonel (temporary Brigadier-General) C. E. D. Budworth, M.V.O., Royal Artillery.
Major-General E. S. Bulfin, C.V.O., C.B.
Colonel (temporary Brigadier-General) C. B. Bulkeley-Johnson, C.B., A.D.C.
Captain F. W. Bullock Marsham, 19th Hussars.
Captain V. R. Burkhardt, Royal Artillery.
Captain H. P. Burn, D.S.O., Gordon Highlanders.
Lieutenant-Colonel R. O. Burne, Army Service Corps.
Major (temporary Lieutenant-Colonel) B. F. Burnett Hitchcock, D.S.O. Nottinghamshire and Derbyshire Regiment.
Lieutenant-Colonel J. T. Burnett-Stuart, D.S.O., Rifle Brigade.
Honorary Brigadier-General (temporary Brigadier-General) H. H. Burney, C.B., retired pay.
Major I. W. Burns-Lindow, D.S.O., South Irish Horse.
Lieutenant-Colonel H. S. Bush, Army Ordnance Department.
Colonel (temporary Brigadier-General) J. E. Bush.
Second Lieutenant (temporary Lieutenant) H. W. Butler, King's Royal Rifle Corps.

MENTIONED IN DESPATCHES

Captain R. B. Butler, 30th Lancers.
Brevet Colonel (temporary Major-General) R. H. K. Butler, Lancashire Fusiliers.
Captain L. G. Buxton, M.V.O., Reserve of Officers.
Captain C. A. E. Cadell, Royal Field Artillery.
Lieutenant-Colonel (temporary Brigadier-General) A. R. Cameron, C.M.G., Royal Highlanders.
Colonel (temporary Brigadier-General) D. G. M. Campbell.
Colonel (temporary Major-General) W. Campbell, C.B., D.S.O.
Major-General J. E. Capper, C.B.
Major-General Sir T. Capper, K.C.M.G., C.B., D.S.O. (died of wounds).
Captain U. E. C. Carnegy, 3rd Dragoon Guards.
Colonel C. M. Cartwright, Indian Army.
Colonel G. S. Cartwright, Royal Engineers.
Major W. F. S. Casson, 27th Light Cavalry.
Colonel (temporary Brigadier-General) C. T. Caulfield.
Major-General F. R. Cavan, Earl of, C.B., M.V.O.
Major F. W. L. S. H. Cavendish, 9th Lancers.
Major (temporary Lieutenant-Colonel) O. K. Chance, 5th Lancers.
Colonel (temporary Brigadier-General) A. J. Chapman, C.B.
Major W. G. Charles, Essex Regiment.
Colonel (temporary Major-General) Sir P. W. Chetwode, Bt., C.B., D.S.O.
Brevet Major (local Lieutenant-Colonel) B. E. W. Childs, Royal Irish Regiment.
Lieutenant-Colonel H. W. A. Christ'e, C.M.G., Royal Field Artillery.
Major (temporary Lieutenant-Colonel) W. E. T. Christie, Army Service Corps.
Lieutenant-Colonel G. R. M. Church, C.M.G., Royal Artillery.
Major A. L. C. Clarke, Argyll and Sutherland Highlanders.
Major M. O. Clarke, Royal Fusiliers.
Brevet Lieutenant-Colonel (temporary Brigadier-General) T. E. Clarke, Royal Inniskilling Fusiliers.
Major E. R. Clayton, Oxfordshire and Buckinghamshire Light Infantry.
Temporary Captain A. E. Clerk.
Lieutenant-Colonel (temporary Brigadier-General) H. F. H. Clifford, D.S.O., Suffolk Regiment.
Colonel (temporary Brigadier-General) A. S. Cobbe, V.C., C.B., D.S.O., Indian Army, A.D.C.
Lieutenant-Colonel H. H. Cobbe, D.S.O., 13th Lancers.
Major J. K. Cochrane, Leinster Regiment.
Captain G. B. Coleman, Army Service Corps.
Brevet Major (temporary Lieutenant-Colonel E. H. E. Collen, D.S.O., Reserve of Officers.

MENTIONED IN DESPATCHES

Major R. J. Collins, Royal Berkshire Regiment.
Major P. R. C. Commings, South Staffordshire Regiment.
Lieutenant-Colonel (temporary Brigadier-General) C. W. Compton, C.M.G., Somerset Light Infantry.
Major (temporary Lieutenant-Colonel) L. J. Comyn, Connaught Rangers.
Captain C. R. Congreve, D.S.O., Durham Light Infantry.
Captain W. La T. Congreve, Rifle Brigade.
Major-General W. N. Congreve, V.C., C.B., M.V.O.
Major E. C. W. Conway-Gordon, 3rd Skinner's Horse.
Lieutenant-Colonel (temporary Brigadier-General) C. E. Corkran, C.M.G., Grenadier Guards.
Captain J. H. M. Cornwall, Royal Artillery.
Brevet Lieutenant-Colonel G. N. Cory, D.S.O., Royal Dublin Fusiliers.
Captain C. B. Costin, West Yorkshire Regiment.
Colonel (temporary Major-General) V. A. Couper.
Major J. G. Courtice, Army Ordnance Department.
Major R. W. Courtney, Army Service Corps.
Captain E. W. Cox, D.S.O., Royal Engineers.
Major E. Craig-Brown, D.S.O., Cameron Highlanders.
Colonel (temporary Brigadier-General) H. L. Croker, C.B.
Captain F. L. M. Crossman, Royal Artillery.
Major G. L. Crossman, D.S.O., West Yorkshire Regiment.
Major J. A. F. Cuffe, Royal Munster Fusiliers.
Captain H. C. Cumberbatch, Yorkshire Regiment.
Captain F. W. M. Cunningham, M.D., Royal Army Medical Corps.
Lieutenant-Colonel (temporary Brigadier-General) A. C. Currie, Royal Artillery.
Major (temporary Lieutenant-Colonel) R. A. M. Currie, Somerset Light Infantry.
Colonel (temporary Brigadier-General) G. J. Cuthbert, C.B.
Colonel (temporary Brigadier-General) A. G. Dallas, C.B.
Second Lieutenant (temporary Captain) Lord A. E. H. M. A. Dalmeny, Reserve of Officers.
Brevet Lieutenant-Colonel (temporary Brigadier-General) A. C. Daly, West Yorkshire Regiment.
Captain V. A. H. Daly, West Yorkshire Regiment.
Captain (temporary Major) L. J. Danby, London Regiment.
Major (temporary Lieutenant-Colonel) F. H. Dansey, Wiltshire Regiment.
Major (temporary Lieutenant-Colonel) W. H. V. Darell, D.S.O., Coldstream Guards.
Captain A. E. Davidson, Royal Engineers.
Captain E. H. Davidson, Gordon Highlanders.
Brevet Lieutenant-Colonel J. H. Davidson, D.S.O., King's Royal Rifle Corps.

MENTIONED IN DESPATCHES

Major N. R. Davidson, Royal Artillery.
Major P. Davidson, D.S.O., M.B., Royal Army Medical Corps.
Colonel (temporary Brigadier-General) H. R. Davies.
Major-General R. H. Davies, C.B.
Lieutenant (temporary Captain in Army) V. C. Davies, Royal Field Artillery, Special Reserve.
Major W. E. Davies, Rifle Brigade.
Major (temporary Lieutenant-Colonel) W. P. L. Davies, Royal Artillery.
Colonel (temporary Brigadier-General) R. Dawson.
Major (temporary Lieutenant-Colonel) H. S. de Brett, D.S.O., Royal Artillery.
Major C. P. Deedes, D.S.O., Yorkshire Light Infantry.
Major (temporary Lieutenant-Colonel) H. V. M. de la Fontaine, East Surrey Regiment.
Temporary Captain W. E. Delves-Broughton, Royal Field Artillery (Lieutenant, Reserve of Officers).
Temporary Captain M. E. Denny.
Lieutenant-Colonel (temporary Colonel) H. D. De Pree, Royal Artillery.
Brevet Colonel (temporary Brigadier-General) F. S. Derhan, retired pay.
Major J. K. Dick-Cunyngham, D.S.O., Gordon Highlanders.
Brevet Colonel W. V. Dickinson, retired pay.
Major E. FitzG. Dillon, D.S.O., Royal Munster Fusiliers.
Captain W. G. S. Dobbie, Royal Engineers.
Captain J. A. Don, Royal Field Artillery.
Major J. C. M. Doran, Army Service Corps.
Major (temporary Lieutenant-Colonel) J. F. I. H. Doyle, Royal Artillery
Second Lieutenant (temporary Lieutenant) H. Drummond, Northumberland Yeomanry.
Major Hon. M. C. A. Drummond, Royal Highlanders.
Colonel N. W. H. Du Boulay.
Major-General J. P. Du Cane, C.B.
Temporary Captain J. S. Duckett (Lieutenant Reserve of Officers).
Brevet Lieutenant-Colonel F. C. Dundas, Argyll and Sutherland Highlanders.
Colonel J. W. Dunlop, C.B., retired pay.
Colonel A. B. Dunsterville, retired pay.
Major A. M. Duthie, Royal Artillery.
Captain H. L. Dyce, 9th Hodson's Horse.
Lieutenant E. G. Earle, D.S.O., Royal Artillery.
Major S. H. Eden, Royal Highlanders.
Colonel (temporary Brigadier-General) FitzJ. M. Edwards, D.S.O., Indian Army.
Major-General R. G. Egerton, C.B., Indian Army.
Brevet Major H. J. Elles, Royal Engineers.
Major (temporary Lieutenant-Colonel) E. L. Ellington, Royal Artillery.

MENTIONED IN DESPATCHES

Lieutenant-General Sir E. L. Elliot, K.C.B., D.S.O., retired Indian Army.
Lieutenant-Colonel (temporary Brigadier-General) F. A. G. Y. Elton Royal Artillery.
Lieutenant M. P. Evans, Royal Artillery.
Major-General R. Fanshawe, C.B., D.S.O.
Colonel (temporary Brigadier-General) W. H. Fasken, Indian Army.
Colonel (temporary Brigadier-General) D. J. M. Fasson, C.B.
Lieutenant-Colonel (temporary Captain in Army) J. C. Faunthorpe, Indian Volunteers.
Lieutenant-Colonel H. B. Fawcus, C.M.G., M.B., Royal Army Medical Corps.
Brevet Colonel (temporary Brigadier-General) G. P. T. Feilding, D.S.O., Coldstream Guards.
Lieutenant (temporary Captain in Army) R. E. A. Viscount Feilding, D.S.O., Coldstream Guards, Special Reserve.
Brevet Colonel (temporary Brigadier-General) R. B. Fell, retired pay.
Captain R. T. Fellowes, Rifle Brigade.
Lieutenant-General Sir C. Fergusson, Bt., K.C.B., M.V.O., D.S.O.
Major V. M. Fergusson, Royal Artillery.
Major (temporary Lieutenant-Colonel) H. C. Fernyhough, D.S.O., Army Ordnance Department.
Major W. A. Fetherstonhaugh, 8th Cavalry.
Major R. G. Finlayson, D.S.O., Royal Artillery.
Major (temporary Lieutenant-Colonel) B. D. Fisher, D.S.O., 17th Lancers.
Major (temporary Lieutenant-Colonel) P.D. FitzGerald, D.S.O., 11th Hussars.
Temporary Captain G. Flemming.
Major A. F. Fletcher, D.S.O., 17th Lancers.
Major R. S. Follett, Rifle Brigade.
Lieutenant-Colonel R. M. Foot, late East Anglian Brigade Royal Field Artillery (Major, Reserve of Officers).
Lieutenant-Colonel (temporary Colonel) A. Forbes, Army Ordnance Department.
Lieutenant-Colonel (temporary Brigadier-General) R. Ford, C.M.G., D.S.O., Army Service Corps.
Major D. Forster, Royal Engineers.
Captain C. C. Foss, V.C., D.S.O., Bedfordshire Regiment.
Captain O. B. Foster, Northumberland Fusiliers.
Colonel (temporary Brigadier-General) C. A. Fowler, D.S.O.
Temporary Captain H. G. Fowler.
Lieutenant-Colonel (temporary Brigadier-General) J. S. Fowler, C.B., D.S.O., Royal Engineers.
Colonel (temporary Brigadier-General) R. F. Fox, C.B., D.S.O.
Captain H. E. Frankyn, Yorkshire Regiment.

MENTIONED IN DESPATCHES

Brevet Colonel (temporary Brigadier-General) G. McK. Franks, Royal Artillery.
Captain A. J. Fraser, Royal Berkshire Regiment.
Captain F. L. Fraser, Seaforth Highlanders.
Lieutenant-Colonel T. Fraser, Royal Engineers.
Major J. C. Freeland, 35th Sikhs (Indian Army).
Major W. H. M. Freestun, Somerset Light Infantry.
Brevet Lieutenant-Colonel G. H. B. Freeth, D.S.O., Lancashire Fusiliers.
Major (temporary Lieutenant-Colonel) J. Fryer, 7th Hussars.
Captain C. G. Fulton, Highland (Howitzer) Brigade, Royal Field Artillery.
Captain M. Furber, Reserve of Officers.
Colonel (temporaary Major-General) W. T. Furse, C.B., D.S.O.
Major (temporary Lieutenant-Colonel) M. F. Gage, 5th Dragoon Guards.
Captain F. H. Gale, Bedfordshire Regiment.
Major (temporary Lieutenant-Colonel) P. W. Game, D.S.O., Royal Artillery.
Captain W. C. Garsia, Hampshire Regiment.
Lieutenant-Colonel H. E. Garstin, Royal Artillery.
Lieutenant-Colonel Hon. J. F. Gathorne-Hardy, D.S.O., Grenadier Guards.
Colonel (temporary Brigadier-General) A. W. Gay, D.S.O.
Colonel (temporary Brigadier-General) J. G. Geddes, C.B.
Major E. C. Gepp, Duke of Cornwall's Light Infantry, Special Reserve (Lieutenant, retired pay).
Lieutenant C. R. Gerard, Grenadier Guards.
Major (temporary Lieutenant-Colonel) R. W. St. L. Gethin, Royal Artillery.
Lieutenant-Colonel (temporary Brigadier-General) G. Gillson, D.S.O. Royal Artillery.
Colonel (temporary Brigadier-General) G. M. Gloster.
Major-General F. M. Glubb, C.B., D.S.O.
Temporary Captain R. FitzG. Glyn, Army Service Corps (Lieutenant, Reserve of Officers).
Major L. Godman, Royal Artillery.
Major (temporary Lieutenant-Colonel) C. A. C. Godwin, 23rd Cavalry.
Major H. D. Goldsmith, Duke of Cornwall's Light Infantry.
Major E. B. Gordon, Northumberland Fusiliers.
Lieutenant-Colonel (temporary Brigadier-General) C. Gosling, King's Royal Rifle Corps.
Major (temporary Lieutenant-Colonel) A. P. G. Gough, D.S.O., Reserve of Officers.
Major-General (temporary Lieutenant-General) H. de la P. Gough, C.B.

MENTIONED IN DESPATCHES

Lieutenant O. Gough, 12th Cavalry.
Major C. A. L. Graham, D.S.O., Royal Artillery.
Captain C. P. Graham, D.S.O., Welsh Regiment.
Major C. J. C. Grant, D.S.O., Coldstream Guards.
Second Lieutenant (temporary Captain) D. L. Grant, The London Regiment.
Captain C. O. V. Gray, Seaforth Highlanders.
Captain E. St. C. Gray, 34th Poona Horse.
Temporary Major J. A. S. Gray.
Lieutenant (temporary Captain) J. N. Gray, Inns of Court Officers' Training Corps.
Major G. C. Grazebrook, Royal Inniskilling Fusiliers.
Major (temporary Lieutenant-Colonel) A. F. U. Green, Royal Artillery.
Temporary Captain F. A. Green, Stationery Services.
Captain S. H. Green, West Yorkshire Regiment.
Brevet Colonel (temporary Brigadier-General) W. H. Greenly, C.M.G., D.S.O., 19th Hussars.
Temporary Second Lieutenant S. W. Griffin.
Major T. T. Grove, Royal Engineers.
Major A. H. W. Grubb, D.S.O., Royal Engineers.
Major R. R. Gubbins, D.S.O., Reserve of Officers.
Major Hon. C. H. C. Guest, 1st Dragoons.
Captain J. R. Guild, Gloucestershire Regiment.
Major R. F. Guy, Wiltshire Regiment.
Major (temporary Lieutenant-Colonel) C. H. Haig, Leicestershire Regiment.
General Sir D. Haig, G.C.B., K.C.I.E., K.C.V.O., A.D.C.-General.
Major-General (temporary Lieutenant-General) R. C. B. Haking, C.B.
Major-General J. A. L. Haldane, C.B., D.S.O.
Major H. Hale, Territorial Force Reserve.
Brevet Lieutenant-Colonel P. O. Hambro, 15th Hussars.
Major C. L. C. Hamilton, Royal Artillery.
Captain E. G. Hamilton, Connaught Rangers.
Lieutenant (temporary Captain) G. G. Hamilton, Lord, K.T., C.V.O., Reserve of Officers.
Captain (temporary Major) F. D. Hammond, Royal Engineers.
Major C. T. M. Hare, Leicestershire Regiment.
Lieutenant-Colonel R. H. Hare, M.V.O., D.S.O., Royal Artillery.
Second Lieutenant (temporary Lieutenant) C. L. Hargreaves, Reserve of Officers.
Brevet Lieutenant-Colonel (temporary Brigadier-General) C. H. Harington, D.S.O., Liverpool Regiment.
Colonel (temporary Major-General) G. M. Harper, C.B., D.S.O.
Temporary Lieutenant-Colonel W. A. Harrison, Royal Engineers (Major, Reserve of Officers).
Temporary Captain H. Hartley.

MENTIONED IN DESPATCHES

Brevet Lieutenant-Colonel (temporary Brigadier-General) W. J. St. J. Harvey, Royal Highlanders.
Major B. J. Haslam, Royal Engineers.
Major C. J. B. Hay, Corps of Guides.
Lieutenant-Colonel P. O. Hazelton, Army Service Corps.
Major (temporary Lieutenant-Colonel) H. R. Hadalam, D.S.O., York and Lancaster Regiment.
Major-General J. E. W. Headlam, C.B., D.S.O.
Colonel (temporary Major-General) G. M. Heath, D.S.O.
Colonel (Territorial Force) (temporary Brigadier-General in Army) Hon. C. S. Heathcote-Drummond-Willoughby (Major Reserve of Officers).
Major K. Henderson, 39th Garhwal Rifles.
Captain A. M. Henderson-Scott, Royal Inniskilling Fusiliers.
Brevet Colonel (temporary Brigadier-General) W. C. G. Heneker, D.S.O., North Staffordshire Regiment, A.D.C.
Major (temporary Lieutenant-Colonel) A. M. Henniker, Royal Engineers
Colonel (temporary Brigadier-General) C. G. Henshaw, Reserve of Officers.
Major (temporary Lieutenant-Colonel) R. Henvey, Royal Artillery.
Major (temporary Brigadier-General) Hon. J. F. Hepburn-Stuart-Forbes-Trefusis, D.S.O., Irish Guards (killed).
Temporary Captain H. V. Hesketh-Prichard.
Captain H. W. O'C. Hewett, 41st Dogras (killed).
Captain A. S. Hewitt, Royal West Kent Regiment.
Major E. Hewlett, Devonshire Regiment.
Major C. P. Heywood, Coldstream Guards.
Second Lieutenant (temporary Lieutenant) M. B. Heywood, Northumberland Yeomanry.
Colonel (temporary Brigadier-General) F. J. Heyworth, C.B., D.S.O.
Colonel (temporary Brigadier-General) G. L. Hibbert, D.S.O.
Colonel (temporary Brigadier-General) W. B. Hickie, C.B.
Temporary Captain C. M. Higgins.
Major (temporary Lieutenant-Colonel) H. W. Higginson, Royal Dublin Fusiliers.
Major H. C. T. Hildyard, Reserve of Officers.
Colonel (temporary Brigadier-General) C. Hill.
Lieutenant-Colonel (temporary Brigadier-General) E. S. Hoare Nairne, Royal Artillery.
Major-General P. E. F. Hobbs, C.B., C.M.G.
Major A. E. Holbrook, Army Service Corps.
Colonel (temporary Major-General) A. E. A. Holland, C.B., M.V.O., D.S.O.
Temporary Colonel G. E. Holland, C.I.E., D.S.O. (temporary Lieutenant-Colonel Royal Engineers).
Major L. B. Holliday, West Riding Regiment (Territorial Force).

MENTIONED IN DESPATCHES

Captain R. J. Holliday, London Regiment.
Major (temporary Lieutenant-Colonel) S. E. Hollond, Rifle Brigade.
Lieutenant-Colonel (temporary Brigadier-General) H. C. Holman, C.M.G., D.S.O., 16th Cavalry.
Major (temporary Brigadier-General) A. F. Home, D.S.O., 11th Hussars.
Brevet Lieutenant-Colonel G. V. Hordern, King's Royal Rifle Corps.
Major Hon. C. M. Hore-Ruthven, D.S.O., Royal Highlanders.
Lieutenant-Colonel Hon. W. P. Hore Ruthven (Master of Ruthven), C.M.G., D.S.O., Scots Guards.
Major-General H. S. Horne, C.B.
Captain (temporary Major) W. T. F. Horwood, Reserve of Officers.
Colonel (temporary Brigadier-General) J. Hotham, retired pay.
Major G. W. Howard, D.S.O., Essex Regiment.
Captain H. C. L. Howard, 16th Lancers.
Lieutenant-Colonel (temporary Brigadier-General) P. Howell, C.M.G., 4th Hussars.
Major-General H. Hudson, C.B., C.I.E., Indian Army.
Major P. Hudson, Liverpool Regiment.
Lieutenant-Colonel T. R. C. Hudson, Royal Artillery.
Captain F. St. J. Hughes, Reserve of Officers.
Brevet Colonel (temporary Brigadier-General) C. P. A. Hull, Middlesex Regiment.
Lieutenant-Colonel F. C. L. Hulton, Reserve of Officers.
Major A. S. Humphreys, Army Service Corps.
Major E. T. Humphreys, Lancashire Fusiliers.
Colonel (temporary Brigadier-General) G. Humphreys, C.B., D.S.O.
Captain H. R. A. Hunt, 25th Punjabis.
Colonel (temporary Major-General) W. Huskisson.
Colonel (temporary Brigadier-General) A. H. Hussey, C.B.
Major (temporary Lieutenant-Colonel) R. Hutchison, D.S.O., 4th Dragoon Guards.
Major A. B. Incledon-Webber, Royal Irish Fusiliers.
Major (District Officer) J. Inder, retired pay.
Major R. J. FitzG. Ingham, Royal Artillery.
Captain A. G. F. Isaac, Royal Berkshire Regiment.
Brevet Lieut.-Colonel H. Isacke, C.M.G., Royal West Kent Regiment.
Brevet Lieutenant-Colonel E. M. Jack, Royal Engineers.
Captain (temporary Major) B. Jackson, Yorkshire Regiment, Territorial Force.
Captain C. B. A. Jackson, York and Lancaster Regiment.
Major H. C. Jackson, Bedfordshire Regiment.
Colonel (temporary Brigadier-General) H. K. Jackson, C.B., D.S.O.
Colonel (temporary Major-General) C. W. Jacob, C.B., Indian Army.
Colonel (temporary Brigadier-General) C. H. L. James.
Colonel W. R. W. James.

MENTIONED IN DESPATCHES

Major (temporary Brigadier-General) R. G. Jelf, D.S.O., King's Royal Rifle Corps.
Major (temporary Lieutenant-Colonel) J. L. Jesse, Army Service Corps.
Colonel (temporary Brigadier-General) H. S. Jeudwine, C.B.
Colonel (temporary Brigadier-General) F. E. Johnson, C.M.G., D.S.O.
Lieutenant-Colonel H. G. Joly de Lotbinière, D.S.O., Royal Engineers.
Colonel H. B. Jones, C.B., Royal Engineers.
Second Lieutenant H. C. F. Jones, Royal Artillery.
Colonel (temporary Brigadier-General) L. Jones.
Colonel O. R. A. Julian, C.M.G.
Major H. Karslake, D.S.O., Royal Artillery.
Major-General C. T. McM. Kavanagh, C.V.O., C.B., D.S.O.
Major-General H. D'U. Keary, C.B., D.S.O., Indian Army.
Major-General (temporary Lieutenant-General) J. L. Keir, K.C.B.
Brevet-Colonel (temporary Brigadier-General) G. C. Kemp, Royal Engineers.
Brevet Colonel (temporary Brigadier-General) A. A. Kennedy, C.M.G., 3rd Hussars.
Major (temporary Lieutenant-Colonel) G. E. R. Kenrick, D.S.O., Royal West Surrey Regiment.
Lieutenant-Colonel K. J. Kincaid-Smith, D.S.O., Royal Artillery.
Second Lieutenant (temporary Lieutenant) M. H. King, West Riding Regiment, Territorial Force.
Brevet Colonel (temporary Brigadier-General) Sir D. A. Kinloch, Bt., C.B., M.V.O., retired pay.
Brevet Lieutenant-Colonel W. M. St. G. Kirke, Royal Artillery.
Major H. H. S. Knox, Northamptonshire Regiment.
Major-General Hon. W. Lambton, C.V.O., C.B., C.M.G., D.S.O.
Major-General H. J. S. Landon, C.B.
Major O. M. Lanyon, Royal Artillery.
Captain Hon. E. C. Lascelles, Rifle Brigade, Special Reserve.
Captain P. R. Laurie, 2nd Dragoons.
Major (temporary Lieutenant-Colonel) W. H P. Law, Army Service Corps.
Captain E. I. Lea, Royal Warwickshire Regiment, Territorial Force.
Colonel (temporary Brigadier-General) H. P. Leader, C.B.
Brevet Major (temporary Colonel) A. H. Lee, M.P., Reserve of Officers.
Colonel (temporary Brigadier-General) R. P. Lee, C.B., Royal Engineers.
Major S. F. Legge, Royal Fusiliers, Special Reserve (Major Reserve of Officers).
Major (temporary Lieutenant-Colonel) W. K. Legge, Essex Regiment.
Major E. H. G. Leggett, D.S.O., Royal Artillery.
Major W. S. Leslie, 31st Punjabis.
Temporary Captain C. E. Levita.
Major L. W. Lewer, Royal Artillery.

MENTIONED IN DESPATCHES

Major E. O. Lewin, Royal Artillery.
Major H. F. E. Lewin, Royal Artillery.
Captain C. G. Liddell, D.S.O., Leicestershire Regiment.
Captain W. G. Lindsell, Royal Artillery.
Major F. H. Lister, Royal Artillery.
Second Lieutenant (temporary Lieutenant) W. B. Little, Durham Light Infantry, Territorial Force.
Captain R. O'H. Livesay, D.S.O., Royal West Surrey Regiment.
Lieutenant-Colonel H. A. A. Livingstone, C.M.G., Royal Engineers.
Major J. E. C. Livingstone-Learmonth, D.S.O., Royal Artillery.
Lieutenant-Colonel (temporary Brigadier-General) Lord E. D. Loch, C.M.G., M.V.O., D.S.O., Grenadier Guards.
Major (temporary Lieutenant-Colonel) F. D. Logan, Royal Artillery.
Colonel A. Long, D.S.O.
Lieutenant (temporary Captain) B. Long, Oxfordshire and Buckinghamshire Light Infantry, Territorial Force.
Captain (temporary Major) E. W. Longden, York and Lancaster Regiment, Territorial Force.
Colonel (temporary Brigadier-General) J. R. Longley.
Lieutenant-Colonel (temporary Brigadier-General) J. C. G., Longmore, D.S.O., Army Service Corps.
Brevet Lieutenant-Colonel J. A. Longridge, 43rd Erinpura Regiment.
Major S. J. Lowe, D.S.O., Royal Fusiliers.
Brevet Colonel (temporary Brigadier-General) H. C. Lowther, C.V.O., C.M.G., D.S.O., Scots Guards.
Captain C. C. Lucas, Royal Artillery.
Temporary Major C. M. Luck, Royal Engineers.
Colonel (temporary Brigadier-General) E. R. O. Ludlow, C.B.
Major R. Luker, Lancashire Fusiliers.
Captain W. V. Lumsden, Argyll and Sutherland Highlanders.
Colonel (temporary Major-General) A. L. Lynden-Bell, C.B., C.M.G.
Major C. H. Lyon, North Staffordshire Regiment.
Lieutenant-Colonel (temporary Brigadier-General) F. Lyon, D.S.O., Royal Artillery.
Major R. L. Macalpine-Leny, 16th Lancers.
Colonel T. T. Macan, retired pay.
Lieutenant-Colonel (temporary Brigadier-General) M. J. MacCarthy, C.M.G., Royal Artillery.
Colonel (temporary Brigadier-General) W. K. McClintock.
Captain (local Captain in Army) J. T. McColl, Australian Commonwealth Military Forces.
Second Lieutenant (temporary Captain in Army) H. McCombie, Worcestershire Regiment, Territorial Force.
Major-General F. W. N. MCracken, C.B., D.S.O.
Major A. G. Macdonald, Royal Berkshire Regiment.
Colonel (temporary Brigadier-General) G. M. W. Macdonogh, C.B.

MENTIONED IN DESPATCHES

Colonel (temporary Brigadier-General) F. A. MacFarlan.
Major W. C. Macfie, Royal Engineers.
Captain D. K. McLeod, Corps of Guides.
Colonel (temporary Brigadier-General) W. K. McLeod.
Brevet Lieutenant-Colonel E. B. Macnaghten, D.S.O., Royal Field Artillery.
Major A. E. McNamara, Royal West Surrey Regiment.
Major-General (temporary Lieutenant-General) Sir C. F. N. Macready, K.C.B., K.C.M.G.
Lieutenant G. N. Macready, Royal Engineers.
Captain J. Macready, D.S.O., Bedfordshire Regiment.
Lieutenant-Colonel W. R. N. Madocks, Royal Artillery.
Major C. L. Magniac, Royal Engineers.
Captain C. A. S. Maitland, Gordon Highlanders.
Captain G. R. Maitland, 14th Lancers.
Major H. C. Makgill Crichton Maitland, Royal Scots Fusiliers.
Major R. H. Mangles, D.S.O., Royal West Surrey Regiment.
Major (temporary Lieutenant-Colonel) A. H. Marindin, Royal Highlanders.
Lieutenant-Colonel H. J. M. Marshall, Royal Engineers.
Major H. de C. Martelli, Royal Artillery.
Major G. H. Martin, King's Royal Rifle Corps.
Brevet Colonel (temporary Brigadier-General) A. Martyn, Royal West Kent Regiment.
Captain F. N. MacFarlane Mason, Royal Artillery.
Brevet Lieutenant-Colonel (temporary Brigadier-General) T. G. Matheson, Coldstream Guards.
Major F. G. Maughan, Durham Light Infantry.
Brevet Colonel G. W. Maunsell, retired pay.
Brevet Colonel (temporary Brigadier-General) F. B. Maurice, C.B., Nottinghamshire and Derbyshire Regiment.
Major-General F. I. Maxse, C.V.O., C.B., D.S.O.
Captain G. A. P. Maxwell, M.V.O., Royal Engineers.
Major-General (temporary Lieutenant-General) Sir R. C. Maxwell, K.C.B.
Major (temporary Lieutenant-Colonel) R. S. May, Royal Fusiliers.
Brevet Lieutenant-Colonel (temporary Brigadier-General) C. C. M. Maynard, D.S.O., Devonshire Regiment.
Major J. G. S. Mellor, Reserve of Officers.
Major-General H. F. Mercer, C.B.
Honorary Lieutenant-Colonel (temporary Major in Army) F. B. Mildmay, Territorial Force Reserve.
Major W. Miller, Middlesex Regiment.
Major-General G. F. Milne, C.B., D.S.O.
Major (temporary Lieutenant-Colonel) A. J. G. Moir, Royal Scots.
Lieutenant-General (temporary General) Sir C. C. Monro, K.C.B.

MENTIONED IN DESPATCHES

Lieutenant F. J. O. Montagu, Reserve of Officers.
Lieutenant-Colonel Lord H. A. Montagu Douglas Scott, D.S.O., London Regiment (Captain, Reserve of Officers).
Major-General Hon. E. J. Montagu-Stuart-Wortley, C.B., C.M.G., M.V.O., D.S.O.
Lieutenant-Colonel (temporary Brigadier-General) A. A. Montgomery, Royal Artillery.
Lieutenant-Colonel H. M. de F. Montgomery, Royal Artillery.
Major F. H. Moore, Royal Berkshire Regiment.
Major H. T. G. Moore, D.S.O., Royal Engineers.
Colonel (temporary Brigadier-General) J. Moore, C.B., F.R.C.V.S.
Major-General (temporary Lieutenant-General) T. L. N. Morland, K.C.B., D.S.O.
Lieutenant D. J. F. Morton, Royal Artillery.
Captain R. A. Mostyn-Owen, Rifle Brigade.
Captain S. A. Mott, Reserve of Officers.
Colonel E. A. Moulton-Barrett, C.M.G., retired pay.
Captain J. A. Muirhead, 1st Lancers.
Colonel (temporary Major-General) R. L. Mullens.
Major B. E. Murray, Shropshire Light Infantry.
Major H. Musgrave, D.S.O., Royal Engineers.
Colonel F. C. Muspratt, Indian Army.
Captain S. F. Muspratt, 12th Cavalry.
Major V. E. Muspratt, 30th Lancers.
Major H. Needham, Gloucestershire Regiment.
Lieutenant (temporary Captain) H. A. H. Newington, London Regiment.
Major C. R. Newman, Royal Artillery.
Major (temporary Lieutenant-Colonel) C. C. Newnham, 6th Cavalry.
Captain L. A. Newnham, Middlesex Regiment.
Captain H. I. Nicholl, Reserve of Officers.
Colonel (temporary Brigadier-General) G. H. Nicholson.
Major O. H. L. Nicholson, D.S.O., West Yorkshire Regiment.
Major W. N. Nicholson, Suffolk Regiment.
Brevet Colonel (temporary Brigadier-General) C. E. de M. Norie, D.S.O., 2nd Gurkha Rifles.
Colonel (temporary Major-General) O. S. W. Nugent, D.S.O., A.D.C.
Major T. H. C. Nunn, D.S.O., Royal West Kent Regiment.
Temporary Captain M. O'Connor.
Major (temporary Lieutenant-Colonel) W. M. Ogg, Royal Artillery.
Captain T. B. Olive, 3rd Hussars.
Colonel (temporary Brigadier-General) W. H. Onslow, C.B.
Captain J. B. Orde, Royal Artillery.
Captain E. A. B. Orr, Royal Berkshire Regiment.
Captain R. H. Osborne, 20th Hussars.
Colonel (temporary Brigadier-General) R. S. Oxley.

MENTIONED IN DESPATCHES

Major E. C. Packe, Royal Fusiliers.
Captain C. A. S. Page, Middlesex Regiment.
Lieutenant H. J. Page, Royal Field Artillery, Special Reserve.
Colonel (temporary Brigadier-General) W. L. H. Paget, C.B., C.M.G., M.V.O.
Temporary Lieutenant-Colonel C. W. Paget, Royal Engineers.
Captain A. E. S. L. Paget, M.V.O., 11th Hussars.
Captain D. Paige, Royal Artillery.
Major G. de la P. B. Pakenham. D.S.O., Border Regiment.
Captain A. E. G. Palmer, Yorkshire Regiment.
Colonel (temporary Brigadier-General) H. D. E. Parsons, C.B., C.M.G., Army Ordnance Department.
Captain C. Parsons, Reserve of Officers.
Temporary Major S. G. Partridge, Stationery Services.
Brevet Colonel (temporary Brigadier-General) Serocold E. Pearce, King's Royal Rifle Corps.
Major-General E. M. Perceval, C.B., D.S.O.
Brevet Colonel (temporary Brigadier-General) C. E. Pereira, Coldstream Guards.
Major J. W. P. Peters, Reserve of Officers.
Major (temporary Brigadier-General) L. F. Philips, D.S.O., King's Royal Rifle Corps.
Lieutenant L. G. Phillips, Worcestershire Regiment.
Colonel (temporary Brigadier-General) E. J. Phipps-Hornby, V.C., C.B.
Major (temporary Lieutenant-Colonel) C. J. Pickering, West Riding Regiment.
Colonel W. W. Pike, D.S.O., F.R.C.S.I.
Major-General T. D. Pilcher, C.B.
Major-General C. P. W. Pirie, Indian Army.
Brevet Colonel W. H. P. Plomer, Reserve of Officers.
Lieutenant-General (temporary General) Sir H. C. O. Plumer, K.C.B.
Lieutenant-Colonel (temporary Brigadier-General) J. Ponsonby, C.M.G., D.S.O., Coldstream Guards.
Major C. L. Porter, East Kent Regiment.
Major A. G. Pratt, Essex Regiment.
Major L. A. E. Price-Davies, V.C., D.S.O., King's Royal Rifle Corps.
Major H. B. Protheroe-Smith, Reserve of Officers.
Brevet Lieutenant-Colonel (temporary Brigadier-General) C. B. Prowse, Somerset Light Infantry.
Major-General (temporary Lieutenant-General) W. P. Pulteney, K.C.B., D.S.O.
Temporary Second Lieutenant P. F. Pyle, Postal Section, Royal Engineers, Special Reserve.
Second Lieutenant A. C. M. Pym, 16th Lancers, Special Reserve.
Major J. Rainsford-Hannay, Royal West Surrey Regiment.

MENTIONED IN DESPATCHES

Major H. A. Ramsay, Royal Artillery.
Honorary Lieutenant-Colonel A. F. Randolph, late 3rd Battalion Suffolk Regiment (Major, Reserve of Officers).
Captain A. L. Ransome, Dorsetshire Regiment.
Captain L. C. Rattray, King's Royal Rifle Corps, Special Reserve.
Lieutenant-Colonel (temporary Brigadier-General) H. S. L. Ravenshaw, C.M.G., Connaught Rangers.
Major S. W. H. Rawlins, D.S.O., Royal Artillery.
Major-General (temporary Lieutenant-General) Sir H. S. Rawlinson, Bt., K.C.B., C.V.O.
Captain E. D. Raymond, 30th Lancers.
Major (temporary Brigadier-General) A. J. Reddie, D.S.O., South Wales Borderers.
Captain H. R. B. Reed, 39th Garhwal Rifles.
Major L. F. Renny, D.S.O., Royal Dublin Fusiliers.
Temporary Captain L. W. Reynolds, C.I.E.
Major-General S. R. Rice, C.B.
Honorary Major C. E. F. Rich, Captain Lincolnshire Regiment, Special Reserve, Captain, Reserve of Officers.
Captain T. S. Riddell-Webster, D.S.O., Scottish Rifles.
Captain D. G. Ridgeway, 3rd Gurkha Rifles.
Lieutenant (temporary Captain) G. Robarts, Northamptonshire Yeomanry.
Second Lieutenant B. H. Robertson, Royal Engineers.
Captain D. E. Robertson, 11th Lancers.
Lieutenant-Colonel (temporary Brigadier-General) P. R. Robertson, C.M.G., Scottish Rifles.
Lieutenant-General Sir W. R. Robertson, K.C.B., K.C.V.O., D.S.O.
Captain D. G. Robinson, 46th Punjabis.
Major P. G. Robinson, Royal Field Artillery.
Major (temporary Lieutenant-Colonel) S. W. Robinson, Royal Artillery.
Major H. S. Rogers, Reserve of Officers.
Major H. S. Rogers, Shropshire Light Infantry.
Captain S. P. A. Rolls, Dorsetshire Regiment.
Lieutenant-Colonel (temporary Brigadier-General) C. F. Romer, C.B. Royal Dublin Fusiliers.
Captain A. R. Dougal Roney, Royal Artillery.
Lieutenant-Colonel H. Rose, Reserve of Officers.
Colonel (temporary Brigadier-General) C. Ross, D.S.O., Reserve of Officers.
Colonel (temporary Brigadier-General) W. C. Ross, C.B., retired pay.
Lieutenant-Colonel (temporary Brigadier-General) C. M. Ross-Johnson, C.M.G., D.S.O., Royal Artillery.
Lieutenant-Colonel (temporary Brigadier-General) J. G. Rotton, Royal Artillery.
Colonel (temporary Brigadier-General) J. W. G. Roy.

MENTIONED IN DESPATCHES

Major (temporary Lieutenant-Colonel) Hon. A. V. F. Russell, M.V.O., Grenadier Guards.
Major (temporary Lieutenant-Colonel) F. D. Russell, 1st Lancers.
Captain T. G. Ruttledge, Connaught Rangers.
Colonel C. M. Ryan, D.S.O.
Captain F. T. Ryan, Royal Artillery.
Captain R. S. Ryan, Royal Artillery.
Lieutenant-Colonel Hon. C. J. Sackville-West, C.M.G., King's Royal Rifle Corps.
Major E. F. St. John, Royal Artillery.
Lieutenant F. J. Salmon, Temporary Staff Lieutenant.
Colonel (temporary Brigadier-General) H. G. Sandilands, C.B.
Colonel (temporary Brigadier-General) H. N. Sargent, C.B., D.S.O.
Major W. E. Scafe, Devonshire Regiment.
Lieutenant-Colonel G. P. Scholfield, Royal Engineers.
Colonel (temporary Brigadier-General) A. L. Schreiber, D.S.O., A.D.C.
Major L. R. Schuster, Liverpool Regiment.
Major S. J. P. Scobell, Norfolk Regiment.
Colonel (temporary Major-General) A. B. Scott, C.B., D.S.O.
Captain H. L. Scott, 1st Gurkha Rifles.
Major J. C. Scott, Argyll and Sutherland Highlanders.
Colonel (temporary Brigadier-General) S. W. Scrase-Dickins.
Colonel A. K. Seccombe, D.S.O.
Lieutenant-Colonel and Honorary Colonel (temporary Brigader-General in Army) Rt. Hon. J. E. B. Seely, D.S.O., Hampshire Yeomanry.
Major B. N. Sergison-Brooke, D.S.O., Grenadier Guards.
Major W. W. Seymour, Rifle Brigade.
Lieutenant-Colonel (temporary Brigadier-General) J. S. M. Shea, C.B., D.S.O., 35th Horse.
Colonel (temporary Brigadier-General) H. P. Shekleton, C.B.
Captain E. Sheppard, 19th Hussars.
Major N. H. C. Sherbrooke, Royal Artillery.
Major D. J. C. E. Sherlock, Royal Artillery.
Lieutenant C. R. Shield, Highland Light Infantry, Special Reserve.
Colonel (temporary Brigadier-General) C. T. Shipley.
Captain S. R. Shirley, 54th Sikhs.
Brevet Lieutenant-Colonel T. H. Shoubridge, D.S.O., Northumberland Fusiliers.
Colonel (temporary Brigadier-General) C. D. Shute.
Captain E. H. Simpson, Liverpool Regiment, Special Reserve.
Captain J. G. Simpson, Cameron Highlanders.
Colonel (temporary Brigadier-General) W. D. Smith, C.B.
Colonel W. H. U. Smith, D.S.O., Army Ordnance Department.
Captain H. W. Snow, Reserve of Officers.
Major-General (temporary Lieutenant-General) T. D'O. Snow, K.C B.

MENTIONED IN DESPATCHES

Captain F. E. Spencer, Royal Artillery.
Major J. A. W. Spencer, Rifle Brigade.
Captain Hon. V. A. Spencer, King's Own Scottish Borderers, Special Reserve.
Lieutenant (temporary Captain) E. L. Spiers, 11th Hussars.
Captain G. W. R. Stacpoole, D.S.O., Reserve of Officers.
Major J. R. Stanhope, Earl, Royal West Kent Regiment, Territorial Force (Captain, Reserve of Officers).
Major H. A. S. Stanton, Royal Scots.
Major F. B. J. Stapleton-Bretherton, late Lancashire Hussars Yeomanry (Captain, Reserve of Officers).
Major (temporary Brigadier-General) J. McC. Steele, Coldstream Guards.
Lieutenant D. J. Steevens, Royal Field Artillery.
Major H. W. Stenhouse, Royal West Surrey Regiment.
Captain G. E. B. Stephens, Reserve of Officers.
Second Lieutenant G. M. Stevenson-Reece, Special Reserve.
Major (temporary Lieutenant-Colonel) A. F. Stewart, Middlesex Regiment.
Lieutenant-Colonel J. A. Stewart, Army Ordnance Department.
Major P. A. V. Stewart, D.S.O., King's Own Scottish Borderers.
Major Sir G. M. H. Stirling, Bt., D.S.O., Essex Regiment.
Colonel (temporary Brigadier-General) A. Stokes, C.B., D.S.O.
Colonel (temporary Brigadier-General) L. A. M. Stopford.
Captain M. G. N. Stopford, Rifle Brigade.
Major H. Street, Devonshire Regiment.
Brevet Colonel (temporary Brigadier-General) E. P. Strickland, C.M.G., D.S.O., Manchester Regiment.
Brevet Lieutenant-Colonel A. G. Stuart, 40th Pathans.
Colonel (temporary Brigadier-General) A. M. Stuart, C.B.
Major G. A. Sullivan, Oxfordshire and Buckinghamshire Light Infantry.
Colonel (temporary Brigadier-General) H. C. Surtees, C.B., M.V.O., D.S.O., retired pay.
Major W. A. W. Swettenham, Royal Artillery.
Major E. V. Sydenham, Royal Warwickshire Regiment, Territorial Force.
Lieutenant-Colonel (temporary Brigadier-General) T. A. Tancred, C.M.G., Royal Artillery.
Major (temporary Lieutenant-Colonel) E. N. Tandy, Royal Artillery.
Major and Honorary Lieutenant-Colonel C. N. Taylor, Territorial Force Reserve.
Lieutenant-Colonel E. F. Taylor, C.B., Army Service Corps.
Major N. McD. Teacher, Royal Scots Fusiliers.
Brevet Lieutenant-Colonel H.S.H. Prince Alexander A. F. W. A. G. of Teck, G.C.B., G.C.V.O., D.S.O., 2nd Life Guards.

MENTIONED IN DESPATCHES

Captain F. R. Teesdale, 25th Cavalry.
Major R. S. Tempest, Scots Guards.
Major R. J. A. Terry, M.V.O., D.S.O., Royal Sussex Regiment (killed)
Brevet Colonel (temporary Major-General) G. H. Thesiger, C.B., C.M.G., Rifle Brigade, A.D.C. (killed).
Major E. G. Thompson, Reserve of Officers.
Colonel H. N. Thompson, D.S.O., M.B.
Cojonel A. G. Thomson, C.B.
Major A. F. A. N. Thorne, Grenadier Guards.
Major L. H. Thornton, Rifle Brigade, Special Reserve (Capt., retired).
Major H. W. B. Thorp, Yorkshire Light Infantry.
Major G. Thorpe, D.S.O., Argyll and Sutherland Highlanders.
Lieutenant-Colonel (temporary Brigadier-General) H. F. Thuillier, Royal Engineers.
Major E. G. L. Thurlow, D.S.O., Somerset Light Infantry.
Lieutenant-Colonel (temporary Brigadier-General) W. Thwaites, Royal Artillery.
Captain E. S. W. Tidswell, D.S.O., Leicestershire Regiment.
Colonel G. F. N. Tinley, C.B., Indian Army.
Honorary Lieutenant-Colonel (temporary Major in Army) A. C. Tompkins, late 7th Battalion Royal Fusiliers).
Major R. H. D. Tompson, D.S.O., Royal Artillery.
Captain W. W. T. Torr, West Yorkshire Regiment.
Captain B. C. B. Tower, Royal Fusiliers.
Captain F. H. E. Townshend, Royal Engineers.
Captain D. le P. Trench, Royal Artillery.
Brevet Colonel (temporary Brigadier-General) H. M. Trenchard, C.B., D.S.O., Royal Scots Fusiliers, A.D.C.
Major H. E. Trevor, D.S.O., Yorkshire Light Infantry.
Captain R. C. Trousdale, D.S.O., Reserve of Officers.
Second Lieutenant J. M. Troutbeck, London Regiment.
Major Hon. J. S. R. Tufton, Royal Sussex Regiment, Special Reserve.
Colonel (temporary Brigadier-General) J. A. S. Tulloch, C.B., Royal Engineers.
Major (temporary Lieutenant-Colonel) J. B. G. Tulloch, Yorkshire Light Infantry.
Lieutenant-Colonel F. C. Turner, Northumberland Fusiliers.
Lieutenant-Colonel H. H. F. Turner, 2nd Lancers.
Lieutenant-Colonel (temporary Brigadier-General) H. D. Tuson, Duke of Cornwall's Light Infantry.
Major-(temporary Lieutenant-Colonel) F. A. Twiss, M.V.O., Royal Artillery.
Captain W. L. O. Twiss, 9th Gurkha Rifles.
Captain A. C. L. Tyrrell, 25th Cavalry.
Major (temporary Lieutenant-Colonel) G. E. Tyrrell, D.S.O., Royal Artillery.

MENTIONED IN DESPATCHES

Major F. St. J. Tyrwhitt, Worcestershire Regiment.
Lieutenant-Colonel (temporary Brigadier-General) C. C. Van Straubenzee, Royal Artillery.
Colonel (temporary Brigadier-General) C. H. C. Van Straubenzee.
Colonel (temporary Major-General) J. Vaughan, C.B., D.S.O.
Major (temporary Lieutenant-Colonel) L. R. Vaughan, D.S.O., 7th Gurkha Rifles.
Captain E. S. Vicary, 16th Cavalry.
Captain (temporary Major) J. E. Viccars, Leicestershire Regiment, Territorial Force.
Major V. Vivian, M.V.O., Grenadier Guards.
Major E. G. Wace, Royal Engineers.
Lieutenant-Colonel W. D. Waghorn, Royal Engineers.
Captain B. Walcot, D.S.O., Royal Engineers.
Brevet Lieutenant-Colonel G. Walker, Royal Engineers.
Captain J. D. G. Walker, D.S.O., Reserve of Officers.
Major R. S. Walker, Royal Engineers.
Colonel (temporary Major-General) W. G. Walker, V.C., C.B., Indian Army.
Major A. W. B. Wallace, Durham Light Infantry.
Colonel F. E. Wallerstein, retired pay.
Lieutenant-Colonel (temporary Brigadier-General) A. E. Wardrop, Royal Artillery.
Temporary Major F. Ware.
Major B. C. Waterfield, retired, Indian Army.
Major C. F. Watson, D.S.O., Royal West Surrey Regiment.
Colonel (temporary Major-General) H. E. Watts, C.B., C.M.G., retired pay.
Major B. A. G. Watts, Royal Australian Garrison Artillery.
Brevet Major N. W. Webber, Royal Engineers.
Major (temporary Lieutenant-Colonel) W. H. F. Weber, Royal Artillery
Lieutenant-Colonel H. W. Weekes, Royal Engineers.
Major H. H. Were, Reserve of Officers.
Major J. L. Weston, Army Service Corps.
Major (temporary Lieutenant-Colonel H. L. Wethered, Army Ordnance Department.
Major J. R. Wethered, Gloucestershire Regiment.
Colonel (temporary Major-General) R. D. Whigham, C.B., D.S.O.
Major H. F. Whinney, Royal Fusiliers.
Brevet Lieutenant-Colonel W. A. White, Connaught Rangers.
Honorary Brigadier-General W. L. White, C.B., retired pay.
Major W. N. White, Army Service Corps.
Lieutenant-Colonel (temporary Brigadier-General) H. D. White-Thomson, C.B., D.S.O., Royal Artillery.
Captain J. Whitehead, 1st Brahmans.
Major K. Wigram, 2nd Gurkha Rifles.

MENTIONED IN DESPATCHES

Colonel (temporary Brigadier-General) M. G. Wilkinson, M.V.O., retired pay.
Major-General P. S. Wilkinson, C.B., C.M.G.
Colonel (temporary Major-General) H. B. Williams, C.B., D.S.O.
Lieutenant-Colonel S. F. Williams, Royal Engineers.
Captain A. H. M. Wilson, 12th Cavalry.
Lieutenant C. M. Wilson, Wiltshire Regiment, Territorial Force.
Captain D. D. Wilson, 17th Cavalry.
Major-General (temporary Lieutenant-General) Sir H. F. M. Wilson, K.C.B.
Major-General (temporary Lieutenant-General) Sir H. H. Wilson, K.C.B., D.S.O.
Colonel J. B. Wilson, M.D.
Major S. H. Wilson, C.M.G., Royal Engineers.
Major G. Windsor Clive, Coldstream Guards.
Major-General F. D. V. Wing, C.B. (killed).
Brevet Major (temporary Lieutenant-Colonel) Hon. M. A. Wingfield, Rifle Brigade.
Major W. J. R. Wingfield, Reserve of Officers.
Honorary Brigadier-General C. V. Wingfield-Stratford, retired pay.
Major H. St. J. L. Winterbotham, Royal Engineers.
Colonel (temporary Major-General) F. Wintour, C.B.
Lieutenant-Colonel C. B. Wood, retired pay.
Major D. Wood, Rifle Brigade.
Lieutenant-Colonel (temporary Brigadier-General) P. R. Wood, C.M.G., Royal Irish Fusiliers.
Captain (temporary Major) R. J. Wordsworth, Nottinghamshire and Derbyshire Regiment (Territorial Force).
Colonel (Territorial Force) (temporary Brigadier-General in Army) J. C. Wray, M.V.O. (Major, Reserve of Officers).
Major H. E. S. Wynne, Royal Artillery.
Major H. W. Wynter, D.S.O., Royal Artillery.
Captain C. M. Yates, M.V.O., Liverpool Regiment.

Intelligence Corps.

Temporary Second Lieutenant C. W. Bell.
Temporary Lieutenant S. P. Best.
Temporary Captain C. A. Cameron.
Temporary Lieutenant A. H. D'Egville.
Temporary Lieutenant K. T. Gemmell.
Temporary Captain M. A. Hall.
Temporary Lieutenant P. Leigh-Smith.
Temporary Lieutenant H. A. Lloyd.
Temporary Lieutenant I. H. McClure.
Temporary Lieutenant W. L. McEwen.
Temporary Lieutenant R. W. A., Earl of Onslow.

MENTIONED IN DESPATCHES

Temporary Lieutenant W. M. Sherring.
Temporary Captain C. M. Smith.
Temporary Second Lieutenant K. W. Tremellen.
Temporary Lieutenant A. V. L. Vigors.
Temporary Major J. A. Wallinger.

ROYAL FLYING CORPS.

Second Lieutenant (temporary Lieutenant) W. H. D. Acland, Royal 1st Devon Yeomanry.
Lieutenant (temporary Captain in Army) W. C. Adamson, Special Reserve.
Second Lieutenant J. O. Andrews, Royal Scots.
Lieutenant-Colonel E. B. Ashmore, M.V.O., Royal Artillery.
Second Lieutenant (temporary Captain) P. Babington, Hampshire Regiment (Territorial Force).
Second Lieutenant (temp. Lieutenant) J. E. A. Baldwin, 8th Hussars.
Lieutenant Hon. M. Baring, Special Reserve.
Captain V. A. Barrington-Kennett, Special Reserve.
Lieutenant (temporary Captain) A. S. Barratt, Royal Artillery.
Brevet Major (temporary Lieutenant-Colonel) J. H. W. Becke, Nottinghamshire and Derbyshire Regiment.
Captain M. McB. Bell-Irving, Special Reserve.
Lieutenant (temporary Captain) W. C. K. Birch, Yorkshire Regiment.
Captain H. Blackburn, Special Reserve.
Major A. G. Board, South Wales Borderers.
Captain (temporary Major) A. E. Borton, D.S.O., Royal Highlanders.
Captain (temporary Major) Hon. J. D. Boyle, Rifle Brigade.
Captain C. R. S. Bradley, 4th Cavalry, Indian Army.
Brevet Lieutenant-Colonel W. S. Brancker, Royal Artillery.
Captain H. Le M. Brock, Royal Warwickshire Regiment.
Brevet Major (temporary Lieutenant-Colonel) C. J. Burke, D.S.O., Royal Irish Regiment.
Second Lieutenant E. Bush, Special Reserve.
Second Lieutenant A. J. Capel, Somerset Light Infantry.
Lieutenant J. Cemlyn-Jones, Royal Welsh Fusiliers (Territorial Force).
Major (temporary Lieutenant-Colonel) L. E. O. Charlton, D.S.O., Lancashire Fusiliers.
Captain A. Christie, Royal Artillery.
Temporary Captain F. H. Cleaver.
Second Lieutenant H. A. Cooper (Special Reserve).
Lieutenant (temporary Captain) C. C. Darley, Royal Artillery.
Captain (temporary Major) G. W. P. Dawes, Royal Berkshire Regiment.
Captain H. de Haviland, Special Reserve.
Lieutenant W. S. Douglas, Royal Field Artillery, Special Reserve.
Captain (temporary Major) H. C. T. Dowding, Royal Artillery.
Temporary Lieutenant A. J. Evans, Special List.

MENTIONED IN DESPATCHES

Major F. L. Festing, Northumberland Fusiliers.
Lieutenant O. D. Filley, Special Reserve.
Second Lieutenant E. M. Gilbert, Essex Regiment, Special Reserve.
Captain H. F. Glanville, West India Regiment.
Second Lieutenant D. A. Glen, Manchester Regiment.
Lieutenant (temporary Captain) E. L. Gossage, Royal Artillery.
Captain E. L. M. L. Gower, Special Reserve.
Temporary Second Lieutenant B. P. Greenwood, Special List.
Lieutenant (temporary Captain) E. O. Grenfell, Royal Artillery.
Temporary Second Lieutenant H. B. R. Grey-Edwards, Royal Artillery.
Captain J. G. Hearson, Royal Engineers.
Lieutenant (temporary Captain in Army) F. E. Hellyer, Hampshire Regiment (Territorial Force).
Brevet Lieutenant-Colonel (temporary Brigadier-General) J. F. A. Higgins, D.S.O., Royal Artillery.
Temporary Captain E. D. Horsfall.
Temporary Second Lieutenant E. L. Hyde.
Temporary Second Lieutenant A. J. Insall.
Captain J. L. Jackson, Connaught Rangers, Special Reserve.
Lieutenant (temporary Captain) B. T. James, Royal Engineers (killed).
Lieutenant (temporary Captain) J. L. Kinnear, Liverpool Regiment.
Lieutenant (temporary Captain) G. A. K. Lawrence, D.S.O., Royal Artillery.
Captain (temporary Major) D. S. Lewis, D.S.O., Royal Engineers.
Second Lieutenant S. H. Long, Durham Light Infantry.
Brevet Major (temporary Lieutenant-Colonel) C. A. H. Longcroft, Welsh Regiment.
Major R. Longstaff, Royal Field Artillery.
Captain R. Loraine, Special Reserve.
Temporary Lieutenant Hon. E. F. P. Lubbock, Army Service Corps.
Captain (temporary Major) E. R. Ludlow-Hewitt, Royal Irish Rifles.
Captain A. Marshall, D.S.O., 28th Cavalry, Indian Army.
Temporary Second Lieutenant H. W. Medlicott.
Lieutenant (temporary Captain) G. D. Mills, Nottinghamshire and Derbyshire Regiment.
Captain W. G. S. Mitchell, Highland Light Infantry.
Second Lieutenant (temporary Captain) E. H. Mitchell, Royal Artillery.
Captain J. T. C. Moore-Brabazon, Special Reserve.
Lieutenant (temporary Captain in Army) H. R. Nicholl, Special Reserve.
Temporary Lieutenant A. H. Parker (Lieutenant Punjab Volunteer Rifles).
Temporary Second Lieutenant R. H. Peck, Dorset Regiment.
Lieutenant (temporary Captain in Army) R. M. Pike, Special Reserve.
Second Lieutenant J. C. W. A. Pinney, Royal Fusiliers.
Lieutenant (temporary Captain) P. H. L. Playfair, Royal Artillery.

MENTIONED IN DESPATCHES

Captain G. T. Porter, Royal Artillery.
Captain (temporary Lieutenant in Army) E. W. Powell, Unattached List (Territorial Force).
Temporary Lieutenant F. J. Powell.
Quartermaster and Honorary Lieutenant (temporary Captain) J. Ramsay.
Lieutenant (temporary Captain) W. R. Read, 1st Dragoon Guards.
Captain L. W. B. Rees, Royal Artillery.
Brevet Major H. R. P. Reynolds, Royal Engineers.
Second Lieutenant R. S. Rumbold, Somerset Light Infantry.
Temporary Lieutenant J. C. Russell, Royal Engineers (Second Lieutenant, Royal Engineers, Territorial Force).
Lieutenant (temporary Captain) C. E. Ryan, Royal Field Artillery.
Major (temporary Lieutenant-Colonel) W. G. H. Salmond, Royal Artillery.
Brevet Major (temporary Lieutenant-Colonel) J. M. Salmond, D.S.O., Royal Lancaster Regiment.
Temporary Lieutenant R. A. Saunders, Royal Field Artillery (Territorial Force).
Second Lieutenant E. R. C. Schofield, Lancashire Fusiliers.
Captain (temporary Major) G. S. Shephard, Royal Fusiliers.
Temporary Second Lieutenant H. S. Shield.
Lieutenant (temporary Captain) F. W. H. Simpson, Royal Garrison Artillery.
Second Lieutenant H. R. D. Simpson, 6th Dragoons.
Temporary Lieutenant H. M. Sison, Army Service Corps.
Captain T. V. Smith, Special Reserve.
Lieutenant A. Somervail, King's Own Scottish Borderers (Territorial Force).
Captain N. C. Spratt, Special Reserve.
Lieutenant J. V. Steel, Royal Garrison Artillery.
Second Lieutenant Symington, D.A.C., Special Reserve.
Second Lieutenant (temporary Captain) A. A. B. Thomaso
Second Lieutenant (temporary Captain) A. A. B. Thomson, Royal Warwickshire Regiment.
Second Lieutenant H. R. Vagg, Somerset Light Infantry.
Temporary Second Lieutenant A. M. Vaucour, Royal Field Artillery.
Lieutenant (temporary Captain) R. H. Verney, Army Service Corps.
Major (temporary Lieutenant-Colonel) T. I. Webb-Bowen, Bedfordshire Regiment.
Second Lieutenant J. W. Woodhouse, Special Reserve.
Second Lieutenant L. W. Yule, Special Reserve.
Acting Serjeant-Major J. P. Angell.
Serjeant A. W. Armstrong.
Serjeant A. Armstrong.
Serjeant A. A. J. Beer.

MENTIONED IN DESPATCHES

Serjeant H. E. Bethell.
Flight Serjeant G. Brown.
Corporal G. S. Chapman.
1st Class Air Mechanic W. Elstow.
Corporal A. Hawley.
Acting Serjeant-Major A. Hunter.
Flight-Serjeant W. C. Ibbott.
Flight-Serjeant F. James.
Acting Serjeant-Major M. Keegan.
Flight-Serjeant E. J. P. Kelly.
Corporal E. J. A. Knight.
Flight-Serjeant T. C. Noble.
Serjeant A. Randle.
Serjeant W. Smith.
1st Class Air Mechanic P. M. Veitch.
Acting Serjeant-Major H. Woods.

1st Life Guards.

Major (temporary Lieutenant-Colonel) Hon. A. F. Stanley, D.S.O.
Major L. E. Barry, Reserve of Officers.

2nd Life Guards.

Captain F. Penn.
Corporal of Horse, J. E. Peel.
Corporal of Horse W. P. Doyle.

Royal Horse Guards.

Brevet Lieutenant-Colonel (temporary Lieutenant-Colonel) D. C. Lord Tweedmouth, C.M.G., M.V.O., D.S.O.
Major C. S. H. Londonderry, Marquis of, M.V.O.
Lieutenant (temporary Captain) Hon. C. E. A. Philipps (killed).

1st Dragoon Guards.

Lieutenant-Colonel (temporary Brigadier-General) J. A. Bell-Smyth.
Major (temporary Lieutenant-Colonel) H. F. Wickham.
Major A. M. Turner.
Captain (temporary Major) G. R. H. Cheape.
Farrier Quartermaster-Serjeant J. Woolley.

2nd Dragoon Guards.

Lieutenant-Colonel A. Lawson.
Major (temporary Lieutenant-Colonel) A. E. W. Harman.
Major G. H. A. Ing, D.S.O.
Major M. C. C. Pinching.
Lieutenant (temporary Captain in Army) W. H. Tapp, Special Reserve.

MENTIONED IN DESPATCHES

Second Lieutenant (temporary Lieutenant) J. J. Kingstone.
Second Lieutenant (temporary Lieutenant) V. H. Misa.
Quartermaster-Serjeant E. A. Hire.
Lance-Serjeant L. Parker.
Lance-Corporal A. Langley.

3rd Dragoon Guards.

Lieutenant-Colonel O. B. B. Smith-Bingham, D.S.O.
Major (temporary Brigadier-General) G. A. Weir, D.S.O.
Major P. G. Mason, D.S.O.
Captain C. W. Brennand, Special Reserve.
Lieutenant (temporary Captain) C. E. R. Holroyd-Smith, Reserve of Officers.
Lieutenant H. A. Grimshaw.
Lieutenant F. B. Katinakis.
Captain N. K. Worthington, Special Reserve.
Second Lieutenant J. K. Greer, Irish Guards, Special Reserve.
Second Lieutenant A. B. P. L. Vincent.
Quartermaster and Honorary Lieutenant J. Donald.
Squadron Serjeant-Major W. Crane.
Private T. C. Lee.

4th Dragoon Guards.

Captain A. Gallaher.
Captain R. K. McGillycuddy.
Captain J. W. Aylmer.
Second Lieutenant R. G. Boosey.
Second Lieutenant M. O'Donnell.
Quartermaster and Honorary Lieutenant F. A. Dunham.
Farrier Serjeant-Major E. Simmons.
Acting-Serjeant A. G. Young.
Lance-Corporal E. Hill.
Acting Lance-Corporal E. Clark.
Private W. Lock.
Private A. W. Steer.

5th Dragoon Guards.

Lieutenant E. S. D. Martin.
Second Lieutenant L. F. Levinson.
Private W. G. Felgate.
Private R. Laidlaw.

6th Dragoon Guards.

Second Lieutenant (temporary Lieutenant) K. S. Hunter.
Second Lieutenant A. F. Creighton.
Second Lieutenant K. L. Gibson.
Private A. F. Bannister.
Private E. Ramsey.

MENTIONED IN DESPATCHES

7TH DRAGOON GUARDS.
Lieutenant J. S. Mellor.

1ST (ROYAL) DRAGOONS.
Lieutenant-Colonel H. D. McNeile.
Major P. E. Hardwick.
Captain A. H. D. Chapman (killed).
Captain W. T. Hodgson.
Captain A. W. Waterhouse.
Captain F. W. Wilson-Fitzgerald.
Temporary Second Lieutenant W. O. Berryman.
Second Lieutenant A. W. Wingate, Special Reserve.
Corporal T. Butler.
Corporal B. Proctor.
Corporal F. J. Allsebrook.
Lance-Corporal C. Durnin.
Private P. McCann.
Private R. Shaw.

2ND DRAGOONS.
Major W. Long, D.S.O.
Captain W. E. Lawrence, Reserve of Officers.
Lieutenant J. G. Crabbe.
Squadron Serjeant-Major J. McWhannel.
Private J. Milligan.

3RD HUSSARS.
Squadron Quartermaster-Serjeant F. S. Hodgson.

4TH LANCERS.
Captain H. K. D. Evans.
Temporary Second Lieutenant C. B. Ainslie.
Second Lieutenant F. D. Sowerby, Special Reserve.
Regimental Quartermaster-Serjeant E. Beadsmore.
Squadron Serjeant-Major J. H. Baron.
Squadron Serjeant-Major B. W. Dudley.
Serjeant J. Alexander.
Lance-Corporal E. Sloane.
Lance-Corporal F. Underwood.
Private R. Bearman.
Private W. Buckler.
Private C. Jack.

5TH LANCERS.
Temporary Lieutenant-Colonel M. F. McTaggart, Gordon Highlanders (Territorial Force) (Major, 5th Lancers).

MENTIONED IN DESPATCHES

Captain B. W. Robinson.
Captain V. de V. M. Vallance.
Second Lieutenant A. W. Carr.
Second Lieutenant A. C. Nugent.
Regimental Serjeant-Major A. Mobey.
Farrier-Serjeant W. Snowdon.
Corporal H. G. Hepworth.
Corporal M. G. Ryan.
Private J. O'Toole.

6TH DRAGOONS.

Lance-Corporal R. Biggadike.

7TH HUSSARS.

Major (temporary Lieutenant-Colonel) C. H. Rankin, D.S.O.

9TH LANCERS.

Major L. W. de V. Sadleir-Jackson, C.M.G., D.S.O.
Captain L. W. Diggle.
Captain A. C. D. Graham.
Captain G. F. Reynolds.
Temporary Lieutenant-Colonel W. R. Greene, County of London Yeomanry.
Temporary Second Lieutenant P. H. Corbett.
Quartermaster and Honorary Lieutenant W. A. Letts.

10TH HUSSARS.

Lieutenant-Colonel C. W. H. Crichton, D.S.O.
Major A. Roddick, Essex Yeomanry (killed).
Lieutenant D. L. G. W., Earl of Airlie.
Lieutenant G. Alexander, Special Reserve.

11TH HUSSARS.

Lieutenant F. V. Drake.
Acting-Serjeant T. Barr.
Corporal A. Dew.
Lance-Corporal H. J. Skipper.
Lance-Corporal W. Christie.
Private S. Knight.
Private J. Walland.

12TH LANCERS.

Captain H. V. S. Charrington.
Lieutenant G. M. Brown, Special Reserve.
Lieutenant H. A. Wernher.
Quartermaster and Honorary Captain H. B. Knop.

MENTIONED IN DESPATCHES

Regimental Quartermaster-Serjeant C. J. Blyth.
Squadron Quartermaster-Serjeant A. E. Swell.
Serjeant F. G. Taylor.
Private A. H. Bates.
Private J. Donnelly.

14TH HUSSARS.

Major Hon. H. E. Joicey.
Regimental Serjeant-Major F. Hill.

15TH HUSSARS.

Major (temporary Lieutenant-Colonel) F. C. Pilkington, D.S.O.
Captain J. Arnott.
Captain J. B. Wheeler.
Temporary Lieutenant P. P. Curtis, 14th Reserve Regiment of Cavalry (Adjutant, Westmoreland and Cumberland Yeomanry).
Temporary Major K. D. L. Maclaine of Lochbuie, Service Battalion, Middlesex Regiment (Captain 15th Hussars, Special Reserve).
Regimental Serjeant-Major J. Ellicock.
Corporal D. T. Holmes.
Private F. Gent.
Private W. Primmer.

16TH LANCERS.

Lieutenant R. L. Loyd.
Temporary Second Lieutenant R. G. Hornyold.
Temporary Second Lieutenant (temporary Lieutenant) J. O. MacBrayne.
Lance-Corporal J. W. Clark.
Private G. E. Taylor.

17TH LANCERS.

Lieutenant-Colonel D'A. Legard.
Lieutenant G. B. Black.
Lance-Corporal W. Clark.

18TH HUSSARS.

Lieutenant-Colonel C. K. Burnett.
Captain A. C. MacLachlan, Reserve of Officers.
Second Lieutenant J. A. B. Lane.
Second Lieutenant G. W. L. Meredith.
Quartermaster and Honorary Lieutenant W. H. Parsons.
Serjeant R. Snowball.
Acting-Serjeant R. Secker.
Private J. Conner.

MENTIONED IN DESPATCHES

19TH HUSSARS.
Major A. W. Parsons, D.S.O.
Captain J. C. W. Francis.
Captain G. Osborne.
Captain H. E. A. Platt.
Lieutenant E. G. Davidson.
Lieutenant C. H. Tremayne.
Quartermaster and Honorary Lieutenant R. E. Bird.
Regimental Serjeant-Major T. Johnson.
Quartermaster-Serjeant J. T. Crewdson.
Serjeant A. A. Farmer.
Saddler Quartermaster-Serjeant J. M. Guy.
Lance-Corporal J. Burchett.
Corporal G. R. G. Hart.
Trumpeter A. Marshall.

20TH HUSSARS.
Major M. E. Richardson.
Captain S. Barne.
Lieutenant W. D'A. Hall.
Regimental Serjeant-Major T. Austin.
Regimental Serjeant-Major W. O. Witherington.
Regimental Quartermaster-Serjeant J. T. Addis.
Corporal R. Poutney.

21ST LANCERS.
Lance-Corporal (temporary Serjeant) J. Wright.

RESERVE CAVALRY.

9TH RESERVE CAVALRY.
Quartermaster-Serjeant W. Fry.

11TH RESERVE CAVALRY.
Private J. J. Lord.

14TH RESERVE CAVALRY.
Temporary Lieutenant R. B. de B. Hodge.
Temporary Second Lieutenant J. M. Grant.

NORTH IRISH HORSE.
Major J. H. M. Viscount Cole.

SOUTH IRISH HORSE.
Major R. Hamilton-Stubber.
Captain A. H. Watt (Captain, retired pay).
Lance-Serjeant J. Spittal.
Serjeant C. L. Taylor.
Private (Acting Quartermaster-Serjeant) R. C. Airey.

MENTIONED IN DESPATCHES

KING EDWARD'S HORSE.
Lieutenant-Colonel M. Cradock, C.B.
Major M. F. Dick.
Major Hon. A. C. Murray.
Serjeant J. F. Bennett.
Private P. F. W. May.

YORKSHIRE HUSSARS.
Temporary Major W. G. Eley (Major, Reserve of Officers).
Lieutenant (temporary Captain) Sir D. Lawson, Bt.

LEICESTERSHIRE YEOMANRY.
Major W. F. Martin (killed).
Major W. F. Ricardo (Major, Reserve of Officers).
Lieutenant W. S. F. Johnson.
Quartermaster and Honorary Captain J. Crowley (Riding Master and Honorary Lieutenant, Reserve of Officers).
Squadron Serjeant-Major H. A. Swain.

NORTH SOMERSET YEOMANRY.
Lieutenant-Colonel G. C. Glyn, D.S.O.
Major G. Lubbock.
Major H. B. Matthews.
Major H. G. Spencer.
Second Lieutenant (temporary Captain) J. A. Garton.
Second Lieutenant S. W. Applegate.
Second Lieutenant O. C. K. Corrie.
Second Lieutenant C. T. O'Callaghan, 1st Dragoons.
Corporal H. Britten.
Private E. J. Buxton.

LANARKSHIRE YEOMANRY.
Captain (temporary Major) W. Macfarlane.
Lieutenant D. F. Jackson.

NORTHUMBERLAND YEOMANRY.
Lieutenant (temporary Captain) J. G. G. Rea.
Second Lieutenant (temporary Lieutenant) C. M. Laing.
Lance-Corporal E. Pigg.

WESTMORELAND AND CUMBERLAND YEOMANRY.
Second Lieutenant (temporary Lieutenant) C. W. Lowther.
Second Lieutenant M. H. J. Burns-Lindow.

OXFORDSHIRE HUSSARS.
Major (temporary Lieutenant-Colonel) C. R. I. Nicholl.
Second Lieutenant A. J. Muirhead.
Lance-Serjeant C. H. Hunt.

MENTIONED IN DESPATCHES

SURREY YEOMANRY.
Lieutenant E. Bell.
Squadron Serjeant-Major H. Hardy.
Farrier-Serjeant J. Phillips.
Serjeant O. C. Packer.

ESSEX YEOMANRY.
Major A. Buxton.
Captain E. A. Ruggles-Brise.
Lieutenant (temporary Captain) R. A. Thomson.
Squadron Serjeant-Major W. C. Howard.
Serjeant A. Frost.
Serjeant H. R. Wardill.
Corporal W. A. V. Schwier.
Lance-Corporal F. Smy.

NORTHAMPTONSHIRE YEOMANRY.
Second Lieutenant F. Litchfield.
Regimental Quartermaster-Serjeant W. R. White.
Squadron Quartermaster-Serjeant W. R. P. Allen.

SCOTTISH HORSE.
Serjeant J. Leonard.

ROYAL ARTILLERY.
Major H. T. Cunningham, attached Army Ordnance Department.
Captain E. V. H. Fairtlough, attached Royal Engineers.
Lieutenant S. S. Forsyth, Trench Mortar Battery.
Lieutenant S. G. B. Marsh, Trench Howitzer Battery.
Major R. M. Powell, Corps Signals.
Captain T. R. Ubsdell, Reserve of Officers, Divisional Ammunition Column.
Major (temporary Lieutenant-Colonel) H. de L. Walters, Reserve of Officers, Divisional Ammunition Column.
Lieutenant-Colonel F. H. Ward, retired pay, attached Railway Transport.
Serjeant (Acting Serjeant-Major) (Artillery Clerk) W. G. Burt.
Serjeant-Major (Artillery Clerk) T. A. Hartgrove.
Quartermaster-Serjeant (Acting Serjeant-Major) J. T. MacIntosh.
Quartermaster-Serjeant (Acting Serjeant-Major) (Artillery Clerk) E. H. Garwood.
Serjeant (Acting Company Serjeant-Major) (Artillery Clerk) J. B. Rosamund.
Corporal J. Thomas.
Gunner W. M. Bartlett.

MENTIONED IN DESPATCHES
Royal Horse Artillery.
Lieutenant-Colonel H. F. Askwith.
Captain W. A. T. Barstow.
Captain A. F. Brooke.
Lieutenant-Colonel (temporary Brigadier-General) C. E. D. Budworth, M.V.O.
Captain R. H. Carrington.
Captain C. J. H. Clibborn.
Lieutenant E. C. B. Dale.
Captain B. L. Duke.
Lieutenant E. D. Evelegh.
Major (temporary Lieutenant-Colonel) A. B. Forman, D.S.O.
Captain Hon. R. E. Grosvenor (killed).
Major W. W. Jelf, D.S.O.
Lieutenant-Colonel W. H. Kay.
Lieutenant-Colonel R. G. Keyworth.
Major (temporary Lieutenant-Colonel) J. W. F. Lamont.
Major R. H. Lascelles.
Lieutenant R. C. Lyons.
Captain M. H. McConnel.
Lieutenant A. H. MacIlwaine.
Lieutenant F. L. McNaughton.
Lieutenant E. H. Mann.
Lieutenant (temporary Captain) J. C. M. Mostyn.
Lieutenant (temporary Captain) P. H. Murray.
Lieutenant P. S. Myburgh.
Lieutenant-Colonel H. Rouse, D.S.O.
Lieutenant O. R. Schreiber.
Lieutenant-Colonel H. S. Seligman.
Major E. J. Skinner.
Lieutenant R. Staveley, D.S.O.
Lieutenant-Colonel H. H. Tudor.
Captain A. W. Van Straubenzee.
Captain J. T. Wallace.
Lieutenant V. Walrond.
Captain R. H. Walsh.
Captain C. L. T. Walwyn.
Lieutenant-Colonel (temporary Brigadier-General) A. E. Wardrop.
Temporary Second Lieutenant F. R. Watson.
Bombardier W. R. Bell.
Corporal C. M. Bromby.
Serjeant J. Campbell.
Serjeant L. Cook.
Fitter G. W. Cook.
Corporal T. Daniels.
Farrier Quartermaster-Serjeant (acting Battery S.-M.) W. H. Gooch.

MENTIONED IN DESPATCHES

Gunner G. G. Goodchild.
Serjeant (acting Battery Quartermaster-Serjeant) F. W. Herbert.
Serjeant J. Hutchinson.
Gunner D. C. Parker.
Serjeant W. J. Phillips.
Serjeant R. J. Rands.
Gunner W. L. Sams.
Serjeant E. Seabrook.
Fitter A. M. Smith.
Gunner H. W. Trusler.
Gunner H. G. Venning.
Bombardier R. R. Wills.

ROYAL FIELD ARTILLERY.

Major R. J. Adams.
Lieutenant-Colonel (temporary Brigadier-General) E. W. Alexander, V.C., C.M.G.
Second Lieutenant S. E. Alford, Special Reserve.
Major J. G. B. Allardyce.
Second Lieutenant (Temporary Lieutenant) J. T. Allen.
Second Lieutenant A. Anderson.
Captain H. O. C. Anne.
Lieutenant R. H. Antrobus.
Captain A. S. Archdale.
Major H. B. C. Arthur.
Second Lieutenant J. S. Arthur.
Captain S. Atkinson.
Captain E. A. C. Attwood, Special Reserve.
Second Lieutenant W. J. Banks.
Lieutenant E. G. Barkham.
Lieutenant B. M. B. Bateman (died of wounds).
Captain C. R. Bates, Reserve of Officers.
Lieutenant R. T. Baxter.
Captain C. W. Bayne-Jardine.
Captain (temporary Major) W. C. H. Bell, Reserve of Officers.
Temporary Second Lieutenant J. L. B. Bentley.
Major J. Berkley, Reserve of Officers.
Temporary Lieutenant R. H. Bingham.
Brevet Colonel (temporary Brigadier-General) C. F. Blane, retired pay.
Major D. G. Blois.
Lieutenant J. R. N. Bolton (died of wounds).
Lieutenant L. E. Booth.
Captain G. E. S. Bowen.
Major C. E. S. Bower.
Captain C. E. Boyce.
Captain C. E. D. Bridge.

MENTIONED IN DESPATCHES

Captain Hon. H. G. O. Bridgeman.
Lieutenant W. H. Brookes.
Major F. Brousson.
Lieutenant-Colonel W. B. Browell.
Lieutenant (temporary Captain) L. Browning.
Lieutenant N. A. Browning-Paterson.
Major C. N. Buchanan-Dunlop, D.S.O. (killed).
Major L. M. Bucknill (died of wounds).
Lieutenant S. D. Bulteel.
Lieutenant (temporary Captain) F. W. Burkinshaw.
Major E. R. Burne.
Captain G. Burrard, D.S.O.
Temporary Second Lieutenant G. B. Burridge.
Lieutenant C. E. V. Buxton, Special Reserve.
Temporary Captain H. J. Cannan.
Brevet Colonel (temporary Brigadier-General) G. G. S. Carey.
Major H. E. Carey.
Major T. Carlyon.
Lieutenant E. F. Carne.
Temporary Second Lieutenant R. W. Carrigan.
Brevet Colonel A. H. Carter, retired pay.
Lieut.-Colonel (temp. Brigadier-General) G. N. Cartwright, D.S.O.
Lieutenant T. F. Cavenagh.
Lieutenant T. C. Chilton.
Major W. E. Clark, D.S.O.
Major (temporary Lieutenant-Colonel) H. C. Clarke, D.S.O.
Second Lieutenant J. A. Clarke.
Second Lieutenant J. E. Clayton.
Lieutenant N. C. Clery.
Lieutenant-Colonel R. C. Coates, D.S.O.
Temporary Captain C. L. Cockell.
Captain L. A. Coker.
Lieutenant A. G. Coles.
Temporary Captain A. E. Cook (Lieutenant Territorial Force Reserve).
Lieutenant R. R. Copeland.
Second Lieutenant R. W. Corbert.
Major (temporary Lieutenant-Colonel) A. R. B. Cossart.
Major (temporary Lieutenant-Colonel) A. S. Cotton, D.S.O.
Temporary Lieutenant G. R. Cowie.
Major M. Crofton.
Temporary Second Lieutenant M. M. Cudmore.
Captain A. G. Cunningham.
Captain (temporary Major) E. W. Cushen, Special Reserve.
Lieutenant H. Cutbush.
Captain J. A. Dane, Special Reserve (Lieutenant, retired pay).
Lieutenant-Colonel H. M. Davison.

MENTIONED IN DESPATCHES

Lieutenant H. W. Deacon.
Lieutenant-Colonel P. P. E. de Berry.
Lieutenant H. G. de Burgh.
Lieutenant-Colonel E. F. Delaforce.
Second Lieutenant H. G. Dewey.
Captain R. C. Dodgson.
Lieutenant J. S. Drennan.
Major H. B. Dresser, Special Reserve.
Temporary Lieutenant C. G. Duffin.
Major O. C. Du Port, Reserve of Officers.
Second Lieutenant W. S. Durward.
Major L. M. Dyson, Reserve of Officers.
Major (temporary Lieutenant-Colonel) W. R. Eden, D.S.O.
Major H. W. T. Elam.
Lieutenant (temporary Captain) H. S. Ellis.
Second Lieutenant W. R. Ellison, Special Reserve (died of wounds).
Lieutenant Colonel (temporary Brigadier-General) F. A. G. Y. Elton.
Colonel C. E. English, Reserve of Officers.
Lieutenant-Colonel C. Evans.
Lieutenant-Colonel W. Evans, D.S.O.
Second Lieutenant E. D. Evelegh.
Captain H. N. Fairbank.
Lieutenant F. H. Fardell.
Lieutenant H. W. F. B. Farrer.
Captain P. H. Ferguson.
Second Lieutenant (temporary Captain) H. B. Fetherston.
Lieutenant (temporary Captain) D. R. D. Fisher.
Major M. J. F. FitzGerald.
Lieutenant-Colonel R. Fitzmaurice.
Temporary Captain T. R. Fletcher.
Second Lieutenant C. F. Forestier-Walker.
Major J. A. C. Forsyth.
Major Sir D. B. Forwood, Bt., Reserve of Officers.
Temporary Lieutenant A. Fox.
Second Lieutenant J. S. Franey.
Temporary Captain A. T. G. Gardner.
Lieutenant R. P. Gatehouse.
Major J. A. Geary.
Captain C. Geldard.
Captain (temporary Major) S. F. Gosling, Reserve of Officers.
Temporary Second Lieutenant L. B. Govan.
Major C. R. Gover.
Lieutenant S. D. Graham.
Captain G. E. A. Granet.
Second Lieutenant I. A. W. Grant.
Captain H. F. Grant Suttie.

MENTIONED IN DESPATCHES

Captain W. W. Green.
Temporary Lieutenant N. E. Haig.
Captain (temporary Major) E. C. Hall.
Lieutenant-Colonel E. F. Hall.
Lieutenant H. R. Hall.
Major H. A. Hamilton.
Captain R. T. Hammick.
Lieutenant S. P. Hannam, Special Reserve.
Major (temporary Lieutenant-Colonel) E. Newman-Harding, D.S.O.
Major J. M. R. Harrison.
Major (temporary Lieutenant-Colonel) C. St. L. G. Hawkes.
Major J. P. V. Hawksley.
Major V. J. Heather.
Lieutenant F. J. Hext.
Major C. R. Hill.
Lieutenant J. W. Hoggart.
Lieutenant John B. Hollwey.
Captain E. T. F. Hood (temporary Major, Lincolnshire Yeomanry).
Lieutenant A. H. Hornby.
Lieutenant (temporary Captain) E. J. T. Housden.
Captain H. O. Hutchison.
Lieutenant C. R. M. Hutchison.
Second Lieutenant A. Ibbitson.
Lieutenant W. S. Ironside.
Lieutenant C. R. Jackson.
Brevet Lieutenant-Colonel R. M. Johnson.
Major W. A. F. Jones.
Lieutenant-Colonel W. H. Kay.
Temporary Second Lieutenant Hon. L. U. Kay-Shuttleworth.
Captain Sir J. Keane, Bt., Reserve of Officers.
Lieutenant J. T. Keay.
Temporary Second Lieutenant C. S. King.
Lieutenant-Colonel B. R. Kirwan.
Second Lieutenant A. Kiteley.
Captain R. M. Knolles.
Temporary Second Lieutenant W. Laing.
Temporary Lieutenant S. Lawrence.
Lieutenant P. N. A. C. Lawton.
Second Lieutenant W. Lead.
Major A. G. Leech.
Captain H. G. Lee-Warner, D.S.O.
Temporary Second Lieutenant G. M. Liddell.
Temporary Second Lieutenant C. E. W. Lockyer.
Lieutenant E. G. Lutyens.
Major C. D. G. Lyon.
Temporary Lieutenant N. Maasdorp.

MENTIONED IN DESPATCHES

Lieutenant J. McBride.
Second Lieutenant A. McDonald.
Major T. McGowan.
Major H. J. A. Mackey, M.V.O., D.S.O.
Major C. W. W. McLean, D.S.O.
Lieutenant (temporary Captain) J. C. Maples.
Lieutenant W. C. Maskell.
Temporary Second Lieutenant J. W. Mason.
Captain C. W. Massy.
Major R. G. Maturin, D.S.O.
Captain E. B. Maxwell.
Lieutenant J. L. Maxwell.
Captain G. W. Meade.
Temporary Second Lieutenant J. McK. Menzies.
Major G. R. Miller.
Major C. A. Mortimore.
Temporary Second Lieutenant H. J. Muir.
Temporary Second Lieutenant J. S. G. Munro.
Major W. A. Murray.
Major A. D. Musgrave.
Lieutenant A. F. Nash.
Major H. W. Newcome, D.S.O.
Lieut.-Colonel (temp. Brigadier-General) G. H. W. Nicholson, D.S.O.
Second Lieutenant R. Hisbet.
Captain S. M. Noakes.
Lieutenant E. Nottidge.
Lieutenant G. T. Nugee.
Lieutenant W. J. Odlum, Special Reserve.
Lieutenant-Colonel L. C. L. Oldfield, D.S.O.
Temporary Lieutenant G. V. Ormsby.
Lieutenant M. R. Orr-Ewing.
Lieutenant (temporary Captain) E. A. Palmer.
Captain R. L. Palmer.
Major J. W. Parrington.
Lieutenant-Colonel C. F. P. Parry.
Temporary Second Lieutenant N. J. Patterson.
Major W. P. Paynter.
Temporary Second Lieutenant H. M. Pearse.
Lieutenant C. H. Peck.
Captain D. R. Peel.
Lieutenant-Colonel A. M. Perreau.
Captain M. A. Phillips (killed).
Captain F. A. Pile.
Lieutenant-Colonel E. W. Plummer.
Major G. L. Popham, D.S.O.
Major W. J. L. Poston.

MENTIONED IN DESPATCHES

Major R. ff. Powell.
Major R. C. Prance.
Captain J. T. Price.
Temporary Major V. E. Pringle (Honorary Major, retired Special Reserve).
Captain R. B. Purey Cust.
Lieutenant B. B. Quiller-Couch, Special Reserve.
Major L. T. Raikes.
Major R. E. Ramsden.
Captain R. N. Rashleigh.
Lieutenant-Colonel (temporary Brigadier-General) F. T. Ravenhill, C.M.G.
Captain R. M. Rendel.
Major D. Reynolds, V.C.
Captain G. C. Richardson.
Captain G. A. Rickards.
Major J. B. Riddell, D.S.O.
Lieutenant (temporary Captain) A. F. M. Riecke.
Temporary Second Lieutenant C. Q. Roberts (killed).
Major C. C. Robertson, Reserve of Officers.
Major F. W. Robinson.
Second Lieutenant W. P. A. Robinson.
Captain A. R. Roney Dougal.
Lieutenant-Colonel C. F. Rugge-Price.
Second Lieutenant A. C. Russell.
Captain (temp. Major) Hon. B. J. Russell, D.S.O., Reserve of Officers.
Major H. K. Sadler.
Captain T. F. Sandeman.
Major Hon. H. R. Scarlett.
Major C. W. Scott.
Major F. R. Sedgwick, Reserve of Officers.
Lieutenant-Colonel F. L. Sharp, C.M.G.
Lieutenant (temporary Captain) R. de V. Shaw.
Captain E. Sherlock, Special Reserve.
Lieutenant P. F. Shier.
Lieutenant-Colonel W. A. Short.
Brevet Colonel C. N. Simpson, retired pay.
Major H. C. Simpson.
Temporary Second Lieutenant W. H. Smith.
Lieutenant-Colonel G. A. Smyth.
Lieutenant-Colonel E. W. Spedding, C.M.G.
Major D. C. Spencer-Smith.
Major D. W. L. Spiller.
Lieutenant F. B. B. Spragge.
Captain Hon. O. H. Stanley, Reserve of Officers.
Major A. G. Staveley.

MENTIONED IN DESPATCHES

Major (temporary Lieutenant-Colonel) E. H. Stevenson, D.S.O.
Brevet Colonel J. W. Stirling, retired pay.
Captain W. A. Stirling (Adjutant, Territorial Force).
Lieutenant-Colonel A. U. Stockley.
Second Lieutenant S. G. Strudwick, Special Reserve.
Lieutenant R. H. Studdert.
Temporary Captain H. E. M. Studdy.
Second Lieutenant E. Swinton, Special Reserve (died of wounds)
Temporary Lieutenant G. A. Syme.
Lieutenant A. R. Tabor.
Major B. W. Taylor.
Captain V. A. H. Taylor.
Major Hon. H. E. Thellusson.
Major A. C. L. Theobald.
Lieutenant R. L. Thompson.
Major W. Thompson, Special Reserve.
Captain J. F. P. Thorburn.
Temporary Second Lieutenant S. D. Timson.
Major G. S. Tovey.
Lieutenant W. Townsend.
Major P. Turnbull.
Major D. K. Tweedie, D.S.O.
Lieutenant-Colonel (temporary Brigadier-General) J. A. Tyler.
Temporary Captain A. J. Usborne.
Temporary Second Lieutenant W. N. C. Van Grutten.
Lieutenant A. N. Venning.
Temporary Second Lieutenant B. H. Vyvyan.
Captain C. E. Walker.
Lieutenant (temporary Captain) J. R. Walker.
Major E. A. Wallinger.
Major B. Walter.
Lieutenant A. J. Wark.
Major W. R. Warren.
Lieutenant W. D. Watson.
Lieutenant J. Wedderburn-Maxwell.
Major F. G. West.
Lieutenant S. M. de H. Whatton.
Major A. K. G. White.
Lieutenant P. G. Whitefoord.
Lieutenant-Colonel E. H. Willis.
Captain E. W. G. Wilson.
Captain H. G. Worsley.
Major H. C. Wray.
Lieutenant M. O. M. Wynne (killed).
Gunner H. L. Avery.
Gunner E. V. Baker.

MENTIONED IN DESPATCHES

Corporal E. A. Bailey.
Bombardier W. J. Barnes.
Gunner (Acting Bombardier) H. H. Barnett.
Serjeant L. Barton.
Gunner G. Beckett.
Bombardier G. W. H. Beckett.
Battery Serjeant-Major B. Belcher.
Corporal C. J. Blackmoor.
Corporal L. Bloomfield.
Bombardier A. E. Bond.
Bombardier E. Brackley.
Battery Serjeant-Major W. C. Briggs.
Acting Bombardier J. J. Brittor.
Battery Serjeant-Major A. H. Bromley.
Acting Serjeant-Major E. Broom.
Battery Serjeant-Major J. H. Budd (killed).
Acting Bombardier G. Bull.
Bombardier T. Burrows.
Serjeant W. J. Byrne.
Corporal J. Caffrey.
Bombardier C. Callaghan.
Battery Serjeant-Major D. A. Campbell.
Acting Bombardier H. Carter, Ammunition Column.
Corporal J. F. Connell.
Corporal Cook.
Driver E. Coy.
Bombardier W. Croghan.
Bombardier C. H. Crowlie.
Serjeant A. Curtis.
Bombardier H. H. Daniels.
Gunner E. V. Davidson.
Bombardier G. A. Davis.
Driver J. T. Davis.
Gunner T. Davies.
Acting Regimental Serjeant-Major E. Dawson.
Serjeant R. M. Dick.
Corporal F. Dillon.
Corporal C. V. Dipnall.
Battery Serjeant-Major H. Dobney.
Driver J. A. Douglas.
Gunner G. W. Duncanson.
Staff Serjeant-Farrier C. Dungey.
Gunner G. H. Dunn.
Corporal W. A. Ede.
Bombardier A. Edwards.
Serjeant W. R. Emmett.

MENTIONED IN DESPATCHES

Battery Serjeant-Major A. Farr.
Serjeant J. Fenn.
Acting-Corporal F. Fields.
Corporal G. P. Fisher.
Battery Serjeant-Major W. G. Fitch.
Regimental Serjeant-Major A. Flowers.
Serjeant L. B. Foster.
Battery Serjeant-Major S. G. Franklin.
Serjeant A. Gardner.
Serjeant J. P. Geeson (killed).
Bombardier (Acting Corporal) T. W. Gibbs.
Corporal E. Gillham, Intelligence Police.
Acting Bombardier F. W. Godden.
Battery Serjeant-Major H. Grant.
Gunner A. J. Green.
Driver G. W. Groom.
Corporal J. R. Handyside.
Regimental Serjeant-Major W. R. Harbar.
Acting Bombardier F. Hawkes.
Driver W. Hepple.
Gunner J. Holland.
Serjeant-Major B. P. Hornby.
Acting-Serjeant W. M. Howard.
Gunner J. A. Hunt.
Bombardier Wheeler F. R. Hurd.
Gunner J. Irvine.
Serjeant P. Jackson.
Corporal R. Jacques.
Bombardier H. Jeffry.
Gunner W. Jennings.
Corporal H. Jenney.
Driver A. E. Jonas.
Bombardier C. A. Jones.
Corporal W. Kelly.
Serjeant G. H. Kendall.
Corporal F. King.
Lance-Corporal I. Lamb.
Serjeant J. J. Lauder.
Gunner W. Lefever.
Serjeant A. Lewis.
Corporal G. J. Lock.
Saddler-Corporal (now Lieutenant) L. Lockwood.
Gunner C. McCarthy.
Serjeant P. McCorkindale.
Battery Serjeant-Major R. H. McGowan.
Farrier-Serjeant D. McNair.

MENTIONED IN DESPATCHES

Battery Quartermaster-Serjeant A. E. Mann.
Driver G. F. Marchant.
Corporal A. Martin.
Driver A. Mason.
Battery Serjeant-Major W. C. Metcalfe.
Acting Bombardier E. Mildenhall.
Gunner C. Mitchell.
Driver H. Monk.
Battery Serjeant-Major G. Moore.
Serjeant E. Morley.
Regimental Serjeant-Major E. J. Munden.
Driver R. F. Myhill.
Gunner T. D. Nagle.
Driver H. W. Nicholas.
Battery Quartermaster-Serjeant C. E. Nichols.
Bombardier W. Nicholson.
Gunner N. Nicholson.
Bombardier F. Nixon.
Corporal C. O'Mahoney.
Gunner P. S. Palmer.
Bombardier A. Parker.
Driver G. Pateman.
Corporal H. T. Pearson.
Battery Serjeant-Major J. Penrose.
Gunner F. Pestell.
Corporal H. Pickup.
Gunner (Acting Bombardier) A. D. Pope.
Serjeant R. Potter.
Driver W. Price.
Serjeant G. Pugh.
Gunner J. T. Pye.
Gunner (Acting Bombardier) T. Rainford.
Regimental Serjeant-Major F. Rawson.
Serjeant W. Rawson.
Corporal T. Rees.
Gunner J. Rix.
Gunner H. E. Roach.
Battery Quartermaster-Serjeant F. J. Rose.
Driver J. Ross.
Driver R. Ross.
Corporal E. G. Rossiter.
Bombardier F. H. Russell.
Bombardier S. E. Russell.
Serjeant A. Sage.
Corporal J. J. Saxby.
Serjeant J. F. Sayer.

MENTIONED IN DESPATCHES

Serjeant-Major F. C. Seymour.
Battery Serjeant-Major J. Shann.
Corporal W. B. Sinclair.
Gunner R. L. Smith.
Gunner F. Spencer.
Serjeant A. H. Spink.
Corporal A. F. Stamp.
Battery Serjeant-Major C. Stocker.
Gunner W. Strachan.
Fitter J. Stribling.
Gunner A. Stubbs.
Corporal C. W. U. Taylor.
Gunner Taylor.
Gunner H. J. Thomas.
Gunner O. E. Thomas.
Acting Bombardier W. Thomas.
Corporal F. R. Tracey.
Gunner E. A. W. Tucker.
Regimental Serjeant-Major J. Vevers.
Battery Quartermaster-Serjeant P. Walker.
Corporal W. H. Ward.
Regimental Serjeant-Major A. F. Watts.
Battery Serjeant-Major E. E. Weinel.
Gunner E. H. Wellard.
Acting Regimental Serjeant-Major C. H. Whitcombe
Serjeant O. M. Wilde.
Serjeant F. Wilkinson.
Serjeant J. E. Wood.
Corporal F. Wood.
Battery Serjeant-Major J. Woodward.
Corporal H. Woolley.
Serjeant H. Wootton.
Gunner J. A. Wright.
Gunner S. Wright.

ROYAL FIELD ARTILLERY (TERRITORIAL FORCE).

Lieutenant C. Abbott, Northumbrian Brigade.
Lieutenant (temporary Captain) K. Anderson, Northumbrian Brigade.
Second Lieutenant G. Armitage, West Riding Brigade.
Major (temporary Lieutenant-Colonel) H. E. Aykroyd, West Riding Divisional Ammunition Column.
Second Lieutenant A. H. Aykroyd, West Riding Brigade.
Lieutenant-Colonel A. M. Balfour, South Midland Brigade (Major, Reserve of Officers).
Second Lieutenant H. B. Barran, West Riding Brigade.
Major H. Bayley, D.S.O., London Brigade.

MENTIONED IN DESPATCHES

Major (temporary Lieutenant-Colonel) H. S. Bell, D.S.O., Northumbrian Brigade.
Second Lieutenant (temporary Lieutenant) R. C. Benson, West Riding Brigade.
Second Lieutenant D. C. Briggs, West Riding Brigade.
Second Lieutenant J. G. P. Browne, West Riding Brigade
Lieutenant-Colonel E. C. Bullock, South Midland Brigade.
Major R. L. Bullock, Territorial Force Reserve.
Captain (temporary Major) B. H. Butler, West Riding Brigade.
Major C. J. Caddick, North Midland Brigade.
Second Lieutenant (temporary Lieutenant) G. Campbell, North Midland Brigade.
Second Lieutenant R. J. Cavill, West Riding Brigade.
Lieutenant (temporary Captain) C. L. Chapman, Northumbrian Brigade.
Major R. Chapman, Northumbrian Brigade.
Lieutenant-Colonel Sir S. H. Child, Bt., M.V.O., North Midland Brigade.
Lieutenant-Colonel C. Clifford, West Riding Brigade.
Lieutenant (temporary Captain) E. C. Clifford.
Major (temporary Lieutenant-Colonel) F. W. Cluff, Northumbrian Divisional Ammunition Column.
Lieutenant (temporary Major) L. A. Common, Northumbrian Brigade.
Second Lieutenant (temporary Lieutenant) E. N. FitzG. de R. Cooper, London Brigade.
Major F. G. Crompton, North Midland Brigade.
Major T. J. Daniel, South Midland Brigade.
Lieutenant L. E. de St. Paër, West Riding Brigade.
Major W. D. Drury-Lowe, North Midland Brigade (Captain, Reserve of Officers).
Lieutenant-Colonel M. M. Duncan, Highland Brigade.
Lieutenant J. H. Eddison, West Riding Brigade.
Lieutenant-Colonel E. H. Eley, London Brigade.
Major E. Eton, London Brigade.
Second Lieutenant (temporary Lieutenant) E. H. Field, South Midland Brigade.
Major F. Fleming, Highland Brigade.
Major C. Fowler, South Midland Brigade.
Captain (temporary Major) H. Fraser, Highland Brigade.
Lieutenant J. A. Gascoyne-Cecil, Home Counties Brigade.
Second Lieutenant (temporary Lieutenant) E. L. Gedye, South Midland Brigade.
Lieutenant W. Golding, Northumbrian Brigade.
Major A. C. Gordon, D.S.O., London Brigade.
Lieutenant A. McD. Gordon, West Riding Brigade.
Second Lieutenant C. Griffin, Home Counties Brigade.

MENTIONED IN DESPATCHES

Temporary Major H. E. Hanson, Northumbrian Brigade (Lieutenant-Colonel, retired Territorial Force).
Second Lieutenant W. B. Haynes, West Riding Divisional Ammunition Column.
Second Lieutenant G. Helps, West Riding Brigade.
Captain (temporary Major) J. H. Hinton, North Midland Brigade.
Lieutenant-Colonel E. A. Hirst, West Riding Brigade.
Second Lieutenant G. B. Howarth, West Riding Brigade.
Lieutenant (temporary Major) W. Howson, West Riding Brigade.
Lieutenant E. C. Hudson, West Riding Brigade.
Lieutenant W. H. H. Hutchinson, Northumbrian Brigade.
Major J. Kent, North Midland Brigade.
Second Lieutenant (temporary Lieutenant) F. P. Kindell, London Brigade.
Second Lieutenant E. A. C. Lawson, West Riding Brigade.
Lieutenant-Colonel R. P. Leach, North Midland Divisional Ammunition Column (Major, retired pay).
Lieutenant-Colonel C. C. Leveson-Gower, North Midland Brigade (Major, retired, Indian Army).
Second Lieutenant (temporary Lieutenant) C. G. Lewthwaite, North Midland Brigade.
Second Lieutenant (temporary Lieutenant) A. Lord, West Riding Brigade.
Lieutenant (temporary Captain) J. Lovegrove, West Riding Brigade (Quartermaster and Honorary Captain, retired pay).
Second Lieutenant (temporary Lieutenant) H. Lowther, Highland Brigade.
Major W. F. Lucey, West Riding Brigade.
Second Lieutenant L. M. Lupton, West Riding Brigade.
Lieutenant-Colonel P. C. Macfarlane, Highland Brigade.
Second Lieutenant (temporary Lieutenant) J. Y. McLean, Northumbrian Brigade.
Lieutenant-Colonel E. C. Massy, London Brigade (Lieutenant-Colonel, Royal Field Artillery).
Major F. Middleton, West Riding Brigade.
Lieutenant A. C. O. Morgan, North Midland Brigade.
Lieutenant C. Morris, North Midland Brigade.
Lieutenant-Colonel F. B. Moss-Blundell, Northumbrian Brigade.
Captain (temporary Major) C. P. Nickalls, South Midland Brigade.
Second Lieutenant N. F. Nickols, West Riding Brigade.
Captain (temporary Major) E. B. Osborn, West Riding Brigade (Major, retired, Territorial Force).
Surgeon-Major E. G. Peck, West Riding Brigade.
Lieutenant (temporary Captain) J. C. E. Pellereau, Royal Field Artillery (Adjutant, West Riding Brigade).
Captain (temporary Major) P. C. Petrie, West Riding Brigade.

MENTIONED IN DESPATCHES

Captain (temporary Major) E. W. Pickering, West Riding Brigade.
Lieutenant-Colonel Hon. S. Pleydell-Bouverie, Home Counties Brigade
Captain (temporary Major) C. A. Pollard, London Brigade.
Captain (temporary Major) J. J. Read, Lowland Brigade.
Lieutenant-Colonel C. McL. Robertson, Highland Divisional Ammunition Column.
Lieutenant S. H. Robinson, South Midland Brigade.
Lieutenant W. O. Ryan, South Midland Brigade.
Captain R. M. Shaw, West Riding Brigade.
Captain (temporary Major) D. K. Smith, Home Counties Brigade.
Temporary Lieutenant-Colonel H. K. Stephenson, West Riding Brigade.
Lieutenant G. V. Stringer, North Midland Brigade.
Major G. H. Taylor, South Midland Brigade.
Major J. C. G. Thompson, Home Counties Brigade.
Captain (temporary Major) C. W. Todd, South Midland Brigade.
Second Lieutenant W. H. Turner, West Riding Brigade.
Major (temporary Lieutenant-Colonel) F. C. B. West, South Midland Brigade.
Second Lieutenant V. Whitaker, West Riding Brigade.
Lieutenant-Colonel E. N. Whitley, West Riding Brigade.
Lieutenant (temporary Captain) D. C. Willock, Highland Brigade.
Lieutenant (temporary Captain) F. J. Wrottesley, North Midland Brigade.
Captain (temporary Major) K. S. Yeaman, Northumbrian Brigade.
Bombardier T. S. Askin, West Riding Brigade.
Serjeant T. E. Bellamy, North Midland Brigade.
Battery Quartermaster-Serjeant G. Bestwick, North Midland Brigade.
Bombardier F. Bowcock, North Midland Brigade.
Gunner W. B. Cannel, Northumbrian (County of Durham) (Howitzer) Brigade.
Battery Serjeant-Major W. Cavanagh, West Riding Divisional Ammunition Column.
Bombardier G. C. Clarke, West Riding Brigade.
Corporal F. R. Clarkson, West Riding Divisional Ammunition Column.
Corporal R. Connor, North Midland Brigade.
Bombardier O. H. Dobson, North Midland Brigade.
Bombardier E. W. Dunn, North Midland Brigade.
Bombardier F. Dunn, North Midland Brigade.
Driver H. Fisher, West Riding Divisional Ammunition Column.
Gunner F. Griffiths, West Riding Brigade.
Gunner L. J. Heveningham, West Riding Brigade.
Serjeant G. P. Hill, Northumbrian Brigade.
Serjeant L. Horsfall, West Riding Brigade.
Gunner L. Hurst, West Riding Brigade.
Bombardier H. Jefferson, Northumbrian Brigade.

MENTIONED IN DESPATCHES

Serjeant A. Jones, North Midland Brigade.
Bombardier P. King, West Riding Brigade.
Corporal C. Lee, West Riding Brigade.
Driver (Acting Bombardier) E. C. Lee Foot, South Midland Brigade.
Gunner H. Locket, North Midland Brigade.
Serjeant-Major W. J. McCann, Northumbrian Brigade.
Serjeant J. McGhee, Highland Howitzer Brigade.
Quartermaster-Serjeant A. B. MacVean, West Riding Brigade.
Battery Serjeant-Major T. B. Martin, Northumbrian (County of Durham) Brigade.
Corporal A. S. Mason, North Midland Brigade.
Corporal B. Mee, North Midland Brigade.
Battery Serjeant-Major J. W. Millar, Northumbrian Brigade.
Serjeant L. G. Mortimer, West Riding Brigade.
Gunner H. Nelson, Northumbrian Brigade.
Acting Bombardier L. Painter, West Riding Divisional Ammunition Column.
Driver W. M. Pearson, Northumbrian Brigade.
Gunner W. F. Powell, South Midland Brigade.
Acting Bombardier J. Reed, Northumbrian (County of Durham) Brigade.
Bombardier R. Rhodes, West Riding Brigade.
Serjeant E. Roberts, West Riding Brigade.
Bombardier A. Robinson, North Midland Brigade.
Bombardier W. Rogers, North Midland Brigade.
Serjeant T. H. Rush (killed), West Riding Brigade.
Gunner A. B. Rushworth.
Serjeant A. Scott.
Bombardier W. Shires, West Riding Brigade.
Bombardier H. Sidley, North Midland Brigade.
Gunner T. E. Simmons, North Midland Brigade.
Gunner E. Singleton, West Riding Brigade.
Gunner H. Smith, North Midland Brigade.
Serjeant J. Stephen, Highland Brigade.
Serjeant J. Stewart, Northumbrian Brigade.
Bombardier E. Stokes, North Midland Brigade.
Gunner S. E. Stott, West Riding Brigade.
Gunner S. Taylor, North Midland Brigade.
Driver A. Thomas, Northumbrian Brigade.
Gunner H. A. Tooley, North Midland Brigade.
Driver E. W. Triffitt, West Riding Brigade.
Bombardier T. W. Vickery, North Midland Brigade.
Bombardier L. Waldron, North Midland Brigade.
Serjeant W. Webb, West Riding Brigade.
Gunner S. White, West Riding Brigade.
Gunner J. A. Whiting (killed), London Brigade.

MENTIONED IN DESPATCHES

Gunner E. Whitfield.
Acting Bombardier C. Whitworth, West Riding Brigade.
Bombardier B. Wilkinson.
Gunner H. Windle, West Riding Brigade.
Battery Serjeant-Major A. J. Winzar, South Midland Brigade.
Corporal A. Wise, West Riding Brigade.
Wheeler E. Woods, South Midland Howitzer Brigade.
Acting Bombardier W. Woolliscroft, West Riding Brigade.

Royal Garrison Artillery.

Captain H. R. Adams.
Captain N. W. Aitken.
Major W. D. Alexander.
Major F. E. Andrewes.
Temporary Lieutenant F. D. Arundel.
Captain H. D. Ashby.
Major W. B. G. Barne.
Lieutenant-Colonel B. M. Bateman.
Lieutenant A. J. Beattie.
Captain L. B. A. Becher.
Lieutenant-Colonel R. P. Benson.
Temporary Lieutenant C. R. Bicknell.
Lieutenant-Colonel (temporary Brigadier-General) W. St. C. Bland.
Lieutenant-Colonel H. E. J. Brake, C.B., D.S.O.
Lieutenant A. W. T. Buckland.
Lieutenant-Colonel C. R. Buckle, D.S.O.
Lieutenant-Colonel P. de S. Burney, C.B., Reserve of Officers.
Captain J. D. Byrne.
Captain C. P. G. Cameron.
Major C. A. H. Campbell.
Captain R. Carson.
Second Lieutenant N. G. Chamberlain, London Brigade (Territorial Force).
Captain C. C. Chambers.
Captain A. H. M. Cherry.
Lieutenant G. M. Churcher.
Major I. S. Cobbe.
Major B. B. Colbeck.
Major C. W. Collingwood.
Second Lieutenant C. F. Cope.
Major R. D. Crawford.
Captain R. T. C. Cream.
Major E. F. Creswell.
Captain (temporary Major) C. S. S. Curteis, Reserve of Officers.
Lieutenant H. B. Dance
Captain C. G. F. Davidson.

MENTIONED IN DESPATCHES

Second Lieutenant J. R. Davies.
Temporary Second Lieutenant H. P. Dick.
Colonel G. C. Dowell.
Major J. T. Dreyer.
Captain W. B. Duncan.
Lieutenant K. G. Dymott.
Lieutenant C. M. Ewan-Smith.
Lieutenant E. G. Evans.
Temporary Second Lieutenant H. Eyden.
Captain O. E. Fane.
Lieutenant-Colonel L. D. Fraser.
Captain W. H. Fry.
Major L. Galloway, D.S.O.
Major C. R. Gillett.
Captain H. W. Goldney.
Lieutenant E. W. Goodman.
Temporary Second Lieutenant C. H. Goulden.
Captain A. D. Greig.
Lieutenant M. N. T. Gubbins.
Captain H. B. L. G. Gunn.
Major A. G. Haig.
Lieutenant K. M. Hamilton-Jones, Special Reserve.
Temporary Captain W. C. Hand.
Lieutenant E. G. W. W. Harrison.
Lieutenant J. C. B. Hawkins.
Major R. L. Haymes, D.S.O.
Captain A. C. Heaslop.
Second Lieutenant A. M. Henderson.
Lieutenant D. A. H. Hire.
Temporary Second Lieutenant H. R. Hood.
Lieutenant-Colonel F. P. Hutchinson.
Captain J. H. Johnston.
Second Lieutenant C. W. Jones.
Major J. H. H. Jones.
Major A. R. Y. Kirkpatrick.
Lieutenant-Colonel K. K. Knapp.
Captain J. H. Knight.
Captain C. P. J. Layard.
Captain J. B. Leefe.
Captain L. K. Leeson.
Lieutenant W. A. A. Leslie.
Captain W. H. Lewis.
Lieutenant-Colonel D. F. H. Logan.
Brevet Lieutenant-Colonel W. Loring.
Major W. M. Macalpine-Leny, D.S.O.
Captain W. A. O. C. Mackintosh.

MENTIONED IN DESPATCHES

Lieutenant-Colonel T. E. Marshall.
Captain M. E. Mascall.
Major F. H. Metcalfe.
Captain E. Miles.
Major H. E. Molesworth.
Lieutenant B. S. K. G. Moores.
Second Lieutenant W. A. Murley.
Lieutenant-Colonel W. J. Napier.
Major C. C. Noott.
Major C. H. W. Owen.
Captain V. H. L. Pellew.
Lieutenant C. Q. L. Penrose.
Major H. R. Poole.
Captain E. R. Pratt.
Lieutenant (temporary Captain) J. A. Pym.
Captain F. H. Reid (killed).
Major J. Y. H. Ridout.
Major H. Rowan-Robinson.
Temporary Lieutenant G. Sainsbury.
Captain D. A. Sandford.
Second Lieutenant J. E. Sargent.
Lieutenant-Colonel A. F. S. Scott.
Second Lieutenant R. J. Shaw.
Captain H. W. T. Smith.
Major L. K. Stanbrough.
Second Lieutenant A. B. Stewart.
Captain C. H. M. Sturges, D.S.O.
Major O. R. Swayne, D.S.O.
Lieutenant-Colonel C. S. Taylor.
Captain C. D. Tod.
Lieutenant (temporary Captain) J. F. H. Tomasson, Reserve of Officers.
Captain S. M. Toppin.
Major H. E. O'B. Traill.
Lieutenant (temporary Captain) B. D. C. Treatt.
Major F. W. Vander Kiste.
Captain J. Way.
Major A. H. Webb.
Temporary Second Lieutenant O. Whitaker (killed).
Major E. Wighton.
Major A. C. Wilkinson, D.S.O.
Temporary Second Lieutenant J. Williams.
Second Lieutenant H. A. S. Wortley, Special Reserve.
Trumpeter W. Bell.
Corporal B. F. Braham.
Serjeant W. Bridle.
Bombardier C. Chadwick.

MENTIONED IN DESPATCHES

Battery Serjeant-Major P. G. Cook.
Corporal E. C. Dartnell.
Corporal W. J. Davis.
Serjeant J. Dixon.
Bombardier J. Downing.
Serjeant W. W. Fenn.
Corporal A. A. Gumbs.
Bombardier W. J. Gutteridge.
Gunner A. J. Hall.
Corporal F. B. Halliwell.
Serjeant (Acting Battery Quartermaster-Serjeant) G. F. Hartley.
Corporal P. H. Holman.
Corporal H. P. Howes.
Serjeant H. D. Jones.
Bombardier R. E. Knightsbridge.
Serjeant J. Lawrence.
Gunner C. McCarthy.
Battery Quartermaster-Serjeant J. B. Mead.
Gunner F. C. Meadows.
Corporal C. W. L. Moser.
Gunner R. Murphy.
Corporal F. W. Newman.
Serjeant T. H. Owen (died of wounds).
Bombardier A. E. Parton (killed).
Gunner H. Petit.
Battery Serjeant-Major F. J. Rees.
Serjeant E. S. Sands.
Gunner E. W. Sharp.
Bombardier H. C. Simmons (deceased).
Gunner A. Stewart.
Acting Bombardier A. V. Taylor.
Bombardier F. Thoresby.
Regimental Quartermaster-Serjeant (Acting Serjeant-Major) P. J Walker, Artillery Clerk.
Gunner H. Warmington.
Battery Serjeant-Major A. W. Webb.
Gunner J. M. Westbrook.
Corporal W. H. T. Whitehorn.
Gunner J. Wilson (killed).
Serjeant W. Timberlake.

ROYAL GARRISON ARTILLERY (TERRITORIAL FORCE).

Temporary Major F. J. Chapple (Captain, North Midland [Staffordshire] R.G.A.).
Captain S. Low, London R.G.A.
Lieutenant G. T. F. Royle, South Midland (Warwickshire) R.G.A.

MENTIONED IN DESPATCHES

Second Lieutenant B. P. Hill, Northumbrian (North Riding) R.G.A.
Battery Serjeant-Major H. Hartley, West Riding R.G.A.
Bombardier H. Grindall, South Midland (Warwickshire) R.G.A.
Bombardier G. Utley, West Riding R.G.A.

Honourable Artillery Company.

Second Lieutenant (temporary Captain) D. G. Collins.
Temporary Captain E. A. Lankester.
Second Lieutenant (temporary Captain) H. P. G. Maule.
Second Lieutenant (temporary Captain) F. P. Morphy.
Second Lieutenant (temporary Captain) C. F. Osmond.
Second Lieutenant (temporary Captain) W. A. Stone.
Second Lieutenant (temporary Lieutenant) E. W. F. Hammond.
Second Lieutenant J. N. Balme.
Second Lieutenant L. W. McArthur.
Quartermaster and Honorary Lieutenant G. H. Mayhew.
Regimental Quartermaster-Serjeant F. A. Caddick.
Company Serjeant-Major (Acting Regimental Serjeant-Major) A. G. S. Huddart.
Serjeant H. E. Hills.
Lance-Serjeant W. H. R. Merriman.
Serjeant R. N. C. Pickering.
Private J. Thompson.
Private D. Clare (killed).
Private E. J. Spanier.
Private E. L. Sprunt (killed).

Royal Engineers.

Lieutenant C. C. Adams.
Lieutenant E. S. R. Adams, Special Reserve.
Temporary Lieutenant J. E. Anderson.
Captain C. J. Aston.
Temporary Lieutenant C. P. L. Balcombe.
Temporary Second Lieutenant A. Barlerin.
Temporary Lieutenant A. H. Barry.
Temporary Captain W. M. Batchelor.
Captain H. H. Bateman.
Lieutenant J. Batho (died of wounds).
Temporary Second Lieutenant F. Bell (New Armies).
Second Lieutenant R. Bennett (Special Reserve).
Major P. K. Betty, D.S.O.
Major H. Biddulph.
Temporary Lieutenant H. D. Bindley.
Lieutenant J. I. F. Bourdillon.
Major O. G. Brandon.
Major (temporary Lieutenant-Colonel) A. G. Bremner.

MENTIONED IN DESPATCHES

Temporary Lieutenant R. W. Brims.
Temporary Second Lieutenant R. B. Brisco.
Lieutenant A. C. Brooks.
Major A. Brough, D.S.O.
Captain A. H. Brown.
Major G. A. P. Brown.
Major C. M. Browne, D.S.O.
Major F. M. Browne, D.S.O. (died of wounds).
Captain W. E. Buckingham.
Temporary Second Lieutenant E. W. Byrde.
Captain A. Campbell.
Captain E. B. Cardew.
Lieutenant R. W. Cardew.
Captain W. L. de M. Carey.
Temporary Lieutenant T. H. Carlisle.
Lieutenant K. MacL. Carnduff.
Temporary Lieutenant G. R. Cassels (New Armies).
Temporary Second Lieutenant N. F. Cave-Brown-Cave.
Captain A. A. Chase.
Temporary Lieutenant W. R. Cloutman (killed).
Temporary Captain G. H. Comport (Captain, Territorial Force Reserve).
Temporary Second Lieutenant W. Cooper.
Major S. H. Cowan.
Major J. E. E. Craster.
Temporary Lieutenant E. Crewsdon.
Temporary Lieutenant N. G. Crompton (killed).
Major S. D'A. Crookshank.
Temporary Lieutenant C. H. Cropper (New Armies).
Major A. B. Cunningham.
Temporary Lieutenant C. A. Currie.
Major B. W. Y. Danford.
Temporary Lieutenant E. C. Daniels.
Captain A. J. Darlington.
Temporary Lieutenant R. H. Davies.
Captain E. F. S. Dawson.
Temporary Captain L. Delphin.
Brevet Major G. E. B. Dobbs.
Captain R. V. Doherty-Holwell, D.S.O.
Captain F. McC. Douie, D.S.O.
Temporary Captain J. E. Drennan (Special Reserve, Postal Section).
Lieutenant H. G. Eady.
Temporary Lieutenant C. H. W. Edmonds.
Colonel J. E. Edmonds, C.B.
Temporary Lieutenant W. N. Elgood.
Lieutenant W. E. Euler.

MENTIONED IN DESPATCHES

Major W. H. Evans.
Lieutenant D. K. Finnimore.
Major J. G. Fleming.
Temporary Lieutenant F. R. Forbes (killed).
Colonel H. R. Gale.
Temporary Second Lieutenant W. Gardner.
Captain W. Garforth.
Captain H. S. Gaskell.
Temporary Second Lieutenant C. Gattens.
Temporary Captain H. G. Gilchrist (Lieutenant, temporary Captain Territorial Force).
Major G. F. B. Goldney, D.S.O.
Lieutenant A. W. Gordon.
Captain J. A. Graeme.
Temporary Captain G. R. Grange (Captain Territorial Force).
Temporary Captain T. H. Grange.
Lieutenant-Colonel P. G. Grant.
Captain A. E. Grassett.
Lieutenant D. H. Green (Special Reserve).
Lieutenant H. G. Greenwood.
Major J. N. Griffiths (King Edward's Horse, Special Reserve).
Lieutenant F. Grundy (Special Reserve).
Lieutenant G. F. Hall (Special Reserve).
Lieutenant W. E. Hamblin.
Lieutenant H. W. R. Hamilton.
Lieutenant D. H. Hammonds (Special Reserve).
Temporary Captain (Army) H. M. Hance (Second Lieutenant Indian Army Reserve of Officers).
Temporary Second Lieutenant G. Hart.
Lieutenant L. V. Hart (Reserve of Officers).
Lieutenant-Colonel R. N. Harvey, D.S.O.
Major G. R. Hearn.
Captain J. T. Heath.
Temporary Second Lieutenant A. Hibbert.
Temporary Captain H. C. B. Hickling.
Temporary Captain F. F. Higginson.
Lieutenant H. Higgs (Special Reserve).
Brevet Lieutenant-Colonel A. B. R. Hildebrand, D.S.O.
Captain R. C. R. Hill.
Lieutenant F. G. Hill (Special Reserve).
Temporary Lieutenant L. C. Hill.
Lieutenant G. E. W. Hitchcock (Special Reserve).
Major C. C. H. Hogg.
Temporary Lieutenant E. E. F. Homer.
Major (temporary Lieutenant-Colonel) F. G. Howard, M.V.O., D.S.O. (killed).

MENTIONED IN DESPATCHES

Lieutenant B. Howorth (Special Reserve).
Temporary Lieutenant E. B. Hugh-Jones.
Major (temporary Lieutenant-Colonel) C. G. W. Hunter, D.S.O.
Lieutenant N. D. R. Hunter.
Lieutenant H. P. W. Hutson.
Captain F. G. Hyland.
Major F. A. Iles.
Temporary Second Lieutenant C. F. S. Jameson.
Temporary Second Lieutenant A. R. C. Jenks.
Major D. C. Jones.
Lieutenant S. H. Joseph.
Temporary Second Lieutenant C. M. Kay.
Lieutenant E. Kaye-Parry (Special Reserve).
Temporary Major P. T. R. Kellner.
Captain E. H. Kelly.
Major T. E. Kelsall.
Lieutenant C. S. C. Kennedy.
Colonel E. R. Kenyon (retired pay).
Lieutenant W. A. FitzG. Kerrich.
Lieutenant J. Kiggell.
Lieutenant S. W. Kirby.
Captain F. H. Kisch.
Major G. S. Knox.
Temporary Second Lieutenant G. T. Labey.
Temporary Second Lieutenant D. E. Laing.
Temporary Lieutenant G. Lambert.
Captain H. P. T. Lefroy.
Captain F. B. Legh.
Lieutenant-Colonel G. A. J. Leslie.
Major H. L. Lewis.
Colonel W. A. Liddell.
Temporary Lieutenant (Army) B. Lightfoot.
Captain C. G. Ling.
Second Lieutenant W. H. Livens (Special Reserve).
Lieutenant N. C. Lowson (Special Reserve).
Major G. Lubbock.
Lieutenant M. Luby.
Temporary Second Lieutenant A. J. McCarraher (Postal Section, Special Reserve).
Temporary Second Lieutenant (Army) D. McKelvie.
Captain P. J. Mackesy.
Lieutenant L. J. MacLean.
Captain H. C. McNeile.
Lieutenant J. W. D. Mallins.
Temporary Second Lieutenant R. C. Manning.
Lieutenant G. E. Mansergh.

MENTIONED IN DESPATCHES

Temporary Lieutenant I. W. Massie.
Second Lieutenant F. V. Merchant.
Major S. Mildred.
Temporary Lieutenant W. M. Miller.
Captain E. M. F. Momber.
Major J. D. Monro.
Temporary Captain E. Moore (Lieutenant Special Reserve).
Lieutenant L. T. Morshead.
Temporary Lieutenant O. F. Morshead.
Captain A. H. L. Mount.
Lieutenant C. F. Mulvany.
Temporary Captain J. D. Murdoch (Captain Territorial Force).
Captain P. Neame, V.C.
Captain N. D. Noble.
Temporary Captain G. T. W. Olver.
Temporary Lieutenant J. F. Ormsby.
Captain E. A. Osborne, D.S.O.
Major G. F. F. Osborne.
Major S. L. Owen.
Second Lieutenant R. F. Parkinson.
Lieutenant E. R. L. Peake.
Lieutenant T. M. M. Penney.
Lieutenant I. S. O. Playfair.
Temporary Lieutenant A. Podmore.
Major H. de L. Pollard-Lowsley, C.I.E.
Temporary Second Lieutenant (Army) W. A. Pope.
Captain F. Preedy.
Lieutenant P. T. Rawlings (Special Reserve).
Captain J. H. Richard.
Temporary Captain T. C. Richardson (Lieutenant Special Reserve).
Temporary Lieutenant A. G. Richardson.
Captain A. V. T. Robinson.
Temporary Second Lieutenant M. W. Salmon.
Major (temporary Lieutenant-Colonel) E. S. Sandys, D.S.O.
Captain A. P. Sayer.
Captain A. H. Scott.
Lieutenant F. H. Seabrooke (Special Reserve).
Lieutenant H. S. Semple.
Lieutenant C. D. Sheldon (Special Reserve).
Lieutenant-Colonel B. A. G. Shelley.
Temporary Second Lieutenant W. D. Shennan.
Captain G. E. H. Sim.
Captain V. H. Simon.
Major (temporary Lieutenant-Colonel) C. W. Singer, D.S.O.
Lieutenant-Colonel G. E. Smith, C.M.G.
Captain G. B. F. Smyth, D.S.O.

MENTIONED IN DESPATCHES

Captain G. E. Sopwith.
Captain P. G. Spackman.
Major D. O. Springfield (Special Reserve).
Major G. H. Stack.
Lieutenant J. H. Stafford.
Major (temporary Lieutenant-Colonel) A. G. Stevenson, D.S.O.
Captain D. MacI. Stewart.
Lieutenant R. S. G. Stokes.
Lieutenant J. S. W. Stone.
Temporary Captain F. J. M. Stratton.
Lieutenant C. V. Strong.
Captain T. A. S. Swinburne.
Temporary Lieutenant E. M. Tabor.
Temporary Lieutenant (Army) J. W. Talbot.
Temporary Second Lieutenant A. J. Taylor.
Captain H. C. Thomas.
Major F. V. Thompson.
Captain J. L. Tomlin.
Major W. S. Traill.
Temporary Second-Lieutenant E. Tulloch.
Captain A. G. Turner, D.S.O.
Captain R. A. Turner.
Temporary Second Lieutenant S. C. Vickers.
Temporary Lieutenant F. G. C. Walker (New Armies).
Major C. Walton.
Temporary Second Lieutenant (Army) J. Warnock.
Captain J. Watson.
Captain E. V. C. W. Wellesley.
Lieutenant W. B. Wishaw.
Temporary Lieutenant H. C. Whitehead.
Captain J. C. Wickham.
Captain B. H. Wilbraham.
Brevet Major G. C. Williams, D.S.O.
Temporary Second Lieutenant R. A. Williams.
Temporary Second Lieutenant R. B. Williams.
Temporary Second Lieutenant H. Williamson.
Temporary Lieutenant R. W. Williamson.
Lieutenant J. C. Willis.
Lieutenant-Colonel C. S. Wilson, C.B.
Temporary Major N. Wilson, D.S.O.
Second Lieutenant D. M. Wilson, General List, New Armies, attached Royal Engineers.
Major H. St. J. L. Winterbotham.
Lieutenant A. V. D. Wise.
Lieutenant R. L. Withington.
Lieutenant C. G. Woolner.

MENTIONED IN DESPATCHES

Temporary Second Lieutenant C. S. Wright (Second Lieutenant, Territorial Force).
Captain F. J. C. Wyatt.
Captain O. E. Wynne.
Captain A. St. J. Yates.
Temporary Second Lieutenant R. Yates.
Temporary Lieutenant H. H. Yuill.
Quartermaster and Honorary Captain W. H. Dale.
Quartermaster and Honorary Lieutenant F. H. Ashford.
Quartermaster and Honorary Lieutenant F. Cutting.
Quartermaster and Honorary Lieutenant W. R. Evans.
Quartermaster and Honorary Lieutenant W. Reid.
Quartermaster and Honorary Lieutenant W. Stoyle.
Serjeant H. Adams.
Acting-Corporal W. O. Aston.
Lance-Corporal (Acting Serjeant) H. Austen.
Quartermaster-Serjeant (Acting Superintending Clerk) J. H. A. Banger.
Sapper J. Barr.
Pioneer J. Barry.
Pioneer W. C. Bartlett.
Quartermaster-Serjeant (Acting Superintending Clerk) G. H. Batty.
Pioneer H. Bayliss.
Sapper W. Beaton.
Company Serjeant-Major A. J. Bellinger.
Sapper R. Bevan.
Sapper E. Blewitt.
Lance-Corporal A. C. Bond.
Sapper A. Boocock.
Corporal R. G. Bowes.
Acting-Serjeant A. J. Brown.
Serjeant G. E. Brown.
Serjeant R. Brown.
Sapper L. Brierly.
Acting-Serjeant W. H. Bultitude.
Sapper R. Bunce.
Engineer Clerk Quartermaster-Serjeant C. H. D. Burrage.
Sapper G. S. Busby.
Serjeant (Acting Company Quartermaster-Serjeant) W. J. Bussell.
Second Corporal F. Cartwright.
Acting Second Corporal J. A. Cashman.
Engineer Storekeeper Quartermaster-Serjeant R. H. Chambers.
Lance-Corporal A. E. Chare.
Serjeant T. Christie.
Serjeant H. W. Clark.
Acting-Corporal W. Clark.
Serjeant T. Comins.

MENTIONED IN DESPATCHES

Sapper J. H. Cook.
Serjeant R. Cosgrove.
Sapper A. Coveney.
Serjeant F. Craig.
Serjeant W. Crout.
Serjeant D. D. Currie.
Company Serjeant-Major H. Curtis.
Engineer Clerk Quartermaster-Serjeant J. A. Cusack.
Sapper C. Darling.
Acting-Serjeant S. J. Davis.
Sapper J. Davis.
Serjeant A. Dawson.
Corporal E. Day.
Sapper D. J. Devonshire.
Pioneer A. G. Doe.
Serjeant R. Dowling.
Sapper R. H. Drummond.
Sapper J. J. Duane.
Engineer Clerk Quartermaster-Serjeant J. Edington.
Pioneer J. O. Evans.
Sapper A. H. Eyre.
Quartermaster-Serjeant S. Farnham.
Serjeant R. S. Farquhar.
Serjeant F. W. Fagager.
Lance-Corporal E. Fear.
Acting-Corporal W. Fearn.
Sapper W. Firth.
Serjeant H. B. Fiske.
Sapper J. T. Fletcher.
Serjeant F. M. Florance.
Serjeant P. H. Forbes.
Quartermaster-Serjeant H. B. J. Franklin.
Corporal F. Fryer.
Sapper F. I. Fuzzens.
Company Serjeant-Major H. Gallagher.
Sapper F. Garbett.
Serjeant W. Gardner.
Serjeant-Engineer-Clerk and Draughtsman R. C. Gibson.
Company Serjeant-Major L. P. Gill.
Sapper G. Grainger.
Engineer Clerk Quartermaster-Serjeant C. F. Grandy.
Sapper A. J. E. Grant.
Serjeant J. Grayston.
Corporal H. J. Grice.
Sapper T. Groom.
Sapper L. Groome.

MENTIONED IN DESPATCHES

Second Corporal W. Hamby.
Sapper F. Hampson.
Corporal J. L. Hanks.
Corporal E. H. J. Hanmer.
Company Serjeant-Major J. F. Hard.
Pioneer J. C. Hardy.
Lance-Corporal E. B. Harris.
Lance-Corporal E. Hartley.
Sapper V. L. Hatton.
Second Corporal F. C. Heath.
Sapper A. J. Heath.
Sapper C. Henderson.
Serjeant H. S. Higgins.
Serjeant C. R. Hill.
Corporal W. R. Hines.
Acting Second Corporal G. V. Hodson.
Staff-Serjeant (Acting Superintending Clerk) G. E. Hogg.
Sapper A. Hunt.
Sapper F. Hunt.
Acting Lance-Corporal H. Hunter.
Corporal W. G. Hunting.
Serjeant J. G. Hutchison.
Serjeant D. S. Hutchinson.
Second Corporal T. Iles.
Superintending Clerk W. R. V. Isaac.
Acting Superintending Clerk M. Jackson.
Sapper F. J. Jakeman, formerly Private F. J. Jakeman, Royal Lancaster Regiment.
Driver W. T. Jeffery.
Quartermaster-Serjeant S. Johnson.
Sapper A. E. Johnson.
Sapper W. S. Joiner.
Acting Lance-Corporal F. V. Jones.
Sapper W. E. Jones.
Quartermaster-Serjeant J. W. Jordan.
Corporal (Acting-Serjeant) E. W. Judge.
Company Serjeant-Major Frederick Keeley.
Acting Company Quartermaster-Serjeant J. Keir.
Sapper J. Kemley.
Sapper S. J. Kenning.
Corporal T. W. E. Kenward.
Serjeant John William Kesterton.
Sapper B. Kiff.
Serjeant J. Kneebone.
Corporal A. E. Knibbs.
Engineer Clerk Quartermaster-Serjeant W. Knott.

MENTIONED IN DESPATCHES

Acting Corporal R. W. Lack.
Company Quartermaster-Serjeant G. Lane.
Acting-Serjeant W. Leach.
Serjeant T. Leath.
Acting-Serjeant E. LeCluse.
Corporal G. Leigh.
Sapper (Acting Lance-Corporal) R. Liddell.
Company Serjeant-Major A. Lillecrapp.
Sapper F. H. Lister.
Sapper A. G. Locke.
Lance-Corporal G. E. Lomas.
Sapper T. Longstaff (killed).
Lance-Corporal H. McBryde.
Sapper E. McCaffery.
Sapper D. McDermott.
Serjeant T. McDickens.
Acting-Corporal H. M. McLaughlin.
Lance-Corporal A. J. McMasters.
Corporal F. P. Mann.
Acting Lance-Corporal F. D. Marshall.
Acting-Serjeant A. W. Matheson.
Sapper G. Mee.
Company Serjeant-Major C. Mepham.
Second Corporal C. H. Milne.
Pioneer A. Mitchell.
Sapper J. Mitchell.
Acting-Serjeant R. Moffat.
Corporal F. J. D. Montgomerie.
Sapper W. Montgomery.
Sapper B. J. Moore.
Engineer Clerk Quartermaster-Serjeant T. Murphy.
Acting-Corporal W. Murphy.
Lance-Corporal W. E. H. Murrell.
Corporal W. Neal.
Sapper W. Nettle.
Acting Company Serjeant-Major W. A. Nicol.
Superintending Clerk R. H. Nixon.
Sapper F. Nunn.
Corporal M. Nyland.
Superintending Clerk T. N. O'Mara.
Corporal W. K. Palmer.
Lance-Corporal J. Parish.
Company Serjeant-Major A. J. Parker.
Sapper C. J. Patmore.
Farrier-Serjeant E. Payne.
Sapper H. Peacock.

MENTIONED IN DESPATCHES

Second Corporal S. Peck.
Serjeant J. Pettit.
Serjeant J. M. Petty.
Sapper E. Phillips.
Second Corporal S. E. Pittock.
Quartermaster-Serjeant (Acting Superintending Clerk) W. W. Popperwell.
Superintending Clerk A. G. Porters.
Sapper F. M. Preece.
Company Serjeant-Major W. G. Prescott.
Corporal C. Pridden.
Acting Corporal R. Radford.
Sapper A. Read.
Sapper A. Reade.
Engineer Clerk Serjeant J. Reddin.
Lance-Corporal W. Reeve.
Engineer Ledger Keeper Second Corporal A. Reid.
Sapper E. W. Rhymes.
Acting Regimental Serjeant-Major E. Richards.
Company Serjeant-Major G. H. Rodwell.
Corporal G. Rowe.
Lance-Corporal R. W. Rowell.
Sapper (Acting Second Corporal) R. Rule.
Serjeant J. W. Russell.
Second Corporal E. J. Samuel.
Sapper G. Scholes.
Private E. V. Sewter.
Lance-Corporal H. S. Shave.
Acting Lance-Corporal C. Scivier.
Acting-Serjeant G. F. Shefford.
Corporal J. Skinner.
Corporal H. H. Skinner.
Sapper W. Skinner.
Company Serjeant-Major P. Small.
Serjeant J. Smeeth.
Quartermaster-Serjeant S. G. Smith, Engineer Clerk.
Serjeant J. Smith.
Acting-Serjeant J. A. Smith.
M.C. Corporal E. U. Smith.
Engineer Clerk Quartermaster-Serjeant A. Snow.
Sapper C. Soutar.
Serjeant P. Stanley.
Serjeant E. N. Stooke.
Corporal W. Street.
Serjeant W. Stuart.
Troop Serjeant-Major M. Sweeney.

MENTIONED IN DESPATCHES

Sapper J. Smetten.
Second Corporal W. J. Symes.
Acting Company Serjeant-Major J. W. Symington.
Sapper A. Tattershall.
Corporal C. A. Taylor.
Sapper J. T. Tedman.
Acting-Serjeant A. Terris.
Serjeant F. Thompson.
Sapper T. R. Tombs.
Serjeant F. A. Tuft.
Engineer Clerk Quartermaster-Serjeant F. Turner.
Serjeant E. Waldron.
Company Serjeant-Major F. Walker.
Sapper M. H. Wallace.
Lance-Corporal (Acting Second Corporal) J. Warren.
Corporal A. Watson.
Serjeant W. S. Weeks.
Corporal T. G. Wells.
Sapper E. H. Whale.
Sapper I. H. Whittle.
Sapper W. J. Whyte.
Corporal A. C. Wilde.
Acting-Corporal H. Williamson.
Sapper W. Wilson.
Sapper W. Winckles.
Sapper J. H. Wintie.
Sapper C. K. Woodford.
Lance-Corporal W. R. Woodgate.
Serjeant F. T. Woodward.
Sapper B. T. Worfolk.
Second Corporal (Acting Corporal) F. J. Worley.
Serjeant F. A. C. Young.
Serjeant V. L. Young.
Acting Second Corporal E. Young.

Special Reserve.

Major (temporary Lieutenant Army, P. Warren (Postal Section).
Major R. S. Forestier-Walker, Royal Monmouthshire.
Major D. J. Lidbury (Postal Section).
Lieutenant J. A. Goodwin.
Captain P. C. R. Moreton, Royal Monmouthshire.
Lieutenant R. J. Barnes (Postal Section).
Serjeant-Major F. W. Anderson (Postal Section).
Quartermaster-Serjeant R. I. Sargent (Postal Section).
Serjeant J. J. Collins (Postal Section).
Serjeant E. Fitzmorris, Royal Monmouthshire.

MENTIONED IN DESPATCHES

Company Serjeant-Major J. Guy, Royal Monmouthshire.
Company Serjeant-Major E. Peto (Postal Service).
Company Serjeant-Major C. Williams, Royal Anglesea.
Serjeant S. Russell, Royal Monmouthshire.
Serjeant T. Walters, Royal Monmouthshire.

ROYAL ENGINEERS, TERRITORIAL FORCE.

Captain (temporary Major) Sir L. C. W. Alexander, Bt., London Regiment (Captain, London Divisional Signal Co.).
Captain (temporary Major) J. G. Allan, Highland Divisional Engineers.
Captain (temporary Major) J. A. Arrowsmith-Brown, South Midland Divisional Signal Company.
Lieutenant (temporary Captain) W. P. Barron, Highland Divisional Engineers.
Second Lieutenant (temporary Lieutenant) E. R. H. Beaman, Home Counties Divisional Engineers.
Captain G. T. Biggs, Glamorgan Fortress Engineers.
Lieutenant (temporary Major) A. G. Birch, London Divisional Engineers.
Second Lieutenant (temporary Major) W. Bisset, Highland Divisional Engineers.
Second Lieutenant (temporary Lieutenant) T. S. Bliss, Wessex Divisional Engineers.
Lieutenant (temporary Major) E. B. Blogg, D.S.O., London Divisional Engineers.
Temporary Captain (Lieutenant, temporary Captain London Divisional Signal Company) W. F. Bruce.
Captain (temporary Major) C. C. Bryan, Home Counties Divisional Engineers.
Captain (temporary Major) E. C. Burnup, Northumbrian Divisional Engineers.
Second Lieutenant (temporary Lieutenant) C. I. Burrell, Northumbrian Divisional Engineers.
Temporary Second Lieutenant C. T. Cadman, Motor Cyclist Section, Special Reserve.
Major H. La T. Campbell, West Lancashire Divisional Engineers.
Second Lieutenant (temporary Lieutenant) L. C. Chasey, Wessex Divisional Engineers.
Second Lieutenant (temporary Lieutenant) G. W. Clark, Lowland Divisional Engineers.
Captain L. J. Coussmaker, North Midland Divisional Engineers.
Captain H. Davies, Hampshire Fortress Engineers.
Lieutenant (temporary Captain) J. Dawson, Wiltshire Fortress Engineers.
Major R. B. Dutton, Wessex Divisional Engineers.

MENTIONED IN DESPATCHES

Captain (temporary Major) G. S. J. F. Eberle, South Midland Divisional Engineers.
Lieutenant (temporary Captain) H. W. Edwards, Royal Warwickshire Regiment and Northumbrian Divisional Signal Company.
Major P. G. Fry, Wessex Divisional Engineers.
Second Lieutenant (temporary Captain) C. M. Gamage, London Divisional Engineers.
Temporary Major J. S. Gardner, North Midland Divisional Engineers.
Lieutenant R. Glegg, Highland Divisional Engineers (killed).
Second Lieutenant (temporary Lieutenant) L. A. Halsall, Welsh Divisional Engineers.
Lieutenant N. C. Harbutt, Wessex Divisional Engineers.
Second Lieutenant (temporary Lieutenant) W. H. Hardman, North Midland Divisional Engineers.
Captain S. L. Harvey, Wessex Divisional Engineers.
Major C. Hatton, North Midland Divisional Engineers.
Lieutenant D. L. Herbert, Home Counties Divisional Engineers.
Second Lieutenant (temporary Major) A. F. Hobson, West Riding Divisional Engineers.
Lieutenant (temporary Captain) F. R. Hybart, Glamorgan Fortress Engineers.
Second Lieutenant (temporary Lieutenant) F. W. Jackson, West Lancashire Divisional Engineers.
Captain O. G. D. Jones, Adjutant West Riding Divisional Engineers.
Second Lieutenant (temporary Lieutenant) L. T. Jordan, North Midland Divisional Engineers.
Major R. H. Joseph, London Divisional Engineers.
Second Lieutenant O. H. Keeling, East Anglian Divisional Engineers.
Brevet Colonel A. H. Kenney, C.M.G., D.S.O., retired pay, London Divisional Engineers.
Temporary Major J. C. M. Kerr, Major Scottish Signal Company.
Second Lieutenant (temporary Lieutenant) G. E. C. Knapp, Wiltshire Fortress Engineers.
Captain (temporary Major) E. A. Lewis, North Midland Divisional Signal Company.
Second Lieutenant (temporary Captain) S. G. Love, London Divisional Engineers.
Lieutenant (temporary Captain) R. H. Mackenzie, London Divisional Engineers.
Second Lieutenant A. G. MacNeill, Highland Divisional Engineers.
Captain J. A. McQueen, Adjutant Northumbrian Divisional Engineers.
Second Lieutenant S. Maurice, Wessex Divisional Engineers (died of wounds).
Lieutenant (temporary Major) W. Middleton, West Riding Divisional Engineers.
Captain J. B. Miller, City of Aberdeen Fortress Engineers.

MENTIONED IN DESPATCHES

Captain (temporary Major) R. Mitchell, Highland Divisional Engineers.
Second Lieutenant (temporary Lieutenant) D. M. T. Morland, London Divisional Engineers.
Second Lieutenant (temporary Captain) R. W. Narracott, London Divisional Engineers.
Lieutenant R. B. Pitt, Wessex Divisional Engineers.
Major G. C. Pollard, D.S.O., Northumbrian Divisional Engineers.
Second Lieutenant (temporary Lieutenant) H. Rhodes, West Riding Divisional Engineers.
Captain (temporary Major) A. Robertson, Highland Divisional Signal Company.
Second Lieutenant (temporary Lieutenant) J. Russell, Highland Divisional Engineers.
Second Lieutenant (temporary Lieutenant) G. C. Sanford, Wessex Divisional Engineers.
Captain (temporary Major) H. C. Saunders, Home Counties Divisional Signal Company.
Second Lieutenant (temporary Lieutenant) C. E. Sherwin, Hampshire Fortress Engineers.
Second Lieutenant (temporary Captain) V. F. Stapleton-Bretherton, West Lancashire Divisional Engineers.
Lieutenant (temporary Captain) W. R. Stowell, Northumbrian Divisional Engineers.
Lieutenant (temporary Captain) D. Sutherland, Seaforth Highlanders, and Highland Divisional Signal Company.
Major S. W. Tonks, North Midland Divisional Engineers (killed).
Second Lieutenant (temporary Lieutenant) W. H. S. Tripp, Northumbrian Divisional Engineers.
Temporary Lieutenant A. W. Vigers (Second Lieutenant London Signal Company).
Temporary Captain G. K. Walker (Second Lieutenant, temporary Lieutenant) Northumbrian Divisional Engineers.
Temporary Lieutenant W. A. B. K. Ward (Second Lieutenant London Signal Company) (died of wounds).
Lieutenant G. F. Watson, Cheshire Field Company.
Second Lieutenant G. F. Watson, Welsh Divisional Engineers.
Lieutenant (temporary Captain) P. E. Welchman, North Midland Divisional Engineers.
Major F. Wilson, East Anglian Divisional Engineers.
Captain C. S. Wilson, Wiltshire Fortress Engineers.
Serjeant J. Armstrong, Welsh Divisional Engineers.
Second Corporal W. H. Baber, Home Counties Divisional Engineers.
Second Corporal V. W. Bailey, Hampshire Fortress Engineers.
Sapper W. J. Bailey, Hampshire Fortress Engineers.
Sapper S. C. E. Bellinger, Wiltshire Fortress Engineers.
Pioneer L. Bramall, London Divisional Signal Company.

MENTIONED IN DESPATCHES

Serjeant A. J. Butler, Home Counties Divisional Signal Company.
Corporal H. D. Caie, Highland Divisional Engineers.
Motor Cyclist Corporal T. G. Campbell, Wessex Divisional Signal Company.
Corporal W. B. Chambers, West Riding Divisional Engineers.
Lance-Corporal W. T. Charleson, Highland Divisional Engineers.
Serjeant G. H. Child, Wessex Divisional Engineers.
Sapper J. Convery, Northumbrian Divisional Engineers.
Acting-Serjeant J. Cunningham, Highland Divisional Engineers.
Second Corporal G. H. Eaton, Wiltshire Fortress Engineers.
Serjeant A. W. Edwards, Wiltshire Fortress Engineers.
Sapper H. Fincham, Home Counties Divisional Engineers.
Sapper A. Forsyth, Highland Divisional Engineers.
Serjeant G. H. Francis, Wessex Divisional Engineers.
Sapper W. N. H. Freeman, London Divisional Signal Company.
Lance-Corporal J. S. R. Gale, Wiltshire Fortress Engineers.
Serjeant W. Green, Northumbrian Divisional Engineers.
Sapper A. Harding, South Midland Divisional Engineers.
Second Corporal J. Harper, Highland Divisional Engineers.
Serjeant R. Heaton, West Lancashire Divisional Engineers.
Acting-Corporal W. N. Higson, Welsh Divisional Engineers.
Corporal J. Hopper, Northumbrian Divisional Engineers.
Lance-Corporal A. Horsfield, Northumbrian Divisional Engineers.
Acting Lance-Corporal E. Hughes, Welsh Divisional Engineers.
Serjeant B. H. D. Hurst, Wessex Divisional Engineers.
Second Corporal H. R. Iliffe, London Divisional Signal Company.
Corporal F. C. Jarvis, Wessex Divisional Engineers.
Corporal J. W. Jones, London Divisional Engineers.
Sapper G. W. Jones, Welsh Divisional Engineers.
Sapper W. H. H. Leaver, London Divisional Signal Company.
Company Quartermaster-Serjeant E. J. Leggatt, Home Counties Divisional Engineers.
Corporal J. M. Lightfoot, West Lancashire Divisional Engineers.
Lance-Corporal G. Lowrie, Northumbrian Divisional Engineers.
Serjeant A. G. Marchant, Wessex Divisional Engineers.
Serjeant T. J. Marchant, Wessex Divisional Engineers.
Corporal J. Martin, Welsh Divisional Engineers.
Serjeant A. Minnis, West Riding Divisional Engineers.
Serjeant A. G. Mogg, Wessex Divisional Engineers.
Serjeant W. Morris, West Lancashire Divisional Engineers.
Lance-Corporal J. Nixey, Wessex Divisional Engineers.
Second Corporal J. Oakford, Wiltshire Fortress Engineers.
Lance-Corporal C. O'Sullivan, London Divisional Engineers.
Company Serjeant-Major E. Pheasey, West Riding Divisional Engineers
Second Corporal H. Philpot, Home Counties Divisional Engineers.
Second Corporal P. Puncher, Wessex Divisional Signal Company.

MENTIONED IN DESPATCHES

Serjeant H. J. Pursey, Wessex Divisional Engineers.
Company Serjeant-Major T. Quigley, Welsh Divisional Engineers.
Corporal (Acting-Serjeant) G. Rankin, Lowland Divisonal Engineers.
Corporal W. Roach, Wessex Divisional Engineers.
Company Serjeant-Major H. C. Rodda, Wiltshire Fortress Engineers.
Field Linesman Serjeant J. F. Ryan, Wessex Divisional Signal Company.
Field Linesman Second Corporal W. S. Sansom, Wessex Divisional Signal Company.
Company Serjeant-Major E. J. Sawyer.
Sapper H. S. Sims, Welsh Divisional Engineers.
Sapper H. J. Shorland, Wiltshire Fortress Engineers.
Serjeant S. Shaw, West Riding Divisional Engineers.
Serjeant W. J. Slade, London Divisional Signal Company.
Company Serjeant-Major W. G. Smith, London Divisional Signal Company.
Serjeant F. J. Sparrow, Home Counties Divisional Engineers.
Serjeant A. E. Stone, London Divisional Engineers.
Sapper J. B. Sullivan, Home Counties Signal Company.
Serjeant W. G. L. Sutherland, Highland Divisional Engineers.
Sapper G. B. Swinbank, Welsh Divisional Engineers.
Sapper W. F. Thorpe, London Divisional Engineers.
Sapper A. Tully, Home Counties Divisional Engineers.
Serjeant W. C. Walker, Highland Divisional Engineers.
Company Serjeant-Major J. W. Western, Wessex Divisional Signal Company.
Serjeant W. Whittle, Wessex Divisional Engineers.
Sapper R. Wilson, Wessex Divisional Signal Company.
Sapper H. Winkle, North Midland Divisional Engineers.

GRENADIER GUARDS.

Lieutenant-Colonel G. E. Pereira, C.M.G., D.S.O. (Reserve of Officers)
Lieutenant-Colonel (temporary Brigadier-General) C. E. Corkran, C.M.G.
Major (temporary Lieutenant-Colonel) G. F. Trotter, M.V.O., D.S.O., Reserve of Officers.
Major C. R. Champion de Crespigny.
Captain C. H. Greville.
Captain J. S. Hughes.
Lieutenant C. Mitchell (Adjutant) (Captain Northumberland Fusiliers).
Second Lieutenant E. O. R. Wakeman, Special Reserve (killed).
Quartermaster and Honorary Lieutenant J. Teece.
Serjeant W. Golding.
Private S. Carpenter.
Lance-Corporal G. Laming.
Private G. Rhodes.

MENTIONED IN DESPATCHES

Private G. Roache (killed).
Private W. Waterman.
Major (temporary Lieutenant-Colonel) Lord H. C. Seymour.
Lieutenant A. V. L. Corry.
Lieutenant J. C. Craigie.
Lieutenant A. K. S. Cuninghame.
Second Lieutenant (temporary Lieutenant) H. A. Clive.
Second Lieutenant M. A. Knatchbull-Hugessen, Special Reserve.
Second Lieutenant H. G. W. Sandeman, Special Reserve.
Quartermaster and Honorary Lieutenant W. E. Acraman.
Company Serjeant-Major R. Gudgin.
Lance-Serjeant (acting Serjeant) F. Jones.
Lance-Serjeant J. Thomas.
Private W. Godfrey.
Private E. Nelmes.
Private P. Smith.
Private P. Murphy.
Captain C. F. A. Walker.
Lieutenant G. G. Gunnis.
Second Lieutenant A. T. Ayres-Ritchie, Special Reserve.
Serjeant R. Dickson.
Lance-Serjeant H. Nuttall.
Private G. Cooke.
Private D. Cronin.
Lance-Corporal W. Latta.
Captain H. L. Aubrey-Fletcher, M.V.O.
Captain J. A. Morrison, Reserve of Officers.
Second Lieutenant (temporary Captain) E. F. Penn, Special Reserve (killed).
Lance-Corporal W. Matthews.
Corporal W. Miller.
Lance-Corporal H. Painter.
Lance-Corporal M. Hartley.
Lance-Corporal J. W. Robinson.

Coldstream Guards.

Quartermaster-Serjeant (temporary 1st Class Staff Serjeant-Major) G. W. Ewings.
Major (temporary Lieutenant-Colonel) A. Egerton (killed).
Lieutenant (temporary Captain) Hon. T. C. R. Agar-Robartes, Special Reserve.
Captain G. M. Darell.
Lieutenant Hon. M. H. D. Browne (killed).
Lieutenant (temporary Captain) Hon. E. K. Digby.
Lieutenant C. J. M. Riley.
Lieutenant (temporary Captain) M. B. Smith, D.S.O.

MENTIONED IN DESPATCHES

Second Lieutenant O. G. Style, Special Reserve.
Serjeant-Major W. H. Barkham.
Company Serjeant-Major T. J. Prosser.
Lance-Serjeant R. W. Blackett.
Private W. Eccles.
Private W. Jones.
Private W. E. Robbins.
Major (temporary Lieutenant-Colonel) P. A. Macgregor, D.S.O.
Captain H. D. Bentinck.
Lieutenant (temporary Captain) H. C. Lloyd.
Lieutenant (temporary Captain) H. W. Verelst.
Lieutenant (temporary Captain) L. M. Gibbs.
Lieutenant (temporary Captain) S. G. F. Taylor (killed).
Serjeant G. S. Finch.
Serjeant A. F. Gough.
Lance-Corporal H. W. Slade.
Lance-Corporal C. Webb.
Lance-Corporal J. F. Carnell.
Private P. H. Marshall.
Private G. Molyneux.
Major (temporary Lieutenant-Colonel) J. V. Campbell, D.S.O.
Captain C. B. Gunston, Special Reserve.
Captain P. R. B. Lawrence.
Lieutenant (temporary Captain) H. A. Cubitt.
Lieutenant (temporary Captain) A. F. Smith.
Lieutenant J. C. Wynne-Finch.
Second Lieutenant R. O. Hambro, Special Reserve.
Second Lieutenant A. O. J. Hope.
Serjeant J. T. McDonagh.
Serjeant C. H. Purnell.
Serjeant C. W. Rabjohns.
Private G. Cockram.
Private C. Richardson.
Private J. T. Richardson.
Private W. J. Richmond.
Captain G. J. Edwards.
Serjeant C. Wilson.

SCOTS GUARDS.

Temporary Lieutenant J. G. Lumsden.
Quartermaster-Serjeant (Acting Serjeant-Major) J. Cook.
Quartermaster-Serjeant (Acting Serjeant-Major) H. G. Shaw.
Major S. H. Godman, D.S.O. (Reserve of Officers).
Captain Sir V. A. F. Mackenzie, Bt., M.V.O.
Captain J. H. Cuthbert, D.S.O. (Reserve of Officers).
Major N. A. Orr-Ewing, D.S.O.

MENTIONED IN DESPATCHES

Captain J. S. Thorpe (Reserve of Officers) (Major, Notts [Sherwoo Rangers] Yeomanry).
Second Lieutenant (temporary Lieutenant) C. Bartholomew.
Lieutenant H. C. Hammersely (Special Reserve).
Lieutenant (temporary Captain) L. Norman, Special Reserve.
Lieutenant A. J. Thompson, Special Reserve.
Serjeant-Major E. T. Cutler.
Serjeant (Acting Serjeant-Major) C. W. Crouch, attached Headquarters, 1st Army.
Company Serjeant-Major (Drill Serjeant) H. W. Hayward.
Serjeant T. P. Brownlow.
Serjeant W. E. Sait.
Serjeant C. W. Clarke.
Lance-Serjeant (Acting Serjeant) F. Harris.
Private R. Low.
Private W. McCulloch.
Private T. B. Mayer.
Private G. Schweitzer.
Major (temporary Lieutenant-Colonel) A. B. E. Cator, D.S.O.
Captain G. J. M. Bagot-Chester (Reserve of Officers).
Captain E. C. T. Warner.
Lieutenant (temporary Captain) W. H. Wynne Finch.
Second Lieutenant (temporary Lieutenant) E. F. W. Arkwright, Special Reserve.
Second Lieutenant E. S. Clarke, Special Reserve.
Second Lieutenant R. E. Warde, Special Reserve.
Quartermaster and Honorary Lieutenant T. Ross.
Serjeant W. Bold.
Serjeant J. M. Lindores.
Serjeant J. P. Sheridan.
Serjeant P. Smart.
Corporal A. L. Taylor.
Lance-Serjeant S. T. Lingley.
Private G. H. Austin.
Lance-Corporal (Acting Lance-Serjeant) J. Litster.
Private J. Stewart.

Irish Guards.

Major (temporary Lieutenant-Colonel) G. H. C. Madden, Reserve of Officers (died of wounds).
Captain M. V. Gore-Langton (killed).
Lieutenant P. H. Antrobus, Special Reserve.
Lieutenant (temporary Captain) J. S. N. Fitzgerald.
Lieutenant Hon. H. B. O'Brien (Special Reserve).
Lieutenant F. L. Pusch, Special Reserve.
Quartermaster and Honorary Lieutenant H. Hickie.

MENTIONED IN DESPATCHES

Orderly Room Quartermaster-Serjeant J. T. Halligan.
Serjeant J. Fawcett.
Serjeant M. Kenny.
Serjeant F. J. Keown.
Drill-Serjeant T. Cahill.
Lieutenant-Colonel Hon. L. J. P. Butler.
Captain (temporary Major) Hon. H. R. L. G. Alexander.

WELSH GUARDS.

Lieutenant-Colonel W. Murray-Threipland.
Captain H. Dene.
Captain R. Williams, D.S.O.
Captain R. C. W. Williams-Bulkeley.
Lieutenant R. W. Lewis.
Superintending Clerk C. E. Woods (late Scots Guards).
Company Serjeant-Major D. Cossey.
Drill-Serjeant W. Bland.
Lance-Corporal J. Gough.
Lance-Serjeant F. Phillips.
Private M. Jones.

INFANTRY.
ROYAL SCOTS.

Captain G. E. Hall.
Major G. H. F. Wingate.
Captain L. S. Farquharson (killed).
Major A. F. Lumsden.
Captain H. E. Stanley-Murray.
Lieutenant C. Wilson Brown, Royal Scots Fusiliers, Special Reserve.
Lieutenant J. D. Scott, Special Reserve.
Second Lieutenant D. C. Thomson.
Serjeant G. Passelow.
Corporal J. Groat.
Private D. Carty.
Lance-Corporal D. R. Millar.
Lance-Corporal P. Robertson.
Private W. Sivier.
Private L. Smith.
Captain J. C. H. Grant, Special Reserve.
Captain B. H. H. Perry.
Captain N. S. Stewart (killed).
Captain R. C. Blackwood, Special Reserve.
Lieutenant (temporary Captain) J. Lamond (Adjutant) South Staffordshire Regiment, Territorial Force.
Temporary Second Lieutenant C. B. Whittaker, Service Battalion.
Regimental Quartermaster-Serjeant J. A. Carleton.
Serjeant P. O'Hara.

MENTIONED IN DESPATCHES

Private D. Martin.
Captain O. M. Crackanthorpe, Special Reserve.
Captain R. R. Nye, Special Reserve.
Lance-Corporal J. Smith.

ROYAL SCOTS (TERRITORIAL FORCE).

Temporary Captain J. F. F. Trelawny.
Lieutenant-Colonel A. Brook, V.D. (killed).
Major (temporary Lieutenant-Colonel) W. Gemmill, D.S.O.
Second Lieutenant (temporary Lieutenant) James Martin, Highland Light Infantry (Territorial Force).
Second Lieutenant A. G. A. Jamieson.
Second Lieutenant (temporary Lieutenant) R. A. D. Ritchie.
Acting Regimental Serjeant-Major A. Thomson.
Company Serjeant-Major A. Smith.
Pipe-Major J. M. McDougall.
Corporal J. Richardson.
Private D. Cairney.
Lieutenant-Colonel A. S. Blair.
Captain P. A. Blair.
Captain J. Ferguson.
Second Lieutenant C. F. Stewart.
Company Serjeant-Major R. Gibson.
Corporal G. A. Gibb.

ROYAL SCOTS (SERVICE BATTALIONS).

Major (temporary Lieutenant-Colonel) R. C. Dundas.
Captain (temporary Major) K. R. McCloughin, 14th Sikhs (killed).
Temporary Major R. W. Campbell.
Captain L. Errington (Adjutant).
Temporary Lieutenant G. Lammie.
Temporary Lieutenant A. W. Morey.
Lance-Corporal J. Briggs.
Private D. Lamond.
Private J. Leitch.
Private W. Lindsay.
Major (temporary Lieutenant-Colonel) G. G. Loch.
Temporary Major J. H. Hutton.
Lieutenant (temporary Captain) G. F. H. Faithfull, 126th Baluchistan Infantry.
Temporary Lieutenant H. E. Sanderson.
Temporary Second Lieutenant R. B. Stewart.
Corporal J. Forrest.
Lance-Corporal P. McKeown.
Private C. Flannigan.
Private J. Fraser.

MENTIONED IN DESPATCHES

Private W. Paterson.
Private A. Renton.
Private R. Rodon.
Lieutenant-Colonel H. Maclear, D.S.O., East Lancashire Regiment.
Captain (temporary Major) E. H. B. Raymond, Reserve of Officers.
Captain K. G. Buchanan (Adjutant).
Temporary Lieutenant R. J. M. Christie.
Temporary Second Lieutenant A. Linton.

Royal West Surrey Regiment.

Lieutenant G. K. Olliver.
Serjeant-Major C. M. Barrett.
Lieutenant-Colonel H. St. C. Wilkins.
Quartermaster and Honorary Lieutenant G. H. Wallis.
Major (temporary Lieutenant-Colonel) M. G. Heath.
Lieutenant-Colonel B. T. Pell, D.S.O. (died of wounds).
Major H. R. Bottomley (died of wounds).
Major H. F. Kirkpatrick, East Kent Regiment, Special Reserve.
Major R. C. Slacke, East Kent Regiment, Special Reserve (killed).
Major C. F. Watson, D.S.O.
Captain J. A. L. Browne (killed).
Captain W. B. Fuller (killed).
Captain W. B. Haddon-Smith (killed).
Captain F. C. Longbourne, D.S.O.
Temporary Second Lieutenant (temporary Captain) R. H. Maddock.
Lieutenant (temporary Captain) R. H. Philpot.
Lieutenant (temporary Captain) E. K. B. Furze.
Lieutenant (temporary Captain) R. K. Ross.
Second Lieutenant T. V. Chapman.
Second Lieutenant A. M. Hiller, Special Reserve (killed).
Second Lieutenant A. McCabe (killed).
Second Lieutenant J. H. Musson (killed).
Temporary Second Lieutenant C. T. Jones.
Company Serjeant-Major E. Sparkes.
Company Quartermaster-Serjeant E. Cox.
Serjeant G. Morris.
Private E. Aldridge.
Private F. Barrett.
Private E. Beazleigh.
Private G. Clarke.
Private F. Cleaver.
Private W. L. Dalton.
Private T. Hardy (killed).
Private A. Kilby.
Private T. Shreeves.
Private A. Williamson.

MENTIONED IN DESPATCHES

Royal West Surrey Regiment (Territorial Force).
Lieutenant (temporary Captain) W. J. Perkins.

Royal West Surrey Regiment (Service Battalions).
Major (temporary Lieutenant-Colonel) H. F. Warden.
Temporary Lieutenant H. C. Cannon.
Temporary Lieutenant A. J. Pike.
Private S. Baker.
Major (temporary Lieutenant-Colonel) W. J. T. Glasgow, Reserve of Officers.
Corporal R. Deane.
Temporary Lieutenant F. C. J. Lofting.

East Kent Regiment.
Captain D. K. Anderson.
Lieutenant W. L. J. Nicholas, Special Reserve.
Captain C. F. Cattley.
Lieutenant (temporary Captain) R. W. Homan (died of wounds).
Temporary Second Lieutenant C. E. Clouting.
Temporary Second Lieutenant P. Dangerfield.
Second Lieutenant B. E. Davies.
Temporary Second Lieutenant D. G. Ferguson.
Corporal W. H. Wren.
Drummer W. G. Duff.
Private A. E. Gunn.
Major (temporary Lieutenant-Colonel) C. A. Worthington.
Captain H. L. Archer-Houblon, Special Reserve.
Captain J. V. R. Jackson.
Lieutenant H. de R. Morgan.
Temporary Second Lieutenant W. T. Williams.
Company Serjeant-Major A. W. Andrews.
Company Serjeant-Major H. J. Martin.
Private T. H. Ferry (killed).

East Kent Regiment (Service Battalions).
Captain C. E. G. Davidson.
Acting Company Serjeant-Major F. H. Page.
Serjeant F. Peattie.
Lance-Serjeant H. W. Neville.
Lance-Corporal G. V. Bray.
Lance-Corporal W. J. Wall.
Private A. H. Forrest (killed).
Private W. Linstead.
Private S. Seath.
Private A. V. Setterfield.

MENTIONED IN DESPATCHES

Lieutenant-Colonel W. F. Elmslie, retired pay.
Temporary Second Lieutenant J. Vaughan.
Lance-Corporal J. Buzzard.

ROYAL LANCASTER REGIMENT.

Lieutenant G. R. R. Beaumont.
Major (temporary Brigadier-General) T. D. Jackson, M.V.O, D.S.O.
Captain W. A. T. B. Somerville, D.S.O.
Captain J. E. E. Packard.
Second Lieutenant R. C. Leach, Reserve of Officers.
Quartermaster and Honorary Major G. Wilson.
Company Serjeant-Major F. C. Lelliot (killed).
Serjeant H. Lindsay.
Lance-Corporal W. Lichfield.
Private F. Randerson.
Lieutenant-Colonel E. M. Morris.
Second Lieutenant E. C. Shone.
Quartermaster and Honorary Lieutenant M. Connell.
Second Lieutenant A. Weatherhead, Special Reserve.

ROYAL LANCASTER REGIMENT (TERRITORIAL FORCE).

Second Lieutenant (temporary Lieutenant) E. H. Hewitt.
Second Lieutenant (temporary Lieutenant) G. F. Taylor.
Second Lieutenant W. A. Wolfendale.

NORTHUMBERLAND FUSILIERS.

Brevet Lieutenant-Colonel (temporary Brigadier-General) C. Yatman D.S.O.
Major W. N. Herbert.
Major H. R. Sandilands.
Captain G. O. Sloper.
Second Lieutenant H. U. Scrutton.
Lieutenant (temporary Captain) E. E. Dorman-Smith.
Company Serjeant-Major M. G. Thorneycroft.
Company Quartermaster-Serjeant H. J. Bracey.
Corporal W. P. Carlin.
Private J. Connor.
Captain E. L. Salier.
Lieutenant C. R. Freeman.
Second Lieutenant W. Watson.
Quartermaster and Honorary Captain W. M. Allan.
Serjeant J. Pickering.

NORTHUMBERLAND FUSILIERS (TERRITORIAL FORCE).

Lieutenant-Colonel A. J. Foster.
Captain (temporary Lieutenant-Colonel) B. D. Gibson.

MENTIONED IN DESPATCHES

Captain W. Robb.
Lieutenant H. H. Bell.
Second Lieutenant (temporary Captain) C. O. P. Gibson.
Second Lieutenant W. W. Varvill, Northumbrian Divisional Royal Engineers.
Company Serjeant-Major R. Rewcastle.
Serjeant R. Amos.
Serjeant N. Cornish.
Serjeant P. Flanagan.
Corporal D. Clarence.
Private H. Newton.
Temporary Lieutenant-Colonel (Brevet Colonel, retired pay) A. H. Coles, C.M.G., D.S.O.
Captain (temporary Lieutenant-Colonel) H. Luhrs.
Captain A. Irwin.
Captain D. Hill.
Lieutenant (temporary Captain) N. M. North.
Second Lieutenant (temporary Captain) F. N. Syms,
Captain I. M. Tweedy.
Second Lieutenant (temporary Lieutenant) R. Ellis.
Second Lieutenant (temporary Lieutenant) W. Keen.
Second Lieutenant J. H. Swan.
Quartermaster and Honorary Lieutenant R. J. Holloway.
Regimental Serjeant-Major W. J. Offord.
Company Serjeant-Major J. Allen (killed).
Lance-Corporal R. Dawson.
Private A. Moat.
Lieutenant-Colonel G. R. B. Spain.
Major J. R. Hedley.
Captain F. R. I. Athill, Northumberland Fusiliers.
Captain L. A. Barrett, Northumberland Fusiliers.
Captain E. Temperley.
Second Lieutenant (temporary Lieutenant) E. A. Fawcus.
Second Lieutenant (temporary Lieutenant) N. B. Ramsay,
Second Lieutenant (temporary Lieutenant) F. C. Clayton.
Acting Company Serjeant-Major H. L. Benson.
Serjeant J. France.
Private R. R. Bell.
Private R. McWilliams.
Captain (temporary Lieutenant-Colonel) G. S. Jackson.
Second Lieutenant (temporary Captain) H. Liddell.
Lieutenant (temporary Captain) V. Merivale.
Captain H. R. Smail.
Second Lieutenant (temporary Captain) G. F. Ball.
Second Lieutenant (temporary Lieutenant) F. B. Cowen
Company Serjeant-Major J. T. Elliott.

MENTIONED IN DESPATCHES

Serjeant R. B. Appleby.
Serjeant W. Moffatt.
Serjeant J. Richardson.
Serjeant G. Renwick.

NORTHUMBERLAND FUSILIERS (SERVICE BATTALIONS).

Lieutenant-Colonel H. St. G. Thomas, Indian Army.
Temporary Major G. P. Westmacott.
Captain J. F. Chenevix-Trench, Northumberland Fusiliers.
Temporary Captain H. R. Gallatly.
Temporary Second Lieutenant R. M. Hill.
Temporary Lieutenant E. W. Shann.
Temporary Second Lieutenant R. Oliver.
Private G. W. Harris.
Private G. E. Dotchin (dead).
Private S. T. Keeling.
Private S. McVay.

ROYAL WARWICKSHIRE REGIMENT.

Captain P. V. Davidson (Adjutant, Royal Warwickshire Regiment Territorial Force).
Major (temporary Lieutenant-Colonel) G. N. B. Forster.
Captain C. E. M. Richards.
Lieutenant (temporary Captain) H. Strevens.
Lieutenant (temporary Captain) J. T. Bretherton.
Lieutenant (temporary Captain) A. H. K. Jackson.
Lieutenant T. L. Besant, Special Reserve.
Second Lieutenant J. W. V. Haskins.
Corporal W. G. Gilkes.
Lance-Corporal J. Dark.
Captain R. J. Brownfield, Special Reserve (killed).
Captain P. S. Brindley, Special Reserve.
Lieutenant H. S. Maunsell (died of wounds).
Lieutenant J. Pennington (killed).
Lieutenant R. F. Richardson (died of wounds).
Lieutenant C. C. H. Chavasse (retired pay).
Second Lieutenant W. L. Dibben.
Lieutenant F. R. Elderton, Special Reserve (killed).
Temporary Second Lieutenant A. Forbes.
Lieutenant A. Hodgkinson, Special Reserve.
Lieutenant A. E. Stehn, Special Reserve.
Quartermaster and Honorary Lieutenant W. N. Hyde.
Serjeant W. Webb.
Lance-Corporal F. W. Crisp.
Private A. Hartley.
Private A. Tattem.

MENTIONED IN DESPATCHES

Private J. Twynham.
Bandsman F. Underwood.
Lieutenant J. S. T. Weston, Special Reserve (killed).
Second Lieutenant R. L. Keller, Special Reserve.

ROYAL WARWICKSHIRE REGIMENT (TERRITORIAL FORCE).

Captain (temporary Major) P. H. Carter.
Second Lieutenant (temporary Lieutenant) H. L. R. J. Groom.
Serjeant G. H. Williams.
Corporal C. Haynes.
Lieutenant-Colonel E. Martineau.
Lieutenant-Colonel F. O. Wethered.
Lieutenant R. H. Astbury.
Second Lieutenant (temporary Lieutenant) R. C. Lowe.
Serjeant S. Harvey.
Serjeant W. Higgs.
Lieutenant-Colonel and Honorary Colonel L. H. Hanbury.
Lieutenant-Colonel A. G. G. Elton.
Major J. M. Knox.
Lance-Corporal P. W. Hancocks.
Lieutenant-Colonel E. A. Innes.
Captain (temporary Major) A. A. Caddick.
Captain (temporary Major) J. N. Townsend.
Temporary Captain G. W. Arnell.
Temporary Captain H. Davies.
Second Lieutenant (temporary Lieutenant) R. Adams.
Second Lieutenant (temporary Lieutenant) P. Docker.
Serjeant A. Nicholls.

ROYAL WARWICKSHIRE REGIMENT (SERVICE BATTALIONS).

Temporary Second Lieutenant J. S. Thain.

ROYAL FUSILIERS.

Major W. B. F. Rayner, Adjutant, The London Regiment (Territorial Force).
Major G. A. Stevens, Adjutant, Durham Light Infantry (Territorial Force).
Captain (temporary Major) J. A. Dunnington-Jefferson.
Captain C. G. Maude.
Serjeant M. J. Clancy, C.I.D., Scotland Yard (attached Intelligence Corps).
Serjeant-Major C. H. Frost, C.I.D., Scotland Yard (attached Intelligence Corps).
Quartermaster-Serjeant B. Hughes (Intelligence Section, General Headquarters).
Major (temporary Lieutenant-Colonel) B. G. Price, D.S.O.
Captain W. H. Tyndall.
Lieutenant (temporary Captain) M. C. Bell.

MENTIONED IN DESPATCHES

Lieutenant K. W. Brewster, Special Reserve.
Serjeant J. Sword.
Lance-Corporal C. W. Chillcott.
Private A. W. Cannon.
Private D. Rush.
Private L. Tovey.
Major (temporary Lieutenant-Colonel) A. C. Roberts.
Major E. M. Baker.
Captain P. G. Barton.
Captain B. W. W. Gostling.
Captain C. H. Sykes, D.S.O., Special Reserve.
Second Lieutenant J. Ball.
Second Lieutenant J. E. French.
Lieutenant H. W. Persse, Special Reserve.
Regimental Serjeant-Major H. F. D. Dockrill.
Company Serjeant-Major A. Sargeant.
Serjeant W. Brereton.
Private A. Lace.
Brevet Lieutenant-Colonel (temporary Lieutenant-Colonel) W. F. Sweny.
Captain H. Lathom-Browne.
Major C. A. H. Palairet.
Second Lieutenant F. A. Hicks.
Quartermaster and Honorary Lieutenant F. C. Cross.
Company Serjeant-Major W. S. Harris.
Corporal S. Jetten.
Corporal J. Lamm.
Private J. Harrington.
Private E. J. Knight.
Private G. McGee.
Captain J. N. de la Perelle, Special Reserve.

ROYAL FUSILIERS (SERVICE BATTALIONS).

Temporary Captain N. G. Darnell (Lieutenant, Reserve of Officers).
Lieutenant A. S. Allen.
Temporary Second Lieutenant D. W. Hanna.
Captain D. E. Estill, Royal Fusiliers.
Temporary Lieutenant G. L. Cazalet.
Company Serjeant-Major H. E. Covington.
Company Quartermaster-Serjeant R. Howse.
Private W. Peverill.
Major (temporary Lieutenant-Colonel) C. C. Carr, Reserve of Officers.
Corporal C. J. Fox.

LIVERPOOL REGIMENT.

Major R. C. R. Jones, Adjutant, Special Reserve.

MENTIONED IN DESPATCHES

Brevet Lieutenant-Colonel (temporary Brigadier-General) C. J. Steavenson.
Major (temporary Lieutenant-Colonel) H. C. Potter.
Captain C. E. Goff.
Captain N. Fleming.
Lieutenant J. P. Hope, Special Reserve.
Lieutenant W. M. Hutchison, Special Reserve.
Lieutenant C. J. Phipps.
Second Lieutenant C. F. V. Fulton.
Second Lieutenant J. H. McErvel.
Lieutenant (temporary Captain) F. J. Roberts, Special Reserve.
Lance-Serjeant J. Lonergan (dead).
Lance-Corporal J. Chambers.
Private J. Duddle.
Private H. L. Hanby.
Private H. Harrington (killed).
Lieutenant-Colonel J. W. Allen.
Major E. M. Beall, D.S.O.

LIVERPOOL REGIMENT (TERRITORIAL FORCE).

Lieutenant-Colonel and Honorary Colonel J. M. McMaster.
Lieutenant (temporary Captain) W. L. Evans.
Quartermaster and Honorary Lieutenant W. Burnett.
Acting-Serjeant G. P. Benbow.
Acting Lance-Corporal R. F. Hoy.
Lieutenant-Colonel H. Davison.
Major (temporary Lieutenant-Colonel) E. J. Harrison.
Second Lieutenant (temporary Lieutenant) G. G. Blackledge.
Quartermaster and Honorary Captain E. S. Goulding.
Second Lieutenant (temporary Lieutenant) H. L. Downes.
Lieutenant (temporary Major) F. S. Evans, D.S.O.
Lieutenant (temporary Major) J. W. B. Hunt.
Lieutenant (temporary Captain) P. G. A. Lederer.
Second Lieutenant (temporary Lieutenant) C. Nott (killed).
Captain (temporary Lieutenant-Colonel) E. G. Thin.
Lieutenant (temporary Captain) R. D. Cunningham.
Second Lieutenant (temporary Lieutenant) L. G. Wall.
Second Lieutenant E. W. Stubbs.
Quartermaster-Serjeant W. Mackay.
Serjeant W. Rathbone.
Serjeant E. P. Ward.
Lance-Corporal J. M. Tomkinson.
Private T. G. Berry.
Private J. C. Darrock.

MENTIONED IN DESPATCHES

LIVERPOOL REGIMENT (SERVICE BATTALIONS).

Major (temporary Lieutenant-Colonel) V. T. Bailey, Liverpool Regiment.
Temporary Second Lieutenant A. L. B. Gray.
Corporal A. Haskayne.
Corporal H. Murray.
Corporal C. Spilling.
Lance-Corporal J. Cook.
Private L. W. Kempson.
Lieutenant-Colonel L. St. C. Nicholson, Reserve of Officers.

NORFOLK REGIMENT.

Major (temporary Lieutenant-Colonel) H. R. Done, D.S.O.
Captain P. V. P. Stone.
Captain P. F. Wall, Special Reserve.
Lieutenant H. R. Kerr, Special Reserve.

NORFOLK REGIMENT (SERVICE BATTALIONS).

Major J. C. Atkinson, Norfolk Regiment.
Temporary Major F. E. Walter (Captain, Reserve of Officers).
Captain R. Otter, Norfolk Regiment.
Temporary Lieutenant T. A. Buckland (killed).
Temporary Second Lieutenant H. V. Franklin.
Serjeant F. G. Symonds.
Private W. Newton.
Brevet Colonel F. C. Briggs, retired pay.
Company Serjeant-Major J. Coe.

LINCOLNSHIRE REGIMENT.

Captain V. de Hoghton, Adjutant, Lincolnshire Regiment (Territorial Force).
Captain G. H. Teall, Adjutant, Liverpool Regiment (Territorial Force).
Major R. H. Johnston, D.S.O.
Captain E. J. de C. Boys.
Captain R. L. Toynbee, retired pay.
Lieutenant (temporary Captain) R. D. Crosby.
Lieutenant (temporary Captain) J. W. G. Hopper.
Lieutenant (temporary Captain) C. Hutchinson.
Temporary Second Lieutenant R. O. Pearson.
Quartermaster and Honorary Lieutenant F. W. Masters.
Serjeant H. E. Davies.
Serjeant A. Ryman.
Lance-Corporal J. W. Ellerby.
Private E. Blount.
Private F. A. Bowler.

MENTIONED IN DESPATCHES

Lieutenant-Colonel S. FitzG. Cox.
Captain E. P. Lloyd.
Captain B. J. Thruston.
Acting-Serjeant J. Senior.
Corporal J. Barringer.
Private (Acting Corporal) O. T. Sharpe.
Lance-Corporal T. E. Horry.

LINCOLNSHIRE REGIMENT (TERRITORIAL FORCE).
Major (temporary Lieutenant-Colonel) G. J. Barrell.
Major O. Cooper.
Lieutenant (temporary Captain) H. M. Bellamy.
Regimental Serjeant-Major W. O. Harrick.
Serjeant W. Bliss.
Lieutenant-Colonel T. E. Sandall.
Captain (temporary Major) H. I. Robinson (killed).
Acting Quartermaster-Serjeant F. King.
Lance-Corporal H. W. Smith.

LINCOLNSHIRE REGIMENT (SERVICE BATTALION).
Major (temporary Lieutenant-Colonel) J. Forrest, retired pay.
Temporary Captain J. A. Graham.
Lance-Corporal F. Fowler.
Private J. E. Short.

DEVONSHIRE REGIMENT.
Second Lieutenant J. Vicary, Gloucestershire Regiment.
Major N. Luxmore.
Major (temporary Lieutenant-Colonel) J. F. Radcliffe, D.S.O.
Captain L. E. L. Maton.
Lieutenant (temporary Captain) C. H. Gotto.
Quartermaster and Honorary Lieutenant S. Downing.
Serjeant-Major E. F. Thole.
Serjeant A. E. Whittey.
Private R. J. Cousins.
Captain J. R. Cartwright.
Captain H. Eardley-Wilmot (Brigade Machine-Gun Officer).
Captain C. H. M. Imbert-Terry.
Quartermaster and Honorary Lieutenant G. Palmer.
Company Serjeant-Major C. H. G. Ward.
Lance-Corporal A. G. Berry.
Private R. Handford.
Major R. F. W. Hill.

DEVONSHIRE REGIMENT (SERVICE BATTALIONS).
Lieutenant-Colonel A. G. W. Grant, West African Regiment (killed).
Temporary Captain M. O. Broadbridge.

MENTIONED IN DESPATCHES

Temporary Captain K. D. H. Gwynn, D.S.O.
Captain A. St. G. M. Kekewich, Devonshire Regiment (Adjutant).
Temporary Second Lieutenant St. B. Goldsmith.
Temporary Second Lieutenant F. W. Trott.
Serjeant R. Northam.
Drummer W. Haymes.
Major (temporary Lieutenant-Colonel) H. I. Storey, Devonshire Regiment.
Temporary Second Lieutenant W. N. Hodgson.
Temporary Second Lieutenant R. H. Smyth.
Serjeant A. G. Brown.
Private A. D. Bugler.
Private L. W. Moody.

Suffolk Regiment.

Lieutenant-Colonel W. B. Wallace.
Lieutenant O. I. Wood (killed).
Second Lieutenant T. Packard.
Regimental Quartermaster-Serjeant F. W. Pye.
Captain C. H. Turner, Reserve of Officers (killed).
Lieutenant T. S. Wynn.
Second Lieutenant T. D. Pickard-Cambridge.
Private J. Bailey.
Private P. McNamee.
Captain C. M. E. Dealtry, Special Reserve.
Captain C. B. Brooke, Special Reserve.

Suffolk Regiment (Territorial Force).

Captain R. A. Parry.
Second Lieutenant J. G. Frere, Suffolk Regiment.
Second Lieutenant (temporary Lieutenant) L. E. Milburn.
Acting-Serjeant J. R. Ennion.

Suffolk Regiment (Service Battalions).

Lieutenant-Colonel C. D. P. Crooke.
Captain H. R. Gadd, Suffolk Regiment.
Captain G. H. Henty (Lieutenant Reserve of Officers).
Temporary Captain T. M. C. Thomas.
Temporary Lieutenant G. W. Deighton.
Temporary Second Lieutenant L. L. Bright.
Serjeant J. Brown.
Temporary Captain A. H. Catchpole (Second Lieutenant, Special Reserve).
Lance-Serjeant J. Hodgson.
Private C. Long.

MENTIONED IN DESPATCHES

Somerset Light Infantry.
Major (temporary Lieutenant-Colonel) R. A. M. Currie (Commandant, Cadet School, General Headquarters).
Lieutenant H. Lane.
Captain G. Fleming.
Captain W. M. Sutton.
Lieutenant (temporary Captain) A. J. Harington.
Temporary Second Lieutenant H. L. Armstrong.
Second Lieutenant G. H. Neville.
Serjeant-Major E. Paul.
Company Serjeant-Major J. A. Wilson.
Serjeant (Acting Company Serjeant-Major) A. H. Bond.
Lance-Corporal J. Hopkins.
Private J. Greenwood.
Bugler R. S. Hayes.
Private C. Whittle.
Lieutenant C. A. Gould, Special Reserve.
Lieutenant J. C. N. Peard, Special Reserve.

Somerset Light Infantry (Service Battalions).
Major (temporary Lieutenant-Colonel) C. G. Rawling, C.I.E., Somerset Light Infantry.
Captain F. D. Bellew, Somerset Light Infantry.
Temporary Second Lieutenant C. Thatcher.
Company Serjeant-Major G. Thorne.
Serjeant E. Williams.
Temporary Second Lieutenant B. E. F. Mitchell.
Temporary Lieutenant-Colonel L. C. Howard.
Major T. F. Ritchie, Somerset Light Infantry.
Temporary Lieutenant A. B. Hatt.
Temporary Second Lieutenant I. S. Brodie-Innes.

West Yorkshire Regiment.
Major (temporary Lieutenant-Colonel) G. D. Price.
Temporary Second Lieutenant (temporary Lieutenant) F. G. Hobson.
Major (temporary Lieutenant-Colonel) G. G. Lang.
Major A. A. W. Spencer.
Captain F. A. W. Armitage.
Lieutenant J. P. Palmes, Special Reserve.
Lieutenant (temporary Captain) K. E. S. Stewart.
Lieutenant J. H. E. Trafford-Rawson.
Quartermaster and Honorary Lieutenant E. G. Butler.
Serjeant J. W. Booth.
Lance-Corporal J. H. Tyson.
Lance-Corporal A. Wilson.
Private F. Gospel.

MENTIONED IN DESPATCHES

Captain J. C. Blackburn.
Lieutenant (temporary Captain) A. E. E. Lowry.
Captain F. P. Worsley, Reserve of Officers.
Second Lieutenant (temporary Lieutenant) E. Howard.
Regimental Serjeant-Major A. Kenyon.
Regimental Quartermaster-Serjeant H. Thornhill.
Serjeant A. Self.
Corporal A. Andrews.
Lance-Corporal E. Stewart.
Private S. Holmes.

West Yorkshire Regiment (Territorial Force).

Lieutenant-Colonel C. E. Wood.
Major (temporary Lieutenant-Colonel) S. J. Wilkinson, West Yorkshire Regiment.
Lieutenant (temporary Captain) G. Sowerby.
Captain P. G. Williamson.
Serjeant R. T. Hastings.
Serjeant J. T. Sim.
Private J. E. Abbott.
Lieutenant-Colonel H. O. Wade.
Captain (temporary Major) R. Clough.
Captain J. Muller.
Captain G. R. Sandeman, Border Regiment (Adjutant).
Quartermaster and Honorary Captain W. H. Hill.
Company Quartermaster-Serjeant C. H. Woodhead.
Serjeant E. Beldon.
Serjeant B. M. Riley.
Serjeant W. Servant.
Serjeant H. C. Speight.
Corporal E. Bradley.
Lance-Corporal T. E. Howlett.
Private G. H. Hodgson.
Lieutenant-Colonel A. E. Kirk.
Major H. D. Bousfield.
Captain J. B. Redmayne.
Captain G. E. St. C. Stockwell.
Lieutenant A. R. Glazebrook.
Company Serjeant-Major E. E. Powell.
Lance-Serjeant R. A. Dalby.
Lance-Serjeant A. Chaplin.
Private J. W. Cooper.
Private W. E. Geldard.
Major (temporary Lieutenant-Colonel) J. W. Alexander.
Major R. A. Hudson.
Captain W. H. Brooke.

MENTIONED IN DESPATCHES

Second Lieutenant (temporary Lieutenant) H. R. Lupton.
Second Lieutenant (temporary Lieutenant) A. G. Rigby.
Second Lieutenant E. F. Wilkinson.
Corporal H. Archer.
Corporal G. B. Baines.
Corporal S. Smith.
Private P. Brooke.
Private F. Townend.

WEST YORKSHIRE REGIMENT (SERVICE BATTALIONS).
Captain (temporary Lieutenant-Colonel) H. K. Umfreville, D.S.O., Reserve of Officers.
Temporary Lieutenant C. J. Busher.
Serjeant J. McLoriman.

EAST YORKSHIRE REGIMENT.
Lieutenant-Colonel J. L. J. Clarke.
Captain A. E. C. Cart de Lafontaine.
Second Lieutenant (temporary Captain) M. Brown.
Second Lieutenant (temporary Lieutenant) G. Willis.
Second Lieutenant (temporary Lieutenant) C. J. Huntriss.
Quartermaster and Honorary Lieutenant J. Horrocks (dead).
Company Quartermaster-Serjeant P. Grieve.
Serjeant A. Powell.
Corporal J. Nolan.
Lance-Corporal T. Slack.
Private A. McCarthy.
Major C. P. Berthon.
Second Lieutenant R. J. H. Gatrell, Special Reserve.

EAST YORKSHIRE REGIMENT (TERRITORIAL FORCE).
Lieutenant (temporary Captain) C. Easton.
Captain E. Holtby.
Lieutenant H. A. Westrope.
Lance-Serjeant J. W. Train.
Lance-Corporal S. Yeaman.
Private F. Russell.

EAST YORKSHIRE REGIMENT (SERVICE BATTALIONS).
Temporary Lieutenant-Colonel N. F. Jenkins,(Captain, Border Regiment), Special Reserve.
Temporary Captain M. S. Cockin.
Corporal A. E. Ashley.
Lieutenant-Colonel B. I. Way, North Staffordshire Regiment, Special Reserve.
Temporary Lieutenant W. B. Richardson (Adjutant).
Temporary Lieutenant L. E. Hill.

MENTIONED IN DESPATCHES

Bedfordshire Regiment.
Lieutenant-Colonel C. R. J. Griffith, C.M.G., D.S.O.
Captain H. Courtenay.
Lieutenant F. Whittemore.
Regimental Quartermaster-Serjeant W. F. Bartlett.
Serjeant F. Stubbings.
Corporal E. B. Spicer.
Acting-Corporal J. Baldwin.
Brevet Lieutenant-Colonel E. I. de S. Thorpe.
Major (temporary Lieutenant-Colonel) J. C. Monteith (killed).
Major C. C. Onslow, C.M.G.
Captain C. C. Foss, V.C., D.S.O.
Temporary Second Lieutenant W. H. George.
Temporary Second Lieutenant R. J. Oldfield.
Temporary Second Lieutenant K. L. Stephenson (killed).
Second Lieut. W. White, Royal West Surrey Regt., Special Reserve.
Company Serjeant-Major A. Aldridge.
Serjeant T. Eustace.
Serjeant G. E. Grant.
Serjeant E. Pepper.

Bedfordshire Regiment (Service Battalions).
Serjeant A. Fountain.

Leicestershire Regiment.
Captain H. B. Brown, D.S.O.
Second Lieutenant (temporary Lieutenant) C. E. Morrison.
Major A. W. S. Brock, D.S.O.
Captain F. Latham.
Major F. Lewis, D.S.O.
Captain F. H. Romilly, D.S.O. (killed).
Second Lieutenant (temporary Lieutenant) D. W. Sutherland.
Quartermaster and Honorary Lieutenant H. C. Brodie.
Captain A. S. McIntyre, Special Reserve.
Captain W. C. Wilson, D.S.O.
Lieutenant N. G. Salmon, Special Reserve.
Serjeant A. E. Raynor.
Lance-Corporal F. W. Plumb.
Serjeant G. Smith.
Lance-Serjeant H. Smith.
Lance-Corporal J. Hewitt.
Lance-Corporal G. Simmonds.
Private G. Lovell.

Leicestershire Regiment (Territorial Force).
Lieutenant-Colonel R. E. Martin.
Lieutenant (temporary Captain) W. B. Jarvis

MENTIONED IN DESPATCHES

Captain (temporary Major) B. F. Newill.
Second Lieutenant J. Emmerson.
Lieutenant-Colonel C. H. Jones.
Major W. S. N. Toller.
Major W. T. Bromfield, Leicestershire Regiment.
Captain J. L. Griffiths.
Temporary Lieutenant (temporary Captain) E. G. Langdale (killed).
Second Lieutenant (temporary Lieutenant) A. G. de A. Moore.
Lieutenant (temporary Captain) C. H. F. Wollaston.
Lance-Corporal W. Fisher.
Private B. S. Alexander.
Private A. E. Lowe.

ROYAL IRISH REGIMENT.

Major (temporary Lieutenant-Colonel) E. C. Lloyd.
Captain A. H. Caldecott.
Captain T. E. H. Taylor.
Quartermaster and Honorary Major J. J. Fox.
Major S. E. St. Leger.
Captain P. J. G. Gordon-Ralph.
Captain F. G. R. Mockler.
Quartermaster and Honorary Lieutenant T. Mahony.
Company Quartermaster-Serjeant T. Croke.
Company Quartermaster-Serjeant J. McGuire.
Serjeant E. Eagar.
Serjeant-Drummer J. McDermott.

YORKSHIRE REGIMENT.

Captain B. T. Burbury (Adjutant, West Riding Regiment, Territorial Force).
Captain S. Grant-Dalton (Adjutant, Yorkshire Regiment, Territorial Force).
Lieutenant-Colonel W. L. Alexander (killed).
Major (temporary Lieutenant-Colonel) B. H. Leatham, D.S.O. (killed).
Major T. W. Stansfeld, D.S.O.
Captain (temporary Major) C. G. Forsyth.
Captain W. H. G. Raley, Special Reserve (killed).
Captain A. E. G. Palmer.
Lieutenant (temporary Captain) N. T. Wright, Special Reserve (died of wounds).
Lieutenant P. A. Forster, Special Reserve.
Lieutenant W. Gray, Special Reserve.
Lieutenant G. F. Hadow (killed).
Lieutenant F. C. Pyman, Special Reserve.
Second Lieutenant W. Sheay (died of wounds).
Temporary Second Lieutenant J. Lloyd-Jones.

MENTIONED IN DESPATCHES

Quartermaster and Honorary Lieutenant E. Pickard.
Serjeant F. Whitlock.
Corporal F. Norfolk.
Lance-Corporal A. E. Irving.
Private E. Beck (died of wounds).
Private C. Champion.
Private E. Gray.
Private E. Skelton.
Private J. W. Nicholson.

YORKSHIRE REGIMENT (TERRITORIAL FORCE).

Lieutenant-Colonel M. H. L. Bell.
Captain B. H. Charlton.
Captain J. Maughan.
Lieutenant (temporary Captain) T. H. Hutchinson.
Second Lieutenant (temporary Lieutenant) D. McLaren.
Temporary Lieutenant (temporary Captain) T. S. Rowlandson.
Temporary Second Lieutenant (temporary Lieutenant) C. Sproxton.
Second Lieutenant (temporary Lieutenant) A. R. Welsh.
Major (temporary Lieutenant-Colonel) J. Mortimer.
Captain G. J. Scott.
Lieutenant (temporary Captain) H. Brown, D.S.O.
Lieutenant F. Woodcock.
Second Lieutenant E. M. Thompson.
Second Lieutenant G. Thompson.
Regimental Serjeant-Major P. D. Denman.
Regimental Serjeant-Major W. Radley.
Company Serjeant-Major J. S. Bainbridge.
Company Serjeant-Major J. Brammall.
Serjeant T. Banks.
Serjeant E. Dent.
Serjeant R. J. Gray.
Serjeant R. Forster.
Serjeant H. E. Potter.

YORKSHIRE REGIMENT (SERVICE BATTALIONS).

Major (temporary Lieutenant-Colonel) R. D'A. Fife, Reserve of Officers
Temporary Lieutenant R. W. S. Croft.
Temporary Lieutenant A. Hollingworth (Adjutant).
Serjeant E. Gray.

LANCASHIRE FUSILIERS.

Lieutenant R. P. A. Helps.
Major (temporary Lieutenant-Colonel) C. J. Griffin, D.S.O.

MENTIONED IN DESPATCHES

Major (temporary Lieutenant-Colonel) A. H. Spooner, D.S.O.
Captain A. J. W. Blencowe.
Lieutenant G. C. Martin.
Second Lieutenant J. Greaves, Special Reserve.
Lieutenant V. F. S. Hawkins.
Quartermaster and Honorary Major W. Bowes.
Company Serjeant-Major E. Martin.
Private E. James.
Private W. Keating.
Private J. W. Warren.
Major (temporary Lieutenant-Colonel) T. S. H. Wade, Lancashire Fusiliers.
Temporary Captain A. H. Thomas.

ROYAL SCOTS FUSILIERS.

Major (temporary Lieutenant-Colonel) M. E. McConaghey.
Captain A. C. Bolton.
Lieutenant (temporary Captain) J. E. Utterson-Kelso.
Major J. C. Whigham.
Second Lieutenant (temporary Captain) R. A. G. Taylor.
Second Lieutenant W. E. S. Gascoigne.
Second Lieutenant (temporary Captain) W. B. Dawson, Special Reserve.
Lieutenant D. R. Gawler, Royal Scots Special Reserve.
Second Lieutenant S. J. K. Thomson, Special Reserve (died of wounds)
Regimental Quartermaster-Serjeant W. L. MacLean.
Serjeant W. R. Morrison.
Company Serjeant-Major C. E. Paynter.
Lance-Corporal T. Smith.
Private W. King.
Private M. Manning.
Private J. Timlin.
Private A. C. Townsend.
Lieutenant-Colonel (temporary Brigadier-General) J. H. W. Pollard.
Captain R. V. G. Horn.
Lieutenant (temporary Captain) G. R. T. Kennedy.
Captain D. G. C. Critchley-Salmonson.
Lieutenant (temporary Captain) M. B. Buchanan.
Temporary Second Lieutenant S. C. Godfrey.
Second Lieutenant A. E. Robinson (killed).
Temporary Second Lieutenant J. L. L. Sweet (killed).
Quartermaster and Honorary Lieutenant A. Spence.
Serjeant T. F. Phillips.
Serjeant T. Hayton.
Serjeant W. Skidmore.
Corporal W. Shand.

MENTIONED IN DESPATCHES

Corporal A. Carroll.
Private J. Inglis.
Private W. Jackson.
Private J. Jones (killed).
Private (Acting Lance-Corporal) P. Madden.

Royal Scots Fusiliers (Service Battalions).

Major (temporary Lieutenant-Colonel) H. H. Northey, Royal Scots Fusiliers.
Captain (temporary Major) G. O. Turnbull, 26th Punjabis.
Lieutenant (temporary Captain) G. D. Begg, Reserve of Officers.
Captain J. Brodie, Royal Scots Fusiliers.
Lieutenant (temporary Captain) G. G. de B. Purves, Reserve of Officers.
Temporary Lieutenant R. C. Galloway.
Company Serjeant-Major J. Bentley.
Company Quartermaster Serjeant J. Williams.
Serjeant J. Wilson.
Private J. Slinn.
Major (temporary Lieutenant-Colonel) C. M. S. Henning, Reserve of Officers.
Temporary Captain A. W. Baker.
Temporary Captain J. W. Nesbitt.
Temporary Second Lieutenant C. McK. McGavin.
Serjeant G. T. Willstrop.

Cheshire Regiment.

Quartermaster and Honorary Lieutenant J. C. Sproule.
Lieutenant (temporary Captain) C. R. Andrews.
Captain N. Freeman.
Captain E. C. Maxwell.
Captain P. G. Villiers Stuart.

Cheshire Regiment (Territorial Force).

Lieutenant-Colonel J. E. G. Groves.
Captain L. Bengough, Cheshire Regiment.
Lance-Corporal J. A. Boardman.
Private C. Flynn.
Private A. H. Hawksford.
Private S. Hayes.
Private J. Bennett.
Private T. Mather (killed).
Private A. Wood.

Cheshire Regiment (Service Battalion).

Temporary Second Lieutenant S. S. John.

MENTIONED IN DESPATCHES
ROYAL WELSH FUSILIERS.
Lieutenant-Colonel (temporary Brigadier-General) R. A. Berners.
Major G. F. H. Dickson, Reserve of Officers.
Captain H. S. Coles, Special Reserve.
Lieutenant (temporary Captain) J. Cottrell.
Captain E. R. Kearsley, D.S.O.
Major C. I. Stockwell, D.S.O.
Lieutenant (temporary Captain) A. Walmsley.
Lieutenant J. M. J. Evans (Adjutant).
Captain F. Jones-Bateman, Special Reserve.
Temporary Second Lieutenant G. S. Barton.
Second Lieutenant R. Gambier-Parry.
Second Lieutenant R. M. C. Ormrod.
Second Lieutenant J. B. Savage (killed).
Regimental Serjeant-Major T. Bluck.
Company Serjeant-Major T. Hannon.
Serjeant C. Dickens.
Serjeant H. Povey.
Serjeant F. Watts (killed).
Lance-Corporal A. Bown.
Private F. Evers.
Private G. Illesley.
Private A. Melia.
Private W. White.
Serjeant J. Stephens.
Major C. S. Owen, D.S.O.
Captain J. Cuthbert.
Second Lieutenant (temporary Captain) W. H. Stanway.
Temporary Second Lieutenant (temporary Captain) P. Moody.
Quartermaster and Honorary Lieutenant H. Yates.
Regimental Serjeant-Major T. Davies.
Company Serjeant-Major W. H. Fox.
Lance-Corporal W. Bale.
Second Lieutenant J. P. Owen, Special Reserve.

ROYAL WELSH FUSILIERS (TERRITORIAL FORCE).
Second Lieutenant R. Richards.

SOUTH WALES BORDERERS.
Major F. G. Lawrence, D.S.O. (Cadet School, General Head-quarters).
Major (temporary Lieutenant-Colonel) R. S. Gwynn.
Lieutenant (temporary Captain) C. K. Steward.
Second Lieutenant L. B. Potts.
Regimental Serjeant-Major J. Shirley.
Regimental Quartermaster-Serjeant F. Wiltshire.
Company Serjeant-Major H. Franklin.
Private W. Lewis.

MENTIONED IN DESPATCHES

SOUTH WALES BORDERERS (SERVICE BATTALIONS).

Private P. T. Newberry.
Temporary Second Lieutenant S. Evans.

KING'S OWN SCOTTISH BORDERERS.

Major (temporary Lieutenant-Colonel) W. T. Wilkinson, D.S.O.
Major E. S. D'E. Coke, C.M.G.
Brevet Major G. Hilton.
Lieutenant (temporary Captain) J. M. Challinor, Special Reserve.

KING'S OWN SCOTTISH BORDERERS (SERVICE BATTALIONS).

Major (temporary Lieutenant-Colonel) H. D. N. Maclean, D.S.O., King's Own Scottish Borderers.
Major W. J. S. Hosley, King's Own Scottish Borderers (killed).
Captain (temporary Major) N. C. Sparling, 54th Sikhs (killed).
Captain A. C. Campbell, King's Own Scottish Borderers.
Temporary Captain J. S. Keith, Quartermaster and Hon. Lieutenant.
Temporary Captain R. P. Hills.
Serjeant-Major J. Devrey.
Company Serjeant-Major J. Denham.
Company Serjeant-Major J. Laurie (killed).
Serjeant (Pipe-Major) R. Mackenzie (died of wounds).
Acting Company Quartermaster-Serjeant W. M. Scott.
Lance-Corporal H. McKenzie.
Lieutenant-Colonel G. de W. Verner, retired pay (died of wounds).
Temporary Major T. A. Glenny.
Temporary Captain M. F. B. Dennis (Lieutenant, retired pay)
Temporary Lieutenant J. Seafield-Grant.
Temporary Second Lieutenant T. K. Newbigging.
Regimental Serjeant-Major C. Cooper.
Private S. Hargreaves.
Major (temporary Lieutenant-Colonel) T. B. Sellar, Reserve of Officers.
Captain (temporary Major) G. M. Hannay, Reserve of Officers.
Temporary Second Lieutenant W. G. Herbertson (killed).
Temporary Second Lieutenant C. K. Thursby-Pelham.
Private J. Bould.

SCOTTISH RIFLES.

Captain R. N. O'Connor.
Major (temporary Lieutenant-Colonel) J. G. Chaplin, D.S.O.
Major H. H. Lee.
Lieutenant (temporary Captain) D. G. Moncrieff Wright.
Lieutenant M. N. Gray, Special Reserve (died of wounds).
Lieutenant C. D. W. Rooke (killed).
Quartermaster and Honorary Lieutenant G. Wood.

MENTIONED IN DESPATCHES

Lance-Corporal A. Johnstone.
Private A. E. Andrews.
Major (temporary Brigadier-General) G. T. C. Carter-Campbell, D.S.O.
Major (temporary Lieutenant-Colonel) V. C. Sandilands.
Major H. C. H. Smith.
Lieutenant (temporary Captain) C. R. H. Stirling.
Second Lieutenant (temporary Lieutenant) E. Brecken.
Second Lieutenant W. E. Roberton, Special Reserve.
Serjeant G. W. Phillips.
Second Lieutenant A. G. Robb, Special Reserve.

SCOTTISH RIFLES (TERRITORIAL FORCE).

Major W. D. Croft, Scottish Rifles.
Captain (temporary Major) A. A. Kennedy.
Second Lieutenant (temporary Captain) J. M. Grierson.
Second Lieutenant G. Gray.
Captain (temporary Major) A. G. Graham.
Captain J. Lusk.
Second Lieutenant (temporary Captain) D. L. Gray.
Lieutenant (temporary Captain) J. C. E. Hay.
Private J. R. Brown.
Private J. Craig.
Private W. Hannah.
Private J. Williamson.

SCOTTISH RIFLES (SERVICE BATTALIONS).

Captain (temporary Major) A. F. Townshend, Reserve of Officers.
Temporary Captain P. W. Gardiner.
Temporary Captain H. P. Mackenzie (killed).
Temporary Captain A. G. Hutcheson.
Quartermaster and Honorary Lieutenant W. Langrish.
Company Serjeant-Major W. Henderson.
Company Serjeant-Major E. Yates.
Serjeant J. McCreadie.
Serjeant J. Walsham.
Lieutenant-Colonel A. V. Ussher, retired pay.
Temporary Captain J. F. Duncan (killed).
Temporary Captain J. C. Grant.
Temporary Lieutenant J. A. Callen.
Temporary Second Lieutenant L. C. Paton.

ROYAL INNISKILLING FUSILIERS.

Lieutenant-Colonel C. A. Wilding, C.M.G.
Major J. N. Crawford.
Captain C. C. Hewitt.

MENTIONED IN DESPATCHES

Lieutenant E. E. J. Moore.
Second Lieutenant J. J. L. Morgan (died of wounds).
Quartermaster and Honorary Lieutenant R. Lumsden.
Regimental Serjeant-Major T. Maguire.
Serjeant (Acting Quartermaster-Serjeant) J. L. Clarke.
Corporal J. A. Dutton.
Lance-Corporal G. Murphy.
Private F. Hutchinson.
Private D. Jones.
Private S. Patterson.
Captain K. H. Crawford, Special Reserve.

GLOUCESTERSHIRE REGIMENT.

Major (temporary Lieutenant-Colonel) R. I. Rawson.
Captain F. A. Breul, Reserve of Officers.
Captain H. F. L. Hilton-Green, Divisional Cyclist Company.
Captain V. N. Johnson.
Lieutenant L. W. D. Lyne, Divisional Cyclist Company.
Major (temporary Lieutenant-Colonel) A. W. Pagan.
Lieutenant (temporary Captain) D. Duncan.
Corporal A. W. Thurlow.
Major R. L. Beasley.
Major (temporary Lieutenant-Colonel) F. C. Nisbet.
Captain A. C. Vicary.
Lieutenant (temporary Captain) C. E. Gardner.
Lieutenant R. M. Grazebrook.
Serjeant W. Smith.
Lance-Corporal C. F. J. Moreman.
Private H. C. Rice.
Lieutenant B. H. Waddy, Special Reserve.

GLOUCESTERSHIRE REGIMENT (TERRITORIAL FORCE).

Temporary Lieutenant-Colonel S. Davenport.
Captain P. G. J. Güterbock.
Lieutenant (temporary Captain) A. L. W. Newth.
Lieutenant E. E. Wookey.
Lance-Corporal T. Stephens.
Lance-Corporal T. Vezey.
Lieutenant-Colonel J. H. Collett.
Captain (temporary Major) N. H. Waller.
Second Lieutenant (temporary Lieutenant) E. Conder.
Serjeant F. Finch.
Serjeant J. W. Watkins.
Second Lieutenant (temporary Major) E. McFarlane.
Second Lieutenant (temporary Lieutenant) D. H. Hartog.
Private C. Jones.

MENTIONED IN DESPATCHES

WORCESTERSHIRE REGIMENT.

Major G. M. C. Davidge.
Captain A. C. Johnston.
Quartermaster-Serjeant (temporary 1st Class Staff Serjeant-Major) E. Pearson.
Major (temporary Lieutenant-Colonel) G. W. St. G. Grogan.
Major T. Fitzjohn.
Lieutenant (temporary Captain) J. M. Monk.
Lieutenant (temporary Captain) E. L. G. Lawrence.
Lieutenant L. G. Phillips.
Second Lieutenant (temporary Captain) A. Pratt.
Serjeant-Major G. Grover.
Serjeant H. W. Ash.
Corporal H. Beniams.
Brevet Lieutenant-Colonel (temporary Lieutenant-Colonel) G. C. Lambton, D.S.O.
Brevet Major C. L. Armitage, D.S.O.
Brevet Major P. S. G. Wainman, Special Reserve (killed).
Lieutenant (temporary Captain) C. H. Ralston (Adjutant).
Temporary Second Lieutenant E. P. Bennett.
Lieutenant C. J. Hart, Special Reserve.
Temporary Second Lieutenant A. E. Prosser.
Second Lieutenant T. N. Wilmot.
Serjeant J. A. Airey.
Corporal A. V. Wells.
Corporal H. Walker.
Corporal T. E. Westwood.
Captain E. W. Buckler, Special Reserve (killed).
Captain A. J. Stephenson-Featherstonhaugh, Special Reserve.
Captain S. A. Gabb.
Captain J. P. S. Maitland, Reserve of Officers.
Quartermaster and Honorary Major A. Whitty.
Company Serjeant-Major S. Macdonald.
Serjeant J. W. Copson.
Corporal W. J. Roberts.
Lance-Corporal J. R. Taylor.
Captain R. D. Temple, Special Reserve.

WORCESTERSHIRE REGIMENT (TERRITORIAL FORCE).

Lieutenant-Colonel A. R. Harman.
Captain F. M. Tomkinson.
Second Lieutenant J. C. Humphries.
Serjeant L. W. Birkett.
Serjeant J. Bow.
Lieutenant-Colonel W. K. Peake.
Major F. A. W. How.

MENTIONED IN DESPATCHES

Second Lieutenant (temporary Lieutenant) C. R. Pawsey.
Second Lieutenant A. Plaistowe.
Company Serjeant-Major W. E. Ward.
Lance-Corporal W. H. Wheeler.

East Lancashire Regiment.

Captain E. C. Hopkinson.
Captain H. T. MacMullen.
Lieutenant J. W. Parks.
Lieutenant W. A. Salt, Special Reserve.
Acting Regimental Serjeant-Major J. Burgess.
Company Quartermaster-Serjeant G. Page.
Serjeant A. Puttick.
Private E. Bolton.
Lieutenant-Colonel T. S. Lambert.
Major (temporary Lieutenant-Colonel) G. E. M. Hill.
Lieutenant R. S. Boothby.
Second Lieutenant (temporary Lieutenant) M. C. Fitch, Reserve of Officers.
Quartermaster and Honorary Lieutenant J. Shaw.
Serjeant-Major F. Duckworth.
Serjeant F. Organ.
Acting-Corporal W. Wallington.
Private F. Burns (killed).
Captain P. E. M. Richards, Special Reserve.

East Surrey Regiment.

Lieutenant-Colonel H. S. Tew.
Serjeant G. F. Brown.
Major (temporary Lieutenant-Colonel) F. S. Montague-Bates.
Captain H. V. Bayliss (Adjutant).
Captain J. Gurdon.
Second Lieutenant H. F. B. Garrett.
Lieutenant C. Mead (killed).
Quartermaster and Honorary Lieutenant H. J. Percy.
Serjeant G. Coomber.
Serjeant S. Wootten.
Lance-Corporal G. Lyon.
Private W. Barker.
Private H. Milan.
Captain A. E. Norman, Special Reserve (died of wounds).

East Surrey Regiment (Service Battalions).

Major (temporary Lieutenant-Colonel) R. H. Baldwin, East Surrey Regiment.
Major A. H. Wilson, Reserve of Officers.

MENTIONED IN DESPATCHES

Captain E. H. J. Nicolls, East Surrey Regiment.
Temporary Lieutenant J. L. Findlay.
Temporary Lieutenant J. S. Hewart.
Temporary Lieutenant R. B. Marshall.
Lance-Serjeant B. Hanscombe.
Lance-Corporal W. J. Rule.
Lance-Corporal A. Saunders.
Private A. Wood.
Captain (temporary Lieutenant-Colonel) H. G. Powell, D.S.O., Reserve of Officers.
Temporary Lieutenant C. Thorne.
Serjeant P. Conquest.
Temporary Captain D. P. O'Connor.

DUKE OF CORNWALL'S LIGHT INFANTRY.

Major H. T. Dobbin.
Major F. H. S. Rendall (Adjutant, West Riding Regiment (Territorial Force).
Captain W. P. Buckley, D.S.O.
Captain (temporary Major) C. B. Norton, Reserve of Officers.
Lieutenant H. C. C. Lloyd.
Second Lieutenant (temporary Lieutenant) R. Phillipps.
Temporary Second Lieutenant B. M. Taylor.
Quartermaster and Honorary Lieutenant W. T. Price.
Serjeant J. H. Symons.
Serjeant R. Blacker.
Brevet Lieutenant-Colonel (temporary Lieutenant-Colonel) H. F. Price.
Major A. P. Dene.
Captain M. Crawley-Boevey.
Second Lieutenant R. C. Jenkins.
Lieutenant E. E. Mulock.
Company Quartermaster-Serjeant A. Ostler.
Serjeant T. Going.
Serjeant C. Moore.
Lance-Corporal W. R. Peters.
Lance-Corporal F. Harvey.
Private F. E. Aguilar.
Private J. Walker.
Captain T. M. Lowry.
Lieutenant A. F. Baker.

DUKE OF CORNWALL'S LIGHT INFANTRY (SERVICE BATTALION)

Major (temporary Lieutenant-Colonel) J. L. Swainson, Duke of Cornwall's Light Infantry.
Temporary Lieutenant R. McG. Barrington-Ward.

MENTIONED IN DESPATCHES

WEST RIDING REGIMENT.
Major (temporary Lieutenant-Colonel) R. N. Bray.
Captain M. N. Cox.
Captain C. W. G. Ince.
Lieutenant (temporary Captain) C. L. Hart, Special Reserve.
Second Lieutenant P. Walsh, Special Reserve.
Quartermaster and Honorary Major A. Ellam.
Company Serjeant-Major C. R. Scurry.

WEST RIDING REGIMENT (TERRITORIAL FORCE).
Captain (temporary Major) R. E. Sugden.
Lieutenant (temporary Captain) M. P. Andrews (killed).
Captain E. E. Sykes.
Second Lieutenant F. A. Innes.
Second Lieutenant T. D. Pratt.
Company Serjeant-Major A. McNulty.
Serjeant J. Wilson.
Lance-Corporal D. Dow.
Lance-Corporal C. Wood.
Private G. H. Holt.
Private J. Shelley.
Private L. Stead.
Captain (temporary Major) G. P. Norton.
Temporary Lieutenant K. Sykes.
Second Lieutenant A. McLintock.
Lance-Corporal T. J. Holland.
Private H. Firth.
Private E. Kay.
Private G. Nowell.
Private T. Wilkinson.
Captain (temporary Major) C. M. Bateman.
Captain N. B. Chaffers.
Captain A. B. Clarkson.
Captain S. F. Marriner, West Riding Regiment (Adjutant).
Lieutenant M. C. M. Law.
Regimental Serjeant-Major O. Buckley.
Corporal J. Bury.
Corporal H. Calvert.
Corporal T. W. Limmer.
Private T. Brook.
Private R. Snowden.
Lieutenant L. G. R. Harris.
Second Lieutenant J. Brierley.
Serjeant-Major H. Smeath.
Serjeant N. Hinchcliffe.
Serjeant A. Pearson.

MENTIONED IN DESPATCHES

Lance-Serjeant W. Gaynor.
Lance-Corporal H. Batley.
Lance-Corporal J. Taylor.
Private H. Mallinson.
Private L. Shaw.

WEST RIDING REGIMENT (SERVICE BATTALIONS).

Lieutenant-Colonel F. A. Hayden, D.S.O., Reserve of Officers.
Captain A. E. Miller, West Riding Regiment.
Temporary Lieutenant H. H. McColl.
Temporary Lieutenant L. H. de Pinto.
Temporary Lieutenant L. G. S. Bolland.

BORDER REGIMENT.

Temporary Captain R. G. Tower.
Lieutenant-Colonel A. S. W. Moffat (killed).
Captain A. P. Blackwood.
Lieutenant (temporary Captain) W. Kerr.
Lieutenant (temporary Captain) A. W. Sutcliffe, Special Reserve.
Second Lieutenant (temporary Lieutenant) R. M. Burmann (Adjutant).
Captain H. F. Chads.
Temporary Second Lieutenant R. M. Goodman (killed).
Second Lieutenant (temporary Captain) J. Horsley, Special Reserve.
Second Lieutenant V. H. Luscombe, Special Reserve.
Second Lieutenant R. Rawlinson, Special Reserve (killed).
Quartermaster and Honorary Lieutenant F. W. Mitchell.
Serjeant T. E. Parkinson.
Lance-Corporal G. Dowden.
Lance-Corporal W. H. Corkish.
Corporal P. Gilmour.
Lance-Corporal W. Graham.
Private A. Philpot.
Lieutenant S. H. H. James.

BORDER REGIMENT (TERRITORIAL FORCE).

Major (temporary Lieutenant-Colonel) T. A. Milburn.
Captain R. C. R. Blair, D.S.O.
Captain A. B. Cowburn.
Captain T. W. MacDonald, Border Regiment.
Second Lieutenant P. W. Maclagan.
Corporal J. Gregg.
Lance-Corporal J. W. Norman.
Private J. Johnston.
Lance-Corporal C. Mossop (died of wounds).

MENTIONED IN DESPATCHES

BORDER REGIMENT (SERVICE BATTALION).
Temporary Lieutenant-Colonel R. L. Norrington.
Second Lieutenant J. W. Tailford, Border Regiment.
Temporary Second Lieutenant J. C. White.
Serjeant J. Cragg.
Private R. O'Maley.

ROYAL SUSSEX REGIMENT.
Lieut.-Colonel (temporary Brigadier-General) E. W. B. Green, D.S.O.
Major C. E. Bond, D.S.O. (attd. Cadet School, General Headquarters).
Major F. W. B. Willett.
Major J. S. Cameron.
Major E. F. Villiers, D.S.O.
Lieutenant (temporary Captain) H. E. H. Blakeney.
Second Lieutenant E. J. Hobbs.
Private H. Jarvis (killed).
Lieutenant G. B. Ramsbotham, Special Reserve (killed).

ROYAL SUSSEX REGIMENT (TERRITORIAL FORCE).
Captain E. A. C. Fazan.
Quartermaster and Honorary Lieutenant H. Plews.

ROYAL SUSSEX REGIMENT (SERVICE BATTALIONS).
Major (temp. Lieut.-Colonel) W. L. Osborn, Royal Sussex Regiment.
Captain (temporary Major) R. M. Birkett, Royal Sussex Regiment.
Temporary Captain G. Woodhams.
Temporary Lieutenant E. G. Sutton.
Company Serjeant-Major A. Nutley.
Serjeant T. Jones.
Major (temporary Lieutenant-Colonel) A. E. Glasgow, Royal Sussex Regiment.
Temporary Captain V. M. FitzHugh.
Temporary Captain H. W. Meade.
Temporary Lieutenant H. C. Lott.
Temporary Lieutenant E. T. H. Godwin.

HAMPSHIRE REGIMENT.
Second Lieutenant E. Ward (attached Machine Gun School).
Lieutenant (temporary Captain) J. W. F. Wyld.
Temporary Second Lieutenant F. J. Dale.
Second Lieutenant C. J. H. Goodford.
Second Lieutenant H. G. Harding.
Lieutenant (temporary Captain) H. N. Hume.
Second Lieutenant H. W. M. May, Special Reserve.
Second Lieutenant A. E. Stevens (died of wounds).
Serjeant S. Lee.

MENTIONED IN DESPATCHES

Serjeant J. J. Paice.
Company Quartermaster-Serjeant H. L. Wheeler.
Second Lieutenant T. E. Rodocanachi, Special Reserve.
Second Lieutenant M. T. Smith, Special Reserve.

SOUTH STAFFORDSHIRE REGIMENT.

Major S. Bonner, D.S.O. (Adjutant).
Captain A. B. Beauman, D.S.O.
Captain A. F. G. Kilby.
Captain R. F. B. Naylor.
Lieutenant-Colonel R. M. Ovens, C.M.G.
Major R. Duckworth.
Captain C. H. Green.
Lieutenant (temporary Captain) C. R. Limbery.
Lieutenant (temporary Captain) H. W. MacGeorge (killed).
Second Lieutenant (temporary Lieutenant) E. Bell.
Second Lieutenant A. W. Lee.
Quartermaster and Honorary Lieutenant S. Bradbury.
Regimental Serjeant-Major J. Snape.
Serjeant W. H. Jordon.
Serjeant F. Thorne.
Acting-Serjeant A. Wilcox.
Serjeant J. Wright.
Serjeant F. Clarke.
Serjeant R. Rankin.
Corporal G. Shepherd.
Corporal W. Vincent.
Corporal E. Chatwin.
Corporal J. Williams.
Lance-Corporal H. Monger.
Lance-Corporal F. Turner.
Private G. Cooper.
Private H. Cooper.
Private J. McHale.
Private C. Milner.
Bandsman W. Neville.
Private W. Price.
Drummer E. Winchester.
Colonel (temporary Brigadier-General) C. S. Davidson, C.B.
Brevet Lieutenant-Colonel L. B. Boyd-Moss.
Brevet Lieutenant-Colonel P. C. L. Routledge (killed).
Major R. W. Morgan.
Lieutenant A. de Hamel, Special Reserve.
Second Lieutenant W. H. Carter.
Second Lieutenant C. R. Hind, Special Reserve.
Second Lieutenant D. M. Williams.

MENTIONED IN DESPATCHES

Serjeant T. Wilkes.
Private J. Green.
Second Lieutenant B. R. Taylor.
Second Lieutenant (temporary Captain) R. B. Gibson, Special Reserve.
Second Lieutenant C. W. Macfie, Special Reserve (killed).

South Staffordshire Regiment (Territorial Force).
Temporary Major (temporary Lieutenant-Colonel) R. R. Raymer.
Major W. Burnett.
Captain C. Lister.
Second Lieutenant (temporary Lieutenant) H. Hawkes.
Lieutenant-Colonel T. F. Waterhouse.
Lieutenant (temporary Captain) H. V. Mander.
Second Lieutenant (temporary Lieutenant) G. H. Smith.

South Staffordshire Regiment (Service Battalion).
Major (temporary Lieutenant-Colonel) G. N. Going, Reserve of Officers
Serjeant H. S. Bird.
Lance-Corporal D. Baker.

Dorsetshire Regiment.
Captain W. B. Algeo (Adjutant, Cambridgeshire Regiment).
Captain S. P. A. Rolls.
Second Lieutenant A. Agelasto.
Second Lieutenant (temporary Lieutenant) R. V. Kestal-Cornish.
Second Lieutenant (temporary Captain) H. G. M. Mansel-Pleydell.
Quartermaster and Honorary Lieutenant W. Alderman.
Serjeant W. J. Bray.
Serjeant A. E. Smith.
Lance-Serjeant A. E. Janaway.
Acting-Corporal W. J. Haggett.
Lieutenant C. P. Whitaker, Special Reserve.
Second Lieutenant J. Bessell, Special Reserve.
Second Lieutenant N. J. Lewis, Special Reserve.
Second Lieutenant M. H. Turner, Special Reserve.

Dorsetshire Regiment (Service Battalion).
Major (temporary Lieutenant-Colonel) C. A. Rowley, D.S.O., Reserve of Officers.
Temporary Lieutenant A. E. Broad.
Company Serjeant-Major J. A. W. MacMullen.

South Lancashire Regiment
Lieutenant (temporary Captain) C. J. Gasson.
Lieutenant J. Muhlig.
Major (temporary Lieutenant-Colonel) H. T. Cotton.
Captain F. A. Bagley (died of wounds).

MENTIONED IN DESPATCHES

Second Lieutenant A. W. Gates, Special Reserve.
Temporary Second Lieutenant W. A. L. Poundall.
Temporary Second Lieutenant J. E. T. Strickland.
Temporary Second Lieutenant (temporary Lieutenant) C. Thompson.
Corporal S. Rushworth.
Lance-Corporal C. Roden.
Private H. Curran.
Private H. Humphries.
Private P. Tubrity.

SOUTH LANCASHIRE REGIMENT (TERRITORIAL FORCE).

Lieutenant-Colonel B. Fairclough.
Major G. R. Crosfield.
Captain Egerton Fairclough.
Second Lieutenant F. J. Barnish.
Second Lieutenant J. S. Frith.
Second Lieutenant S. T. Quint.
Quartermaster and Honorary Lieutenant G. H. Ingram.
Serjeant H. I. Creamer.
Serjeant T. Widd.
Corporal J. A. Vale.
Private Clark.
Private G. Harding.
Lieutenant-Colonel L. E. Pilkington.
Lieutenant (temporary Captain) J. H. Dickinson.
Second Lieutenant (temporary Captain) L. Hammill.
Quartermaster and Honorary Lieutenant E. Doolan.
Private J. H. Clarke.
Private J. E. Lynn (died of wounds).

THE WELSH REGIMENT.

Captain D. P. Dickinson.
Acting Serjeant-Major A. E. Holley.
Major (temporary Lieutenant-Colonel) R. T. Toke.
Lieutenant (temporary Captain) W. Owen.
Lieutenant (temporary Captain) G. P. de B. Monk.
Lieutenant (temporary Captain) E. W. Bryan.
Quartermaster and Honorary Lieutenant A. Holt.
Company Serjeant-Major E. Gallop.
Lieutenant W. G. Hewett.
Lieutenant B. U. S. Cripps.
Lieutenant (temporary Captain) B. M. Dunn.
Regimental Serjeant-Major C. S. Hampton.

ROYAL HIGHLANDERS.

Captain F. G. Chalmer.
Brevet Major V. M. Fortune.

MENTIONED IN DESPATCHES

Major L. P. Evans, D.S.O.
Major W. Green.
Lieutenant (temporary Captain) J. Millar.
Lieutenant A. Wanliss.
Quartermaster and Honorary Lieutenant W. Fowler.
Acting-Serjeant John Brown.
Corporal J. McMillan.
Private W. Morison.
Private J. Scully.
Private J. Valentine.
Second Lieutenant J. I. Buchan, D.S.O.
Lieutenant (temporary Captain) M. E. Park, D.S.O.
Lieutenant N. McMicking.
Captain A. H. C. Sutherland.
Quartermaster and Honorary Lieutenant J. Anderson.
Serjeant Drummer (Local Serjeant-Major) H. R. Large (employed with Military Mounted Police).
Lance-Corporal A. Rodman.
Private (Local Serjeant) H. Telford (employed with Military Mounted Police).
Second Lieutenant M. S. Gunn, Special Reserve.
Lieutenant R. Macfarlane, Special Reserve.

ROYAL HIGHLANDERS (TERRITORIAL FORCE).

Lieutenant (temporary Captain) R. W. McIntyre.
Second Lieutenant (temporary Lieutenant) T. Stevenson.
Regimental Serjeant-Major W. Charles.
Captain J. B. McNab.
Second Lieutenant (temporary Lieutenant) G. A. Grant.
Second Lieutenant F. N. E. Kitson.
Quartermaster and Honorary Lieutenant A. Hall.
Lance-Corporal W. Keen.
Private A. Redford.
Private D. Smart.
Captain (temporary Major) W. Alexander.
Captain J. A. Durie, Royal Highlanders.
Captain A. Innes.
Lieutenant R. B. Ellis.
Second Lieutenant (temporary Lieutenant) W. P. Wrathall.
Corporal W. Gibbs.
Lance-Corporal F. W. Deane.
Piper A. Macdonald.
Lieutenant-Colonel (local Colonel in Army) H. M. Allen, D.S.O.
Captain D. Beveridge.
Second Lieutenant G. D. H. Fullerton-Carnegie.
Second Lieutenant (temporary Lieutenant) E. D. H. Thomson.

MENTIONED IN DESPATCHES

Serjeant J. Lumsden.
Lance-Corporal W. Drylie.
Lance-Corporal W. Halley.
Private (Acting Lance-Corporal) D. Birrell (killed).

ROYAL HIGHLANDERS (SERVICE BATTALIONS).

Honorary Colonel J. Lord Sempill, Highland Divisional Transport and Supply Column, Army Service Corps (Captain, retired pay).
Captain (temporary Major) J. G. Collins, Reserve of Officers.
Temporary Captain R. N. Duke.
Captain J. L. S. Ewing, Royal Highlanders.
Temporary Captain G. B. McClure.
Temporary Second Lieutenant P. H. Forrester (died of wounds).
Private A. Fairhurst.
Major (temporary Lieutenant-Colonel) T. O. Lloyd, Reserve of Officers.
Temporary Captain C. S. Tuke (killed).
Captain (temporary Major) J. Stewart, Reserve of Officers.
Temporary Lieutenant E. R. Wilson.
Serjeant J. Henderson.
Private G. Boak.
Lance-Corporal A. Brown.
Lance-Corporal R. Ledlie.

OXFORDSHIRE AND BUCKINGHAMSHIRE LIGHT INFANTRY.

Major (temporary Lieutenant-Colonel) J. A. Ballard.
Captain A. J. N. Bartlett (Adjutant, Oxfordshire and Buckinghamshire Light Infantry) (Territorial Force).
Brevet Lieutenant-Colonel (temporary Lieutenant-Colonel) A. J. F. Eden.
Major C. G. Higgins.
Lieutenant (temporary Captain) R. M. Owen.
Lieutenant E. H. Whitefeld.
Second Lieutenant (temporary Lieutenant) G. Field.
Temporary Lieutenant V. V. Jacob, Service Battalion.
Acting-Serjeant H. Benford.
Lance-Corporal W. Johnson.
Private T. R. Walter.
Lieutenant C. A. F. Fowke, Special Reserve.

OXFORDSHIRE AND BUCKINGHAMSHIRE LIGHT INFANTRY (TERRITORIAL FORCE).

Major R. L. Ovey.
Lieutenant (temporary Captain) P. Pickford.
Second Lieutenant (temporary Captain) G. K. Rose.
Serjeant A. J. Shurvell.
Corporal A. Cook.

MENTIONED IN DESPATCHES

Lieutenant (temporary Captain) N. S. Reid.
Second Lieutenant (temporary Lieutenant) A. D. B. Brown.
Lance-Corporal W. E. Reeves.
Private F. Tipping.

OXFORDSHIRE AND BUCKINGHAMSHIRE LIGHT INFANTRY (SERVICE BATTALIONS).

Major (temporary Lieutenant-Colonel) C. H. Cobb.
Captain (temporary Lieutenant-Colonel) W. F. R. Webb, 22nd Punjabis.
Temporary Captain N. F. Barwell.
Captain B. C. T. Paget, Oxfordshire and Buckinghamshire Light Infantry.
Temporary Lieutenant W. R. Birch.
Temporary Second Lieutenant H. J. Cupper.
Temporary Second Lieutenant L. S. Lee.
Serjeant F. Godfrey.
Serjeant C. A. Hill.
Private H. W. Lockwood.
Lieutenant-Colonel E. D. White.

ESSEX REGIMENT.

Captain A. E. Maitland (Machine Gun Officer).
Lieutenant (temporary Captain) N. M. S. Irwin.
Lieutenant W. P. Spooner, Special Reserve.
Serjeant W. R. Couzens.
Lance-Corporal F. J. Baudains.
Lance-Corporal F. J. Gooch.
Lance-Corporal C. Moss.
Lance-Corporal E. Thompson.
Second Lieutenant K. N. Bion, Nottinghamshire and Derbyshire Regiment.
Lieutenant F. Steel, Special Reserve.

ESSEX REGIMENT (SERVICE BATTALIONS).

Major (temporary Lieutenant-Colonel) C. G. Lewes, Essex Regiment.
Major H. C. Copeman, Reserve of Officers.
Temporary Captain N. J. Sievers.
Captain C. C. Spooner, Essex Regiment.
Temporary Lieutenant C. R. Brown.
Acting Lance-Serjeant E. W. Short.
Lance-Corporal E. J. Chilvers (killed).
Temporary Captain F. Western.
Private C. W. Halsley.

NOTTINGHAMSHIRE AND DERBYSHIRE REGIMENT.

Captain E. N. T. Collin (Adjutant, Nottinghamshire and Derbyshire Regiment) (Territorial Force).
Major L. St. H. Morley.

MENTIONED IN DESPATCHES

Captain R. T. Foster (attached The London Regiment) (Territorial Force).
Captain R. L. Sherbrooke.
Lieutenant (temporary Captain) C. Chambers.
Lieutenant (temporary Captain) A. T. Miller.
Quartermaster and Honorary Lieutenant F. A. W. Coman.
Serjeant-Major H. Morton.
Corporal F. Sutton.
Major (temporary Lieutenant-Colonel) C. J. W. Hobbs.
Captain R. B. Tower.
Lieutenant H. M. Gleave, Special Reserve.
Lieutenant G. P. Walsh, Special Reserve (killed).
Second Lieutenant H. Carter.
Second Lieutenant A. S. Edwards.
Second Lieutenant R. Palmer (died of wounds).
Company Serjeant-Major J. Sephton.
Acting Company Quartermaster-Serjeant W. Allingham.
Serjeant T. B. Kirk.
Lance-Serjeant F. Johnson.
Corporal F. Messom.
Lance-Corporal E. Mortimer.
Lance-Corporal W. Samson.
Private C. Whibberley.
Private J. H. Curtis.
Captain E. R. Street, D.S.O., Special Reserve.

NOTTINGHAMSHIRE AND DERBYSHIRE REGIMENT (TERRITORIAL FORCE).
Major (temporary Lieutenant-Colonel) G. A. Lewis.
Captain F. W. Wragg.
Serjeant A. L. Jones.
Major (temporary Lieutenant-Colonel) G. D. Goodman.
Lieutenant (temporary Captain) V. O. Robinson.
Acting Regimental Serjeant-Major H. H. Jackman.
Private J. E. Hamer.
Lieutenant-Colonel C. W. Birkin.
Captain (temporary Major) L. A. Hind.
Second Lieutenant (temporary Captain) R. M. Gotch.
Second Lieutenant (temporary Lieutenant) H. H. Walton.
Second Lieutenant (temporary Captain) J. C. Warren.
Second Lieutenant N. E. Webster.
Company Serjeant-Major J. W. Herod.
Corporal G. Cooke.
Serjeant R. Mills.
Private E. Banks.
Major (temporary Lieutenant-Colonel) G. H. Fowler (killed).
Captain (temporary Major) J. P. Becher, D.S.O.

MENTIONED IN DESPATCHES

Lieutenant (temporary Major) A. L. Ashwell.
Second Lieutenant (temporary Lieutenant) A. Hacking.
Second Lieutenant (temporary Captain) E. C. A. James.
Second Lieutenant (temporary Captain) B. W. Vann.
Second Lieutenant (temporary Captain) J. S. C. Oates.
Serjeant A. Phillipson.
Corporal J. T. Templeman.
Private E. Grantham.
Private F. Holland.

NOTTINGHAMSHIRE AND DERBYSHIRE REGIMENT (SERVICE BATTALION).
Lieutenant-Colonel W. E. Banbury, Indian Army.
Temporary Lieutenant J. A. Meads.
Corporal C. G. Wyld.
Lance-Corporal E. H. Johnson.
Private A. Hollingsworth.
Private E. Morgan.

LOYAL NORTH LANCASHIRE REGIMENT.

Lieutenant-Colonel W. D. Sanderson.
Major A. J. Carter, D.S.O. (killed).
Captain J. F. Allen (killed).
Captain A. W. Colley.
Captain A. L. Prince (killed).
Captain S. T. Lucey.
Captain D. H. Garden, East Kent Regiment, Special Reserve.
Lieutenant E. W. P. Haymen, East Kent Regiment.
Company Serjeant-Major Thompson.
Serjeant J. J. Cockerell.
Serjeant E. Cully.
Serjeant-Drummer J. Durkin.
Serjeant J. Hardman.
Serjeant H. R. Roberts.
Serjeant C. W. Whittaker.
Acting-Serjeant F. Mossford.
Lance-Serjeant F. Burge.
Lance-Corporal G. Rigby.
Lance-Corporal J. Jones.
Lance-Corporal C. S. Nicholls.
Lance-Corporal C. F. Puttrell.
Private J. Finlinson.
Private J. McDermott.
Captain V. L. Henderson, Special Reserve.

LOYAL NORTH LANCASHIRE REGIMENT (TERRITORIAL FORCE).
Second Lieutenant H. Lindsay.
Second Lieutenant P. Parker.
Major (temporary Lieutenant-Colonel) G. Hesketh.

MENTIONED IN DESPATCHES

Captain (temporary Major) C. K. Potter.
Captain P. A. O. Read.
Second Lieutenant H. Chronnell.
Company Serjeant-Major W. Parker.
Serjeant J. T. Ball.

NORTHAMPTONSHIRE REGIMENT.

Major (temporary Lieutenant-Colonel) L. G. W. Dobbin.
Major G. A. Royston-Pigott.
Captain G. M. Bentley (died of wounds).
Captain C. G. Buckle.
Lieutenant (temporary Captain) W. J. Jervois.
Lieutenant H. F. Pitcher.
Quartermaster and Honorary Lieutenant A. Hofman.
Private B. Tebbutt.
Major C. R. J. Mowatt.
Captain (temporary Major) L. A. Haldane.
Captain S. G. Latham, Special Reserve.
Lieutenant O. K. Parker.
Lieutenant E. B. L. Rushton.
Quartermaster and Honorary Lieutenant R. Mayes.
Serjeant-Major G. Lee.
Company Serjeant-Major A. Drage.
Serjeant A. Foster.
Lance-Corporal Clarke.
Private A. G. Mullerhausen.

NORTHAMPTONSHIRE REGIMENT (SERVICE BATTALIONS).

Major E. A. B. Alston, Northamptonshire Regiment.
Temporary Captain F. W. Butler.
Lieutenant (temporary Captain) A. C. Pickering, Northamptonshire Regiment.
Acting Company Quartermaster-Serjeant G. Colver.
Honorary Colonel G. E. Ripley (late 4th Battalion).
Second Lieutenant (temporary Captain) R. W. Beacham, West Yorkshire Regiment.

ROYAL BERKSHIRE REGIMENT.

Captain A. G. M. Sharpe.
Captain (temporary Major) L. W. Bird.
Captain E. M. Allfrey.
Captain C. W. Frizell.
Captain M. C. Radford, D.S.O. (killed).
Lieutenant (temporary Captain) J. H. Woods.
Temporary Second Lieutenant (temporary Lieutenant) E. L. Jerwood.
Lieutenant D. E. Ward, Special Reserve.

MENTIONED IN DESPATCHES

Second Lieutenant E. K. Colbourne, Special Reserve (died of wounds).
Serjeant H. Crutch.
Serjeant J. Harris.
Lance-Corporal B. A. Gurney.
Private P. W. Combley.
Private W. Sparrow.
Major (temporary Lieutenant-Colonel) G. P. S. Hunt.
Captain G. H. Sawyer.
Temporary Second Lieutenant G. G. Paine.
Temporary Second Lieutenant B. Russell.
Lieutenant N. West.
Quartermaster and Honorary Captain H. S. Lickman.
Serjeant (Acting Company Serjeant-Major) F. Vockins.
Serjeant F. Pearce.

ROYAL BERKSHIRE REGIMENT (TERRITORIAL FORCE).
Brevet Colonel C. Pearce-Serocold.
Captain G. A. Battcock.
Lieutenant O. B. Challenor.
Second Lieutenant (temporary Lieutenant) G. M. Gathorne-Hardy.
Company Serjeant-Major (Acting Serjeant-Major) W. C. Hanney.
Corporal H. G. Collyer.

ROYAL BERKSHIRE REGIMENT (SERVICE BATTALIONS).
Temporary Lieutenant R. T. Pollard (killed).
Lance-Corporal A. Histead.
Private L. W. Perris.

ROYAL BERKSHIRE REGIMENT (SERVICE BATTALIONS).
Lieutenant Colonel A. J. W. Dowell.
Temporary Captain W. P. Hewetson.
Serjeant G. H. Thomas.
Temporary Captain D. Tosetti.
Temporary Second Lieutenant T. B. Lawrence.

ROYAL WEST KENT REGIMENT.
Captain B. Johnstone (Adjt., Royal Warwickshire Regt.) (Terr. Force).
Temporary Major A. H. Pullman.
Brevet Lieutenant-Colonel (temporary Brigadier-General) P. M. Robinson, C.M.G.
Major (temporary Lieutenant-Colonel) H. D. Buchanan, D.S.O.
Major (temporary Lieutenant-Colonel) E. H. Norman.
Quartermaster and Honorary Lieutenant H. G. Rogers.
Major R. L. White.
Private J. Hissey.
Private H. Newell.
Captain S. H. Lewis, Special Reserve.

MENTIONED IN DESPATCHES

ROYAL WEST KENT REGIMENT (SERVICE BATTALIONS).

Major (temporary Lieutenant-Colonel) E. F. Venables, Reserve of Officers.
Temporary Major H. C. W. Beeching.
Temporary Captain A. B. C. Francis.
Captain G. E. Wingfield-Stratford, Royal West Kent Regiment.
Temporary Second Lieutenant M. H. Carre.
Quartermaster and Honorary Lieutenant E. Mills.
Serjeant-Major G. Allen.
Serjeant A. Mitchell.
Corporal G. Tutt.
Lance-Corporal E. Baker.
Lance-Corporal W. E. Norburn.
Private J. Linge.
Private A. Perrin.
Brevet Colonel A. W. Prior, retired pay.
Temporary Lieutenant B. McKenzie.
Temporary Lieutenant W. K. Tillie.
Temporary Second Lieutenant V. G. Don.
Private A. Scarratt.

KING'S OWN YORKSHIRE LIGHT INFANTRY.

Major E. F. W. Barker.
Major F. J. G. Agg.
Captain J. A. Jervois (Adjutant).
Major H. Mallinson, D.S.O.
Quartermaster and Honorary Captain J. C. Brasier.
Regimental Quartermaster-Serjeant H. J. Knight.
Lance-Serjeant (Acting Company Serjeant-Major) F. G. Setterfield.
Corporal R. Hill.
Lieutenant-Colonel (temporary Brigadier-General) W. M. Withycombe, C.M.G.
Captain C. S. Buckle, Reserve of Officers.
Captain M. F. Day.
Captain C. E. D. King.
Lieutenant R. Oxspring, Special Reserve.
Quartermaster and Honorary Lieutenant A. E. Bentham.
Corporal A. Holding.

KING'S OWN YORKSHIRE LIGHT INFANTRY (TERRITORIAL FORCE).

Lieutenant-Colonel H. J. Haslegrave.
Major H. Moorhouse.
Captain A. C. Chadwick (killed).
Lieutenant (temporary Captain) W. B. Creswick.
Captain H. S. Kaye, Yorkshire Light Infantry.
Captain L. M. Taylor.

MENTIONED IN DESPATCHES

Quartermaster-Serjeant H. Stafford.
Company Serjeant-Major J. Grice.
Company Serjeant-Major W. Jones.
Company Serjeant-Major F. W. McKay.
Company Serjeant-Major E. Pollard.
Serjeant S. P. Shippam.
Lance-Corporal E. Pearson.
Private T. Chappel.
Private A. Punyer.
Private J. Smith.
Lieutenant-Colonel C. C. Moxon.
Major C. G. Bradley.
Captain T. G. Mackenzie.
Captain G. K. Sullivan, Yorkshire Light Infantry (Adjutant).
Second Lieutenant (temporary Lieutenant) H. E. H. Clayton-Smith.
Company Serjeant-Major R. Suthers.
Private G. Hall.
Private A. Parr.

KING'S OWN YORKSHIRE LIGHT INFANTRY (SERVICE BATTALIONS)
Temporary Quartermaster and Honorary Lieutenant T. Shearwood.
Temporary Lieutenant F. Else.
Serjeant J. T. Evans.
Private L. Lawton.
Captain (temporary Lieutenant-Colonel) C. W. D. Lynch, Reserve of Officers.
Captain C. K. Butler, Yorkshire Light Infantry.
Temporary Captain H. Greenwood.
Temporary Lieutenant A. N. Richardson.
Temporary Lieutenant H. E. Yeo.
Temporary Second Lieutenant E. R. Nott.
Temporary Captain A. M. Dale.
Temporary Second Lieutenant A. de C. Meade.

SHROPSHIRE LIGHT INFANTRY.
Major (temporary Lieutenant-Colonel) E. B. Luard, D.S.O.
Lieutenant (temporary Captain) R. Bryans.
Lieutenant R. H. Marriott.
Regimental Serjeant-Major J. Skirving.
Serjeant J. Blud.
Private J. T. Coton.
Private W. A. Hyson.
Major (temporary Lieutenant-Colonel) J. H. Bailey.
Lieutenant J. W. Hallowes.
Second Lieutenant (temporary Captain) H. E. Steer.
Temporary Second Lieutenant H. K. Turner.

MENTIONED IN DESPATCHES

Serjeant G. Hirst.
Serjeant T. Fletcher.
Corporal F. W. Jones.
Lance-Corporal W. A. Meredith (killed).
Private A. E. Cowles.
Private W. Openshaw.

Shropshire Light Infantry (Service Battalion).
Lance-Serjeant C. F. Cowper.
Lance-Corporal G. Morris.
Lance-Corporal A. King.
Private J. Crawshaw.
Private R. Lloyd.
Private R. Lloyd.

Middlesex Regiment.
Acting Staff Serjeant-Major W. Blackwood.
Lieutenant-Colonel F. G. M. Rowley, C.M.G.
Major W. C. C. Ash.
Captain H. W. B. Warneford.
Lieutenant H. W. M. Paul.
Temporary Second Lieutenant B. U. Hare, Service Battalion (killed).
Temporary Second Lieutenant J. L. Henry.
Temporary Second Lieutenant A. D. Hill.
Lance-Corporal J. Bolton.
Private C. Levett.
Private W. S. Rough.
Major (temporary Lieutenant-Colonel) F. W. Ramsay.
Major H. P. F. Bicknell.
Lieutenant (temporary Captain) R. J. Young.
Quartermaster and Honorary Lieutenant H. A. Wiemers.
Company Serjeant-Major F. J. Fane.
Acting Regimental Serjeant-Major J. Shearstone.
Serjeant C. A. Green.
Private J. L. Court.
Major (temporary Lieutenant-Colonel) G. H. Neale (killed).
Lieutenant (temporary Captain) A. D. Gordon.
Second Lieutenant (temporary Lieutenant) F. Defries.
Acting Regimental Serjeant-Major J. W. G. Reddick (killed).
Serjeant J. Everingham.
Lance-Corporal J. M. Ifold.
Lance-Corporal T. Medway.
Private A. Browne.
Major (temporary Lieutenant-Colonel) G. A. Bridgman.
Major C. D. K. Greenway, Reserve of Officers.
Temporary Second Lieutenant H. L. Gilks.
Temporary Second Lieutenant R. P. Hallowes, V.C.

MENTIONED IN DESPATCHES

Second Lieutenant H. M. Lepper.
Captain H. W. M. Potter, Special Reserve.
Serjeant C. Law (died of wounds).
Acting-Serjeant T. Wilkins.
Serjeant E. F. Remnant.
Acting-Corporal M. Chappell (killed).
Lance-Corporal W. Simmons.
Lance-Corporal J. R. Tandy.
Private J. E. Matthews (killed).

Middlesex Regiment (Territorial Force).

Lieutenant-Colonel E. J. King.
Captain G. A. H. Bower.
Lieutenant (temporary Captain) S. H. Gillett.
Second Lieutenant (temporary Lieutenant) C. Ashby.
Second Lieutenant (temporary Lieutenant) A. G. Groser.
Second Lieutenant (temporary Lieutenant) G. B. Tait.
Serjeant C. A. Clarke.
Serjeant E. J. King.
Lance-Serjeant C. F. Reynolds.
Major E. D. W. Gregory.
Captain T. F. Chipp.
Captain (temporary Major) A. H. Woodbridge.
Corporal A. Mills.

Middlesex Regiment (Service Battalions).

Major (temporary Lieutenant-Colonel) W. D. Ingle, Middlesex Regiment.
Temporary Captain H. Peploe.
Temporary Second Lieutenant G. B. Anderson.
Temporary Second Lieutenant J. O. Leach.
Serjeant A. Brown.
Private H. Hagley.
Colonel R. F. B. Glover, D.S.O., retired pay, Reserve Battalion, Royal Fusiliers.
Captain M. C. Scarborough, Middlesex Regiment.
Temporary Lieutenant L. H. Methuen.
Temporary Second Lieutenant G. Pigache.
Temporary Second Lieutenant E. C. Scott.

King's Royal Rifle Corps.

Captain A. C. Oppenheim, D.S.O.
Captain H. C. M. Porter.
Captain E. D. Shafto.
Second Lieutenant (temporary Captain) E. A. Pearson, Special Reserve.
Second Lieutenant E. W. Fane-de Salis.

MENTIONED IN DESPATCHES

Major (temporary Lieutenant-Colonel) G. A. Armytage.
Captain E. B. Denison.
Captain S. H. Ferrand.
Second Lieutenant T. R. Reid, Special Reserve.
Second Lieutenant A. E. Dent.
Temporary Second Lieutenant S. A. S. Goodwin.
Temporary Second Lieutenant L. E. Hall.
Second Lieutenant (temporary Lieutenant) R. S. H. Stafford, Special Reserve.
Company Serjeant-Major G. H. Floater.
Lance-Corporal L. Robinson.
Lance-Corporal H. V. Smith.
Private L. Alderson.
Private E. R. Bryant.
Private G. Teahan.
Private J. H. Todd.
Brevet Colonel (temporary Brigadier-General) E. Pearce Serocold.
Brevet Lieutenant-Colonel H. C. Warre, D.S.O.
Major J. E. N. Heseltine.
Lieutenant (temporary Captain) P. J. R. Currie.
Captain Hon. E. E. M. J. Upton (killed).
Second Lieutenant (temporary Captain) R. E. Bullen.
Second Lieutenant (temporary Captain) L. C. Nash (died of wounds).
Second Lieutenant A. W. Symington.
Lance-Corporal A. Little.
Lance-Corporal L. Bostock.
Major (temporary Lieutenant-Colonel) W. J. Long.
Major (temporary Lieutenant-Colonel) H. F. W. Bircham, D.S.O.
Major A. F. C. Maclachlan, D.S.O.
Captain H. B. Nicholson, Reserve of Officers.
Lieutenant (temporary Captain) A. H. Brocklehurst.
Lieutenant (temporary Captain) N. C. H. Macdonald-Moreton (killed).
Second Lieutenant D. C. O'Rorke.
Quartermaster and Honorary Lieutenant A. C. Watkins.
Serjeant E. Sands (Meerut Signal Company), attached.
Lance-Corporal W. L. Wheeler.
Lance-Corporal F. J. Curtis.
Private J. Nolan.
Major (temporary Lieutenant-Colonel) B. F. Widdrington.
Major (temporary Lieutenant-Colonel) B. J. Majendie.
Lieutenant (temporary Captain) G. S. Oxley.
Major H. W. M. Watson.
Second Lieutenant D. Morton.
Second Lieutenant J. S. Poole.
Company Serjeant-Major G. Wells.

MENTIONED IN DESPATCHES

Serjeant V. H. Gray.
Acting-Serjeant T. Medhurst.
Corporal R. Wilson.
Lance-Corporal W. Brooks.
Lance-Corporal H. W. Walker.
Private H. Bowen.
Private E. Heath.
Private G. Keats.
Private E. Kitchen.

KING'S ROYAL RIFLE CORPS (SERVICE BATTALIONS).

Major (temporary Lieutenant-Colonel) G. A. P. Rennie, D.S.O., King's Royal Rifle Corps.
Captain H. M. B. de Sales La Terriere, King's Royal Rifle Corps.
Temporary Captain J. Wormald.
Acting-Serjeant G. Houghton.
Acting-Serjeant G. Spears.
Private A. H. Mead.
Major (temporary Lieutenant-Colonel) H. C. R. Green, King's Royal Rifle Corps.
Major C. H. N. Seymour, King's Royal Rifle Corps.
Temporary Captain E. W. Benson.
Temporary Captain J. Christie.
Temporary Captain N. J. Exell (died of wounds).
Temporary Captain M. Mallalue.
Temporary Lieutenant F. G. Dansey.
Temporary Second Lieutenant C. D. Lacey.
Company Serjeant-Major J. Kent.
Serjeant E. F. Warren.
Lance-Corporal H. Mitchell.
Private E. Knight.
Private R. Rickards.
Private G. E. Smart.
Temporary Major C. A. Blacklock.
Temporary Lieutenant R. de H. M. Bell.
Major (temporary Lieutenant-Colonel) W. H. L. Allgood, Reserve of Officers.
Temporary Second Lieutenant I. S. Drysdale.
Temporary Lieutenant C. D. White.

WILTSHIRE REGIMENT.

Lieutenant (temporary Captain) R. L. Knubley, Special Reserve.
Temporary Lieutenant (temporary Captain) S. S. Ogilive.
Lieutenant G. E. George, Special Reserve.
Temporary Lieutenant J. H. V. Barker-Mill.
Second Lieutenant F. S. Gregory, Special Reserve.

MENTIONED IN DESPATCHES

Temporary Lieutenant E. T. Peel.
Temporary Second Lieutenant J. T. Snelgar.
Lance-Corporal J. G. Staples.
Private C. H. Dobson.
Private W. Voyle.
Major R. M. T. Gillson.
Major E. L. Makin, D.S.O.
Second Lieutenant (temporary Lieutenant) P. P. Legg.
Lieutenant (temporary Captain) W. T. Sargeaunt, Special Reserve.
Second Lieutenant J. H. Clark, Special Reserve (killed).
Second Lieutenant C. F. B. Hodgins (killed).
Temporary Lieutenant A. J. Samut.
Temporary Second Lieutenant L. E. Schultz (killed).
Serjeant J. Hounsell.
Corporal R. H. Williams.
Lance-Corporal W. U. Collins.
Private E. Ong.
Private E. J. Stevens.
Second Lieutenant J. G. C. Jones, Special Reserve.

WILTSHIRE REGIMENT (SERVICE BATTALION).
Temporary Lieutenant J. K. W. Trueman.

MANCHESTER REGIMENT.
Brevet Lieutenant-Colonel W. P. E. Newbigging, D.S.O.
Lieutenant-Colonel W. H. E. Hitchins (killed).
Lieutenant (temporary Captain) G. T. Ewen, Special Reserve.
Lieutenant (temporary Captain) G. S. Henderson.
Lieutenant (temporary Captain) W. N. Shipster.
Serjeant (Acting Serjeant-Major) C. Yeates.
Lance-Corporal J. H. Worcester.
Captain J. R. Gwyther, Special Reserve.
Lieutenant V. A. Albrecht.
Lieutenant (temporary Captain) Close-Brooks, Special Reserve.
Company Serjeant-Major J. Harrison.
Major C. M. Thornycroft, Special Reserve.
Captain H. J. Gwyther, Special Reserve.
Second Lieutenant L. Findlater, Special Reserve.

MANCHESTER REGIMENT (SERVICE BATTALION).
Brevet Major (temporary Lieutenant-Colonel) E. G. Harrison, C.B., D.S.O., retired pay.
Serjeant C. Ross.
Private P. Logan.

NORTH STAFFORDSHIRE REGIMENT.
Major A. S. Conway.
Second Lieutenant H. C. Pickering, Special Reserve (killed).

MENTIONED IN DESPATCHES

Private T. Kirkland.
Captain H. I. Allen.
Second Lieutenant (temporary Lieutenant) C. A. N. Fox, Special Reserve.
Lieutenant G. D. Chew, Special Reserve.
Second Lieutenant Sidney Jepson, Special Reserve.

NORTH STAFFORDSHIRE REGIMENT (TERRITORIAL FORCE).

Lieutenant-Colonel (Honorary Colonel) J. H. Knight.
Temporary Lieutenant A. J. Campbell.
Corporal J. Hand.
Lance-Corporal J. Stone.
Private H. Emony.
Private W. Ryles.
Major (temporary Lieutenant-Colonel) R. F. Ratcliff.
Lieutenant H. T. Bostock.

NORTH STAFFORDSHIRE REGIMENT (SERVICE BATTALION).

Lieutenant (temporary Captain) R. F. Wynne, Reserve of Officers.

YORK AND LANCASTER REGIMENT.

Major H. A. B. Salmond.
Major (temporary Lieutenant-Colonel) G. E. Bayley, D.S.O.
Lieutenant (temporary Captain) T. K. Shaw, Special Reserve.
Captain E. Buckley, Special Reserve.
Lieutenant C. G. Burge.
Second Lieutenant B. A. Bates, Special Reserve.
Second Lieutenant H. Sharpe.
Second Lieutenant F. G. Sherriff.
Serjeant J. Cutts.
Lieutenant-Colonel (temporary Brigadier-General) W. F. Clemson, D.S.O.
Captain H. A. W. Cole-Hamilton.
Captain H. P. Philby, D.S.O.
Captain R. P. Wood.
Lieutenant F. N. Houston.
Lieutenant (temporary Captain) J. A. Reid.
Lieutenant E. H. Moore, Special Reserve.
Company Serjeant-Major M. J. Aithwaite.
Company Serjeant-Major R. Spink.
Serjeant J. Gray.
Captain A. C. Cameron, Special Reserve.
Captain (Honorary Major) J. E. Forster, Special Reserve (killed).

YORK AND LANCASTER REGIMENT (TERRITORIAL FORCE).

Lieutenant (temporary Captain) H. G. Barber.
Captain J. L. Marsh (killed).

MENTIONED IN DESPATCHES

Captain R. M. Williams, York and Lancaster Regiment (Adjutant).
Second Lieutenant (temporary Lieutenant) P. N. Johnson.
Second Lieutenant S. Brooke.
Second Lieutenant (temporary Lieutenant) W. Tozer.
Quartermaster and Honorary Major M. J. Duggan.
Quartermaster-Serjeant M. H. Deakin.
Serjeant P. Skelton.
Lance-Corporal J. Barlow.
Lance-Corporal C. Brown.
Private R. Crow.
Major T. W. Parkinson, York and Lancaster Regiment (Adjutant).
Captain E. D. B. Johnson.
Lieutenant (temporary Captain) C. V. Monier-Williams.
Second Lieutenant (temporary Lieutenant) J. M. L. Hess.
Second Lieutenant V. G. Southern.
Serjeant T. F. Bellamy.
Corporal A. L. Carpenter.
Lance-Corporal E. Ford.
Private E. Brook.
Private A. B. Fearn.
Private H. Petty.
Private F. Warriner.
Private J. Wilde.

York and Lancaster Regiment (Service Battalions).

Brevet Colonel H. N. Byass, retired pay.
Captain (temporary Major) W. McG. Armstrong, Reserve of Officers
Temporary Captain H. Gilbert.
Captain (temporary Major) C. H. Taylor, retired pay.
Private C. W. Binns.

Durham Light Infantry.

Major J. W. Jeffreys.
Lieutenant C. H. Green.
Second Lieutenant H. D. Beadon, Special Reserve.
Lieutenant-Colonel M. D. Goring-Jones.
Captain W. H. Godsal.
Lieutenant T. M. Layng, 10th Jats.
Lieutenant (temporary Captain) L. S. Briggs.
Lieutenant G. Sopwith, Special Reserve.
Lieutenant G. I. Wiehe.
Second Lieutenant J. D. Cartwright (killed).
Temporary Second Lieutenant K. Storey.
Serjeant-Major J. Watson.
Serjeant H. Pickering.
Serjeant T. Temple.

MENTIONED IN DESPATCHES

Corporal T. Fairbairn.
Corporal W. Riley (killed).
Corporal N. Pratt.
Lance-Corporal T. Hunton.
Private H. Hudson.
Private J. McGurk.
Private J. Tynan.

DURHAM LIGHT INFANTRY (TERRITORIAL FORCE).

Lieutenant-Colonel G. O. Spence.
Lieutenant (temporary Captain) V. F. Gloag.
Captain H. R. Wilson.
Lieutenant (temporary Captain) P. Wood, D.S.O.
Second Lieutenant (temporary Lieutenant) W. N. J. Moscrop.
Serjeant N. E. Brown.
Serjeant J. Wilkes.
Lance-Corporal T. Cant.
Private E. A. Bezant.
Private W. Clark.
Private W. F. Flitcroft.
Second Lieutenant (temporary Lieutenant) W. P. Gill.
Second Lieutenant (temporary Captain) T. B. Heslop.
Lieutenant-Colonel E. Vaux, D.S.O.
Second Lieutenant (temporary Major) W. D. Carswell-Hunt.
Corporal J. Tweddle.
Temporary Lieutenant-Colonel J. Turnbull.
Captain T. A. Bradford.
Captain J. A. S. Ritson.
Lieutenant W. Johnson.
Lance-Corporal T. Stokoe.
Major (temporary Lieutenant-Colonel) A. Henderson.
Captain A. F. Hebron.
Second Lieutenant (temporary Captain) E. Dryden.
Second Lieutenant (temporary Captain) E. A. Abraham.
Lance-Corporal J. W. Carr.

DURHAM LIGHT INFANTRY (SERVICE BATTALIONS).

Captain W. T. Wyllie, Durham Light Infantry.
Temporary Lieutenant C. E. Pumphrey.
Quartermaster and Honorary Lieutenant J. P. Cherry.
Lance-Corporal W. Laverick.
Private D. Anderson.
Private J. W. Taylor.
Temporary Captain G. White.
Temporary Lieutenant G. F. Stringfellow.
Serjeant E. Handy.

MENTIONED IN DESPATCHES

Temporary Captain A. E. Babbage.
Acting-Serjeant P. Brass.
Private A. Lauder.
Private T. Laing.

HIGHLAND LIGHT INFANTRY.

Lieutenant-Colonel (temporary Brigadier-General) E. R. Hill.
Captain W. P. Stewart.
Lieutenant J. R. Cowan.
Captain D. M. Murray-Lyon.
Quartermaster and Honorary Captain A. Stevens.
Bugler P. Maloy.
Lieutenant-Colonel A. A. Wolfe-Murray, C.B.
Captain C. W. Hooper (killed).
Captain C. J. Wallace (Adjutant).
Second Lieutenant B. Crossley, Special Reserve (killed).
Lieutenant H. W. Whitson (killed).
Second Lieutenant H. McCulloch.
Second Lieutenant B. A. Medley (Special Reserve).
Quartermaster and Honorary Captain J. E. Taylor.
Company Quartermaster-Serjeant (Acting Serjeant-Major) A. Hauxwell.
Serjeant R. Dearie.
Private P. Higgins.
Private J. Marchant.
Lieutenant G. A. F. Tyler, Special Reserve.

HIGHLAND LIGHT INFANTRY (TERRITORIAL FORCE).

Lieutenant-Colonel C. C. Murray, C.M.G.
Major H. J. R. Bock.
Captain S. Acklom, Highland Light Infantry (Adjutant).
Captain W. M. Todd.
Captain G. Wingate.
Second Lieutenant (temporary Lieutenant) J. K. T. Glen.
Quartermaster and Honorary Lieutenant A. W. Clark.
Lance-Serjeant J. M. Hay.
Lance-Corporal R. C. Reid.
Private A. J. Brown.
Private T. M. Burton.

HIGHLAND LIGHT INFANTRY (SERVICE BATTALIONS).

Major (temporary Lieutenant-Colonel) J. C. Grahame, D.S.O., Highland Light Infantry.
Captain (temporary Major) H. C. Stuart, D.S.O., Reserve of Officers.
Captain (temporary Major) C. H. T. Whitehead, 56th Rifles (killed).
Captain H. G. N. de Berry, Reserve of Officers.
Temporary Captain J. Reid (killed).
Temporary Second Lieutenant J. A. McKinlay.

MENTIONED IN DESPATCHES

Serjeant E. J. Liddiard.
Serjeant F. L. Liddiard.
Lieutenant-Colonel H. C. Fergusson, Argyll and Sutherland Highlanders, Special Reserve.
Major C. E. Andrews, Reserve of Officers.
Captain (temporary Major) J. J. Ronald, D.S.O., Reserve of Officers.
Captain (temporary Major) R. F. Forbes, Highland Light Infantry.
Temporary Captain R. Nasmith (Adjutant).
Temporary Captain O. Lyle.
Serjeant-Major F. W. McSorley.
Company Serjeant-Major E. Eves.
Serjeant J. Cumming.
Serjeant J. Milroy.
Private W. Irvine.
Private R. Wilson.
Brevet Major (temp. Lieut.-Colonel) J. H. Purvis, Reserve of Officers.
Temporary Captain P. W. Torrance.
Temporary Second Lieutenant G. S. Laird.
Temporary Second Lieutenant N. H. MacNeil.
Temporary Second Lieutenant D. G. Watson.
Corporal A. McNicol.

Seaforth Highlanders.

Captain D. B. Burt-Marshall, D.S.O.
Major (temporary Lieutenant-Colonel) C. P. Doig.
Captain F. R. G. Forsyth.
Captain Sir J. E. Fowler, Bt. (Adjutant, Seaforth Highlanders, Territorial Force) (killed).
Major J. E. Thornhill (Adjutant, The London Regiment, Territorial Force).
Second Lieutenant (temporary Lieutenant) I. Anderson.
Second Lieutenant D. Lindsay.
Quartermaster and Honorary Lieutenant J. Macrae.
Private W. Barry.
Private D. Graham.
Lieutenant-Colonel (temp. Brigadier-General) R. S. Vandeleur, C.M.G.
Captain G. N. Alison.
Captain F. Anderson.
Captain J. O. Hopkinson.
Second Lieutenant H. W. Houldsworth.
Second Lieutenant S. H. Macculloch.
Second Lieutenant G. S. Rawstorne.
Serjeant-Major A. N. Dunton.
Serjeant (Acting Serjeant, Acting Serjeant-Major) A. Sutherland.
Acting-Corporal R. Stewart.
Captain F. J. Rigby (Special Reserve).

MENTIONED IN DESPATCHES

SEAFORTH HIGHLANDERS (TERRITORIAL FORCE).
Second Lieutenant (temporary Lieutenant) L. Fraser.
Drummer E. F. Lawrence.

SEAFORTH HIGHLANDERS (SERVICE BATTALIONS).
Major (temporary Lieutenant-Colonel) W. T. Gaisford, Seaforth Highlanders (killed).
Captain F. W. I. V. Fraser, Seaforth Highlanders.
Temporary Captain W. T. Henderson.
Quartermaster and Honorary Lieutenant (temporary Captain) K. K. McLeod, Seaforth Highlanders.
Temporary Lieutenant G. H. W. Green.
Temporary Quartermaster and Honorary Lieutenant J. Allan.
Serjeant J. Taylor.
Lance-Corporal T. Cropper.
Private A. Niccols.
Private H. Wallace.
Major (temporary Lieutenant-Colonel) N. A. Thomson, Seaforth Highlanders.
Temporary Captain D. W. P. Strang.
Temporary Lieutenant E. K. O. Fergusson.
Acting Company Serjeant-Major A. H. Fraser.
Acting-Serjeant M. Eaglesham.
Acting-Serjeant F. Edwards.
Acting Lance-Serjeant J. O'Donnell.
Major (temporary Lieutenant-Colonel) T. Fetherstonhaugh, Reserve of Officers.
Temporary Captain H. T. Allen (died of wounds).
Temporary Captain S. F. Sharp.
Company Serjeant-Major T. Anderson.
Corporal D. Henderson.
Corporal C. Barnicle.
Private J. Isbister (died of wounds).
Private C. Paterson.

GORDON HIGHLANDERS.
Major (temporary Lieutenant-Colonel) P. W. Brown.
Captain Hon. W. Fraser.
Second Lieutenant (temporary Captain) W. Morrison.
Second Lieutenant A. R. Davidson.
Temporary Second Lieutenant O. Horsley.
Temporary Second Lieutenant A. M. Thom.
Quartermaster and Honorary Captain J. W. MacLennan.
Private G. Cowe.
Private J. Everet (killed).
Lieutenant-Colonel A. F. Gordon, C.M.G., D.S.O.

MENTIONED IN DESPATCHES

Major (temp. Lieut.-Col.) J. R. E. Stansfeld, D.S.O. (died of wounds).
Captain H. A. Ross, D.S.O.
Captain L. Carr (Adjutant).
Captain D. Mactavish, Special Reserve.
Lieutenant G. H. Gordon, Special Reserve.
Temporary Second Lieutenant T. C. Scoones.
Quartermaster and Honorary Captain J. Mackie.
Company Serjeant-Major L. Gordon.
Company Serjeant-Major T. Lawrence.
Company Serjeant-Major J. Macdonald.
Corporal A. Blacker.
Lance-Corporal H. Keys.
Private W. Gilchrist.
Private E. Kelly.
Private W. Lawson.
Piper H. Munro.
Private D. Nimmo.
Private G. Smith.
Captain M. Dinwiddie, Special Reserve.
Captain G. M. Monteith, Special Reserve.

GORDON HIGHLANDERS (TERRITORIAL FORCE).

Lieutenant-Colonel J. Dawson, D.S.O.
Captain (temporary Major) A. Lyon.
Second Lieutenant (temporary Captain) N. C. S. Down.
Second Lieutenant F. W. Bain.
Temporary Second Lieutenant G. P. Geddes, Service Battalion.
Second Lieutenant D. A. Waddell.
Serjeant A. Allardyce (killed).
Serjeant W. Forrest.
Private D. McLean.
Captain (temporary Major) S. McDonald.
Lieutenant (temporary Captain) J. L. Low.
Second Lieutenant M. M. Jack.
Quartermaster and Honorary Lieutenant J. Marr.
Serjeant C. Dickie.
Serjeant J. S. Taylor.
Corporal J. Stuart.
Temporary Lieutenant-Colonel J. E. Macqueen (killed).
Second Lieutenant (temporary Captain) W. H. Newson.
Second Lieutenant (temporary Lieutenant) A. G. Petrie-Hay.
Second Lieutenant T. A. Henderson.
Second Lieutenant (temporary Lieutenant) J. Scott.
Company Serjeant-Major J. Forbes.
Serjeant R. Alexander.
Serjeant A. Archibald.

MENTIONED IN DESPATCHES

Private J. Chree.
Private J. Elder.
Private W. Morrison.
Private J. Stuart.
Lieutenant-Colonel G. H. Bower.
Major R. Bruce.
Second Lieutenant (temporary Lieutenant) R. Ross.
Quartermaster and Honorary Lieutenant A. J. Kennington.
Private A. Donald.
Private A. Lees.
Private G. A. Reid.

GORDON HIGHLANDERS (SERVICE BATTALIONS).

Brevet Colonel H. Wright, D.S.O., retired pay.
Captain (temporary Major) G. J. G. Cumine, Reserve of Officers.
Captain (temporary Major) D. MacLeod, D.S.O., Reserve of Officers.
Temporary Captain J. E. Adamson, D.S.O.
Temporary Lieutenant Q. C. D. Bovey.
Captain W. G. Maxwell, Gordon Highlanders.
Temporary Lieutenant G. E. Burney (died of wounds).
Quartermaster and Honorary Lieutenant W. Drummond.
Serjeant E. Marquis.
Lance-Serjeant R. G. Gray.
Corporal J. Sellar.
Lance-Corporal A. McLean.
Private D. Mooney.
Brevet Colonel W. A. Scott, C.B., retired pay.
Temporary Major E. H. H. Gordon.
Captain (temporary Major) W. W. MacGregor, Reserve of Officers.
Temporary Captain T. MacWhirter.
Temporary Lieutenant-Colonel H. R. Wallace.
Lieutenant (temporary Captain) H. K. Longman, Reserve of Officers.
Temporary Second Lieutenant P. B. Boyd.
Temporary Second Lieutenant F. W. Gordon.
Temporary Second Lieutenant J. S. Husband.
Temporary Second Lieutenant L. G. Robertson.
Temporary Second Lieutenant J. B. Wood.
Company Serjeant-Major J. Rodger.
Company Serjeant-Major J. Young.
Serjeant A. J. Young.

CAMERON HIGHLANDERS.

Captain R. M. Dudgeon (Adjutant, Royal Scots, Territorial Force).
Private J. Cobban.
Major (temporary Lieutenant-Colonel) L. O. Graeme.
Lieutenant (temporary Captain) J. Pringle.

MENTIONED IN DESPATCHES

Second Lieutenant Andrew Fraser.
Second Lieutenant E. McIntyre.
Serjeant D. Pollock.
Lieutenant-Colonel (temporary Brigadier-General) J. D. McLachlan.
Captain R. L. McCall.
Captain A. C. Lampson.
Second Lieutenant Alexander Fraser.
Regimental Serjeant-Major E. Fraser.
Company Serjeant-Major G. Draper.
Company Serjeant-Major G. S. Fraser.
Captain C. L. Patton-Bethune, Special Reserve.
Captain C. C. K. Campbell, Special Reserve.
Second Lieutenant N. Martin, Special Reserve.
Lieutenant C. M. Mills, Special Reserve.

CAMERON HIGHLANDERS (TERRITORIAL FORCE).

Temporary Lieutenant-Colonel A. Fraser (killed).
Major G. B. Duff, Cameron Highlanders (Adjutant).
Lieutenant (temporary Captain) J. Campbell.
Second Lieutenant (temporary Captain) J. D. MacPherson.
Temporary Lieutenant (temporary Captain) R. McErlich.
Second Lieutenant (temporary Lieutenant) F. E. Laughton.
Second Lieutenant M. Roemmele.
Quartermaster and Honorary Major J. Lockie.
Company Serjeant-Major W. Ross (killed).
Corporal W. F. Jenkins.
Corporal D. McPherson.
Lance-Corporal A. Reid.
Private W. Macpherson.

CAMERON HIGHLANDERS (SERVICE BATTALIONS).

Lieutenant-Colonel D. W. Cameron of Lochiel, Special Reserve.
Major N. J. M. Archdall, Special Reserve.
Captain and Brevet Major (temporary Major) H. R. Brown.
Captain J. S. Drew, Cameron Highlanders (Adjutant).
Temporary Lieutenant J. Macdonald.
Quartermaster and Honorary Lieutenant D. Cameron.
Serjeant C. M. Drever.
Lance-Corporal J. Gilchrist (killed).
Private D. H. Muir.
Private G. Paterson.
Private G. M. Robertson.
Temporary Lieutenant A. F. P. Christian.
Temporary Lieutenant H. B. Rowan.
Temporary Second Lieutenant D. C. H. Watson.
Temporary Second Lieutenant J. Wilson.

MENTIONED IN DESPATCHES

Serjeant T. Clapperton.
Serjeant J. Porter.
Major (temporary Lieutenant-Colonel) J. W. Sandilands, D.S.O., Cameron Highlanders.
Temporary Lieutenant W. G. S. Stuart.
Temporary Second Lieutenant R. R. Anderson.
Company Serjeant-Major D. Adam.

Royal Irish Rifles.

Major A. D. N. Merriman.
Captain C. J. Newport.
Lieutenant F. Workman, Special Reserve.
Second Lieutenant G. W. Panter.
Quartermaster and Honorary Lieutenant G. W. Edwards.
Lieutenant C. J. Wakefield.
Second Lieutenant (temporary Lieutenant) C. H. H. Eales, Indian Army.
Lieutenant E. B. Kertland, Royal Irish Fusiliers, Special Reserve.
Second Lieutenant (temporary Captain) R. J. O'Lone (killed).
Acting-Serjeant J. Coleman.
Serjeant J. Quinn.
Corporal P. Humpson.
Lance-Corporal S. Harbinson.
Lance-Corporal D. Lorimer.
Lance-Corporal C. Morley.
Lance-Corporal J. Thompson.
Private J. Lynskey.
Private T. J. Mitchell.

Royal Irish Fusiliers.

Major R. J. Kentish.
Lieutenant-Colonel A. R. Burrowes, C.M.G.
Captain G. V. W. Hill.
Captain P. Penn.
Lieutenant G. F. Gough.
Lieutenant A. Low.
Company Serjeant-Major G. Reeve.
Bandsman E. Pass.
Major R. C. Dobbs.
Major H. B. Holmes.
Major (temporary Lieutenant-Colonel) H. B. H. Orpen-Palmer.
Captain H. W. D. McCarthy O'Leary.
Lieutenant (temporary Captain) G. E. G. Cockburn.
Captain W. A. Colhoun, Special Reserve.
Company Serjeant-Major J. Carroll.
Serjeant C. Dempsey.

MENTIONED IN DESPATCHES

Private F. McLoughlin.
Private J. Welsh.
Second Lieutenant R. Brennan, Special Reserve.
Lieutenant E. Workman, Royal Irish Rifles, Special Reserve.

CONNAUGHT RANGERS.
Major (temporary Lieutenant-Colonel) H. R. G. Deacon.
Captain G. F. Callaghan.
Captain R. D'Arcy, Special Reserve.
Captain T. F. V. Foster.
Lieutenant L. C. Badham.
Quartermaster and Honorary Lieutenant J. T. Gorman.
Lance-Corporal (Acting Corporal) J. Whelan.
Private R. Brady.
Captain J. J. Kavanagh, Special Reserve.
Second Lieutenant H. H. Lyons.

ARGYLL AND SUTHERLAND HIGHLANDERS.
Major J. C. Scott.
Lieutenant-Colonel H. L. Henderson.
Brevet Lieutenant-Colonel H. B. Kirk.
Major W. G. Neilson, D.S.O.
Captain J. Mackay.
Second Lieutenant J. Neill.
Second Lieutenant S. G. Rome.
Quartermaster and Honorary Lieutenant J. Heatly.
Regimental Serjeant-Major James Gilmour.
Serjeant Thomas Kerr.
Lieutenant-Colonel R. C. Gore.
Major J. Kennedy.
Captain H. de B. Purves.
Lieutenant (temporary Captain) J. C. Aitken (killed).
Lieutenant E. P. Buchanan.
Serjeant-Major F. R. Walker.
Corporal J. Ogilvie.
Acting-Corporal R. Kennedy.
Lance-Corporal E. Lynch.
Captain I. F. C. Bolton.
Lieutenant (temporary Captain) P. Y. Lyle.
Second Lieutenant T. B. Erskine (temporary Captain) (died of wounds).
Second Lieutenant L. F. S. Sotheby (killed).

ARGYLL AND SUTHERLAND HIGHLANDERS (TERRITORIAL FORCE).
Piper W. Carlyle.
Captain J. F. Jones.
Lieutenant (temporary Captain) J. M. Scott, D.S.O.

MENTIONED IN DESPATCHES

Lieutenant (temporary Captain) A. Stein.
Temporary Lieutenant S. F. Butchart.
Company Serjeant-Major G. Smith.
Private A. Heddleston.
Second Lieutenant (temporary Lieutenant) A. Fraser-Campbell.
Major G. J. Christie, D.S.O., temporary half-pay.
Second Lieutenant (temporary Captain) W. G. Wright.
Lieutenant (temporary Captain) P. A. Kirsop.
Second Lieutenant D. J. Dunbar.
Acting-Corporal G. Crawford.
Private W. Barlas.
Private T. Towie.
Private H. Watson.

Argyll and Sutherland Highlanders (Service Battalions).

Lieutenant-Colonel A. F. Mackenzie, M.V.O.
Major G. W. Muir.
Temporary Captain J. H. Beith.
Captain W. G. Campbell (Adjutant).
Major R. N. Macpherson.
Temporary Captain R. V. C. Cavendish.
Temporary Lieutenant N. R. Colville.
Serjeant-Major H. T. Bunnett.
Serjeant J. Smith.
Lance-Corporal W. Debavey.
Temporary Lieutenant-Colonel M. McNeill, D.S.O.
Temporary Major A. J. Campbell.
Captain N. C. Bennett.
Temporary Second Lieutenant J. F. C. Cameron.
Temporary Second Lieutenant C. R. Davidson.
Serjeant M. Campbell.
Private T. McGovern.

Leinster Regiment.

Captain G. B. Scott, Adjutant, The London Regiment (Territorial Force).
Major H. G. R. Wakefield (Cadet School, General Headquarters).
Major (temporary Lieutenant-Colonel) B. J. Jones.
Major E. H. Wildblood.
Second Lieutenant H. McCormick.
Second Lieutenant (temporary Lieutenant) P. McEnroy.
Lieutenant H. F. Otway.
Lieutenant A. J. M. Pemberton.
Lieutenant C. G. Snelling.
Company Serjeant-Major H. Brown.
Company Serjeant-Major P. Kennedy.

MENTIONED IN DESPATCHES

Company Serjeant-Major P. Mahon.
Private J. Kenny.
Captain L. D. Daly.
Lieutenant (temporary Captain) A. D. Murphy.
Second Lieutenant T. H. Poole.
Quartermaster and Honorary Lieutenant H. O. Squire.
Company Serjeant-Major R. Boyer.
Corporal P. McNally.
Private G. Locke.

Royal Munster Fusiliers.

Major J. A. F. Cuffe.
Captain T. W. Filgate (died of wounds).
Temporary Second Lieutenant A. M. Horsfall (presumed dead).
Captain J. P. M. Ingham, D.S.O.
Second Lieutenant (temporary Lieutenant) J. O'Brien.
Second Lieutenant T. Price (missing).
Regimental Quartermaster-Serjeant R. Jones.
Serjeant P. Harte.
Serjeant A. O'Donoghue.
Corporal J. Kavanagh.
Private C. Barry.

Royal Dublin Fusiliers.

Major (temporary Lieutenant-Colonel) J. P. Tredennick.
Captain R. J. H. Carew.
Captain T. J. Leahy.
Captain B. Maclear (killed).
Lieutenant G. W. B. Tarleton.
Lieutenant F. Treacher.
Temporary Second Lieutenant R. H. Ingoldby.
Second Lieutenant W. J. Shanks.
Lance-Corporal T. Brennan.
Private P. Hayden.

Rifle Brigade.

Major (temporary Lieutenant-Colonel) H. C. Buller, D.S.O.
Major G. M. Lindsay.
Captain (temporary Lieutenant-Colonel) J. Micklem.
Captain (temporary Lieutenant-Colonel) G. C. Sladen.
Farrier Quartermaster-Serjeant W. Webber.
Major W. W. Seymour.
Captain O. C. Downes, D.S.O.
Captain T. H. P. Morris.
Captain H. G. M. Railston, D.S.O.
Second Lieutenant B. Gibbs (killed).

MENTIONED IN DESPATCHES

Second Lieutenant R. I. V. Birkeck.
Second Lieutenant G. L. Jackson.
Company Serjeant-Major A. Scrase.
Serjeant F. G. Eade.
Corporal J. W. Brooks.
Private H. Wood.
Major (temporary Lieutenant-Colonel) F. H. Nugent.
Captain Hon. R. Brand.
Lieutenant (temporary Captain) R. C. J. Chichester-Constable.
Captain F. E. M. Roe, Special Reserve.
Second Lieutenant (temporary Captain) W. E. Gray.
Quartermaster and Honorary Captain J. H. Alldridge.
Serjeant (Acting Quartermaster-Serjeant) C. G. P. Pionchon.
Serjeant H. R. Bull.
Corporal C. R. Garner.
Corporal L. Pinnock.
Private T. Davey.
Major E. R. Meade Waldo.
Captain (temporary Major) R. Pigot.
Lieutenant (temporary Captain) The Honourable M. T. Boscawen.
Captain Hon. T. G. B. Morgan-Grenville.
Lieutenant R. O. Skeggs.
Company Serjeant-Major T. Cox.
Company Serjeant-Major W. Vine.
Serjeant W. H. Hearn.
Serjeant W. J. Mash.
Serjeant F. W. Wright.
Acting-Corporal J. W. Heritage.
Major J. Harrington, D.S.O.
Major F. H. A. Wollaston.
Captain R. L. H. Collins.
Second Lieutenant H. C. Costobadie.
Quartermaster and Honorary Lieutenant H. E. Worthing.
Acting-Serjeant W. J. Jackson.
Acting-Corporal H. C. Crowe.
Acting-Corporal A. Meads.
Private J. Hopkins.
Private H. Vincent.
Lieutenant C. N. C. Boyle (attached Special Reserve).
Second Lieutenant J. G. M. Henderson.
Second Lieutenant H. M. Ramsay Fairfax-Lucy.
Major R. Haig, D.S.O.
Lieutenant H. Law (died of wounds).

RIFLE BRIGADE (SERVICE BATTALIONS).

Lieutenant-Colonel J. D. Heriot-Maitland, D.S.O.

MENTIONED IN DESPATCHES

Major H. D. Ross (Reserve of Officers).
Temporary Second Lieutenant R. H. Lawson.
Temporary Captain C. G. Norbury.
Private F. R. Freer.
Captain A. L. C. Cavendish.
Temporary Captain L. Woodroffe (Captain, Unattached List Territorial Force).
Temporary Captain A. C. Sheepshanks, D.S.O.
Temporary Lieutenant C. R. Gorell-Barnes.
Serjeant C. Vickers.
Major (temporary Lieutenant-Colonel) G. J. Davis, Indian Army.
Temporary Lieutenant R. F. E. R. d'Erlander.
Company Serjeant-Major G. Goodey.
Serjeant J. R. Peacock.
Corporal J. Smith.
Private W. Bennett.
Temporary Captain G. H. Gilbey.
Temporary Lieutenant M. L. Cope.

ARMY CYCLIST CORPS.

Captain A. B. Gracie, Northumberland Fusiliers (Territorial Force) (Northumbrian Division Cyclist Company).
Temporary Second Lieutenant M. Tucker.
Temporary Second Lieutenant R. N. Chubb.
Second Lieutenant W. Watson, Highland Division Cyclist Company.
Company Serjeant-Major F. Bumstead.
Company Serjeant-Major J. Parish.
Serjeant R. H. Barrs.
Serjeant C. H. Rawlings.
Company Serjeant-Major R. Ray.
Lance-Serjeant S. Rogers.
Lance-Corporal F. Southcott.
Corporal A. Wordsdell.
Private G. W. Glayton.
Private A. Walden.

ARMY CYCLIST CORPS (TERRITORIAL FORCE).

Temporary Lieutenant J. H. I. Hankin, Army Cyclist Corps (Captain, Huntingdonshire Cyclist Battalion).
Second Lieutenant K. G. H. R. Gunn, London Div. Cyclist Company.
Second Lieutenant F. G. Truscott, Suffolk Regiment (London Division Cyclist Company).
Serjeant T. A. Richards.
Corporal H. P. Wood, South Midland Divisional Cyclist Company.

MONMOUTHSHIRE REGIMENT.

Lieutenant (temporary Captain) A. L. Evans.
Captain W. C. Hepburn, D.S.O.

MENTIONED IN DESPATCHES

Quartermaster and Honorary Lieutenant R. H. Martin.
Serjeant J. W. Crump (killed).
Private W. Shaw.
Lieutenant-Colonel E. B. Cuthbertson, C.M.G., M.V.O.
Captain (Honorary Major) P. G. Pennymore.
Captain (temporary Major) A. J. H. Bowen, D.S.O.
Second Lieutenant (temporary Captain) C. Comely.
Quartermaster and Honorary Major A. Sale.
Company Serjeant-Major J. S. Granger.
Private F. Leek.
Temporary Major (temporary Lieutenant-Colonel) W. S. Bridge.
Temporary Major O. W. D. Steel.
Lieutenant (temporary Captain) J. M. Jones.
Quartermaster and Honorary Lieutenant A. A. Fry.
Serjeant W. Allen.
Serjeant W. T. Pritchard.
Private J. Wyatt.

CAMBRIDGESHIRE REGIMENT.

Captain (temporary Major) E. T. Saint.
Second Lieutenant (temporary Captain) Sir H. G. T. Butlin, Bt.
Captain M. C. Clayton.
Second Lieutenant (temporary Lieutenant) K. C. Gill.
Second Lieutenant (temporary Lieutenant) W. Shaw.
Second Lieutenant (temporant Lieutenant) E. H. Hopkinson.
Second Lieutenant (temporary Lieutenant) F. M. Platt-Higgins.
Corporal J. B. Death.
Lance-Corporal R. Lambert.
Private G. Allen.
Private P. Painter.

THE LONDON REGIMENT.

Lieutenant-Colonel E. G. Mercer.
Major D. V. Smith.
Captain (temporary Major) R. B. G. Glover.
Company Serjeant-Major G. Bond.
Acting-Corporal S. Cave.
Corporal A. Munro.
Captain (temporary Major) G. A. Stacey.
Lieutenant (temporary Captain) L. H. R. Inglis.
Lieutenant (temporary Captain) F. J. T. Moon.
Second Lieutenant A. G. Jepson.
Serjeant A. Smith.
Private W. Reynolds.
Private J. Stufford.
Major F. D. Samuel .
Captain A. L. B. Agius.
Temporary Lieutenant C. W. Hammerton.

MENTIONED IN DESPATCHES

Company Serjeant-Major D. Cooper.
Private W. H. Whitaker.
Major (temporary Lieutenant-Colonel) L. T. Burnett.
Captain (temporary Major) W. G. Clark, D.S.O.
Second Lieutenant (temporary Captain) J. R. Pyper.
Major (temporary Lieutenant-Colonel) A. S. Bates, D.S.O.
Captain J. R. Somers-Smith.
Second Lieutenant (temporary Captain) C. W. Trevelyan.
Second Lieutenant A. K. Dodds.
Second Lieutenant (temporary Lieutenant) R. Russell.
Serjeant-Major B. K. Mamby.
Major (temporary Lieutenant-Colonel) W. F. Mildren.
Temporary Major W. Whitehead.
Captain W. Hughes.
Captain G. N. F. Powell.
Captain E. W. Hughes.
Serjeant C. Rush.
Lieutenant-Colonel and Honorary Colonel E. Faux.
Captain W. Casson (killed).
Captain C. J. S. Green.
Captain A. D. Laurie.
Second Lieutenant H. O. B. Roberts (died of wounds).
Lieutenant-Colonel J. Harvey, D.S.O.
Second Lieutenant (temporary Lieutenant) A. S. Thomas.
Second Lieutenant O. J. Lawrence (killed).
Second Lieutenant B. O. Moon (died of wounds).
Second Lieutenant (temporary Lieutenant) H. Peel.
Serjeant W. A. G. Heather.
Serjeant C. R. Tapsfield (killed).
Private W. G. H. Clark.
Major (temporary Lieutenant-Colonel) V. W. F. Dickins.
Lieutenant (temporary Captain) J. C. Andrews.
Captain R. H. Lindsey-Renton.
Second Lieutenant R. B. Murray.
Lieutenant (temporary Captain) J. K. Dunlop.
Lieutenant-Colonel (temporary Brigadier-General) F. G. Lewis, C.M.G.
Captain E. G. Kimber, D.S.O.
Second Lieutenant (temporary Lieutenant) H. Holland.
Second Lieutenant R. G. Malby (killed).
Regimental Serjeant Major A. Lock.
Company Serjeant-Major J. R. Davis.
Captain C. J. Low, D.S.O.
Second Lieutenant (temporary Captain) H. L. Syer.
Second Lieutenant (temporary Captain) N. L. Mackie (died of wounds).
Second Lieutenant (temporary Lieutenant) I. E. Snell.

MENTIONED IN DESPATCHES

Quartermaster and Honorary Captain W. E. Webb.
Serjeant R. McLagan.
Temporary Captain (temporary Major) H. H. Kemble.
Lieutenant R. Chalmers (died of wounds).
Private G. Oliver.
Private C. W. Beadel.
Major N. B. Tyrwhitt.
Lieutenant (temporary Captain) J. B. Baber.
Second Lieutenant (temporary Lieutenant) S. G. L. Bradley.
Lieutenant (temporary Captain) P. E. Harding.
Lieutenant (temporary Captain) S. R. Savill.
Company Serjeant-Major H. M. Masson.
Serjeant A. Maas.
Private A. M. Wingfield.
Lieutenant-Colonel J. Godding.
Captain (temporary Major) F. E. Evans.
Second Lieutenant (temporary Captain) E. A. B. Chandler.
Second Lieutenant (temporary Lieutenant) H. C. Wright.
Second Lieutenant (temporary Lieutenant) H. D. Withers.
Serjeant G. T. Garnham.
Lance-Corporal A. J. Barnes.
Private B. Parry.
Captain A. P. Hamilton, Royal West Surrey Regiment (Adjutant).
Second Lieutenant (temporary Captain) H. U. Mann.
Captain J. R. Trinder.
Lieutenant J. H. B. Rich.
Second Lieutenant C. E. Ashby.
Acting Regimental Serjeant-Major T. J. Crome.
Corporal F. J. Shelton.
Temporary Lieutenant-Colonel P. T. Westmorland, D.S.O., Lincolnshire Regiment, Territorial Force.
Lieutenant (temporary Captain) S. C. Haskins.
Lieutenant (temporary Captain) J. de Mexa.
Temporary Lieutenant (temporary Captain) J. H. Whitby.
Serjeant W. G. J. Parker.
Serjeant W. C. Gates.
Temporary Lieutenant-Colonel A. B. Hubback.
Temporary Major W. H. Matthews.
Lieutenant (temporary Captain) W. M. L. Escombe, D.S.O.
Lieutenant (temporary Captain) F. Thorne.
Lieutenant (temporary Captain) G. Williams.
Lieutenant W. F. Dyer.
Second Lieutenant A. E. Young (killed).
Private E. Carrington.
Second Lieutenant (temporary Captain) S. F. Corby.
Captain A. Hutchence.

MENTIONED IN DESPATCHES

Second Lieutenant C. H. H. Roberts.
Second Lieutenant M. H. Gilkes.
Second Lieutenant S. H. Persse.
Second Lieutenant (temporary Lieutenant) N. A. Taylor.
Company Serjeant-Major W. C. Burrow.
Private R. S. Salmon (killed).
Private T. A. Taylor.
Lieutenant-Colonel E. J. Previte.
Captain L. J. Woolley.
Second Lieutenant (temporary Lieutenant) A. Baswitz.
Second Lieutenant (temporary Lieutenant) T. S. Belshaw.
Serjeant P. J. Spencer.
Lance-Serjeant W. S. Porter.
Corporal H. E. Gosling.
Lance-Corporal S. Starkey (killed).
Private G. Lipscombe.
Major T. G. W. Newman.
Captain (temporary Lieutenant-Colonel) H. S. J. Streatfield.
Captain A. T. Fearon.
Lieutenant L. S. Clinton.
Lieutenant F. Entwistle.
Lieutenant K. E. Wood (died of wounds).
Temporary Second Lieutenant R. C. Barkworth.
Quartermaster-Serjeant A. Green.
Private E. J. Doran.
Private M. G. Galloway (killed).
Lieutenant-Colonel W. G. Simpson.
Second Lieutenant (temporary Captain) D. W. Figg, D.S.O.
Captain J. T. Harley.
Captain G. E. Millner.
Second Lieutenant (temporary Lieutenant) E. N. Carr.
Second Lieutenant (temporary Lieutenant) H. I. P. Hallett.
Lieutenant W. H. S. Morrison (killed).
Second Lieutenant (temporary Lieutenant) C. G. Davies.
Second Lieutenant L. W. Mobberley.
Lance-Serjeant F. H. Newcomb (died of wounds).
Private P. A. Guest.
Lieutenant (temporary Captain) H. K. E. Ostle.
Lieutenant (temporary Captain) F. K. Simmons, M.V.O.
Second Lieutenant (temporary Lieutenant) A. A. Tyer, M.V.O.
Serjeant C. R. Willis.
Private J. Strode.
Private A. S. Wallis.

HERTFORDSHIRE REGIMENT.

Captain A. G. Clerk.
Second Lieutenant (temporary Lieutenant) B. Milburn.

MENTIONED IN DESPATCHES

Second Lieutenant K. Oliphant.
Regimental Serjeant-Major F. Young.
Lance-Corporal R. Evans.
Corporal G. Callow.
Private G. A. Dunn.
Private R. Stevens.

Motor Machine Gun Service.

Temporary Major C. H. T. B. Hall.
Temporary Major A. W. Tate (Captain, Royal Highlanders, Special Reserve).
Temporary Captain A. S. Le Rossignol.
Temporary Lieutenant E. C. Barclay (killed).
Temporary Lieutenant E. W. Bennett.
Temporary Lieutenant G. Campbell.
Temporary Lieutenant W. W. Honywood.
Temporary Lieutenant S. A. Westrop.
Temporary Second Lieutenant C. O. D. Anderson.
Acting Battery Serjeant-Major D. W. Herd.
Acting Battery Serjeant-Major P. D. Taylor.
Acting Battery Quartermaster-Serjeant E. Jones.
Serjeant B. Adair.
Acting-Serjeant A. Miller.

Army Service Corps.

Temporary Captain C. G. Allen (Captain, Home Counties Divisional Train, Territorial Force).
Temporary Major T. W. A. Bagley (dead).
Temporary Captain E. S. Baring-Gould.
Captain (temporary Lieutenant-Colonel) F. P. Barnes.
Temporary Major C. A. Barron (Major, South Midland Divisional Supply Column, Territorial Force).
Major (temporary Lieutenant-Colonel) A. Berger.
Temporary Major W. M. Bicket.
Major E. H. Blamey.
Temporary Lieutenant S. Bradbury.
Temporary Captain C. D. Branch.
Temporary Lieutenant J. L. P. F. Brewer.
Temporary Major M. A. Caldwell.
Temporary Major C. W. Cochrane (Major, Highland Divisional Supply Column, Territorial Force).
Lieutenant-Colonel J. Coulson.
Major (temporary Lieutenant-Colonel) R. P. Crawley, M.V.O.
Temporary Major E. H. Crispin (Captain (temporary Major) London Divisional Supply Column, Territorial Force).
Lieutenant W. E. Crossby.

MENTIONED IN DESPATCHES

Temporary Lieutenant C. R. J. Day.
Temporary Major R. W. Day.
Temporary Lieutenant W. E. Dickson (Second Lieutenant, London Divisional Train, Territorial Force).
Lieutenant-Colonel F. F. Duffus.
Temporary Major C. P. W. F. R. Dugmore (Captain, Reserve of Officers)
Second Lieutenant (temporary Lieutenant) T. B. M. Egleston, Special Reserve).
Captain (temporary Major) J. E. Fasken.
Lieutenant-Colonel E. C. L. Fitzwilliams.
Second Lieutenant (temporary Lieutenant) B. C. Frederick.
Captain (temporary Major) J. C. L. Godfray.
Second Lieutenant (temporary Captain) A. Grant, Special Reserve.
Temporary Lieutenant C. L. Green (Second Lieutenant, Home Counties Divisional Train, Territorial Force).
Temporary Captain G. H. B. Hanbury.
Captain (temporary Major) C. H. Hart.
Temporary Captain J. H. B. Hesse.
Temporary Second Lieutenant D. S. Hewett.
Temporary Captain R. V. Hunt.
Major T. M. Hutchinson.
Temporary Captain H. E. S. Huth.
Temporary Lieutenant L. Ingram.
Temporary Captain F. W. Jackson.
Temporary Captain E. Jecks.
Lieutenant-Colonel T. P. Johnson.
Second Lieutenant (temporary Lieutenant) H. A. Kelsall.
Temporary Major D. S. Kennedy.
Temporary Captain J. R. King.
Temporary Major H. V. Kitson (Major, West Riding Divisional Supply Column, Territorial Force).
Second Lieutenant (temporary Major) H. Knothe, Special Reserve.
Temporary Captain T. E. Laing.
Major F. W. G. Leland.
Temporary Captain A. E. Lloyd.
Temporary Honorary Lieutenant S. Lyne-Stephens.
Lieutenant (temporary Captain) S. G. McBride.
Second Lieutenant (temporary Major) F. de C. McCracken, Special Reserve.
Temporary Major F. C. J. Macdermot.
Temporary Captain S. C. Mead.
Lieutenant-Colonel E. L. Mears.
Temporary Lieutenant A. G. Mitchell.
Temporary Captain J. F. Moody.
Temporary Major J. J. Murphy.
Temporary Captain J. C. O'Kell.

MENTIONED IN DESPATCHES

Temporary Major H. W. Peebles (Captain, Reserve of Officers).
Temporary Major H. S. W. Pennington.
Major G. L. Peterson.
Temporary Second Lieutenant R. H. C. Plews.
Temporary Captain R. B. Prust.
Temporary Captain C. H. Rawson.
Major A. H. Roberts (temporary Lieutenant-Colonel, South Midland Divisional Train, Territorial Force).
Temporary Captain W. H. C. Rowe.
Temporary Major R. G. F. Saunders.
Major G. T. Savage.
Temporary Captain L. Smales.
Temporary Captain I. C. V. Smith.
Lieutenant (temporary Captain) P. L. Spafford.
Temporary Major G. S. Spurrier.
Temporary Lieutenant A. W. Squirl.
Temporary Lieutenant R. A. Starbuck-Williams.
Temporary Major A. L. Stewart.
Temporary Lieutenant H. J. D. Stokes.
Lieutenant (temporary Captain) J. B. Stubbs.
Temporary Major H. P. B. Tayler.
Temporary Lieutenant R. H. Thomas.
Temporary Lieutenant H. R. Tuppen.
Lieutenant (temporary Captain) D. Turnbull.
Lieutenant (temporary Captain) E. S. Unwin.
Temporary Major T. P. Wansbrough.
Temporary Captain F. D. Wilson.
Major (temporary Lieutenant-Colonel) B. J. G. Woods.
Temporary Major E. T. L. Wright.
Quartermaster and Honorary Captain H. G. Beaumont, retired pay.
Quartermaster and Honorary Lieutenant E. C. Boulter.
Quartermaster and Honorary Major J. Caddy.
Quartermaster and Honorary Major J. J. G. Donnelly.
Quartermaster and Honorary Lieutenant J. W. Hickson.
Third Class Inspector of Mechanical Transport and Honorary Lieutenant H. G. Hoare.
Quartermaster and Honorary Lieutenant J. L. Hutchinson.
Quartermaster and Honorary Lieutenant S. Knight.
Quartermaster and Honorary Lieutenant J. Moore.
Quartermaster and Honorary Lieutenant A. E. Notley.
Quartermaster and Honorary Lieutenant T. G. Spain.
Quartermaster and Honorary Lieutenant F. Way.
Quartermaster and Honorary Lieutenant W. J. White.
Serjeant E. L. Abbey.
Acting Farrier Staff-Serjeant T. Ahern.
Acting-Corporal T. H. Airey.

MENTIONED IN DESPATCHES

Serjeant A. Allen.
Corporal S. Allen.
Acting Company Serjeant-Major H. Andrews.
Mechanist Staff-Serjeant W. H. Archer.
Farrier Quartermaster-Serjeant A. Arlett.
Staff-Serjeant A. Arthur.
Corporal G. Ashworth.
Staff Quartermaster-Serjeant C. R. Aspden.
Acting-Serjeant S. F. Aston.
1st Class Staff Serjeant-Major B. W. Badcock.
Corporal W. J. Bailey.
Serjeant J. Bange.
First Class Staff-Serjeant Major D. Barry.
Staff-Serjeant W. A. B. Bartholomew.
Serjeant A. C. Bassett.
Acting Company Serjeant-Major R. A. Beckingham.
Wheeler-Serjeant R. J. Beer.
Private C. D. Bell.
Mechanist Serjeant-Major P. Bennett.
Serjeant A. Bennett.
Staff Serjeant-Major W. A. Bird.
Wheeler Staff-Serjeant B. C. Blowers.
Serjeant W. Boakes.
Mechanist Serjeant-Major A. C. Booth.
Mechanist Serjeant-Major J. Bradburn.
Company Serjeant-Major W. F. Brake.
Corporal P. J. Bricknell.
Driver E. Bristow.
Acting Lance-Corporal S. W. Brown.
Serjeant V. E. Browne.
Mechanist Serjeant-Major W. Buckle.
Corporal E. V. Budd.
Lance-Corporal D. Calder.
Farrier Quartermaster-Serjeant A. Carter.
Serjeant R. S. Cathery.
Private R. Chadwick.
Staff-Serjeant F. V. Chandler.
Private J. Chatterton.
Farrier Staff-Serjeant J. Cheveralls.
Staff Quartermaster-Serjeant H. E. Clegg.
Acting Mechanist Staff-Serjeant W. E. Coles.
Staff-Serjeant F. J. Coplin.
Acting-Serjeant F. J. G. Costello.
Acting Staff-Serjeant W. Crook.
Serjeant F. Crosby.
Driver Wheeler T. Crutchley.

MENTIONED IN DESPATCHES

First Class Staff Sergeant Major J. Cullen.
Acting Farrier Quartermaster-Serjeant O. Cuthbert.
Serjeant A. J. Daborn.
Farrier Quartermaster-Serjeant G. Davies.
Staff-Serjeant R. A. Death.
Corporal W. R. Desmond.
Serjeant W. Devlin.
Staff Serjeant-Major W. Digby.
Acting-Corporal W. Donoghue.
Corporal W. Doole.
Acting-Corporal R. J. Down.
Serjeant W. F. Dyas.
Staff Serjeant-Major E. O. Eagleton.
Acting Company Quartermaster-Serjeant T. Edwards.
Acting Company Quartermaster-Serjeant A. E. England.
Staff-Serjeant C. R. Fitzpatrick.
Staff Serjeant-Major W. G. Fitzwater.
Serjeant G. E. Fletcher.
Staff-Serjeant A. W. Flood.
Acting Company Quartermaster-Serjeant T. F. Flood.
Farrier Staff-Serjeant J. Franks.
Company Serjeant-Major W. Freeman.
Acting Company Serjeant-Major J. T. B. Gale.
Staff-Serjeant A. W. Galpin.
Saddler Quartermaster-Serjeant J. I. Gifford.
Mechanist Serjeant-Major C. F. Goff.
Staff Serjeant (Acting Staff Serjeant-Major) W. R. A. Gooding.
Acting Company Serjeant-Major F. J. Gray.
Staff-Serjeant Major A. C. Grimwood.
Serjeant J. Guilfoyle.
Saddler Serjeant J. M. Guy.
Staff Quartermaster-Serjeant T. G. Hackett.
Acting Mechanist Serjeant-Major W. H. Hamilton.
Staff Serjeant-Major J. Harold.
Staff Serjeant-Major G. Harrison.
Staff Serjeant P. Harvey.
Acting-Serjeant J. Harvey.
Acting Staff Serjeant-Major G. H. Hatfield.
Staff Serjeant-Major R. E. Hayward.
Acting Serjeant J. S. Heathcote.
Acting Serjeant J. E. Hedges.
Staff Serjeant-Major S. Hellier.
Private H. T. Henry.
Staff Serjeant-Major A. Hewett.
Corporal G. A. Hewitt.
Acting Staff Serjeant-Major C. C. Hewlett.

MENTIONED IN DESPATCHES

Staff Serjeant-Major E. C. Hickie.
Corporal J. N. Hingle.
Staff Serjeant W. A. Hipperson.
Staff Serjeant E. Hobson.
Acting Serjeant-Major W. E. Hopkins.
Acting Staff Serjeant-Major C. W. Hopkins.
Corporal F. Horsfield.
Corporal C. T. Hughes.
Company Quartermaster-Serjeant T. E. Hulme.
Acting Serjeant R. Hume.
Staff Serjeant-Major H. E. Humphries.
Company Quartermaster-Serjeant W. S. Hushar.
Company Serjeant-Major F. W. C. Hutchings.
Serjeant W. A. Huxtable.
Driver Wheeler E. A. Ingleton.
Staff Serjeant W. H. M. Ives.
Farrier Quartermaster-Serjeant S. W. Izzard.
Mechanist Serjeant-Major V. Jackson.
Acting Serjeant W. James.
Staff Serjeant F. T. Johnson.
Mechanist Serjeant-Major L. C. Johnstone.
Mechanist Serjeant-Major T. W. Jones.
Corporal F. Jones.
Acting Serjeant H. S. Justice.
Serjeant R. J. Kennaway.
Corporal H. D. King.
Private C. J. King.
Staff Serjeant H. J. Knight.
Acting Serjeant W. J. Knights.
First Class Staff Serjeant-Major F. E. Lane.
Staff Serjeant-Major J. G. Lane.
Company Quartermaster-Serjeant A. Lambert.
Acting Staff Quartermaster-Serjeant M. Livesey.
Staff Serjeant-Major W. Locke.
Company Quartermaster-Serjeant W. Lord.
Corporal C. E. Lowen.
Lance-Corporal G. Lowne.
Serjeant J. McCrory.
Corporal R. McDonald.
First Class Staff Serjeant-Major J. H. Mayes.
Private R. McDonald.
Acting Corporal T. Mackie.
Serjeant J. Martin.
Acting Company Serjeant-Major P. W. Mayl.
Saddler Staff Serjeant W. Meehan.
Company Serjeant-Major M. Metcalfe.

MENTIONED IN DESPATCHES

Farrier Quartermaster-Serjeant H. Miles.
Corporal T. Miller.
Acting Corporal J. B. Mitchell.
Acting Lance-Corporal W. A. Morgan.
Acting Lance-Corporal D. Moriarty.
Mechanist Staff Serjeant-Major A. Musgrave.
Corporal H. P. Newberry.
Acting Serjeant E. A. Newbon.
Acting Company Serjeant-Major J. Nicholas.
Driver R. J. Nicholls.
Private H. Nickless.
Wheeler Corporal F. Nye.
Corporal W. F. Oram.
Corporal R. A. Oxley.
Acting Mechanist Serjeant-Major E. Packman.
Serjeant F. H. Padfield.
Company Quartermaster-Serjeant E. Parker.
Staff Serjeant D. Parry.
Corporal W. G. Payne.
Acting Lance-Corporal S. F. Payne.
Serjeant A. H. Peake.
Company Serjeant-Major C. G. Pedder.
Company Quartermaster-Serjeant H. F. Phillips.
Staff Quartermaster-Serjeant (Acting Serjeant-Major) T. Pollock
Private A. L. Pratt.
Private R. Preston.
Serjeant F. W. Price.
Acting Lance-Corporal W. L. M. Price.
Corporal E. Prince.
Serjeant C. Prince-Cox.
Farrier Staff Serjeant J. W. Pullen.
Staff Serjeant-Major C. E. Quarrier.
Acting Serjeant W. Ragan.
Serjeant H. Reakes.
Staff Serjeant-Major, 1st Class, E. Record.
Serjeant E. W. Redknap.
Serjeant A. R. Reynolds.
Lance-Corporal G. A. Reynolds.
Serjeant C. A. Ricketts.
Serjeant A. Ridgeon.
Acting Company Serjeant-Major R. W. Ridout.
Acting Company Serjeant-Major C. Robinson.
Company Serjeant-Major E. Rogers.
Staff Serjeant-Major A. W. Rouse.
Serjeant P. Rowden.
Serjeant F. Rowe.

MENTIONED IN DESPATCHES

Serjeant W. J. Rowe.
Acting Mechanist Serjeant-Major A. Rudd.
Lance-Serjeant C. J. Saunders.
Staff Serjeant J. C. Saunders.
Company Serjeant-Major P. Scott.
Acting Company Serjeant-Major W. J. Searle.
Mechanist Serjeant-Major F. Sharp.
Acting Mechanist Serjeant-Major G. H. Sharp.
Staff Quartermaster-Serjeant W. Sharp.
Staff-Serjeant S. F. Sharp.
Private (Acting Staff-Serjeant) H. Sharpe.
Company Quartermaster-Serjeant R. H. Simpson.
Staff Serjeant-Major J. T. Skipper.
Staff Serjeant (Acting Serjeant-Major) F. Slade.
Staff Serjeant-Major W. F. Smith.
Lance-Corporal F. D. Smith.
Staff Serjeant V. C. Soggee.
First Class Staff Serjeant-Major S. P. Stock.
First Class Staff Serjeant-Major W. J. Stroud.
Acting Mechanist Serjeant-Major A. G. Sweet.
Company Serjeant-Major C. Sweetman.
Staff Serjeant-Major T. A. Tacey.
Acting Company Serjeant-Major J. Thompson.
Acting Company Serjeant-Major A. J. Timoney.
Serjeant H. Tovell.
Staff-Serjeant J. L. Treweek.
Corporal E. Trowbridge.
Staff Serjeant-Major A. E. Tucker.
Acting Corporal R. Venes.
Private L. T. Vickers.
Company Serjeant-Major W. C. Walker.
Driver J. Wall.
Serjeant G. T. Walter.
Mechanist Staff Serjeant G. H. Ward.
Serjeant W. Ward.
Acting Serjeant H. S. Ward.
Mechanist Serjeant-Major J. Watcham.
Acting Quartermaster-Serjeant C. L. Willis.
Mechanist Serjeant-Major A. P. Wills.
Mechanist Serjeant-Major W. Wilson.
Farrier Staff Serjeant H. Wood.
Acting Serjeant J. T. Wright.
Farrier Serjeant B. Wyatt.
Staff Serjeant-Major A. J. Yates.
Acting Mechanist Serjeant-Major L. W. Yates.

MENTIONED IN DESPATCHES

ARMY SERVICE CORPS (TERRITORIAL FORCE).

Lieutenant-Colonel C. F. T. Blyth, London Divisional Train.
Lieutenant-Colonel J. C. Chambers, West Riding Divisional Train.
Lieutenant-Colonel H. D. Henderson, Highland Divisional Train.
Lieutenant-Colonel E. W. R. Pinkney, Northumbrian Divisional Train.
Captain (temporary Major) E. H. Crispin, 47th (London) Divisional Supply Column (temporary Major, Army Service Corps).
Major T. Dowling, Northumbrian Divisional Train.
Major W. C. Galbraith, London Divisional Train.
Major R. A. E. H. Kearns, London Divisional Train (temporary Major, Army Service Corps).
Major A. G. Nicol-Smith, Highland Divisional Train.
Captain (temp. Major) R. T. Pemberton, N. Midland Divisional Train.
Major R. H. Whitcombe, junr., South Midland Divisional Train.
Temporary Captain C. G. Allen, Home Counties Divisional Train (temporary Captain, Army Service Corps).
Lieutenant (temporary Captain) J. Milner, West Riding Divisional Train.
Staff Serjeant-Major E. Bustard, Northumbrian Divisional Train.
Serjeant W. J. Cooper, Northumbrian Divisional Train.
Staff Serjeant L. A. Grint, London Divisional Train.
Staff Serjeant J. R. Long, West Riding Divisional Train.
Corporal R. McDonald, Northumbrian Divisional Train.
Company Serjeant-Major F. Pilgrim, London Divisional Train.
Company Serjeant-Major G. W. Ross, Northumbrian Divisional Train.
Serjeant B. Thompson, West Riding Divisional Train.
Farrier-Staff Serjeant H. Wood, Northumbrian Divisional Train.

ARMY SERVICE CORPS (ATTACHED ROYAL ARMY MEDICAL CORPS).

Temporary Lieutenant J. W. Shephard.
Temporary Captain J. Cooper.
Serjeant D. Cochrane.
Serjeant A. Summerscale.
Serjeant J. Sumner.
Acting Serjeant F. W. W. Watkins.
Corporal H. B. Rogers.
Driver W. McLay.
Driver D. Rees.
Private F. Rhodes.

ARMY MEDICAL SERVICE.

GENERAL HEADQUARTERS STAFF, &c.

Surgeon-General W. G. Macpherson, C.B., C.M.G., M.B., K.H.P.
Surgeon-General T. J. O'Donnell, D.S.O.
Surgeon-General M. W. O'Keefe, C.B., M.D.
Surgeon-General R. Porter, M.B.
Surgeon-General H. Treherne, C.M.G., F.R.C.S. Edin.

MENTIONED IN DESPATCHES

Surgeon-General T. P. Woodhouse, C.B.
Colonel G. H. Barefoot, C.M.G.
Temporary Colonel W. C. Beevor, C.M.G., M.B., Territorial Force (Lieutenant-Colonel, retired pay).
Colonel E. G. Browne.
Colonel C. H. Burtchaell, C.M.G., M.B.
Colonel G. Cree, C.M.G.
Colonel R. H. Firth, F.R.C.S.
Colonel M. P. C. Holt, C.B., D.S.O.
Colonel G. D. Hunter, D.S.O.
Colonel R. Kirkpatrick, C.M.G., M.D.
Colonel S. MacDonald, M.B.
Colonel R. L. R. MacLeod, M.B.
Colonel C. E. Nichol, D.S.O., M.B.
Colonel D. M. O'Callaghan.
Colonel G. T. Rawnsley.
Colonel J. J. Russell, M.B.
Colonel B. H. Scott.
Colonel B. M. Skinner, M.V.O.
Colonel W. H. Starr.
Colonel H. C. Thurston, C.M.G.
Lieutenant-Colonel (temporary Colonel) N. Tyacke, M.B., R.A.M.C.
Colonel T. du B. Whaite, M.B.
Colonel C. A. Young.
Lieutenant-Colonel E. T. F. Birrell, C.M.G., M.V., R.A.M.C.
Lieutenant-Colonel F. J. Brakenridge, R.A.M.C.
Lieutenant-Colonel A. Chopping, R.A.M.C.
Lieutenant-Colonel S. L. Cummins, C.M.G., M.D., R.A.M.C.
Lieutenant-Colonel H. E. M. Douglas, V.C., D.S.O., R.A.M.C.
Lieutenant-Colonel L. N. Lloyd, D.S.O., R.A.M.C.
Lieutenant-Colonel C. K. Morgan, M.B., R.A.M.C.
Lieutenant-Colonel F. S. Penny, M.B., R.A.M.C.
Lieutenant-Colonel H. S. Roch, R.A.M.C.
Lieutenant-Colonel J. M. Sloan, D.S.O., M.B., R.A.M.C.
Major C. G. Browne, D.S.O., R.A.M.C.
Major B. B. Burke, R.A.M.C.
Major J. M. H. Conway, F.R.C.S.I., R.A.M.C.
Major P. Davidson, D.S.O., M.B., R.A.M.C.
Major P. G. Easton, R.A.M.C.
Major C. C. Fleming, D.S.O., M.B. (Reserve of Officers).
Major J. A. Hartigan, M.B., R.A.M.C.
Major T. E. Harty, R.A.M.C.
Major P. H. Henderson, M.B., R.A.M.C.
Major H. C. Hildreth, F.R.C.S. Edin., R.A.M.C.
Major J. D. Richmond, M.D., R.A.M.C.
Major M. B. H. Ritchie, M.B., R.A.M.C.

MENTIONED IN DESPATCHES

Major A. B. Smallman, M.D., R.A.M.C.
Major R. N. Woodley, R.A.M.C.
Captain J. J. H. Beckton, R.A.M.C.
Captain R. Gale, D.S.O., M.B., R.A.M.C.
Captain F. D. G. Howell, R.A.M.C.
Captain W. P. MacArthur, M.D., F.R.C.P.I., R.A.M.C.
Captain J. W. L. Scott, M.B., R.A.M.C.

ARMY MEDICAL SERVICE.
CONSULTANTS.

Temporary Colonel Sir B. E. Dawson, K.C.V.O., M.D. (Captain, London General Hospital, R.A.M.C., Territorial Force).
Temporary Colonel H. McI. W. Gray, M.D., F.R.C.S. Edin. (Major, Scottish General Hospital, R.A.M.C., Territorial Force).
Temporary Colonel W. T. Lister, M.B., F.R.C.S.
Temporary Colonel H. A. Thomson, M.D., F.R.C.S. (Captain, Scottish General Hospital, Royal Army Medical Corps, Territorial Force).
Temporary Colonel C. S. Wallace.

ROYAL ARMY MEDICAL CORPS.

Lieutenant-Colonel L. Addams Williams.
Lieutenant-Colonel J. E. Brogdon.
Lieutenant-Colonel T. H. M. Clarke, C.M.G., D.S.O., M.B.
Lieutenant-Colonel R. W. Clements, M.B.
Lieutenant-Colonel V. J. Crawford, D.S.O.
Temporary Lieutenant-Colonel T. C. English, M.B., F.R.C.S. (Captain London General Hospital, Royal Army Medical Corps, Territorial Force).
Lieutenant-Colonel G. H. Goddard.
Lieutenant-Colonel (temporary Colonel) H. A. Hinge.
Lieutenant-Colonel A. W. Hooper, D.S.O.
Lieutenant-Colonel W. E. Hudleston.
Lieutenant-Colonel E. T. Inkson, V.C.
Lieutenant-Colonel F. Kiddle, M.B.
Lieutenant-Colonel J. W. Langstaff.
Lieutenant- Colonel J. W. Leake.
Lieutenant-Colonel J. R. McMunn.
Lieutenant-Colonel C. W. Mainprise.
Lieutenant-Colonel E. W. P. V. Marriott.
Lieutenant-Colonel H. G. Martin.
Lieutenant-Colonel G. A. Moore, M.D.
Lieutenant-Colonel W. H. S. Nickerson, V.C., M.B.
Lieutenant-Colonel H. H. Norman, M.B.
Lieutenant-Colonel M. MacG. Rattray, M.B.
Lieutenant-Colonel J. P. Silver, M.B.
Lieutenant-Colonel and Brevet Colonel F. Smith, D.S.O.

MENTIONED IN DESPATCHES

Lieutenant-Colonel A. A. Watson (Special Reserve) (Lieutenant-Colonel, Royal Army Medical Corps, Territorial Force).
Lieutenant-Colonel A. O. B. Wroughton.
Major R. B. Ainsworth.
Major E. G. Anthonisz.
Major R. B. Black, M.B., Reserve of Officers.
Major G. H. J. Brown, M.B.
Major J. H. Campbell, M.B.
Major K. A. C. Doig.
Major FitzG. G. Fitzgerald.
Major A. W. Gibson.
Temporary Major E. L. Gowlland, M.B.
Major P. J. Hanafin.
Major D. L. Harding, F.R.C.S.I.
Major H. Harding, M.B.
Major G. W. G. Hughes, D.S.O.
Major A. E. S. Irvine.
Major E. F. Q. L'Estrange.
Major R. P. Lewis.
Major S. E. Lewis, M.B.
Major N. Low.
Major J. T. McEntire, M.B.
Major A. A. Meaden.
Major S. M. W. Meadows.
Major A. H. McN. Mitchell.
Major J. S. Pascoe.
Major L. M. Purser, M.B.
Major J. M. B. Rahilly, M.B.
Major W. Riach, M.D.
Major T. F. Ritchie, M.B.
Major F. E. Roberts.
Major E. Ryan.
Major F. C. Sampson, M.B.
Major H. F. Shea, M.B.
Major M. Sinclair, M.B.
Major R. S. Smyth, M.D.
Major H. Stewart, M.B.
Major R. Storrs.
Major R. J. C. Thompson.
Major J. A. Turnbull.
Major C. H. Turner.
Major W. J. Waters.
Major J. W. West, M.B.
Major R. K. White.
Major W. Wiley, M.B.
Captain J. Adams, M.B. (Special Reserve).

MENTIONED IN DESPATCHES

Captain J. E. Allan, M.B. (Special Reserve).
Temporary Captain J. A. Andrews, M.B.
Captain R. R. G. Atkins (Special Reserve), M.B.
Captain J. H. Baird, M.B. (Special Reserve).
Captain D. C. G. Ballingall, M.B.
Temporary Captain J. H. Barry.
Captain H. C. Bazett, M.B., F.R.C.S. (Special Reserve).
Captain W. K. Beaman.
Captain F. A. Bearn, M.B. (Special Reserve).
Captain E. C. Beddows.
Temporary Captain D. Bell, M.B.
Captain W. J. E. Bell, D.S.O., M.B.
Captain J. E. Black, M.B. (Special Reserve).
Temporary Captain L. G. Bourdillon.
Captain J. E. M. Boyd.
Captain A. B. H. Bridges.
Temporary Captain A. E. Bullock (killed).
Captain W. K. Campbell, M.B. (Special Reserve).
Temporary Captain E. W. Carrington, M.B. (killed).
Temporary Captain R. Charles, F.R.C.S.I.
Captain A. G. W. Compton (Special Reserve).
Temporary Captain R. E. Cree, M.B.
Captain A. R. Dale (Special Reserve).
Temporary Captain W. S. Danks, M.D.
Captain E. C. Deane (killed).
Captain G. De La Cour, M.B.
Temporary Captain J. W. Dew, M.B.
Captain R. M. Dickson, M.B.
Captain M. G. Dill, M.D.
Temporary Captain M. Donaldson, M.B., F.R.C.S.
Captain J. S. Dockrill, M.B. (Special Reserve).
Captain J. A. C. Dowse, M.B. (Special Reserve).
Captain A. C. Elliott, M.B.
Captain E. J. Elliot, M.B.
Captain P. Elvey, G.M.
Captain D. B. Chiles-Evans, M.B. (Special Reserve) (Captain, Welsh Field Ambulance, Royal Army Medical Corps, Territorial Force).
Captain A. J. Ewing, M.B. (Special Reserve).
Temporary Captain G. D. Ferguson, M.B.
Temporary Captain P. Ferguson, M.B., F.R.C.S.
Captain F. G. Flood, M.B. (Special Reserve).
Temporary Captain W. Foot, M.B.
Captain R. Forgan, M.B. (Special Reserve).
Captain W. Fotheringham, M.B. (Special Reserve).
Captain H. R. Friedlander (Special Reserve).
Captain J. K. Gaunt, M.B.

MENTIONED IN DESPATCHES

Captain A. J. Gilchrist, M.B. (Special Reserve).
Temporary Captain J. M. Gillespie, M.B.
Temporary Captain R. H. C. Gompertz, M.B.
Captain T. O. Graham, M.D., F.R.C.S.I. (Special Reserve).
Temporary Captain G. L. Grant (killed).
Captain J. W. Gray, M.B. (Special Reserve).
Temporary Captain J. R. C. Greenlees, D.S.O., M.B.
Temporary Captain E. H. Griffin, M.D.
Captain J. B. Grogan.
Captain B. Goldsmith (Special Reserve).
Temporary Captain S. Gurney-Dixon.
Captain O. Hairsine (Special Reserve).
Temporary Captain C. S. P. Hamilton, D.S.O.
Captain T. Hampson, M.B. (Reserve of Officers).
Temporary Captain F. A. Hampton, M.B.
Captain H. A. Harbison, M.B. (Special Reserve).
Captain J. W. P. Harkness, M.B. (Special Reserve).
Captain R. Hemphill, M.B.
Captain A. H. Heslop, M.B.
Captain J. W. Houston, M.B.
Captain B. Hughes, M.B., F.R.C.S., West Riding Field Ambulance, Royal Army Medical Corps, Territorial Force.
Temporary Captain E. B. Jardine.
Captain A. C. Jebb, M.B. (Special Reserve).
Temporary Captain H. J. R. Jones.
Captain K. W. Jones, D.S.O., M.D. (Special Reserve) (Captain, East Lancashire Field Ambulance, Royal Army Medical Corps, Territorial Force).
Temporary Captain W. Kelsey-Fry.
Temporary Captain R. Kennon, M.D.
Captain F. R. Kerr, D.S.O., M.B. (Special Reserve).
Captain D. R. King, M.B. (Special Reserve).
Temporary Captain H. R. Knowles, M.B.
Temporary Captain D. A. Laird, M.B.
Captain S. D. Large.
Temporary Captain T. A. Lawder, M.B.
Captain N. V. Lothian, M.B.
Temporary Captain E. F. W. MacKenzie, M.B.
Captain W. H. L. McCarthy, M.D. (Special Reserve).
Captain W. McK. H. McCullagh, M.B. (Special Reserve).
Captain C. McN. McCormack, M.B. (Special Reserve).
Captain J. R. McCurdie, M.B. (Special Reserve).
Temporary Captain S. F. McDonald, M.B.
Captain D. Mackie, M.B. (Special Reserve).
Temporary Captain J. M. McLaggan, N.B.
Temporary Captain I. C. MacLean, M.D.

MENTIONED IN DESPATCHES

Temporary Captain J. A. MacLeod, M.B.
Temporary Captain J. W. McLeod, M.B.
Captain J. W. McNee, M.B. (Special Reserve).
Temporary Captain J. H. McNicol, M.B.
Captain C. McQueen.
Temporary Captain D. McVicker, M.B.
Captain J. J. Magner, M.B. (Special Reserve).
Captain D. M. Marr, M.B. (Special Reserve).
Temporary Captain E. K. Martin, F.R.C.S.
Captain A. J. A. Menzies, D.S.O., M.B.
Temporary Captain G. Millar, M.B.
Captain S. Miller, M.B. (Special Reserve).
Captain T. MacK. Miller (Special Reserve).
Captain J. P. Mitchell, M.D. (Special Reserve).
Captain T. J. Mitchell, M.B.
Captain H. G. Monteith, D.S.O.
Captain G. T. Mullaly, M.B., F.R.C.S. (Special Reserve).
Temporary Captain W. G. Mumford, M.B., F.R.C.S.
Temporary Captain F. L. Nash-Wortham, F.R.C.S. Edin.
Temporary Captain G. E. Neligan, M.B., F.R.C.S.
Captain R. E. U. Newman, M.B.
Captain C. M. Nicol, M.B.
Captain A. P. O'Connor, M.B.
Captain J. A. O'Driscoll (Special Reserve).
Captain J. J. O'Keeffe, M.B.
Captain E. M. O'Neill, M.B.
Temporary Captain C. J. R. P. O'Reilly.
Temporary Captain C. J. O'Reilly, M.D.
Captain W. H. O'Riordan.
Captain K. L. O'Sullivan (Special Reserve).
Captain R. C. Ozanne, M.B. (Special Reserve).
Temporary Captain T. E. Parker, M.B.
Captain G. S. Parkinson.
Temporary Captain H. W. Parnis, M.D.
Captain H. M. J. Perry.
Captain G. Petit.
Temporary Captain M. Peto, M.B.
Captain E. Phillips, M.B.
Temporary Captain W. B. Purchase.
Captain W. T. Quinlan (Special Reserve).
Captain A. Ramsbottom, M.D. (Special Reserve) (Captain, East Lancashire Field Ambulance, Royal Army Medical Corps, Territorial Force).
Temporary Captain G. Rankine, M.B.
Temporary Captain E. L. N. Rhodes.
Temporary Captain O. Richards, D.S.O., M.D., F.R.C.S.

MENTIONED IN DESPATCHES

Temporary Captain J. E. H. Roberts, M.B., F.R.C.S.
Temporary Captain R. E. Roberts.
Temporary Captain Robert Cecil Robertson, M.B.
Captain E. Robinson, M.B. (Special Reserve).
Temporary Captain H. A. Ronn, M.B.
Captain A. W. Russell, M.B. (Special Reserve).
Captain E. U. Russell.
Temporary Captain W. A. Russell, M.B.
Captain P. Sampson, D.S.O.
Captain H. B. Sherlock (Special Reserve).
Captain W. C. Smales.
Captain Herbert Smith (Special Reserve).
Temporary Captain J. F. Smith, M.B.
Temporary Captain P. Smith.
Captain S. H. Smith.
Temporary Captain T. V. Somerville.
Captain C. W. Sparks (Special Reserve).
Temporary Captain D. B. Spence.
Temporary Captain D. J. S. Stephen, M.D.
Captain G. H. Stevenson, M.B. (Special Reserve).
Temporary Captain James S. Stewart, M.B.
Temporary Captain G. Stiell.
Captain E. A. Sutton.
Captain R. G. H. Tate, M.D.
Captain M. R. Taylor, M.B. (Special Reserve).
Temporary Captain F. R. Thornton, M. B.
Captain W. O. Tobias, M.B. (Special Reserve).
Captain F. T. Turner.
Captain W. Tyrrell, M.B. (Reserve of Officers).
Captain T. Walker, M.B. (Special Reserve).
Temporary Captain S. L. Walker, M.B.
Captain Q. V. B. Wallace, M.D. (Special Reserve).
Captain S. J. A. H. Walshe, D.S.O. ,M.B. (Special Reserve).
Captain H. K. Ward, M.B. (Special Reserve).
Captain J. H. Ward, M.B. (Special Reserve).
Captain A. G. Wells.
Temporary Captain A. W. Weston, M.B.
. Captain M. J. Williamson, M.B.
Temporary Captain I. S. Wilson, M.D., F.R.C.S.
Temporary Captain C. G. L. Wolf, M.D.
Captain F. Worthington, M.B.
Captain A. R. Wright, M.B.
Captain T. W. Wylie, M.B. (Special Reserve).
Temporary Captain R. F. Young, M.B.
Temporary Lieutenant D. C. Alexander, M.B.
Temporary Lieutenant J. E. Barnes, M.B.

MENTIONED IN DESPATCHES

Temporary Lieutenant C. M. Bernays.
Temporary Lieutenant J. H. Boag, M.B.
Temporary Lieutenant H. E. A. Boldero.
Temporary Lieutenant C. A. Boyd, M.D.
Late Temporary Lieutenant A. E. Brown.
Temporary Lieutenant B. S. Browne, M.B.
Late Temporary Lieutenant P. Cagney.
Temporary Lieutenant J. Caton-Shelmerdine.
Late Temporary Lieutenant H. P. Costobadie, F.R.C.S. Edin.
Temporary Lieutenant W. E. David, M.B.
Temporary Lieutenant C. G. Douglas, M.D.
Temporary Lieutenant J. Dunbar, M.B.
Temporary Lieutenant J. C. Dunn, M.D.
Late Temporary Lieutenant B. V. Dunne, M.B.
Temporary Lieutenant J. D. Driberg.
Temporary Lieutenant R. H. Fothergill, M.B.
Temporary Lieutenant H. C. Godding.
Late Temporary Lieutenant R. J. Harley-Mason.
Temporary Lieutenant R. A. Hughes, M.D.
Late Temporary Lieutenant P. W. James, M.D.
Temporary Lieutenant C. A. Kenny.
Temporary Lieutenant J. T. Kirkland, M.B.
Temporary Lieutenant M. MacKenzie.
Temporary Lieutenant O. G. Maginness.
Temporary Lieutenant R. H. McGillycuddy.
Temporary Lieutenant T. Meagher, M.B.
Temporary Lieutenant A. F. Menzies, M.D. (Lieutenant, Canadian Army Medical Corps).
Temporary Lieutenant C. S. L. Roberts.
Temporary Lieutenant A. R. Roche.
Temporary Lieutenant H. A. Rowell.
Temporary Lieutenant L. D. Saunders.
Temporary Lieutenant C. A. Smallhorn.
Late Temporary Lieutenant A. C. S. Smith.
Temporary Lieutenant J. F. Steven, M.B.
Temporary Lieutenant J. K. Stewart.
Temporary Lieutenant T. Strain, M.D.
Temporary Lieutenant R. H. Tribe.
Temporary Lieutenant H. B. Walker, M.B.
Temporary Lieutenant D. G. Watson, M.B. (died of wounds).
Temporary Lieutenant W. N. Watson, M.B.
Temporary Lieutenant J. R. M. Whigham.
Temporary Lieutenant N. S. Whitton, M.B.
Temporary Lieutenant G. S. Williams, M.D. (Lieutenant, Canadian Army Medical Corps).
Late Temporary Lieutenant J. B. Wood, M.B.

MENTIONED IN DESPATCHES

Temporary Lieutenant A. F. Wright, M.B.
Quartermaster and Honorary Major H. W. Glover.
Quartermaster and Honorary Major J. B. Short.
Quartermaster and Honorary Captain G. A. Benson, Reserve of Officers
Quartermaster and Honorary Captain E. J. Buckley.
Quartermaster and Honorary Lieutenant A. P. Barnard.
Quartermaster and Honorary Lieutenant E. Birch.
Quartermaster and Honorary Lieutenant T. D. Conway.
Quartermaster and Honorary Lieutenant C. H. Cooper.
Quartermaster and Honorary Lieutenant F. Davis.
Quartermaster and Honorary Lieutenant C. A. Figg.
Quartermaster and Honorary Lieutenant W. H. Giddings.
Quartermaster and Honorary Lieutenant R. H. Green.
Quartermaster and Honorary Lieutenant J. Jackson.
Quartermaster and Honorary Lieutenant E. O'Hara.
Quartermaster and Honorary Lieutenant E. V. Saunders.
Quartermaster and Honorary Lieutenant E. H. Senior.
Quartermaster and Honorary Lieutenant W. A. Taylor.
Serjeant-Major H. J. Angell.
Quartermaster-Serjeant R. C. Blair.
Serjeant-Major H. S. Boxshall.
Acting Serjeant-Major W. H. Brown.
Serjeant-Major J. B. Cantrell.
Serjeant-Major W. H. Chudleigh.
Acting Serjeant-Major J. Davis.
Serjeant-Major F. W. Goodread.
Serjeant-Major J. H. Jones.
Serjeant-Major W. Merchant.
Serjeant-Major W. A. Muirhead.
Acting Serjeant-Major C. Williams.
Quartermaster-Serjeant W. C. Prince.
Quartermaster-Serjeant A. Bell.
Quartermaster-Serjeant J. E. Crawley.
Quartermaster-Serjeant L. S. Ellis.
Quartermaster-Serjeant S. M. Gawthorne.
Quartermaster-Serjeant R. E. Halford.
Quartermaster-Serjeant R. G. Leggett.
Quartermaster-Serjeant W. H. Parr.
Quartermaster-Serjeant T. C. Prewett.
Quartermaster-Serjeant C. E. Rouse.
Quartermaster-Serjeant F. Sparks.
Quartermaster-Serjeant R. Sproule.
Quartermaster-Serjeant W. Stokes.
Quartermaster-Serjeant J. G. Thomas.
Staff-Serjeant J. J. Abbott.
Staff-Serjeant E. Alexander.

MENTIONED IN DESPATCHES

Staff-Serjeant W. A. Beckett.
Staff-Serjeant R. R. Benham.
Staff-Serjeant L. V. Bilbee.
Staff-Serjeant R. Boddy.
Staff-Serjeant C. E. Bull.
Staff-Serjeant S. Collins.
Staff-Serjeant E. Connor.
Staff-Serjeant W. A. Clenshaw.
Staff-Serjeant E. Cragg.
Staff-Serjeant W. G. Delamare.
Staff-Serjeant J. G. Eves.
Staff-Serjeant T. French.
Staff-Serjeant A. F. Gibbs.
Staff-Serjeant W. C. Hampson.
Staff-Serjeant R. Herbert.
Staff-Serjeant L. Higgins.
Staff-Serjeant M. W. Hutchings.
Staff-Serjeant C. H. Hyde.
Staff-Serjeant W. Lawson.
Staff-Serjeant T. Lythgoe.
Staff-Serjeant H. Mayes.
Serjeant (Acting Staff-Serjeant) F. J. R. Money.
Staff-Serjeant W. C. Savegar.
Staff-Serjeant W. T. Stovold.
Staff-Serjeant C. B. Symes.
Staff-Serjeant E. A. Young.
Serjeant G. H. Botten.
Serjeant J. T. Brown.
Corporal (Acting Serjeant) G. Burdett.
Serjeant W. G. W. Clark.
Serjeant G. Coleman.
Corporal (Acting Serjeant) W. J. Collins.
Serjeant J. Cooper.
Serjeant A. G. Cripps.
Serjeant J. Douglas.
Serjeant E. Dugmore.
Serjeant G. Dunn.
Serjeant J. T. Emerson.
Serjeant H. E. Fawden.
Serjeant J. Fenton.
Serjeant C. K. Grigg.
Serjeant T. H. Harding.
Serjeant E. Hardy.
Serjeant J. W. Hastings (Special Reserve).
Serjeant F. Horn.
Serjeant J. Howitt.

MENTIONED IN DESPATCHES

Serjeant J. G. Julyan.
Serjeant H. Langley.
Serjeant F. H. Lucas.
Serjeant W. J. McClay.
Serjeant J. P. Makeham.
Serjeant G. Oliver.
Serjeant F. H. Perkins.
Corporal (Acting Serjeant) J. B. Purvis.
Serjeant H. W. Selden.
Corporal (Acting Serjeant) V. Smith.
Serjeant J. A. Stoney.
Serjeant E. Suckling.
Serjeant E. F. Taylor.
Serjeant F. C. Weare.
Corporal W. Ahearn.
Corporal R. Atkinson.
Corporal H. P. Bird.
Private (Acting Corporal) G. W. Bradford.
Corporal G. A. Doyle.
Corporal H. A. Ely.
Corporal J. A. Hewitt.
Corporal F. G. Marrable.
Corporal G. T. Platford.
Private (Acting Corporal) A. Pullen.
Private (Acting Corporal) T. Roberts.
Corporal A. J. Sage.
Corporal A. J. Stirk.
Corporal W. Strachan.
Corporal W. J. Twidell.
Corporal W. Walton.
Lance-Corporal A. Avery.
Private (Acting Lance-Corporal) C. A. Banyard.
Private (Acting Lance-Corporal) F. Clapton.
Private V. H. Andrews.
Private F. Bailey.
Private F. J. Baxter.
Private F. Best.
Private E. W. Bowsher.
Private E. J. Biggins.
Private J. R. Bray.
Private C. J. Brooks.
Private T. H. Brooke.
Private G. Brown.
Private W. O. Browne.
Private R. Buckly.

MENTIONED IN DESPATCHES

Private F. G. Bush.
Private F. Capes.
Private J. Carleton.
Private R. W. Cathrine.
Private R. J. Coles.
Private G. H. Cotterell.
Private W. Craib.
Private E. Dew.
Private H. Dodsworth.
Private G. Dunlop.
Private G. Falkner.
Private T. Foreman.
Private T. Gray.
Private T. Hackett.
Private G. Harding.
Private M. Hardingham.
Private W. R. Harris.
Private W. Henry.
Private W. T. Herrick.
Private C. E. Heywood.
Private J. Higham.
Private C. A. T. Hughes.
Private W. Hughes.
Private H. Kearney.
Private T. Kelly.
Private R. Laws.
Private F. Leakey.
Private J. Lewis.
Private J. Ludlow.
Private W. Marchant.
Private W. H. Marklew.
Private G. Marsh.
Private J. Masters.
Private R. G. Meades.
Private G. Mercer.
Private J. Morris.
Private R. New.
Private J. W. Nicholson.
Private M. Ogden.
Private W. Orme.
Private W. Owen.
Private J. Peacock.
Private R. Pemberton.
Private J. Reed.
Private G. C. Richards.
Private C. M. H. Richardson.
Private V. T. Roberts.
Private A. T. Rose.
Private H. Saunders.
Private R. R. Sturrock.
Private H. Scandrett.
Private H. Shaw.
Private W. Smith.
Private E. Strangeways.
Private R. Treglown.
Private W. Valentine.
Private G. Waller.
Private E. Walton.
Private F. G. Whitbread.
Private S. W. White.
Private L. Whitaker.
Private A. Y. Williamson.
Private F. W. Woolnough.
Private C. Wright.

ROYAL ARMY MEDICAL CORPS (TERRITORIAL FORCE).
Colonel J. V. W. Rutherford.
Colonel E. O. Wight (Lieutenant-Colonel, retired pay).
Lieutenant-Colonel L. J. Blandford, M.D.
Lieutenant-Colonel T. F. Dewar, M.D.
Major C. J. Martin, M.B.
Major F. Whalley, M.B., West Riding Field Ambulance.
Lieutenant-Colonel S. G. Barling, M.B., F.R.C.S., South Midland Field Ambulance.
Temporary Lieutenant-Colonel W. A. Benson, Northumbrian Field Ambulance.
Lieutenant-Colonel W. K. Clayton, Yorkshire Mounted Brigade Field Ambulance.

MENTIONED IN DESPATCHES

Temporary Lieutenant-Colonel H. Collinson, M.B., F.R.C.S., West Riding Field Ambulance.
Temporary Lieutenant-Colonel L. P. Demetriadi, M.D., F.R.C.S. Edin., West Riding Casualty Clearing Station.
Lieut.-Colonel F. Hawthorn, M.D., Northumbrian Field Ambulance.
Lieutenant-Colonel C. H. Howkins, South Midland Field Ambulance.
Temporary Lieutenant-Colonel E. Lloyd-Williams, London Field Ambulance.
Temporary Major (temporary Lieutenant-Colonel) H. G. G. Mackenzie, M.D., Home Counties Field Ambulance.
Lieutenant-Colonel A. Milne-Thomson, Wessex Field Ambulance.
Lieutenant-Colonel W. M. O'Connor, M.D., London Field Ambulance.
Lieutenant-Colonel R. Pickard, M.D., Wessex Field Ambulance.
Lieutenant-Colonel W. Ranson, F.R.C.S., Edin., Northumbrian Field Ambulance (Captain, Royal Army Medical Corps, Special Reserve).
Lieutenant-Colonel A. D. Sharp, West Riding Field Ambulance.
Lieutenant-Colonel A. B. Soltau, M.D., Wessex Field Ambulance.
Major (temporary Lieutenant-Colonel) J. Ward, Home Counties Field Ambulance.
Captain, Territorial Force Reserve, C. G. Watson, F.R.C.S. (temporary Honorary Lieutenant-Colonel, Royal Army Medical Corps).
Lieutenant-Colonel J. Young, M.D., South Midland Field Ambulance.
Major W. B. Armstrong, M.B.
Temporary Major J. W. Bird, D.S.O., London Field Ambulance.
Major J. P. Brown, M.B.
Temporary Major J. C. S. Burkitt, M.D., North Midland Field Ambulance.
Major H. L. de Legh, M.D.
Major A. Don, M.B., F.R.C.S., Edin., Highland Casualty Clearing Station.
Major A. D. Ducat, M.B.
Captain (temporary Major) C. H. S. Frankau, M.B., F.R.C.S., London Casualty Clearing Station.
Major G. H. L. Hammerton, Yorkshire Mounted Brigade Field Ambulance.
Major T. Kay, M.B.
Major A. E. Kidd, M.B., Highland Field Ambulance.
Major W. B. Mackay, M.D.
Major E. C. Montgomery-Smith, London Field Ambulance.
Temporary Major T. H. Peyton, M.D., Home Counties Field Ambulance.
Major T. P. Puddicombe, Wessex Field Ambulance.
Major W. F. Roe.
Major J. S. Y. Rogers, M.B.
Captain (temporary Major) H. B. Sproat, M.D., West Riding Field Ambulance.

MENTIONED IN DESPATCHES

Surgeon-Major A. R. Stoddart, M.B., West Yorkshire Regiment, Territorial Force.
Surgeon-Major E. G. Stocker, Wessex Divisional Engineers, Royal Engineers, Territorial Force.
Captain J. W. Anderson, M.B.
Captain M. H. Barton.
Captain H. T. Bates, M.B., West Riding Casualty Clearing Hospital.
Captain F. G. Bennett, North Midland Field Ambulance.
Captain J. M. Bowie, M.D.
Surgeon-Captain R. W. Branthwaite, Territorial Force Reserve.
Captain T. Carnwath, M.B.
Captain F. S. Carson, M.B., London Sanitary Company.
Captain N. G. Chavasse, M.B.
Captain S. Clark, London Field Ambulance.
Captain E. A. Cooper, London Sanitary Company.
Captain M. Coplans, M.D., London Field Ambulance.
Temporary Capt. J. W. Craven, M.B., Northumbrian Field Ambulance.
Captain T. W. Crowley, Northumbrian Field Ambulance.
Captain J. Dale, M.B.
Captain S. H. Daukes, M.B., London Sanitary Company.
Captain H. B. F. Dixon, M.B., London Field Ambulance.
Captain J. Downie, M.B., Yorkshire Mounted Brigade Field Ambulance
Captain C. N. Draycott, London Sanitary Company.
Captain R. Errington, M.B., Northumbrian Field Ambulance.
Temporary Captain J. H. Fletcher, R.A.M.C.
Captain J. Golding, London Sanitary Company.
Captain C. W. Greene, M.B., F.R.C.S., Home Counties Field Ambulance.
Captain H. S. Hollis, M.B., Home Counties Field Ambulance.
Captain G. H. Hunt, M.B., London Casualty Clearing Station.
Captain D. M. Johnston, M.B., Home Counties Field Ambulance.
Captain W. B. Keith, M.B., Home Counties Field Ambulance.
Captain G. Q. Lennane, F.R.C.S.I., London Sanitary Company.
Captain H. Lightstone.
Captain H. B. Low, M.D., Northumbrian Field Ambulance.
Captain J. MacMillan, M.B., London Field Ambulance.
Temporary Captain J. R. Marrack, M.B., R.A.M.C.
Captain G. S. Melvin, M.B., Highland Field Ambulance.
Captain F. Metcalfe, M.B., Northumbrian Field Ambulance.
Captain J. Murdoch, M.B., F.R.C.S. Edin.
Captain A. W. Nuthall, F.R.C.S., South Midland Casualty Clearing Station.
Captain W. J. C. B. Pitt, South Midland Casualty Clearing Station.
Captain J. A. C. Scott, M.B.
Captain H. J. D. Smythe, South Midland Field Ambulance.
Captain R. E. T. Tatlow, M.D.

MENTIONED IN DESPATCHES

Captain R. M. Vick, London Field Ambulance.
Captain J. A. Watt, M.B., London Field Ambulance.
Captain G. White, London Sanitary Company.
Captain H. F. Wilkin, F.R.C.S. Edin.
Captain G. S. Williamson, South Midland Field Ambulance.
Captain W. L. R. Wood.
Lieutenant S. R. Foster, M.B., North Midland Field Ambulance.
Quartermaster and Honorary Lieutenant E. H. Beeton, West Riding Field Ambulance.
Quartermaster and Honorary Lieutenant M. Cohen, Northumbrian Field Ambulance.
Quartermaster and Honorary Lieutenant G. W. Harris, Home Counties Field Ambulance.
Quartermaster and Honorary Lieutenant E. T. Jones, West Riding Field Ambulance.
Quartermaster and Honorary Lieutenant J. Keogh, Home Counties Field Ambulance.
Quartermaster and Honorary Lieutenant R. D. Matthews, West Riding Field Ambulance.
Quartermaster and Honorary Lieutenant J. H. Maunder, Wessex Field Ambulance.
Quartermaster and Honorary Lieutenant H. C. O'Kill, Home Counties Field Ambulance.
Quartermaster and Honorary Lieutenant C. T. Ross, West Riding Field Ambulance.
Quartermaster and Honorary Lieutenant D. P. Taylor, South Midland Casualty Clearing Station.
Serjeant-Major E. T. Moxham, Welsh Field Ambulance.
Staff-Serjeant G. E. Bellairs, London Sanitary Company.
Staff-Serjeant J. Clough, Northumbrian Field Ambulance.
Serjeant E. T. Baker, Home Counties Ambulance.
Serjeant H. C. Blench, London Sanitary Company.
Serjeant W. Brooks, West Riding Field Ambulance.
Serjeant W. G. Carroll, London Field Ambulance.
Serjeant W. T. Charlton, Northumbrian Field Ambulance.
Serjeant W. W. Cowans, Northumbrian Field Ambulance.
Serjeant J. H. Cross, Wessex Field Ambulance.
Serjeant J. R. Ellison, Northumbrian Field Ambulance.
Serjeant J. W. Embleton, West Riding Field Ambulance.
Serjeant (Acting Staff-Serjeant) J. J. Gordon, Highland Casualty Clearing Station.
Serjeant A. Holtum, Home Counties Field Ambulance.
Serjeant C. R. Lee, Welsh Field Ambulance.
Serjeant A. T. Price, Wessex Field Ambulance.
Serjeant P. W. Tighe, Wessex Field Ambulance.
Serjeant M. H. F. Williams, Wessex Field Ambulance.

MENTIONED IN DESPATCHES

Serjeant H. Willmore, South Midland Casualty Clearing Station.
Serjeant G. W. Wright, Northumbrian Field Ambulance.
Corporal W. J. Howell, Wessex Field Ambulance.
Corporal J. R. Leadbetter, London Sanitary Company.
Acting Corporal S. C. Rigg, London Sanitary Company.
Corporal (Acting Serjeant) P. Smith, Highland Field Ambulance.
Lance-Corporal D. Brook, West Riding Field Ambulance.
Lance-Corporal E. C. Dolton, Home Counties Field Ambulance.
Lance-Corporal W. Rae, Highland Field Ambulance.
Lance-Corporal A. Stratton, London Sanitary Company.
Private W. Bailey, West Riding Field Ambulance.
Private W. Bailey, Home Counties Field Ambulance.
Private G. S. Beaton, Highland Casualty Clearing Station.
Private F. Y. Bodger, Northumbrian Field Ambulance.
Private W. Cambourne, Home Counties Field Ambulance.
Private E. Coleman, Home Counties Field Ambulance.
Private H. D. Dodd, Welsh Border Mounted Brigade Field Ambulance.
Private J. F. Duffy, West Riding Field Ambulance.
Private S. T. Eeles, attached 93rd Field Ambulance.
Private G. C. Goode, South Wales Mounted Brigade Field Ambulance.
Private P. Harvey, West Riding Field Ambulance.
Private A. E. Holmes, Yorkshire Mounted Brigade Ambulance.
Private F. Jackson, West Riding Casualty Clearing Station.
Private D. T. Y. Middleton, Wessex Field Ambulance.
Private H. J. Osborne, London Sanitary Company.
Private R. Rowden, Home Counties Field Ambulance.
Private N. Russell, Yorkshire Mounted Brigade Ambulance.
Private G. R. Todd, London Field Ambulance.
Private E. J. Witherstone, South Wales Mounted Brigade Field Ambulance.
Private R. T. Wood, London Field Ambulance.

Nursing Service.
Queen Alexandra's Imperial Military Nursing Service.

Matron Miss M. M. Blakeley.
Matron Miss M. Mark.
Matron Miss A. B. Smith, R.R.C.
Acting Matron Miss E. Barber.
Acting Matron Miss E. C. Cheetham.
Acting Matron Miss E. M. Denne.
Acting Matron Miss E. C. Fox.
Acting Matron Miss E. H. Hordley.
Acting Matron Miss E. M. Lyde.
Acting Matron Miss L. E. Mackay.
Acting Matron Miss E. J. Minns.
Acting Matron Miss B. F. Perkins.

MENTIONED IN DESPATCHES

Acting Matron Miss C. G. Stronach.
Acting Matron Miss M. M. Tunley.
Acting Matron Miss A. L. Walker.
Sister Miss J. S. G. Gardner.
Sister Miss M. O'C. McCreery.
Sister Miss A. C. Mowat.
Sister Miss K. Roscoe.
Sister Miss L. M. Toller.
Sister Miss M. B. Williams.
Acting Sister Miss M. R. Casswell.
Acting Sister Miss M. T. Casswell.
Acting Sister Miss G. H. Caulfeild.
Acting Sister Miss W. E. Eardley.
Acting Sister Miss A. H. Esden.
Acting Sister Miss M. G. C. Foley.
Acting Sister Miss M. Hale.
Acting Sister Miss K. H. M. Holmes.
Acting Sister Miss G. M. Jones.
Acting Sister Miss E. M. Long.
Acting Sister Miss J. D. C. Macpherson.
Acting Sister Miss C. Sandbach.
Acting Sister Miss M. H. Smyth.
Acting Sister Miss M. E. Stewart.
Acting Sister Miss C. V. E. Thompson.
Acting Sister Miss A. P. Wilson.
Acting Sister Miss M. Wood.

Queen Alexandra's Imperial Military Nursing Service Reserve.

Miss A. I. Baird.
Miss A. J. Bailey.
Miss M. S. Barwell.
Miss I. E. Church.
Miss M. A. Cain.
Miss C. Cameron.
Miss G. E. Custance.
Miss A. B. Denton.
Miss L. Evans.
Miss M. Gow.
Miss M. D. E. Knight.
Miss K. E. Luard.
Miss M. J. L. Lyons.
Miss C. Macleod.
Miss V. M. Marsh.
Miss M. Plaskett.
Miss H. F. Starbuck.
Miss M. R. Thomson.
Miss M. E. Vernon-Harcourt.
Miss E. Ward.
Miss E. F. Watkins.
Miss E. Wilson-Jayne.
Miss E. Willoughby.

Australian Nurses working on Queen Alexandra's Military Nursing Service Reserve.

Miss B. G. Cheeseman.
Miss M. Cumming.
Miss E. M. Hamilton.
Miss K. R. Heriot.
Miss M. A. Raye.

MENTIONED IN DESPATCHES

New Zealand Nurses working on Queen Alexandra's Military Nursing Service Reserve.

Miss E. L. Craig. Miss E. C. Jordan.

TERRITORIAL FORCE NURSING SERVICE.

Miss M. E. Atkins.
Miss M. D. Bain.
Miss A. Charlesworth.
Miss K. Davidson.
Miss E. Dodd.
Miss M. Edwards.
Miss M. E. Gregory.
Miss J. E. Hills.
Miss M. Hendry.
Miss M. G. Keene.
Miss A. M. Kelson.
Miss E. Kerr.
Miss M. C. Laing.
Miss D. A. Laughton.
Miss K. M. Martin.
Miss A. Lofthouse.
Miss J. M. Murray.
Miss A. Pear.
Miss F. M. Rice.
Miss M. E. Ruck.
Miss E. V. Scott.
Miss E. D. Smaill.
Mrs. M. Walker.
Miss A. C. Watson.
Miss M. Wharton.
Miss M. E. Williamson.
Miss I. C. Woodford.

CIVIL HOSPITAL RESERVE.

Miss M. Alexander (Birmingham General Hospital).
Miss W. H. Amos (London Hospital).
Miss E. E. Appleton (St. Bartholomew's Hospital).
Miss A. C. Binnian (St. Bartholomew's Hospital).
Miss H. L. Brakefield (St. Bartholomew's Hospital).
Miss K. A. Brothwell (The London Hospital).
Miss S. B. Burrell (The London Hospital).
Miss K. M. Carthew (The London Hospital).
Miss A. E. Casserley (Royal Southern Hospital, Liverpool).
Miss N. G. Clements (The London Hospital).
Miss H. Daly (The London Hospital).
Miss A. Duncan (Glasgow Royal Infirmary).
Miss E. J. Evans (King Edward VII Hospital, Cardiff).
Miss B. D. Ford (Westminster Hospital).
Miss E. V. Gascoigne (St. Bartholomew's Hospital).
Miss M. Gow (Royal Infirmary, Edinburgh).
Miss C. M. Hogarth (St. Thomas's Hospital).
Miss M. Hopton (Charing Cross Hospital).
Miss S. A. Jarvis (St. Bartholomew's Hospital).
Miss K. Latham (St. Bartholomew's Hospital).
Miss G. D. McCrae (Cheltenham General Hospital).
Miss E. H. Morley.
Miss R. M. Phillips (The London Hospital).
Miss J. W. Walker (Kilmarnock Infirmary).
Miss E. Ward (St. Bartholomew's Hospital).

MENTIONED IN DESPATCHES

Miss A. Weatherstone (Edinburgh Royal Infirmary).
Miss L. Winpenny (Royal Victoria Hospital, Newcastle-on-Tyne).
Miss M. Wolsey (The London Hospital).

Scottish Red Cross.

Miss K. F. Young.

British Red Cross Society.

Lady Gifford.
Temporary Honorary Lieutenant-Colonel E. Stewart, M.D., Royal Army Medical Corps.
Major A. Y. G. Campbell.
Captain A. S. Collard.
Temporary Honorary Captain in Army P. C. Dickens.
Temporary Honorary Captain in Army E. Duveen.
Temporary Honorary Lieutenant in Army R. K. Rumford.
Doctor R. Pryce-Mitchell.
H. D. Bayley.
Section Officer G. B. Marshall.
C. Clipperton.
J. B. Maxwell.
Driver H. T. Martin.
Section Leader J. Innes.
Miss A. M. Bailey.
Miss R. E. Crowdy.
Miss E. J. Densham.
Miss F. Law.
Miss M. Whitson.
Mrs. A. de Winton.
Miss E. Williams.

MISCELLANEOUS.

Officers attached to R.A.M.C.

Captain E. E. Austen, London Regiment, Territorial Force.
Quartermaster and Honorary Captain J. H. Redstone (Reserve of Officers).
Temporary Quartermaster and Honorary Lieutenant in Army G. Kerns.

MEDICAL SERVICES.

Members of the American, Chicago and Harvard Units attached to Nos. 22 and 23 General Hospitals, Etaples.

Doctor P. S. Chancellor.
Doctor W. J. Dodd.
Doctor W. E. Faulkner.
Doctor V. Kazanjian.
Doctor J. M. Neff.
Matron Miss M. G. Parsons.
Matron Miss I. M. Patton.
Sister Miss M. K. Adams.

MENTIONED IN DESPATCHES
Army Veterinary Corps.
Major H. E. Gibbs.
Major (temporary Lieutenant-Colonel) R. H. Holmes, F.R.C.V.S.
Major H. Kirby.
Major J. A. B. McGowan.
Major K. McL. McKenzie.
Major H. S. Mosley.
Major J. S. Nimmo.
Major A. Olver, F.R.C.V.S.
Major F. C. O'Rorke, F.R.C.V.S.
Major E. J. Wadley.
Temporary Major A. S. Head, F.R.C.V.S. (Captain, Reserve of Officers)
Captain E. Hearne.
Captain (temporary Major) A. B. Mattinson, F.R.C.V.S. (Special Reserve).
Temporary Captain C. W. Makinson.
Lieutenant J. G. T. Edwards (Special Reserve).
Temporary Captain W. B. De Vine.
Temporary Quartermaster and Honorary Lieutenant J. Fisher.
Temporary Quartermaster and Honorary Lieutenant J. F. Ives.
Temporary Quartermaster and Honorary Lieutenant W. H. Mawdsley.
Serjeant-Major F. H. Young.
Farrier Staff-Serjeant R. Woolley.
Staff-Serjeant C. H. Barrow (Special Reserve).
Staff-Serjeant H. Carrigan.
Staff-Serjeant G. Langley.
Staff-Serjeant J. G. Robertson.
Staff-Serjeant R. W. Vane.
Staff-Serjeant P. J. Wellings (Special Reserve).
Serjeant C. V. D. Hay.
Serjeant W. Knowler.
Serjeant F. Nelson.
Serjeant C. Roberts.

Army Veterinary Corps (Territorial Force).
Major E. M. Perry, F.R.C.V.S.
Captain (temporary Major) J. Abson, F.R.C.V.S.
Captain C. Hartley, F.R.C.V.S.
Lieutenant T. Bagshaw.
Serjeant D. B. Douglas, Northumbrian Division.
Corporal F. Lucas, South Midland Division.
Lance-Corporal C. Taylor, South Midland Division.
Shoeing-Smith A. Webb, South Midland Division.

Remount Service.
Honorary Colonel (temporary Brigadier-General) C. L. Bates, D.S.O., Northumberland Yeomanry.

MENTIONED IN DESPATCHES

Brevet Colonel W. G. Massy, retired pay.
Temporary Lieutenant-Colonel A. D. Acland (Lieutenant-Colonel, Territorial Force Reserve).
Lieutenant-Colonel J. W. Yardley, retired pay.
Major F. H. Eadon, Reserve of Officers.
Riding Master and Honorary Major E. G. Tomblings, retired pay.
Temporary Major (Lieutenant, Reserve of Officers) W. P. C. Cantrell-Hubbersty.
Regimental Serjeant-Major F. T. Nash.
Squadron Serjeant-Major M. W. Tyler.

Army Chaplains' Department.

Rev. F. I. Anderson, M.A., Chaplain to the Forces, 3rd Class.
Rev. P. O. Ashby, M.A., Chaplain, 4th Class (Territorial Force).
Rev. C. F. Baines, M.A., Chaplain to the Forces, 1st Class.
Rev. J. H. Baynham, M.A., Chaplain to the Forces, 3rd Class.
Rev. H. W. Blackburne, M.A., Chaplain to the Forces, 3rd Class.
Rev. T. Brook, B.D., LL.D., Chaplain to the Forces, 3rd Class.
Rev. D. F. Carey, M.A., Chaplain to the Forces, 3rd Class.
Rev. J. Clayton, Temporary Chaplain to the Forces, 4th Class.
Rev. M. W. T. Conran, Temporary Chaplain to the Forces, 4th Class.
Rev. D. S. Corkey, Temporary Chaplain to the Forces, 4th Class.
Rev. J. J. M. Cowper, M.A., Chaplain to the Forces.
Rev. E .R. Day, M.A., Chaplain to the Forces, 1st Class.
Rev. W. Donlevy, Temporary Chaplain to the Forces, 4th Class.
Rev. F. H. Drinkwater, Temporary Chaplain to the Forces, 4th Class.
Rev. J. L. O. B. Findlay, Chaplain to the Forces, 3rd Class.
Rev. J. Firth, Temporary Chaplain to the Forces, 4th Class.
Rev. E. A. Fitch, Chaplain to the Forces, 4th Class.
Rev. H. J. Fleming, M.A., Chaplain to the Forces, 3rd Class.
Rev. A. S .G. Gilchrist, Temporary Chaplain to the Forces, 4th Class.
Rev. T. S. Goudge, B.A., Chaplain to the Forces, 3rd Class.
Rev. L. Green, Temporary Chaplain to the Forces, 4th Class.
Rev. H. V. Griffiths, Temporary Chaplain to the Forces, 4th Class.
Rev. P. Grobel, Temporary Chaplain to the Forces.
Rev. T. Harris, Temporary Chaplain to the Forces, 4th Class.
Rev. A. L. Helps, Temporary Chaplain to the Forces, 4th Class.
Rev. F. A. Hill, B.A., Chaplain to the Forces, 1st Class.
Rev. R. J. B. Irwin, Ecclesiastical Establishments, Bengal.
Rev. W. S. Jaffray, C.M.G., Chaplain to the Forces, 1st Class.
Rev. W. Keatinge, C.M.G., Chaplain to the Forces, 1st Class.
Rev. J. D. Kelly, Temporary Chaplain to the Forces, 4th Class.
Rev. J. C. Kinnear, M.A., Chaplain to the Forces, 4th Class.
Rev. S. S. Knapp, Temporary Chaplain to the Forces, 4th Class.
Rev. J. Lane-Fox, Temporary Chaplain to the Forces, 4th Class.
Rev. W. P. G. McCormick, Temp. Chaplain to the Forces, 4th Class.

MENTIONED IN DESPATCHES

Rev. A. M. Maclean, B.D., Chaplain, 2nd Class (Territorial Force) (Temporary Chaplain to the Forces, 4th Class, Army Chaplains' Department).
Rev. H. G. Marshall, Chaplain to the Forces, 4th Class.
Rev. C. L. Money-Kyrle, Temporary Chaplain to the Forces, 4th Class.
Rev. E. M. Morgan, Chaplain to the Forces, 1st Class, retired pay.
Rev. A. W. Morrow, Temporary Chaplain to the Forces, 4th Class.
Rev. H. L. Parker, B.A., Chaplain to the Forces, 4th Class.
Rev. J. D. S. Parry-Evans, Chaplain to the Forces, 3rd Class.
Rev. W. R. Paterson, M.A., Chaplain to the Forces, 4th Class.
Rev. S. B. Pelling, Temporary Chaplain to the Forces, 4th Class.
Rev. M. G. J. Ponsonby, Temporary Chaplain to the Forces, 4th Class
Rev. J. Pringle, Canadian Chaplain.
Rev. T. W. Pym, Temporary Chaplain to the Forces, 4th Class.
Rev. C. I Radford, Chaplain to the Forces, 3rd Class.
Rev. B. S. Rawlinson, Temporary Chaplain to the Forces, 4th Class (Assistant Principal Chaplain and temporary Chaplain to the Forces, 2nd Class).
Rev. J. M. Rodger, Temporary Chaplain to the Forces, 4th Class.
Rev. W. H. Sarchet, Temporary Chaplain to the Forces, 4th Class (Honorary Chaplain to the Forces, 3rd Class).
Rev. F. G. Scott, Canadian Chaplain.
Rev. J. M. Simms, C.M.G., D.D., K.H.C., Principal Chaplain (Chaplain to the Forces, 1st Class).
Rev. F. F. S. Smethwick, B.A., Chaplain to the Forces, 4th Class.
Rev. Canon H. K. Southwell, M.A., Chaplain, 1st Class (Territorial Force).
Rev. J. Stack, Temporary Chaplain to the Forces, 4th Class.
Rev. G. Standing, Temporary Chaplain to the Forces, 4th Class (United Board).
Rev. R. A. Stewart, Temporary Chaplain to the Forces, 4th Class.
Rev. N. S. Talbot, Temporary Chaplain to the Forces, 4th Class.
Rev. T. N. Tattersall, Temporary Chaplain to the Forces, 4th Class.
Rev. J. G. W. Tuckey, M.A., Chaplain to the Forces, 1st Class.
Rev. O. S. Watkins, Honorary Chaplain to the Forces, 2nd Class.
Rev. H. M. Webb-Peploe, M.A., Chaplain to the Forces, 3rd Class.
Rev. R. C. L. Williams, B.A., Chaplain to the Forces, 4th Class.
Rev. C. T. T. Wood, Chaplain, 4th Class (Territorial Force).
Rev. A. R. Yeoman, M.A., Chaplain to the Forces, 3rd Class.

STAFF FOR ROYAL ENGINEER SERVICES.
Inspector of Works and Honorary Captain G. H. Bryant.

ARMY ORDNANCE DEPARTMENT.
Lieutenant-Colonel N. B. Bainbridge, D.S.O.
Lieutenant-Colonel H. W. G. Keddie.

MENTIONED IN DESPATCHES

Major (temporary Lieutenant-Colonel) A. R. Oldfield.
First Class Inspector of Ordnance Machinery and Honorary Major (temporary Chief Inspector and Honorary Lieutenant-Colonel) D. Paul.
First Class Inspector of Ordnance Machinery and Honorary Major O. Brown.
First Class Inspector of Ordnance Machinery and Honorary Major J. R. Collacott.
First Class Inspector of Ordnance Machinery and Honorary Major (temporary Chief Inspector and Honorary Lieutenant-Colonel) P. G. Davies.
First Class Inspector of Ordnance Machinery and Honorary Major A. J. Last.
Deputy Commissary of Ordnance and Honorary Captain G. J. Gay.
Assistant Commissary of Ordnance and Honorary Lieutenant (temporary Deputy Commissary of Ordnance and Honorary Captain) A. H. Badcock.
Conductor G. A. Mathews.
Serjeant (Acting Sub-Conductor) W. Carolan.
Staff-Serjeant (Acting Sub-Conductor) G. Pritchard.
Armament Quartermaster-Serjeant (Acting Armament Serjeant-Major) W. Bennett.
Armament Quartermaster-Serjeant (Acting Armament Serjeant-Major) P. Moth.
Armament Staff-Serjeant (Acting Armament Serjeant-Major) T. F. Collier.
Serjeant (Acting Staff-Serjeant) R. Gatenby.
Armament Staff-Serjeant (Acting Armament Serjeant-Major) J. W. Longstaff.
Second Corporal (Acting Staff-Serjeant) H. Cufley.
Private (Acting-Serjeant) T. B. Daniels.
Lance-Corporal (Acting Serjeant) F. J. Webb.
Lance-Corporal (Acting Lance-Serjeant) C. L. Bell.
Private (Acting Corporal) A. Cruickshank.
Private (Acting Corporal) H. W. Pearce.

Army Ordnance Corps.
Armament Staff-Serjeant A. W. Hammant.
Armament Staff-Serjeant W. S. Lesslie.
Private (Acting Staff-Serjeant) H. F. Patrick.

Army Pay Department.
Lieutenant-Colonel P. de S. Bass.
Major H. T. Arnold.
Major C. V. Isacke.
Lieutenant W. J. H. Bilderbeck.

MENTIONED IN DESPATCHES

Temporary Lieutenant R. Blair.
Temporary Lieutenant W. Holman.
Lieutenant G. A. C. Ormsby-Johnson.
Lieutenant H. G. Riley.
Staff-Serjeant-Major W. Moran.
Staff Quartermaster-Serjeant L. V. Carter.
Acting Staff-Serjeant R. J. Warneford.

STATIONERY SERVICES.
Temporary Captain W. H. Clifford.
Temporary Lieutenant R. A. Grieve.
Temporary Lieutenant J. O. Richens.

MILITARY MOUNTED POLICE.
Serjeant-Major A. Baverstock.
Serjeant-Major S. Bennett.
Serjeant A. Ginn (killed).
Quartermaster-Serjeant G. Sherring.
Serjeant R. W. Carr.
Serjeant J. J. Castaldini.
Serjeant A. W. Bray.
Serjeant J. Bulman.
Serjeant C. J. Harris.
Serjeant W. Hay.
Serjeant A. W. Lee.
Serjeant J. T. C. Williams.
Serjeant W. J. Willis (killed).
Serjeant A. Sharp.
Corporal A. M. Scott.
Lance-Corporal S. Allaker.
Lance-Corporal A. H. Butterworth.
Lance-Corporal T. French.
Lance-Corporal E. Thomas.
Acting Serjeant W. Thomas.

MILITARY FOOT POLICE.
Acting Serjeant C. Dale.
Lance-Corporal E. Brace.
Private (Acting Lance-Corporal) W. Gibson.
Lance-Corporal C. Tullett.

AUSTRALIAN ARMY SERVICE CORPS.
Lieutenant-Colonel W. H. Tunbridge, C.B.
Captain J. Hamilton.

AUSTRALIAN NURSING SERVICE.
Miss A. Wyllie.

MENTIONED IN DESPATCHES

Australian Voluntary Hospital.
Miss A. B. Cabriell.   Miss J. B. Buckham.   Miss C. V. Reay.

CANADIAN FORCES.
Canadian Staff.
Lieutenant-Colonel (temporary Brigadier-General) C. J. Armstrong.
Lieutenant-Colonel (temporary Brigadier-General) D. Watson, Canadian Local Forces.
Brevet Colonel (temporary Brigadier-General) T. B. Wood.
Colonel A. E. Ross.
Lieutenant-Colonel C. H. Mitchell.
Brevet Lieutenant-Colonel G. R. Frith, Royal Engineers.
Temporary Major A. B. Cutcliffe.
Major J. H. Elmsley.
Major (temporary Lieutenant-Colonel) G. C. W. Gordon-Hall, Yorkshire Light Infantry.
Major E. de B. Panet, Canadian Local Forces.
Major J. S. Brown, Royal Canadian Regiment.
Captain R. P. Clark, Canadian Local Forces.
Captain J. E. Hahn.
Captain K. A. Murray, Canadian Postal Corps.
Captain R. R. Napier.
Captain A. S. Wright, Canadian Artillery.
Lieutenant R. C. Lalor, Canadian Contingent.
Lieutenant D. McGugan, Canadian Contingent.
Serjeant-Major G. E. Berry, Canadian Contingent.

Canadian Field Artillery.
Lieutenant-Colonel (temporary Brigadier-General) E. W. B. Morrison D.S.O.
Lieutenant-Colonel C. H. Maclaren.
Major C. F. Constantine.
Major E. T. B. Gillmore, 1st Canadian Division, Ammunition Sub-Park.
Major L. C. Goodeve.
Major E. W. Leonard.
Major F. C. Magee.
Captain H. McD. Dunlop, 1st Canadian Division, Ammunition Column.
Lieutenant C. S. Craig.
Lieutenant R. J. Leach, Canadian Heavy Battery.
Lieutenant (temporary Captain) A. T. Paterson.
Lieutenant F. H. Tingley.
Paymaster and Honorary Captain L. S. G. Kelly.

MENTIONED IN DESPATCHES

Serjeant J. R. Langford.
Bombardier G. Quilter.
Gunner V. A. Bleakney.

ROYAL CANADIAN ENGINEERS.

Lieutenant-Colonel W. B. Lindsay.
Captain E. R. Vince.
Lieutenant E. A. Baker.
Lieutenant J. R. Cosgrove.
Lieutenant E. F. Lynn.
Lieutenant J. C. Macdonald.
Lieutenant D. M. Mathieson.
Quartermaster and Honorary Captain C. Shergold (temporary Second Lieutenant, Royal Engineers).
Regimental Serjeant-Major S. A. Ridgwell.
Serjeant W. H. B. Bevan.
Serjeant A. Melville.
Corporal G. Law.
Corporal J. F. Norton.
Lance-Corporal D. B. Jones.
Sapper W. Sinclair.
Sapper F. T. Spencer.

ROYAL CANADIAN DRAGOONS.

Lieutenant-Colonel C. M. Nelles.
Captain F. H. McD. Codville.

LORD STRATHCONA'S HORSE.

Lieutenant-Colonel A. C. Macdonell, D.S.O.
Major J. A. Hesketh, D.S.O.
Captain J. A. Critchley.
Lieutenant D. J. MacDonald.
Corporal J. S. Hewitson.
Private J. M. Dunwoody.

PRINCESS PATRICIA'S CANADIAN LIGHT INFANTRY.

Major (temporary Lieutenant-Colonel) R. T. Pelly (Captain, Loyal North Lancashire Regiment, Special Reserve).
Major D. F. B. Gray.
Lieutenant G. C. Carvell.
Lieutenant R. G. Crawford (died of wounds).
Lieutenant N. A. Edwards (killed).
Company Serjeant-Major A. E. Cordery.
Company Quartermaster-Serjeant S. Godfrey.
Serjeant M. Allan.
Corporal J. M. Christie.
Private A. G. S. Fleming.
Private J. McAllister.

MENTIONED IN DESPATCHES

1st Canadian Infantry Battalion.
Lieutenant-Colonel F. W. Hill.
Captain W. J. A. Lalor.
Lieutenant G. A. Metcalfe (killed).
Private W. C. Large.
Private J. F. Murray.
Private C. D. Smith.

2nd Canadian Infantry Battalion.
Temporary Lieutenant-Colonel A. E. Swift.
Serjeant G. G. Winterbottom.
Serjeant J. K. Young.
Lance-Corporal J. Maxwell.

3rd Canadian Infantry Battalion.
Lieutenant-Colonel (temporary Brigadier-General) R. Rennie, M.V.O.
Captain J. B. Rogers.
Captain F. O. W. Tidy.
Lieutenant G. E. Reid.
Serjeant H. K. Clifton.
Serjeant H. V. Spence.
Lance-Corporal E. H. Jones.

4th Canadian Infantry Battalion.
Lieutenant-Colonel M. A. Colquhoun.
Serjeant H. Hickey (killed).
Lieutenant W. D. Sprinks.
Private J. Millar.

5th Canadian Infantry Battalion.
Lieutenant-Colonel E. Hilliam.
Lieutenant-Colonel G. S. Tuxford.
Major H. M. Dyer.
Captain S. J. Anderson, D.S.O.
Captain J. F. P. Nash, D.S.O.
Lieutenant J. G. Anderson.
Regimental Serjeant-Major A. G. Mackie.
Corporal E. G. McFeat.
Corporal S. Saunders.

7th Canadian Infantry Battalion.
Lieutenant-Colonel V. W. Odlum.   Lieutenant H. H. Owen.
Captain S. D. Gardner.   Serjeant J. J. Fyles.
Captain A. Brooks.   Corporal R. M. Allison.
Lieutenant W. D. Holmes.   Corporal A. E. Hall.
Serjeant J. Holland.   Private W. Paterson.
Private W. McQueen.

8th Canadian Infantry Battalion.
Major G. W. Andrews.   Captain J. M. Prower.   Private H. Tate

MENTIONED IN DESPATCHES

9TH CANADIAN INFANTRY BATTALION.
Major E. J. Ashton.

10TH CANADIAN INFANTRY BATTALION.
Lieutenant-Colonel J. G. Rattray.
Serjeant C. Morrison.
Corporal D. O'Rourke (died of wounds).
Corporal H. R. Smith.

13TH CANADIAN INFANTRY BATTALION.
Major W. H. Clark-Kennedy.   Corporal O. Kranchel.
Lance-Serjeant W. N. Jones.   Private B. J. Connor.

14TH CANADIAN INFANTRY BATTALION.
Regimental Serjeant-Major W. A. Bonshor.
Serjeant E. Cowen.

15TH CANADIAN INFANTRY BATTALION.
Signalling Serjeant W. B. Venner.   Serjeant R. Gilpin.

16TH CANADIAN INFANTRY BATTALION.
Regimental Serjt.-Major J. Kay.   Serjeant W. Le Maitre.
Major W. Rae.   Private E. Appleton.
Captain V. J. Hastings.   Private P. M. Grant.
Major F. Morison, D.S.O.   Private C. Payne.

17TH (RESERVE) CANADIAN INFANTRY BATTALION.
Captain W. Mavor.

22ND CANADIAN INFANTRY BATTALION.
Major A. Roy (killed).   Private A. Deblois.
Private P. A. Lambert.

27TH CANADIAN INFANTRY BATTALION.
Private A. V. Bonner.   Private J. J. Milne.

28TH CANADIAN INFANTRY BATTALION.
Lieutenant A. W. Northover.

29TH CANADIAN INFANTRY BATTALION.
Lance-Corporal A. J. Hourston.   Private W. B. Harris.

CANADIAN ARMY MEDICAL CORPS.
Colonel J. W. Bridges.   Captain R. H. Macdonald.
Colonel M. McLaren.   Captain S. A. Smith, D.S.O.
Lieutenant-Colonel K. Cameron.   Lieutenant W. M. Hart.
Lieut.-Colonel G. G. Nasmith.   Serjeant-Major R. Robart.
Major W. T. M. Mackinnon.   Staff-Serjeant W. Hogg.
Major C. A. Young.   Lance-Corporal R. Horne.
Captain G. H. R. Gibson.   Private F. McKeegan.

CANADIAN NURSING SERVICE.
Matron Miss E. M. Charleson.
Matron Miss M. O. McLatchey.
Nursing Matron Miss V. C. Nesbitt.

MENTIONED IN DESPATCHES

Nursing Matron Miss E. C. Rayside.
Nursing Matron Miss E. B. Ridley.
Nursing Sister Miss A. C. Strong.
Nursing Sister Miss V. A. Tremaine.

CANADIAN ARMY SERVICE CORPS.
Lieutenant-Colonel W. A. Simson.   Corporal M. S. Purton.
Driver F. Sutcliffe.

CANADIAN ARMY VETERINARY CORPS.
Captain T. C. Evans.   Serjeant O. C. White.

CANADIAN ORDNANCE CORPS.
Lieutenant H. R. Northover.

CANADIAN OVERSEAS RAILWAY CONSTRUCTION CORPS.
Lieutenant-Colonel C. W. P. Ramsey.
Major C. L. Hervey.

1ST NEWFOUNDLAND CONTINGENT.
Major W. H. Franklin.

NEW ZEALAND LOCAL FORCES.
Lieutenant F. A. Hellaby (attached Devonshire Regiment).

GENERAL LIST.
Temporary Captain G. G. Armstrong.
Temporary Captain C. L. Lindeman.

GENERAL LIST (NEW ARMY).
Temporary Captain F. V. Lister.
Temporary Captain J. W. Oldfield, Brigade Machine-Gun Officer.
Temporary Second Lieutenant E. W. Mackay-White, Royal Engineers.
Temporary Lieut. G. Gray, Trench Warfare, Ministry of Munitions.
Temporary Lieutenant C. Romer.

SPECIAL LIST.
Temporary Captain E. Gold, Meteorological Section.
Temporary Second Lieutenant E. B. Howell, Indian Mail Censorship Staff.
Temporary Second Lieutenant R. W. Maude, Interpreter 2nd/8th Gurkha Rifles.
Temporary Second Lieutenant N. Wilks, Corps of Interpreters.

DEPARTMENT OF THE FINANCIAL ADVISER.
H. G. Goligher, Esq. (relative precedence as Brigadier-General).
J. Toplis (relative precedence as Lieutenant-Colonel).

CORPS OF MILITARY STAFF CLERKS.
Staff-Serjeant A. P. Sprange.

MISCELLANEOUS LIST.
Ex-Soldier Clerk J. B. Price.

MENTIONED IN DESPATCHES
INDIAN ARMY.
CAVALRY.

3RD SKINNER'S HORSE.
Risaldar Nur Muhammad Khan.

4TH CAVALRY.
Captain R. Johnston.

6TH CAVALRY.
Risaldar Fateh Singh.

9TH HODSON'S HORSE.
Lieutenant T. W. Corbett.
Temporary Lieutenant in Army T. L. W. Stallibrass.
Jemadar Tek Singh.

10TH LANCERS (HODSON'S HORSE).
Major A. D. Strong.

11TH LANCERS (PROBYN'S HORSE).
Lieutenant (temporary Captain) H. G. A. Fellowes.
Lieutenant E. S. MacL. Prinsep.

13TH LANCERS (WATSON'S HORSE).
Captain F. H. Moody. Lieutenant D. Pott.

15TH LANCERS (CURETON'S MULTANIS).
Captain A. C. K. S. Clarke.

16TH CAVALRY.
Captain W. H. Lang.

17TH CAVALRY.
Lieutenant C. G. Y. Skipwith.

18TH LANCERS.
Honorary Captain Hon. Malik Umar Hyat Khan, C.I.E., M.V.O.

19TH LANCERS (FANE'S HORSE).
Risaldar Hira Singh.

20TH DECCAN HORSE.
Captain R. B. Worgan. Jemadar Sher Singh.

28TH LIGHT CAVALRY.
Sowar Ward Orderly Bal Singh.

29TH LANCERS (DECCAN HORSE).
Captain G. W. Hemans.
Risaldar Ghulam Dastaghir Khan.

36TH JACOB'S HORSE.
Risaldar Major Muhammad Nasir Khan.

39TH CENTRAL INDIA HORSE.
Captain W. A. K. Fraser.

MENTIONED IN DESPATCHES

QUEEN VICTORIA'S OWN CORPS OF GUIDES (FRONTIER FORCE) (LUMSDEN'S).

Captain P. D'A. Banks (killed).

1ST KING GEORGE'S OWN SAPPERS AND MINERS.

Captain L. A. Bartlett, Royal Engineers (died of wounds).
Lieutenant H. S. Trevor, Royal Engineers (killed).
Lieutenant E. O. Wheeler, Royal Engineers.
Quartermaster Serjeant H. T. Henley.

3RD SAPPERS AND MINERS.

Captain A. D. S. Arbuthnot, Royal Engineers.
Captain F. H. Kisch, Royal Engineers.
Captain M. Rawlence, Royal Engineers.
Lieutenant H. W. R. Hamilton, Royal Engineers.
Lieutenant A. Mason, Royal Engineers.
Serjeant M. Sprinks.
Havildar Sardar Khan.
Driver Havildar Amir Ali Shah.
Sapper Hyder Khan.

INFANTRY.

6TH JAT LIGHT INFANTRY.

Captain A. B. McPherson.   Captain R. C. Ross.

12TH PIONEERS.

Lance-Naik Teja Singh.

15TH LUDHIANA SIKHS.

Major H. S. E. Franklin.

19TH PUNJABIS.

Major F. T. Duhan (killed).

21ST PUNJABIS.

Captain J. R. Cook (killed).

22ND PUNJABIS.

Captain (temporary Lieutenant-Colonel) W. F. R. Webb.

24TH PUNJABIS.

Captain C. M. Thornhill.

31ST PUNJABIS.

Lieutenant R. B. Deedes.

34TH SIKH PIONEERS.

Lieutenant-Colonel E. H. S. Cullen, M.V.O., D.S.O.
Brevet Lieutenant-Colonel H. F. Cooke.
Captain G. F. J. Paterson.

37TH DOGRAS.

Captain R. M. Brind.

MENTIONED IN DESPATCHES

39TH GARHWAL RIFLES.
Captain P. T. Etherton.

40TH PATHANS.
Captain J. F. C. Dalmahoy (killed).
Lieutenant F. C. G. Campbell.
Sepoy Mukhtiara.

41ST DOGRAS.
Brevet Lieutenant-Colonel C. A. R. Hutchinson.
Lieutenant-Colonel C. W. Tribe.

42ND DEOLI REGIMENT.
Captain R. F. D. Burnett.   Captain R. M. F. Patrick.

46TH PUNJABIS.
Lieutenant F. L. R. Munn.

47TH SIKHS.
Captain S. B. Combe.   Captain W. H. Ralston.
Captain R. F. Francis.   Lieutenant A. E. Drysdale.

54TH SIKHS (FRONTIER FORCE).
Captain G. N. Mackie (killed).

55TH COKE'S RIFLES (FRONTIER FORCE).
Captain A. E. Mahon.   Lieutenant D. B. Mein.

56TH PUNJABI RIFLES (FRONTIER FORCE).
Captain C. J. S. Le Cornu.

57TH WILDE'S RIFLES (FRONTIER FORCE).
Lieutenant D. Bainbridge.

58TH VAUGHAN'S RIFLES (FRONTIER FORCE).
Second Lieutenant J. H. Milligan.
Jemadar Hawinda.

59TH SCINDE RIFLES (FRONTIER FORCE).
Captain R. D. Inskip.

62ND PUNJABIS.
Captain L. H. Morse.

67TH PUNJABIS.
Lieuteannt J. de la H. Gordon.

74TH PUNJABIS.
Captain H. W. Milne (killed).

89TH PUNJABIS.
Lieut.-Colonel L. W. Y. Campbell.   Naick Harnam Singh.
Captain J. D. Crawford.   Naick Issar Singh.
Captain W. R. James.   Sepoy Indar Singh.

MENTIONED IN DESPATCHES

90TH PUNJABIS.
Lieutenant-Colonel H. A. Carleton.

107TH PIONEERS.
Lieutenant F. H. F. Hornor.
Lieutenant B. H. Wallis.

121ST PIONEERS.
Major E. N. Heale.

125TH NAPIER'S RIFLES.
Lieutenant-Colonel A. H. Dennys.

127TH BALUCH LIGHT INFANTRY.
Major H. Hulseberg.

129TH BALUCHIS.
Captain M. A. Hamar.

130TH BALUCHIS (JACOB'S RIFLES).
Captain E. C. Kensington.

1ST GURKHA RIFLES.
Lieutenant-Colonel W. Christian Anderson.

2ND GURKHA RIFLES.
Major E. H. Sweet.
Captain J. E. Cruickshank.
Lieutenant G. A. P. Scoones.

4TH GURKHA RIFLES.
Captain W. A. Gardiner.
Captain C. D. Roe, D.S.O.

8TH GURKHA RIFLES.
Captain G. C. B. Buckland, D.S.O.

9TH GURKHA RIFLES.
Subadar Bakht Bahadur Adhikari.

SUPPLY AND TRANSPORT.
Colonel A. W. Cripps.
Major H. A. Douglas.
Major W. N. Lushington.
Major H. N. Young.
Captain B. H. H. Barrett, Army Service Corps.
Captain A. E. E. Sargent.
Commissary and Honorary Major R. Orr, Indian Army Departments.
Conductor A. Bartram.
Conductor W. J. Edgerley.
Conductor W. J. Kemp.
Conductor C. Payne.
Sub-Conductor J. F. Bolland.
Sub-Conductor J. Eagles.
Sub-Conductor W. B. Hughes.

MENTIONED IN DESPATCHES

Sub-Conductor J. Ingram.
Sub-Conductor H. Jones.
Staff-Serjeant L. J. Addison.
Staff-Serjeant C. Durham.
Staff-Serjeant E. Grindley.
Staff-Serjeant J. W. Hewson.
Staff-Serjeant A. Jennings.
Staff-Serjeant A. Norton.
Staff-Serjeant J. R. K. Taylor.
Staff-Serjeant C. E. Terry.
Staff-Serjeant J. M. Tingey.
Serjeant F. E. Dann.

QUEEN ALEXANDRA'S MILITARY NURSING SERVICE FOR INDIA.

Miss C. H. Anderson.
Miss M. D. Knapp.
Miss S. G. Mills.
Miss R. L. Neville.
Miss H. A. M. Rait.
Miss L. A. White.

INDIAN MEDICAL SERVICE.

Colonel B. B. Grayfoot, M.D.
Lieutenant-Colonel A. E. Berry, M.B.
Lieutenant-Colonel J. A. Hamilton, M.B., F.R.C.S. Edin.
Lieutenant-Colonel A. J. MacNab, F.R.C.S.
Major H. Boulton, M.B.
Major R. J. Bradley, M.B.
Major G. Browse, M.D.
Major H. M. Cruddas.
Major A. N. Fleming, M.B., F.R.C.S. Edin.
Major J. Good, M.B.,
Major C. Hudson, D.S.O., F.R.C.S. Edin.
Major W. W. Jeudwine, M.D.
Major G. C. L. Kerans.
Major R. A. Needham, M.B.
Captain F. B. Shettle.
Captain H. S. Carmack, M.B., F.R.C.S. Edin.
Captain V. B. Green-Armytage.
Captain S. H. Middleton-West, M.B.
Captain R. B. Nicholson.
Captain W. C. Paton, M.B.
Captain J. Scott, M.B.
Captain J. Smalley, M.B.
Captain C. H. Smith, M.D. F.R.C.S.
Captain V. N. Whitamore.
Captain C. A. Wood, M.B.

INDIAN SUBORDINATE MEDICAL DEPARTMENT.

First Class Sub-Assistant Surgeon Bal-Mukand.
First Class Sub-Assistant Surgeon P. Hira-Lal.
First Class Sub-Assistant Surgeon Rai Bahadur Hira Singh.
First Class Sub-Assistant Surgeon S. Jassudasam.
First Class Sub-Assistant Surgeon Kishan Singh.
First Class Assistant Surgeon W. C. McMillan.
First Class Assistant Surgeon W. J. S. Maine.
First Class Sub-Assistant Surgeon Pohlo Ram.

MENTIONED IN DESPATCHES

Subadar and First Class Senior Sub-Assitant Surgeon Shaikh Hussain Ali.
First Class Sub-Assistant Surgeon Bishan Singh.
Second Class Assistant Surgeon R. F. Browne.
Second Class Sub-Assistant Surgeon Culpankum Virasami Rajagopal Pillai.
Second Class Sub-Assistant Surgeon Kishan Singh.
Second Class Sub-Assistant Surgeon Pargan Singh.
Third Class Assistant Surgeon E. H. Boilard.
Third Class Sub-Assistant Surgeon Mathurapershad Sarswit.
Third Class Assistant Surgeon E. B. Messinier.

INDIAN SUBORDINATE MEDICAL DEPARTMENT AND ARMY BEARER CORPS.
Third Class Assistant Surgeon J. M. Rodrigues.
Fourth Class Sub-Assistant Surgeon W. A. Browne.
Serjeant E. Clements (Packstore). Grade Ward Servant Ghainda.
Private J. T. Rowland. Bearer Beni.
Havildar Abdul Qadir (Packstore). Bearer Bhujjoo.
Havildar Fateh Ali (Packstore). Bearer Chabi.
Havildar Nikka. Bearer Madan Singh.
Naik Ram Charan. Bearer Mastan Singh.
Lance Naik Kundan. Bearer Mulloo.
Lance Naik Ram Charan. Bearer Narain.
Ward Orderly Mahomed Shah.
Temporary First Class Hospital Storekeeper Dorabji Mehrjibhoy.
Temporary First Class Hospital Storekeeper Shiv Ram.

MILITARY WORKS SERVICE.
Conductor A. D. McDonough. Sub-Conductor A. A. Inward.

INDIAN MILITARY ACCOUNTS DEPARTMENT.
Major R. E. Carr-Hall. Captain S. G. V. Ellis.
First Grade Accountant Lalla Hukam Chand.
Third Grade Accountant Nand Lall Khanna.

IMPERIAL SERVICE TROOPS.
Major Hati, Gwalior Transport.

INDIAN ARMY.
Second Lieutenant (temporary Captain) A. C. Curtis (attached Bedfordshire Regiment).
Second Lieutanant (temporary Lieutenant) A. F. Logan (attached Bedfordshire Regiment).
Second Lieutenant (temporary Lieutenant) F. Powell (attached Bedfordshire Regiment).
Second Lieutenant (temporary Lieutenant) C. S. Searle (attached Royal Berkshire Regiment).

MENTIONED IN DESPATCHES

INDIAN UNATTACHED LIST.
Serjeant J. H. Lanfear, Military Staff Clerk.
Serjeant G. McDermott.
Serjeant W. Prescott.

INDIAN NATIVE LAND FORCES.
Second Lieutenant Rana Jodha Jang Bahadur (Commandant, Tehri Sappers and Miners) (attached Garhwal Rifles).

INDIAN ARMY (RESERVE OF OFFICERS).
Captain A. R. Mellis (attached Gurkha Rifles).
Second Lieutenant C. M. Durnford (attached Vaughan's Rifles, Frontier Force).
Second Lieutenant C. C. E. Manson (attached Gurkha Rifles).
Second Lieutenant C. C. Nott-Bower (attached Gurkha Rifles).

VETERINARY CORPS.
Serjeant-Major R. Ford.

POSTAL SERVICE.
Subadar Kanshi Ram.
Conductor G. F. Fressanges.
Sub-Conductor M. H. Coombs.
Sub-Conductor T. G. Wilson.
Staff-Serjeant W. Morris.
Staff-Serjeant E. Pay.
Staff-Serjeant E. W. Smith.
Staff-Serjeant T. Terry.
Staff-Serjeant J. E. Walsh.
Sub-Conductor R. T. Waugh.
Staff-Serjeant A. E. Whicker.

ORDNANCE DEPARTMENT.
Conductor R. W. Hughes.
Conductor J. L. N. Macdougall.

REMOUNT DEPARTMENT.
Lieutenant-Colonel C. F. Templer.

REMOUNT SECTION.
Salutri Kesar Shah (attached to Headquarters Staff, Indian Army).

SPECIAL LIST.
Lieutenant-Colonel W. Donnan (Indian Mail Censorship Staff).
J. C. Coldstream, Supernumerary List (Indian Mail Censorship Staff).
Honorary Lieutenant in Army Qadir Bakhsh Khan, Maler Kotal Sappers (attached 3rd Sappers and Miners).

X. HOHENZOLLERN REDOUBT

X: Whitehall, S.W., 31*st July*, 1916.

To the Secretary of State for War.

Sir,

I HAVE the honour to forward a despatch covering the operation of the military forces under my command in France between the date of my last despatch (15th October) and 19th December, the date upon which I left France and assumed the command of the Forces in the United Kingdom.

The exhaustion in men and material, which results after a great battle, necessarily leads up to a time of comparative inactivity, and the period under review was, therefore, somewhat barren in incidents of military importance.

Up to the end of October the most important operation was an attack, which commenced about noon of the 13th, by troops of the 11th and 4th Corps against Fosse No. 8, the Quarries, and the German trenches on the Lens-La Bassée Road.

The Divisions chiefly engaged were the 1st Division (4th Corps) and the 12th and 46th Divisions (11th Corps).

Speaking generally, the objective of the 1st Division was the enemy's trenches on the Lens-La Bassée Road; that of the 12th Division was the Quarries; whilst the troops of the 46th Division attacked the Hohenzollern Redoubt and Fosse No. 8. The day's fighting commenced with an artillery bombardment of the objectives of the attack, and in this bombardment the French artillery on our right collaborated.

Shortly before the attack was launched at 2 p.m. smoke was turned on all along our front from the Behune-La Bassée Road southwards, and under cover of this smoke the attack was delivered. At the same time the heavy artillery lifted to further objectives while the enemy's front trench system was subjected to shrapnel fire.

At 2.10 p.m. it was reported that our infantry had passed the Hohenzollern Redoubt and were bombing up a trench towards the dump of Fosse 8; they were, however, opposed by heavy machine-gun fire from that point and such success as the original attack gained at the Fosse was only of a temporary nature.

At 2.45 p.m. the 4th Corps reported having captured 1,200 yards of trenches on the Lens-La Bassée Road, but as the left battalion of this corps had failed to get possession of the enemy's trenches the General Officer Commanding did not think it practicable to undertake any further offensive towards Hulluch.

The information received during the remainder of the day was very conflicting, and at nightfall the General Officer Commanding 1st Army was unable to define the exact position of the leading troops of the 1st Division.

One battalion of the 12th Division had gained the south-westerly edge of the Quarries. The fight for the Hohenzollern Redoubt and Fosse No. 8 was still proceeding with varying fortunes, but it appeared clear that none of our troops were in the Fosse or on the dump.

In the course of the next two days the whole attack died down without attaining the objective aimed at, and the situation in that part of the line remained much the same throughout the period covered by the present despatch.

During the night of October 16th-17th the enemy made two bombing attacks against the Guards Division in the vicinity of the Hohenzollern Redoubt. Both these attacks were easily repulsed.

On the 19th October the enemy was seen to be massing in the Quarries near the Hohenzollern Redoubt, and after artillery preparation made a determined attack against our lines to the south-west of the former place.

AIR RAIDS

This attack was repulsed with heavy loss to the enemy. A bombing attack of two hours' duration in the same vicinity met with a similar fate.

On 16th November the 2nd Canadian Infantry Brigade carried out a brilliant little operation near La Petite Douve Farm in raiding the enemy's trenches with bombing parties. They caused considerable damage to the enemy, brought away 12 prisoners, and only suffered one accidental casualty themselves.

On 25th November the Royal Flying Corps carried out an effective raid on the enemy's cantonments at Achiet Le Grand, and this was followed a few days later by a similar raid on Don Station and the adjoining stores, in the course of which several fires and an explosion were observed.

Another air raid against the quay and stores near Miraumont was also reported as having been effective on 30th November.

Throughout the period under review mining activity was constant on both sides; this, as well as almost continuous shelling of varying intensity, has become a practically permanent condition of warfare along the entire length of the line which we now occupy.

I do not propose, in this short despatch, written only in order that the official published narrative of the war may be continuous, to make special mention of the services of individuals under my command, other than those which have already appeared.

The encomiums passed in my despatch of 15th October are proved to be more than justified by the conduct of all ranks of the Army in France up to the time of my handing over the command.

I have the honour to be, Sir,
Your most obedient Servant,
FRENCH, Field-Marshal,
Commanding-in-Chief.

www.ingramcontent.com/pod-product-compliance
Lightning Source LLC
Chambersburg PA
CBHW071352300426
44114CB00016B/2035